The Cultural Patronage
of Medieval Women

THE CULTURAL

PATRONAGE OF

MEDIEVAL WOMEN

EDITED BY JUNE HALL McCASH

THE UNIVERSITY OF GEORGIA PRESS *Athens & London*

© 1996 by the University of Georgia Press
Athens, Georgia 30602
All rights reserved
Designed by Louise OFarrell
Set in 10/13 Aldus by Tseng Information Systems, Inc.
Printed and bound by Thomson-Shore, Inc.
The paper in this book meets the guidelines for permanence and durability
of the Committee on Production Guidelines for Book Longevity of the
Council on Library Resources.

Printed in the United States of America

00 99 98 97 96   C   5 4 3 2 1

00 99 98 97 96   P   5 4 3 2 1

Library of Congress Cataloging in Publication Data
The cultural patronage of medieval women / edited by June Hall McCash.
p.   cm.
Includes bibliographical references (p.) and index.
ISBN 0–8203–1701–2 (alk. paper). — ISBN 0–8203–1702–0 (pbk. : alk.
paper)
1. Women benefactors—Europe—History.   2. Women—History—
Middle Ages, 500–1500.   I. McCash, June Hall.
CB353.C837   1996
920.72'094—dc20   94–13063

British Library Cataloging in Publication Data available

Frontispiece: Vincent de Beauvois, *Speculum historiale.* Walters Art
Gallery, Baltimore.

To my mother, WILLIEMAYE STONE HALL,
in celebration of her strength, courage,
and indomitable spirit, and to all those
generations of women who have left so
rich a legacy despite the odds.

Contents

ix   Preface

xi   Foreword
STEPHEN G. NICHOLS

1   The Cultural Patronage of Medieval Women: An Overview
JUNE HALL MCCASH

50   The Empress Theodora and the Tradition of Women's
Patronage in the Early Byzantine Empire
ANNE L. MCCLANAN

73   Women's Role in Latin Letters From the Fourth to the
Early Twelfth Century
JOAN M. FERRANTE

105   Anchoress, Abbess, and Queen: Donors and Patrons or
Intercessors and Matrons?
MADELINE H. CAVINESS

155   *"Proclaiming her dignity abroad":* The Literary and Artistic
Network of Matilda of Scotland, Queen of England
1100–1118
LOIS L. HUNEYCUTT

175   Of Queens, Courts, and Books: Reflections on the Literary
Patronage of Thirteenth-Century Plantagenet Queens
JOHN CARMI PARSONS

202   Piety, Politics, and Power: The Patronage of Leonor of
       England and Her Daughters Berenguela of León and
       Blanche of Castile
       MIRIAM SHADIS

228   Patterns of Women's Literary Patronage: England,
       1200–ca. 1475
       KAREN K. JAMBECK

266   Elizabeth de Burgh: Connoisseur and Patron
       FRANCES A. UNDERHILL

288   Some Norfolk Women and Their Books, ca. 1390–1440
       RALPH HANNA III

306   The Patronage of Isabel of Portugal
       CHARITY CANNON WILLARD

321   Bibliography

373   Contributors

375   Index

Preface

Fewer than twenty years ago Rita Lejeune bemoaned the lack of "une bonne oeuvre générale" on the patronage of medieval women.[*] Since then, a new focus on women in the Middle Ages has resulted in a number of studies of women's patronage and related topics. In fact, a virtual explosion in patronage studies has recently taken place, as evidenced by the number of conferences devoted in whole or in part to the topic that have been held during the last several years. Despite current interest in the subject, however, it has still not been the sole focus of a single book or monograph. The present volume, the first to deal exclusively with the question, is broadly based, exploring women's patronage from wide geographical and temporal perspectives and examining their contributions as patrons of writers, artists, craftsmen, musicians, and architects, as well as of religious and educational institutions. It also seeks to test the limits of what can legitimately be considered patronage, and it is my hope that it will open a productive debate on a number of the issues raised within the book.

Patronage lends itself especially well to an interdisciplinary inquiry of the type this book undertakes, in which literary scholars, historians, and art historians come together to explore the many ways in which female patrons of the Middle Ages have impacted our cultural heritage. Because women's patronage is a legitimate field of inquiry for all these areas, we clearly have much to share

---

[*] Rita Lejeune, "La Femme dans les littératures française et occitane du XIe au XIIIe siècle," in *La Femme dans les civilisations des Xe–XIIIe siècles: Actes du colloque tenu à Poitiers les 23–25 septembre 1976* (Poitiers: Centre d'Etudes Supérieures de Civilisation Médiévale, Université de Poitiers, 1976), 114 (204). Scattered nineteenth-century publications, primarily on female bibliophiles and women's education, have provided important background information for contemporary patronage studies. See, for example, Vallet de Viriville, "La Bibliothèque d'Isabeau de Bavière, *Bulletin du bibliophile* 14 (1858): 663–87; Ernest Quentin-Bauchart, *Les Femmes bibliophiles de France* (Paris: Morgand, 1886); and Charles Jourdain, "Mémoire sur l'éducation des femmes au moyen âge," *Mémoires de l'Institut national de France. Académie des inscriptions et belles lettres* 28 (1874): 79–133.

and much to learn from each other in our various approaches and methodologies. The opening essay seeks to provide an overview of women's patronage and represents a sort of *précis* of the current state of patronage studies. The remaining essays delve into the contributions of a single woman patron or specific groups of patrons from the early Middle Ages through the fifteenth century and from the Byzantine Empire throughout western Europe. Taken together, they provide a broad picture of women's patronage in the Middle Ages. It is my hope that readers will examine each essay on its own merit as well as within the context of the whole.

I would like to thank the many people who have helped with this project, first and foremost, the Middle Tennessee State University Research Committee for grants that allowed me time and travel opportunities to prepare my own essay and do the necessary editorial work for the book. I am grateful as well to the able staff at the Centre d'Etudes Supérieures de la Civilisation Médiévale in Poitiers who provided me not only with a delightful place to work but with all the assistance I required. I am deeply indebted for the help of those who read all or part of the manuscript and made helpful suggestions and comments, especially Donald Maddox, Sara Sturm-Maddox, and Stephen G. Nichols, and to my colleagues at Middle Tennessee State University, Patrick Conley, Nancy Goldberg, and Margaret Ordoubadian. No one was more valuable to the completion of this project than Betty McFall, who greeted my endless stream of interlibrary loan requests and bibliographical inquiries with cheerful and efficient assistance. I am also grateful to my graduate research assistants Sarah Young and Kathy Dotts for their willing help with the bibliography. To Richard Gleaves, my husband, for both his ongoing encouragement and his assistance with various computer problems, I owe a special word of thanks. Their aid has been invaluable in the final assembling of this project. They have contributed greatly to its strengths though are in no way responsible for its weaknesses. I am grateful as well to the able staff at the University of Georgia Press and especially to Karen Orchard for her interest in the project and her counsel throughout its preparation.

Foreword

Jeanne of Burgundy, queen of France from 1328 to 1348, proudly crowned by a gold, fleur-de-lys diadem, a retinue of ladies-in-waiting behind her, stands as patron of the work that follows a magnificent frontispiece illumination of a *Speculum historiale* (*Mirror of History*) at the Walters Art Gallery in Baltimore (see frontispiece of this volume).[1] Regally, Jeanne commands with her raised hand, index extended in the consecrated gesture of authority. Before her sits Jean de Vignay in his robes of the Order of Hospitalers of Saint Jacques de Haut Pas, the man whom Queen Jeanne has commissioned to undertake the work. He gazes down at the open book resting on his lap while his right hand inscribes the opening words of the text, words in fourteenth-century French. Queen Jeanne, her ladies-in-waiting, and Jean de Vignay are not alone in this frontispiece, and this juxtaposition of her role with the other half of the miniature makes the Walters manuscript pertinent for the question of female patronage.

On the left-hand side of the folio, over the first column of text, we see literally a mirror image of the right-hand scene, this time showing a nimbed Saint Louis (Louis IX) commissioning the original Latin *Speculum historiale* from the Dominican scholar, Vincent de Beauvais. Like Queen Jeanne, Saint Louis stands with retainers behind him, facing the seated monk who holds the open book on a lap desk, the words "Deus adiuua me" visible to the viewer. Vincent and Jean de Vignay sit back to back, each facing his patron and thus Saint Louis and Jeanne of Burgundy face one another.

Subtle details suggest that this is Jeanne of Burgundy's book, and that Saint Louis's image simply recalls the origins of the project and thus serves as an

---

1 The manuscript is Walters 140, Vincent de Beauvais, *Speculum historiale* (French translation by Jean de Vignay, pt. 3, bks. 17–24), Paris, fourteenth century. Walters 140 is a later copy of the original presentation manuscript. One may find the miniature reproduced as fig. 129, catalog entry no. 64 in Lilian M. C. Randall's *Medieval and Renaissance Manuscripts in the Walters Art Gallery*, vol. 1, *France, 875–1420* (Baltimore: Johns Hopkins University Press, 1989). For a thorough, perceptive description of the manuscript and miniatures see pp. 165b–173a.

auctoritas rather than asserting his primacy. The round halo over Saint Louis's head lets the viewer know that this is a retrospective so far as the king's patronage is concerned: the time portrayed in his half of the miniature is not the year of commissioning, 1251, for then he would have worn the rectangular halo that distinguished saints portrayed as though during their lifetime. No, the time of both parts of the frontispiece illumination is some eighty years later, during Queen Jeanne's reign, which explains why she occupies the central position in her painting (Saint Louis is crowded more to the margin of his space) and why her chamber is actually somewhat larger than is Saint Louis's. This accords with the architectural setting: the whole illumination is a cutaway of private rooms in a Gothic structure characteristic of later Gothic; the borders of the painting suggesting outer walls and crenellated roofline.

These scenes attest the extent to which the book itself by the fourteenth century had become a collector's item, a commodity whose very existence ever depended upon a complex set of services requiring both trained professionals and patrons to pay them. Book production involved such varied craftsmen as those who made the vellum (or paper), the scribes who did the actual writing, and the artists responsible for the miniatures, the decorated or historiated initials, and the rubrications that served both as legends for the miniature paintings and as an ordering structure in the visible text to help readers find their way through the finished book. The scribes' writing could readily be distinguished from the rubricators' by the different-colored inks (rubrics were usually red, whence the term from Latin *rubr-, ruber* "red"), the different handwriting, and usually the different style of lettering used in the rubric as compared with the text.

The work of all of these artists and scribes imparted an iconic or visual dimension to the book, reinforcing its status as a precious object. An early commentator on the art of reading and learning from books, Hugh of Saint Victor, advised his students to make full use of the iconic elements on the pages of their books to help them remember the information contained in the text set forth on the folio. Hugh taught that by visualizing the place on the page where a certain fact or passage was recorded and the particular time when the student read the page that one could more efficiently memorize information. Such testimony illustrates just how pervasive material aspects of bookmaking were in the Middle Ages.

As the product of so many different competences the book as an expensive object required a wealthy class who could underwrite and appreciate such things. The images of Saint Louis and Queen Jeanne in the Walters *Speculum historiale* intentionally testify to the high regard in which enlightened monarchs held books and their subject matter, especially when the matter was history. Still this is but a secondary sense of patronage that does not capture the main dynamic of the frontispiece miniature in the Walters manuscript.

The author portraits of Vincent de Beauvais and Jean de Vignay do, to be sure, stand for the whole art of bookmaking that begins with the "invention" or "finding" (*trouver*) of the subject matter and subsequent shaping of it into the form of the work. The full import of patronage, however, associates the patron with the process by giving her a role in the discovery and propagation of knowledge that afforded both patron and author a special status in the divine order that transcended economics and may be said to be largely without precedent in modern culture.

The patron who commissioned a work and the author who wrote it—let us note that the same may be said for the other arts, especially architecture—were linked in a common effort to demonstrate divine purpose and thus human deviation from or adherence to that plan. Bounded by Creation in the beginning and Apocalypse at the end, human knowledge had to look deep into and study the "mirror of history" to discover for humans what God (medieval culture believed) already knew. Sponsoring such an endeavor and executing it were both acts of participation in the quest for the secrets of life and history, yes, but also a demonstration of how history, theology, philosophy could map contemporary life onto the matrix of the one book that represented, for medieval Christianity, the key to existence.

Unlike classical culture, Christianity was a religion of one book; it was to plot the meaning of this one book on the immediate world that the many books were dedicated. Authorship and patronage were, in consequence, an active collaboration in generation and government of a sort. Although God alone could create *ex nihilo*, according to medieval theology, humans could create and rule only in collaboration, collectively and in pairs. Chrétien de Troyes, of course, makes this point suggestively when evoking his and Marie de Champagne's collaboration to produce the romance in his well-known prologue to *Le Chevalier de la Charrete*:

Puis que ma dame de Champaigne
vialt que romans a feire anpraigne,
je l'anprendrai molt volentiers
come cil qui est suens antiers

. . . .

Mes tant dirai ge que mialz oevre
ses comandemanz an ceste oevre

que sans ne painne que g'i mete.
Del CHEVALIER DE LA CHARRETE
comance Crestïens son livre;
matiere et san li done et livre
la contesse, et il s'antremet
de panser, que gueres n'i met
fors sa painne et s'antancïon.[2]

[Since my lady of Champagne wishes me to undertake to make a romance,
I will do so willingly, like one who is altogether hers . . . but if I do say
it, I work her commands better into this work than any wit or effort that
I myself provide. Chrétien begins his book of the *Knight of the Cart;* the
countess gives him and indeed imparts the subject and the conceit, and he
undertakes to think it through, but still he scarcely contributes more than
his effort and his understanding (i.e., compared to her).]

Patronage not only was a practical arrangement in which each party contributed a necessary element lacking in the other for realizing the project; it also
enacted a symbolic statement in two dimensions.

Hierarchically, it reinforced the concept of an asymmetry of power inherent in the divine order by which God ruled humans and the world; that same
asymmetry inhered in the patronage compact, with the important difference
that in the human version power was not uniform but divided (for example,
into artistic ability and economic means). Socially, patronage affirmed the
need for humans to work together to accomplish, dimly, what God could do
resplendently alone. In these senses patronage as symbolic creation reflected
medieval social organization.

But power may not always lie where one expects to find it in the asymmetries of patronage. So it is in the Walters frontispiece, where the pairing of
Latin original and French translation linked to male and female royal patronage bears closer examination. Saint Louis commissioning a Latin work, Jeanne
of Burgundy inspiring the Old French translation: together they betoken the
gendering of language associations into Latin, the father tongue, and the vernacular mother tongue spoken in the intimacy of the family before the (male)
child departs to be trained by the church in Latin.

The concept of the mother tongue developed on the frontier between France
and Germany in the ninth century. By the twelfth it still denoted, as Ivan

---

2 Chrétien de Troyes, *Le Chevalier de la Charrete,* ed. Mario Roques (Paris: Champion, 1958), lines
1–4, 21–29.

Illich recently remarked, "a speech form, *sermo*, as distinct from *lingua*, the Latin Language."[3] It did not have the status of a formal language, for it was not yet a visual cultural entity, something boldly laid out on a page, something that vernacular speakers could visualize as the tongue they spoke and in which they expressed moral, religious, and intellectual constructs of all kinds. When Dante eulogized Arnaut Daniel as the *miglior fabbro del parlar materno*[4] at the beginning of the fourteenth century, he used the troubadour as a historical pretext for asserting the status of the vernacular as a language, not just a *sermo* or speech form, possessing a determinate cultural tradition reaching from Arnaut's Occitan, the founding Romance literary vernacular, to Dante's own more sophisticated and ambitious Tuscan. This is precisely the status of visualized language capable of expressing abstraction and complexity that we find at the end of the thirteenth century in Saint Louis's own chronicle: Jean de Joinville's *Histoire de Saint Louis*.

Joinville presents his history both as an oral record—"Et autant que je vous conte de ses grans faiz . . . vous conterai-je ce que je vi et oy de ses saintes paroles et de ses bons enseignemens . . . pour édifier ceus qui les orront" [And as much as I recount for you his high deeds . . . I will recount what I saw and heard of his holy words and his worthy teachings . . . to edify those who will hear them][5]—and as a written document whose text will be visualized as well as heard: "Je Jehans sires de Joinville, seneschaus de Champaigne, faiz escrire la vie notre saint roy Loois, ce que je vi et oy par l'espace de sis anz que je fu en sa compaignie" [I, John Lord of Joinville, seneschal of Champagne, cause to be written the life of our holy king Louis, what I saw and heard in the space of the six years that I was in his company]; "En nom de Dieu le tout puissant, avons ci arière escriptes partie de bonnes paroles et de bons enseignemens nostre saint roy Looys" [In the name of God the all powerful, we have written above a part of the good words and the worthy teachings of our holy king Louis].[6]

Female patronage played a key role in the evolution of the mother tongue from the status of purely informal speech to a stage where, without losing consciousness of its role as discourse, it also functioned as a language, *langue*, in the sense that Latin was a language, *lingua*. Saint Louis's words in Joinville's *Histoire* were meant to be seen as moral philosophy, as *enseignemens* or ethical teachings.

3 Ivan Illich, *In the Vineyard of the Text: A Commentary to Hugh's "Didascalicon"* (Chicago: University of Chicago Press, 1993), 67 n. 2.
4 *Purgatorio* 26.117.
5 Joinville, *Histoire de Saint Louis*, chap. 3.
6 *Ibid.*, chaps. 3, 15.

The status of the vernacular as a moral force different from but capable of comparison with church Latin emerges dramatically in a confrontation between Louis IX and the assembled hierarchy of the French church as recounted by Joinville in chapter 13 of his *Histoire*. Saint Louis's responses to a long, self-interested disquisition by the assembled prelates encapsulates succinctly in French a model moral teaching that articulates divine law as higher than ecclesiastical law in a manner deliberately reminiscent, one suspects, of Christ's responses to the Pharisees and Saducees. More significantly, we see the unmistakable assertion that divine law may be articulated in a language other than Latin, for it is Saint Louis's French teaching that silences the prelates: "Et lors se soufrirent li prelat; ne onques puis nen oy parler que demande fust faites des choses desus dites" [The prelates had to be content with this; nor did one ever again hear mention of the request regarding these matters discussed above].

Perhaps because this had always been their linguistic domain, women had no little hand in establishing the independence of the vernacular from Latin with an authority of its own. Joinville himself tells us at the beginning of his work that Jeanne de Navarre, wife of Philip the Fair, had commissioned his *Histoire*: "Madame la royne . . . qui mout m'amoit (a cui Dieus bone merci face!), me pria si à certes comme ele put, que je li feisse faire un livre des saintes paroles et des bons faiz nostre roy saint Looys" [My lady the queen . . . who held me dear (may God have mercy on her), begged me fervently to make a book of the holy words and the good deeds of our king, Saint Louis].

Froissart tells us that his very first venture into history as a youth was a rhymed chronicle (now lost) written for his patron, Queen Philippa of Hainaut, wife of Edward III of England. Dante takes Beatrice for his posthumous patron and divine intecessor for his vernacular *Commedia*. We have already seen the role of Queen Jeanne in commissioning the vernacular translation of Vincent de Beauvais's *Mirror of History*. Her pairing with Saint Louis in the Walters manuscript brings to mind her reputation in the fourteenth century as the real power during Philip VI's reign.

One might argue that like such allegorical figures as Fortune, Reason, and Nature, in the medieval pantheon of personifications, Patronage also was a woman. Consider the case of the fabulously worked presentation manuscript in the J. Pierpont Morgan Library (New York) of the French translation of Boethius's *De consolatione philosophiae* attributed to Jean de Meun (Morgan 332). Jean de Meun's prologue tells us that the translation was commissioned not by Jeanne de Navarre, Joinville's patron, but by her husband, Philip the

Fair, thus making the enterprise a seemingly male affair: Boethius, Jean de Meun, Philip the Fair.

Again the asymmetries of power make appearances deceiving. We must consider the visual components of the physical manuscript, for they alter considerably this apparent hierarchy in Morgan 332. Boethius's Latin text faces Jean de Meun's French on each double folio so the Latin is on the left and the French is on the right. While this might intuitively seem to give primacy to the Latin, we must remember that the left side of a double folio is actually the verso of that folio, whereas the right side is the recto or front. This means that the Latin text is always on the back of the folio that has the previous page of Old French. Conversely, the Old French is on the front of each folio, and it is to the recto or right-hand side that one's eye instinctively turns when opening the quarto-sized volume, or when turning the page.

The physical layout undermines to a certain extent the expected primacy of father tongue (Latin) vis-à-vis mother tongue (French), so that the mother tongue turns out to dominate, as the prologue leads us to expect when Jean makes it clear that although the king may understand Latin, French is easier and more agreeable for him: in short, French is the real language of power. The iconographic program of miniatures reinforces the dominance of the feminine, mother tongue, reminding us that visual images, like the vernacular, had a feminine valence in medieval treatises.

The Walters Vincent de Beauvais may once more prove instructive in showing how the Morgan Boethius–Jean de Meun inflects patronage in feminine terms even when the principal author and patron figures are male. Queen Jeanne of Burgundy presides over the actual writing of the translation in the Walters manuscript. Jean de Vignay does not offer her a closed and completed volume as Jean de Meun does to Philip the Fair. Rather, Jean de Vignay bends over the page, writing while Queen Jeanne points commandingly at the work, exactly as though she were dictating the translation that Jean takes down. The miniature sends an unambiguous message: without Queen Jeanne's physical and spiritual presence in the project, the work would not exist: Queen Jeanne embodies both patron *and* creative genius.

Morgan 332, however, makes a distinction between the physical patron, Philip the Fair, and an allegorical personification of patronage who is also the tutelary genius of the work. In terms understood by medieval philosophy, the manuscript distinguishes between the material cause of the translation, its immediate historical, contextual stimulus, and the efficient cause, the real "power" that brings the work into existence. These distinctions underlie the iconographic program of miniatures, though they are also implicit in Jean de Meun's prologue and the picture that stands at its head.

The latter depicts Jean de Meun kneeling before Philip the Fair and offering him the closed and completed book, one end of which Philip grasps in his left hand. Like Joinville, who dedicates his book to the prince, son of Philip the Fair and Jeanne of Navarre, Jean de Meun offers his translation to King Philip, its material cause. The higher or efficient cause of the work must be found elsewhere, in a feminine allegorical persona represented by the iconographical program within the manuscript in historiated initials that open the translation proper on folio 4 and appear again at the beginning of books 2 and 4 on folios 29 and 100.

In the first instance a crowned and robed Lady Philosophy (much the same attributes as for Queen Jeanne in the Walters miniature) appears to the sleeping author; in the second initial the same crowned and robed female figure sits enthroned, instructing the author seated below her; and in the third (fol. 100) Lady Philosophy appears engaged in lively discussion with the author, now seated opposite her and at the same level.

There is no doubt that although the text would lead us unhesitatingly to identify the "author" figure in each instance as Boethius, iconographically the author figure is identical in the three historiated initials with the presentation miniature portrait of Jean de Meun and a historiated initial portrait of the translator at work, both found on folio 1. Clearly, the miniatures suggest a permeability between Boethius and Jean de Meun: they become interchangeable. Just as the French language supplants the Latin, and Jean de Meun replaces Boethius for Philip the Fair and fourteenth-century French readers of the *De consolatione*, so Lady Philosophy reveals herself as the true and enduring figure of patronage: Philip the Fair, Jeanne of Navarre, Jeanne of Burgundy, Philippa of Hainaut, even Beatrice are the vernacular, worldly personae of Lady Philosophy. Or might we not say that patronage, the collaborative venture of revealing divine wisdom to the world, was an amalgamation of a variety of feminine personae of which Boethius's Lady Philosophy was simply the most logical?

Acting in the best medieval tradition, then, June McCash has assembled in the present volume a number of excellent inquiries into the precise nature and range of female patronage in the Middle Ages. Despite their overwhelming importance for the evolution of medieval culture, particularly vernacular culture, woman have not previously been recognized by a book dealing exclusively with their role, not simply in France and England but throughout Europe; not simply as patrons of letters but of the visual and decorative arts, of architecture, and of religious and educational foundations. With the appearance of this book, the formal and dynamic role of women as patrons has been set forth clearly and unmistakenly. Professor McCash thus not only has cast herself as patron of what should in the coming years become an important aspect of medieval studies; she also exemplifies the difference between the Middle Ages and our own era: for unlike their medieval counterparts, June McCash and her colleagues are not simply patrons but authors.

Stephen G. Nichols

The Cultural Patronage
of Medieval Women

The Cultural Patronage of Medieval Women: An Overview

✸ ✸ ✸ JUNE HALL MCCASH

As discussions of power in the Middle Ages have expanded in recent years beyond the predominantly masculine realms of politics, law, and war to include such areas as the domestic, social, and cultural, scholars have given greater scrutiny to women's modes of self-empowerment. As a consequence, the cultural patronage of medieval women, a subject long ignored and veiled in shadows, has become a ripe field of inquiry. Because it was one of the few domains in which a public role for women was sanctioned, patronage was an area that provided rich opportunities for women to make their voices heard. They spoke with varying degrees of intensity and sometimes quite eloquently through the works they supported, the projects they sponsored, and the causes they embraced. Studying their patronage allows us to hear once again voices that might otherwise have remained forever silent.[1] Except for the occasional female writer, the rare extant letter, and the vocalization given to women by male authors, the multiple voices of medieval women had by the seventeenth century been effectively eradicated. Only now are we beginning to rediscover them for the richness they disclose.

The patronage of medieval women is proving to be far more widespread than anyone could have expected a decade ago, and scholars are discovering that female influence on the cultural developments of the Middle Ages was considerable. Studying the patronage that women extended to writers, artists, craftsmen, musicians, and religious institutions is significant, however, not only for its illumination of the contributions women made to their society, but also for what it reveals about their enthusiasms, concerns, and aspirations. It

1

allows us to discern female strategies of self-empowerment in a world that was unconcerned with women's self-actualization, offering them little as a rule beyond a meager education and custodial or paternalistic care. It also sheds light on patterns of wealth and influence among females during the Middle Ages. Because engaging in patronage was one of the few ways in which women were permitted to assert their power openly and in a public forum, they took full advantage of it, using it effectively toward a variety of ends—not only cultural but political, religious, social, and educational as well. In short, the study of patronage provides another important brick in (re)constructing women's history and in understanding how medieval women were able to overcome at least some of the obstacles that blocked their way to full participation in their own society and how they acquired an audible voice.

Determining which women engaged in cultural patronage, therefore, becomes a matter of importance. In some cases patrons may be easily identified because of the clues left for us in various texts and documents; many, however, remain unknown because writers and artists are not always helpful in clearly identifying their benefactors. How then does one discover cultural patrons? According to Karl Julius Holzknecht, author of an early work on literary patronage, "It is evident . . . that when a book is addressed to a prince or noble in a position to become a patron of letters or who is addressed as one, patronage undoubtedly exists, and dedications, therefore, in all ages have been generally recognized as an indication of this relationship." [2] Some have questioned such an assumption. Diana Tyson contends that, although "dedication alone is not sufficient to prove active patronage," it does indicate "that the person must have been interested in letters and in the subject of the work, and this goes at least some way towards indicating that he (or she) may have actually commissioned the work or encouraged its writing." [3] Throughout this volume the writers have made every effort to follow her sound conclusion: "The safest method to determine patronage is to take together as many indices of it as are available: dedication, mention by the author of payment, record of payment, praise of the patron, introduction or epilogue addressed to him [or her], internal evidence such as structure or treatment of the subject matter, existence of a presentation copy, illumination [indicating the author presenting the work to a patron], and, most important of all, a statement by the author that he was asked to write the work" (185). We might also add to the list third-party writings (for example, troubadour *vidas*) attesting to the patronage. At best we can say that dedication is an important clue, sometimes perhaps the only one, and probably stronger for women than for men, for writers would have little else to gain from most female dedicatees than their patronage. We must always keep in mind the possibility that the work may have been commissioned by someone else as a gift to the dedicatee, but wherever such a probability can be set aside, we are surely on firmer ground. Literary composition and the copying of manuscripts were laborious and time-consuming projects before the introduction of the printing press. Dedications, therefore, would scarcely have been made lightly, and works were certainly dedicated to either current or prospective patrons, in hope of continued patronage or in an effort to curry favor or honor a benefactor. In the best of cases, a poet or artist is clear in stating either verbally or visually that a work was commissioned by a patron, but to poet and patron alike such clarification may have seemed unnecessary.

Sometimes poets not only attest to a lady's patronage bestowed upon themselves, but also to her more comprehensive interest in the arts. For example, Adela, the daughter of William the Conqueror and wife of Etienne de Blois, was praised by Hugues de Sainte-Marie, a monk of Fleury, who composed a Latin chronicle for her and described her as a patron with astute literary tastes:

Una tamen restat quâ praesit filia Patri,
    Versibus applaudit, scitque vacare libris.
Haec etiam novit sua merces esse Poëtis,
    A probitate sua nemo redit vacuus.
Rursus inest illi dictandi copia torrens.
    Et praeferre sapit carmina carminibus.[4]

[There is one matter in which the daughter surpasses the father;
She applauds poems, and she knows and appreciates books.
She rewards poets; with her generosity none goes away empty-handed.
She has a natural ease and abundance in expressing her thoughts;
Moreover, she knows how to distinguish good from bad verse.]

Many materials available to us do not make it so easy to identify female patrons or to determine precisely what their roles were in the artistic process.[5] Even defining patronage in the Middle Ages is not a simple task, for the patron's role tended to take various forms. In fact, one of the purposes of this volume is to explore the varieties and to test the limits of women's patronage. Some patrons, as we shall see, were active participants in the creative process, directing writers or artists to sources and prescribing subjects and interpretations, while others played a more passive role, becoming patrons only after the fact by compensating an artist for a work already completed. A number of women were able to enjoy the role of patron only indirectly and by virtue of their ability to further the works they supported by imposing their will upon the male figure (usually the husband) on whom they depended for financial support. At its most essential level patronage can be defined as the support or backing of a prosperous or powerful benefactor for an artist, an artifact, or an institution in the form of gifts, money (sometimes in the form of a household position for an artist), political influence, personal encouragement, or assistance in helping to gain currency for a particular work, idea, or project.[6]

In the early medieval period, when a gift-giving economy prevailed, patronage manifested itself most often as support and encouragement, rewarding artists with gifts rather than money for their work. As the shift began in the twelfth century toward a mercantile economy, artists and performers tended to be more frequently compensated with money.[7] An interesting scene composed by Chrétien de Troyes in the latter half of the twelfth century describes the reward system for jongleurs at the marriage of Erec and Enide, no doubt reflecting practices of the time:

Ce jor furent jugleor lié,
car tuit furent a gré paié:
tot fu randu quanqu'il acrurent,
et molt bel don doné lor furent:
robes de veir et d'eminetes,
de conins et de violetes,
d'escarlate, grise ou de soie;
qui vost cheval, qui volt monoie,
chascuns ot don a son voloir
si boen com il le dut avoir.[8]

[On that day the jongleurs were happy, for all were paid whatever they asked. All were given whatever was due them, and they received many beautiful gifts—robes of *vair* and ermine and rabbit, of purple, scarlet, gray, or silk. Whoever asked for a horse or wanted money, each had the gift of his choice as was his due.]

The text suggests that, although in some cases cash payments were made, in Champagne they were still considered gifts in the same category with horses and fine garments, thus reflecting the rewards of patronage for an economy in transition.

In England, however, payment for literary services seems to have been as early as 1135 an accepted form of patronage. Geoffrey Gaimar tells us that his patron Constance Fitzgilbert had in her possession a copy of a metrical history that a certain David had composed for Queen Adeliza of Louvain. Constance paid Geoffrey a silver mark ("un marc d'argen ars e pesé") to copy the work for her.[9] She also commissioned him to write his lengthy *Estoire des Engleis*, a vernacular verse history of England from 495 until the death of William Rufus in 1100, a task he began in the spring and took a full year to complete, sometime between 1147 and 1151.[10] In that work he stresses the active role of "Dame Cunstance la gentil" (line 6437), depicting the *Estoire* as a collaborative endeavor with his patron. Not only does she assign the topic, she also helps him locate sources, sending him to borrow a book from Walter Espec, founder of the Abbey of Rievaulx, who was living at that time at Helmsley in Yorkshire.[11] According to Geoffrey, "If his lady had not helped him, he would never have completed it" [Si sa dame ne li aidast, / Jà à nul jor ne l'achevast, [lines 6445–46].

Throughout the Middle Ages writers, particularly clerics, often became a part of the household of the patron, perhaps performing routine duties in the chancery or scriptorium, as well as providing creative services (for example, songs, love treatises, fabliaux, or *beaux dittiés*) for the entertainment of the court or the edification of the patron. In all likelihood, they were most satisfied when, like Jean Froissart, writing for Philippa of Hainault, wife of Edward III, they could profit in a number of ways from the patronage accorded to them. Having prepared for her a volume of an early draft of his chronicles, he writes of his voyage to England, where he could present it her personally: "Ce non obstant si empris-je assez hardiment, moi issu de l'escole, à rimer et à dicter les guerres dessus dites, et pour porter le livre en Angleterre tout compilé, si comme je fis, et le présentay adont à très-haute et très-noble dame madame Phelippe de Haynaut, royne d'Angleterre, qui liement et doulcement le receut de moy et m'en fist grand prouffit."[12] [Howbeit, I took on me, as soon as I came from school, to write and recite the said book, and bare the same compiled into England and presented the volume thereof to my Lady Philippa of Hainault, noble Queen of England, who right amiably received it to my great profit and advancement.][13] He is elsewhere more specific about the various ways in which he profited, indicating that she took him into her court where he served as a clerk, writing amusing and amorous verses for her and gaining thereby a widespread admiration and "grand prouffit" from others in the nobility.[14] Gaining currency among the nobility because of his exposure at Philippa's court was for Froissart particularly noteworthy. Their initial poet-patron relationship, however, exemplifies the more passive role a patron could play, rewarding an artist after the fact if the work pleased her.

In the later Middle Ages, when the gift-giving economy had given way to a system of monetary exchange, artists, if they were not members of the patron's household, were more frequently paid outright a price agreed upon in advance, with the patron reserving the right to reject the work if it was found unsuitable.[15] Although evidence suggests that some earlier writers received monetary "gifts" from the patron, these tended to be but token payments. No eleventh- or twelfth-century poet that we know of was able to support a household by the pen as was Christine de Pizan three centuries later. Although some poets may have buttered their bread by their talents, it was because they were taken into the patron's household and nurtured as a consequence of their ability to stimulate the courtly atmosphere or of the patron's love of song or story, but they do not seem to have been paid a particular sum for their literary work.

Just who were the women who sought to make their voices heard through their cultural patronage? The one medieval woman whose patronage has been extensively studied is Eleanor of Aquitaine. Groundbreaking work was done by such scholars as Rita Lejeune and René Labande in the 1950s, and a collection of symposium papers edited by William W. Kibler under the title *Eleanor of Aquitaine: Patron and Politician* represents what is probably the most comprehensive effort in the English language to bring together available information on the patronage of a powerful woman. Eleanor was certainly extraordinary in many respects, and, as Lejeune points out in her study on the influence of Queen Eleanor and her descendants,[16] she spawned an entire generation of literary patrons. However, as Margaret Schaus and Susan Mosher Stuard note in a recent bibliographical essay, "powerful women like Eleanor of Aquitaine . . . were often treated as anomalies whose achievements could reveal nothing about female agency and influence in general."[17]

The present volume does not include an article on Eleanor of Aquitaine. Its intent is rather to provide a context for such "anomalies," to determine, in fact, whether their accomplishments within the domain of cultural patronage are truly unique or whether they fit into a broader or even a typical context of women's contributions. There is little question that Eleanor was extraordinary in the political arena. Her unique role as queen of two kings, her longevity of eighty-one years, her exceptional good health and energy, and her irrepressible interest in politics were sufficient to assure the special place that she holds in medieval history. But was she extraordinary insofar as her patronage was concerned? While her cultural influence may have been far-reaching, was she in fact an anomaly or did she merely do what was expected of any woman of wealth and cultured background?[18] With the systematic study of the contributions of a wider sampling of female patrons we can begin to evaluate in a more realistic way the cultural legacy of such a remarkable woman as Eleanor of Aquitaine.

Women who practiced patronage tended to be, like Eleanor, women of means and relative independence who could control their own fortunes to a significant extent. They had the resources or the prestige to commission or command artists or writers to create for them beautiful works. Most were of the nobility, although toward the end of the Middle Ages some wealthy bourgeois women also had the means to engage in patronage. Most frequently, important female patrons were widows who had gained control of their dower properties; sometimes they were regents for their minor children and, as such, held temporary control over the financial affairs of the territory under their supervision; sometimes they were women of the church, abbesses, nuns, or wealthy noblewomen who for a variety of reasons had retired to a convent.

Relatively few married women were able, like Eleanor, to assert their individual influence through cultural patronage without the assistance of their husbands. There were, however, notable exceptions. One who, despite being twice married, ruled in her own right and thereby controlled her own fortune even during the lifetime of her husbands was Viscountess Ermengarde de Narbonne, one of the few female patrons of the troubadour poets. Despite her marriages, she nonetheless maintained authority over her own lands, personally administering justice and participating in various political struggles, both to quell her rebellious vassals and to maintain her political sovereignty in the face of repeated attempts by the counts of Toulouse, Alphonse I and later his son Raymond, to seize control of the *vicomté*, initially under the guise of "protecting" Ermengarde during her minority.[19] The territories she had inherited from her father, Aymeri II, remained under her supervision for nearly fifty years.[20] With such freedom and authority, she chose to devote some of her resources to cultural activities. While she bestowed generous patronage on various religious organizations in her region, among them the Abbey of Silvanès, it was her interest in the secular lyric that best assured her reputation as a cultural patron.[21] Her protection of the troubadour Peire Rogier is attested to in some detail by his *vida* as well as by six of his nine extant poems in which he addresses her under the *senhal* of *Tort-n'avetz*. He makes it clear in one of these, "Per far esbaudir mos vezis" that it was she who encouraged him to sing.[22] The *vida* of Sail d'Escola indicates that he, too, was a poet welcomed at the court of one "N'Ainermada de Nerbona," a name generally recognized as a garbled rendering of that of Ermengarde. She was evidently widely recognized as a significant patron of the poetic arts, for a number of other poets seem to address her in their works, among them Bernard de Ventadorn, Giraut de Bornelh, Peire d'Alvernhe, and the trobairitz Azalaïs de Porcairagues.[23] Ermengarde's reputation may well have spread beyond her native Provence, for the Viking tale the *Orkneyinga Saga* recounts a stopover of a fleet of ships led by Earl Rognvald journeying to Galicia in Spain at a seaport called Nerbon ruled by a lady named Ermingerda. She greeted them with "lavish hospitality," and during their stay her visitors, apparently aware of her love of the troubadour lyric, entertained the court with love songs in her honor.[24]

Married women, however, rarely had the personal control of such large resources as those that were at Ermengarde's and Eleanor's disposal. Laws in the south of France at the time were more favorable to women's inheritance and agency than they were in most other regions and gave such women a decided advantage.[25] More frequently, however, and in other areas such as Germany or the northern French *pays des coutumes*, wives were compelled to rely on their influence over their husbands in order to provide patronage to others, for they were by law unable to act independently.[26] Thus, their patterns of patronage are inevitably different from those of more independent widows or nuns. Married women are most often included in joint husband-wife patronage acts such as commissions of literary works or donations to religious institutions. Although these commissions or gifts may have been attributed to both parties (or sometimes to the husband alone), the wife, as legal co-actor, was, not infrequently, the driving force behind them, especially those involving the foundation of convents.[27] For example, although scholars generally note that the Saxon convent at Gandersheim was founded in 852 by Duke Liudulf, Hrotsvit makes it quite clear in her history of the convent, *Primordia Coenobii Gandeshemensis*, that, although Liudulf and his son Otto may have paid the bills, it was his mother-in-law, Aeda, and his wife, Oda, who were in truth responsible for its founding. According to Hrotsvit's account, John the Baptist appeared to Aeda in a vision announcing that "your illustrious descendant shall found a cloister for saintly virgins."[28] It was her daughter Oda who enacted the prophecy of her mother's vision to build the convent. Fortunately, Oda's husband, Liudulf, was "in harmonious agreement" ("consensuque suae dilectae coniuges Odae") with his wife, giving the necessary orders and providing the means that made it possible.

Another case in point was the founding of the Cistercian convent at Trebnitz in 1202 by Hedwig of Silesia and her husband, Duke Henry I, who together endowed five religious institutions. It is described by Jeffrey Hamburger both as "the oldest foundation for monastic women in Silesia" and as "the staging point for the expansion of the.Cistercian order into eastern Europe."[29] The copy of the *Legenda maior*, which recounts both the patronage and the piety of Hedwig that led to her canonization in 1267, contains drawings that clearly depict *her* as the patron overseeing the convent's construction. The caption accompanying the image tells us that Hedwig *"prevailed on her husband* to build from his own means a monastery for Cistercian nuns at Trebnitz," and the legend notes that *"on the advice of his wife, the holy Hedwig,* Duke Henry richly endowed the monastery when it was completed and provided it with revenues sufficient for the support of one thousand persons and for the ongoing management of a hospice and hospital."[30]

Like Hedwig, Queen Sancia of Naples, who with her husband, Robert the Wise, endowed the construction of the Church of Santa Chiara in 1310, was clearly the impetus behind the project, which resulted in significant building and art patronage.[31] Her spiritual devotion to the Franciscans was well attested in her own times.[32] She has been described as the order's "mater, soror, protectrix, patrona et auxiliatrix." In fact, she openly claimed her role as mother of the Franciscans in a letter to the General Chapter of Assisi in 1334 written in her own hand and signed with her secret seal: "Although I am not worthy on my own, nevertheless through the grace of God I can be called the true mother of the order of blessed Francis, not only in word or writing, but by works that I have performed continuously and that I intend to do with his help all the days of my life" [Licet ego non sim digna ex me, tamen per gratiam Dei ego multipliciter possum dici vera mater Ordinis beati Francisci, non solum verbo vel scripto, sed operibus, quae feci continue et intendo facere cum adiutorio suo toto tempore vitae meae].[33]

More typically, women did not engage in significant independent programs of patronage until after their husbands' deaths, for only then did most control their own fates and fortunes. An Angevin charter describes the widespread legal status enjoyed only by widows, by which a female donor would be "constituted in widowhood and in unrestricted power" [in viduitate et in libera potestate constituta].[34] As Robert Hadju has described the widow's status, she was "emancipated from the legal tutelage of a male for the first time,"[35] and many women took full advantage of it.

Patronage early in a woman's widowhood usually came about quite naturally, even predictably, in the form of efforts to honor her deceased husband or aggrandize her family by preserving a record of their past deeds, thereby enhancing the reputations of her minor children, who, without a father to see to their rights and futures, could otherwise be politically disadvantaged. As we shall see below, Blanche de Navarre, Gertrude of Brunswick, and Queen

Fig. 1. Saint Radegund. Poitiers, Bibliothèque Municipale. MS 250, fol. 43v. By permission of the Centre d'études supérieures de civilisation médiévale.

Emma of England were all women who undertook patronage for such a reason. A second reason for the cultural patronage of widows was the need for solace or spiritual comfort and for the salvation of her husband's soul, assurance of which frequently took the form of endowments and embellishments to religious institutions or support for the composition of religious texts. Yet another factor was the need for cultural diversion, which was often greater during the lonely time of widowhood and provided a means of surrounding the widow with interesting, creative people. Most important, however, she had, often for the first time in her life, fiscal resources at her disposal adequate to undertake such projects.

A third group consists of holy women, nuns, abbesses, and even recluses, many of whom played a significant role as literary and artistic patrons as well, particularly in the encouragement of religious works, such as hagiographic texts, books of hours and other devotional manuals, or artifacts suitable for use in the contemplative life. It was the only way by which women other than widows might obtain some degree of autonomy free from the direct custody of a male figure. One of the earliest of these holy women to make a reputation for herself as an important patron was Queen Radegund (see figure 1), the so-called "Mother of France," who left her brutal husband, Clothar, to become a nun and found the Abbey of Sainte-Croix in Poitiers. It is important to note that in her letter of foundation to the bishops she indicated that her goal in establishing the abbey was to benefit other women. "I asked myself, with all the ardour of which I am capable, how I could best forward the cause of other women, and how, if our Lord so willed, my own personal desires might be of advantage to my sisters."[36] Once settled there, she used her influence and what Jo Ann McNamara has called "the bounty of her royal fortune"[37] both to encourage the writing of Venantius Fortunatus (see figure 2), who would later become bishop of Poitiers, and to give continued support to her convent. With her considerable resources, to which Fortunatus himself has attested in his *De vita Sanctae Radegundis*, she provided an abundance of daily banquets and generosity to all who presented themselves at Sainte-Croix.[38] Yet her specific encouragement of Fortunatus and his poems, many of which tell of his

Fig. 2. Fortunatus. Poitiers, Bibliothèque Municipale. MS 250, fol. 21v. By permission of the Centre d'études supérieures de civilisation médiévale.

love, presumably spiritual in nature, for Radegund and her protégée Agnes, the first abbess of Sainte-Croix, appears to have taken the form of friendship, small gifts of food, or personal tokens, rather than the bounteous monetary payments that later queens would bestow.[39] Along with her encouragement of Fortunatus and her maintenance to the fledgling convent, Radegund's bounty was also used to enrich Sainte-Croix with "a store of world-famous relics."[40] At her death Gregory of Tours reports that some two hundred grieving nuns wept for the loss not only of the Blessed Radegund but also for the source of the gold and silver she had represented to the monastery.[41]

The case of Queen (and later Saint) Radegund is significant, for it demonstrates that women in this period who had not found freedom for such generosity through the benevolence of their husbands could sometimes do so within the female world behind convent walls. Even though "the *cura monialium* was designed to ensure that women and the images produced for them were anchored to systems governed by men,"[42] wealthy women who came to the convent to find a place of refuge were afforded not only protection but also a greater degree of liberty to make their own decisions. At least they were freed from the kinds of constraints that Radegund had experienced in her roles as wife and queen. It is, therefore, not surprising that many women, among them those who found themselves in difficult domestic situations as well as those who were widowed, elected to enter the convent.

Following in the footsteps of Radegund was the seventh-century abbess Dedimia at Sainte-Croix, who encouraged the nun Baudonivia to write a second *De vita Sanctae Radegundis* to fill some of the gaps that she felt Fortunatus had left in his own account of Radegund's life.[43] Without the encouragement and permission of Dedimia, Baudonivia, who constantly apologizes for her stylistic and personal shortcomings ("Baudonivia, humilis omnium . . . pusillanimis . . . parven habens intelligentiae eloquium . . . minima omnium minimarum . . . non polito sed rustico"),[44] would never have been bold enough to undertake the task. We cannot assume that Dedimia's patronage took any other form than encouragement and permission for Baudonivia to free herself from other tasks in order to write. Nevertheless, without the support, and above all permission, of their abbesses, as representatives of the convent that functions as corporate patron, no nuns would have written saints' lives or illuminated manuscripts. Holy women who played the role of cultural patrons are numerous, including the abbess Gerberga II, the mentor and patron of Hrotsvit who charged her to write the *Gesta Ottonis*; Hildegard of Bingen, abbess of the Benedictine convent at Bingen-am-Rhein and a writer, composer, and artist herself, who was patron of Elisabeth of Schönau;[45] and Hild, the abbess of Whitby, whom Bede credits with having encouraged Caedmon to write "in his own English tongue."[46]

Female patrons in the convent were not, of course, always abbesses. Despite the rules of any specific monastic order against owning private property, it seems to have been acceptable in some convents for individual nuns to acquire books or art objects suitable for contemplative purposes, for evidence exists to indicate that nuns sometimes used whatever resources they had to commission books, reliquaries, crosses, and the like. Hamburger cites the example of Heluis d'Ecouffans, a nun at the Benedictine convent of Sainte-Benoîte-d'Origny in northern France, who in 1312 commissioned the *Vie de Sainte Benoîte* (Berlin, Kupferstichkabinett, MS 78 B16). The next to the last miniature in the manuscript depicts Heluis kneeling at the altar in supplication for herself and her community. The manuscript is "a liturgical handbook for the 'trésorière,' or keeper of the treasury, probably none other than Heluis herself," Hamburger surmises, and, as such, it is "both the product and a record of her patronage."[47] He also cites the examples of Jeanne Bernard and Jeanne de la Poterne the Younger, nuns at the Franciscan abbey of Longchamp,[48] who purchased golden reliquaries to contain relics of Saint Cecilia and Saint Martin. The only condition placed on such patronage was apparently that "sacred objects not leave the convent except under the most pressing circumstances, and that proceeds remain within the community."[49]

These patterns of female patronage by which widows and nuns seem to have had more freedom in patronizing artists are clearly reflected in an interesting late Italian document. The *Ricordanze* of Neri di Bicci, a fifteenth-century Florentine artist,[50] is an extensive and detailed record of the artist's business transactions from 1453 to 1475. Neri's patrons listed in the work include 183 men and 20 women. Ten of the female patrons are nuns; 7 are widows; only 1 is identified as a married woman, and 2 are presumably single. The single women are involved in joint commissions with men, and both they and the married woman have male guarantors. Although one must be somewhat cautious in dealing with the *Ricordanze,* for it is a late document and deals only with the work of a single artist, it nonetheless substantiates patterns that are well evident in the data of the earlier periods.

Despite such evidence, we must not dismiss too quickly the majority of married women as patrons and promoters of culture. Their patronage sometimes follows a different and more indirect pattern than that of widows, nuns, and men. Because of the legal status of married women and the husband's control in most cases over both his property and hers, the probability was far greater that *her* patronage would be recorded in acts of donation as *their* or

simply *his* patronage. By virtue of being the guarantor or payer of the financial commitment, the husband's name inevitably became attached to the work
and sometimes no doubt *replaced* that of the wife, who may have been the real
force behind the project. Nevertheless, though many of their names may be
forgotten, married women who did not control their own finances often found
ways to further the projects to which they wished to lend their support.

Although financial resources are critical in determining which women engaged in patronage, wealth alone can explain the penchant for patronage only
in part. A second factor, which is of equal if not greater importance, is the value
the women's family placed on education and a cultural legacy. Women who
engaged in important patronage, particularly of literary works, almost always
came from cultured backgrounds where learning was valued and where encouragement and support of the arts was a familial expectation. Some wealthy
families made only paltry contributions to our cultural heritage, engaging not
at all in secular patronage and making only routine and token donations to
religious establishments.

Matrilineal paradigms of patronage, as scholars both in this volume and
elsewhere have noted, were exceedingly important.[51] That her mother had
patronized writers and artists provided a particularly strong incentive for a
daughter to do so. Such matrilineal patronage, however, fits within the broader
spectrum of social and cultural expectations in the family as a whole. The tradition could also be passed from father to daughter, from husband to wife, or
from brother to sister, just as a woman, in turn, could influence her husband
or her son to engage in cultural patronage. Dhuoda, the ninth-century duchess
of Septimania, an educated woman herself, reminded her son in her manual
of advice, the *Liber manualis*, not to be reluctant "among your worldly cares
to acquire for yourself a great many volumes of books" [Admoneo te etiam, o
mi fili Wilhelme pulchre et amabilis, ut inter mundanas saeculi curas, plurima
volumina librorum tibi acquiri non pigeas].[52] Likewise, other women were
conscious of passing their cultural traditions on to their children, regardless of
the interest and abilities of their husbands.

Such was the case with Gisela, the wife of Conrad II (990–1039), the first
emperor of the Salian dynasty. She was a well-educated woman who found
herself wedded to an illiterate man. Despite her husband's limitations Gisela
encouraged at their court the traditions of her own family rather than those
of Conrad. She commissioned copies of Notker's German translations of the
Psalms and the book of Job for her own use.[53] She also made certain that her
son Henry III was provided not only with a good education, as befitted a mon-
arch and a future patron of literature, but also with a wife whose intellectual

heritage would match his own. His bride, Agnes of Poitou, daughter of Guillaume V of Aquitaine, came from a family known for its rich and cultured background, and both were subsequently recognized as cultural patrons of the first order. John the Poor, abbot of Fécamp, wrote for Agnes's edification his *De contemplatione* so that she might perceive there a "normam bien vivendi," a pattern for living well.[54] She was sufficiently schooled to correspond with such cultured men as Peter Damian and Albert of Fructuaria. Also written for her was the now lost *Libellus Agnetis imperatricis*, by the Anonymous Haserensis, but to the existence of which the author himself attests in his *De episcopis Eichstentensibus*.[55] Arnulf dedicates his *Delicie cleri* to both Henry and Agnes.[56]

Another such case was that of Saint Margaret, the wife of Malcolm III of Scotland and the mother of Queen Matilda. Although she was well educated, enjoyed books, and was able to engage in subtle and intelligent discourse with the most learned men in her entourage, her husband was unable to read.[57] Women like Agnes and Gisela often found themselves in positions of being what Susan Groag Bell has called "cultural ambassadors."[58] Sent from the court of their parents to that of a betrothed, often in a distant land, noble women were among the best possible disseminators of culture. From their homeland they brought stories and songs, an awareness of styles of architecture, gold work, and manuscript illumination, and sometimes an entourage that included craftsmen and artists capable of executing fine works at the lady's request.

It was in such a manner that the daughters of Eleanor of Aquitaine took into courts in France, Spain, and Germany the Arthurian materials that Eleanor had encountered in England as well as the *fin'amors* that originated in her native Aquitaine. Her eldest daughter, Marie de Champagne, ensured her place in literary history as the patron of Chrétien de Troyes, the first writer to use the Arthurian materials on the continent and to infuse them with the champenois version of *fine amor*. Marie was not the only one of Eleanor's daughters who disseminated these materials. Her half-sister Matilda of Saxony is acknowledged by her husband's biographer as having been responsible for introducing into Henry the Lion's circle "the new style of courtly poetry" that "led to the composition, after French models, of two major poems that are among the first specimens of the early courtly epic to have originated on German soil": Konrad's *Rolandslied* and Eilhart von Oberg's *Tristant und Isalde*.[59] Similarly, the court of their sister Leonor of England and her husband, Alfonso VIII of Castile, was known as a haven for troubadours. The *vida* of Peire Rogier indicates that, when he left the city of Narbonne and the protection of Viscountess Ermengarde, he went first to the court of Raimbaut d'Aurenga and then to that of Alfonso of Castile, where he was no doubt welcomed with hospitality by Leonor and her husband.[60] She is also said to have hosted Guiraut de Calanso, the Gasconese troubadour who composed a now-lost *Lansolet* and demonstrated his awareness of Arthurian materials in a lament written at the death of Leonor's son Fernando in 1211.[61] Such "cultural ambassadorship" may merely have been an attempt by young women who found themselves in an alien environment to render it more familiar and to their liking. Nonetheless, it had the effect of contributing to an increasingly homogeneous culture throughout western Europe.

Patronage was typically a social expectation of important noble dynasties, as is evidenced by the family of Emma of Normandy, queen of England from 1002 to 1035, who learned well that it could also be used for political ends. The Norman dukes became a major political force with the concomitant expectation of cultural patronage during the reign of her father, Richard I, but according to Lucien Musset, it was his son Richard II (996–1026) who became the "true initiator of a large-scale patronage program" [véritable initiateur d'un mécénat de grande échelle].[62] Emma was not to be left behind in this emerging familial tradition in which patronage would be "envisaged as a means of displaying their success within their lands and of affirming their prestige abroad" [envisagé comme un moyen d'étaler leur réussite à l'intérieur de leur état et d'affirmer leur prestige à l'extérieur].[63] Political rivalry drove her to compete with her brother Richard, particularly in her generosity to religious sanctuaries on the Continent. For example, she is known to have sent to her brother Robert, archbishop of Rouen, a splendid illuminated psalter which eventually became a part of the library of the Abbey of Saint-Evroul,[64] and she aided in the reconstruction of Saint-Hilaire-le-Grand in Poitiers, providing an architect, one Gautier Coorland, to assist in the building program.[65]

Her most obvious use of patronage for political ends, however, was the commissioning of the *Encomium Emmae Reginae*. Emma had been first the wife of King Aethelred, after whose death in 1016 she married Cnut, the son of a long-standing enemy whose invasions had briefly forced Emma, Aethelred, and their sons into refuge in her homeland of Normandy. It was a political marriage for Cnut, designed to gain favor with Emma's brother Richard II of Normandy.[66] After Cnut's death in 1035, a struggle for the throne ensued between Harthacnut, Cnut's eldest son by Emma, and Harold Harefoot, his son by a previous liaison. Emma, forced again into exile, commissioned the *Encomium*, which is widely interpreted as a propaganda piece composed after the death of Harold in 1040 to establish the claims of Harthacnut over those of his elder half-brother Edward, Emma's son by Aethelred.[67] When Harthacnut did eventually come to the throne, in a gesture of familial harmony he designated Edward as his heir. Upon Edward's ascension to the throne, however, he apparently took revenge on his mother by seizing her lands. Although some have questioned Emma's political motives in sponsoring the work, the timing and content, as well as Edward's behavior toward his mother, seem to justify no other equally plausible interpretation.[68] In short, for Emma, patronage was both a dynastic responsibility and an occasional political tool.

Women's reasons for engaging in cultural patronage are as varied as the women themselves; one can, however, discern certain recurring patterns. It was, as Emma's example shows, a means by which disempowered but determined women could articulate clear and well-defined political agendas. Although overt efforts to assert political authority were more often than not met with staunch resistance from men,[69] cultural authority remained a realm open to women, a socially sanctioned way for them to activate their quest for power. On the surface it seemed harmless enough, yet hidden behind the innocuous façade of a promotion of the arts were often serious and determined political goals. Two of those who had similar objectives and techniques, albeit widely separated in time and geography, were the eleventh-century Countess Gertrude of Brunswick and the thirteenth-century countess of Champagne, Blanche de Navarre. Both women commissioned artifacts, a portable altar in the case of Countess Gertrude and her husband's tomb in the case of Countess Blanche, that bear purportedly religious images but contain not-so-subtle political messages. In a study of Countess Gertrude's altar, conserved in the Museum of Cleveland along with various other treasures of the Welf family, Patrick Courbet demonstrates that the artifact underscores the nobility of the counts of Brunswick, connecting it by its iconography with a glorification of the empire and the royal house and underscoring several themes of Salian ideology.[70] Courbet contends that the altar reveals "the latent hopes of the lineage, ready, if the occasion presents itself, to transform themselves into demands. It is the promise of a future capable of leading them to the highest destinies" [les espérences latente du lignage, prêtes, si l'occasion se présente, à se transformer en revendications. Il est promesse d'un futur susceptible de les conduire aux plus hautes destinées].[71] The claims to the throne of the empire, which the altar images express, would manifest themselves in political conflict not too many years later when Gertrude's grandson Egbert II would try to seize the throne from his cousin Henry IV. And her great-grandson Henry the Lion, whose estates centered in Brunswick, became the well-known rival of Frederick Barbarossa.

Similarly, Blanche de Navarre had erected at Saint-Etienne de Troyes a magnificent enameled bronze tomb for her husband, Thibaut III de Champagne. Unfortunately, the tomb did not survive the French Revolution, but Jean Hugot, writing in 1704, has left a detailed description of it.[72] Like the artwork on Gertrude's altar, the tomb commissioned by Blanche expressed the political ambitions and unfulfilled pretensions presumably of her husband, but it was certainly reflective of Blanche's own ambitions for her son. Rare in its extensive collection of silver images representing family figures that decorated its four sides, the tomb is a clear political statement on the part of Blanche de Navarre of her son's connections to four crowns: that of France, where his great-uncle Philip Augustus reigned; that of England, where his great-uncle John sat on the throne; that of Jerusalem, which had been held by his uncle Henri de Champagne and to which he would, in fact, eventually lay claim in opposition to the rights of his female cousins; and, finally, that of Navarre, the one crown Blanche's son Thibaut IV would, in fact, inherit.[73]

While political goals were sometimes an important motive for women's patronage, works were also commissioned for more personal reasons. Queen Matilda, first wife of Henry I of England, had been reared, somewhat unhappily, by an aunt at the convent of Wilton and orphaned prior to her marriage. When commissioned to write the *Life of Saint Margaret*, a biography of her mother, the author of the piece, probably Turgot, suggests that her motives were largely personal ones: "You desire not only to hear of the queen your mother . . . but also to have it constantly before you in writing: so that although you knew but little of your mother's face, you may have more fully the knowledge of her virtues" [non solum audire, sed etiam litteris impressam desideratis iugiter inspicere; ut quae faciem matris parum noveratis, virtutum eius notitiam plenius habeatis].[74] The work also served the practical purpose of setting forth and praising the lineage of the queen.[75]

Marie de Champagne's cultural contributions provide us with another example of a patronage program that seems to have had a more personal agenda. Her important patronage did not begin until after her husband departed on crusade in 1179. During this time and her subsequent widowhood, she encountered various problems because of her sex, exemplified by her difficulty in collecting tolls that had been paid without complaint during her husband's lifetime and in enforcing the marriage agreements that Henri had made for their children.[76] Perhaps because of these, she seems to have taken a special interest in sponsoring works that enhanced the power or reputation of women. Chrétien de Troyes attests to the collaborative effort of patron and poet, claiming that he is merely elaborating the basic material (*matière*) and the interpretation (*sens*) that she wishes to have expressed. She was not a passive patron but one who participated in the artistic process, imposing her will upon the poet. An examination of other works she sponsored will bear that out. The subservient role of the male lover, his love service to the queen, and the propulsion of the action by female characters all suggest Marie's attitudes about women's worth, which I have explored elsewhere in greater detail.[77]

A concern for the status and reputation of women is evident even in the religious literature she sponsored during her widowhood. For example, not long before her death she commissioned a translation of the book of Genesis by Evrat, a clerk at the Church of Saint-Etienne, which adjoined her palace in Troyes. Even in this book, which contains the story of Eve, the primordial negative model for medieval women, Marie seems to have been determined to see women depicted favorably. Frances Henderson, who has studied the work in depth, concludes that there were two basic versions of the poem. "Most conspicuous is the first version's bitter misogyny, which gives way in the second version to positive praise of womankind."[78] Of the revised version, which contains "a burst of feminism unusual in medieval literature" (69), Henderson concludes that the change in tone must result from Marie's influence. Evrat himself seems to attest to her concern for the reputation of women in this remarkable passage:

A li doivent prendre exemplaire
Totes les dames ki or vivent,
Car de li tuit bien se derivent.
Totes sunt par li honorees
Les altres, c'a grans demorees
Venist honors en lor pooir
Mais ceste les a fait seoir
En lor delivre poeste.
Ceste a le malvaiz blasme oste
Des altres dames par le munde,
Si ki granz honors lor habunde.[79]

[All women now living should take her as an example, for from her all good things are derived. All other women are honored by her. Honor was delayed in coming into their power, but she has caused it to reside there and gives strength to them. She has taken away the wicked blame the world bestows on other women, so that great honor abounds in them.]

Patronage may have been a socially acceptable way for women to assert power, but it was not without obstacles. Women faced the inevitable double standard and were sometimes castigated for excessive generosity as patrons. Although generosity was considered a great medieval virtue in men, it could quickly be interpreted as prodigality in women, even in a dynasty with strong traditions of patronage. Marie de Champagne was one such case. Even though, ironically, she had been married to a man who was so well known and admired for his generosity that he was called Henri le Libéral, the author of the *Eructavit* chides her for "largece et li hauz despans" [generosity and great expenditures].[80] He does not specifically mention that she overspent in rewarding the writers at her court, but if the translator in question was Adam de Perseigne, as T. Atkinson Jenkins thought, he was known to have had outspoken views on excessive luxury and lavish gifts to minstrels at the expense of the poor. It *is* generally recognized that the writer of the work was a Cistercian, a member of an order that typically condemned such "excess."

William of Malmesbury does not tiptoe around the issue in his vivid description of the patronage of Queen Matilda: "Erat ei in audiendo servitio Dei voluptas unica ideoque in clericos bene melodos inconsiderate provida; blande quoscumque alloqui, multa largiri, plura polliceri. Inde, liberalitate ipsius per orbem sata, turmatim huc adventabant scholastici tum cantibus tum versibus famosi; felicemque se putabat qui carminis novitate aures mulceret dominae. Nec in his solum expensas conferebat, sed etiam omni generi hominum, praesertim advenarum: qui, muneribus acceptis, famam ejus longe per terras venditarent."[81] [Her one love was of hearing divine service; and therefore she *recklessly* provided for sweet-singing clerks, speaking well of them all, making generous gifts, promising more. Thence, as news of her liberality spread world-wide, clerks famed in song and poetry flocked thither; he who charmed the queen's ears with the novelty of song considered himself lucky. She contributed payment not only to these, but also to all kinds of men, especially foreigners: so that, having accepted the rewards, they might sing her praises in all lands.][82] He clearly disapproves of what he calls her "lust for glory" (*cupiditas gloriae*), contending that it created hardships for her dependents.

In addition to political and personal agendas, women also engaged in patronage for religious reasons. They sought spiritual guidance in their books of hours, saints' lives, and religious treatises, and they sought to ensure the salvation of their souls or the souls of those they loved through good works and generosity to the church. Sometimes they promoted a particular institution or embraced a religious movement through support of its works. Although religion played an important role for medieval women throughout their lives, the devotion reflected in their patronage activities often became stronger with age. Women who in their younger days may have commissioned secular works would frequently turn to religious texts as they grew older and after they had suffered losses in their lives. For example, we see Mahaut, the fourteenth-century countess of Artois, ordering books of history and romance in her younger days, but after the death of her only son in 1316 she turned to commissioning books on religion and meditative philosophy, biblical translations, saints' lives, books of hours, and a French translation of Boethius's *Consolation of Philosophy*.[83] The patronage of Marie de Champagne followed a similar pattern, with secular patronage predating her husband's death in 1181 and sponsorship of religious literature coming after.

The Virgin Mary was, without question, the most popular figure to whom women dedicated churches, abbeys, or chapels and whom they accepted as the ideal model for the aspirations of noble women. Typical of their devotion is Catherine of Cleves's Book of Hours (ca. 1430), where, in one manuscript illumination, Catherine herself stands with the Virgin Mary, one on either side of the cross. The Virgin's breast flows with milk, "reminding Catherine of her expected duty as a merciful and chaste mother."[84] Judith of Flanders also had herself depicted in an eleventh-century book of Evangiles in place of Mary Magdelene, at the foot of the cross.[85] The articles of both Shadis and Jambeck in this volume underscore women's particular devotion to the Virgin, and examples abound in literature, art, and architecture.[86]

The religious fervor of women with its concomitant patronage to ecclesiastical or monastic institutions and for personal devotion was, however, by no means limited to the figure of the Virgin Mary. The lives of other female saints also drew their special attention. Although women sometimes sponsored the composition of male saints' lives, it was female hagiography that both secular and religious women favored. Typical of this phenomenon is the *Vie de Sainte Marthe* composed by Wauchier de Denain for Jeanne of Flanders after 1210.[87] Religious patrons tended to prefer the lives of female saints who were of special importance to their orders or their convents. One example is that of the abbess of Nazareth, located in the region of Antwerp, who about 1275 commissioned an unknown author, probably a monk from Saint Bernard's Abbey in nearby Hemiksem, to compose a biography of Beatrice of Nazareth, a former prioress at the convent and a well-known mystic. The author, identifying himself in the text only as a chaplain to the abbey, is possibly Fulgerius, who served off and on for thirty years as chaplain to the convent at Nazareth. He based his Latin *Vita Beatricis* on Beatrice's now-lost vernacular autobiography.[88] Such hagiographic texts which portrayed the lives of strong and devout women of courage and conviction were particularly important in providing models for medieval women.

In terms of their religious patronage, women also contributed significantly to the establishment and enrichment of churches and monasteries, particularly female monastic houses. Like Radegund and Hedwig of Silesia, those who founded convents recognized the special need for monastic establishments to house increasing numbers of women who chose the medieval ideal of virginity or who required a place to retire during widowhood or refuge from misfortunes in marriage. Another early example, pointed out by Suzanne Wemple, is the northern Italian Benedictine monastery of Saint Salvatore (or Saint Giulia) in Brescia, founded for female monastics in the mid-eighth century by Ansa, queen of the Lombards, and richly endowed by Ansa, her husband, Desiderius, and her son Adelchis, who gave "sacred vases and mantles, all things that pertain to the ministry of the altar, . . . gold, silver, bronze, iron, wood, and earthen vessels," along with such essential endowments as buildings, vineyards, and pasture lands.[89] By the same token, Agnes of Prague in 1231 founded the convent of Saint Francis, said to be "the earliest Gothic structure in Prague,"[90] thus bringing both a new architectural style and the new order of the Poor Clares into eastern Europe. Agnes herself entered the order on 11 July 1234 and engaged in an extended correspondence with its founder, Clare of Assisi, the only woman ever to have written a female monastic rule that was officially approved by the pope.[91]

Another significant motive for women's patronage was a desire for knowledge and the need to provide learning materials for their children, as Susan Groag Bell so well demonstrates in her important study of women book owners in the Middle Ages. One such work was Vincent de Beauvais's *De eruditione filiorum nobilium*, composed between 1247 and 1249 at the request of Marguerite de Provence, wife of Louis IX of France and mother of two children, Louis and Isabelle. Marguerite clearly asserted her right to say what should be included within the book; for example, at her request Vincent de Beauvais wrote chapters that dealt particularly with the education of noble daughters.[92] Such books were frequently requested by noble mothers for their children. Anne of Brittany ordered a primer for her daughter Claude in 1505, when the child was six. It began with the alphabet, followed by "the Lord's Prayer, the creed, grace to be said before meals, the story of the creation, and other short details from the New Testament."[93] Similarly, Blanche of Castile commissioned a psalter, currently in the Morgan Library, as a reading primer for her son, the future Louis IX.[94] Isabeau of Bavaria ordered the preparation of a small illuminated book of hours for her seven-year-old daughter, Jeanne, in 1398 and an alphabet Psalter for another daughter, Michelle, in 1403, just before her eighth birthday.[95] She also acquired and in all likelihood used for the instruction of her own children a copy of Christine de Pizan's *Enseignements moraux*, written originally for the benefit of the author's son Jean.[96] Such women were interested, above all, in being good mothers and in using their wealth and power to assure their children's education. As Bell points out, "By commissioning books and by instructing children they were able to influence both artistic and ideological developments. The choice between an alphabet Psalter, a Gospel, a Book of Hours, or an educational treatise may indicate steps in the growth of the student reader or the commissioner."[97] There can be little question that in selecting the types of books their children read, and especially in influencing their content, these women were of tremendous importance in molding future leaders and generations to come.

Finally, the social responsibility to provide entertainment for the court must not be excluded as a major motive for female patronage, particularly for the support and encouragement of writers, jongleurs, dancers, and singers. While there was unquestionably some overlap in the types of entertainment enjoyed by the two sexes, women, according to Dominica Legge, showed specific preference for certain types of literature.[98]

Epic belonged to the Great Hall, romance to what the French called the Chamber, the Anglo-Norman and English more often the Solar—the Bower of our ballads. One was chanted or recited to a large mixed assembly, the other read aloud to a small homogeneous company. The former was predominantly masculine, the other predominantly feminine. The romance did not begin to exist side by side with the epic until houses began to have several comfortable rooms built on to or near the Great Hall, and this coincided with the spread of refinement, physical and moral, from the South at the time of the Crusades.[99]

Legge associates love songs with the patronage of married women in the *chambre des dames*, and romances and lays with the inclusion of unmarried women. Such a hypothesis is difficult to test, for we have so little data on the women who populated the ladies' chambers at any given medieval court. That women enjoyed and sponsored the genres in question, however, is undeniable. Along with Ermengarde de Narbonne's support for the troubadour *canso* and that of Marie de Champagne for the romance, we may also cite the patronage of the latter's sister Alix de Blois for the romance *Partonopeu de Blois* and that of Marie de Brabant for both the *Enfances Ogier* and for Adenet le Roi's *Cleo-*

madés.[100] Nevertheless, despite the fact that women doubtless enjoyed these genres, Legge's generic assessment is unquestionably oversimplified. Men enjoyed them too and were patrons of romance writers. Interestingly enough, the best-known writer of *lais*, Marie de France, dedicated her work not to a woman but to a "noble king," most likely Henry II. On the other hand, some women took pleasure in the epic poems traditionally associated with men, as Robert de Greatham, writing for "sa trechere dame, Aline," attests, noting that she delighted in hearing, reading, and even sometimes committing to memory "Chancon de geste e d'estoire."[101] Nonetheless, Legge is, no doubt, generally correct in assuming that some genres, among them the *lais*, were especially enjoyed by women, while men tended to prefer others. She is supported in that assumption by Marie de France's contemporary Denis Piramus, author of the *Vie seint Edmund le Rei*:

> Les lais solent as dames pleire,
> De joie les oient e de gré,
> Qu'il sunt sulum lur volenté.
> Li rei, li prince e li courtur,
> Cunte, barun e vavasur
> Aiment cuntes, chanceuns e fables
> E bons diz, qui sunt dilitables.[102]

> [The *lais* most usually please women;
> with joy they hear them willingly
> for they are in accordance with their desire.
> Kings, princes, courtiers,
> counts, barons, and vavasseurs
> like tales, songs, and fables
> and good verses which are amusing.]

The issue of women's social responsibility for providing entertainment for their courts in the form of story and song is an interesting one that deserves greater attention from scholars. What was appropriate for courtly diversions was, in fact, a question of some debate in the Middle Ages. The writer of a prose translation of the *Vies des Pères*, composed for Blanche de Navarre sometime between 1199 and 1229, takes on the issue with gusto (ironically in a rhymed prologue to the work), cautioning the countess against the lies of rhymed fiction, particularly in the form of romances:

> Si font les mençonges rimer
> Et les paroles alimer

Pour les cuers mielz enrooillier
Et pour honesté avillier.
Dame, de ce n'avez vos cure:
De mençonge qui cuers oscure,
Corrompent la clarté de l'ame,
N'en aiez cure, douce dame.
Leissiez Cligès et Perceval,
Qui les cuers tue et met a mal,
Et les romanz de vanité;
Assez trouverez vérité.
Jeroimes dit que cuers entiers
N'ot pas mençonge volentiers.
Toute mençonge Dieu desplest;
Et ce que Dieu het, si vous plest,
C'est granz maux et grant vilenie.[103]

[Thus, they cause lies to rhyme and join together words to harden hearts
and scorn honesty. Lady, you do not care for this: they corrupt the bright-
ness of the soul with a lie that darkens the heart. Do not give protection to
them, sweet lady. Put aside *Cligès* and *Perceval* and the shallow romances;
which destroy hearts and set one to evil. You will find much truth. Jerome
says that the pure heart does not willingly listen to lies. Every lie displeases
God; and if something pleases you that God detests, it is great evil and
great villainy.]

Fortunately for the development of secular literature, such caveats were ignored at a good number of medieval courts, which continued to be amused by
a variety of genres, rhymed and otherwise.

To sum up, women's motives for patronage included the assertion of political and personal agendas, religious concerns, education for themselves and
their children, and courtly diversion. Their thirst for works in the vernacular,
which they could read more easily, may initially have marginalized them in
terms of Latinate literature, but ultimately it was to give them extraordinary
power in the shaping of the secular culture of the High and late Middle Ages.
Because they were less concerned with Latin traditions, women were at the
forefront in supporting the development of new vernacular genres. As Legge
points out, the "first extant poem which can be regarded as the ancestor of the
courtly romance is *St. Brendan's Voyage*, written by Benedeit l'apostoïle for a
Queen of England [Queen Matilda, first wife of Henry I] in the first half of
the twelfth century."[104] While this is still a quasi-religious work, it opened

the generic door for more secular romances to follow. Marie de Champagne was the first known patron of an Arthurian romance. For Adeliza of Louvain, the second wife of Henry I of England, Philippe de Thaon wrote the first French bestiary between 1121 and 1135 (Oxford, Merton College, MS 249). Bestiaries went on to become what Xenia Muratova has called one of the "peculiar manifestations of the twelfth-century Renaissance," serving especially as "entertaining and moralizing reading for the royal ladies."[105] After the death of her husband in 1135, Adeliza also commissioned the first known historical work in the vernacular, a metrical history celebrating her husband's exploits, written by one David, as we learn from Geoffrey Gaimar, who refers to the work as a "chançon" with musical notation ("Le primer vers noter par chant," line 6492).[106]

It took a while longer for vernacular histories to become fashionable on the Continent, and again it was a woman who led the way. The earliest translation into the vernacular of the quasi-historical work the *Pseudo-Turpin* was sponsored by Yolande, countess of Saint-Pol, who sought access to the knowledge that her brother Baudouin VIII was able to glean from the Latin manuscripts in his possession. An ardent admirer of Charlemagne, Baudouin had sought and found a copy of the Latin *Pseudo-Turpin Chronicle*, which he sent to his sister Yolande before his death, asking her to preserve it as long as she lived. It was she who commissioned Nicolas de Senlis to render it in the vernacular sometime between 1195 and 1205, as he himself tells us: "La bona contessa ha gardé le livre jusqu'a ore; or me proie que je le metra de latin en romanz [The good countess has kept the book until now; now she requests that I translate it from Latin into *roman*].[107] Both the prologue and the colophon to the work make it clear that the translation was requested for the use of one who could not read Latin ("qui de latin ne seüst eslire") in order that she might better understand ("por mieuz entendra"). Perhaps the idea had come to her from her sister Laurette d'Alsace, for whose benefit a vernacular prose commentary on the Psalms had been written not long before.[108] During the first quarter of the thirteenth century, a similar vernacular rendering of the *Pseudo-Turpin* was composed by William of Braine, who prepared the work for its only Anglo-Norman patrons, Alice de Curcy and her husband Warin Fitzgerold, chamberlain at the court of the Plantagenets, who accompanied Richard the Lion-Hearted on crusade.[109]

Thus, the first quasi-romance, the first Arthurian romance, the first vernacular bestiary, and some of the earliest biblical translations into the vernacular were all written for women. John Benton notes the "avant-garde" quality of the patronage of Marie de Champagne at a time when "even the idea of translating Scriptural material into French was new and exciting in the twelfth century."[110] It is an important point. Even if women's desire for translations and works in the vernacular evolved, as Diana Tyson has suggested, from the fact that their "erudition was not up to taking advantage of what there was in Latin,"[111] it should in no way undermine the historical importance of the phenomenon, for it demonstrates the strategies women used in overcoming obstacles that blocked their participation in mainstream culture. Where they could not break them down, they sought a new avenue for exploitation of their abilities and achievement of their goals. Their encouragement of the vernacular is such a case.

One of the earliest women to recognize the value of the vernacular for religious instruction was Hild, the seventh-century abbess of Whitby, a wealthy double monastery. Hild herself was well educated, having been taught by the monk Aidan, and she could read Latin, no doubt, with a fair amount of ease. Nevertheless, she encouraged Caedmon to developed his special talent for writing religious poetry in the vernacular. Not unlike her secular counterparts, Hild, whose abbey "played a major intellectual role in a newly-literate society" recognized that the vernacular was an important medium for reaching the widest audience.[112]

To be sure, a knowledge of Latin was notable in such women as Hild, Héloïse, who became abbess at the Paraclete after her reluctant marriage to Abelard, and Hildeli, abbess at the Abbey of Barking, another double monastery noted for its learning.[113] But such educated women who were able to hold their own in Latin with male intellectuals of their day tended to be the exception rather than the rule. More typical were the sister of Aelred de Rievaulx, a recluse whose brother felt the need to simplify his Latin in preparing a religious manual for her, and the anchoresses for whom Austin, canon of Wigmore, always provided a translation for Latin citations in his *Ancrene Wisse* (ca. 1230), a manual based upon that of Aelred. Even women who lacked the Latin and ecclesiastical training of their male counterparts were capable of recognizing the implicit value of cultural patronage in achieving their goals. Thus, when they had difficulty with Latin, they requested vernacular texts, prompting some of the earliest translations into *roman* in the twelfth century, thereby providing not only to themselves but to other women a greater opportunity for cultural participation.

We have already noted some women's patronage that demonstrated a specific concern for other women. The fourteenth century saw a significant increase in literary works about women sponsored by women, depicting them in a positive light. One of the most famous examples is Boccaccio's *De mulie-*

ribus claris, written in 1360–61 for Andrea Acciaiuoli, countess of Altaville, daughter of a wealthy Florentine banker and sister of Niccolò Acciaiuoli, grand seneschal at the court of Robert of Anjou, king of Naples.[114] Even earlier, we find the development of a motif that will eventually affect both art and literature—that of the *speculum dominarum*, the mirror of ladies. The *speculum* per se was far from an innovative genre, for it had existed in one form or another throughout the Middle Ages. In its relationship to women, however, the iconography of the mirror had been often cautionary and frequently negative. This type of mirror was new, held up to women at their own request to define appropriate and positive female behavior among the noble class. Toward the end of the thirteenth century or possibly the beginning of the next, Durand de Champagne, Franciscan monk and confessor of Queen Jeanne de Navarre, wife of Philippe le Bel, wrote a Latin *Speculum dominarum*, a manual of Christian moral behavior for noble women.[115] Diane Bornstein sees it as the "first mirror for the princess" and a belated acknowledgment of her political importance. As the prestige and power of the monarchy increased, her social and symbolic roles became more important. Even though the real power of the queen had diminished since the early twelfth century, "a more elaborate coronation ceremony, an increasingly autonomous and extensive household, and a personal seal all added to [her] prestige."[116] It was perhaps to underscore her importance and buttress the queen's image that Jeanne requested the work.[117] She had it translated into French as well, also by a Franciscan, possibly Durand himself. Jeanne d'Evreux, widow of Charles le Bel, owned a copy of it.[118] Watriquet de Couvin, a minstrel at the court of Blois, dedicated major portions of his *Mireoirs as Dames* (ca. 1319–29) to Jeanne d'Evreux, who very likely commissioned him to write this allegorical version.[119]

The *speculum dominarum* tradition continues into the sixteenth century with the *Miroir des dames* by Bouton, lord of Corbeveau near Beaune, a squire at the Burgundian court and captain of the guard for Charles V. Unfortunately, we do not know for whom it was written and can only speculate that it was very likely composed at the behest of a woman at one of these courts.[120] We do know, however, that, between 1526 and 1531 a priest named Ysambert de Saint-Léger composed a new translation of the *Miroir des dames*, dedicating it to Marguerite de Navarre and her daughters.[121] Thus, the *speculum dominarum* represents a tradition in literature for women that spanned more than two hundred years.

The *speculum* image is a particularly appropriate one in the flood of literature written for women during the later Middle Ages that sought to display their positive capabilities and to represent at the very least a groping toward a uniquely feminine system of values. As Luce Irigaray has suggested, male writers of the traditional canon have tended to depict women only as the mirror of masculine values. The *speculum dominarum,* on the other hand, becomes what Tilde Sankovitch has called "an active instrument of female self-discovery."[122] The self-conscious use of the image itself suggests that women's gender awareness was heightened during the period in which these works were composed, even though it existed to some extent, as Sankovitch and others have shown, much earlier. One interesting illumination in a French translation of Boccaccio's *De mulieribus claris* dating from about 1402 depicts a female painter Marcia, holding a mirror in her hand in order to paint a self-portrait (see figure 3).[123] Symbolically, the portrait represents what women were seeking to accomplish with the *speculum dominarum.* For the first time in European literature women, through their patronage, were seeking to clarify that which was unique to them. That their self-portraits were filtered through a set of masculine values and rendered most frequently by the hand of a male writer is undeniable, but they had, nonetheless, begun a process that has continued into our own time.

At least one female author, Christine de Pizan, writing at the end of the fourteenth and beginning of the fifteenth century, entered into the process.

Fig. 3. Marcia painting her self-portrait, using a mirror. Bibliothèque nationale. MS français 12420, fol. 101v. By permission of the Bibliothèque nationale, Paris.

Fig. 4. The Mirror of Reason in Christine de Pizan's *Livre de la cité des dames*. London, British Library, Harley MS 4431, fol. 290. By permission of the British Library.

She too used the iconography of the mirror, which figures prominently in her *Livre de la cité des dames* in both text and image. In the illumination in the Harley manuscript 4431 (folio 290) depicting Reason, Rectitude, and Justice, who have come to help Christine build her city of ladies, Reason holds a mirror up to the writer (see figure 4), who, having read of the abominations heaped upon women by many famous men, had begun to wonder "how such a worthy artisan [God] could have deigned to make such an abominable work" [124] [comment si digne ouvri[e]r daigna oncques faire tant abominable ouvrage].[125] She had concluded that she and the "entire feminine sex . . . were monstrosities in nature" [tout le sexe feminin . . . fust monstre en nature, 620]. The appearance of the three Virtues reassures her. Reason explains the importance of her mirror, which will allow one to achieve "clear self-knowledge" [il n'est quelconques personne qui s'i mire, quel que la creature soit, qui clerement ne se congnoisse, 627] and learn "the essences, qualities, proportions, and measures of all things" [les essances, calités, proporcions et measures de tout choses,

628]. In short, Christine herself is holding up the mirror of Reason to all women, to empower them to become more self-reflective and more willing to define themselves and their own capabilities, thereby refusing the definitions of misogynistic males. The *Livre de la cité des dames* provides them with positive models, women capable of noble deeds and courage in the face of adversity. The iconography of the mirror continues in Christine's later *Trésor de la cité des dames*, also known as the *Livre des trois vertus*, a book of advice for medieval women that should, according to Bornstein, be included among the "mirrors" composed for them. In fact, one of its modern translators, Charity Cannon Willard, entitles the text *A Medieval Woman's Mirror of Honor: The Treasury of the City of Ladies*.

Not surprisingly, Christine's work inevitably attracted an extensive female following. In fact, the outpouring of female patronage for her writing is unprecedented in literary history. She had clearly struck a responsive chord by giving voice to praise of women and by offering renewed dignity to those who were, like her, weary of the ceaseless negative outpourings of gynophobic writers. The *Livre des trois vertus* was dedicated and presented to Marguerite of Burgundy, the youthful bride of the French dauphin, Louis of Guyenne. It enjoyed extraordinary popularity with a number of powerful women, who, as Willard points out, read it "for more than a hundred years after she wrote it."[126] Some eighteen manuscripts of the work are extant, and several were owned by women, including Agnes of Burgundy, Louise of Savoy, and Margaret of Austria, the latter two having ruled as regents for their son and nephew respectively. Anne of France, daughter of Louis XI and coregent during her son's minority, "drew inspiration from it in writing her own book of advice for her daughter, Suzanne de Bourbon" (43). The work continued to be popular well into the Renaissance, when the three French printings of the *Trésor* were all done under the patronage of the French queen Anne of Brittany, wife first of Charles VIII then of Louis XII, and the sixteenth-century Portuguese translation was completed under the patronage of Leonor, widow of King João II.[127]

The *Livre de la cité des dames* was equally popular with women, and manuscripts of the work were acquired by a number of Christine's female patrons, among them Queen Isabeau of Bavaria, Marie de Bourbon; Marguerite of Bavaria, duchess of Burgundy; and Jeanne of Auvergne, the duchess of Berry, along with her husband, Jean. Marie de Berry, Jean's daughter by a previous marriage and another of Christine's known patrons, would inherit the copy that belonged to her father and stepmother.[128]

It is interesting to note that in the late medieval period when women seem to have become more self-reflective in much of their patronage, we also have more evidence of their support for female authors and artists. The model existed, of course, much earlier in a monastic setting, but we know far less about earlier female-to-female patronage in the secular world. The twelfth-century relationship between the trobairitz Azalaïs de Porcairagues and Ermengarde de Narbonne is at best shadowy, but the patronage relationships between women of the later period are on firmer ground. Christine de Pizan herself was the patron of a female artist named Anastaise and engaged her to illuminate her work. Her appraisal of the female artist was glowing, and she judged her to be "so skillful and experienced in painting borders and miniatures of manuscripts that no one can cite an artist in the city of Paris, the center of the best illuminators on earth, who in these endeavors surpasses her in any way. . . . And this I know from my own experience, for she has produced some things for me which are held to be outstanding among the vignettes of the great masters."[129] [Tant est experte a faire vigneteures d'enlumineure en livres et champaignes d'istoires qu'il n'est mencion d'ouvrier en al ville de Paris, ou sont les souverains du monde, qui point l'en passe. . . . En ce sçay je par experience: Car pour moy meismes a ouvré aucunes choses qui sont tenues singulieres entre les vignettes des autres grans ouvriers," 759–60]. Theirs was, to be sure, a business arrangement, for the manuscripts that the artist illuminated were presentation copies. Nonetheless, this relationship contributed to the support and success of the "enlumineresse de livres." Not long after her marriage in 1353, Yolande of Flanders, countess of Bar, also engaged a female illuminator named Bourgot and Bourgot's father, Jean le Noir, to prepare for her a book of hours, now in the British Museum.[130] Such patronage relationships merely add evidence to support the fact that women frequently used their patronage to benefit other women, both by the types of activities they supported and by direct patronage to female artists or poets.

Women were not, of course, even in the late Middle Ages, single-mindedly centered on feminist patronage activities, for they also supported male writers and artists as well as institutions for the benefit of men. They played a significant role, for example, in the founding of colleges and universities where only men could study. Jeanne of Navarre was founder and benefactress of the College of Navarre; Margaret of Anjou, wife of Henry VI, and Elizabeth, wife of Edward IV, were founders and benefactors of Queens' College, Cambridge; Lady Margaret Beaufort, mother of Henry VII, founded both Christ's College and St. John's College, Cambridge; Elizabeth de Burgh founded Clare College, Cambridge.[131]

The last major accomplishment of medieval women patrons, which benefited both sexes, took place on the threshold of the Renaissance when women served as patrons of some of the earliest printers. Margaret of York, duchess of Burgundy and sister of the king of England, used her influence to support William Caxton in the translation into English and printing in 1476 of a *Recuyell of the Histories of Troy*, the first book printed in English.[132] He makes it clear that he serves at her command:

Y durst in no wyse disobey because
y am a seruant vnto her sayde grace
and resseiue of her yerly ffee and
other many goode and grete benefetes.[133]

Isabella d'Este, whose vast library in the Grotta of the Corte Vecchia was famous for its collection of manuscripts, ranging from medieval Arthurian romances to such classical texts as the works of Virgil, Pliny, and Terence, was also a supporter of printers. She commissioned Aldo Manutio of Venice, to print on vellum or parchment a variety of books, including works by Petrarch, Dante, and Virgil. She also commissioned a copy of Jerome's *Letters* to be printed at Mantua in 1497, insisting on good quality at reasonable prices.[134] Just as women, eager for knowledge, had supported vernacular literature that they could read with relative ease, they now championed printed texts, which were less expensive than manuscripts, both affording easier access to learning.

What conclusions can be drawn from the examples of female patronage we have explored? First of all, in response to the question of whether Eleanor of Aquitaine was an "anomaly" in her role as a female patron, we must conclude that, despite her prominence, she was not truly exceptional. Throughout the Middle Ages women were active patrons engaging in a great variety of cultural activities, often at the forefront of literary and artistic developments. While their special problems and agendas dictated to some extent the nature of their contributions, their motives for literary and artistic patronage frequently overlapped with those of their male counterparts. We see female patrons interested in preserving the past, frequently for blatant political reasons, sometimes to preserve the memory of an ancestor, commemorate an occasion, or glorify their lineage. We see them focusing on instructional and religious texts, for their own or their children's edification. (The concern for the education of young children in particular was women's domain.) And, finally, they commissioned works that would provide entertainment and diversion for the ladies and knights of their courts and to bolster their own reputation and image, either as individuals or as a sex.

Women's cultural patronage, like men's, supported a vast variety of literary and artistic activities as well as a large number of religious and educational institutions. What women chose or were able to sponsor seems to have been limited not so much by their sex per se as by its concomitant economic or legal constraints and educational disadvantages. While institutions, laws, and social structures were defined to reinforce male values, medieval women patrons nevertheless found ways to overcome obstacles to their cultural participation in order to insert and validate their own perspectives, thereby helping to shape the cultural milieux of their own times and of future generations. The materials explored here suggest clearly that women patrons, who spoke to us not directly but through the works they sponsored, were conscious from the outset of the disadvantages of being female in a male-defined world and were concerned for the well-being of other women. They became increasingly outspoken in the late Middle Ages. Although much of their patronage fell within established categories similar to those of their male counterparts, other aspects of it were especially directed at the betterment of their own sex. Evidence of this concern is seen in their founding of women's monastic institutions, even within religious orders that resisted the involvement of females; in their sponsorship of literary works that showed women in a positive light in counterpoint to the misogynistic outpourings from male clerics; in their enthusiasm for the cult of the Virgin; and in their efforts to disseminate information about other female saints whose lives demonstrated the goodness and fortitude of which women were capable. Thus it is not surprising that women embraced and supported enthusiastically the fourteenth- and fifteenth-century outpouring of literary works that openly praised women, thereby preparing the way for the antimisogynistic arguments of Christine de Pizan in the famous Quarrel of the Rose and the even more famous and enduring debate that her works ignited—the *querelle des femmes*.[135]

Certainly these women patrons were not inured against the prevalent attitudes of their own times, and they accepted without question the notion that they had biological limitations that separated their roles from those of men. Nevertheless, despite these societally defined gender restrictions and the negative attitudes of many male clerics, the pattern of female cultural patronage provides evidence of a growing awareness of women's worth and intrinsic value to society. This is not to make the argument that women were, through their patronage, consciously subversive; yet a clear underlying motive and impetus for a great deal of women's patronage in the Middle Ages, whether conscious or unconscious, was the need to influence societal attitudes and make their voices heard. There is no question that they did so. Without their relentless efforts, we would be deprived today of many splendid visions and artistic achievements that have inestimably enriched our cultural heritage.

NOTES

1. The general editors, Georges Duby and Michelle Perrot, of a recent series called *A History of Women in the West*, aptly entitle the second volume, which deals with medieval women, *Silences of the Middle Ages* (Cambridge: Belknap Press of Harvard University Press, 1992), ed. Christiane Klapisch-Zuber.

2. Karl Julius Holzknecht, *Literary Patronage in the Middle Ages* (Philadelphia: Collegiate, 1923). Issues raised in Madeline Caviness's article in this volume suggest the problems inherent in viewing dedication alone as a clear indication of patronage. Given her argument, one must also question whether either the "donor portrait" or the presentation copy alone could be considered any more definite as an indicator of patronage without other corroborating evidence.

3. Diana B. Tyson, "Patronage of French Vernacular History Writers in the Twelfth and Thirteenth Centuries," *Romania* 100 (1979): 184–85.

4. *Histoire Littéraire de la France* (Paris: Imprimerie Nationale, 1733–1898), 7:153 (hereafter referred to as *Hist. litt.*); the translation that follows is from Holtzknecht, *Literary Patronage*, 218. According to the poet Baudri, Adela's sister Cécile, a nun at the abbey of La Trinité in Caen and eventually its abbess, was also noted for her literary tastes (*Hist. litt.*, 7:153). So, in fact, was their mother, Matilda of Flanders, of whom Orderic Vital wrote, "Reginam hanc simul decoravere forma, genus, litterarum scientia, cuncta morum et virtutum pulchritude." See *Historiae ecclesiasticae*, ed. Auguste Leprévost (Paris: Renouard, 1840), 2:189. For other information on Adela see also *Hist. litt.*, 10:131, 11:282. According to the former source, Adela was also a poet.

5. In their introduction to *Interpreting Cultural Symbols: Saint Anne in Late Medieval Society*, Kathleen Ashley and Pamela Sheingorn suggest that the "meaning of patronage needs to be broadened to include not only elite patrons but also such patrons as convents and guilds (since so many cultural artifacts were produced for corporate groups during the Middle Ages)." (Athens: University of Georgia Press, 1990), 6. Such an expansion is beyond the scope of this book, although I do touch on the patronage of the convents, usually supervised by the abbess. In the cases of the life of Saint Radegund by Baudonivia and that of Beatrice of Nazareth, both discussed below, the convent is by their definition the "corporate" sponsor of the work, with the abbess functioning as its representative. Another example that might be cited is that of Herrad of Landsberg's *Hortus deliciarum*, written for the nuns of the Abbey of Hohenburg but unfortunately destroyed in a military bombardment during the Franco-Prussian War.

6. Joan Ferrante posits yet another patronage role for women: "requests from friends or colleagues which led to the composition of particular works," such as Heloïse's requests for specific information from Abelard. See Ferrante's article in this volume.

7. For a fuller discussion of these shifting values in the medieval economy, see Judith Kellogg, *Medieval Artistry and Exchange: Economic Institutions, Society, and Literary Form in Old French Narrative* (New York: Lang, 1989).

8. Chrétien de Troyes, *Erec et Enide*, ed. Mario Roques (Paris: Champion, 1981), lines 2055–67. The following translation and all other translations are my own unless otherwise indicated.

9. *The Anglo-Norman Metrical Chronicle of Geoffrey Gaimar*, ed. Thomas Wright (1850; reprint, New York: Franklin, 1976), lines 6495–98.

10. Ibid. See preface, 9.

11. Ibid., 225n, for line 6447. It is evident from Gaimar's text, however, that other vernacular works of history existed at this time. He speaks of his sources in some detail, indicating that he used "maint esamplaire, / Liveres Engleis, e par gramaire, E en Romanz e en Latin" (lines 6441–42).

12. Jean Froissart, *Oeuvres de Froissart, Chroniques*, ed. Kervyn de Lettenhove (Brussels: Devaux, 1867), 2:5.

13. Jean Froissart, *The Chronicles of Jean Froissart in Lord Berners' Translation*, ed. Gillian and William Anderson (Carbondale: Southern Illinois University Press, 1963), 2.

14. He writes of Philippa of Hainaut "à laquelle en ma jeunesse je fus clerc, et la servoie de beaulx dittiers et trettiés amoureux, et pour l'amour du service de la noble et vaillant dame à qui j'estoie, tous autres grans seigneurs, ducs, contes et barons, chevalliers et nobles hommes, de quelconques nations qu'ils fuissent, m'amoient et me veoient voulentiers, et me faisoient grant prouffit" (*Oeuvres*, 14:2).

15. Neri di Bicci, a fifteenth-century Italian artist, kept careful records of patronage and remuneration, which have been preserved in *Le ricordanze di Neri di Bicci, 10 marzo 1453–24 aprile 1475*, ed. Bruno Santi (Pisa: Marlin, 1976). His patrons will be discussed below. Isabella d'Este was one of those who commissioned but rejected whatever was not to her liking or was too expensive. See Julia Cartwright, *Isabella d'Este* (1903; reprint, New York: Dutton, 1923), 2:25.

16. Rita Lejune, "Rôle littéraire d'Aliénor d'Aquitaine et de sa famille," *Cultura Neolatina* 14 (1954): 5–57.

17. Margaret Schaus and Susan Mosher Stuard, "Citizens of No Mean City: Medieval Women's History," *Choice* 30 (December 1992): 588.

18. The essay of Elizabeth A. R. Brown in Kibler's volume takes issue with Eleanor's role as a literary patron altogether, arguing that she was far too interested in politics to take much interest in promoting the arts. However, the evidence seems overwhelmingly on the other side of the issue. Because many male patrons, including Eleanor's astute and energetic husband Henry II, were also powerful political figures, as Brown readily admits, describing Henry as one who "enjoyed preeminence as a promoter of culture" ("Eleanor of Aquitaine," 19), the two can hardly be seen as mutually exclusive endeavors. Surely a woman could balance the two roles as well as a man. It is interesting to note in this context that Eleanor's tombal effigy at Fontevrault depicts her holding not a symbol of political power but a book.

19. Ermengarde was officially recognized by Louis VII in 1163 as having the right to administer justice. See Fritz Bergert, *Die von den Trobadors genannten oder gefeierten*

Damen: Beihefte zur Zeitschrift für romanische Philologie 46 (Halle: Niemeyer, 1913): 6–10.

20. Ermengarde, born about 1125 (some sources date her birth as early as 1120), inherited from her father (d. 1134) when she was still a child. She must have assumed personal control at age twenty-one about 1146, not long after her second marriage to Bernard of Anduze. Thus she would have maintained authority over her own lands from 1146 until she abdicated control to her nephew Peter of Lara in 1192, approximately forty-six years.

21. See Constance Berman, "Women as Donors and Patrons to Southern French Monasteries in the Twelfth and Thirteenth Centuries," in *The Worlds of Medieval Women: Creativity, Influence, and Imagination*, eds. Constance H. Berman, Charles W. Connell, and Judith Rice Rothschild (Morgantown: West Virginia University Press, 1985), 58. See also P. -A. Verlaguet, ed., *Cartulaire de l'abbaye de Silvanès* (Rodez: Carrere, 1910), no. 396 (1152).

22. See *The Poems of the Troubadour Peire Rogier*, ed. Derek E. T. Nicholson (Manchester: Manchester University Press, 1976), 60, lines 6–10.

23. Bernard sends his poem "La dousa votz ai auzida" to "midons a Narbona" (line 58). Giraut de Bornelh also speaks of "Midons de Narbona" in his *canso* "La flors del verjan" as one who should be consulted about a question of love. Such attributions have been questioned because of the vagueness of the wording, but Ermengarde's fame as an arbiter in such cases was fixed forever by Andreas Capellanus in his *De amore*, where she renders judgments in five love disputes. Peire d'Alvernhe's poem "Ab fina joia comensa" also contains a probable allusion to Ermengarde as does "Ar em al freg temps vengut," the one extant lyric of the trobairitz Azalaïs de Porcairagues, who also sends her poem to Narbonne.

24. Nicholson, *Poems of Peire Rogier*, app. 2, 160–64. This appendix provides an excellent summary of all that is known about Ermengarde's relationship with the troubadour poets as well as the incident recounted in the *Orkneyinga Saga*. See also Nicholson's introduction as well as the commentaries on the various poems for additional pertinent information about Ermengarde; Claude de Vic and Joseph Vaissète, *Histoire générale de Languedoc* (Toulouse: Privat, 1872) 6:152; Camille Chabaneau, "Poésies inédites des troubadours du Périgord," *Revue des langues romanes* 25 (1884): 218–19; Jean Boutière and A. -H. Schutz, eds., *Biographies des troubadours: Textes provençaux des XIIIe et XIVe siècles* (1950; reprint, New York: Franklin, 1972), 231; Stephen G. Nichols, Jr., et. al., *The Songs of Bernart de Ventadorn*, revised edition (Chapel Hill: University of North Carolina Press, 1965), 105; Peire d'Auvergne, *Peire d'Auvergne: Die Lieder*, ed. Rudolf Zenker (1900; reprint, Geneva: Slatkine, 1977), 739–42; *Sämtliche Lieder des Trobadors Giraut de Bornelh*, ed. Adolf Kolsen (Halle: Max Niemeyer, 1910), 1:138–39; Oskar Schultz-[Goya], *Die provenzalischen Dichterinnen* (Leipzig: Fock, 1888), 17. I am grateful to Hans-Erich Keller for allowing me to read his unpublished paper "Ermengarda of Narbonne and Beatrice of Este: A Study in Contrasts," which focuses on these patron-poet relationships.

25. Laws and customs of southern France and Catalonia, for example, were significantly more accepting of women as property owners and heirs than were those of other parts of Europe. See David Herlihy, "Land, Family, and Women in Continental Europe, 701–1200," in *Women in Medieval Society,* ed. Susan Mosher Stuard (Philadelphia: University of Pennsylvania Press, 1976), 13–45.

26. See Robert Hadju, "The Position of Noblewomen in the Pays des Coutumes, 1100–1300," *Journal of Family History* 5 (1980): 122–44; see also Pierre Petot and André Vandenbossche, "Le statut de la femme dans les pays coutumiers français du XIIIe au XVIIe siècle," in *La Femme: Recueils de la Société Jean Bodin pour l'histoire comparative des institutions* (Brussels: De Boeck, 1952–62), 12:243–54.

27. See Penny Shine Gold, *The Lady and the Virgin: Image, Attitude, and Experience in Twelfth-Century France* (Chicago: University of Chicago Press, 1985). Gold indicates that, although married women in France found themselves most frequently in the role of consenter, they could exercise some influence. "She might encourage her husband to make a donation, . . . insist on her inclusion in a transfer of property, or . . . withhold consent when her husband wanted to alienate property from her" (147–8).

28. See Marcelle Thiébaux, *The Writings of Medieval Women* (New York: Garland, 1987), 86; Hrotsvit, *Hrotsvithae opera,* ed. Helene Homeyer (Munich: Paderborn Schöningh, 1970), 450–59. The first three abbesses of Gandersheim were all daughters of Liudulf and Oda: Hathumoda, Gerberga I, and Christine. See Anne Lyon Haight, ed., *Hroswitha of Gandersheim* (New York: Hroswitha Club, 1965), 4–8.

29. Jeffrey F. Hamburger, "Art Enclosure and the *Cura Monialium:* Prolegomena in the Guise of a Postscript," *Gesta* 31, no. 2 (1992): 116.

30. The translation is from Hamburger, "Art Enclosure," 117 (italics mine). The Hedwig Codex is from the court of Ludwig I of Leignitz and Brieg, Silesia, 1353, Malibu, J. Paul Getty Museum, MS Ludwig XI 7 (83.MN.126.), fol. 56.

31. Ronald G. Musto has pointed out that between 1328 and 1334 "Giotto was commissioned to complete a cycle of frescoes for the church that were white-washed in the seventeenth century and are now destroyed." See "Queen Sancia and the Spiritual Franciscans," in *Women of the Medieval World,* eds. Julius Kirschner and Suzanne F. Wemple (Oxford: Blackwell, 1985), 193.

32. Ibid., 192.

33. The letter is quoted in its entirety in Musto, "Queen Sancia," 214. See also Luke Wadding, *Annales minorum,* ed. J. M. Fonesca (1731; reprint, Florence: Claras Aquas [Quaracchi], 1932), 7:172–73. The entire letter is preserved in Latin in *Analecta Franciscana,* ed. Bernardo A. Bessa (Florence: Collegio St. Bonaventura, 1897), 3:508–14.

34. Gold, *The Lady and the Virgin,* 130.

35. Hadju, "The Position of Noblewomen," 130. Even so, "being of the weaker sex, she was still thought to be in need of a male protector, an *advocatus,*" who became her advisor and representative in legal proceedings (ibid.). Such legal proceedings did not, apparently, extend to patronage where most widows seem to have acted independently.

36. Letter in Gregory of Tours, *History of the Franks*, trans. Lewis Thorpe (New York: Penguin, 1974), 9.42 (p. 535).

37. Jo Ann McNamara, "Hagiography and Nunneries in Merovingian Gaul," in *Women of the Medieval World*, 47.

38. Venantius Fortunatus, *De vita Sanctae Radegundis*, in *De vita Sanctae Radegundis libri duo*, ed. B. Krusch, *Monumenta Germaniae Historica, Scriptorum rerum Merovingicarum* (hereafter referred to as MGH, SRM) II, 17–18.

39. See Jean Leclercq, "Les relations entre Venance Fortunat et Sainte Radegonde," in *La riche personnalité de Sainte Radegonde* (Poitiers: Comité du XIVe centenaire, 1988), 68. On relations between Fortunatus and the two women, Judith W. George points out that, although the "passionate friendship" had many precedents in the church, the relationship of Fortunatus and Agnes apparently gave rise to gossip, which Fortunatus denies in poem 11.6, contending that his love was chaste and that she was like a sister. See her *Venantius Fortunatus: A Latin Poet in Merovingian Gaul* (Oxford: Clarendon, 1992), 161–77. Radegund was also a poet herself, as Fortunatus makes clear in his writings. "In brevibus tabulis mihi carmina magna dedisti, / quae vacuis ceris reddere mella potes" ["On small tablets you have given me great poetry, you who are able to make honey on empty wax"]. (Original and translation cited in George, *Venantius Fortunatus*, 198–99).

40. McNamara, "Hagiography and Nunneries," 47.

41. Gregory of Tours, *Liber in gloria Confessorum*, ed. W. Arndt and B. Krusch, MGH, SRM I/II (Hanover, Germany: Hanian, 1884–85), 106, 364–66.

42. Hamburger, "Art Enclosure," 109.

43. See Louise Coudanne, "Baudonivie, Moniale de Sainte-Croix et biographe de Sainte Radegonde," in *Etudes mérovingiennes: Actes des journées de Poitiers ler-3 mai 1953* (Paris: Picard, 1953), 45–51.

44. Quoted in Coudanne, "Baudonivie," 46.

45. For details on the relationship between Hildegard and Elisabeth, see Barbara Newman, *Sister of Wisdom: St. Hildegard's Theology of the Feminine* (Berkeley and Los Angeles: University of California Press, 1987), 36–39.

46. Bede, *Historia ecclesiastica*, in *Venerabilis Baedae opera historica*, ed. Charles Plummer (Oxford: Clarendon, 1896), 4:24.

47. Hamburger, "Art Enclosure," 118–19. See also H. Ormont, "Anonyme, auteur du 'Livre de la Tresoye,' de l'abbaye d'Origny," in *Hist. Litt.*, 35:640–41.

48. The Abbey of Longchamp was founded in 1255 by Isabella, sister of Louis IX.

49. Hamburger, "Art Enclosure," 118.

50. See n. 15. The statistical analysis of the *Ricordanze* was presented by Rosi Gilday in her paper "The Women Patrons of Neri di Bicci," presented at the Twenty-eighth International Congress on Medieval Studies in Kalamazoo, Michigan, in May 1993. I am grateful to her for sharing with me the results of her work and allowing me to read her paper. Her analysis tends to substantiate the patterns of women's patronage suggested herein.

51. I do not belabor this point because several articles in this volume, notably those of Karen Jambeck and Miriam Shadis, address the issue of matrilineal patronage at some length.

52. Dhuoda, *Manuel pour mon fils,* ed. Pierre Riché (Paris: Cerf, 1975), 114.

53. See James Westfall Thompson, *The Literacy of the Laity in the Middle Ages* (New York: Franklin, 1963), 88. It is interesting to note that German translations of the Scriptures preceded translations into *Roman* by two centuries.

54. Ibid., 89. See also John the Poor, *De contemplatione,* ed. F. Richter, in *Archiv für Kunde österreicher Geschichtsquellen* (1849), 3:369.

55. Chap. 36, MGH SS, 8:264.

56. See J. Huemer's "Zur Geschichte der mittellateinischen Dichtung: Arnulfidelicie cleri," *Romanische Forschungen* 2 (1886): 211–12, 216–17. See also J. Thompson, *Literacy of the Laity,* 88–89 and 106–7, nn. 71 and 72.

57. Joan Ferrante, "The Education of Women in the Middle Ages in Theory, Fact, and Fantasy," in *Beyond Their Sex: Learned Women of the European Past,* ed. Patricia H. Labalme (New York: New York University Press, 1980), 11. David Herlihy in the preface to his *Opera Muliebria: Women and Work in Medieval Europe* (New York: McGraw-Hill, 1990) writes, "In the social world of the central Middle Ages, the clerics or clerks read Latin, noble women read the vernacular, and noble men read nothing at all" (xii). Although this statement may have a kernel of truth, many noblemen throughout the Middle Ages were literate. Malcolm, however, was not among them.

58. Susan Groag Bell, "Medieval Women Book Owners: Arbiters of Lay Piety and Ambassadors of Culture," in *Women and Power in the Middle Ages,* eds. Mary Erler and Maryanne Kowaleski (Athens: University of Georgia Press, 1988), 173.

59. Karl Jordan, *Henry the Lion: A Biography,* trans. P. S. Falla (Oxford: Clarendon, 1986), 200. The author states in the epilogue of the *Rolandslied* that a Duke Henry procured the original French text in order to have it translated into German at the request of his noble spouse, the daughter of a great king. Internal evidence makes clear that the parties in question are Henry the Lion and his wife, Matilda. The case of the *Tristant* is a little less certain, although John of Oberg, the father of Eilhart, was known to be in the immediate entourage of Henry the Lion, and Eilhart himself turns up as a witness to a number of charters for the Count Palatine Henry, son of Henry the Lion and Matilda. Jordan concludes that "although no patron is mentioned as in the case of the *Rolandslied,* we may assume that the ducal couple commissioned this work also" (211).

60. See Boutière and Schutz, 233. Raimbaut died in 1173. If Peire Rogier came to Castile after Raimbaut's death, Leonor would have been already married to Alfonso for three years.

61. See Julio Gonzales, *El reino de Castilla en la epoca de Alfonso VIII: Documentos,* vol. 1 (Madrid: Escuela de Estudios Medievales, 1960), 210. The court is associated as well with the poet Ramón Vidal de Besalú, who in his *Castia gilós* described in some detail the elegant garb of Queen Leonor (see Gonzales, *El reino de Castillo,* 203); how-

ever, in his recent work on Ramón, Hugh Field has questioned whether the work is correctly attributed to Ramón. See Hugh Field, ed., *Ramón Vidal de Besalú* (Barcelona: Curial, 1991), 2:203.

62. Lucien Musset, "Le mécénat des princes normands au XIe siècle," in *Artistes, artisans, et production artistique au Moyen Âge*, vol. 2 of *Commande et travail*, ed. Xavier Barral I Altet (Paris: Picard, 1987), 121–34.

63. See also Georges Bataille, "The Notion of Expenditure," in *Visions of Excess: Selected Writings, 1927–1939*, trans. Allan Stoekl, Carl R. Lovitts, and Donald M. Leslie, Jr. (Minneapolis: University of Minnesota Press, 1985), 116ff. He contends that attaining wealth is less important than publicly spending it in order to demonstrate "nobility, honor, and rank in a hierarchy" (122).

64. See Orderic Vital, *Historiae ecclesiasticae*, ed. Auguste Le Prévost (Paris: Renouard, 1838–55), 2:41.

65. Musset, "Le mécénat," 125; see also Marie-Thérèse Camus, "La reconstruction de Saint-Hilaire-le-Grand de Poitiers à l'époque romane: La marche des travaux," in *Cahiers de civilisation médiévale* 25 (1982): 101–20. See especially pages 108–9.

66. On the life of Queen Emma, see Miles W. Campbell, "Emma, Reine d'Angleterre, mère dénaturée ou femme vindicative?" *Annales de Normandie*, 23 (1973): 99–114. See also Alistair Campbell, ed., *Encomium Emmae Reginae* (London: Royal Historical Society, 1949), 33. At the time of their marriage Cnut and Emma had a contract drawn up that stated that her sons by Cnut would succeed him on the throne. Although many scholars have interpreted this contract as a protection of her as yet unborn children by Cnut at the expense of her children by Aethelred, Campbell sees it rather as a political expedient to make certain that her sons, and not those of Aelfgifu, Cnut's mistress before their marriage, would rule after their father's death. There is little question that Cnut was concerned to provide these illegitimate sons, Harold Harefoot and Svein, with kingdoms. He would later defeat Olaf Haraldson for Norway, where he set his son Svein up as king and Aelfgifu as regent. After Cnut's death in 1035, Harold Harefoot struggled with Harthacnut, the son of Emma and Cnut, for the throne of England, despite the agreement. He also captured Alfred, Emma's oldest son by Aethelred, and had him tortured and murdered.

67. See Sten Körner, *The Battle of Hastings, England, and Europe, 1035–1066* (Lund: Gleerup, 1964), 64–74. For additional artistic patronage on the part of Queen Emma, see Caviness's article in this volume.

68. See Campbell's article for an alternate reading. It should be noted that, after the death of Emma's brother Richard, his widow, Gonnor, also continued the tradition of family patronage, providing unspecified gifts to the Abbaye de Saint-Père at Chartres, aiding the bishop of Coutances in constructing his cathedral, and providing resources toward the completion of Mont Saint-Michel. See the "Livre noir de la cathédrale de Coutances," in *Gallia Christiana* (Paris: Ex Typographia Regia, 1716–1865), 11, instr. col. 218: "Hujus tamen temporibus incoepta et ex parte constructa est Coustantiensis ecclesia, fundante et coadjuvante Gonorra comitissa, auxiliantibus

etiam canonicus, reditibus medietatis altaris ad tempus operi concessis, cooperantibus quoque baronibus et parochianis fidelibus, quod usque hodie contestantur aliquot ipsorum nomina insculpta lapidibus in ecclesiae arcubus." On her donations to Mont Saint-Michel see Jean Huynes, *Histoire générale de l'abbaye du Mont Saint-Michel*, ed. Eugène de Robillard de Beaurepaire (Rouen: A. Le Brument, 1872–1873), 2:6. See also Emile Molinier and Auguste Longnon, eds., *Obituaires de la province de Sens, 2, Diocèse de Chartres* (Paris: Imprimerie nationale, 1906), 2:18.

Matilda, the wife of William the Conqueror, also continued this program of family patronage by funding such constructions as the refectory of the abbey of Marmoutier and founding, in conjunction with her husband, the abbeys of La Trinité and Saint-Etienne at Caen. To La Trinité, where their daughter Cécile was a nun and eventually abbess, they gave a variety of magnificent liturgical garments, among them a hooded robe from a Winchester workshop, a sleeveless ceremonial robe finely woven with golden threads, golden chains decorated with a cross to be used to suspend a lamp over the altar, great candelabras made at Saint-Lô, a crown, a scepter, a chalice, and other unspecified jewels and vases. Outside of Normandy they made significant donations to the cathedrals at Chartres and Le Man, the abbeys of Saint-Denis, Saint-Corneille de Compiègne, Saint-Florent de Saumur, and Cluny. To Saint-Corneille Matilda herself gave a vase decorated with gold, gems, and precious stones; to Saint-Florent she gave a golden chalice, and to Cluny she gave a liturgical robe that was said to be so rigid with metal, possibly gold, that it could not be bent. Finally, Queen Matilda, described in the *vida* of Saint Simon of Crespy as *dives et prepotentissima*, sent gold and silver to Rome for the construction of the sepulcher of the saint, with whom she claimed a family connection. The tomb was constructed of polished stones and encrusted with various colors of marble. See Musset, "Le mécénat," 127–28. On Cécile's role at La Trinité, see *Hist. litt.*, 7:153. See also *Vita Sancti Simeonis comitis Crespeiensis*, in *Patrologia Latina* [hereafter *PL*], 156, col. 1222, charte 14.

69. A case in point was the effort of Matilda, daughter of Henry I of England, to assume the throne to which her father had named her as his successor. Male resistance, particularly among the Norman barons, to having a woman on the throne led to the coronation of Etienne de Blois, known in England as Stephen, the king's nephew. Matilda's determined struggle to regain the throne of England ultimately led to a compromise, whereby Stephen kept the throne during his lifetime but was forced to name her son, the later Henry II, as his heir. See also note 64.

70. See Patrick Courbet, "L'autel portatif de la comtesse Gertrude de Brunswick (vers 1040): Tradition royale de Bourgogne et conscience aristocratique dans l'Empire des Saliens," *Cahiers de civilisation médiévale*, 34 (1991): 117.

71. Ibid., 119.

72. The description of Thibaut's tomb is quoted in Henri d'Arbois de Jubainville, *Histoire des ducs et des comtes de Champagne* (Paris: Durand, 1859–67), 4:90–98.

73. See Michel Bur, "Les comtes de Champagne et la 'Normanitas': Sémiologie d'un tombeau," *Proceedings of the Battle Conference on Anglo-Norman Studies* 3 (1980),

24. Two of the figures on the tomb are disputed. The most interesting is that of the king of England, who is depicted with his crown in his hand and without a scepter. Jean Hugot identified him as Henry II of England; Arbois de Jubainville, like his seventeenth-century predecessor Nicolas Camuzat, proposes Richard the Lion-Hearted, Countess Marie's half-brother. Michel Bur takes issue with both identifications, seeing the uncrowned figure as the younger brother of Thibaut le Grand, King Stephen, who had assumed the throne after the death of Henry I. Refusing Henry's daughter Matilda as their queen, the Norman vassals had called Count Thibaut from Champagne to accept the crown. Before he could reach England, however, his younger brother Stephen had already assumed the throne. Although the two brothers worked out what appeared on the surface to be an amicable solution, with Stephen paying heftily into Thibaut's coffers and promising never to lay claim to Champagne or Blois in exchange for Thibaut's allowing him to keep his English crown without a family struggle, some lingering pretension to the English throne seems to have remained in Thibaut's descendants. Thus the uncrowned figure, still open to interpretation, seems to me an unlikely depiction of King Stephen, who in fact wore the crown, even though he was later forced to leave it not to his own son but to Matilda's. It would appear, rather, a more accurate depiction of Thibaut le Grand himself who might have been king had communications been better and steeds swifter, but who would remain forever emblazoned on his grandson's tomb as the older brother who never wore the crown.

The other disputed figure is that of the king of Spain, identified by scholars as both Countess Blanche's father and her brother. Bur argues that Blanche, finding herself in a position of isolation after her husband's death, would have sought the support of her brother, the current King Sancho, particularly in the protection and education of her children. An equally good case, however, could be made for interpreting the figure of the king of Navarre as Blanche's father, from whom a direct line of descent would be established in the following generation from Sancho to Blanche to her son, Thibaut IV, who would become king of Navarre.

74. See Derek Baker, " 'A Nursery of Saints': St Margaret of Scotland Reconsidered," in *Medieval Women: Essays Presented to Rosalind M. T. Hill on the Occasion of Her Seventieth Birthday* (Oxford: Blackwell for the Ecclesiastical History Society, 1978), 124.

75. See Janet Nelson, "Perceptions du pouvoir chez les historiennes du Haut Moyen Age," in *La Femme au Moyen Age*, edited by Michel Rouche and Jean Heuclin (Maubeuge: Touzot, 1990), 76–77. See also the article by Lois Huneycutt in this volume.

76. She complained in a letter to her father, Louis VII, of her difficulties in collecting the toll on one of her dower properties at Coulumière. The men of Saint-Denis, passing through Coulumière, had paid the toll without complaint when her husband was alive. Count Henri had received seven to ten pounds income from the toll, whereas she had been able to collect only forty to sixty sous. "Now," she writes, "because I have the aforementioned toll . . . they run to you and complain for very little" ["Nunc

vero, ad vos concurrent et vobis pro minimo conqueruntur."] She knew that they were trying to take advantage of her, and she clearly found it intolerable. See *Recueil des historiens des Gaules et de la France*, vol. 16, ed. M. J. J. Brial (Paris: Imprimerie royale, 1806–22), cclv, 15–16. Similarly, her brother Philip Augustus, evidently thinking that the regency of a woman weakened the strength of Champagne, took the bold step, in order to consolidate his support in Flanders, of precipitously marrying a niece of Philip of Flanders, to whom Marie's minor son Henri was already betrothed. He underestimated Marie's resolve, and the incident provoked a brief war between the armies of Champagne and those of the king.

77. See June Hall McCash, "Marie de Champagne's 'Cuer d'ome et cors de fame': Aspects of Feminism and Misogyny in the Twelfth Century," in *The Spirit of the Court: Selected Proceedings of the Fourth Congress of the International Courtly Literature Society, Toronto 1983*, ed. Glyn S. Burgess and Robert A. Taylor (Cambridge: Brewer, 1985), 234–45.

78. Jane Frances Anne Henderson, "A Critical Edition of Evrat's *Genesis:* Creation to the Flood" (Ph.D. diss., University of Toronto, 1977), 63.

79. See Reinhold R. Grimm, *Shöpfung und Sündenfall in der altfranzösischen Genesisdichtung des Evrat* (Bern: Lang, 1976), MS A, lines 174–84.

80. See T. Atkinson Jenkins, "*Eructavit:* An Old French Metrical Paraphrase of Psalm XLIV," *Gesellschaft für Romanische Literatur* 20 (Dresden, 1909), line 11.

81. William of Malmesbury, *De gestis regum Anglorum*, ed. William Stubbs, Rolls Series 90 (London: Eyre and Spottiswoode, 1887–89), 2:494. Elizabeth Salter seems to see this as a favorable comment, contending that William of Malmesbury writes "respectfully of the learning, piety and generosity of Maud." See *English and International: Studies in the Literature, Art and Patronage of Medieval England*, ed. Derek Pearsall and Nicolette Zeeman (Cambridge, England: Cambridge University Press, 1988), 12. The key word, however, is *inconsiderate*, defined unequivocally by the *Oxford Latin Dictionary* as "without due care or consideration, thoughtlessly, injudiciously." There can be little question, particularly considering the comments that follow about the hardship it placed on her descendants, that William intends to rebuke her actions.

82. Translation quoted in Lawrence Wright, "The Role of Musicians at Court in Twelfth-Century Britain," *Art and Patronage in the English Romanesque*, eds. Sarah Macready and F. H. Thompson (London: Society of Antiquaries, 1986), 98.

83. Bell, "Medieval Women Book Owners," 157.

84. Ibid., 161. See also John Plummer, ed. *The Hours of Catherine of Cleves* (New York: Braziller, 1966), 96.

85. Information comes from Chiara Frugoni, "L'iconographie de la femme au cours des Xe-XIIe siècles," in *La femme dans les civilisations des Xe-XIIIe siècles: Actes du colloque tenu à Poitiers les 23–25 septembre 1976* (Poitiers: Centre d'études supérieures de la civilisation médiévale, 1977).

86. On the devotion of both women and men to the Virgin, see Marina Warner, *Alone of All Her Sex: The Myth and Cult of the Virgin Mary* (London: Wiedenfeld and Nicholson, 1976), esp. 103–17.

87. See Brian Woledge and H. P. Clive, *Répertoire des plus anciens textes en prose française depuis 842 jusqu'aux premières années du XIIIe siècle* (Geneva: Droz, 1964), 127. Of the thirty English women whose patronage she examines in this volume, Karen Jambeck shows that eight requested the composition of the lives of female saints, but only three of male saints.

88. See the bilingual edition of *The Life of Beatrice of Nazareth*, trans. Roger DeGanck, (Kalamazoo, Mich.: Cistercian, 1991): xxii–xxiii.

89. See Suzanne F. Wemple, "S. Salvatore/S. Giulia: A Case Study in the Endowment and Patronage of a Major Female Monastery in Northern Italy," in *Women of the Medieval World: Essays in Honor of John H. Mundy*, ed. Julius Kirshner and Suzanne F. Wemple (Oxford: Blackwell, 1985), 86–88. Concerning the endowment, see also *Historiae patriae monumenta*, ed. Caroli Alberti (Augustae Taurinorum: Regio typographeo, 1836), 13; *Codex diplomaticus Langobardiae* (Torino, 1873), 36–37, n. 18, and 41, n. 20. The convent's first abbess was Anselberga, daughter of Ansa and Desiderius. She was also generous toward the community, although her endowments, such as the canal system to conduct water to the convent fountains, appear to have been primarily practical. Even the decorative iron doors for the convent's church had the useful function of protecting the treasury.

90. Hamburger, "Art Enclosure," 115. Agnes also founded a church and a hospital in Prague. For more information on Agnes of Prague (also known as Agnes of Bohemia), see Marie Fassbinder, *Die Selige Agnes von Prag* (Werl: Dietrich-Coelde, 1957), translated by G. Daubié as *Princesse et moniale Agnès de Bohème, amie de Sainte Claire* (Paris: Editions franciscaines, 1962; Walter W. Seton, *Some New Sources for the Life of Blessed Agnes of Bohemia* (Aberdeen: Aberdeen University Press, 1915). I am indebted to Sister Beth Lynn, O.S.C., for these last two references.

91. For the correspondence between Agnes and Clare, see Regis J. Armstrong and Ignatius C. Brady, trans., *Francis and Clare: The Complete Works* (New York: Paulist, 1982), 189–206. Note that Clare had followed the lead of Francis of Assisi in embracing a rule of poverty. Agnes, like Clare, sought approval for her own rule, but the request was denied. Clare's rule was approved in 1253, two days before her death on 11 August.

92. See Vincent de Beauvais, *De eruditione filiorum nobilium*, ed. Arpad Steiner (Cambridge, Mass.: Mediaeval Academy of America, 1938), and Astrik L. Gabriel, *The Educational Ideas of Vincent of Beauvais* (Notre Dame, Ind.: University of Notre Dame Press, 1962). According to Bell, Vincent's ideas on the education of girls "relied almost entirely on Jerome's letters concerning girls' education, insisting that by busying themselves in reading and writing, girls could escape harmful thoughts and the pleasures and vanities of the flesh." ("Medieval Women Book Owners," 162).

93. Bell, "Medieval Women Book Owners," 183 n. 57. This and subsequent examples are found in Bell's work.

94. Ibid., 163.

95. See Vallet de Viriville, "La bibliothèque d'Isabeau de Bavière," *Bulletin du bibliophile* 14 (1858): 668–69; Bell, "Medieval Women Book Owners," 163.

96. Bell, "Medieval Women Book Owners," 163; Christine de Pizan, *Oeuvres poétiques de Christine de Pisan*, ed. Maurice Roy (Paris: Firmin-Didot, 1886–96), 3:iv–ix and 3:27–57; and MS Harley, 4431, British Library, London.

97. Bell, "Medieval Women Book Owners," 163–65.

98. Mary Dominica Legge, "The Influence of Patronage on Form in Medieval French Literature," in *Stil- und Formprobleme in der Literatur*, ed. Paul Böckmann (Heidelberg: Winter, 1959), 136–41.

99. Ibid., 136.

100. I am grateful to Charity Cannon Willard for calling the patronage of Marie de Brabant to my attention. Donald Maddox and Sara Sturm-Maddox have also pointed out that the countess of Bar was one of the patrons of Jean d'Arras's *Mélusine*.

101. Prologue, line 5, cited in Marion Y. H. Aitken, ed., *Etude sur "le miroir ou les évangiles des domnées" de Robert de Gretham* (Paris: Champion, 1922), 105. See also Salter, *English and International*, 33.

102. Denis Piramus, *La "Vie seint Edmund le rei": Poéme anglo-normand du XIIe siècle*, ed. Hilding Kjellmann (1935; reprint, Geneva: Slatkine, 1974), 4–5, lines 46–52.

103. *Hist. litt.*, 33:293 and 33:295. See also Woledge and Clive, *Répertoire*, 30. One finds a similar connection drawn between "lies" and poetry in the prologue of Nicolas de Senlis to his prose translation of the *Pseudo-Turpin Chronicle*. See n. 108 below. See also Gabrielle Spiegel, *Romancing the Past: The Rise of Vernacular Prose Historiography in Thirteenth-Century France* (Berkeley and Los Angeles: University of California Press, 1993), 56.

104. Legge, "Influence of Patronage on Form," 137. See also the article by Lois Huneycutt in this volume.

105. Xenia Muratova, "Bestiaries: An Aspect of Medieval Patronage," in *Art and Patronage in the English Romanesque*, ed. Sarah Macready and F. H. Thompson, Society of Antiquaries of London, Occasional Paper, n.s. 8 (London: Burlington House, 1986), 121.

106. See Geoffrey Gaimer, *Anglo-Norman Metrical Chronicle*, 227, lines 6485–90.

107. See Tyson, "Patronage of History Writers," 189. See also Theodor Auracher, "Der sogenannte poitevinische Pseudo-Turpin," in *Zeitschrift für romanische Philologie* 1 (1877): 263. See also André de Mandach, *Chronique dite saintongeaise* (Tübingen: Niemeyer, 1970), 256; and Woledge and Clive, *Répertoire*, 25, 28. While the work's prologue is quite specific in stating that it was Yolande who requested the translation, it should be noted that the colophon names not the "contessa" but the "conta de saint Po," or her husband, Hugh IV. Most likely we have here an example of the husband's name replacing that of the wife, who is dependent upon him to provide payment to the poet. Possibly they commissioned the translation jointly, but if she was, in fact, the sole patron, it is possible that the scribe, concerned about his payments, decided to include Hugh at this belated point in the work. It is also possible that he simply made an error in the colophon, since the prologue is very specific in indicating that it was Yolande, not Hugh, who ordered the work. On the history of translations of the *Pseudo-Turpin*

Chronicle, see Spiegel, *Romancing the Past,* 55–98. Yolande de Saint-Pol was also patron of romance. *Guillaume de Palerne* was written for her. See Joan Ferrante, "Whose Voice?" The Influence of Women Patrons on Courtly Romances," in *Literary Aspects of Courtly Culture. Selected Papers from the Seventh Triennial Congress of the International Courtly Literature Society, University of Massachusetts, Amherst, USA, 27 July–1 August 1992,* edited by Donald Maddox and Sara Sturm-Maddox (Cambridge, Eng.: Brewer, 1994), 12–13.

108. Woledge and Clive, *Répertoire,* 25.

109. Tyson, "Patronage of History Writers," 202; see also Woledge and Clive, *Répertoire,* 27.

110. John Benton, The Court of Champagne as a Literary Center," *Speculum* 36: 4 (1961): 587.

111. Tyson, "Patronage of History Writers," 220. It is imperative to point out that many men also lacked the training in Latin that allowed them to read with ease, with the consequence that vernacular histories as well as other forms of vernacular literature were written for both sexes.

112. Derek Baker, *Medieval Women* (Oxford: Blackwell, 1978): 17. See Bede, *Historia ecclesiastica in Opera historica,* 24. Caedmon may well have been a reluctant though nonetheless talented poet, for it was said that he "fled to the stables rather than take his turn at singing to the harp in entertainments at dinner." See Joan Nicholson, "Feminae Gloriosae: Women in the Age of Bede," in Baker, *Medieval Women,* 17. See also Angela M. Lucas, *Women in the Middle Ages: Religion, Marriage, and Letters* (New York: St. Martin's, 1983), 170–71.

113. The Abbey of Barking was particularly noted for its library and eventually for its authors, among them Clemence and an unnamed nun who composed with a sure literary hand the *Life of Edward the Confessor.*

114. See Vittore Branca, *Boccaccio: The Man and His Works,* trans. Richard Monges (New York: New York University Press, 1976), esp. 110. The tendency took root particularly in France, where, according to Joan Kelly, women may have reacted negatively to the enactment of the so-called Salic Law of 1328, which officially barred women from inheritance of the French crown. In fact, the law changed nothing, for male rule had been a customary practice for centuries. Even before the law was passed, however, women had begun to lose ground in political and social realms. See Joan Kelly, "Early Feminist Theory and the Querelle des Femmes, 1400–1789," in *Women, History, and Theory: The Essays of Joan Kelly* (Chicago: University of Chicago Press, 1984), 85.

115. See *Hist. litt.,* 30:302ff. Only one manuscript of the Latin text survives (Paris, Bibliothèque nationale, fonds latins 6784), but the French translation, of which six manuscripts are extant, seems to have been more popular. In fact, according to the account in the *Hist. litt.,* "Au moyen âge, le *Miroir des Dames* devait être entre les mains de la plupart des reines et des princesses." Quoted in Alice A. Hentsch, *De la littérature didactique au Moyen Age s'adressant spécialement aux femmes* (1903; reprint, Geneva: Slatkine, 1975), 102.

116. Diane Bornstein, *The Lady in the Tower: Medieval Courtesy Literature for Women* (Hamden, Conn.: Archon, 1983), 78. Bornstein points out that in the mid-twelfth century the "ruling partnership" of the king and queen in France had come to an abrupt end and that the queen "was no longer granted any official status in the government of the kingdom."

117. Jeanne also encouraged Joinville to write the *Vie de Saint Louis*.

118. See Hentsch, *Littérature didactique*, 99–104. It should be noted that Queen Jeanne de Navarre was a very active literary patron whose contributions deserve special study.

119. See Auguste Scheler, ed., *Dits de Watriquez de Couvin* (Brussels: Devaux, 1868).

120. Hentsch, *Littérature didactique*, 161. See Francisque Thibaut, *Marguerite d'Autriche et Jehan Lemaire de Belges* (Paris: Leroux, 1888), 119.

121. Hentsch, *Littérature didactique*, 103. The work is found in Paris, Bibliothèque nationale, fonds français 1189. The manuscript, as Hentsch describes it, contains in its entirety only the first of the three treatises that make up the *Miroir*. She speculates that Ysambart never completed it.

122. Tilde Sankovitch, "Lombarda's Reluctant Mirror: Speculum of Another Poet," in *The Voice of the Trobairitz: Perspectives on the Women Troubadours*, ed. William D. Paden (Philadelphia: University of Pennsylvania Press, 1989), 183. See Luce Irigaray, *Speculum de l'autre femme* (Paris: Minuit, 1974).

123. Paris, Bibliothèque nationale, ms. fr. 12420, fol. 101 verso.

124. Christine de Pizan, *The Book of the City of Ladies*, trans. Earl Jeffrey Richards (New York: Persea, 1982), 5. All other English quotations from this work are between pages 5 and 9.

125. The Middle French text is taken from Maureen Lois Cheney Curnow, "*Le livre de la cité des dames*: A Critical Edition" (Ph.D. diss., Vanderbilt University, 1975), 2:620. All other Middle French citations of the work are from this source, and page numbers will be noted in the text.

126. Charity Cannon Willard suggests the possibility that the work may have been commissioned by Marguerite's parents, Marguerite of Bavaria and Jean sans Peur, although she indicates that such patronage is by no means certain. See Christine de Pizan, *A Medieval Woman's Mirror of Honor: The Treasury of the City of Ladies*, trans. Charity Cannon Willard (Tenafly, N.J.: Bard Hall, and New York: Persea, 1989), 39–40, 43. It is interesting to note that Christine herself was determined that her *Trésor* reach its intended audience, and she states her intention to "multiply this work throughout the world in various copies, whatever the cost might be, and present it in particular places to queens, princesses, and noble ladies." See Christine de Pizan, *Mirror of Honor*, 224.

127. Ibid., 43.

128. See Curnow, "*Cité des dames*."

129. Quoted by Dorothy Miner, *Anastaise and Her Sisters: Women Artists of the*

Middle Ages (Baltimore: Walters Art Gallery, 1974), 8. See also Henry Martin, *Les miniaturistes français* (Paris: Leclerc, 1906), 164; and Millard Meiss, *French Painting in the Time of Jean de Berry* (London: Phaidon, 1967), 1:362 n. 3.

130. British Museum MS Yates Thompson, 27. See Miner, *Anastaise and Her Sisters,* 19; Meiss, *French Painting,* 160ff., figs. 363–66. The pair were later lured away from Yolande's court by the future Charles V, probably during his regency at the time of Jean II's captivity. After the death of Charles V in 1380, the father-daughter team went to the court of Jean de Berry, who was known to have engaged only the best.

131. See the article by Francis Underhill in this volume. The name of Mechthild von der Pfalz is also connected with the founding of the universities of Freiburg and Tübingen. In earlier times the Byzantine empress Eudokia had been involved in the founding or reorganization of the University of Constantinople. For information on her patronage, see Anne McClanan's article in this volume.

132. It is interesting to note that one of Caxton's earliest printed texts was his own translation of one of the works of Christine de Pizan, whom he called "the mistress and mirror of intelligence." See Madeleine Pelner Cosman, "Christine de Pizan's Well-Tempered Feminism," in Christine de Pizan, *Mirror of Honor,* 14–15.

133. See Holzknecht, *Literary Patronage,* 105. See also Norman Francis Blake, *William Caxton and His World* (London: Deutsch, 1969).

134. See Cartwright, *Isabella d'Este,* 2:25ff. On Isabella's library, see 1:20 and 1:76ff.

135. For information on the literary debate surrounding the Quarrel of the Rose, see Joseph L. Baird and John R. Kane, eds., *La Querelle de la Rose: Letters and Documents* (Chapel Hill: University of North Carolina Department of Romance Languages, 1978, distributed by the University of North Carolina Press). On the *querelle des femmes,* see Kelly, "Early Feminist Theory."

The Empress Theodora and the Tradition of Women's Patronage in the Early Byzantine Empire

ANNE L. McCLANAN

Evidence of the patronage of the Byzantine empress Theodora (d. 548) has been neglected in scholarly literature, although contemporary sources demonstrate its variety and extent.[1] Records of the beneficence of the Emperor Justinian's wife appear in several sixth-century sources, the best known being those of the court historian Procopius, namely the *Buildings* and the *Anecdota*. Both texts conform to a distinct rhetorical genre that, as we shall see later, molded his account.[2] We are not, however, compelled to rely on Procopius alone. Other contemporary writings, typically relegated to a subordinate position, provide valuable information that augments our understanding of the empress's patronage. Furthermore, Theodora was represented as a donor in the Church of San Vitale in Ravenna, and we have record of other important monuments in which she was depicted.

Before undertaking an analysis of these sources for what they reveal about Theodora's patronage, we must first consider the patronage tradition established by previous Byzantine imperial women. These earlier patrons determine the patterns by which the representation of Theodora's patronage was formulated and elucidate her particular significance. The powerful empresses of the Houses of Constantine and Theodosius set important precedents in both patronage and other public displays of authority during the fourth and fifth centuries. The overview of these antecedents that follows shows consistent patterns in the patronage of these women. They gravitated toward traditional Christian *philanthropia*, often establishing poorhouses, hospitals, and religious establishments. These projects perhaps were seen as extensions of typical Byzantine women's interest in their families and immediate communities. Not limited to just these charitable enterprises, some of the period's most remarkable buildings were built by early Byzantine empresses.

Helena (d. between 330 and 336), the mother of Constantine the Great, was seen as the first great Christian female patron in the imperial family. Although even her most famous act—the discovery of the True Cross—was almost certainly a legend, this unearthing was considered an undisputed truth during the early Byzantine period.[3] After domestic unrest in the imperial court in Rome that possibly implicated her in the murder of Fausta, Helena did make a pilgrimage to the Holy Land, but her patronage is a murky issue. Her visit overlapped Constantine's main phase of building in the area, and, not surprisingly, the activities of the two are not carefully differentiated in most sources.[4] Eusebius does, however, cite the churches on the Mount of Olives and in Bethlehem as her initiatives.[5] The magnitude of her patronage was gradually exaggerated, to the point that she was said to have built over thirty churches throughout the Holy Land, and later empresses were eulogized as the "new Helena."[6]

Aelia Flavia Flaccilla (d. 387) was represented as fulfilling all of the traditional ideals of *basileía* (imperial dominion).[7] As the first wife of Theodosius I and descended from Spanish aristocracy, her historical position at the beginning of the Theodosian period enhanced the importance of her example. In his *oratio consolatoria* upon her death in about 387, Gregory of Nyssa sets forth her fundamental attributes, one of the most prominent features being her *philanthropia*, manifested through her generous largess to the poor.[8] The terms for the description of imperial women become conventionalized so that the charitable deeds and foundations of later empresses are framed in the same topoi.

The patronage of the wife of Theodosius II, Aelia Eudokia Augusta (d. 460), in addition to following the traditional patterns of patronage, reflected her personal interests and background. She built in Constantinople the Church of Saint Polyeuktos, later sumptuously reestablished in the sixth century by her descendant Anicia Juliana. Some versions of the *Chronicle of John Malalas* record that when she made her first pilgrimage to the Holy Land in 438 she stopped in Antioch, where she delivered an encomium on her birthplace. Proudly establishing kinship, she states, "I boast that I am of your race and blood," endowing the corn supply of the city and paying for the restoration of the burned Bath of Valens.[9] The grateful citizens commemorated her generosity with a bronze statue in the Mouseion that was still standing when Malalas wrote almost a century later.[10] She may also have been responsible for the emperor's extension of Antioch's city walls to include the suburbs.[11]

In 441 or 442 Eudokia separated from Theodosius, yet she managed to retain *basileía* while living in Jerusalem until her death in 460. The origin of her journey in domestic unrest is reminiscent of the suspect inception of Helena's equally acclaimed pilgrimage. Eudokia's impressive list of foundations includes the Church of Saint Stephen, the Church of Saint Peter, several hospices, and a tower in honor of her Euthymius on Mount Muntar. Finally she was buried in the Church of Saint Stephen near the martyr, a common mortuary practice in the period. She rebuilt the south wall of Jerusalem, reportedly saying, "It was for me that the prophet David spoke when he said, 'In thy good pleasure [*eudokia*], O Lord, the walls of Jerusalem shall be built.'"[12] The allusion to David effectively reinforces her connection to *basileía*. Her patronage in the Holy Land was so extensive that she is frequently considered one of its greatest builders, surpassing even the earlier female patrons of ancient Palestine, Flaccilla and Helena.[13]

In addition to her momentous works of philanthropic Christian piety, the Empress Eudokia may also have influenced the enlargement and reorganization of the "university" in Constantinople.[14] Her extensive training in classical literature was exceptional, so she is sometimes considered the impetus behind the reforms made by Theodosius II. Several of the changes include a sharp increase in the rank of senior professors as well as the expansion of facilities. Even well-known pagans received these new distinctions, such as the grammarian Helladios, who claimed to have killed nine Christians in a clash between the pagans and Christians of Alexandria.[15] Eudokia's personal inclinations are evident in the literary project she sponsored while in Palestine, the *Homerocentones*, Bible stories retold in the Homeric idiom.[16]

Eudokia's rival in court politics was Pulcheria (d. ca. 453), the sister of Theodosius II. This sister avowed celibacy early in life, ostensibly from piety, but this move proved quite effective as well for solidifying her personal power.[17] One of the primary tools that she employed for the display of her carefully cultivated authority was patronage. Through a series of well-chosen projects, she selectively emphasized aspects of her public identity. Her foundations reflect the predictable range of ventures, including churches, poorhouses, hospitals, and hostels.[18] She fashioned herself a "bride of Christ," an affinity underscored by building a series of churches dedicated to the Virgin Mary, the Virgin of the Blachernai, the Virgin of the Hodegetria, and the Virgin of the Chalkoprateia.[19] To draw attention to her recently acquired relics, Pulcheria built the Church of Saint Lawrence to house relics that her sister-in-law,

Eudokia, had brought back from the Holy Land. In addition, she also initiated the Church of the Prophet Isaiah and the Chapel of Saint Stephen. These displays of singular privilege solidified her position of strength and gave her a very visible edge in her controversial maneuvers for influence at court.

One final contemporary example of female patronage of which Theodora would have been aware was that of the Princess Anicia Juliana (d. 527 or 529), the sole patron of one of the most impressive buildings in Constantinople, the now-destroyed Church of Saint Polyeuktos. This building was just being completed at the time of Justinian's ascent to sole rulership and Theodora's rise to empress rank. Located in the heart of the capital in the Constantianae quarter, the church was constructed from 524 to 527. Anicia Juliana was the only heir of her wealthy and illustrious parents, Anicius Olybrius and Placidia the Younger. Her father, who was one of the last emperors of the western portion of the Byzantine Empire, traced his family back through seven centuries of Roman statesmen. Both of her mother's grandparents furthermore were the descendants of Theodosius I.[20] This venerable lineage offers a strong contrast to that of the illiterate former peasant Emperor Justin I, who had managed to acquire the Byzantine throne in 518 instead of Anicia Juliana's son, Flavius Anicius Olybrius. Because of this rivalry Anicia's patronage requires scrutiny; it could not have escaped the attention of Theodora. Anicia clearly possessed vast resources and a strong inclination to demonstrate both her wealth and her lineage. The lavish decoration of the Church of Saint Polyeuktos, therefore, served to illustrate her imperial prerogative.

Archeological excavation has revealed a great deal about the Church of Saint Polyeuktos. The main plan is square, with the typical eastern apse and western narthex. The interior was further divided by a side aisle along the north and south walls. Given the size and arrangement of the foundations, the structure probably had a large dome, indicating the grandiose nature of Anicia's church.[21] Marble revetments adorned the interior, accented by elaborately carved and inscribed architectural ornament.

Part of the decoration was in fact what allowed the church to be identified, for inscribed fragments contained a few pieces from the dedicatory inscription of Saint Polyeuktos preserved in the *Greek Anthology,* a collection of ancient and Byzantine epigrams.[22] This poem offers a revealing image of female aristocratic patronage, because Anicia Juliana's church is the continuation of a tradition established by her female forebears. With typical encomiastic flourish, the text reads:

Eudokia the empress, eager to honour God, first built here a temple of Polyeuctus the servant of God. But she did not make it as great and as beau-

tiful as it is, not from any economy or lack of possessions—what doth a
queen lack?—but because her prophetic soul told her that she should leave
a family well knowing how better to adorn it. Whence Juliana, the glory of
her blessed parents, inheriting their royal blood in the fourth generation,
did not defeat the hopes of the Queen, the mother of a noble race, but raised
this from a small temple to its present size and beauty, increasing the glory
of her many-sceptered ancestors."[23]

Thus the patronage of Anicia is carefully shown in the light of her rarefied
ancestry, tacitly commenting by force of the contrast on the parvenu Emperor
Justin I.

The imperial potency of her patronage is further expanded through allusion to Solomon: "She alone did violence to Time and surpassed the wisdom
of renowned Solomon by raising a habitation for God."[24] Based on the "royal"
cubit of 0.518 meters, the church was built to be a hundred cubits square,
trying to match in size and grandeur Solomon's Temple. Likewise the decoration of the church derives from descriptions of the Temple, including palm
trees, lilies, and vines.[25] In scale and costliness Anicia's church exceeded any
other church in the capital at the time of construction; Hagia Sophia, built
shortly thereafter, seems like a response of one-upmanship, especially in view
of Justinian's apocryphal remark on entering his church for the first time,
"Solomon, I have outdone thee!"[26]

The Greek Anthology provides other examples of Anicia's patronage, such
as the Church of Saint Euphemia at Olybrius. As in the case of the Church of
Saint Polyeuktos, here she also constitutes her philanthropia in terms of her
female ancestors. The building was founded by Eudokia, adorned by Placidia,
and then further enhanced by Anicia.[27]

Anicia Juliana's patronage is also shown in a luxurious manuscript, which
may have been a gift. One of the finest surviving late antique manuscripts, the
Vienna Dioscurides, portrays Anicia in a dedication miniature (fig. 1).[28] Significantly, her image in the manuscript alludes to her architectural patronage
by surrounding the eight-pointed star with putti, still faintly visible, at work
building. Seated between classically inspired personifications of Prudence and
Magnanimity, she powerfully vaunts her cultivated background.

Theodora's patronage emulates aristocratic models set by women such as
Anicia Juliana. In keeping with the tradition, she extended her charity to poorhouses, convents, and new churches. Her need to engage in patronage may
have been strengthened by the fact that her own background is somewhat
dubious, for Procopius states that she came from a disreputable family tied to

the circus and had been a notorious prostitute before marriage to the Emperor Justinian. A standard insult in the tradition of antique rhetoric was to accuse one's opponent whenever possible of having embarrassing origins, so it is debatable how scurrilous her background actually was. Procopius's construction of Theodora's scandalous past must be evaluated in light of his rhetorical tradition. Although she may not have originated in the aristocracy, she could have otherwise had a reputable, though modest, past and still be vulnerable to the *Anecdota*'s insinuations. The previous neglect of Theodora's work as a patron was partially the outcome of Procopius's ad hominem attack in the *Anecdota*, which has diverted attention from her conventional charitable deeds.

Procopius begins the *Anecdota* with an account of his reasons for writing the book, which in turn shape his representation of Theodora's patronage. He explicitly puts himself within the tradition of the invective or antiencomium: "For what men of later times would have learned of the licentious life of Semiramis or of the madness of Sardanapalus and of Nero, if the records of these things had not been left behind by the writers of their times?"[29] After briefly feigning great reluctance at performing such an unsavory task, he thereupon dives into his exposé with obvious relish. The actual means by which he kept his text secret during his lifetime and then made it accessible once dead are unknown, for there are no Byzantine references to the work before the tenth century.[30]

Fig. 1. Vienna Dioscurides. Cod. med. graec. 1, fol. 6 verso. Princess Anicia Juliana. ca. 512 A.D. Bild-Archiv der Österreichischen Nationalbibliothek, Wien.

The education of Procopius grounded him firmly in classical rhetoric, so he could proficiently argue both sides of an argument with equal adroitness.[31] Although now questioned, the long-standing critique of rhetoric focused on its disregard for the truth.[32] Thus Menander's handbook of rhetoric, which was widely used in Byzantium, delineates the contents and form of genres such as the encomium.[33] The rhetor teaches how to praise one set of features as well as its inverse set; thus the aspiring Byzantine writer and statesman learned how to fit any fact into the desired structure of interpretation.[34] The dramatically different viewpoints of the *Buildings* and the *Anecdota* illustrate the force of these rhetorical practices.

Procopius's *Buildings* provides the most detailed and geographically comprehensive account of imperial patronage during the period of Justinian and Theodora.[35] It records an extensive program of building throughout the empire, the magnitude of which notoriously emptied the imperial treasuries. The work as a whole is uneven and incomplete; for instance, all of Italy is omitted. The later sections of *Buildings* seem skeletal, and in place of stock encomia there are merely long lists of public works. Book 1, however, appears substantially more complete and polished; the whole piece is devoted to Theodora's and Justinian's patronage in Constantinople. It differs to such an extent from the later books that Glanville Downey concluded that it may well have been written as "a literary show-piece designed to be presented orally before the Emperor and the Court."[36] It describes the efforts of Theodora and Justinian to rebuild Constantinople after the devastating Nike Riots of 532. The burden that this extensive construction placed on the people of the city, the former rioters, was immense. The almost punitive pace of construction hints at a rather brutal side to this extraordinarily rich phase of patronage.

In addition to rebuilding what had been lost, Theodora made entirely new foundations. The Church of Hagia Irene and its neighboring hospice were lavishly rebuilt after the riots on a substantially grander scale than the original structures. The empress cosponsored the House of Isodorus and the House of Arcadius, two hospices next to Hagia Irene.[37] Almost as an aside at the end of book 1, Procopius mentions that she also helped found another "very large" hospice specifically for the destitute who had come to Constantinople to petition the imperial court and those "led to come either by some errand of business or by some hope or by chance."[38] These projects parallel the typical acts of patronage performed by the Theodosian empresses to demonstrate their *philanthropia*. As Procopius describes Theodora's patronage, he almost duplicates a list of Pulcheria's good works: churches, hospices, and hostels. In Theodora's case, she funded these projects by means of the income from estates in Asia Minor, which Justinian had given to her upon their marriage and later augmented.[39]

Procopius mentions another example of Theodora's patronage in both the *Anecdota* and the *Buildings*, a comparison of which affords a prime example of the duplicitous nature of rhetoric. She had built the Convent of Repentance as a refuge for former prostitutes of the Constantinopolitan marketplace, who would sell their services for the pittance of three obols. Located on the Asiatic shore of the Bosporus, the convent accommodated over five hundred women. In the *Anecdota* Procopius describes it as a sadistic move to punish the women "for sins against the body."[40] The motivation in the *Buildings* is, as one would expect given its rhetorical genre, much more innocuous. Lavishing money on the institution, she "added many buildings most remarkable for their beauty and costliness, to serve as a consolation to the women, so that they should never be compelled to depart from the practice of virtue."[41] The moral status of the prostitutes is likewise inverted in the two accounts. Whereas the *Anecdota* indicated that the women had to be forcibly compelled to leave prostitution and live in the convent, the *Buildings* describes Byzantine prostitution as a form of slavery the women entered "not of their own free will, but under force of [the patrons'] lust."[42]

The *Anecdota* version of such events has been seized upon as fodder for the sensationalizing picture of Theodora prevalent since the acceptance of Procopius's invective as authentic. It has yielded a series of popular biographies, making Theodora one of the best-known figures from Byzantine history, albeit in this form warped by the antiencomium. Their titles, such as *The Female*, *Empress of the Dusk*, and *The Bearkeeper's Daughter*, divulge the ready acceptance of Procopius's slander.[43]

Lopsided appraisals fixated on the salacious aspect of the empress's representation neglect other contemporary evidence that balances the image of Theodora. John of Ephesus's Syriac text *Lives of Eastern Saints* compiles a wide range of lives of holy men, women, and Christian communities. That John of Ephesus even included Theodora in his hagiographical compilation is exceptional. In his account of the "blessed virgin" Susan, he prefaces his history with a justification for her inclusion: "The strong power of Christ . . . is wont to display its operation not only through men of great size or mighty strength, but also in weak, feeble, powerless women."[44]

John of Ephesus describes the haven Theodora created within the Hormisdas Palace in Constantinople for over five hundred persecuted former stylites, desert solitaries, and heads of convents.[45] Their geographic origin represents the heartland of Monophysite belief, covering a wide-ranging stretch of the eastern Byzantine territories.[46] Once established in Constantinople under the protection of "the believing Theodora," these holy men organized themselves on the model of a convent/monastery, with an archimandrite and a steward. According to John of Ephesus, our only source mentioning this palatial asylum, the Monophysites filled every area of the palace; "their marvellous canticles and their melancholy voices . . . were performed and uttered in all the chambers and courts [πλατεῖα] and cells and halls [τρίκλινος] of that palace [παλάτιον]."[47] In addition to the description given in the forty-seventh unit of the *Lives*, which is devoted to this Monophysite community under Theodora's protection, John of Ephesus alludes to it within the other lives he includes in his collection. The lives of the Egyptian bishop John from Hephaestu, the Edessene monk Hala, and the holy man Mare, for example, all refer to the special shelter the Empress Theodora offered them.[48]

Having a sizeable presence of Monophysites in the palace was problematic for the Chalcedonian community around them both in the capital city and court. John claims that some orthodox believers were so impressed by the holy men that they converted to Monophysitism and took communion with them. What caused even more resentment, however, was no doubt the active support that the empress showed for the heretics: "The believing queen also would regularly once in every two or three days come down to them to be blessed by them, being amazed at their community and their practices, and admiring their honoured old age, and going round among them and making obeisance to them, and regularly being blessed by each one of them."[49] In return for these spiritual favors, Theodora "provided the expenses required for them liberally in every thing."[50]

Cyril Mango has convincingly argued that Theodora's patronage of the Monophysite community extended even to the construction of the lavish church in the Hormisdas Palace, Saints Sergius and Bacchus. Theodora's power may well have been sufficiently great for her to build this church as a martyrium for the holy men. Although the inscription engraved inside the church mentions Justinian as well as Theodora, the empress is eulogized to a greater extent in the standard phrasing for appropriate *philanthropia:* "God-crowned Theodora whose mind is adorned with piety, whose constant toil lies in unsparing efforts to nourish the destitute."[51] Because both Sergius and Bacchus were Syrian saints, they would be very suitable choices for serving the Monophysite community. If Mango's theory is correct, then the church is contemporary with Hagia Sophia and not its predecessor.[52] The simultaneous construction of the two churches makes them an intriguing pair, for in Turkish the Church of Saints Sergius and Bacchus is appropriately called "Little Hagia Sophia"

(Küçük Aya Sofya Camii). Having similar plans but vastly different scales, Theodora's church parallels Justinian's grandiose endeavor. Her monogram is on some of the column capitals of several important Justinianic commissions, such as Hagia Sophia in Constantinople and the Church of Saint John in Ephesus.

Justinian had been a particularly vigorous persecuter of many groups deviating from Chalcedonian orthodoxy, including Manicheans, Jews, homosexuals, and above all the Monophysites who were so popular in Egypt and the Levant. Theodora's family probably originated in the Levant, and the sources agree that she was very protective of the Monophysites. The Chalcedonian Justinian, in contrast, was clearly more ambivalent about the horde of former stylites encamped in the palace, although he would sometimes receive their blessings. When she died in 548, Theodora had commanded that this Monophysite community continue to be supported. The account given in the *Lives of the Eastern Saints* then offers two conflicting views of the extent to which Justinian perpetuated her patronage. Although in one passage John of Ephesus states that Justinian continued their special protection, he later says that the emperor was persuaded by their adversaries to transfer the holy men to a less prominent location.[53] The Monophysite community was further dissolved by the introduction of married couples and "others who were not chaste" into their midst. The hagiographer next tells how God showed his anger at this defilement by setting the building and some of the women on fire.[54]

Procopius alludes to this conflict between Theodora's and Justinian's religious views in *Anecdota*: "They set the Christians at odds with each other in the matters under dispute, they succeeded in rending them all asunder." Whereas Procopius's writing in positive rhetorical modes emphasizes the couple's harmony and common faith, the necessary opposite is an image of discord: "Now in all this trickery they were always in full accord with each other, but openly they pretended to be at variance and thus succeeded in dividing their subjects and in fortifying their tyranny most firmly."[55] This reversal of representation offers a perverse inversion of the traditional values of marital and social harmony: "the potency of *basileía*, and with it peace and order in the Empire, depended on the fiction that all holders of dominion, female as well as male, acted from a single imperial will."[56] His speculation was transformed when he wrote the *Buildings*. Procopius, in typical panegyrical terms, describes the imperial couple, "who always shared a common piety in all that they did," carefully planning their projects.[57]

Theodora's ability to sustain this Monophysite community within the Hormisdas Palace and the construction of the Church of Saints Sergius and Bacchus testifies to her status as an independent patron. Although some of her other projects were joint foundations with Justinian, she pursued a distinct agenda of building and cultural support. The sanctuary for the holy men, if John of Ephesus is to be believed at all, seems to contravene directly the policies initiated by her husband.[58]

The influence of a woman in government affairs seems to have galled the court historian, who, typically for his society, considered women's proper sphere of activity to be limited to the home.[59] Procopius writes approvingly, for example, of the former empress Euphemia, for "she was quite unable to take part in government, but continued to be wholly unacquainted with affairs of State."[60] This seclusion is used as evidence that she was "far removed from wickedness."[61] Euphemia is in this way set up as the positive example and a foil for the negative portrayal given Theodora. Procopius's ability to employ Euphemia as a counterexample demonstrates the degree of manipulation in his representations. Earlier in the *Anecdota* he claims that she was previously a concubine of Justin I, but for the purposes of his forced contrast between her and Theodora, he is quite willing to describe her when it suits his rhetorical needs in terms of conventional feminine virtues.[62] He depicted Theodora's action's necessarily indirect nature as base conniving and willfulness: "This woman [Theodora] claimed the right to administer everything in the State by her own arbitrary judgment."[63]

A contemporary of Theodora and Procopius, John of Lydus, represents her influence in a more flattering light. In *De magistratibus* he depicts Theodora's contribution to the ouster of John the Cappodocian as an act of almost saintly disinterest. Lydus claims that everyone knew of the Cappodocian's corruption except the emperor himself, but that nobody had the courage to inform Justinian of the situation. Then "the emperor's wife and helpmeet, who was most vigilant in her sympathy towards those suffering injustice, found it intolerable to ignore the destruction of the state" and told the emperor "grievances that were of the utmost severity."[64]

The *Chronicle of John Malalas* enumerates rather blandly the pious acts of Justinian and Theodora, citing their patronage and specifically mentioning the work of the empress that was directed towards helping other women. In sixth-century Byzantium young girls from poor families would be sold to brothelkeepers and forced to become prostitutes for the rest of their lives. A standard act of charity lauded by Christian sources was to buy the women back from the brothelkeepers and provide them with bridal dowries. In Malalas's *Chronicle* Theodora freed many prostitutes of Constantinople in this way from what was justly described by Malalas as "the yoke of their wretched slavery."[65]

Glimpses such as this reveal the grim reality of the institution of prostitution in the sixth-century capital city, countering the sordid sensationalism with which it is typically handled.

Theodora's patronage extended even to the frontier of the Byzantine Empire at Antioch. Although one of the most culturally and economically important cities of the Roman Empire, in the second quarter of the sixth century it experienced a series of disasters after which it never fully recovered its previous eminence. A ravaging fire in 525 and then the two earthquakes of 526 and 528 crippled the city so that the Persian sack in 540 ended any hope of recovery.[66]

Theodora's acts as a patron are enumerated in the *Chronicle* of Malalas: "The most devout Theodora also provided much for the city [Antioch]." She had built "what is known as the basilica of Anatolius, for which the columns were sent from Constantinople."[67] The prestige of imported materials marked the building as an important foundation. She also had a church founded and dedicated to Saint Michael in Antioch. Both buildings were started in 527, the year that Justinian became coemperor in April and then sole ruler in August upon the death of Emperor Justin I. Perhaps these examples of Theodora's patronage were designed partially to mark this occasion, although the earthquake of 526 that devastated Antioch may also have been a factor. The concentration of her activity in Antioch is reminiscent of Eudokia's, but this preponderance in the case of Theodora is the result of Malalas's regional interests.

Procopius's eulogy in the *Buildings* of Justinian's construction in Antioch does not corroborate the account of Malalas. The court historian speaks only of the patronage of the emperor as he rebuilt the walls, cleared debris, and had the city center rebuilt after its destruction by Chosroes.[68] Procopius does not even mention Theodora's patronage within Antioch, however substantial according to Malalas. Procopius's description of Antioch, though, must be viewed as a set piece, much like his rhetorical recital of Justinian's heroically proportioned building patronage at Daras.[69] The most thorough commentator on this passage concluded that Procopius lacks even the minimal accuracy or "circumstantial information" that one might reasonably expect from a panegyric that would customize the routine rhetorical tropes to the particular subject at hand.[70] Procopius not only misrepresents features of Antioch in *Buildings* but also contradicts the account he himself gave of Antioch in his *Wars*.[71] In addition, Malalas is a more reliable source than Procopius for evaluating Theodora's patronage of Antioch, because he lived there until 532, the period when Theodora's Antiochene building projects there were being executed.

Although Procopius is routinely privileged as the most dependable source on the Justinianic period, the case of Thedora's patronage in Antioch is but one

Fig. 2. Theodora and Retinue. Apse Mosaic. ca. 540–50 A.D. San Vitale, Ravenna. Alinari/Art Resource, New York.

example of an instance in which an alternate source such as Malalas should be favored. Each document presents its own problems and strengths, so that in particular circumstances Malalas offers the best source we have. Detailed analysis of Procopius's and Malalas's treatment of Arethas, king of the Ghassanids, has led Irfan Shahîd to rely on Malalas and not Procopius for portions of his account.[72]

Malalas briefly mentions several other acts of patronage by Theodora in his chronicle. Theodora had made and sent to Jerusalem "a very costly cross, set with pearls."[73] A few other charitable acts are described, such as an excursion she made to the mineral springs of Pythion in which she and her "4,000" companions made donations to the churches, poorhouses, and monasteries en route.[74] These displays of *philanthropia* mirror very closely the precedent set by the Theodosian empresses.

The flattering depictions conform to a typology, of course, just as the invective does. Although numerous accounts of the Byzantine and classical imperial milieu survive in this propagandistic mode, the rhetorical type represented by the *Anecdota* is rarer. There are commonsense reasons for this. The author of a document composed to incriminate the current rulers is obviously put in

Fig. 3. Justinian and Retinue. Apse Mosaic. ca. 540–50 A.D. San Vitale, Ravenna.
Alinari/Art Resource, New York.

a dangerous position, whatever the degree of accuracy of its contents. More
commonly, these indictments were invented after the death of their subject
as a justification of a new regime. The infrequency of surviving texts of this
genre in Byzantium might help to explain the reluctance on the part of some
historians to acknowledge its conventions of form.

The vocabulary of rhetoric, so easily molded to the requirements of context, also has a visual equivalent. The standard set of forms offered by the
encomium parallel the conventions deployed in the portrait of Theodora and
her courtiers in the apse of San Vitale in Ravenna. The portrait is, above all
else, an offering scene (fig. 2). With the pendant portrait of Justinian and court
(fig. 3), her image has multiple layers of meaning because of its context in
the church and its complex imagery. The themes of offering and kingship that
appear elsewhere in the program are emphasized in these two prominent portraits of the emperor and empress accompanied by separate retinues, in the act
of presenting gifts to the church. Although Julian Argentarius was actually
the chief donor of the church, the couple are marked as founders in a symbolic
sense. Justinian holds a gold paten bearing the eucharistic bread; his wife, the
chalice that contained the wine offered at the altar. This act is uniquely ap-

propriate to the location, the apse, as it parallels in some sense the eucharistic sacrifice taking place below. This central theme of San Vitale's iconography, eucharistic sacrifice, is coherently reinforced by the imperial presence.[75]

The exact classification of the depicted imperial offering is questionable. On the basis of the Emperor Constantine Porphyrogenitos's *Book of Ceremonies*, compiled in the tenth century yet containing much earlier material, the scene can be interpreted as a representation of the Great Entrance. From the customs described in Porphyrogenitos and the fourteenth-century treaty by Pseudo-Kodinos, Theodora seems to be depicted in the prothesis of the church in the act of preparing gifts with her attendants.[76] A contrasting theory also derived from the *Book of Ceremonies* suggests that she is to be seen participating in an offering ceremony of the church donors.[77]

Within the context of the tumultuous history of Ravenna during the period, the imperial portraits affirmed the newly regained Byzantine power in the city in a charged political scenario. The mosaics were made soon after the reconquest of the city, most likely during the period when Victor held the episcopal see, 537/38–544/45.[78] The formulation of the two mosaics, with the Byzantine emperor and empress placed firmly in pendant positions in the most sacred area of the church, solidifies the claim to Byzantine imperial authority being made in Ravenna at that time.

Official representations of Theodora were probably widespread. Byzantine writers mention several very prominent public images of the empress in and near Constantinople. The now-destroyed Chalke Gate was decorated with an elaborate mosaic celebrating recent military triumphs. Procopius tells us that at the center of the whole decorative program was shown "the Emperor and the Empress Theodora, both seeming to rejoice and to celebrate the victories over both the King of the Vandals and the King of the Goths, who approach them as prisoners of war to be led into bondage. Around them stands the Roman Senate, all in festal mood. This spirit is expressed by the cubes of the mosaic, which by their colors depict exultation on their very countenances."[79] Thus in a secular context as well as the religious setting of San Vitale, it was considered appropriate to include the Empress Theodora in a joint emblem of imperial authority.

Procopius describes another official representation of Theodora slightly later in the *Buildings* as the conclusion of his discussion of the public bath called Arcadianae, located outside the city. The court historian renders it as an idyllic scene. Along the side by the sea were arrayed marble pavements, columns, and statues. Though he conventionally mentions that the sculptures were all extraordinarily beautiful—so fine, in fact, that they could be mistaken for the work of Phidias, Lysippus, or Praxiteles—the only statue that he singles out for further comment is the one of the empress: "There also the Empress Theodora stands upon a column, which the city in gratitude for the court dedicated to her. The statue is indeed beautiful, but still inferior to the beauty of the Empress . . . the column is purple, and it clearly declares even before one sees the statue that it bears an Empress."[80] This monument corresponds to one made for Eudoxia, wife of Arcadius. Sozomen writes, "The silver statue of the empress . . . was placed upon a column of porphyry; and the event was celebrated by loud acclamations, dancing, games, and other manifestations of public rejoicing, usually observed on the erection of the statues of emperors."[81] By lingering on the monument's imperial signifier, the purple color reserved for Byzantine royalty, Procopius adeptly incorporates Theodora into the visual language that was used to promulgate imperial ideology.

A surviving fragment of sculpture might give us some indication of how such a statue of Theodora would have appeared (fig. 4).[82] Found inside the medieval wall of Milan, this piece is attributed on stylistic grounds to the sixth-century Constantinopolitan school.[83] The distinctive crown comprises

Fig. 4. Head of Theodora? Sixth century. Museo archeologico, Milan. Alinari/Art Resource, New York.

Fig. 5. Detail of Fig. 2. Theodora and Retinue. Apse Mosaic. ca. 540–50 A.D. San Vitale, Ravenna. Alinari/Art Resource, New York.

a pearl- and jewel-laden diadem encircling a snooded hairstyle. Within the study of comparable images of Byzantine empresses, the headdress type is not known to predate ca. 500 in any of these confirmed examples.[84] If it is a sculptural portrait of Theodora, then presumably it was installed in Milan during the early 540s during the limited period of Byzantine control, that is, fairly soon after the devastating massacre there in 539. The specific identification of the sculpture with Theodora is founded only on its likeness with her San Vitale portrait (fig. 5). The image of the empress in Ravenna was clearly not intended to be a precise portrait; it was to have a much more important role in the iconographic program than the documentation of an individual's appearance. Given the idealized nature of both sculpture and the mosaic, their superficial correspondence thus does not seem very conclusive.[85] For lack of any more substantive proof, it is difficult to maintain that it is Theodora rather than another woman, such as Galla Placidia or one of the other identifications sometimes made for this work. Despite these uncertainties, one author in his identification of it as Theodora went so far as to assert that it is "convincing not only as to physical similarity but psychological truth as well."[86]

The verbal descriptions in the *Buildings* of Theodora's official imagery substantiate the observations made about her role in the San Vitale ideological program. She was tightly incorporated into the structures used to display imperial dominion. The marginalized status that Procopius seeks to give her in his invective in the *Anecdota* must be seen as an unabashedly conventional retort to the equally mannered official depiction.

The traditions of rhetoric and female imperial patronage shaped the way Theodora's *philanthropia* was represented. The active patronage of Helena, the Theodosian empresses, and Anicia Juliana set an impressive standard by which to assess the work of Theodora. In the full range of textual sources, however, Theodora was clearly an active patron in her own right. Her sanctuary and church for the heretical Monophysites inside an imperial palace in Constantinople demonstrate that she possessed enough latitude to pursue policies that conflicted with those of the Emperor Justinian. Furthermore, her building projects both within the capital city and at the borders of the Byzantine Empire show considerable command of resources. The type of *philanthropia* in which she engaged, moreover, evidenced a shrewd awareness of the practices and precedents of aristocratic female patronage. It would seem, therefore, that her capabilities as a cultural patron have often been underrated, primarily because of scholars' overdependence on Procopius as a source for the period. Once we recognize Theodora's achievements, however, her patronage offers a fascinating example of the display of female *basileía* in early Byzantium.

NOTES

1. This research was begun in a graduate seminar entitled "The Age of Justinian," taught in the spring term of 1991 at Harvard University by Professors Ioli Kalavrezou and Clive Foss. In the preparation of this article, I have benefited from the valuable advice of June McCash, Jeff Johnson, Nicolette Trahoulia, and the University of Georgia Press's anonymous readers. I would also like to express my appreciation for the ongoing guidance and encouragement of my advisor, Ioli Kalavrezou, as well as for the intellectual stimulus and financial support of the Department of Fine Arts of Harvard University.

2. The Greek name *Anecdota* simply means "unpublished things," but this too may be a later name. The title *Secret History* adopted for some English translations of the

text has naively sensationalistic overtones, with the implicit assumption that the scandalous "secret" history must be more truthful than the more easily recognized rhetoric of the *Buildings* or *Wars*. The translations of Procopius used in this article are *Anecdota*, trans. H. B. Dewing, Loeb Classical Library (Cambridge, Mass.: Harvard University Press, 1935) and *Buildings*, trans. H. B. Dewing, Loeb Classical Library (Cambridge, Mass.: Harvard University Press, 1940).

3. Not included in Eusebius, the first mention is over sixty years after her visit, in the sermon by Ambrose, *De obitu Theodosii*, ed. Otto Faller, in *Corpus scriptorum ecclesiasticorum Latinorum*, vol. 73 (Vienna: Hoelder-Pichler-Tempsky, 1955).

4. E. D. Hunt, *Holy Land Pilgrimage in the Later Roman Empire, A.D. 312–460* (New York: Oxford University Press, 1982), 37.

5. Eusebius, *Vita Constantini*, ed. Friedhelm Winkelmann, *Griechischen Christlichen Schriftsteller der ersten Jahrhunderts* (Berlin: Akademie, 1975), iii, 43.

6. Hunt, *Holy Land Pilgrimage*, 29 and 48.

7. Kenneth G. Holum, *Theodosian Empresses: Women and Imperial Dominion in Late Antiquity* (Berkeley and Los Angeles: University of California Press, 1982), 3.

8. Ibid., 27.

9. John Malalas, *The Chronicle of John Malalas*, trans. Elizabeth Jeffreys, Michael Jeffreys, and Roger Scott (Melbourne: Australian Association for Byzantine Studies, 1986), 195.

10. Glanville Downey, *Ancient Antioch* (Princeton, N.J.: Princeton University Press, 1963), 217.

11. Holum, *Theodosian Empresses*, 118, for full citations.

12. Malalas, *Chronicle*, 195.

13. Yizhar Hirschfeld, *Judean Desert Monasteries in the Byzantine Period* (New Haven, Conn.: Yale University Press, 1992), 242.

14. Alan Cameron argues that Eudokia's classical pagan predilections have been exaggerated, "The Empress and the Poet: Paganism and Politics at the Court of Theodosius II." *Yale Classical Studies* 27 (1982): 217–90. Previous scholarship on the "university" has allowed her influence as a possibility: Michael J. Kyriakis, "The University: Origin and Early Phases in Constantinople," *Byzantion* 41 (1971): 168; and Paul Lemerle, *Byzantine Humanism: The First Phase*, trans. Helen Linday and Ann Moffat (Canberra: Australian Association of Byzantine Studies, 1986), 66.

15. Lemerle, *Byzantine Humanism*, 127.

16. *Eudociae Augustae*, ed. Arthur Ludwich, Bibliotheca scriptorum Graecorum et Romanorum Teubneriana (Leipzig: Teubner, 1897).

17. Holum's overly generous assessment of her precocious role in Constantinopolitan politics has recently been revised by Alan Cameron and Jacqueline Long, *Barbarians and Politics at the Court of Arcadius* (Berkeley and Los Angeles: University of California Press, 1993), 399–401.

18. W. Ensslin, "Pulcheria 2," *Paulys Real-Encyclopädie der classischen Altertumswissenschaft* 23 (Stuttgart: Metzler, 1959), 1961.

19. Holum, *Theodosian Empresses*, 142.

20. Martin Harrison, *A Temple for Byzantium* (Austin: University of Texas Press, 1989), 36.

21. Ibid., 131.

22. Cyril Mango and Ihor Sevçenko, "Remains of the Church of Saint Polyeuktos at Constantinople," *Dumbarton Oaks Papers* 15 (1961): 243–47.

23. *Greek Anthology*, trans. W. R. Paton, Loeb Classical Library (Cambridge, Mass.: Harvard University Press, 1916), 1:10.1–11.

24. Ibid., 1:10.47–48.

25. Harrison, *A Temple for Byzantium*, 138.

26. Ibid., 139.

27. *Greek Anthology*, 1:12.

28. Kurt Weitzmann, *Late Antique and Early Christian Book Illumination* (New York: Braziller, 1977), 61.

29. Procopius, *Anecdota*, 1.9.

30. Cameron does not name it, but this tenth-century source is the Souda lexicon. Averil Cameron, *Procopius and the Sixth Century* (Berkeley and Los Angeles: University of California Press, 1985), 50.

31. Hans-Georg Beck, *Kaiserin Theodora und Prokop: Der Historiker und sein Opfer* (Munich: Piper, 1986), 18.

32. Plato provides the classic example of this skepticism, for even the earliest proponents of rhetoric were perceived as interested not in "what is truly good or noble, but what will be thought so; since it is on the latter, not the former, that persuasion depends" [*Phaedrus*, trans. R. Hackforth [Indianapolis: Bobbs Merrill, 1952], 119). An extreme example of the recent positive reassessment of the value of rhetoric is Renato Barilli, *Rhetoric*, trans. Giuliana Menozzi (Minneapolis: University of Minnesota Press, 1989).

33. Menander, *Menander Rhetor*, trans. and ed. D. A. Russell and N. G. Wilson (Oxford: Oxford University Press, 1981), xi.

34. For example, Menander discusses how to laud with equal fervor the aristocratic or humble origins of an emperor. Menander, *Menander Rhetor*, "Treatise II," 81.

35. The date of the text is widely disputed, although its composition within the decade of the 550s seems fairly certain. For recent discussion see Averil Cameron, *Procopius and the Sixth Century*, 86.

36. Glanville Downey, "Notes on Procopius, *De Aedificiis*, Book I," in vol. 2 of *Studies Presented to David Moore Robinson on His Seventieth Birthday*, ed. George E. Mylonas and Doris Raymond (St. Louis: Washington University Press, 1953), 722.

37. Procopius, *Buildings*, 1.2.17.

38. Ibid., 1.11.24–35.

39. John Bagnell Bury, *History of the Later Roman Empire*, vol. 2 (1923; Reprint, New York: Dover, 1958), 2:31.

40. Procopius, *Anecdota*, 17.5.

41. Procopius, *Buildings*, 1.9.10.

42. Procopius, *Buildings*, 1.9.2. The *Anecdota*, in contrast, tells us that the former prostitutes were so unhappy with their new life that "some of them threw themselves down from a height at night and thus escaped the unwelcome transformation" (17.6).

43. Paul I. Wellman, *The Female: A Novel of Another Time* (New York: Doubleday, 1953); John W. Vandercook, *Empress of the Dusk: A Life of Theodora of Byzantium* (New York: Reynal and Hitchcock, 1940); and Gillian Bradshaw, *The Bearkeeper's Daughter* (Boston: Houghton Mifflin, 1987).

44. John of Ephesus, *Lives of the Eastern Saints*, ed. and trans. E. W. Brooks, in *Patrologia Orientalis*, vol. 18, fasc. 4. (Paris: Firmin-Didot, 1924), 541. He bolsters this assertion with the stock quotation from Paul, "In Christ Jesus is no male or female, nor bond nor free" (542). Likewise his hagiography of "the Blessed Mary the Anchorite" begins with "Therefore neither was the history of this holy Mary unworthy of admiration, a woman who by nature only bore the form of females, but herself also too bore in herself the character and soul and will not only of ordinary men, but of mighty and valiant men" (559).

45. Ibid., 677.

46. "Syria and Armenia, Cappodocia and Cilicia, Isauria and Lycaonia, and Asia and Alexandria and Byzantium" (Ibid., 677).

47. Ibid., 678.

48. Ibid., 529, 533–36, 600.

49. Ibid., 680.

50. Ibid.

51. Cyril Mango, "The Church of Saints Sergius and Bacchus at Constantinople and the Alleged Tradition of Octagonal Palatine Churches," *Jahrbuch der Österreichischen Byzantinistik* 21 (1972): 190. Several of Mango's arguments were challenged in Thomas F. Mathews, "Architecture et liturgie dans les premières églises palatiales de Constantinople," *Revue de l'art* 24 (1974): 22–29, and by Richard Krautheimer, "Again Saints Sergius and Bacchus," *Jahrbuch der Österreichischen Byzantinistik* 23 (1974): 251–53. I believe Mango successfully refutes these issues in "The Church of Sts. Sergius and Bacchus Once Again," *Byzantinische Zeitschrift* 68 (1975): 385–92.

52. Mango, "Alleged Tradition," 192.

53. John of Ephesus, *Lives of the Eastern Saints*, 680 and 683.

54. Ibid., 684.

55. Procopius, *Anecdota*, 10.23.

56. Holum, *Theodosian Empresses*, 175.

57. Procopius, *Buildings*, 1.9.5.

58. Harvey argues that, despite Theodora's initiative, the credit should go to Justinian for the protection of the Monophysites, although their amnesty was continued after her death "because of his love for her and devotion to her memory." Susan Ashbrook Harvey, *Asceticism and Society in Crisis: John of Ephesus and the Lives of the Ancient Saints* (Berkeley and Los Angeles: University of California Press, 1990), 82.

59. Menander represents this traditional view when he gives instructions for an encomium on a city: many "thought wrong—for a woman to keep shop or do any other market business. At some festivals, as at Olympia, women do not appear at all. These points should therefore be observed in encomia." Menander, *Menander Rhetor*, "Treatise I," 67.

60. Procopius, *Anecdota*, 9.49.

61. Ibid., 9.48.

62. Procopius relates "Justinus . . . had a wife named Lupicina (Euphemia) who, as being a slave and barbarian, had been concubine of the man who had previously bought her" (Ibid., 6.17).

63. Ibid., 17.27.

64. John of Lydus, *De magistratibus*, in *John Lydus and the Roman Past*, by Michael Maas (New York: Routledge, 1992), 95.

65. Malalas, *Chronicle*, 255.

66. Downey, *Ancient Antioch*, 254.

67. The verb rendered as "the columns were sent" is noted as being an active masculine participle, although it here clearly refers to the empress. The panegyrical form in this way seems to presuppose a male subject. Malalas *Chronicle*, 17.19 (423), n. 19.

68. Procopius, *Buildings*, 2.10.19–25.

69. Ibid., 2.1.11–27.

70. Glanville Downey, "Procopius on Antioch: A Study of Method in the *De Aedificiis*," *Byzantion* 14 (1939): 369.

71. Averil Cameron, *Procopius and the Sixth Century*, 106.

72. Irfan Shahîd, "Procopius and Arethas," *Byzantinische Zeitschrift* 50 (1957): 45.

73. Malalas, *Chronicle*, 243.

74. Ibid., 256.

75. Otto G. Von Simson, *Sacred Fortress: Byzantine Art and Statecraft in Ravenna* (1948; reprint, Princeton: Princeton University Press, 1987), 29.

76. Djordje Stričević, "The Iconography of the Compositions Containing Imperial Portraits in San Vitale," *Starinar* 9–10 (1958–59): 75.

77. André Grabar, "Quel est le sens de l'offrande de Justinien et de Théodora sur les mosaïques de Saint-Vital?" *Felix Ravenna* 81 (1960): 64 ff.

78. This dating is based on the assumption that the Theodora panel was made at approximately the same time as the Justinian panel. Recent technical study suggests that the Justinian panel was altered upon Maximian's appointment to Victor's position in 546. The head of the bishop was changed to accommodate the new individual in that prominent role and the name "MAXIMIANUS" was added at this point to mark the changed identity of the portrait. Irina Andreescu-Treadgold and Warren Treadgold, "Dates and Identities in the Imperial Panels in San Vitale," *Byzantine Studies Conference Abstracts of Papers* 16 (1990): 52.

79. Procopius, *Buildings*, 1.10.17.

80. Ibid., 1.11.9.

81. Sozomen, *Ecclesiastical History*, trans. Edward Walford (London: Bohn, 1855), chap. 10.

82. Delbrück suggested the identification of other anonymous portraits of late antique imperial women with Theodora: two ivory plaques (one is in Florence; the other, in Vienna) and a diptych in Berlin. "Porträts byzantinischer Kaiserinnen," *Mitteilungen des kaiserlich deutschen archäologischen Instituts, Römische Abteilung* 28 (1913): 341–43. A recent catalog entry on the Berlin diptych is in Arne Effenberger and Hans-Georg Severin, *Das Museum für Spätantike und Byzantinische Kunst: Staatliche Museen zu Berlin* (Mainz am Rhein: von Zabern, 1992), 138.

83. James D. Breckenridge, *Age of Spirituality*, ed. Kurt Weitzmann (New York: Metropolitan Museum of Art, 1978), 33.

84. Siri Sande, "Zur Porträtplastik des sechsten nachchristlichen Jahrhunderts," *Acta ad archaeologiam et artium historiam pertinentia* 6 (1975): 95.

85. This identification is problematic in terms of the general issue of likeness in medieval as well as royal portraiture. As stated by Richard Brilliant, "The typological representation of royalty predetermined the viewer's cognitive response to the individual ruler portrayed. Thus the general propositional attitude took precedence over the particular, even if the king or queen had a face and name that could be recognized" (*Portraiture* [Cambridge, Mass.: Harvard University Press, 1991], 104).

86. Breckenridge, *Age of Spirituality*, 33.

Women's Role in Latin Letters from the Fourth to the Early Twelfth Century

✳ ✳ ✳ Joan M. Ferrante

In the course of reading through correspondence involving women in the Middle Ages, I was struck by the number of times men mention that the commentary or treatise they are sending was written at the request of the woman. Without the man's letter, we would often have no idea of the source. I began to expand my notion of patronage beyond dedications and commissions to include collaboration, requests from friends or colleagues that led to the composition of particular works. Then I looked further at the kinds of works medieval men wrote at the request of women to see what they might reveal about the nature of the relationship between them, and the author's attitudes towards particular women and their roles. I found that the religious texts were often the result of a close collegial relationship or friendship, in which the woman might determine the content by the questions she raised but both author and audience were involved in the effort to further knowledge or establish truth. In secular works, on the other hand, particularly histories, that were commissioned by or dedicated to a woman in a position of greater power or influence than the author, the author might well slant the content in order to favor her political interests.

In this study I include under literary patronage both the active inspiring of works by setting specific subjects for composition or by asking questions that require treatises to answer them, and also the passive acceptance of works dedicated to or composed for the favor of a patron. I consider three categories of texts—religious works, secular lyric poetry, and historic narrative—and I limit my discussion to those works which specify the woman for whom they

73

are written, either by accompanying letter or by direct address within the work.[1] The women addressed are either close friends for whom the text is part of an ongoing exchange, or women in powerful positions whose favor is being sought through the text, though some women seem to be both.

Among the religious texts, I concentrate on commentaries, theological treatises, and attacks on heresy, written for women who are treated as intellectual equals, colleagues, and friends, rather than on the more obvious Rules and the kinds of spiritual advice or sermons that are addressed from a person in authority to those in his care. In the section on Latin lyrics, I discuss both verse letters, which are primarily exchanges between friends whose mutual affection and respect are quite evident, and more formal lyrics of praise or request addressed to traditional patrons, where the woman is in the position of authority. The secular histories dedicated to women, like the formal lyrics, are mostly written for patrons who are being courted, either by direct compliments to themselves and their families or by implied analogies with the powerful women whose actions and influence are emphasized within the history.

RELIGIOUS LITERATURE

In the early centuries of the Latin church, Roman women of wealth and education provided financial, intellectual, and moral support to major figures.[2] Jerome, Ambrose, Augustine worked with and sometimes through women and wrote texts for them or at their request. Both Jerome and Augustine wrote about theological questions and heresy to women they expected to help uphold their views of orthodoxy. Jerome, who worked very closely with women in Rome and in Jerusalem and corresponded regularly with them—a third of his extant letters, an unusually high proportion, are to women—wrote frequently in answer to questions that came up in their work. Indeed, it has been noted that most of Jerome's important treatises were inspired by Marcella and her friends.[3]

Marcella was a close friend who posed difficult questions: "You provoke us with great questions and make our wit numb with inactivity; while you ask, you teach" (Ep. 59); "You write nothing except what tortures me and compels me to read scriptures" (Ep. 29). Jerome responds to her questions on textual matters and on interpretation.[4] When Marcella and two of Jerome's male friends, Pammachus and Oceanus, were distressed by Rufinus's misleading statements about Jerome in his translation of Origen, they sent it to Jerome with a request for information; he responded with a more accurate

translation of his own, and he addressed one of his counterdefenses to Rufinus's subsequent attack to Pammachus and Marcella (*PL* 23, col. 415–514).[5]
Jerome spoke warmly of Marcella's teaching what he had taught her and what
she worked out for herself, even to priests, and of her public battles against
heresy (Ep. 127, to her companion Principia). Jerome wrote less frequently to
another close friend, Paula, because she worked with him in Jerusalem. But
he wrote a commentary on Hebrew letters in the Psalms for her (Ep. 30), and
a detailed bibliography of Origen's works (Ep. 33), which he secretly compiled
for her at night by his own hand—he "would not have dictated [it] with cautious speech" because of the "rabid dogs" who attack Origen. He also wrote
commentaries on some of the books of the Prophets at her request but completed them after her death, dedicating them to her daughter Eustochium and
her granddaughter Paula.

Jerome wrote to women he scarcely knew as well as women he knew well,
provided their questions were of some interest. He responded at some length
to Hedybia's twelve questions about the New Testament, with a show of hesitation because of her distinguished family of scholars and teachers, wondering
if she was only testing to see if his opinion agreed with what she had already
learned from others (Ep. 120). He answered Algasia's eleven questions with
similar care, citing Greek passages and complaining that some of the subjects
would require "many and large volumes" to be answered; he felt she had
not sufficiently studied the Old Testament but compared her in her zeal for
learning to the queen of Sheba (Ep. 121). To Fabiola, who ran through the
Prophets, the Gospels and the Psalms, raising questions, refusing to accept his
ignorance, and shaming him into writing (Ep. 77 to her friend Oceanus), he
wrote all night, dictating from memory about Aaron's vestments so his letter
could catch a departing boat (Ep. 64). Unable to answer her questions about
the mansions of Israel during her lifetime, he dedicated that work to her memory (Ep. 78). At Principia's request Jerome wrote a commentary on Psalm 44,
which he prefaced with a defense of his writing to women about Scripture: "If
men asked about scripture, I would not speak to women; if Barach had wished
to go to war, Debora would not have triumphed over conquered enemies . . .
if to be taught by a woman was not shameful to an apostle [Acts 18 : 24–26],
why should it be to me to teach women?" (Ep. 65).[6]

Augustine, who according to Peter Brown (396) "moved in a monochrome,
all-male world," compared to Jerome and Ambrose, wrote at least one of the
main sources of the Augustinian Rule for a group of virgins (Ep. 211).[7] Augustine also wrote to women in answer to their questions about prayer (Ep. 130,
to Proba), and about heresy and theology, encouraging women to fight against

heresy. He wrote a tract on Pelagius and original sin for Albina, her son Pinian, and his wife, Melania, who had followed him to Africa. Pelagius too worked through women; when Demetrias, granddaughter of Proba, became a nun, he sent her a letter that was a statement of his teachings, a letter that Brown calls "a calculated and widely-publicized declaration of his message" (*Biography*, 342). Distressed at the news, Augustine wrote to Demetrias's mother, Juliana, warning against Pelagius's teachings, asking her to protect her daughter and her servants from them, to look for ambiguities in the work, but at the same time to note any indication that Pelagius might accept the teaching of grace, and if she found it, to let Augustine know (Ep. 188).

At least two works that are preliminary studies toward the last book of the *City of God* were written at the request of women. In answer to a question from Italica, Augustine discussed whether God can be seen with the physical eye now or after the Resurrection (Ep. 92), asking her to read it to those who think differently and be sure to write back to him what answer they make. To Paulina, also at her request, he wrote at greater length (Ep. 147, fifty-four chapters) about whether the invisible God can be seen. He emphasizes the difficulty of the question (chaps. 1, 17) and tells her not to depend on his authority but to find truth in Scripture and in her interior sense of truth (2). Distinguishing between Scripture, which must be believed, and other witnesses or evidence, which she can choose to believe or not as she weighs their value (4), he repeatedly warns her against taking anyone's writings, including his, on faith, without the evidence of her own senses and mind or the authority of Scripture (5). He speaks as to a student of philosophy: "Examine what you have seen, what you have believed, what you still do not know, either because I have not spoken of it, or you have not understood, or you have not judged it credible. Among the points which you have seen to be true, distinguish further . . . [38], after you have carefully examined and distinguished . . . assess the actual weight of evidence" (39). If she has doubts, he tells her to look carefully within herself and find the light (40–43). At the end, he promises to get to the spiritual body in another work, presumably the *City of God*.[8]

From Augustine's teacher, Ambrose, we have no extant letters to women, except the three he sent to his older sister, Marcellina, a consecrated virgin, describing important events and including the texts of sermons.[9] "For it was through Marcellina that Ambrose chose to speak to Rome," Brown declares (*Body and Society*, 343); "we know about some of Ambrose's most heroic confrontations with the Emperors in Milan only because he wrote about them in great detail to Marcellina" (342). Ambrose wrote in response to her letters of concern for the church and for him; he described the attempt by Arian forces to take over a church in Milan, the defense of the people, his own refusal to submit to force, his appropriate readings and comments to the congregation during the siege, the emperor's threat and his own heroic response (Ep. 20), the discovery of the bodies of two martyrs (Ep. 22), the burning of a synagogue by a Christian bishop and monks, their punishment and the ordered rebuilding of the synagogue, and his conversation with the emperor after preaching a sermon before him (Ep. 41).[10]

Though there were similar requests and responses in the intervening centuries, the next period of interest for women's patronage of religious texts is the Carolingian. In the English missions to Germany, as in the early centuries of the church, works were written for colleagues, women similarly engaged in study and teaching. Some of the women came to Germany; others remained in England, from which place they provided books for the mission.[11] Many letters are still extant from the early eighth century, of which two are relevant here because they mention requests for the composition of texts: in one Boniface apologizes to his frequent correspondent, Bugga, that urgent labors and journeys have kept him from finishing the text of the opinions she asked for (Ep. 27);[12] in the other he responds to the request of Abbess Eadburg for an account of an otherworld vision (Ep. 10). The vision had occurred to a man who died and came back to life in the monastery of Abbess Milburga, and the story was told to Boniface by Abbess Hildelida; it is Hildelida's version that was requested by the third abbess, Eadburg, but Boniface meanwhile met the man who had the vision and so was able to send her a transcription of the eyewitness account in considerable detail.

In the Carolingian courts a number of intellectuals wrote on religious subjects for women, sometimes in verse.[13] Alcuin, who corresponded with many women religious, including members of Charlemagne's family, also wrote theological works for them. In response to Gundrada, Charlemagne's granddaughter, he wrote a treatise on the reason of the soul ("De ratione animae"), recommending that she read Augustine and others, indeed that she do some research on the question for him: he mentions a brief but sharp response of Jerome's to Augustine, which Alcuin read in Britain but cannot find here, along with four other related books he does not have, but which she may be able to find in the king's collection; if so, he asks her to read them and send them on to him (Ep. 309).[14] Charlemagne's sister Gisla and his daughter Rotruda requested a commentary on the gospel of John, which at first Alcuin could only answer in brief (Ep. 195), but eventually he wrote the full commentary and dedicated it to them. He appended their letter of request with his of assent as a prologue so future readers would recognize the zeal of their devotion and the occasion of his obedience, providing us with one of the few such requests from women extant (Ep. 196). In it they tell how the desire of holy readings burned in them after they "drank something of the mellifluous knowledge of scripture from Alcuin's expositions"; how they are troubled that they came late to this study, and that now they are into it, he is so far from them, but they beg him to make up for it in letters. Though they have Augustine's sermon on John, it is in places more obscure and decorated with circumlocutions than can enter "the feeble intellect of our smallness." Reminding him that Jerome did not scorn to dedicate many works on prophetic obscurities to women, they ask him not to put his lantern under a bushel, but to place it on the highest stand, to light all in the house of God. Finally, in a striking analogy to Christ on the road to Emmaus, who joined the two disciples on the road and opened senses to them to understand Holy Scripture, they assure him of God's grace on the road of this labor (Ep. 196). In his letter of dedication Alcuin says he had wanted to do this commentary for thirty years but did not get to it until their good intention excited his pen and called it back to the zeal of writing (Ep. 214). He sends them his only copy and asks them, if they deem it worthy, to have it transcribed, that is to publish it for him, sending instructions for the copying.

Hrabanus Maurus dedicated two commentaries to empress Judith, second wife of Louis the Pious: one on Judith, a biblical heroine and her namesake; the other on Esther, a biblical queen—"one your equal in name, the other in dignity"—whose extraordinary virtues make them models for men as well as women. In the dedicatory letters he praises her wit, her imitation of holy women, and her learning. He alludes to Hebrew sources, omitting Greek references whose sense a zealous reader might fill in after examining the preceding: "You, most noble queen, since you well understand divine mysteries in expositions, will rightly assess what is to be perceived in the rest" (Ep. 17a, 17b).[15]

In the eleventh century Peter Damian included so much material on the Bible in his letters to women (royal and noble women, some of whom became nuns), that excerpts from them are cited among his biblical commentaries (PL 145, col. 1021ff).[16] But the most intellectual of his letters to women is one he wrote to one of his sisters in response to her weighty questions about what existed before Creation and what would exist after the end of the world (Ep. 93). He says she draws him to unknown things and compels him to teach what he has not yet learned, but he does not discourage such questions. Indeed he seems to approve her curiosity, saying it is fruitful to inquire, because the mind cannot be free from thoughts, which must be either serious or vain, and wickedness cannot hold a mind that is engaged in sober cogitation on useful things. He talks about infinity and the finite and refers her to Augustine's *City of God*, Jerome on Daniel and the Apocalypse, and his own letter to Blanche (Ep. 66).

In the same period Goscelin wrote a *Liber confortatorius* in four books for a recluse of Angers, Eve, whom he had known well from her earliest years at Wilton.[17] Their friendship was a close one, in which he helped to educate her and she lent him books he wanted, and they corresponded through a series of separations. He worried about her moving to the austerity of the recluse life, but he eventually came to see it as the right decision and wrote this book to support and praise her. The book is filled with classical as well as biblical allusions, including "our" Boethius, Horace, Seneca, and Virgil, who teach the joys of the austere life and the liberty to be attained in it. Her tiny room may be a tomb, but her window can provide a library, which should include the lives of the Fathers, the *Confessions* of Augustine, the histories of Cassiodorus and Eusebius, the *City of God*, Orosius, Boethius. The book abounds in examples of women and men, saints, martyrs, hermits (including one recluse not other-wise known [2.8], according to Wilmart). Goscelin suggests that Eve follow the models of Paula and Eustochium, who were scholars as well as saints of the simple life, citing Jerome's letters on "sancta rusticitas et docta sanctitas" (3.6). Eve apparently had her own living model, a woman recluse who, Gosce-lin says, prepared the place for her and watches over her, "Benedicta domina," perhaps the same Benedicta for whom Baudri of Bourgeuil wrote an epitaph.[18]

At the end of the twelfth century, Adam, abbot of Perseigne, sent sermons or the equivalent to several women in response to their requests for his words: to Agnes, a virgin, he sent one, as best he could reconstruct it, which she had heard him give to a convent of virgins (Ep. 22).[19] He also sent Latin texts to secular women, countesses of Champagne and Chartres, perhaps because he resisted the contemporary tendency to compose in the vernacular; he suggests that they can have someone expound the text to them, though it is not clear whether he refers to the surface meaning or to underlying subtleties.[20] To Blanche, countess of Champagne, he sent the sermons she requested in Latin because they were given in Latin and would lose by translation ("barely will the savor or composition remain in a pilgrim idiom, for liquor when poured from a vessel is altered somewhat in color or savor or odor," Ep. 30). To a countess of Chartres, after an impassioned two-day conversation about sin and contempt of the world, he wrote to encourage her mind to the desire he sensed in her for a religious life: drawn by the "alacrity of your devotion, a certain pious violence compelled me to remain with you two days. The sweet words of new friendship come into my mind, the colloquies in which we conferred equally on hatred of sin" (Ep. 27).

The most famous collaboration between a religious writer and the woman who requested his (Latin) works in the twelfth or perhaps in any century is that of Héloïse and Abelard. She persuaded him to write a series of works for the education of her convents, a history of nuns, a Rule suitable to women, sermons, hymns, and answers to theological and scriptural questions that came up during their studies, so she is directly responsible for many of Abelard's extant writings. Two of her letters of request are extant: the one that asks for the history and the Rule, and the one that accompanies the questions (the *Problemata*), and we also have a good idea what she said in the one requesting the hymns because Abelard discusses it in some detail in his answer.[21] What one derives from her letters is a sense of a highly educated woman, learned in classical as well as religious literature, with a sharp mind and a clear sense of practical reality. Héloïse supports her request for the history and the Rule with a lengthy, erudite, and sensible discussion of the problems the Benedictine Rule poses for women, with quotes from Ovid's *Ars amatoria* and Macrobius's *Saturnalia*, as well as Jerome, Gregory, Chrysostom, Augustine, and the Bible (Ep. 5). Abelard responds with a treatise on the authority or dignity of the order of nuns (Ep. 6), emphasizing the role women played in the Old Testament and in early Christianity, and noting the Fathers of the church who gave particular care to the instruction of women, Origen, Ambrose, and Jerome. The Rule emphasizes learning, though it covers other aspects of life as well.

In a separate and long letter to the virgins of the Paraclete about their studies, Abelard particularly emphasizes the study of biblical languages (Ep. 9, *PL* 178, col. 325–36). He cites Jerome frequently and at length on his involvement in women's studies of Scripture; on the importance of the biblical languages, Hebrew, Greek, and Latin; on the part his women disciples played in fighting heresy; and on their examining and questioning what he taught them. Noting the problems translations raise about the meaning of a text, Abelard encourages Héloïse's nuns while they have a mother, a "worthy queen of Sheba" expert in the three languages, to learn them well enough to be able to resolve any doubts they might have about translated texts: "Let us recover in women what we have lost in men."[22] Héloïse seems to have shared Abelard's concern for textual authenticity. She raised the issue of translation quite persuasively in her request for hymns. In his response he says that he had been hesitant to compose new hymns when there were ancient hymns of saints, but she argued that the Latin church, and the French church in particular, follow customary usage rather than authority, that they do not know who did the translation of the psalter they use in the French church, that it is of doubtful authority and they have no way of deciding among the various translations. Abelard sent them 133 hymns in three groups with accompanying letters.[23]

In the letter Héloïse sent with her forty-two questions, the *Problemata*, she too cites Jerome: his commendation of Marcella for her study of holy letters, her questions about her studies, her unwillingness to accept authority without thinking everything through, so that he felt himself to have not so much a pupil as a judge, and her teaching. It is clear that Héloïse identifies with Marcella as Abelard does with Jerome. She asks Abelard to pay the debt he owes her and her nuns, he who brought them, handmaids of Christ and his own spiritual daughters, together in his oratory and exhorted them to the study of Scripture. Now that they have given themselves to this work, that they are caught up in the love of letters, they are perturbed by many questions and cannot get on with their reading; they are less able to love what they do not understand, and their labor seems fruitless. So they ask and beg him as teacher and father to answer their questions, which they put down as they occur in their daily reading; his responses are published with the questions (*Opera*, 1:237–38). Héloïse's arguments in this letter echo those of Gisla and Rotruda to Alcuin, the women reminding the man that he is responsible for their interest in studies, as if they needed authority to begin such a pursuit and now that they are involved it is up to him to continue to advance their knowledge. In both cases they refer to Jerome, whose model justifies men working on and composing religious texts for women.

Lyric Poetry

The only poetic works Abelard wrote for Héloïse at the Paraclete, as far as we know, are the hymns. Earlier, during their affair, he had written love poems, which she says made her the envy of other women, but these poems seem to have disappeared. If she wrote poems in response, she does not mention it, though women were still doing that in the early twelfth century, as we know from the collections of Hildebert of Lavardin and Baudri of Bourgeuil. The metric epistles and lyrics that are part of an ongoing conversation between poets and friends provide yet another indication of intellectual camaraderie between men and women in different periods of the Middle Ages.

From the sixth century to the twelfth, there are exchanges of occasional poems between religious men and women, poems that express affection and respect, sometimes emotional dependence, sometimes appreciation of a colleague's technical skill. Many of the late-Roman bishops were not only literate but accomplished practitioners of Latin letters, prose and poetry, and engaged in exchanges of occasional verse with their friends, male and female. At the request of Euprepia, Ennodius (d. 521) composed epitaphs of women they both admired and sent them to her, expecting her to detect the flaws, since she often points out the poverty of his wit (Ep. 5.7); whether she sent poems to him we do not know, but because we know she sent letters which are not extant, and because Ennodius acknowledges her technical knowledge, it is at least possible.[24]

Venantius Fortunatus exchanged poems and gifts with his close friends Radegund, a queen who left her husband and throne for a monastery, and her abbess, Agnes. They shared religious devotion, the love and intimacy of a family, and the mutual respect and pleasure of poetic conversation.[25] Many of the short poems Fortunatus sent them celebrate little things: their birthdays (11.3), their Daedalan art in decorating tables (11.11), gifts of food (11.9, 19, 20, 22). Sometimes their honey makes poetry flow from his mouth (11.12); sometimes the food pervades his dreams, so the savor is with him sleeping and eating (11.23); sometimes his poetry excuses his small gifts of violets (8.6, 8), or chestnuts (11.13). Often it expresses his concern. Both Fortunatus and Agnes beg Radegund to drink wine for her health: "Fortunatus and Agnes pray in verses that you, exhausted, drink benign wine . . . we ask, suppliants both . . . that you relieve your two children . . . so also Paul ordered Timothy to take wine, lest his stomach grow weak" (11.4). Fortunatus laments separations from them and rejoices at their meetings, but he particularly reproves them for not sending him poems: "Did passing time so distract you that you did not . . . give sweet melodies of the lady tongue to one who, while you speak words, is fed by your mouth?" (11.5); "Like a lamb thrust from the udder, who wanders in the fields, striking the air with his bleets . . . so am I without your words" (app. 21). And when the verses come, he is delighted: "The flattering teacher recreates with words and foods and sates with various, enticing play" (11.23a).[26]

British missionaries to Germany in the eighth-century circle of Boniface and Lull also exchanged poems as well as letters with their friends, though we have fewer of the poems. There is one, probably from Lull to an abbess and a nun who cared for him when he was very sick. He celebrates them in verse, confident that they will not judge the verses too harshly, although they may be filled with errors, and asks the nuns to correct anything that is contrary to the rule of grammatical art. The verses are playfully designed so that the subjects can read their names in a pattern of first letters (Ep. 98). Another letter from an unknown man to his beloved sister about the approaching end of the world offers poems, "not arrogantly commending mine, but humbly asking yours" (Ep. 140).[27]

A number of intellectuals in contemporary Carolingian courts wrote poems for women, some of them religious, mentioned above, some more secular. The same Theodulf who wrote an epistolary poem of spiritual advice to his daughter wrote to a queen, praising her and asking her to send balsam liquor (PL 105, Carmina 3.5). Walafrid Strabo, who tutored Charles, the son of the empress Judith, second wife of Louis the Pious, wrote many poems in her praise. In a poem about the Dietrich statue in Aachen, "De imagine Tetrici," he describes Judith as "rich in doctrine, powerful in reasoning, pious, sweet in love, strong in spirit, clever in speech."[28] Sedulius sent verses about Peter to the empress Ermengard, wife of Lothar I, to be inscribed on a pallium that she and her ladies embroidered with scenes from the life of the saint; the verses were accompanied by a poem of elaborate praise.[29]

In the late eleventh and early twelfth century, there were bishops who wrote secular as well as religious poetry, some of it to women, in some cases to the same women. Both Hildebert of Lavardin and Baudri of Bourgeuil wrote epistolary poems to Cecilia, probably the daughter of William I, who became an abbess of Caen in 1113, and to a nun named Muriel.[30] Hildebert and Baudri also wrote poems in praise of their secular lord, Countess Adela of Blois, another daughter of William the Conqueror.[31] There seems to have been a literary circle of bishops and abbesses or nuns who corresponded at least in part in verse, and who offer an enthusiastic and knowing audience for each other's verse.[32]

Hildebert has a range of addresses to women. He is capable of worldly flattery, as in a verse to the countess: "He is foolish and sins who equates you to mortals. It is small praise, but you will be to me first among goddesses" (10); and of courtly sentiments, in his poem in praise of the abbess Cecilia: "Who is accustomed to be more skillfull at speaking before men than Cicero, is less eloquent when he comes before Gods. So I, while in the midst of the people I speak with a skillful mouth, to your face can say little" (46). But he is equally capable of misogynist clichés: "Woman is a fragile thing, never constant except in crime, never failing to be harmful of her own will."[33] His greatest enthusiasm seems to be expressed in his response to a poem from Muriel, a nun who wrote to him when he was in exile. Hildebert says: "Former times boasted ten sibyls, and there was great glory to your sex. Present times rejoice in the wit of one. . . . Whatever you breathe out is immortal, and the world adores your work as divine. You put down by your wit celebrated poets and bards, and both sexes are stunned by your eloquence. Looking ten times over at the songs sent to me, I am amazed. . . . The cares of exile and the harsh weight of labors you, virgin, can alleviate with your song. . . . Do not deny your words to me" (26). As with all but one of the women poets addressed by Hildebert, Marbod, and Baudri, we do not have any of the poetry that inspired such praise.

Baudri of Bourgeuil (1046–1130) is reminiscent of Fortunatus in his playful and affectionate tone. Most of his poems to women are letters in verse to fellow poets, nuns, with whom he exchanges, or hopes to exchange, verses: the Cecilia and Muriel to whom Hildebert wrote, as well as Agnes, Beatrice, Emma, and Constantina, the one woman whose answering poem we have. Muriel has long attracted Baudri by her fame, but now he has heard her recite—"With what honeyed charm are your words anointed. How sweet sounds your voice when you recite . . . the words sound a man, the voice a woman."[34] He longs for a time when they can speak together, asking and answering each other's questions; meanwhile "let mutual songs commend us to us," let us be the first to know each other's secrets (72–73). To the virgin Agnes, Baudri writes a play on her name ("little lamb because milder than a lamb"); he encourages her in her virginity—because the one thing Christ, who can do anything, cannot do is restore violated virginity—and in her studies and poetry. He will return the tablets she asked for, as soon as he gets them back; meanwhile he asks her to return his greetings in verses (74–75).

To Beatrice, Baudri writes a complaining poem that she never responds in song despite his requests, and he attempts to coax her with mockery: she puts her finger over her mouth and pretends to hide behind her veil; he begins to see an ass before the lyre; men are often at a loss for words before a virgin, but no woman is before a man (a courtly rather than religious view); "Let her praise or damn our songs in song, but not be a mute and mutilated sheep" (77–78). He praises the poems of Emma as flavored with nectar, her wisdom sustained with honey, her breasts pouring out milk, so swarms of disciples (female) rush to be revived by the honey of the parent bee; if her order allowed male disciples, he would be one (75–76). In a longer poem he wonders if up to now she has read his poems with love or laughter, deceiving him with her praise; now he sends his whole little book and asks her to read it studiously, solicitously, to censure rather than flatter. Describing himself as a raucous cricket who makes noise day and night, as a rustic without eloquence, he asks her to read through, to extol, correct, or add (80–82).

To Constantina, the one woman from whom we have an answering poem, and who was apparently in the same house as Emma, we have two extant poems. In one Baudri says he greets everyone in verse, using his poems to cover his rusticity, and jests in writing; but in fact he speaks quite seriously about her vow of virginity and her sacrifice to God (78–79). At the end he asks her to renew the covenant of friendship, to commit anything she wants to convey to tablets, and to greet Emma for him (78–79). In another, longer poem (179 lines) written by his own hand, Baudri declares his love for Constantina, protesting its innocence, perhaps too frequently, in the language of romantic love, and aware that others might interpret his words differently. He begins: "Read through and cautiously embrace the sheet you've read, lest a malign tongue harm my fame." Assuring her that there is no poison in it, that she can place it in her bosom, he wishes she knew as his guts (*viscera*) know how much she is with him, that she is more and greater to him than a goddess, a virgin, more than the daughter of Leda to Paris, Venus to Mars. He insists, "Foul love never drove me; with you I wish to live a fellow-citizen in virginity. . . . I swear by all that is, I do not wish to be a man to you, nor that you be a woman to me." But he describes her eyes brighter than Venus, her hair more red-yellow than gold, her neck lighter than lilies or snow; her lips heat and swell with a fiery color, and her body suits her face. She might bring down the highest Jove from heaven, if Greek fable were true. At the end he says he must return to greater study, his poem on Genesis—which his companions think he should be writing instead of trifles to her—but he encourages her to write to him and promises not to be silent for long (83–87).

Constantina answers with a poem of the same length and the same kind of language: "I touched your songs with my naked hand. Rejoicing, I unfolded the volume, two, three, four times. . . . I consumed the day, reading [it] often; night was hateful . . . compelling me to cease my study. I refolded in my lap and placed the sheet under my left breast, which they say is closer to the heart. . . . O how gifted this poet, with how divine a mouth he sings, what savor in his words, what wisdom." She compares him to Cato in deeds, Cicero in words, another Homer; "he alone is worth many Aristotles." His beauty of body and mouth is "more pleasing than dawn and more light than sun." She cherishes the poem because "I see him in verse, for I cannot otherwise. . . . A year has passed since I have not been able to see him whom I wish for, and yet I often read his songs." Writing gives her not the opportunity to speak but a way to say what she could not otherwise: "I shall attack wax, since wax does not know modesty. . . . Many things indeed I may write which I do not wish to say to him present." She asks him to come to her, because the obstacles are fewer for him ("I would come if I could") and ends with the plaintive: "Awaited one, come; don't delay long. I have often called you; come."

Baudri also wrote two poems to a formal patron, Adela, countess of Blois, one asking directly for a gift, a cope (*cappa*), the other only mentioning the desired gift at the end of a long poem of elaborate praise.[35] In the shorter one, which seems to be following up the modest request made in the longer, he asks specifically for a cope that will suit both the giver and the receiver, which will turn her from a countess to a queen for him. He promises that his song will spread her fame through the wide world, that she has already furnished the matter for the song: "You yourself furnish the song to me, you the pen, you will give the breath, the mouth, you will fill the void; you pay the deserved rewards to the poet. You compel taciturn bards to be loquacious; therefore come back to your speaking bard, countess, and restore, O lady, to the writer, his rewards, the cope." He describes the cope he expects, with gold and gems, implying that her honor rests on its value, that she should adorn it as she does ministers and churches, and he reminds her at the very end not to forget the fringe ("Cave ne desit etiam sua fimbria cappae" (*Epistole metriche*, 69– 70).[36] The longer poem (1,365 lines; *Oeuvres*, 196–231) flatters the countess with flights of fancy that might be at home in a romance. After comparing her with her illustrious father—no less in virtue though greater in her knowledge of poetry and her interest in books—Baudri describes her room, which he imagines as decorated with themes to suggest her great learning: tapestries of the Old Testament and ancient history; a mosaic map of the world on the floor, with the heavens on the ceiling; a bed draped in hangings showing her father's conquest of England, surrounded by life-sized figures of the seven liberal arts and medicine, which could recite the material of their disciplines. This poem graphically sets Adela at the center of the world, its history, its culture, and implicitly its power.

HISTORICAL NARRATIVE

Hugh of Fleury's *Historia ecclesiastica*, dedicated to Adela of Blois, also im- plicitly sets her and women like her at the center of culture and power by giving an unusual amount of attention to the role of women, rulers as well as saints, in history. Latin histories were still being written for women in the early twelfth century, though in a few decades most women patrons would be commissioning the translation of histories from Latin to French, or the com- position of romances in the vernacular, primarily French, and these women would influence the direction of vernacular narrative. Histories were written in Latin for important women from at least the eighth century, and within a variety of national traditions—Lombard, Frank, Saxon, Angle, Northern

Italian, and French. All gave some attention to the role of women in history. I shall take a brief look at some of them, beginning with Paul the Deacon's *Historia Romana* in the late eighth century, and ending with Hugh of Fleury's *Historia ecclesiastica* in the twelfth.[37]

Paul the Deacon dedicated his *Historia Romana* to Adelpurga, duchess of Benevento and daughter of King Desiderius, because she had urged him to write it. Paul had apparently tutored her at the royal court at Pavia, and perhaps followed her to Benevento after her marriage. Continuing to encourage her studies, which he praises in his dedicatory letter—"You search the secrets of the prudent with subtle wit and very wise zeal so that the golden eloquence of philosophers and jewels of poets speak readily to you; you engage also in divine as well as worldly histories"—he gave her Eutropius's history to read. She examined it avidly, as was her custom, but was displeased by its brevity and failure to mention divine history. She wanted him to extend the history with additions from Scripture and elsewhere, so he wrote the *Historia Romana*, expanding the early books and adding six books to bring it up to Justinian.[38] Scattered through his history, not necessarily playing a major role but always there, are mothers, sisters, wives, and daughters, who are named and whose fate is at least briefly alluded to. Whether active or passive agents in world politics, they are a part of history by virtue of their positions and connections. And many of them are active, taking part in government directly, choosing their husband's successors, plotting, and advising. Bad, good, strong, weak, clever, foolish, ineffective, or neutral, they are, like men, a presence in Paul's history.

Paul gives most attention to women in the last books of his history, where he is no longer following Eutropius, though he also interpolates passages about women in other books, particularly the first, from different sources. Even Aeneas's mother, Venus, is mentioned, as well as his wives, Creusa and Lavinia. Lavinia, it is implied, controlled her father's kingdom after Aeneas's death, after "Ascanius left the kingdom of his stepmother" to found Alba Longa (1.1). Paul tells of the rape of Lucretia, which led to the fall of Tarquinius, and connects the event in time as well as in theme with Judith's killing of Holofernes (1.8).[39] In book 5 Paul adds from Orosius the hard time the Cimbrian women gave the Romans in battle and their heroic self-destruction in the face of defeat. But it is in the last books of the history, which Paul added at Adelpurga's request, that women are most in evidence in a wide variety of roles: Fausta foiled her father's plot to murder her husband (10.3); the widowed empress Dominica kept the Goths from destroying Constantinople by distributing money and thus preserved the kingdom "faithfully and virilely" for her kin (11.11). Galla Placidia, who was captured by the Goths and married to their king, Athaulf, moved her husband by her "very sharp wit" and subtle flattery to seek peace from the Romans (12.15); later, when her son Valentinian was appointed as "Caesar" to the western empire, she was sent with him as "Augusta" (13.9). The very beautiful Digna threw herself from her tower on the walls of her city, Aquileia, rather than be dishonored by the conquering enemy (14.10). Another widowed empress saved her son from his enemy by secretly making him a cleric and substituting someone similar in form (15.7). Two empresses abused their position: Theodora drove Pope Silverius from Rome because he would not reinstate a heretic bishop (16.18), and Sophia taunted her husband's ministers and plotted against his successor, but though her treasure was confiscated and her servants removed, she remained a force to be reckoned with, to be consulted about his successor (17.14).

Women also played the traditional roles of marriage partner and devoted Christian. Theodoric stabilized his kingdom by arranging a series of political marriages for the women of his family: his sister and his legitimate daughters to kings of the Vandals, the Franks, and the Thuringians, and his daughters by a concubine to the rulers of the Visigoths, the Burgundians, and the Amals, so "there were no people near Italy to whom Theodoric was not connected by family or by treaty" (15.20). The daughter whose son succeeded Theodoric, Amalsuntha, retained the throne when her son died but chose to associate her cousin Theodatus with her in the government, to strengthen her position (16.11–12). The move did not work—he had her murdered—but she had had the foresight to commend herself to Emperor Justinian, who eventually sent his armies against her murderer, and legitimacy of rule was carried through her daughter, who was seized and married by Theodatus's successor (16.15).[40] The most striking example of religious devotion is Cesara, wife of a Persian king; she came to Constantinople from Persia disguised as a private person, because of her love for the Christian faith, and refused to share her husband's bed unless he believed in Christ, so he followed her to Constantinople and was baptized with the emperor as godfather (17.27).

There was another spate of historical writing around the Ottonian court, some of it dedicated to or commissioned by women, some of it written by a woman. Widukind of Corvey dedicated his *Sachsengeschichte* to Mathilde, abbess of Quedlinburg, daughter of Otto I; Hrotsvit of Gandersheim wrote both her historical epics for her abbess, Gerberga, niece of the emperor.[41] For the *Gesta Ottonis*, commissioned by Gerberga but presented to Otto I (d. 973) and his son Otto II (d. 983), Hrotsvit has no written model; that is, hers is the first life of the emperor. She gives a lot of attention to the women in the imperial family, to marriages, and to human emotions, intentionally giving short shrift to military operations. She uses the excuse that it is not for a frail woman in a monastery to talk of war, but she had not hesitated to talk of brothels in her dramas, presumably without direct experience of them, so it seems more likely that she prefers to emphasize Otto's gifts and virtues as a ruler over those of the warrior. She is anxious to show him as a wise and merciful king who forgave his enemies and eventually won them over.

Hrotsvit begins the history with the first king in the line, Otto's father, Henry, and his wife and coruler ("conregnante") Matilda, whom none can now surpass in the highest merits (22–24). When Henry decided to find a bride for Otto, he sought a worthy friend ("dignam amicam," 71) among the Angles. Edith, sister of the king (Athelstan), "outstanding daughter of an illustrious mother," beautiful and good, considered the best of all women in her land (81–92), was chosen. Her death left her people distraught (403–4)—she had treated them more as a loving mother than as a stern ruler—and her children bereft (a son, Liudulf, and a daughter, Liudgard, "sweet progeny of the female sex," 420). Otto cared for his children's future with paternal affection and benign piety, raising his son to worthy honors and marrying him to the daughter of an illustrious duke; his daughter, "the only hope he had of the female sex" (445), whom he cherished and loved, he married to a distinguished and powerful duke.

Otto himself remarried. His second wife was Adelheid, the widow of King Lothar of Italy, whose husband left the kingdom in her hands. Her dramatic story is told in some detail. Descended from a long line of great kings, noble, beautiful, and "so shining in wit that none would have ruled the kingdom more worthily, had it not been for treachery" (478–80), she lost her throne and treasures to a usurper, Berengar, who removed her ministers and attendants and imprisoned her with no companions but a girl and a priest. A bishop offered help if she could get to him, so she and her companions plotted to dig a secret tunnel through which she escaped, hiding in caves and grainfields, protected by God from searching armies, until the bishop found her and took her in. Meanwhile, Saxons who had known her kindness when they went to Italy, told Otto her story, saying there could be no worthier successor to Edith. Otto hesitated because of all the conspiracies around her, but remembering that she had helped him sympathetically when he was in exile, and aware of the advantage of joining the Italian lands to his, he made the necessary arrangements and expedition and invited her to join him.

Hrotsvit mentions a number of rebellions against Otto in the course of the poem. The first is by his brother Henry, who is also the father of Hrotsvit's abbess and patron, Gerberga. Hrotsvit therefore does her best to play down his treacherous role, presenting him first as victim, then as protagonist, and finally as a penitent. She hopes he did not agree with the rebellions in his heart but was compelled by force (223–24), though she offers no evidence of force. In the latter part of the poem, there are two large lacunae that probably described the rebellion of Otto's first son, Liudulf; the ensuing civil war; and Liudulf's death, which left the way open to Adelheid's son, Otto II. The poem ends with the raising of Otto II to imperial dignity.

Hrotsvit's second epic, the *Primordia coenobii Gandeshemensis*, begins by attributing the foundation of the monastery (a century before the events of the *Gesta*) to the Saxon chiefs, an earlier Liudulf and his son Otto (grandfather of the emperor Otto I), but the story swiftly moves to the maternal line and concentrates on the role of women throughout the poem. Aeda, the mother of Liudulf's wife, Oda, had a revelation of the imperial future of her posterity from John the Baptist, who also prophesied the foundation of a cloister for virgins. Though Aeda was "overcome by terror at the vision in the way of women" (50–51), she instilled in her daughter the mission to build the convent. Oda, following the example of her venerable mother, persuaded her husband to construct the monastery, and they destined their daughter, Hathumoda, who had been instructed by a venerable abbess, to be its first abbess. Before the building was complete, Liudulf died, leaving his wife and sons with the responsibility to finish it; perhaps, Hrotsvit conjectures, God took him so that the mind of the illustrious lady Oda might be free to devote itself to God's affairs. Oda turned her persuasive powers on her son Otto, who finished the building. God also helped by making Oda's daughter, Liutgard, queen of France, giving her access to even more wealth for the monastery. Indeed, Oda continued to wrest money from children, grandchildren, and in-laws to support the monastery throughout her long life.

When Abbess Hathumoda died, she left her sister Gerberga in charge, but Gerberga, who was a secret nun, had to get free of her betrothal to a man who refused to give her up. Torn between her desire for Christ and her fear of civil war, she continued to live in the world, richly clothed, that is, giving no outward appearance of her profession; even her reluctant encounter with her fiancé was carried out with more royal diplomacy than saintly obstinacy, despite his brutal threats. God intervened once again, dispatching the unwanted and unworthy husband in the war, and Gerberga was able to fulfill her vow. Gerberga was a devoted abbess, and her mother, Oda, kept a watchful eye on all the activities within the convent, setting an example with the sweet love of a prudent mother. When Gerberga died, she entrusted her sheep pen to a third sister, Christine, who followed the others in way of life and virtue, with her mother's constant encouragement. Oda continued to be solicitous for the needs of the nuns and to encourage Otto to help. He never refused to carry out what his mother ordered for them (514), treating them as a kind father. His death was deeply felt by the nuns, who wept for three days beside his body, as if their tears could restore it. Eight days before he died, his grandson, Otto, destined to fulfill the destiny prophesied to Aeda at the beginning of the poem, was born. Six months later, Oda, aged 107 years, died, having seen the monastery built and enriched through several generations of her family. Her life spans and dominates the history of the monastery in the poem.

In the middle of the eleventh century, an unknown author prepared a history of Cnut, king of Denmark and England (*PL* 141, col. 1373–98), at the order of his second wife, the English queen Emma (d. 1052). The author claims that the work praises Emma by praising Cnut as Virgil praised his emperor in the *Aeneid*, even though Virgil scarcely mentioned Augustus. Who could deny, he asks, that this work gives praise to the queen, when not only is it written for her glory, but she also seems to obtain the greater part of that glory in it? As a circle is drawn around a point, which is always at the center, so her praise is to be found in all parts of the story. The author indeed writes his history so as to attribute a key role in the succession to his patron, often giving a very false impression of historic data. Amidst lavish praise, he carefully establishes her influence over the text: "As you order, I shall speak the remembrance of things done"; "since I cannot avoid writing, I believe I must choose either to be subject to the various judgments of men or to remain silent about those things which are ordered to me by you, lady queen" (col. 1375, 1376). He asserts the need for a historian to tell the truth, because any error or embellishment of truth makes the audience suspicious, and he insists he would rather be accused of chattering ("loquacitatis") by the envious than let the truth be hidden. It is difficult to know if this is simply a topos or if he is trying to disguise the propagandistic nature of his assignment. Does he believe what he writes because he was not on the scene when it happened, even though the events are recent, or is he consciously distorting history to present his patron and her sons in the most favorable light? In either case the work presents history as she sees it. The author asks the reader at the end of the prologue to scrutinize the text with the perspicacious eye of the mind and understand that it resounds in every way with praise of Queen Emma.

According to this version Emma agreed to marry Cnut, whose exploits are featured in the early part of the story, only after he swore that no son of his by anyone else would succeed him, which the author approves as prudent on her part and providing for her own.[42] After a happy marriage with much joy on both sides, the king died. Emma was left alone in England, because her son by Cnut, Harthacnut, was on the throne in Denmark, and her other two sons were in Normandy with her brother, the duke. Cnut's oldest son, Harold, whose paternity the author denies, succeeded his father in England.[43] But the archbishop refused to consecrate Harold while Emma's sons were living, making no distinction among them and reinforcing the idea that they were all Cnut's as well as Emma's: "Cnut committed *them* to my faith, I owe this faith to *them*, and I will keep it to *them* faithfully" (col. 1391). Harold lured one of them, Alfred, to England with a forged letter from Emma and had him horribly murdered. The author apologizes to the mother for adding to her pain by describing the murder, but he is in fact glorifying the death as a martyrdom ("finemque hujus martyrii," "innocenter enim fuit martyrisatus," col. 1394), complete with miracles at the tomb. Thus he not only gives Alfred's mother a patron in heaven in place of the son on earth, but also provides political ammunition against her enemies.[44] He also gives a heroic cast to her flight and maneuvers in favor of her other sons, describing them as a battle against the persecutors of the Christian faith and religion (col. 1394). Emma fled to Normandy, from which she sent for her son Harthacnut, and together ("Hardecnuto materque," col. 1396) they returned to England and were received by the Angles as king and queen, and Harold conveniently died. Harthacnut sent for Edward with fraternal love, and together the brothers assumed royal power, ruling harmoniously with their mother. The covenant of maternal and fraternal love flourishes inviolable (col. 1398).[45]

There is a striking contrast between the story of Emma, who put all her political efforts into securing the throne for her sons (not without an eye to power for herself), and the life of a woman born shortly before Emma died, Countess Matilda of Tuscany. Matilda's life is also filled with details of political and diplomatic maneuvers, but they are carried out in her own name as heir to and ruler of vast lands in northern Italy. Matilda's role as mediator between pope and emperor has been noted, if questioned, even by later historians, and it is a major though not exclusive interest of her biographer, Donizo. Donizo, a monk of Canossa, inscribes himself as priest and monk in an acrostic at the end of the two books (2.1358–99); he had inscribed Matilda at the beginning as the daughter of Boniface and Beatrice, handmaid of God and worthy daughter of Peter (1.1–61). Matilda is both patron and subject of his biography. Donizo's intent was to glorify in verse her life and deeds and the deeds of her ancestors so that posterity could know such a lady (1.57), but she died before he could present it to her, as he sadly explains in an epilogue added after her death. In Matilda's case there is no question of her story being told in the shadow of a husband or a son—she was married twice but not for long, and neither marriage interfered with her public life. Donizo does not mention the marriages, preferring to present her as a kind of virgin queen. She is the hero, the heir to large and strategic lands that she ruled first jointly with her mother and then alone. Closely related to the German/Roman emperors and a force in imperial politics by virtue of her holdings, she was also a devoted supporter of the church, particularly the reform papacy of Gregory VII, whose letters declare his reliance on her and her mother.[46]

Donizo gives the history of Matilda's family (noting the women in each generation, one a learned and prudent "gubernatrix," another a pious "ducatrix"), and of her home fortress, Canossa, which literally speaks in the poem for the family and may well represent the formidable countess herself— Canossa too is a woman besieged but never taken (1.279–429). Protected by the relics of two saints, a man and a woman (Victor and Corona), Canossa begins her role in family history by providing refuge to a wronged queen, Adelheid, the widow of Lothar.[47] The family is presented as devoted to justice and peace, loyal to kings and emperors who are not always grateful or deserving, constant in support of their religion. Matilda's parents, Boniface and Beatrice, are described as a comparable pair: just as their names begin with the same letter, they are equal in goodness ("pares," 1.789, 790); they resemble each other in nobility, and both are blessed by Olympus (787–94); he enriches her and is enriched by her; he holds servants, male and female, castles, and towns through her and is lord of Gaul through her (1.813–15). Matilda resembles both parents, with her mother's features and her father's color (1.835); the honor of her father, the love of her mother, she is the glory of both (1.839).

Since Beatrice ruled for twenty-four years after the death of Boniface, Donizo gives some attention to her achievements: her prudent rule; her founding of monasteries with her daughter, whom she carefully nurtured; her opposition to the emperor's antipope; and her support of the (reform) pope, Gregory VII. Donizo blames the young Henry IV for antichurch acts that might well have been committed by his mother, Agnes, when she was regent. But he prefers to credit Agnes and Beatrice with working for peace in the kingdom (1.1226–1354), emphasizing Agnes's later work as mediator between the pope and her son, though he gives the major credit to Beatrice and Matilda. Whatever others did, Donizo says, the great countesses ("Comitissae / Magnae," 1.1348–49, emphasizing the epithet with enjambment) remained firm as a rock; as mediators and friends of the king, they were saddened when he went the wrong way, but they never deserted the pope.

The first book ends with the death of Beatrice; the second is all Matilda's:

"Although the first may flower and shine with what was written about the renowned dukes, the deeds of the *ducatrix* Matilda which are to be written will flower and shine more vehemently" (2.9–12). The book begins with a description of Matilda: her love for Christ and his modest servants; her hatred for vice; her ability to soothe the pious and terrify the evil, acting always with discretion; her fame extending to all kingdoms, from the Middle East and Russia to Britain; and her learning. She composes letters (she is literate in Latin); she knows the German language and speaks it as well as French (2.42–43). She is presented as a major force in the relations between emperor and pope, not only hosting their meeting at Canossa but acknowledged as the only one who can break the impasse (2.92–97). The conflict, however, continues, with Matilda in the middle, learning of new plots and foiling them, always having good sources of information. Donizo presents the conflict as between the emperor, goaded to evil by a bishop, Guibert of Parma, and the pope, supported in the right action by Matilda, a conflict in which Guibert and Matilda are the active figures. She is a Debora and a Jahel, defeating Sisara (2.743–44, 749); a Judith, defeating Holofernes (2.799); an Esther to Henry IV's Haman (2.851). She is also both Martha and Mary, serving the church actively by protecting the pope and attentive to the teachings of the pope and Christ (2.169–72); the wise countess listens like the queen of Sheba to the blessed words of Solomon (2.188–89). Her home is a refuge for religious enemies of the empire, the threatened pope, the fleeing empress, Praxedes; even Henry's son Conrad leaves his father and puts himself under Matilda's wings (2.846–48). She resists Henry and Guibert with arms, with money, and with writings: "To the Germans and princes dear to her, she writes to shun the errors of the rebel king (2.296–97).[48] When cities of Lombardy and Italy rebel against Matilda, she puts down their revolt: "Illustrious Matilda was a terror to them all" [Inclita Mathildis terror fuit omnibus illis, 2.365]. She finally makes peace with the young Henry V, with whom she meets and confers in German; he makes her viceroy for Liguria and helps persuade even the rebellious Mantuans to return to her rule (2.1252–1269).

Though Donizo understandably concentrates on the most public, political, and military of Matilda's actions, he occasionally mentions other aspects of her life, including her literary patronage. After the death of Anselm, bishop of Lucca, Matilda had books composed about him, lives by Bardone and Rangerius, and records of miracles that occurred at his tomb; Donizo quotes at length Rangerius's dedication of a second book (*Liber de anulo et baculo*) to Matilda (2.395–434). At the end of the life, Donizo talks about Matilda's religious devotion, her help to the poor, her conquest of priests by love, her studious attention night and day to sacred psalms and religious offices, in which she was expert; not even bishops were more zealous (2.1369). But her learning was not only religious; she also had a large supply of good books in all the arts and sciences (2.1370–71). She made gifts to monasteries and churches of land, books, pallia, and jewels, and she left her possessions to the papacy ("sua cuncta relinquet," 2.1376). After her death Donizo remembers her religious zeal; her desire to fast, weak with love, until priests forbade it; her generous charity; her orders that numerous servants be freed after her death (2.1487–88); her long illness (seven months); and her death at sixty-nine (in 1115) with the crucifix in hand, offering herself to God.

Donizo's last words are an exhortation to the emperor and his wife (the English Matilda, and he calls attention to the name), when they came to Canossa in 1116. The empress Matilda was the daughter of Henry I of England and niece of yet another patron of Latin history, Adela of Blois.[49] Countess Adela was a woman for whom many works of poetry and prose were written.[50] Like the countess Matilda of Tuscany, Adela was a formidable woman in her own right. Daughter of William the Conqueror, born after he had assumed the English throne and thus royal from birth like her brother Henry I, Adela coruled the Thibaudian lands with her husband, Stephen, from 1089, ruled as regent for him while he was on crusade and then as regent for her minor son after Stephen's death in 1102. She continued in that role until the majority of her second son, her chosen heir, Thibaud, and remained in power, working with him until she retired to Marcigny in 1120.[51]

During her years in power, Hugh of Fleury wrote his *Historia ecclesiastica* for her, explicitly slanting it toward her interests, sending it to her in 1110 with the assertion that "members of the female sex should not be deprived of knowledge of deep things, for great industry of mind and the elegance of most upright morals have always existed among women."[52] As LoPrete shows in her study, Hugh emphasizes the role of ruling and otherwise notable women, good and bad, in his history, selecting, using, or omitting appropriate details from his sources. He begins with Semiramis, who has to dress as a man in order to govern an unruly populace, who surpasses men as well as women in *virtus*, extends the borders of her realm, and rules long after the majority of her son, until he kills her. The Amazons, Scythian women who fought and governed their own lands under the rule of two queens, also expanded their territory, through Europe and Asia, where they founded cities as well. Despite the occasional defeat—by Hercules in battle, by Alexander in bed—they had a long and glorious history, including Penthesilea's exploits in the Trojan War and Thamyris's revenge on Cyrus for her son's death.

In Hugh's Roman history, as in his sources, women's roles are less active, but he emphasizes the part they play in the dynastic succession of the imperial family by marriage, many of them formally recognized as Augustae, acting with their husbands or for minor sons. Justina, the Arian, was ultimately unsuccessful in her fight against orthodoxy and Ambrose, but she had been in power as recognized regent for some years. Irene ruled jointly with her son Constantine VI, making peace with the Arabs, defeating the Slavs, and negotiating with Charlemagne. Then she fell out with her son, imprisoned him, and ruled on her own for five years; he came back with foreign help but was so inept she was able to return once again as empress in her own name for five more years. When she was finally deposed, Hugh let her make a rather heroic speech, accepting God's will and defying the faithless usurper. As LoPrete points out, it is thus a woman who voices "Hugh's oft-depicted moral of the divine source of all legitimate earthly rulership," in contrast to most western historians, who saw her as an illegitimate ruler, allowing the Roman imperial dignity to be transferred to the Franks. Hugh also gives some attention to the religious role played by empresses: Helen, the mother of Constantine, finding the true crosses and working miracles with them; Pacilla, the wife of Theodosius, caring for the sick and advising her husband on his moral responsibility.

Many of the women Hugh uses as models of power and action in world history appeared in the histories that Paul the Deacon and Freculf wrote for women patrons. Like the biblical heroines who take matters into their own hands, fighting to save their people in God's cause (Judith, Debora, Esther) or seeking wisdom (the queen of Sheba), the Amazons and Byzantine empresses show women effectively engaged in a man's world, governing, negotiating, manipulating, plotting, even fighting. And the more contemporary women who appear in the various biographies written for women, even when the work is nominally about their husbands, are also shown to take an active part in diplomacy, in religious and cultural patronage, and in government. All these histories not only accept the fact of women in power but seem to argue at least implicitly that women in power can be beneficial to society. Clearly the women patrons, but to some extent perhaps also the men who wrote for them, admire active, forceful women who play a role in the destiny of their people. The patrons are themselves active women, both in the public sphere and in the patronage of letters, commissioning works that implicitly or explicitly support their positions. Not as directly involved perhaps in producing the literary work as the women who inspired religious tracts by their questions, or lyric poems by their own poetry, the women for whom the histories and lives were written also influenced the content of those works. In virtually all the cases discussed here, the literary work is a collaborative effort between the writer and the woman for whom he wrote.

NOTES

1. I focus on direct address because I have come on much of this material in the course of my research on women's correspondence, for a forthcoming book on medieval women of letters (correspondents, patrons, and writers), for the Indiana University Press series Women of Letters. There are certainly other works that were written for women or dedicated to them but have lost all trace of the addressee. We know, for instance, of one dedication of a life of Anselm of Lucca to Matilda of Tuscany by Rangerius, because Donizo cites the dedication in his life of Matilda, though it is not in the published edition because it was not in the manuscript on which the edition was based. See Donizo, *Vita Mathildis*, ed. Luigi Simeoni (Bologna: Zanichelli, 1930–34), 2:389–438; and 69 n., in which Simeoni says that Donizo's dedicatory epistle was also omitted by copyists. I am limiting myself here to works in which some connection between the author and the patron is explicit. And I am omitting saints' lives, where the original impetus may come from a convent, indeed the first life might well be written by a nun, but a male author was ultimately preferred for the official life. See Jane Schulenberg, "Saints' Lives as a Source for the History of Women, 500–1100," *Medieval Women and the Sources of Medieval History*, ed. Joel T. Rosenthal (Athens: University of Georgia, 1990), 290–91.

2. I do not include the Greek church in my studies, although there, too, women were involved. See Elizabeth A. Clark, *Jerome, Chrysostom, and Friends; Essays and Translations* (New York: Edwin Mellen, 1979); and Peter Brown, *The Body and Society, Men, Women, and Sexual Renunciation in Early Christianity* (New York: Columbia, 1988).

3. Jerome, *Select Letters of Saint Jerome*, trans. F. A. Wright (London: Heinemann, 1933), introduction. For the Latin text see Jerome, *Sancti Eusebii Hieronymi epistulae*, ed. Isidorus Hilberg (1910; reprint, New York: Johnson, 1970).

4. He writes to her about the names for God in Hebrew with Greek and Latin equivalents (Ep. 25), on the reason some words were not translated from Hebrew (Ep. 26), on metrics in the Hebrew Psalms (Ep. 28), on the Hebrew *ephod* (Ep. 29), on interpretations of passages from the Psalms (Ep. 34), on five questions from the New Testament (Ep. 59), and on blasphemy against the Holy Spirit (Ep. 42); and he criticizes the work of other teachers (Ep. 37, 40, 41). Marcella remained in Rome (where, according to P. Brown, *The Body and Society*, 369, she had an unusually large library of Greek texts) when Jerome established himself in the Holy Land; hence the many letters to her.

5. See Henri de Lubac's introduction to Origen, in Origen, *On First Principles*, trans. G. W. Butterworth (New York: Harper and Row, 1966), xlii, xlv. The translation was not then made public, but it survived and is now the only source for correction of Rufinus, since the original is not extant. Butterworth cites a letter of Jerome to Hedybia (120.10) to elucidate a passage in Origen about souls before birth (228). And Peter Brown says Jerome's translation of Origen's *Homilies on the Song of Songs*, which was dedicated to Pope Damasus, was in fact intended for his "new circle of female spiritual charges," which then included Marcella and Paula (*The Body and Society*, 367).

6. Jerome wrote directions for a virginal life for Demetrias (Ep. 130), forty-one chapters on virginity for Eustochium (Ep. 22), and a rule culled from Scripture for a holy married life at the urgent request of Celantia (Ep. 148). He also wrote on widowhood for Furia (Ep. 54) and for Salina (Ep. 79), and on monogamy for Geruchia (Ep. 123). To Paula's daughter-in-law, Laeta, in response to her request and Marcella's, he sent a program of instruction for her daughter, based on languages and religious texts; he took her seriously as a student—a learned man should not blush to do for a noble virgin what Aristotle did for Philip's son—but he also recognized a child's need for pleasure and play, and suggested alphabet blocks to teach her letters (Ep. 107).

7. Indeed, of his nine basic texts on the subject, four addressed to men, five to women, it is impossible to determine which came first; see George Lawless, *Augustine of Hippo and his Monastic Rule* (Oxford: Clarendon, 1987), 65–69. Lawless includes Ep. 211 among the documents that "constitute the basic dossier for the Regula" (x), though he thinks the male version is older. For the text of Augustine's letters, see Alois Goldbacher, *Sancti Augustini epistolae*, Corpus Scriptorum Ecclesiasticorum Latinorum 57 (Vienna: Tempsky, 1911), and *PL* 33; for translations, Sister Wilfrid Parsons, *Saint Augustine: Letters* (New York: Fathers of the Church, 1951–56).

8. In the Retractions he does mention this work on the vision of God (2.41), "in which I undertook a careful examination of the future nature of the spiritual body at the resurrection of the saints, and whether and how God, who is a spirit, can be seen by a body, but that very difficult question at the end I explained as best I could in Book 22 of *The City of God*" (cited by W. Parsons, *Saint Augustine*, 3 : 224).

9. The letters are in *PL* 16, Ep. 20, col. 994–1002; Ep. 22, col. 1019–26; Ep. 41, col. 1113–21.

10. Ambrose included the text of the sermon in the letter. More than a century later, Caesarius of Arles wrote a sermon and a Rule for Virgins at the request of his sister, Caesaria, whom he had installed as abbess of a community he founded. He sent the sermon with great diffidence: "Not that I can confer anything on your learning or perfection . . . fearing to incur a note of boasting or imprudence, especially that I know you spend time in assiduous meditation on divine volumes and ignore nothing that pertains to your perfection" (*PL* 67, Ep. 1, col. 1125).

11. Many of the English religious were trained in double monasteries under abbesses. Aldhelm wrote his *De virginitate* as a long letter to the nuns of Barking, a double monastery, in the seventh century, and apparently expected the monks to hear as well, according to Janemarie Luecke, "The Unique Experience of Anglo-Saxon Nuns," *Medi-*

eval Religious Women, vol. 2, *Peaceweavers,* ed. Lillian T. Shank and John A. Nichols (Kalamazoo, Mich.: Cistercian Publications, 1987), 61.

12. *Epistolae Merovingici et Karolini Aevi,* vol. 6, *Sancti Bonifacii et Lulli Epistolae,* MGH, ed. Societas Aperiendis Fontibus Rerum Germanicarum Medii Aevi (Berlin: Weidmann, 1892). For translations, see Edward Kylie, *The English Correspondence of Saint Boniface* (New York: Cooper Square, 1966).

13. Alcuin sent poems on the Creator with pious wishes and advice, to accompany a theological treatise which Charlemagne's granddaughter Gundrada had requested. Prudentius, palace chaplain and later bishop of Troyes, sent versified psalms to a certain noble matron, who had asked for them so that they could be said when troubles and dangers did not permit the recitation of the entire psalter. The noble matron might be the Empress Judith, according to the editor, Ernst Dümmler, because Prudentius was palace chaplain (*Epistolae Karolini Aevi,* 3, MGH, p. 323). Theodulf wrote an epistolary poem to his daughter Gisla to accompany a psalter he had copied for her; the poem comments on Jerome's corrections, which he enjoins her to study, though he also recommends domestic duties, husband, and children (*PL* 105, Carmina 3.4).

14. Alcuin's letters are in *Epistolae Karolini Aevi,* 2, *Alcuini Epistolae,* ed. Ernst Dümmler, MGH (Berlin: Weidmann, 1895). He sent a work on the Adoptionismus heresy to an unnamed virgin with questions and answers she could use in her arguments against it (Ep. 204). The virgin may be Gundrada; that she is a member of the royal circle is clear from Alcuin's use of nicknames.

15. The text is in *Epistolae Karolini Aevi,* 3, ed. Ernst Dümmler and Karl Hampe (1898–99; reprint, München, 1978), 420–22. The reader referred to ("studiosus lector") may be any reader, but the knowledge of divine mysteries is specifically referred to the queen: "Tu autem, o nobilissima regina, cum sacramenta divina in expositis bene agnoveris." Hrabanus later rededicated the commentary on Esther to Empress Ermengard, adding a poem in which he compares her care for others directly to Esther's (Ep. 46), which suggests that he was seeking favor in both cases, rather than responding to requests.

16. Peter Damian's letters are being edited by Kurt Reindel, *Die Briefe der deutschen Kaiserzeit,* 4, *Die Briefe des Petrus Damiani* (Munich: MGH, 1983, 1988, 1989). Three volumes have so far appeared, going through Ep. 150. Peter's letters can also be found in *PL* 144.

17. For a detailed discussion of the text and excerpts, see André Wilmart, "Eve et Goscelin," *Revue bénédictine* 46 (1934) : 414–38, and 50 (1938): 42–83. I am endebted to Megan McLaughlin for this reference. Wilmart dates the work ca. 1080.

18. There was another woman recluse at Saint Laurent, where Eve had retired, Petronilla, and Wilmart suggests that the three might have shared the life of sacrifice, reinforcing each other (ibid., 75 n. 1). There was also a male recluse, Herveus, at least later, who shared Eve's life and grieved for her after her death. Their close connection is suggested by a letter addressed to them, "Herveo et Evae inclusis," by Geoffrey of Vendôme (Ep. 48) and by Hilarius in a poem in praise of Eve.

19. Adam de Perseigne, *Lettres.* I have seen only the first volume. Some of the

letters are also in *PL* 211. Marie of Champagne, a patron of French poets, was his protector, according to Bouvet, but I know of nothing that he wrote for her. She died in 1198; the letter to Blanche of Champagne is after 1201.

There are other Latin religious texts written for women in the twelfth century, among them Bernard of Clairvaux on virginity for a virgin, Sophia (Ep. 113); Aelred of Rievaulx, *De institutione inclusarum*, addressed to the sister who requested it; not to mention the letters from Hildegard of Bingen and Elisabeth of Schönau to other women.

20. I assume that they had enough knowledge of Latin to get the gist of his sermon, since it would be tactless, not to say pedagogically dubious, to answer a request for edification with a text in a language that could not be understood.

21. The Latin texts of their letters are in J. T. Muckle, ed., "Abelard's Letter of Consolation to a Friend and Letters 1–7," *Mediaeval Studies* 12 (1950): 163–213; J. T. Muckle, ed., "The Personal Letters Between Abelard and Heloise," *Mediaeval Studies* 15 (1953): 47–94; J. T. Muckle, ed., "The Letter of Heloise on Religious Life and Abelard's First Reply," *Mediaeval Studies* 17 (1955): 240–81; T. P. McLaughlin, ed., "Abelard's Rule for Religious Women," *Mediaeval Studies* 18 (1956): 241–92; Peter Abelard, *Petri Abaelardi Opera*, ed. Victor Cousin (Paris: Imprimerie Royale, 1849); and *PL* 178. For a translation of many of them, see Betty Radice, trans. *The Letters of Abelard and Heloise* (Middlesex, England: Penguin, 1974).

22. Although there is no proof beyond Abelard's words that Héloïse knew Hebrew, scholars have argued for a "flourishing interest in Hebrew" among some twelfth-century students of the Bible, indeed among some in Abelard's circle or in contact with it. See D. E. Luscombe, *The School of Peter Abelard* (Cambridge: Cambridge University, 1969), particularly 236–37. Luscombe also cites Beryl Smalley, *The Study of the Bible in the Middle Ages* (Oxford: Blackwell, 1952; reprint, Notre Dame, Ind.: Notre Dame University Press, 1964). Smalley (chap. 4) talks about contact between Christian and Jewish scholars of the Bible in northern France in the twelfth century. Knowledge of Greek sufficient to read the New Testament is also not impossible, given contacts with the Eastern empire, trade with the East, and the Crusades. It seems odd that Abelard should have made this extraordinary claim so often if there were no substance to it at all. The third time he mentions it in this letter, he points out how unusual it is: "You have in your mother mastery which is sufficient for you, as much in the example of virtues as in knowledge of letters: who is expert in letters not only of Latin but also of Hebrew and Greek, she seems alone at this time adept in the experience of the three tongues" (*PL* 178, col. 335).

23. Peter Abelard, *Hymnarius Paraclitensis*, ed. Joseph Szövérffy (Albany, N.Y.: Classical Folia, 1975), 2v.

24. He also wrote short poems to a friend, Firminia, about her ring and her mouse (Carminum liber, 2.46, 98). Ennodius, *Magni Felicis Ennodii Opera omnia*, ed. William Hartel, Corpus Scriptorum Ecclesiasticorum, vol. 6 (Vienna: Geroldi, 1882).

25. Fortunatus, *Venanti Fortunati Carmina*, ed. Friedrich Leo, MGH AA 4 (1961, reprint of 1881).

26. This may be a reference to the kind of wordplay that appears in his poems, like puns on Agnes: "Agnen hanc vobis agnus in orbe dedit" (11.3), "Fortunatus agens, Agnes quoque versibus orant" (11.4). Cf. "In brief tablets you gave me great songs, you were able to give honey to empty wax" (app. 31), a reference to the wax tablets they wrote and sent the poems on.

27. Among the other verses that appear attached to letters in this collection are some from a woman, Bergyth, to her brother Balthard (Epp. 147, 148); describing her loneliness, her desire to see him, and the love that joins them, she acknowledges his message and gifts, and sends religious poems.

28. MGH, *Poetae Latini Aevi Karolini*, vol. 2. Of Judith's patronage, F. J. E. Raby says, "It was during this happy period, when he enjoyed the friendship of the accomplished 'Augusta,' that Walafrid composed many of those occasional poems which are worthy to rank beside the best productions of the court circle of Charles the Great" (*A History of Christian Latin Poetry* [Oxford: Clarendon, 1927], 184–85). For a comprehensive study of Judith's role as literary patron, see Elizabeth Ward, "Caesar's Wife, The Career of the Empress Judith, 819–29," in *Charlemagne's Heir, New Perspectives on the Reign of Louis the Pious (814–40)*, ed. Peter Godman and Roger Collins (Oxford: Clarendon, 1990).

29. *Seduli Scotti carmina quadraginta, ex Codice Bruxellensi*, ed. Ernst Dümmler (Halis: Hendeliis, 1869), 11, 12. Hrabanus Maurus sent a poem comparing the same empress to Queen Esther, along with his recycled biblical commentary (see above).

30. Serlo also wrote a poem to Muriel; see Thomas Wright, ed., *The Anglo-Latin Satirical Poets and Epigrammatists of the Twelfth Century* (London: Longman, 1872), 2: 233–40.

31. Anselm, who corresponded with many women in power at the turn of the twelfth century, sent "flowers of psalms" to Adela at her request, appending seven orations and telling her to hold the little book as a pledge of his faithfulness and prayers (Ep. 10). *Sancti Anselmi Cantuariensis archiepiscopi opera omnia*, ed. Francis S. Schmitt (1946–61; reprint, Stuttgart: Fromann, 1968). For discussion of a history dedicated to Adela by Hugh of Fleury, see below.

32. Marbod of Rennes (1035–1123), is another of the poet-bishops. Like Hildebert a cathedral-trained poet and churchman, a bishop comfortable with classical as well as Christian texts, like him divided in his view of women as dangerous snares and holy models, he wrote poems of spiritual advice and praise to virgins (*PL* 171, col. 1654–55), poems to aristocratic if spiritually inclined women, and "love poems." See *PL* 171 and Walther Bulst, "Liebesbriefgedichte Marbods," in *Liber Floridus, Mittellateinische Studien Paul Lehmann Gewidmet*, ed. Bernhard Bischoff and Suso Brechter, (St. Ottilien: Eos, 1950), 287–301. At least one of these poems suggests an exchange, though we cannot know if the letter was in verse: "I read rejoicing, dearest, what you sent me, / for there it is held that I pleased you / . . . Happy the tablets, happy the stylus and the hand / the right hand when your letter was made" (290).

33. A. B. Scott, ed., *Carmina minora* (Leipzig: Teubner, 1969). Scott suggests that Cecilia may be a daughter of William I who was an oblate in 1066, became abbess in

1113, and died in 1127. Hildebert's poems and letters are also in *PL* 171, including an epitaph for an abbess, whom he praises for her virtue—she is completely virile, and there is nothing womanly in her actions, "nil muliebre gerens, tota virilis erat" (col. 1305–6)—as high a compliment as a medieval man could pay a woman. The misogynous passage is in *PL* 171, col. 1428: "Femina res fragilis, nunquam nisi crimine constans, / nunquam sponte sua desinit esse nocens."

34. *Le epistole metriche di Baldericus Burguliensis*, ed. M. Teresa Razzoli (Milan: SAEDA, 1936). The answering poem from Constantina and the long poem to Countess Adela are in *Les Oeuvres poétiques de Baudri de Bourgeuil*, ed. Phyllis Abraham (1926; reprint Paris: Slatkine, 1974).

35. Kimberly LoPrete, who has written a dissertation and a number of papers on Adela, suggests that Baudri wrote this poem seeking her support after he had failed to be made bishop of his native see of Orléans (despite attempts at simony, according to Ivo of Chartres), "The Latin Literacy of Adela of Blois," read at the International Congress of Medieval Studies, Kalamazoo, Mich., May, 1991. I am most indebted to LoPrete for sharing this paper and other material on Adela with me.

36. I suggest that Chrétien was echoing this poem in his prologue to *Lancelot* in "Whose Voice? The Influence of Women Patrons on Courtly Romances," in *Literary Aspects of Courtly Culture*, ed. Donald Maddox and Sara Sturm-Maddox (Cambridge, Eng.: Brewer, 1994), 3–18.

37. A number of other histories have been written for women, histories which emphasize the roles of women in history in some manner, which I discuss in the forthcoming book. They include Freculf's *Chronicon*, a world history dedicated to Empress Judith, second wife of Louis the Pious; Ermold's verse biography, *In honorem Hludowici*; Æthelweard's *Chronicle*, written in the tenth century for his cousin Matilda, abbess of Essen and granddaughter of Otto I (which features women only in the genealogy of their family); William of Malmesbury's *History of the Kings of England*; and a life of Edward the Confessor written for his queen, Edith, which puts her and her family at the center. The life may have been written to further the claims of her brother Harold, but the author's stated aim is to praise Edith, which he certainly does.

38. *Pauli Diaconi historia Romana*, ed. Amedeo Crivellucci (Rome: Tipografia del Senato, 1914). Crivellucci dates the work between 761 and 774, when Adelpurga's father, Desiderius, was defeated by Charlemagne and the Franks and the Lombard kingdom fell. At the end Paul promises to bring the work up to their time, if Adelpurga wills and he lives, and he did eventually write the *History of the Lombards* but did not go beyond Liutprand (d. 744). Because the historians I cite in this section are talking about the past and using past tenses for the most part, though not exclusively, I use the past tense. The major exception is Donizo's life of Matilda, which uses the present more frequently than other works, presumably because she was alive when he wrote it.

39. Paul's source, Jerome, had mentioned Judith, but not the murder (*Pauli Diaconi historia Romana*, 16n.).

40. Similarly, if more formally, Maurice, a Cappadocian, received the empire by

marriage to Tiberius's daughter wearing royal ornaments, that is bearing and trans-
mitting the imperial dignity (17.14).

41. Widukind may have drawn on Hrotsvit's *Gesta Ottonis* for his history; see
Katharina Wilson, *Hrotsvit of Gandersheim, The Ethics of Authorial Stance* (Leiden:
Brill, 1988), 156. For the text of Hrotsvit's epics, see *Hrotsvithae Opera*, ed. Helene
Homeyer (Paderborn: Schöningh, 1970); and *"Hrosvithae liber tertius,"* text w. translation, Mary Bernardine Bergman (Covington, K.Y.: Sisters of St. Benedict, 1943).
Wilson says Hrotsvit is the only Saxon/Ottonian historian to depict female members
of the dynasty in some detail, the only tenth-century historian who knows or mentions
that two English princesses were sent to Henry's court to provide a choice for Otto's
bride (though Æthelweard, not a major historian but writing for a woman, mentions
it), and the first historian to provide intimate details of Adelheid's escape (114).

42. This is a striking condition, because she herself had already been married to
Aethelred, by whom she had had two sons, who had a claim to the throne; one of them,
Edward the Confessor, would eventually succeed her son by Cnut. The author does not
mention her previous marriage, indeed refers to her twice as a virgin (col. 1388); nor
does he mention that she was the second wife to her first husband, King Aethelred,
who had yet another son with a claim to the throne (Edmund Ironside, Cnut's rival).
Emma's other sons appear in the story, but without reference to their father. The author
either did not know they were Aethelred's sons or suppresses the fact. He allows us to
think they are Cnut's. He mentions the parents' special love for their son, Harthacnut,
whom they kept with them as the future heir of the kingdom, while they sent the
others to be educated in Normandy, as if all three were Cnut's sons.

43. The author comments that Harold was falsely thought to be the son of Cnut by
a concubine, whereas it is more believable that he was the son of a handmaid, stolen
from her and furtively placed in the concubine's chamber (col. 1391). In fact, Harold
was recognized as Cnut's heir and succeeded his father, ruling from 1035 to 1040.

44. Alfred was captured by Godwin, who would later be the father-in-law of
Emma's son Edward, and who became a man of great power in England and certainly a
threat to Emma's position. Indeed, Edward may have used some of his mother's dower
lands to pay for Godwin's support or neutrality (C. W. Previté-Orton, *The Shorter
Cambridge Medieval History* [Cambridge: Cambridge University, 1953], 1:399). Godwin's role in Alfred's death is denied in the anonymous life of King Edward written for
his widow, 'Edith (*Vita Æduuardi Regis qui apud Westmonasterium Requiescit*, in *Lives
of Edward the Confessor*, ed. Henry Richard Luard, Roll Series 3 (London: Longman,
Brown, Green, Longmans, and Roberts, 1858).

45. This is at best a telescoped view: Harold did die conveniently as Harthacnut
returned, and Harthacnut succeeded him (1040–42), but it was only when he died
that the English chose Edward, who had remained in Normandy.

46. Her importance in the history of northern Italy (partly because of the long
battle over the nature of the donation of her holdings to the church) is evident in the
earliest Dante commentaries, over two and a half centuries after her death, which take

it for granted that the Matelda in Dante's earthly paradise is this countess. See my *Political Vision of the Divine Comedy* (Princeton: Princeton University, 1984), 246–47. Giovanni Villani includes various details of her life in his fourteenth-century history of Florence.

47. Donizo, like Hrotsvit, tells this story in detail, though with differences. Here the priest makes a hole in the wall and supplies the two women with men's clothes for their escape. But Adelheid takes control, deciding whom to ask for help and suggesting to the pope that she be married to Otto.

48. Simeoni cites Hugh of Flavigny's *Chronicle of Verdun*: "At this time only Countess Matilda was found among women, who scorned the king's power, who countered his shrewdness and power even with martial conflict and deservedly was called 'virago,' who surpassed even men by the virtue of her spirit" (MGH, SS, 8, 463); and Bardone's life of Saint Anselm: "The single and only one who remains in the faith, with zeal for God and obedient to pope Gregory, is the Duke and Marchioness, Matilda" (MGH, SS, 12, 16).

49. In fact, Hugh of Fleury dedicated to Matilda the *Modernorum regum Francorum liber*, in which he mentions that he had dedicated a work on the exploits of Roman emperors and French kings, presumably the *Historia ecclesiastica*, to her aunt, Adela of Blois (cited by Reto R. Bezzola, *Les origines et la formation de la littérature courtoise en occident. 500–1200*, [Paris: Champion, 1944, 1960, 1963], 2 : 379).

50. Besides the poems noted above, Ingelram wrote a poem for her about her father, William the Conqueror, which is cited in part by Wilhelm Wattenbach, "Lateinische Gedichte aus Frankreich im elften Jahrhundert," *Sitzungsberichte der Akademie der Wissenschaften* (Berlin, 1891), 97–120.

51. See Kimberly A. LoPrete, "The Anglo-Norman Card of Adela of Blois," *Albion* 22, no. 4 (1990): 569–89, for a detailed discussion of Adela's role in Thibaudian government and diplomacy. Adela apparently disposed of enormous wealth in her own name, which certainly strengthened her position.

52. Hugh cites Jerome and Gregory as authorities who wrote for women. I owe my material in this section on Hugh's history to a paper by Kimberly LoPrete, "Exemplary Women Rulers in Hugh of Fleury's *Historia Ecclesiastica* Written for Adela of Blois," which she presented at the Medieval Academy in March 1992.

Anchoress, Abbess, and Queen: Donors and Patrons or Intercessors and Matrons?

✳ ✳ ✳ MADELINE H. CAVINESS

Patronage of the visual arts in the modern era involves commissioning and financing the production of works.[1] The relationship of patron to artist runs counter to modern (and originally Romantic) ideas about artistic freedom and inspired individual creation, in that a patron can maintain a high degree of control over all aspects of the commission, whether it be a house or a portrait. Yet the concept of artistic freedom has prevailed only since the late nineteenth century, when galleries began to act as brokers between the producers of art (who risked not finding a buyer for their finished product) and the collectors. It has only recently been questioned whether there is any such thing as creative genius, or free expression.[2] Art historians have also begun to reflect on the complexity of the relationships that have always existed between the production of art objects and their first owners, an area that is especially fertile for those of us who are concerned with the intersection of class and gender.

The Middle Ages is a rich period for subtle reflection on decision-making roles in relation to the production of art, differing we may assume from the modern model I have outlined. If there were "brokers," they served an ideological rather than a financial role. Although it appears that works were always commissioned (or at least made with a specific use in mind), the patron's control was seldom absolute; even the images in a prayer book for the private use of a secular were likely to be selected by a cleric. Works in public view, such as statues and windows donated to religious foundations, must have been even more subject to clerical control. "Art" was not yet a commodity (which means it was not yet art), and if its users/owners thought of these objects at all in terms of a system of exchange, they would have put them on the side of production, for their affective powers.[3] Religious art, especially, could be apotropaic, miracle working, expiatory, or instructive of spiritual and moral truths. It was seldom openly valued (even in addition) for entertainment or aesthetic pleasure. That being the case, even for male patrons, what were the parameters of control exercised by a female donor or patron? Difference is inscribed in our very language, which provides the passive-sounding form *donatrix* in the one case, and which refuses symmetry to the female equivalent of the patriarchal paying-and-controlling male *patron* by ascribing other meanings to *matron* (much as we assign unequal roles to major/majorette and master/mistress; even patron/patroness is asymmetric).[4]

No single set of conditions for commissioning works prevailed throughout the Middle Ages, especially in light of the shift toward a monetary exchange system around 1200 and the concomitant rise of a professional class of artist-craftsmen. I propose therefore to sift some documentary and visual material that spans the early eleventh to the early fourteenth centuries in northern Europe, and to see where a range of case studies leads in providing an assessment of women's roles as sponsors (another masculine word). The models I have chosen are necessarily selective, and complement recent studies that have concentrated on some of the buildings and devotional images that served women's monastic houses, or on Italian late Medieval and Renaissance "lady-patrons."[5] Whereas women as artists are not a very fruitful subject in this period (though only slightly less than men—the problem is lack of documentation), women's ownership of works of art (especially books) has been increasingly acknowledged in very recent times, and ownership begins to sound like patronage.[6] If one adds to that the frequency with which women are represented holding books, suppositions may begin to be made about the rate of literacy among women, and about their autonomy as critical readers and as controlling patrons. Yet the books women owned, and which were even made for them, were often given to them by men, who are the real donors and patrons; it follows that images of the women owners in such books do not constitute self-representations, any more than the images in modern so-called women's magazines; there are cases where one might prefer to say they were made "against" rather than "for" women. Books made for the personal use of women will thus provide us with a wide range of possibilities. Another category is the works for public viewing, such as stained-glass windows, that are associated in some way (normally by an inscription and/or a "donor portrait") with a woman. Both categories raise the essential Marxist question: To what extent did those particular women (or women of their generation, location, and class) own or control the means of production? In terms of medieval categories of class, those who fought and those who prayed had access to wealth (the third class, those who work, were not predominantly even wage earners), yet women did not fully share the prerogatives of the ruling classes—they could not be priests, and their legal rights to inherit and rule land varied greatly.

Some notable examples of books made for the private use of female religious have so far been scrutinized in relation to authorship within houses for men, rather than in terms of adaptation to female recipients. The matter of financing has scarcely been broached. The first case study concerns the claim that an anchoress was the intended recipient of a sumptuously illuminated early twelfth-century book, the so-called Saint Albans Psalter. These claims were elaborated in a major collaborative publication, though the male authors kept the title Albani-Psalter that traditionally binds the book to a male house.[7] The revisionist title used in print by at least one woman scholar, the Psalter of Christina of Markyate, is being resisted.[8] Especially in the context of the present paper, therefore, it is necessary to recapitulate the evidence for the association with Christina.[9] Although she has never been credited as the patron who commissioned the book, she does appear to have been its first owner, and Wormald concluded that it was made for her while she was still an anchoress. Additions to the calendar include the obits of people close to her, notably her spiritual father, the hermit Roger (d. 1121/22) who had incarcerated her in a cell adjacent to his, and her parents and brothers; departures from Saint Albans's use in the original calendar are explained by Christina's origin in Huntingdon; a final addition is that of the consecration of the Priory of Markyate, of which she became first prioress ca. 1145.[10] Holdsworth has argued that the book was not made until about 1140.[11] Although it might be argued that the Psalter came into Christina's possession after the foundation of the priory, when she was thus no longer an anchoress, Openshaw has very recently remarked on the aptness to the anchoritic life of the scene of individual combat against evil, on the Beatus page.[12] The obit of Roger the hermit associates him rather vaguely with the Psalter, implying that it was found in his cell, without crediting him with its commission.[13] There is ample evidence that the abbot of Saint Albans helped with the construction of buildings for Christina and her associates, including eventually the priory at Markyate.[14]

The claim of Abbot Gregory (1119–47) to the patronage and donation of the book is more tenuous, though his aid to the priory is documented, and it is unlikely Christina had any financial means to pay for a book, at least when she was an anchoress.[15] Certainly she was extremely close to him, receiving many visits and providing prognostications (and even new underwear) for his journeys; he might be supposed to have reciprocated with the gift of a sumptuous psalter, but no such gift is recorded in her *Vita*.[16] Only the internal evidence of the pictures can help us to decide whether their messages were encoded for, and perhaps by, or "against" a female virgin.

One of the most unusual features of Christina's Psalter is the inclusion of an historiated initial at every psalm. The general tone of these is masculine, since they depict over and over the intimate relationship of God to the psalmist and, even more, to tonsured monks. A dramatic example is at Psalm 110, where two priests in mass vestments, one of them with the cross nimbus of Christ, hold a chalice over the psalmist with his open book (fig. 1).[17] Benedictine tenets, such as humility and chastity, are emphasized as an aid to monastic discipline, and the prayers maintain the masculine forms appropriate to male reading. Viewed this way, the textual and pictorial discourse seems male to male, with little room for women's voices or readings. Indeed, women are represented gynephobically, in their common role as temptresses. Even an image of the separation of male and female religious places God and the psalmist on one side of the letter bar, and labels the book held by a heavily draped female figure as the "delights of the world" (fig. 2). More extreme is the use of a kissing couple to illustrate the epitome of Evil at Psalm 51, where the young woman blocks the young man's access to Christ (fig. 3).[18]

On the other hand, it has been noted that these images of earthly love had a particular resonance for Christina, because she had resisted her parents and husband in seeking freedom from her marriage vows to become an anchoress. Virginity and chastity were always emphasized for women religious, who could hope to be freed of female taint by assuming the male part of *virgo* and *virtus*. As if to justify Christina's act, the *Life of Saint Alexis* was appended to the psalter; he too broke his wedding vows to live a celibate life.

Even more personal is an acknowledgment of Christina's authority as a prophet and visionary. Holdsworth suggested that the drawings of the Emmaus cycle, added with the Alexis life, referred to her vision of Christ in the guise of a pilgrim.[19] And Nilgen observed that the opening initial to the litany shows a group of nuns kneeling before the Trinity, which is configured as it had been revealed to Christina in a vision (fig. 4).[20] Nonetheless, the female community is overwhelmed by the monk who stands over them

Fig. 1. Initial to Psalm 110, Psalter of Christina of Markyate (Albani-Psalter). Dombibliothek Hildesheim, MS God. 1, p. 300. Property of the Parish of Saint Godehard Hildesheim; reproduced by permission of the Dombibliothek.

Fig. 2. Initial to Psalm 36, Psalter of Christina of Markyate (Albani-Psalter). Dombibliothek Hldesheim, MS God. 1, p. 140. Property of the Parish of Saint Godehard Hildesheim; reproduced by permission of the Dombibliothek.

Fig. 3. Initial to Psalm 51:3, Psalter of Christina of Markyate (Albani-Psalter). Dombibliothek Hildesheim, MS God. 1, p. 173. Property of the Parish of Saint Godehard Hildesheim; reproduced by permission of the Dombibliothek.

Fig. 4. Initial to the Litany, Psalter of Christina of Markyate (Albani-Psalter). Dombibliothek Hildesheim, MS God. 1, p. 403. Property of the Parish of Saint Godehard Hildesheim; reproduced by permission of the Dombibliothek.

as if to instruct them in their reading of the liturgy.[21] This image was "corrected" in an initial pasted in at Psalm 105, which seems to show Christina leading a group of monks to Christ (fig. 5). Even if it was an afterthought, this self-representation is not entirely at variance with the tenor of the original prefatory cycle, in which the authority of Mary Magdalene is attested to when she sees Christ risen and informs (that is, preaches to) the disciples (fig. 6), and in which the Virgin Mary/Ecclesia is depicted prominently in the center of the Apostles at Pentecost, receiving with them the gift of tongues (as in fig. 8).[22] Even the scene of the Magdalene bowing to the ground as she dries Christ's feet with her hair might be read by an anchoress as an expression of her special relationship to the Savior: The Magdalene is one of the examples of holy women Abelard relied on most heavily as a persuasion of the validity of the conventual life for women, especially emphasizing her sacramental role in anointing Christ's head with oil and her apostolic role in telling the disciples Christ had risen from his tomb.[23] But in that case reading as a woman inserts a cautionary note, since the argument was used against a former mistress and

Fig. 5. Initial pasted in at Psalm 105, Psalter of Christina of Markyate (Albani-Psalter). Dombibliothek Hildesheim, MS God. 1, p. 285. Property of the Parish of Saint Godehard Hildesheim; reproduced by permission of the Dombibliothek.

Fig. 6. Mary Magdalene telling the Apostles Christ has risen, prefatory page, Psalter of Christina of Markyate (Albani-Psalter). Dombibliothek Hildesheim, MS God. 1, p. 51. Property of the Parish of Saint Godehard Hildesheim; reproduced by permission of the Dombibliothek.

unwilling nun.[24] Christina, who has no voice of her own, has been differently represented, because her biographer asserted she herself desired a celibate life.

What then are we to conclude was the relationship between Christina and her book? Its male-to-male discourse may be seen to inscribe the symbiosis of male and female monastic ideals that dictated Christina's life as a disciple of the hermit Roger; the ideology works for both groups to the extent that gender becomes irrelevant: Alexis and Christina are interchangeable. One might imagine the Psalter made in a monastic house where Christina was much admired, and in which she was upheld as the perfect example of chastity; possibly it was made in the monastic scriptorium for Roger to use in her instruction. No doubt Saint Albans Monastery profited from having a famous holy anchoress living nearby, like a sacred mascot. With the right textualization of her life she might become a saint, like Alexis. The additions to the calendar and the added initial suggest that when she became prioress of the newly founded cell at Markyate, the book was used by her, as fitting her new station. Though neither the patron nor the donor who initiated the grand project of illumination, she had nonetheless been in the mind of the men who did so, and as the recipient of a book already informed by the ideals of virgin and visionary that she embodied, she—or her sisters—had only a few corrections to add in order to make it definitively "Christina of Markyate's Psalter."

My first case-study was deliberately chosen to indicate the constant blurring of boundaries among patrons, donors, recipients, and users. Such cases serve to emphasize that wherever the documenting texts allow a variety of interpretations, most men will hold to his-story, while a feminist critique at least allows the alternate possibility of her-story. In fact, books custom designed for women religious may not have been rare in the early Middle Ages, when such women were held in great esteem. For instance, Abbess Uta of Niedermünster, Regensburg, approaches the Virgin and Child from their right, offering her book to them, in a full-page miniature in her famous prayer book; her monogram forms a symmetrical pendant to that of Maria.[25] Yet historians have hypothesized that it was possibly Bishop Fulbert (of Chartres), through his student Hartwic (abbot of Saint Emmeram, 1028–30), who designed the elaborate images of the Mass.[26] The point is of considerable interest, because this representation of Christ as a priest is paralleled (in concept, though not in composition) in the later English psalter I have been discussing. Although without further documentation it cannot be ascertained whether the abbess herself commissioned the Uta Codex, this seems likely, because it was made in Regensburg.

Another case that remains open to interrogation is that of the Shaftesbury Psalter.[27] It has long been noticed that a "nun" prays at the feet of Christ in Majesty, or before a vision of him (fig. 7). Farley suggested an abbess of Shaftesbury as a likely first owner, on the basis of the calendar, which is that of the Abbey of Saint Edward Martyr.[28] Furthermore, this psalter shares with Christina of Markyate's book the prominent position of the Virgin at Pentecost; and whereas it lacks the Magdalene cycle, it introduces another subject that I have come to consider very frequently associated with women, the Tree of Jesse. The question must remain open for the time, however, whether the nun for whom this book was made commissioned it herself. We would do well to refrain from using the standard term *donor figure* (let alone *donor portrait*) for owners until we are sure that they controlled the means of production.[29]

Two case studies provide an alternative way of thinking about the patronage of abbesses in the twelfth century, but they intersect with another dimension of the question, that of authorship. One is the fully illustrated recension of Hildegard of Bingen's *Scivias*; the other is Herrad of Landsberg's *Hortus deliciarum*. They have much in common: both were unique copies (in contrast

Fig. 7. Christ in Majesty with suppliant "patron," Shaftesbury Psalter. London. British Library, Lansdowne MS 383, fol. 14v. By permission of the British Library.

to more widely disseminated works like the *Liber floridus* of Lambert of Saint Omer), both were created by or for abbesses at the height of their careers, and both are lost to us in the original by acts of modern warfare.

Hildegard has recently risen to such heights of scholarly interest that it is impossible to do justice here to the new ideas about her literary work and its implications for women's history. Once marginalized as a mystic, she is now claimed as a philosopher equal to any of the schoolmen whose attention to

Aristotelian logic had given them privileged status in the canon.[30] The illustrations in the lost recension of the *Scivias* from Rupertsberg, however, have only recently begun to be fully considered in this light.[31] My sense of them is that they are so close to the text in spirit (but not in the literal way that illustrations depend on the word for their genesis) that the compositions must have come from the visionary's own stylus and should therefore be given the same status as her verbal or musical compositions.[32] Her pictures are extraordinarily original, avoiding all the conventions of depiction in the visionary mode, and many may indeed have had a basis in the blinding lights and fractured vision of migraine auras. Furthermore, images of feminine beings are preferred whenever the Latin allowed. Indeed, such powerful and immense female figures are imaged in frontal view that it is hard not to think of them as goddesses, so the pictures are more subversive than the text. And again, some of the details in the pictures follow tenets that are expressed elsewhere in Hildegard's writings, but not in the *Scivias*; a case in point, as Allen has remarked, is the avoidance of depicting a flesh-and-blood Eve, and instead identifying her with air and water in the form of a cloud, following Hildegard's revision of the role of the elements in men and women.[33]

Yet it should not be surprising that characterization of Hildegard's literary and artistic prowess was hampered by a too-ready acceptance of her own protestations of ignorance or weakness (such as her self-representation as "the small sound of the trumpet")—tropes that were necessary to her survival as a woman writer.[34] At the same time, not enough credit has been given to the author portraits/self-representations in the *Scivias* manuscript illuminated in her lifetime, images that are reflected in the Lucca recension of the *Liber de divinorum operum*, which postdated her death by about a generation.[35] These show the abbess receiving inspiration from the heavens like the tongue of flame at Pentecost (reminding us again of the central placement of the Virgin/Ecclesia at Pentecost in the English abbess's books we were just examining, cf. also fig. 8) and dictating to Volmar in an antechamber (fig. 9). The Ottonian antecedent for this iconographic type is the famous depiction of Pope Gregory observed by his scribe/biographer, Peter the Deacon, as he receives the Holy Spirit's inspiration (fig. 10).[36] Only in Hildegard's case, just as she says in her account of the occurrence of the visions, the light streams from the heavens to her open eyes. Volmar writes to her dictation while she draws on wax tablets; the clearest explanation for the duplication of records is that he writes as she repeats what voices say to her, and she draws the pictorial compositions; her exegetical commentary would later expand the text, perhaps also dictated to Volmar.[37] Yet the iconographic resonance for her attribute is the tables of the Law given by God to Moses. Small wonder Hildegard could put an anathema

Fig. 8. Pentecost, prefatory page to the Ingeborg Psalter, ca. 1195. Chantilly, Musée Condé, MS 1695, fol. 32v. Photo: Art Resource, by permission of the Musée Condé.

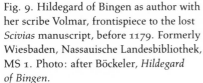

Fig. 9. Hildegard of Bingen as author with her scribe Volmar, frontispiece to the lost *Scivias* manuscript, before 1179. Formerly Wiesbaden, Nassauische Landesbibliothek, MS 1. Photo: after Böckeler, *Hildegard of Bingen.*

Fig. 10. Saint Gregory as author observed by his biographer, Peter the Deacon, leaf from a *Registrum Gregorii,* ca. 983. Trier, Stadtbibliothek. 171/1626. Photo: Art Resource.

on anyone who alters an iota of these revealed truths. The question may remain whether this hagiographic depiction of the "Sibyl of the Rhine" was made under Hildegard's direction, in a book where she controlled the pictures as well as the text, but the style of the pictures in the Rupertsberg *Scivias* would certainly suggest they were done, as has always been said, well before her death in 1179.

The unique manuscript of the *Hortus deliciarum,* produced under the direction of Herrad of Landsberg, abbess of Hohenburg (1167–95) was fortunately copied before its destruction in the bombardment of Strasbourg in the Franco-Prussian War of 1870.[38] It was an elaborate instructional book, culling texts from a variety of sources and borrowing or adapting existing formulae in most of its illustrations. Several themes mark it as a women's book, made by and for the nuns of Hohenburg, with little sign of patriarchal control. It contains a Tree of Jesse, with the Virgin seated very prominently above a group of bust-length kings, and some rare female subjects such as the Daughters of Jerusalem.[39] Several compositions privilege nuns—as virgins they are given the highest place in heaven, above the apostles and martyrs, prophets and patriarchs, the chaste and the married; elsewhere a group of nuns approaches their virginal patrons, John the Evangelist and Mary (fig. 11).[40] Charity (as a woman) tries to lead a nun up the ladder of salvation, but male churchmen leave it for the sins of the world—a priest even offers the nun money (fig. 12).[41] This scene, however, is more anxiety-ridden and more conventional than the comparable one in the *Scivias*, where three women are protected in their energetic ascent by enthroned females on either side (fig. 13). Elsewhere in the *Hortus*, Virtues, looking much like the nuns at the end of the book, surround Christ with the chalice in a wheel of the New Covenant (whereas the Old Law is all male), and in an extended *Psychomachaea* series, Virtues are represented as women wearing helmets and coats of mail over their veils and long skirts.[42] These warriors are reminiscent of the theme of spiritual jousting in Christina of Markyate's Psalter. There is also a cycle for the Old Testament warrior woman, Judith.[43] The wheel of knowledge shows Philosophy and the seven Liberal Arts as full-length female personifications with attributes,

Fig. 11. The Virgin with Saint John the Evangelist, patrons of virgins, Herrad of Landsberg's *Hortus deliciarum*. Nineteenth-century copy of destroyed original, fol. 176v, ca. 1180–95. Photo: after Straub and Keller, *Herrad of Landsberg*, reproduced by permission of Caratzas Bros.

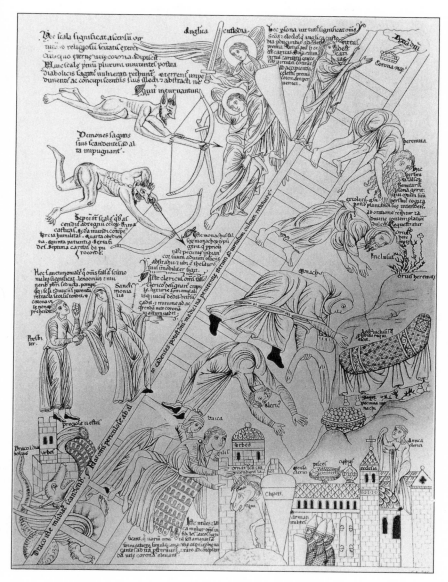

Fig. 12. The Ladder of Virtues, Herrad of Landsberg's *Hortus deliciarum*. Nineteenth-century copy of destroyed original, fol. 215v, ca. 1180–95. Photo: after Straub and Keller, *Herrad of Landsberg*, reproduced by permission of Caratzas Bros.

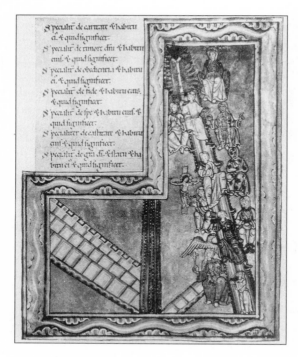

Fig. 13. The Pillar of the Humanity of the Savior, book 3, vision 8 of Hildegard of Bingen's lost *Scivias* manuscript, before 1179. Formerly Wiesbaden, Nassauische Landesbibliothek, MS 1. Photo: after Böckeler, *Hildegard of Bingen.*

dwarfing Socrates and Plato, and in a realm above the bearded secular writers who are inspired by evil (fig. 14). A few cautionary images of women are included, such as a kissing couple signifying fornication, and a very rare depiction of the dream of Pilate's wife, Procula, when Satan told her to tell her husband not to lay a hand on Christ.[44] The manuscript closes with a double-page spread commemorating the foundation of the abbey, under imperial patronage and the protection of the "perpetual" Virgin Mary and the foundress, Saint Odilia. The abbess Rilinda turns to greet the nuns presented by Abbess Herrad, with their names inscribed, on the facing page (figs. 15, 16). This is a medieval schema of patronage, allowing identification of the recipients and users of the book so that their souls could be prayed for by the next generation.[45] This complex image is another warning against the term *donor portrait;* the nuns belong to the ranks of those who pray, especially for the dead, and these hierarchical images show the continuous servitude of that role. Nonetheless, for a moment they are named and made visible, even if disembodied.

Herrad's book of instruction for her nuns demonstrates both her own learning and her acceptance of the social and theological conventions of her time.

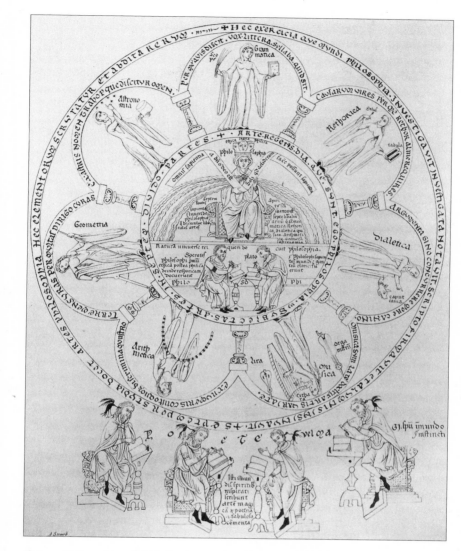

Fig. 14. Philosophy and the Liberal Arts, Herrad of Landsberg's *Hortus deliciarum*. Nineteenth-century copy of destroyed original, fol. 32r, ca. 1180–95. Photo: after Straub and Keller, *Harrad of Landsberg*, reproduced by permission of Caratzas Bros.

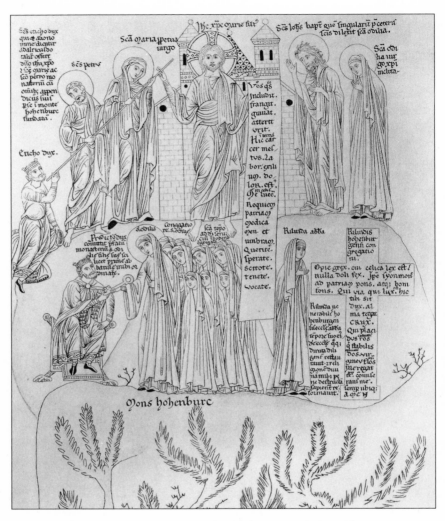

Fig. 15. The foundation of the Monastery of Hohenburg, Herrad of Landsberg's *Hortus deliciarum*. Nineteenth-century copy of destroyed original, fol. 322v, ca. 1180–95. Photo: after Straub and Keller, *Harrad of Landsberg*, reproduced by permission of Caratzas Bros.

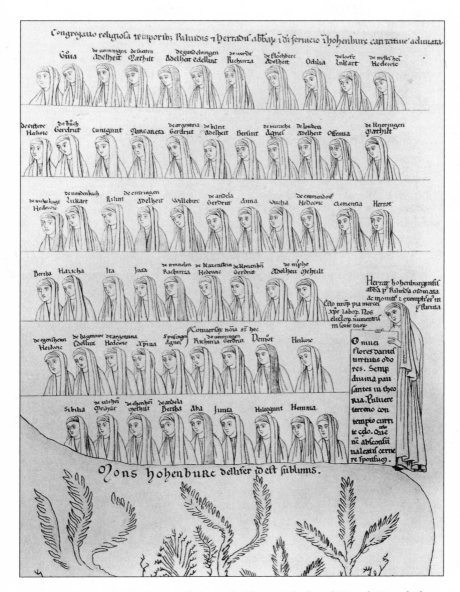

Fig. 16. The nuns of Hohenburg at the time of Abbesses Rilinda and Herrad, Herrad of Landsberg's *Hortus deliciarum*. Nineteenth-century copy of destroyed original, fol. 323r, ca. 1180–95. Photo: after Straub and Keller, *Harrad of Landsberg*, reproduced by permission of Caratzas Bros.

Her position, and the wealth of the monastery, probably gave her autonomy in the creation of her book. Abbesses in German lands seem to have had a privileged existence into the twelfth century; the imperial foundations for aristocratic women (like Quedlinberg, which was ruled successively by Mathilda, sister to Otto II, and Adelaide, sister to Otto III; or Gandersheim, which sheltered Hrotsvit, in an earlier century) continued to flourish under female direction. Even in France rare women like Héloïse could get an excellent education in classical and biblical Latin, in logic and theology.

By the turn of the century, with the shift of education definitively into the all-male cathedral schools, abbesses could not compete, for learning or other resources, with the canons.[46] Instead it is to queens, dowagers, and heiresses that we must look for female patronage of the arts. As seculars, they are associated with public as well as private works.

A contested "donor portrait" is that of Judith, countess of Flanders in her own right (1032–94), represented in one of the three Gospel books she eventually gave to Weingarten Abbey (fig. 17).[47] A veiled woman in an elegant long-sleeved gown clasps the foot of the cross at the Crucifixion so ardently that at least one scholar has misidentified her as Mary Magdalene, despite the lack of nimbus and the fact that no such representation of the saint is known before the fourteenth century. The unmistakably Anglo-Saxon character of script and illumination suggests Judith had these Gospels made in England during her marriage to Tostig Godwinson, earl of Northumbria (1051–64) or immediately after she was widowed. She appears to be the sole instigator of the commission, and the books may have been for her private chapel. The image is a very interesting one in that it not only attests to the autonomy of a secular woman as patron, but also introduces the concept that married women belonged with the class that prayed, rather than with their husbands who fought.

Donations of art to churches are more often documented in the early Middle Ages than are commissions, but the case of Judith of Flanders warns us not to assume that works were made for that immediate purpose; they might well become gifts, or even legacies, later. A major donor who emerges in Anglo-Saxon England is Queen Emma Aelfgifu. She made gifts of two richly woven altar cloths, of purple and green with bands of gold, and coverings of silk, set with gold and gems, for the tombs of the saints, to the Abbey Church of Ely.[48] Weaving textiles for the household was considered an important activity for royal wives to oversee; hence such sumptuous gifts must have been their prerogative. Some left embroidered cushions to the church in their wills.[49]

The *Abingdon Chronicle* documents the royal gift to the abbey of a reliquary. The chronicler describes it as having been commissioned by King Cnut,

Fig. 17. Judith, countess of Flanders, at the foot of the cross, Gospel Book, ca. 1050–65. New York, Pierpont Morgan Library, MS 709, fol. 1v. Photo: The Pierpont Morgan Library.

but he goes on to record the inscription engraved on it, which clearly states that "King Cnut *together with Queen Aelfgifu* ordered this reliquary to be made"—his first account is a blatant case of the silencing of women.[50] The evidence is complicated by the fact that Cnut had two wives called Aelfgifu: a mistress or common-law wife who bore him two sons, often distinguished from his later spouse as Aelfgifu of Northumbria; and Emma, sister of the duke of Normandy and widow of Cnut's predecessor on the English throne, Aethelred II, whom he married in 1017 and who is called Aelfgifu-Emma in some versions of the chronicle. Since he encouraged his first wife to rule in the north after this marriage and in 1030 sent her to rule in Norway as their son's regent, it is possible a joint gift came from them; the more likely case, though, is that the reliquary of Abingdon, and the cross being presented to New Minster, Winchester, in the *Liber vitae*, were joint gifts with Queen Emma, who resided in Winchester. The drawing in the Book of Life (that is, the necrology) of New Minster is inscribed with their names, Aelfgyfu Regina and Cnut Rex, which does not identify the lady (fig. 18).

Fig. 18. Queen Aelfgifu (Emma) and King Cnut presenting a cross to New Minster, Winchester, *Liber vitae*, 1031. London, British Library, Stowe MS 944, fol. 6r. Reproduced by permission of the British Library.

The most enigmatic aspect of this representation, however, is that the queen is positioned on the honored dexter side of the cross and Christ. The date of 1031 that appears elsewhere in the manuscript is now accepted as that of its facture; in that year Aelfgifu of Northumbria was already serving as regent in Norway, and Cnut traveled to Rome as well as campaigning successfully in Scotland; on his return he gave the port of Sandwich to Canterbury. It might be conjectured that the Winchester cross was also an *ex voto*, but an intriguing possibility is that Emma gave it in his absence when she had control of the treasury there. Most significant is the fact that rights at Winchester (and Exeter) were dowered to her for life by her marriage to King Aethelred II; thus when Cnut was in either town he was in his wife's domain and would correctly be represented on the sinister side.[51] Evidently Emma brought in her own administrators to these towns, in that the *Anglo-Saxon Chronicle* blamed a Frenchman appointed by her as reeve for the fall of Exeter in 1003.[52] It was to Winchester that the queen withdrew on Cnut's death in 1035, attempting to hold the royal treasure as well, and she returned to residence there after her Norman son Edward ascended the throne and took a wife.[53] We will shortly see two other cases where wives held their own property independently of their husbands.

The high esteem that Emma-Aelfgifu claimed for herself is indicated by the image of her, enthroned alone, receiving from a monk of Saint-Omer a copy of the biography she had commissioned about 1040, the *Encomium Emmae Reginae* (fig. 19).[54] Like the author portrait of Hildegard later, this pictorial configuration has a prestigious history in the empire, in the presentation pages of imperial manuscripts, where, however, the recipient of the book was always male; the appropriation by a queen mother is all the more powerful.[55] The text serves the dynastic interests of Emma's son by Cnut by making no mention of her previous marriage to Aethelred, as if in respect for her marriage agreement to support Cnut's heirs' rights over those of her prior sons by the English king, Alfred and Edward (although Edward may be one of the sons portrayed here). It also questions the legitimacy of Cnut's sons by Aelfgifu of Northumbria in order the further the claim of Emma's son, Harthacnut. The "Lady Dowager" 's control of wealth, and her independent conduct, appear to make her a significant patron of the arts, even though she has been reviled as an unnatural mother by later historians.[56]

Similar behavior might be expected of Eleanor of Aquitaine. The two queens are alike in marrying two rival kings and bearing each one heirs. Eleanor, however, had the added distinction of being heiress to her father's domains, over which she maintained sovereignty. Her divorce from the Capetian king Louis VII in 1152 and swift remarriage to Henry II of England changed the map of Europe. There has been much speculation about her patronage of the arts, but at least two donations are well substantiated. One is the rock crystal vase which she had received from her grandfather, William IX of Aquitaine, and gave to Louis VII when they were newly wed; he in turn gave it to the Abbey of Saint-Denis, and Abbot Suger had its provenance inscribed on the new mount; in his description of the circumstances of the gift, Suger refers to Eleanor as *"Aquitaniae regina."*[57]

Fig. 19. The book presented to the Queen Mother Emma-Aelfgifu, *Encomium Emmae Reginae,* ca. 1040. London, British Library, Add. MS 33241, fol. 1v. Reproduced by permission of the British Library.

Eleanor's other donation is the great east window of the Cathedral of Poitiers, in which she kneels at the bottom with her offspring, across from a king. In her own domain she is placed on the dexter of the cross (fig. 20). It is often speculated that Henry II gave the window as an act of penance for the death of Thomas Becket (1170), but this hypothesis makes the presumption that the king is the donor. But it was Eleanor who had her ancestral residence in Poitiers, and she had to agree to any decrees issued in her realms by her first husband (Louis VII) even though she owed him fealty. Later, as queen of England, she could issue charters in her own name, though not *sui juris* as a married woman.[58] If the window was glazed on Eleanor's initiative, the date could be left more open (though before 1152 appears too early).[59] She was frequently in residence, especially in 1167/68–1174, after her estrangement from Henry, and it has recently been suggested that she contributed to the reconstrucion of the cathedral that was begun under Bishop Jean Belmain (1162–82).[60]

More tenuous is Eleanor's association with the three Tree of Jesse windows in Saint-Denis (1144), York Minster (about 1170), and Canterbury Cathedral (about 1195), which despite their span in time are remarkably close in composition.[61] I have suggested elsewhere that she is the common link: she was certainly familiar with the Saint-Denis window, and its unique glorification of the genealogical role of a woman in a patrilinial society would not escape a queen who wore a crown in her own right. The York window might have been a royal gift to acknowledge the archbishop's role in crowning the young King Henry in 1170. The Canterbury window provided a royal corrective to the genealogy of Christ, which had been represented in the clerestory windows by all the male ancestors from the Old Testament; its affinity with the Great Seal that Richard I had made in that year, and the fact that he and his widowed mother gave thanks in Canterbury on his delivery from prison in 1194, makes it very likely that the window was their donation.[62] In particular, though, it is the subversive aspect of the Tree of Jesse—its claim to matriliny and even

Fig. 20. Queen Eleanor of Aquitaine and King Henry II of England as donors, lowest panel, Great East Window of Poitiers Cathedral, ca. 1155–70. Photographed in Steinheil's studio before restoration. After the print in the archives of the Glencairn Museum, Bryn Athyn, Pennsylvania.

matriarchy—that I suspect appealed to women such as the unidentified abbess of Shaftesbury, Eleanor of Aquitaine, Herrad of Landsberg, and especially to queens.[63] In a later form it even celebrated the immaculate conception of the Virgin by depicting her with Saint Anne.[64]

Tombs were often commissioned during the lifetime of royalty, and this may have been Eleanor of Aquitaine's intention when in 1185–86, past the age of sixty, she issued a charter endowing the Abbey of Fontevrault.[65] But from its style it appears that the effigy at Fontevrault was prepared after her death in 1204.[66] She lies with her eyes closed, and yet with an open book propped before her as if still reading her prayers. A German psalter of about the same date attests to the fact that an open book had virtually become the attribute of queens and aristocratic women; paired figures at the top of the page show the kings with crowns and scepters (fig. 21).[67] Eleanor no doubt read, since she was acknowledged as a literary patron in a number of dedications at the height of her powers.[68] Yet there is little evidence to indicate that secular women were

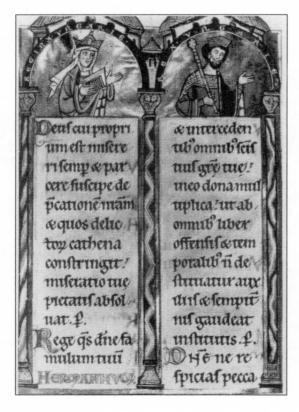

Fig. 21. The king and queen of Hungary, page with prayers, *Landgrafenpsalter*, first half of the thirteenth century. Stuttgart, Wüttembergische Landesbibliothek, HB II 24, fol. 175v. Reproduced by permission of the Württembergische Landesbibliothek.

celebrated or praised for their literacy outside the texts dedicated to them; their normal duty seems to have been to own the family prayer book and keep its memorials. I will return later, however, to the question of women's books.

Eleanor of Aquitaine's sister-in-law during her marriage to Louis VII has proved to be a considerable patron of the arts. Heiress of Braine and dowager countess of Bar, Agnes appears to have maintained control of her revenues during her second marriage to the king's brother Robert, count of Dreux; he took her title (in addition to that of his first dowager-countess wife), and he and Agnes of Braine made gifts together during his lifetime. Agnes, however, is to be credited with financing most of the building of the new church for the Premonstratensian canons at Braine, between about 1179 at the earliest and her death in 1204; during much of this time, from 1188 when she was probably approaching fifty years old, she lived as a devout widow in proximity to the church.[69] She continued to use her seal as countess of Bar (fig. 22); her regal stance contrasts with that of her crusading husband and with the image of her daughter-in-law Isabelle de Coucy on a pony on her seal of 1202, and it seems that the lady dowager, like Aelfgifu nearly two hundred years before, maintained control even after her son's majority (fig. 23).[70] Agnes's husband's wishes for burial elsewhere were respected, but she was buried in the new church of the Virgin and Saint-Yved, in a privileged position behind the main altar, so that her tomb stood literally at the head of the necropolis of the house of Dreux.[71] Above her burial place, in the axial window, was her image, with that of Robert, kneeling at the feet of the Virgin, presenting the church to her; unfortunately these panels have disappeared, and the eighteenth-century descriptions do not specify whether Agnes was on the dexter or sinister, but she can nonetheless be claimed as the patron of the new church. The significant programs of stained glass and sculpture at Braine were associated with Agnes's patronage in the chronicles, which even suggest she obtained glass from England through her relative the queen; this is borne out to some degree by the close resemblance of the surviving windows to some in Canterbury, but I believe the atelier originated in Reims.[72] The clerestory windows repeated, in abbreviated form, the genealogy of Christ from Canterbury, but the west portal had an extended Jesse Tree in the voussoirs. The south rose window had a program resembling the calendar pages of a psalter, with labors of the months and signs of the zodiac, and these were supplemented by female personifications of the liberal arts.[73] The church may be read like a great liturgical book, and it served Agnes as such in her widowhood. Her piety was renowned, and, like her grandmother of the same name, who was given the title Beata, she went down in the necrology as a pious donor.

Fig. 22. Seals of Count Robert I of Dreux and Agnes of Braine, countess of Bar, copied with a document of 1158. Paris, Bibliothèque nationale, MS lat. 5479 fol. 39r (by permission of the Bibliothèque nationale).

Fig. 23. Seal of Isabelle de Coucy, wife of Robert II of Dreux, 1202. Paris, Archives nationales (Douet d'Arcq #723).

A less fortunate contemporary of Agnes was her nephew's Danish wife, Ingeborg, who was married to Philip Augustus in 1193, thirteen years after he ascended the throne.[74] Yet one of the most famous of a long line of books that belonged to Capetian queens is the Psalter of Queen Ingeborg. Another is the Psalter of Blanche of Castile, queen of Louis VIII (m. 1200) and regent to her son Louis IX during his minority (1223–26). These two women fared rather differently at court, in that Ingeborg was repudiated by her bridegroom immediately after their wedding, on the grounds that he found her intimacy and secret vices repulsive—or according to other rumors, that he was in the spell of the devil; his attempts to annul the marriage in favor of another match paralyzed the realm for several years, bringing about an interdict when he persisted with a second marriage (1196; the interdict was 1199–1200) and according to some chroniclers causing crop failures and famine. These circumstances are crucial to my reading of the imagery in the Ingeborg Psalter; indeed the pictorial program seems to support the argument, made by Deuchler, Grodecki, and others on the basis of style, that the book was made for Ingeborg when she was living in a monastic house for women at Cysoing, close to one of her clerical protectors, the bishop of Tournai.[75]

The sumptuously illuminated book opens with a prefatory cycle with identifying inscriptions in Parisian French added to some of the scenes.[76] The pictures include some of our by now familiar subjects: a Tree of Jesse, with only two kings so that the Virgin's role in the genealogy of Christ is enhanced, a Magdalene cycle including Mary telling the disciples that she had seen Christ risen ("Si come la Madelaine dist as apostles qe ele avoit veu dieu"), and the Virgin/Ecclesia receiving the tongue of fire in the center at Pentecost (fig. 8).[77] Among some of the usual prophets flanking the Jesse Tree is a sibyl, precursor to the Magdalene in her prophetic role (fig. 24). Other unusual subjects seem to refer to the queen's painful circumstances: A full page (two scenes, fol. 21r) is given to the adulterous woman brought before Christ, a sequence that could be taken either as a vindication of Ingeborg's innocence, or—with a gender reversal—as a sign of Philip Augustus's possible reconciliation with the church despite his adulterous marriage (fig. 25).[78] Furthermore, the Virgin's rescue of Theophilus from his pact with the devil, which occupies four scenes of an opening (fols. 35v–36) might allude to the king's possession, certainly the preferable cause of rejection for Ingeborg. The coronation of the Virgin (f. 34r) appears in other royal contexts and resonates here with the uncompleted crowning of Ingeborg.[79] Overall, the psalter seems replete with the wishful thinking of the repudiated queen, or her defenders. As with the psalter that belonged to Christina of Markyate, there is no secure

Fig. 24. Jesse Tree, prefatory page to the Ingeborg Psalter, ca. 1195. Chantilly, Musée Condé, MS 1695, fol. 14v. Photo: Art Resource, by permission of the Musée Condé.

Si come li iudeu acuserent la fame qi fu reprise en auourere.

Si come li giu sen partirent 7 ele remeist.

Fig. 25. Christ and the woman accused of adultery, prefatory page to the Ingeborg Psalter, ca. 1195. Chantilly, Musée Condé, MS 1695, f. 21r. Photo: Art Resource, by permission of the Musée Condé.

evidence that the book was made for the owner whose family memorials were included in the calendar, but the cycle of pictures seems in both cases to be specifically adapted to their circumstances. Whether Ingeborg commissioned and paid for her book, and even if so, to what extent its program was selected by an ecclesiastical advisor, must remain open questions.

In the thirteenth century another Capetian queen emerged who was as dominant as her grandmother Eleanor of Aquitaine had been: Blanche of Castile, daughter of Henry II's daughter Eleanor and of Alphonse VIII of Castile, was brought to Paris in 1200 as the bride of the future Louis VIII. Under Castilian law she could succeed to the throne, and she probably received an education to fit her for rulership.[80] Matthew Paris referred to her in his *Chronica majora* as "a woman in sex, but a man in counsels."[81] From 1223 to 1226 she ruled as regent for her son Louis IX. His biographers credit her with teaching him to read, and she oversees his education in a scene included in his illustrated life in the early-fourteenth-century Psalter of Jeanne II de Navarre (fig. 26). As if to confirm that tradition, the so-called Psalter of Saint Louis in Leyden is inscribed to the effect that this is the book Blanche taught him to read.[82] The psalter she gave the royal capella, now in the Bibliothèque de l'Arsenal in Paris, MS 1186, fits the pattern of several women's psalters we have already seen, in having a Tree of Jesse among the prefatory pages; these also include Christ's appearance to Mary Magdalene, and a prominent regal Ecclesia at the Crucifixion. Blanche's role as instigator of a lavish picture cycle seems to be acknowledged (or claimed) in the frontispiece to the recension of the *Bible moralisée*, now divided between Toledo and the Morgan Library in New York, which was produced in Paris about 1230.[83] A queen is seated in the upper tier, with a young king, and the clerical advisor and scribe or illuminator work below (fig. 27). Like Agnes of Braine, the "Lady Dowager" Blanche seems to have eclipsed her daughter-in-law during her lifetime, so the identification of Blanche rather than Margaret of Provence here is quite likely.

Blanche of Castile was remembered as the founder of the Cistercian monastery for women at Maubuisson, to which she eventually retired.[84] More

Fig. 26. Queen Regent Blanche of Castile directing her son's education, Hours of Saint Louis, Psalter of Jeanne II de Navarre, ca. 1335–40. Paris, Bibliothèque nationale, MS lat. 3145, fol. 85v. Reproduced by permission of the Bibliothèque nationale.

Fig. 27. A queen (Blanche of Castile?) and king (Louis IX?) presiding over the production of the *Bible moralisée*, ca. 1230. New York, Pierpont Morgan Library, MS 240 fol. 8. Photo: The Pierpont Morgan Library.

problematic is the role Blanche of Castile may have played in the glazing of the north transept of Chartres Cathedral. The display of the arms of France and Castile in several openings of this gigantic window composition is generally taken as a sign of patronage, as most recently argued by Brenk, who dates the windows about 1226.[85] Yet Blanche herself is not figured in the foot of any of the lights, in contrast to the Dreux dynasty, who appear in the facing south-transept composition.[86] The shield of France at the feet of Saint Anne and the Virgin in the central light below the rose window, however, may refer to the role of the queen mother as regent. Possibly the heraldic bearings were placed there in her honor rather than as her gift. An analogous case may be the stained-glass program of the Sainte Chapelle in Paris, though it is better documented as a work patronized by Louis IX in his majority (1241–48).[87] Yet the subjects in the windows, as only recently perceived, reflect the queen mother's interests, providing biblical role models for a widow's heroism and a queen's devotion (Judith and Esther).[88] As at Chartres, but here in the context of the royal court, only the heraldic bearings of France and Castile seem to attest to her probable role.

Several other female donors of windows are known: Eleanor of Saint-Quentin is credited in the necrology of Soissons Cathedral with the gift of a needed window.[89] And in the upper windows of the inner choir aisle of Bourges Cathedral, Matilda, countess of Nevers (d. 1257), kneels at the feet of Saint William of Bourges, her name prominently inscribed on the window she offers (fig. 28).[90] Such donor figures would not only be remembered in the annual prayers of the church, but their visibility would remind others to pray for them. One very interesting document from the early thirteenth century suggests, however, that tainted money was not acceptable to at least some churchmen, who it thus appears had control over the acceptance of donations: Thomas of Chobham (fl. 1200–1233), in a treatise on penance, recounted how the bishop of Paris refused a gift of money from prostitutes because he did not want the inference that they had earned the money honestly.[91] The same author, incidentally, suggested elsewhere that priests should encourage wives "to be preachers to their husbands, and sway them through eloquence and feminine wiles, to be more just, merciful, and generous" [*suscitet in eum largitatem*].[92] This practice would presumably give the "spiritual credit" for the donation to the husband, helping to save *his* soul, whereas the *largitas* of prostitutes was apparently of no help to them. Yet a century later the *Piers Plowman* poet expresses skepticism that the mere act of paying for a window, and having one's name in it, could (or should) ensure salvation; it is implied that the friars tried this persuasion, but that such transactions should be

Fig. 28. Matilda of
Courtenai, countess of
Nevers (d. 1257), as donor
of a window with Saint
William, archbishop of
Bourges, upper window of
inner choir aisle, Bourges
Cathedral, ca. 1215–30.
S.P.A.D.E.M.

discontinued.[93] Ironically, the prostitutes of Paris are the only group of professional women encountered as possible donors; exactly what role the craftsmen
represented in the windows of Chartres and Bourges played in their financing
is debated, but they do not include women's work. The existing scenes, of men
making wheels and barrels, shoeing horses and sculpting tombs, selling furs
and wine, changing coin and slaughtering cattle, valorize their activities in
much the same way the traditional labors of the months had valorized peasant
work. Women's work goes unsung (as even in Marxist theory).[94] The only
exception at Chartres are the voussoir figures of women spinning as expo-
nents of the active life, on the north transept; their contemplative companions
have books.[95] Not only are the images personifications, but they also represent
upper-class occupations—women had been spinning since Eve, but as we have
seen it was the female household manager who provided luxury textiles.

My recent research has led to a reevaluation of books made "for" or
"against" women in the early fourteenth century. By then it seems that most
illuminated books were made for the use of women, and they have all too
easily been characterized as sources of delight and symbols of learning. A
closer examination of the fashionable marginalia that teem on the pages of
private devotional books has demonstrated that grotesque motifs were selected
to repel the female reader, constantly reminding her of the depravity of sexual
pleasure—a message rendered potent by the fact that many books of hours
were apparently wedding gifts from husband to wife; they carry the double
message that she must ardently desire a male child, but she must conceive
without pleasure and be faithful to her husband to ensure the purity of his
line. My case studies began with the Hours of Jeanne d'Evreux in the Cloisters, a tiny book assigned on good evidence to the Parisian artist Jean Pucelle.[96]
More important, it is a Dominican book and reflects the repressive teaching
that Jeanne would have had from her confessor. Although she is encouraged
to desire a male child (a Capetian heir to the throne was desperately needed
by Charles le Bel in 1324), by being represented kneeling before the Virgin
at the Annunciation, and she is reminded again by a large hare, symbol of
fertility, at the Visitation, there are numerous instances of warning against
carnal appetites. For instance, a monkey climbs toward her on the Annunciation page, and a young man is aroused by a flirtations game of hot cockles
in the lower margin, but the royal bride is sheltered in the initial letter of
the Lord, concentrating on her prayers. A similar page was made by Pucelle's
follower Jean le Noir in a book of hours for Jeanne d'Evreux's niece and close
contemporary, Jeanne II de Navarre, before 1349 (Paris, Bibliotèque nationale,
MS n. acq. lat. 3145, fig. 29); this version even has four hares in the foliage

Fig. 29. Annunciation, and initial with Jeanne II de Navarre, Hours of the Virgin, Psalter of Jeanne II de Navarre, ca. 1335–40, Paris, Bibliothèque nationale, MS n. acq. lat. 3145, fol. 39r. Reproduced by permission of the Bibliothèque nationale.

behind the Angel Gabriel's back, and the Virgin appears with the Christ Child
in the initial with Jeanne. Repulsive grotesques with men's faces and torsos
and bestial hairy hindparts with phallic tails appear in great numbers in the
margins of a group of nine related women's books I have tabulated, whereas
in three contemporary men's prayer books there are proportionately more
female and boyish grotesques.[97] These latter are often alluring rather than repulsive, serving as more rational reminders of the wiles of Eve, Salome, and
Delilah. The collusion of confessor and husband in the preparation and gift
of a bride's book renders it especially effective as an ideological carrier, an
agent in the construction of female gender and in the control of female sexuality. Jeanne d'Evreux's nonexistent role as patron of her own book of hours,
in which she is imaged more as a hostage than as a lady with authority over
her household, may be contrasted with that implied in her gift to the Abbey
of Saint-Denis of a silver, gilt, and enameled statue of the Virgin and Child.
Preserved in the Louvre, the inscription that records Jeanne as the donor gives
the year as 1349, when she had long been widowed; apparently even without
being able to assume the role of queen mother at the court she had control of
sufficient revenues to be a substantial patron.[98]

   The wide range of material objects associated with women donors, patrons
and or owners that I have reviewed here were symbiotically related to women's
piety. It seems that books were especially associated with secular women and
that before the great royal libraries of the late fourteenth century, they may
have owned more books than did men.[99] Yet when a book became the preferred
attribute of well-bred women, what did this mean in regard to their literacy or
to the use they might make of books? Did it empower them to share knowledge, or did it merely label them as imperfect members of the class that prays?
Ward has commented on the piety of such wives, "living what amounted to a
virtually monastic life."[100] Sheingorn has recently brought together numerous late medieval representations of Saint Anne teaching the Virgin Mary to
read, emphasizing that they are witness to existing social practice (mothers
teaching daughters) and thus to women's literacy.[101] There was a long tradition
of depicting the Virgin at the Annunciation holding a book (possibly a reference to the Word that became flesh in Christ)—for instance, in the Psalter of
Christina of Markyate, and in the Hours of Jeanne II de Navarre (fig. 29); in
other cases she may hold a spindle, reminiscent of Eve after the fall and con-
noting women's roles in providing church vestments.[102] Significantly, it is in
the same historical period that women's books of hours became controlling in
the ways I have indicated, that the question was raised how the Virgin learned
to read, and that the answer was found in her mother's teaching. To what

extent this should be considered an empowering image has to be seen in the context of its prolonging the exclusion of women from the schools. Indeed the numbers of books made for women decreased in the late Middle Ages.[103] There are strong indications that by mid-fourteenth century no more was allowed or intended than that women learn to read their prayer books.

The previous generation may have come to regard extensive book holdings by women as dangerous. Charles le Bel's first mother-in-law, the powerful and autonomous widow Mahaut of Artois, was one of the few women of the period to own a significant library, as well as to decorate her castle at Hesdin with sculpture.[104] Although they are not mentioned in the records of works ordered by her, she most probably had books on herbal medicine and gynecology, because both were still practiced by women. This would account, in part, for the accusations of sorcery leveled against her; it was suggested she used some sort of potion to influence Philippe le Long to pardon her daughter Jeanne for adultery, and of poisoning Louis X le Hutin for not reinstating his erring wife, Marguerite, who was Mahaut's niece.[105] Yet, as in the later persecutions of witches, the underlying motivation was surely fear of women armed with learning and a patriarchal desire to control the field of medicine, in which they were by then engaged at the universities.

The historical perspective I have offered here is sobering. It seems that abbesses and queens had sufficient power and command of wealth in the eleventh and twelfth centuries to determine the contents of the books they owned and to make substantial documented gifts to the church. Their names or arms inscribed by their images made their patronage public, and the chronicles indicate that their initiatives were respected. With one exception, they did not use art to subvert existing patriarchal structures, nor should one expect them to reach outside the very class system which allowed them power. The one exception is Hildegard of Bingen, whose powerful depictions of the feminine divine remained visible to a mere handful of her followers and were thus silenced. The powers accorded to some women began to be eroded in the thirteenth century, with something like a nadir in the fourteenth. Blanche of Castile may be the last of the great "Lady Dowagers" to influence the programs of learned books and more visible windows, yet the more public the work the less specific is her trace in it. The theologians were already inveighing against the public display of named images, just as they were also encouraging women to stay home and read their prayer books. Thus women became subject to the very works that were made "for" them.

NOTES

1. For the sake of simplicity, I am leaving collecting off this modern list; there was scarcely any commerce in works of art in the Middle Ages. I note, though, that the role of women patrons as modern collectors is also in need of recognition, as recently emphasized in a review that highlights the role of Louise Havemeyer as collector and that of Mary Cassatt as her advisor: Michael Kimmelman, "Havemeyer Collection: Magic at the Met Museum," *New York Times,* 26 March 1993, sec. C1, p. 30.

2. Linda Nochlin, "Why Are There No Great Women Artists?" in *Women in Sexist Society: Studies in Power and Powerlessness,* ed. Vivian Gornick and Marbara Moran (New York: Basil, 1971), 480–510; reprinted in *Art and Sexual Politics,* ed. Thomas B. Hess and Elizabeth C. Baker (New York: Macmillan, 1971). Stanley Fish, "There's No Such Thing as Free Speech, and It's a Good Thing Too," *Boston Review* 17, no. 1 (February 1992): 3–4, 23–26, has discussed the politicization of the First Amendment.

3. As described in relation to tribal arts: Monni Adams, *Designs for Living: Symbolic Communication in African Art* (Cambridge, Mass.: Carpenter Center for the Visual Arts in cooperation with the Peabody Museum of Archeology and Ethnology, Harvard University, 1982), 9.

4. Francine Frank and Frank Anshen, *Language and the Sexes* (Albany: State University of New York, 1983), 63–93; on the ending *-ess,* see also Robert Graves, *But It Still Goes On: An Accumulation* (London: Cape, 1930), 115–18.

5. Caroline Bruzelius and Constance H. Berman, eds., "Monastic Architecture for Women," *Gesta* 31, no. 2 (1992): 73–134; and Catherine King, "Medieval and Renaissance Matrons, Italian-style," *Zeitschrift für Kunstgeschichte* 55 (1992): 372–93, an article that appeared after I had drafted this chapter, and which raises comparable questions for the later period.

6. Susan Bell, "Medieval Women Book Owners: Arbiters of Lay Piety and Ambassadors of Culture," in *Women and Power in the Middle Ages,* eds. Mary Erler and Maryanne Kowaleski (Athens: University of Georgia Press, 1988), 149–187, and in *Sisters and Workers in the Middle Ages,* eds. Judith M. Bennett, Elizabeth A. Clark, Jean O'Barr, B. Anne Vilen, and Sarah Westphal-Wihl (Chicago: University of Chicago Press, 1989). For some additions: Nicholas Rogers, "The Original Owner of the Fitzwarin Psalter," *Antiquaries Journal* 59 (1989): 257–60; Suzanne Lewis, "The Apocalypse of Isabella of France," *Art Bulletin* 72 (1990): 224–60; Adelaide H. Bennett, "A Book Designed for a Noblewoman: An Illustrated *Manuel des Péchés* of the Thirteenth Century," in *Medieval Book Production: Assessing the Evidence,* ed. Linda L. Brownrigg (Los Altos Hills, California: Anderson-Lovelace, 1990), 163–81; by Alison Stones, review of *Early Gothic Manuscripts, 1250–1285,* by Nigel Morgan, *Speculum* 68 (1993): 215.

7. Otto Pächt, C. R. Dodwell, and Francis Wormald, *The St. Albans Psalter (Albani Psalter)* (London: Warburg Institute, 1960).

8. Ursula Nilgen, "Psalter der Christina von Markyate (sogenannter Albani-

Psalter)," in Diözesan-Museum Hildesheim, *Der Schatz von St. Godehard* [exhibition catalog] (Hildesheim: Diözesan-Museum, 1988), no. 69, 152–65. The curator of the manuscript insists that "every publication must include the following correct description: Albani-Psalter. Dombibliothek Hildesheim," etc. (letter of 25 May 1993); Jonathan Alexander, a prominent male art historian, has suggested to me that a neutral solution is to refer instead to the Hildesheim Psalter, but both the cathedral and the parish church of Saint Godehard (which owns the manuscript) are male institutions.

9. The question was reviewed by Christopher J. Holdsworth, "Christina of Markyate," in *Medieval Women: Essays Presented to Rosalind M. T. Hill on the Occasion of Her Seventieth Birthday,* Studies in Church History, Subsidia 1, ed. D. Baker (Oxford: Blackwell for the Ecclesiastical Society, 1978), 185–204.

10. Pächt, Wormald, and Dodwell, *The St. Albans Psalter,* 23–30, 278–80.

11. Holdsworth, "Christina of Markyate," 194–95. This scholar displays a clear propensity for reading as a man when, having recounted how Christina's own parents tried to get her drunk so that she could be raped by her husband, but he found her "sitting sober on the bed where she regaled him with the story of St. Cecilia," he admits feeling sympathy for the husband (187)! The various dates proposed concern me here only insofar as they intersect with Christina's biography.

12. Kathleen M. Openshaw, "Weapons in the Daily Battle: Images of the Conquest of Evil in the Early Medieval Psalter," *Art Bulletin* 75 (1993): 17–18, 34–38, fig. 1.

13. "ii. Idus Septembris Rogeri heremete monachi Scti Albani. Apud quemcumque fuerit hoc psalterium fiat eius memoria maxime hac die." Charles H. Talbot, *The Life of Christina of Markyate* (Oxford: Clarendon, 1959), 22–23.

14. Sally Thompson, "Why English Nunneries Had No History: A Study in the Problems of the English Nunneries Founded After the Conquest," in *Distant Echoes,* ed. John A. Nichols and Lillian Thomas Shank (Kalamazoo, Mich.: Cistercian, 1984), 141, with references to published charters, 148 n. 82; and Ann K. Warren, "The Nun as Anchoress: England, 1100–1500," in the same work, 200.

15. A. Goldschmidt, *Der Albanipsalter in Hildesheim* (Berlin: Siemens, 1895), 34, claimed this was the psalter mentioned in the *Gesta abbatum,* but this has been identified elsewhere: Talbot, *Christina of Markyate,* 22 n. 3.

16. For their relationship: Talbot, *Christina of Markyate,* 134–39, 142–45, 160–61 (the underwear), 168–69, 180–81, 192–93. Christina is credited with persuading the abbot to give up worldly things (160–61), but this is hardly proof he gave her his psalter.

17. P. 300; Pächt, Dodwell, and Wormald, *The St. Albans Psalter,* 247, pl. 74a.

18. Another case is the courting couple in the initial to Psalm 118:33, where the psalmist holds a book over them inscribed, "Averte oculos meos": 315, ibid., 250, pl. 77.

19. Holdsworth, "Christina of Markyate," 192.

20. Nilgen, "Psalter der Christina von Markyate," 162–63.

21. Another such mixed message is given in the initial to Psalm 149, where the

body of the church is represented by a group of nuns, yet they are overwhelmed by the warriors who defend the church against demons: P. 370; Pächt, Dodwell, and Wormald, *The St. Albans Psalter*, pl. 91b.

22. This depiction differs markedly from the one in the Cluny Lectionary of about the same date (Paris, Bibliothèque nationale, MS Nouv. acq. 2246, fol. 79v), in which Saint Peter as head of the church in Rome (and of the Cluniac order) is placed in the center and the Virgin omitted: Reproduced in Michael D. Taylor, "The Pentecost at Vézelay," *Gesta*, 19 (1980): fig. 2.

23. J. T. Muckle, "The Letter of Heloise on Religious Life and Abelard's First Reply," *Mediaeval Studies* 17 (1955): 252–75; cf. *Petri Abaelardi Opera*, ed. Victor Cousin, 1 (Paris: Imprimerie Royale, 1849), ep. 7, pp. 122, 125, 127. Unfortunately the long passage concerning Mary Magdalene's special status in letter seven is abbreviated in the most easily available translation: Betty Radice, trans., *The Letters of Abelard and Heloise* (Harmondsworth, England: Penguin, 1974), "Letters of Direction," no. 6, p. 180. Abelard's appellate for the three Marys at the tomb, "sanctas mulieres quasi-apostolas super apostolos," and his term "apostola apostolorum" for the Magdalene (Muckle, "Heloise on Religious Life," 258, 271) give authority to preach; he deftly skirts Saint Paul's injunctions against women preaching (I Corinthians 14:34 and I Timothy 2:12) by interpreting his statement on the eligibility of widows to be elected (I Timothy 5: 9–11) to the ministry (263).

24. The issue of gender difference is of course much deeper than I imply here. It has been called a "disagreement between a woman student and her male philosophy teacher" extending to "differences regarding thought and language:" Andrea Nye, "A Woman's Thought or a Man's Discipline? The Letters of Abelard and Heloise," *Hypatia* 7 (1992): 2.

25. Munich, Bayerische Staatsbibliothek, Clm 13601, fol. 2r, illustrated in Florentine Mütherich and Karl Dachs, eds., *Regensburger Buchmalerei von frühkarolingischer Zeit bis zum Ausgang des Mittelalters*, Ausstellung der Bayerischen Staatsbibliothek München und der Museen der Stadt Regensburg (Munich: Prestel, 1987), pl. 96.

26. Bernhard Bischoff, "Literarisches und künstlerisches Leben in St. Emmeram während des frühen und hohen Mittelalters," *Studien und Mitteilungen zur Geschichte des Benediktiner Ordens* 51 (1933): 106–10. John Beckwith, *Early Medieval Art: Carolingian, Ottonian, Romanesque*, (New York: Oxford University Press, 1975), 116–18, nonetheless allows that the abbess was "a woman of considerable intellectual abilities and exacting taste." The iconography of the Crucifixion and mass pages are discussed in Madeline H. Caviness, "Images of Divine Order and the Third Mode of Seeing," *Gesta* 22 (1983): 106–7, fig. 18.

27. London, British Library, MS Lansdowne 383. A full description is in Claus Michael Kauffmann, *Romanesque Manuscripts, 1066–1190: A Survey of Manuscripts Illuminated in the British Isles* (London: Miller, 1975), 82–84, no. 48, col. pl. p. 29, figs. 131–34; and the same in Arts Council of Great Britain, *English Romanesque Art, 1066–1200*, exhibition catalog, Hayward Gallery (London: Weidenfeld and Nicolson, 1984), 99, no. 25, with a date about 1130–40.

28. Mary Ann Farley and Francis Wormald, "Three Related English Romanesque Manuscripts," *Art Bulletin* 22 (1940): 157–58.

29. Corine Schleif, "Hands That Appoint, Anoint and Ally: Late Medieval Donor Strategies for Appropriating Approbation Through Painting," *Art History* 16 (1993): 1–3, makes some useful comments about the neglected subject of "donor portraits." She demonstrates several cases of self-representation, arguing from the attitudes of the figures as appropriate to late medieval art.

30. Elizabeth Gössmann, "Hildegard of Bingen," in *Medieval, Renaissance and Enlightenment Women Philosophers*, vol. 2 of *A History of Women Philosophers*, ed. Mary Ellen Waithe (Dordrecht, Netherlands, and Boston: Kluwer, 1989), 27–65; Helen John, "Hildegard of Bingen: A New Medieval Philosopher?" *Hypatia* 7 (1992): 115–23; Madeline H. Caviness, "The Rationalization of Sight *and* the Authority of Visions? A Feminist (Re)vision," *Museu Nacional d'Art de Catalunya Bulletin* (forthcoming), a revision of the historical narrative I presented in " 'The Simple Perception of Matter' and the Representation of Narrative ca. 1180–1280," *Gesta* 30 (1991): 48–64.

31. Formerly, Wiesbaden, Nassauische Landesbibliothek, MS 1, which disappeared in Dresden in 1945. Black-and-white photographs are preserved in the Rheinische Bildarchiv in Cologne, and these were published twice: "Les miniatures du 'Scivias' de Sainte Hildegarde, conservées à la Bibliothèque de Wiesbaden," *Académie des inscriptions et belles lettres: Monuments et mémoires*, vol. 18 (Paris: Leroux, 1911), 49–149; Maura Böckeler, *Hildegard of Bingen, Wisse die Wege, Scivias* (Berlin: Sankt Augustinus, 1928). A complete copy was handmade in the monastery of Eibingen about the same time, and the illuminations may be close to the original in colors, though in cases where the original was rubbed and detail was invented by the copyist, the style exhibits a period shift toward the Secession. Most unfortunately, all later editions have depended on the copy, or even copies of it, for illustrations. Some recent opinion has assumed Hildegard had a role in directing the illumination of the original manuscript, e.g., Barbara Newman, *Sister of Wisdom: St. Hildegard's Theology of the Feminine* (Berkeley and Los Angeles: University of California Press, 1987), 17–18.

32. Madeline H. Caviness, "Gender Symbolism and Text Image Relationships: Hildegard of Bingen's *Scivias*," in *Medieval Translation Theory and Practice*, ed. Jeanette Beer (Kalamazoo, Mich.: Center for Medieval Studies, forthcoming), paper read in a session at the International Colloquium on Medieval Studies, Kalamazoo, 1993, and expanded for "Hildegard of Bingen: A Symposium," Yale Divinity School, 4 February 1994.

33. Prudence Allen, *The Concept of Woman: The Aristotelian Revolution, 750 BC–AD 1250* (Montreal: Eden, 1985), 293–97. See also Newman, *Sister of Wisdom*, 100–107; and Elizabeth Gössmann, "The Image of the Human Being According to Scholastic Theology and the Reaction of Contemporary Women," *Ultimate Reality and Meaning* 11 (1988), 190–92.

34. Anne Clark Bartlett, "Miraculous Literacy and Textual Community in Hildegard of Bingen's 'Scivias,' " *Mystics Quarterly* 18 (1992): 43–55. The topos has been examined in light of contemporary theology by Barbara Newman, "Divine Power Made

Perfect in Weakness: St. Hildegard on the Frail Sex," in *Medieval Religious Women,* vol. 2: *Peaceweavers,* ed. Lillian Thomas Shank and John A. Nichols (Kalamazoo, Mich.: Cistercian, 1987), 103–21.

35. Good color reproductions of the manuscript in Lucca, Biblioteca Governativa, MS 1942 of about 1220–1230 are available in: Matthew Fox, *Illuminations of Hildegard of Bingen* (Santa Fe: Bear, 1985), 38, 42, 46.

36. Trier, Stadtbibliothek, single leaf from a *Registrum Gregorii* (originally facing one in Chantilly, Musée Condé) of about 983. Both are illustrated in Hans Holländer, *Early Medieval Art* (New York: Universe, 1974), figs. 108–9.

37. The instruction she says she received at the outset, "Dic et scribe quae vides et audis," may be translated "Speak and delineate [or inscribe]" rather than "Speak and write," since the primal meaning of *scribere* was associated with incising lines. This process is far more straightforward cognitively than writing down what she heard and describing aloud what she saw.

38. The copies were reproduced by A. Straub and G. Keller in their edition of Herrad of Landsberg, *Hortus Deliciarum (Garden of Delights)* (New Rochelle, N.Y.: Caratzas, 1977). An excellent scholarly reconstruction with complete illustrations is Herrad of Landsberg, *Hortus Deliciarum,* ed. Rosalie Green, Michael Evans, C. Bischoff, and M. Curschmann (London: Warburg Institute, 1979).

39. Pls. 25bis, 58.

40. Pls. 65, 41.

41. Pl. 56.

42. Pls. 43–52; the Vices are generally sensual, unruly women in tight dresses, though once they are armed like the Virtues (pl. 51).

43. Pl. 17.

44. Pls. 40, 37. Also the two women at the mill who illustrate sudden death (Luke 17:34) look like nuns.

45. Pl. 80.

46. See Penelope D. Johnson, *Equal in Monastic Profession: Religious Women in Medieval France* (Chicago: University of Chicago Press, 1991), on the demise of the once-equal monastic houses for women, eventually in modern times belittled by the term *convent.*

47. The discussion and dates that follow depend largely on Elzbieta Temple, *Anglo-Saxon Manuscripts, 900–1066* (London: Miller, 1976), nos. 93, 94 (New York, Pierpont Morgan Library, MSS 709, 708), pp. 108–111, Pl. 289 (col). I am also grateful to Jane Rosenthal for sharing her views with me; she is working on a forthcoming publication.

48. Charles Reginald Dodwell, *Anglo-Saxon Art: A New Perspective* (Ithaca, N.Y.: Cornell University Press, 1982), 141, 145, 287 nn. 81–84, 288 n. 97.

49. Ibid., 141. Pauline Stafford, *Queens, Concubines, and Dowagers: The King's Wife in the Early Middle Ages* (Athens: University of Georgia Press, 1983), 106–9, comments particularly on the treasure that the eleventh-century Anglo-Saxons had at their disposal, and the many references to their provision of rich cloth.

50. "thecam de argento et auro . . . fieri fecit. In qua etiam apices sculptae erant, quorum forma haec est: Rex Cnut hanc thecam, necnon Aelfgiva regina, cudere jusserunt" (as quoted by Dodwell, *Anglo-Saxon Art*, 25, 246 n. 8).

51. Stafford, *Queens, Concubines, and Dowagers*, 102–3. For Ottonian examples of the norm—the king on the dexter side—see Beckwith, *Early Medieval Art*, figs. 103, 104, 109. I am grateful to Corine Schleif for letting me read her unpublished paper "The Man on the Right and the Woman on the Left: Place and Displacement in Sacred Iconography and Donor Imagery," which explores the normative positions from multiple perspectives.

52. *The Anglo-Saxon Chronicle*, tr. and ed. G. N. Garmonsway (London: Dent, 1954), 134–35.

53. Stafford, *Queens, Concubines, and Dowagers*, 105, 110. Edward the Confessor deprived her of her other lands, but she lived on at Winchester until her death in 1052: Peter Hunter Blair, *An Introduction to Anglo-Saxon England* (Cambridge: Cambridge University Press, 1956), 104–5.

54. London, British Library, Add. MS 33241; see Janet Backhouse, D. H. Turner, and Leslie Weber, *The Golden Age of Anglo-Saxon Art 966–1066* (Bloomington: Indiana University Press, 1984), no. 148, pp. 144–45 (with reproduction of the frontispiece opening, ff. 1v–2).

55. The tradition may have been initiated by the Vivian Bible of Charles the Bald, ca. 845: Charles Reginald Dodwell, *Painting in Europe, 800–1200* (Harmondsworth, England: Penguin, 1971), pl. 38.

56. Miles W. Campbell, "Emma, Reine d'Angleterre, mère dénaturée ou femme vindicative?" *Annales de Normandie* 23 (1973): 97–114. The title "lady dowager" and its complement, lady for queen, appear in the *Anglo-Saxon Chronicle*, e.g., 172.

57. Danielle Gaborit-Chopin, in *Le trésor de Saint-Denis*, exhibition, Musée du Louvre, Paris, 12 March–17 June 1991 (Paris: Réunion des musées nationaux, 1991), no. 27, 168–71. See also George T. Beech, "The Eleanor of Aquitaine Vase, William IX of Aquitaine, and Muslim Spain," *Gesta* 32 (1993): 3–10.

58. Henry Gerald Richardson, "The Letters and Charters of Eleanor of Aquitaine," *English Historical Review* 74 (1959): 193–213, takes a minimal view of her powers to act autonomously before her widowhood and is as much concerned with her male chancery officers as with her role. Cf. the more detailed analysis of Edith Ennen, "Zur Städtepolitik der Eleonore von Aquitanien," in *Civitatum Communitas. Festschrift für Heinz Stoob zum 65. Geburtstag*, ed. H. Jäger, F. Petri, and H. Quirin (Cologne: Böhlau, 1984), 42–55, who, however, admits that only one charter, of 1146, was signed by Eleanor alone, as queen of France and duchess of Aquitaine (46); in a document of 1155 she and Henry, as *Rex Henricus et Alienordis regina*, are both credited with contributions to the new town wall.

59. Louis Grodecki, *Le vitrail roman* (Fribourg: office du livre, 1977), 71, with bibliography.

60. Edith Ennen, *The Medieval Woman*, tr. Edmund Jephcott (Oxford: Oxford Uni-

versity Press, 1989), 139–42, gives a useful summary of her life. For the cathedral construction: Alain Erlande-Brandenburg, *Gothic Art*, tr. I. Mark Paris (New York: Abrams, 1989), 519.

61. I leave aside the question whether the wall paintings in the rustic chapel of Saint Radegonde, in Chinon, depict Eleanor with her son King John and his bride (and whether if so she is to be implicated in the commission): Marc Thibout, "Chronique: Peinture murale," *Bulletin monumental* 125 (1967): 95–96, with bibliography. I am grateful to Eckehard Simon for slides of these paintings.

62. Madeline H. Caviness, "Sugar's Glass at Saint-Denis: The State of Research," in *Abbot Suger and Saint-Denis: A Symposium*, ed. Paula Gerson (New York: Metropolitan Museum of Art, 1986), 267, with bibliography.

63. Whereas Jesse Trees went out of fashion in France by about 1300, patrilineal cycles celebrating earthly kings became prevalent—in an era when women's rights to rule were denied: Uwe Bennert, "Art et propagande politique sous Philippe IV le Bel: Le cycle des rois de France dans la Grand'salle du palais de la Cité," *Revue de l'art* 97 (1992): 46–59.

64. Kathleen Ashley and Pamela Sheingorn, *Interpreting Cultural Symbols: Saint Anne in Late Medieval Society* (Athens: University of Georgia Press, 1990), 13–16, fig. 2 (English psalter, after 1204, Imola, Bibliotheca Comunale, MS 100, fol. 10v).

65. Alfred Richard, *Histoire des comtes de Poitou, 778–1204*, vol. 2 (Paris: Picard, 1903), 133–34.

66. *The Year 1200: A Centennial Exhibition* (New York: Metropolitan Museum of Art, 1970), no. 19, 15–16 (illus.).

67. Alfred Büchler, "Zu den Psalmillustrationen der Haseloff-Schule II. Psalter mit eklektischen Programmen," *Zeitschrift für Kunstgeschichte* 54 (1991), figs. 18–19. Ennen, *The Medieval Woman*, 268, remarked on the books given to Eleanor of Aquitaine and to Beatrix of Tuscia as attributes.

68. Mary Dominica Legge, "La littérature anglo-normande au temps d'Aliénor d'Aquitaine," *Cahiers de civilisation médiévale* 29 (1986), 113–18. See also the essays in *Eleanor of Aquitaine: Patron and Politician*, ed. William W. Kibler (Austin: University of Texas Press, 1976).

69. Madeline H. Caviness, "Saint-Yved of Braine: The Primary Sources for Dating the Gothic Church," *Speculum* 59 (1984): 526–41.

70. Analogous situations in England are described by Linda E. Mitchell, "Noble Widowhood in the Thirteenth Century: Three Generations of Mortimer Widows, 1246–1334," in *Upon my Husband's Death: Widows in the Literature and Histories of Medieval Europe*, ed. Louise Mirrer (Ann Arbor: University of Michigan Press, 1992), 169–90. See also Michael Altschul, *A Baronial Family in Medieval England: The Clares, 1217–1314* (Baltimore: Johns Hopkins University Press, 1965), esp. 36–37. (Maud de Lacy, as widow of Richard, earl of Gloucester, from 1262 until her death in 1289, controlled a third of the revenues of the Clares, despite the protests of their son. She

chose to provide annual support for the abbess and forty Augustinian canonesses at Canonsleigh, which she had founded.)

71. The positions of the other tombs, as established in the nineteenth century, are shown on the plan by Paul Duroche, reproduced in Madeline H. Caviness, *The Sumptuous Arts at the Royal Abbeys in Reims and Braine* (Princeton: Princeton University Press, 1990), fig. 9; see also p. 73, Pl. 62a.

72. Ibid., 98–128.

73. Ibid., 87–97, pls. 189–244.

74. Chantilly, Musée Condé, MS 1695. A monograph with complete black-and-white illustrations was published by Florens Deuchler, *Der Ingeborgpsalter* (Berlin: de Gruyter, 1967). He argued for a date in the 1190s, refuting other scholars who claimed that the obits are original to the calendar.

75. The arguments and historical details are reviewed by Marilyn Beaven, Elizabeth Pastan, and Madeline H. Caviness, "The Gothic Window from Soissons: A Reconsideration," in *Fenway Court, 1983* (Boston: Gardner Museum, 1983), 6–25. The late-twelfth-century date has since been reaffirmed by François Avril, "L'atelier du Psautier d'Ingeburge: Problèmes de localisation et de datation," in *Hommage à Hubert Landais* (Paris: Blanchard, 1987), 16–21.

76. According to Deuchler, *Ingeborgpsalter*, 132–33, the gold script of these vernacular *tituli* is the same as that of the calendar additions and would date from one of the queen's moments of reinstatement in the capital, either 1195 or 1213.

77. Ff. 14v, 29r, Deuchler, *Ingeborgpsalter*, pls. 18, 33 (illus. fol. 3v, D pl. 34).

78. A ninth-century instance of the use of biblical iconography to comment upon a contemporary adultery trial is the Lothar Crystal, carved with the story of Susanna and the elders apparently to commemorate the reconciliation of Lothar with Theutberga: Genevra Kornbluth, "The Susanna Crystal of Lothar II: Chastity, the Church, and Royal Justice," *Gesta* 31 (1992): 25–39.

79. The chrism in the beak of the dove at the Baptism of Christ (fol. 19r) is another specific reference to the Capetians, as Deuchler notes (*Ingeborgpsalter*, 112–13, pl. 23): The Sainte Ampoule used in Reims for the coronations was alleged to have been brought from heaven in this manner at the baptism of Clovis.

80. Castilian widows also had special status. See Clara Estow, "Widows in the Chronicles of Late Medieval Castile," in *Upon My Husband's Death*, ed. Mirrer, 153–55.

81. Quoted by Frances Gies and Joseph Gies, *Women in the Middle Ages* (New York: Crowell, 1978), 119. Their chapter "A Reigning Queen: Blanche of Castille," contains useful information.

82. Leyden, BPL MS 76A, of English origin. For this and Blanche's commissions: Robert Branner, *Manuscript Painting in Paris During the Reign of St. Louis: A Study of Styles* (Berkeley and Los Angeles: University of California Press, 1977), 3–4 n.11.

83. For the date and an attribution to the atelier that produced this manuscript, see

Branner, *Manuscript Painting in Paris*, 49–57, 64–65. He is reluctant to identify the king and queen, regarding them as "symbolic," but suggests that Blanche initiated the work (4 n. 12).

84. Elizabeth M. Hallam, *Capetian France, 987–1328* (London: Longman, 1980), 232–33, 282.

85. Beat Brenk, "Bildprogrammatik und Geschichtsverständnis der Kapetinger im Querhaus der Kathedrale von Chartres," *Arte medievale*, 2d ser., 5 (1991): 71–96.

86. For differing views of the date of this "donation" by Agnes of Braine's grandson, Pierre Mauclerc, see Caviness, *Sumptuous Arts*, 134; and François Perrot, "Le vitrail, la croisade, et la Champagne: Réflexion sur les fenêtres hautes du choeur à la cathédrale de Chartres," in *Les champenois et la croisade: Actes des quatrièmes journées remoises, 27–28 Novembre, 1987*, ed. Yvonne Bellanger and Danielle Quéruel (Paris: Amateurs du Livre, 1989), 116–19.

87. Robert Branner, *St. Louis and the Court Style in Gothic Architecture* (London: Zwemmer, 1965), 64. For the king's role in the glass, see Marcel Aubert, Louis Grodecki, Jean Lafond, and Jean Verrier, *Les vitraux de Notre-Dame et de la Sainte-Chapelle de Paris (Corpus vitrearum Medii Aevi, France I)* (Paris: Nouvelles editions latines, 1959), 73–74.

88. Jennifer Fidlon, a Tufts University student in a course on women in medieval art and literature, 1991, argued in these and other instances that the stained-glass program was likely influenced by Blanche. Alyce A. Jordan, "The Crafting of a King: Politics and Poetics in the Old Testament Windows of the Sainte Chapelle in Paris," paper presented at the joint meeting of the Medieval Academy of America and the Medieval Association of the Pacific, Tucson, 1993, has argued from drawings of lost glass that the "Relic of the True Cross" window contained scenes of the birth of Louis IX as a prelude to the Crusades.

89. Caviness, *Sumptuous Arts*, 148.

90. Amédée Boinet, *La cathédrale de Bourges* (Paris: Laurens, 1952), 83, pl. 17.

91. F. Broomfield, ed., *Thomae de Chobhem summa Confessorum* (Louvain: Nauwelaerts, 1968), 349: "Vidimus tamen quod in eadem civitate volebant meretrices fenestram vitream nobilem facere in maiori ecclesia, et non permittebat episcopus parisiensis hoc fieri, ne videretur earum approbare vitam quarum acciperet pecuniam." The episode is commented upon by Ennen, *The Medieval Woman*, 196–97.

92. Also in the *Summa Confessorum*, cited by Barbara Newman, "Flaws in the Golden Bowl: Gender and Spiritual Formation in the Twelfth Century," *Traditio* 45 (1989–90): 118.

93. [William Langland], *Piers the Plowman: A Critical Edition of the A-Version*, ed. Thomas A. Knott and David C. Fowler (Baltimore: Johns Hopkins University Press, 1952), 85, passus 3, lines 47–63. See also *Piers Plowman, the B. Version: Will's Visions of Piers Plowman, Do-Well, Do-Better, and Do Best*, ed. George Kane and E. Talbot Donaldson (London: Athlone Press, University of London, 1975), 23–24, 153, passus 3, lines 47–75, and passus 14, lines 195–200. See also *A Companion to "Piers Plow-*

man," ed. John A. Alford (Berkeley and Los Angeles: University of California Press, 1988), 36–39. I am grateful to John Fyler for help with this text. For a discussion of the use of transaction as the "controlling metaphor" of satire in the Lady Mede episode, see Wendy Scase, *Piers Plowman and the New Anticlericalism* (Cambridge: Cambridge University Press, 1989), 32–35.

94. Among feminist critiques of Marx, see Mary O'Brien, *Politics of Reproduction* (Boston: Routledge and Kegan Paul, 1981); Jane Flax, "Do Feminists Need Marxism?," in *Building Feminist Theory*, ed. the *Quest* staff (New York: Longman, 1981), 174–85.

95. For reproductions, see Willibald Sauerländer, *Gothic Sculpture in France 1140–1270* (New York: Abrams, 1972), pl. 105.

96. Madeline H. Caviness, "Patron or Matron? A Capetian Bride and a *Vade Mecum* for Her Marriage Bed," *Speculum* (special issue, *Studying Medieval Women: Sex, Gender, Feminism,* edited by Nancy F. Partner) 68, no. 2 (1993): 333–62.

97. A preliminary comparative study was circulated in a conference proceedings: Madeline H. Caviness, "(En)gendering Marginalia in Books for Men and Women," *A Conference on Medieval Archaeology in Europe: Art and Symbolism: Pre-printed Papers,* no. 7, (York, 1993), 97–101. Eight of the nine women's books tabulated are related to the Pucelle shop, but books of this kind made for men are scarce. I have made a detailed study of the Belleville Breviary (Paris, Bibliothèque Nationale, MSS lat. 10483–84) and of some slightly earlier East Anglian and Flemish books, notably the Psalter of Guy de Dompierre (Brussels, Bibliothèque Royale, MS 10607). The study will constitute a chapter in my book in preparation, on reading medieval art as a woman.

98. Gaborit-Chopin, *Le trésor de Saint-Denis,* 246–54.

99. For instance, Clemence of Hungary (d. 1328), widow of the Capetian king Louis X le Hutin, owned eighteen books in Latin and twenty-one in French, including works on government, law, and theology, a moralized Ovid, and a Jewish almanac; on her death Philippe IV bought most of the Latin works, and Jeanne d'Evreux the French; Jeanne bequeathed many of her books to Charles V. See Léopold Delisle, *Le cabinet des manuscrits de la Bibliothèque impériale,* vol. 1 (Paris: Imprimerie Impériale, 1868), 12–15.

100. Jennifer C. Ward, *English Noblewomen in the Later Middle Ages* (London: Longman, 1992), 145.

101. Pamela Sheingorn, " 'The Wise Mother': The Image of St. Anne Teaching the Virgin Mary," *Gesta* 32 (1993): 69–80.

102. A spindle is seen, for instance, in the Annunciation of the Berthold Missal of about 1200–1230 from Weingarten Abbey in the Rhineland (New York, Pierpont Morgan Library, MS 710, fol. 86 verso). For further literature, see Sheingorn, "Wise Mother," 79 n. 9.

103. Brigitte Buetter, "Profane Illuminations, Secular Illusions: Manuscripts in Late Medieval Courtly Society," *Art Bulletin* 74 (1992): 75–90.

104. Bell, "Medieval Women Book Owners," 750; and Jules-Marie Richard, *Une petite-nièce de Saint Louis, Mahaut, comtesse d'Artois et de Bourgogne (1302–1329)*

(Paris: Champion, 1887), 331ff. See also Françoise Baron, "Les sculpteurs de Mahaut, comtesse d'Artois et de Bourgogne (1302–1329)," *Positions des thèses et des mémoires des élèves de l'Ecole du Louvre 1953–1959* (Paris: Musées de France, 1959), 18–22.

105. Paul Lehugeur, *Histoire de Philippe le Long, roi de France, 1316–1322* (Paris: Hachette, 1897), 168–70; also Denys Charles Godefroy-Ménilgaise, "Mahaut comtesse d'Artois," *Mémoires de la Société des antiquaires de France* 28 (1865): 181–230. I am indebted to Suzanne Wemple for this reference.

"Proclaiming her dignity abroad": The Literary and Artistic Network of Matilda of Scotland, Queen of England 1100–1118

Lois L. Huneycutt

Recent work on King Henry I of England has done much to dispel the myth that he was nothing more than a brutal tyrant who achieved order through terror during his thirty-five-year reign over England and Normandy.[1] Although some scholars have been reluctant to go as far as C. Warren Hollister, who sees Henry as almost a medieval reflection of the biblical *rex pacificus,* nearly all now agree that Henry's innovations in the judicial and administrative realms were overwhelmingly successful. These innovations created a centralized and effective state that did much to stabilize the realm after several generations of disputed succession, upheaval, and foreign invasion.[2] But although a great deal has recently been accomplished in reevaluating the political and administrative sides of the reign, there has been much less focus on reassessing the cultural importance of Henry and his queens. I stress Henry *and* his queens quite deliberately, for it has long been recognized that the familiar epithet "Henry Beauclerc" is something of an exaggeration, and that the credit for court-sponsored literary and artistic activity in the first quarter of the twelfth century belongs to Henry's wives rather than to the king himself.[3] Both of Henry's wives were responsible for the production of literary works, but in this essay I focus only on the first of Henry's queens, Edith, renamed Matilda, who played an active part in the political and cultural life of England from her marriage in November 1100 until her death on 1 May 1118.[4]

Claiming that Matilda played an active, public role in governmental affairs

is itself something of a revisionist stand, for until recently the standard historiographical line has been more or less that devised by Matthew Paris in the
thirteenth century. The Saint Albans historian concocted a romantic mix of
fact and fiction that cast Matilda as one of the last survivors of the Anglo-
Saxon royal line who, though preferring to remain as a nun in the monastery
where she had been brought up, reluctantly agreed to leave the convent in
order to marry the cruel Norman king Henry.[5] Matilda was persuaded to
leave the convent only so that, like the biblical Esther with whom she was
often compared, she could intercede to save her suffering race from further
oppression.[6] In the writings of the nineteenth and early twentieth centuries,
Matilda was often portrayed as an overly pious nonentity who, disapproving
of the rollicking lifestyle of the lascivious Normans, lived a semiretired life at
Westminster. Eventually she turned toward patronage of the arts as a way of
expressing her energies and compensating for her unhappy marriage.[7]

Some of the elements of this story are true—for instance, as the daughter of
King Malcolm Canmore and Saint Margaret of Scotland, Matilda was a valuable marriage pawn. Besides carrying the prestige of having been "born to the
purple," Matilda also was a descendant of the Anglo-Saxon kings of Wessex.
And since she had spent part of her childhood being educated in monasteries
and had sometimes appeared in public dressed in a nun's habit, the marriage
was indeed an occasion of controversy.[8] But the overall picture of Matilda is
completely distorted. This distortion is not entirely the fault of later commen-
tators. Her contemporary William, the talented monk of Malmesbury, did
much to establish her reputation as a reclusive patron of the arts. His vivid
description of the queen's activities needs to be quoted in full:

> Enduring with complacency, when the king was elsewhere employed, she
> lived many years at Westminster, but nothing of royal magnificence was
> lacking for her; but at all times crowds of visitors and messengers were,
> in never-ending multitudes, entering and leaving from her superb dwell-
> ing. . . . Her generosity becoming universally known, crowds of scholars,
> equally famed for verse and singing, came over; and happy was he who
> could soothe the queen's ears with the novelty of his song. Nor on these
> only did she lavish money, but on all sorts of men, especially foreigners,
> that through their presents they might proclaim her dignity abroad. For
> the desire for fame is so rooted in the human mind that hardly anybody
> is satisfied with the reward of a good conscience, but is fondly anxious, if
> he does anything worthy of praise, to have it generally known. Thus it was
> justly observed that the queen seemed to want to reward as many foreigners
> as possible, while others were kept in suspense, sometimes with effectual,

but more often with empty promises. So it arose that she fell into the error of prodigal givers; bringing many claims on her tenantry, exposing them to injuries, and taking away their property; but since she became known as a liberal benefactress, she scarcely regarded their outrage.[9]

Because this text has been so formative in shaping the historical image of the queen, it is worth pausing to consider it in context. It is true that, at least for a period in the reign, Matilda did tax her demesne property, including churches, quite harshly. But after drawing a severe reprimand from her spiritual counselor, Archbishop Anselm, she seems to have mended her ways. She became a patron of the church and earned for herself the cognomen *Bona Regina* from those who wrote of her reign and influence.[10] Also, as one of Matilda's tenants himself, William was hardly an objective commentator. Indeed, later in the century, when Malmesbury had been taken over by the rapacious bishop of Salisbury, William looked back on the queen's rule with nostalgia and wrote to her daughter requesting that she take her rightful place as Malmesbury's secular overlord. William himself benefited from the queen's patronage, for it was probably she who inspired and paid for the writing of his greatest work, *The Deeds of the Kings of England*.[11] Finally, William's overall attitude toward Matilda was highly favorable. He firmly stated that her marriage was legal and praised her literacy, kindness, affability, and piety. He was willing to blame her faults on the greediness of her servants rather than her own rapaciousness. When writing of Matilda's death he even hinted at her possible sanctity when he described how she made known "by no trivial signs" that she was now resident in heaven.[12]

Matilda administered the Abbey of Malmesbury as part of her extensive dower lands over which she maintained personal control. These lands gave her the means to influence public policy as well as to follow her own inclinations when it came to secular and ecclesiastical patronage.[13] Especially toward the beginning of the reign, Henry and Matilda seem to have enjoyed an easy and complete trust in each other's abilities. Matilda was one of the most frequent attestors of the king's charters, was present at meetings of the royal *curia*, and most significantly, was left behind to serve as regent in England during most of Henry's trips to Normandy. During her periods of regency, Matilda exercised control over royal administration, although as the bureaucracy grew and began to function independently, her role in the day-to-day business of government probably declined accordingly.[14] By 1100 Westminster, undoubtedly the queen's favorite palace, was rapidly becoming the ceremonial center of the kingdom.[15] Even if Matilda had spent all of her time there—which she did not—she would have been well placed to interact with the secular and ecclesiastical lords who influenced the political and cultural tone of the kingdom. In short, as Henry's queen consort, Matilda was not a pious nonentity but rather a true partner in the administration of his realms. However, with Matilda moved from the periphery to center stage in political affairs, we must now call into question the motives for the extensive artistic and literary activity she sponsored. If she was not a wealthy dilettante trying to fill empty hours, what was she?

Perhaps not surprisingly, most of the projects about which we have any records are ecclesiastical, and many involved the rebuilding of various English monastic or episcopal foundations under the Normans. From these records the queen's passion for building projects of all kinds clearly emerges. Indeed, in her enthusiasm for architectural achievement, she looks less and less like an Anglo-Saxon princess and more and more like a Norman queen. She favored the large-scale and technically daring buildings epitomized by the cathedral at Durham. On her demesne property within and just outside the city of London, she erected an up-to-date hospital for lepers as well as a new and elaborate priory of Augustinian canons, Holy Trinity Aldgate. Neither the leprosarium nor the priory is extant, but surviving descriptions indicate that they were of the fashionable style and formidable scale introduced by the Normans.[16] The same is true of other buildings associated with the queen. Matilda's demesne abbey at Waltham, although founded by the unquestionably Anglo-Saxon king Harold, had been ceded to the bishop of Durham immediately after the Conquest and had undergone extensive rebuilding by Durham-influenced artisans. The same was true of other churches that received substantial gifts from Queen Matilda, such as Abingdon Abbey, Merton Priory, Selby Abbey, and the church of Saint Albans, all of which, following the Conquest, were either founded by Normans or rebuilt in the Norman style.[17]

In addition to her purely ecclesiastical projects, the queen also sponsored practical improvements for her subjects and tenants. She was responsible for the erection of at least three bridges on roads leading in and out of London. One of these, an arched bridge over the Lea, was built out of stone and was extremely well engineered for its day. Known as Bow Bridge, it provided the major crossing linking London and Essex well into the nineteenth century and gave its name to the village of Stratford-le-Bow.[18] Matilda also built an elaborate bathhouse with piped-in water to serve the population of Queenhithe, an area alongside London's wharves. This bathhouse evidently contained London's first public toilets and was hailed as a substantial improvement to the hygienic condition of the area.[19]

Matilda's interest in practical improvements may have come out of conversations with some of her closest friends and advisors, among whom were the episcopal architect Gundulph of Rochester and the physicians Faritius and Grimbald. It is likely that William of Malmesbury was among those English and Norman churchmen who resented Faritius, an Italian who was perceived as enjoying undue influence at the court of Henry and Matilda.[20]

Although at first glance the queen's patronage interests appear to be totally Norman, a closer reading of the sources indicates that Matilda also favored the kinds of crafts at which her Anglo-Saxon ancestors excelled. Chief among these were needlework and metalwork, both of which became increasingly popular on the Continent after the conquest of England in 1066.[21] Matilda sent gifts of needlework and metalwork to favored continental correspondents and institutions. Her gifts were often solicited by a bishop or other high-ranking churchmen who knew of her ancestry and interests and who coveted the kinds of precious liturgical objects that were becoming commonplace in Normandy in the late eleventh and early twelfth centuries.[22] Almost as soon as she was married, Matilda began receiving letters and emissaries from continental churchmen. Typically, she was approached by a bishop who paid tribute to her reputation for piety and generosity, then requested some benefit for himself or his church. In many cases her correspondents shared her literary interests and rewarded or encouraged her gifts by providing her with panegyric poetry or epistles that furthered her reputation as a patron of song. In this manner Matilda, the Anglo-Saxon artisans, and the continental churchmen who approached her participated in a three-way patronage network. The Anglo-Saxon artisans received commissions and court patronage, the continental churches received luxury liturgical objects crafted in the latest style, and Matilda and the new Anglo-Norman monarchy benefited by receiving the recognition and approval of leading members of the continental church. Let us turn now to some specific instances of Matilda's continental patronage and speculate further about the reasons she engaged in that patronage.

Bishop Ivo of Chartres was among the many who wrote to the queen shortly after her marriage and coronation. He rejoiced in the reports of her prudence and holiness, and suggested that they had interests in common that would make it fitting that they learn to esteem each other with a mutual love. He requested that she send, as a seal of their new friendship, "a chasuble or some other liturgical garment, of a quality that is fitting for a queen to give and a bishop to wear in the celebration of divine services."[23] It has been suggested that such requests for clothing are a medieval topos, meant to recall or reinforce a patron/client relationship rather than to be taken literally.[24] In this case, however, the Chartres necrology confirms that Ivo was requesting a garment of the famed *opus anglicanum*. A fifteenth-century inventory from Westminster Abbey, if accurate, attests that Matilda sometimes gave liturgical garments to favored institutions, for it records a black woven girdle with the words of the hymn "Nesciens mater" and the prayer "Deus qui salutis" embroidered in gold letters upon it among the gifts given by *Matildis bona regina*.[25]

When Ivo approached the new queen, he evidently had reasonably sure hopes of a substantial gift, for he went to the expense of sending two canons from Chartres to England to deliver the letter, adding that "they will acquaint you with the needs of our church, and will accept as a blessing the gift which God will inspire you to give."[26] That Matilda took the hint is evident from a later letter of Ivo's that thanked her for the church bells she had sent and for promising to provide a new roof for the church. Ivo assured her that her gift would not go unnoticed: "I will cause them [the bells] to be set up in a much-frequented location, for crowds of people to hear," he wrote, "and daily, as often as they are rung to mark the canonical hours, your memory will be renewed in the hearts of the hearers."[27] Gifts to ecclesiastical institutions were usually given in return for prayers for the soul of the giver, and Ivo's words may simply have been meant to assure the queen that her soul would profit from her material gifts, although the tone of the letter is certainly in keeping with William of Malmesbury's allegations that Matilda was concerned with "proclaiming her dignity abroad."

Two other gifts to continental churches provide further evidence of the queen's patronage of metalworkers. Matilda sent a pair of brass candlesticks for the altar of LeMans Cathedral to Bishop Hildebert of Lavardin, a frequent correspondent and spiritual advisor to the royal couple.[28] It was also a candlestick commissioned by Matilda that drew special venom from Bernard of Clairvaux in his tirade against the lavish lifestyle of the monks at Cluny. Bernard opined that the Cluniacs used, instead of candlesticks, "great trees of brass, fashioned with wondrous skill, glittering with jewels as much as with candlelight."[29]

When Matilda provided luxury items for churches, was it simply because of a desire, conscious or not, to continue the insular traditions with which she was familiar? It is true that this type of gift had a long history, but reading the letters that responded to these gifts makes it clear that other factors were also at work. Women in the medieval world were primary producers of food and clothing, and in one sense Matilda was fulfilling an age-old female role when she provided liturgical garments and objects for the altar, which after all, was a table upon which a meal was prepared.[30] But assisting in the preparation of this particular meal gave a woman a special sacral significance. Both Ivo and Hildebert emphasized that in giving gifts used in God's service, Matilda became an active participant in the liturgy. Ivo compared Matilda to the Hebrew women of old, who supplied gold, silver, gems, and rich dyes that were used for making vestments. According to Ivo, Matilda ought especially to value being recalled to memory when the bells were rung to commemorate the exact moment when "that unique sacrificial lamb" was consecrated on the Lord's table, a time when God was especially inclined toward mercy. Ivo asserted that the benefit of mercy would, without doubt, "extend to the ministers of God who are rich in goods, which for His honor and love, they use to supply those who are lacking."[31] Going further along the same lines, Hildebert asserted that, because the queen provided the objects for the table where the Eucharist was prepared, she took part in the eucharistic service. Her role, although different from that of a priest, was of no less value. And, like Ivo, Hildebert offered a biblical analogy. In presenting Christ with the candlesticks, he said, Matilda acted in the manner of the women who offered Christ their tears at the Crucifixion and who brought spices to the tomb. "You also," he wrote, "are present when Christ is sacrificed."[32] In the reform era, when members of both the laity and the clergy were struggling to redefine their roles in religious life, these kinds of sentiments may have gone a long way toward defining an active and meaningful role for women of the upper classes.[33]

I do not want to push this line of reasoning too far, for the correspondence between Matilda and the continental bishops also provided tangible worldly benefits for all parties. The writings addressed to Matilda served the purposes of panegyric and spiritual instruction and probably also helped her to create an aura of legitimacy and prestige in the queenly office. And, in attempting to guide Matilda's spiritual life, these churchmen were not merely acting as priestly counselors but were also expressing opinions about the political situation in England during the opening years of the twelfth century. Matilda was devoted to Anselm, the exiled archbishop of Canterbury, and during the English Investiture Contest both Pope Paschal II and Anselm recognized her influence over her husband and wrote several letters urging her to persuade Henry to come to terms. A letter from Hildebert of Lavardin, evidently written just after the birth of one of her children, also praised the queen and expressed confidence in her ability to guide the English church:

My spirit rejoices and is made glad about the health of [the one] whose safety preserves reverence for the laws and the undamaged state of the church. For there is nothing greater which ought to gladden the Christian soul above the safety of [the one] through whom the integrity of the law and the state of the church continue uninjured. I rejoice, therefore, and what is more, I shall rejoice as often as Heaven breathes upon my ears, announcing that you are unharmed, as often as I shall hear that the queen, to whom the power of judging crimes has been conferred, whose character is an example of honesty, lives and prospers.[34]

Hildebert's focus on the proper law of the land and the "undamaged state of the church" is duplicated in much of the didactic literature aimed at Queen Matilda. A poem by an unknown author praises Matilda as one who persuaded her husband to bring about a change in legislative policy and praised Henry as the Caesar who listened to his wife, answered her prayers, and abolished the unjust laws of the kingdom.[35] The preface to the Anglo-Norman *Voyage of St Brendan*, which most scholars now accept as written for Matilda, also praises her as the queen who seeks and encourages peace, through whose wisdom and counsel human and divine law are strengthened.[36] Finally, about one-third of the text of the biography of Matilda's mother, written specifically for Matilda to serve as a mirror of proper queenly behavior, is dedicated to a description of Queen Margaret's attempts to bring the Scottish church into conformity with the dictates of Rome.[37]

The benefits that Matilda derived from her extensive correspondence and literary patronage went far beyond the practical advice and spiritual admonitions that she received. Almost all of the literature addressed to her serves also to create an aura of legitimacy and prestige that surely enhanced her position as England's queen. Some of the writing addressed to her even creates an image that foreshadows the "courtly lady" who appeared in all her glory later in the century. Hildebert and the anonymous authors several times referred to Matilda's beauty and noble lineage, and Marbod of Rennes also praised her excellent manners and "fluent, honeyed speech."[38] In a poem remarkable for its explicit description of contemporary female fashion, Marbod praised the queen for not adopting the artifices used by other ladies of the court. Although other ladies painted their faces with false colors and bound up their prominent breasts to appear more slender, Matilda used no artificial means to enhance what nature had given her: "You, O queen," wrote the bishop, "because you are, fear to seem, beautiful."[39]

Authors varied in their degree of approval of the lavish lifestyle adopted by royalty, but all agreed that some display of worldly pomp was necessary to maintain royal dignity. Hildebert's poems and letters are full of warnings not to let worldly wealth become an end in itself. He reminded the queen that her wealth and beauty were gifts from God, in themselves neither good nor evil but made good or evil by the use to which they were put.[40] The *Life of St Margaret of Scotland* carries many of the same didactic messages: besides being an effective agent for the church, the good queen is one to whom her subjects can turn for material aid and in whom her husband has confidence.[41] And, according to her biographer, Margaret enjoyed the perquisites of queenship but always kept in mind that, underneath it all, she was but dust and ashes.[42]

Perhaps the most pervasive element in all the literature addressed to Queen Matilda is the commemoration of her illustrious bloodline. Authors pointed out that she was "sprung from kings on both sides" and rejoiced in the fact that the offspring of her marriage would unite the line of the pre-Conquest kings with that of the Conqueror.[43] The first section of the biography of Matilda's mother refers to Margaret's ancestry and celebrates her ties to the holy King Edward the Confessor.[44] Although it is certainly true that noble women were often valued by others because of their bloodlines, it is much less frequently that we can glimpse women themselves celebrating their lineage. Janet Nelson and Elisabeth Van Houts have brought it to our attention that many medieval women, the *matronae* of royal and aristocratic houses, read and even commissioned works of history that commemorated the deeds of their blood relatives.[45] Matilda's literary commissions demonstrate that she certainly saw herself as a member of an ancient lineage whose deeds were worth recording. These commissions, along with the benefactions recorded in her charters, confirm that the queen valued her natal family and relished the status that came with being the daughter of a crowned king.[46] The continental recognition of the royal marriage of Henry I and the Anglo-Saxon/Scottish princess could not help but elevate the status of the Anglo-Norman monarchy within the European nobility. Perhaps the greatest symbol of the new prestige of Henry's line was the marriage of his and Matilda's daughter to the German emperor Henry V in January 1114.[47]

Although Matilda of Scotland has often been portrayed as a reluctant bride to Henry I, a trembling virgin who left the convent only when duty demanded, nothing could be further from the truth. Matilda received the finest education available to eleventh-century girls in the monastery. She clearly had no vocation, nor had her parents intended to dedicate her as an oblate. She left the monastery, probably permanently, a full seven years before she married Henry. Contemporary chroniclers indicate that the two were acquainted and may even have been fond of one another.[48] When rumors about her convent past emerged before her wedding, Matilda aggressively fought to be allowed to marry Henry and become England's queen. As soon as Anselm returned to England following the accession of Henry I, Matilda arranged to meet with him to affirm that she had never taken monastic vows. When Anselm called an episcopal council to discuss her status, Matilda insisted on testifying on her own behalf and argued compellingly that she was eligible for marriage.[49]

As queen Matilda represented the blending of the Anglo-Saxon and Norman people. When her son was born, the birth was celebrated throughout the kingdom as the fulfillment of a deathbed prophecy made by Edward the Confessor, who predicted that the mixing of the blood of conqueror and conquered would signal a long period of peace and prosperity for England.[50] Far from forgetting her forebears, Matilda actively encouraged literary works that celebrated the history of pre-Conquest England and the glory of her ancestors. Her literary commissions included numerous works of biography and history, chief among which was William of Malmesbury's masterpiece, *The Deeds of the Kings of England*, considered even today as the finest piece of historical writing in England since the days of the Venerable Bede.[51]

It also seems that Matilda commissioned the Anglo-Norman version of *The Voyage of St Brendan*, a poem that introduced the popular insular saint to an Anglo-Norman audience. If we accept the premise that the poem was written for Queen Matilda, it can probably be dated to the years between 1106 and 1108.[52] R. L. G. Ritchie first proposed the 1106 date, arguing that the author's praise of the queen's role in bringing peace and order to the realm would not have been appropriate until after the Battle of Tinchebrai in September of that year.[53] Pointing out that the poem is divided into three parts of approximately six hundred lines each, R. N. Illingworth speculated that "the tripartite structure imposed by the repetition of large- and small-scale themes arises from the contingencies of performance . . . a segment of some 600 lines ending on a suitable climax would provide the material for one evening's recitation, the whole being performed in three separate sessions."[54] Because of the subject matter and the length of the poem, it is likely to have been first sung over the course of one of the formal seasonal courts attended by both the king and the queen. The Easter feast is most likely, because the celebration of Easter is a prominent theme in the poem, which describes the seven-year quest of Brendan and his companions, who are seeking a glimpse of heaven. In the story the passage of time is marked only by the annual Easter feast.[55] The poem, which provides a lively story with an edifying theme, would be perfect for the three nights of entertainment during the festivities that culminated with the Easter Sunday crown wearings accompanied by the singing of the *laudes regiae*. Since Henry celebrated Easter in Normandy in 1109 and then discontinued regular, formal crown wearings shortly after that time, the poem was most likely first performed during the Easter festivities in either 1107 or 1108.[56] The number of surviving manuscripts as well as the fact that the poem was ultimately rededicated to Matilda's successor confirms its popularity among twelfth-century audiences.

St Brendan is not likely to have been the only work composed to be performed at the court of Henry I and Matilda. William of Malmesbury makes it clear that music was one of Matilda's chief interests and claims that musicians from far and wide visited the English queen in the hope of gathering fame and riches.[57] Unfortunately for our purposes, little is known about the musicians or even the type of music that flourished at the Anglo-Norman court. Tentative evidence suggests that Adelard of Bath may have played his cithara for the English queen when she was in Normandy in 1106.[58] Only two other court musicians from the era are known by name, and neither can be specifically associated with Queen Matilda. The first, William LeHarpur, benefited from court patronage through receiving favorable taxation rates on four and a half bovates of land granted him by Henry I.[59] The second, Rahere, was a Norman tenant of Richard Belmeis, bishop of London. Rahere had been a minstrel for William Rufus but appears in the records as a prebendary canon of Saint Paul's shortly after 1115, and he is known to have made a pilgrimage to Jerusalem in 1120. Other than his ties to the bishop of London and Rufus, there is nothing to link him to Henry's court, and no evidence that he was favored by the queen.[60] On the basis of the earliest manuscript of the *Song of Roland*, which dates from the turn of the twelfth century, John Southworth has recently suggested Matilda as the poem's patron. There is no evidence for his position other than the queen's known love of music, and the subject matter of the poem differs greatly from what is known of Matilda's tastes. Stronger arguments have been made for other candidates as patrons of the poem, but it is probably the case that the *Song of Roland* was performed at Henry and Matilda's court.[61] It is also likely that Matilda had some interest in the poet and hagiographer Goscelin of Canterbury, a frequent visitor to the monastery at Wilton, where Matilda was brought up. Goscelin's many accounts of the saints of the house of Wessex may even have stimulated Matilda's interest in her own ancestry.[62] Unfortunately, these few names are all that is known of the literary and musical entertainment that Queen Matilda favored and that undoubtedly accompanied the courtly activity in the royal palace in the early years of the twelfth century.

Medieval panegyric addressed to women often celebrated their roles as "peaceweaver," and the works provided for Matilda prove no exception. Several poems commemorate her marriage as the event that consolidated the Conquest by drawing together the best of the two nations. Nowhere is this consolidation better illustrated than in her artistic patronage. Despite William of Malmesbury's complaints about Matilda's extravagance and preference for foreigners, her cosmopolitan tastes in poetry, music, architecture, and literature and her willingness to make the Anglo-Norman court a center for these activities helped to create a climate in which England flourished. Her patronage of Anglo-Saxon artisans fed the continental taste for English embroidery and metalwork, and the recipients of her gifts worked to enhance the prestige of their patron, the Scottish/Anglo-Saxon princess who became England's queen. Orderic Vital, the monk of Saint Evroul, perhaps summed up the accomplishments of Henry and Matilda's reign most eloquently. Henry, he said, "from the beginning of his reign had the wisdom to conciliate all groups, drawing them to himself by his royal munificence." [63] It was to Henry's further credit that he chose a consort capable of following the same policy.

Notes

1. I delivered a preliminary version of this paper at the Pennsylvania Medieval and Renaissance Studies Symposium, University of Pittsburgh, October 1991. I wish to thank the organizers of the conference and also the members of the panel and audience whose responses helped to improve the finished version of the paper. Some of the preliminary research for the paper was financed by grants from the University of California Santa Barbara Graduate Division and the Interdisciplinary Humanities Center at UCSB.

2. Austin Lane Poole's treatment of Henry in his *From Domesday Book to Magna Carta, 1087–1216*, 2d ed. (Oxford: Clarendon, 1955) is typical of the school that saw Henry as the worst of a bad race of kings. This view has been largely modified in recent scholarship, notably in the work of C. Warren Hollister; see "Royal Acts of Mutilation: The Case Against Henry I" (1978; reprinted in *Monarchy, Magnates and Institutions in the Anglo-Norman World* [London: Hambledon, 1986], 291–301. Unless otherwise noted, all further page references to Hollister's work are to this volume). See also "Henry I and the Invisible Transformation of Medieval England," (303–15). Marjorie Chibnall's *Anglo-Norman England 1066–1166* (Oxford: Blackwell, 1986) also reflects the new generation of scholarship and paints a much more attractive portrait of Henry than that provided in many earlier works.

3. Matilda's impact on the art and architecture of twelfth-century England has been discussed only in passing, but her literary patronage and that of her successor, Adeliza

of Louvain, has been well explored by such writers as Reto R. Bezzola, in *Les origines et la formation de la littérature courtoise en Occident, 500–1200*, 3 vols. (Paris: Champion, 1944, 1960, 1963), and Mary Dominica Legge, in her studies of Anglo-Norman literature. See especially *Anglo-Norman Literature and Its Background* (Oxford: Clarendon, 1963), 7–26. Marcelle Thiébaux included a chapter on Matilda and an excellent translation of her letters to Anselm and Pope Paschal II in her *The Writings of Medieval Women* (New York: Garland, 1987), 165–79.

4. For general discussions of Henry's literacy and that of his wives, see James Westfall Thompson, *The Literacy of the Laity in the Middle Ages* (New York: Franklin, 1963), 170–71; C. W. David, "The Claim of Henry I to Be Called Learned," in *Anniversary Essays in Medieval History by Students of Charles Homer Haskins*, ed. Charles Holt Taylor (Boston: Houghton Mifflin, 1929), 45–56; and V. H. Galbraith, "The Literacy of the Medieval English Kings," *Proceedings of the British Academy* 21 (1935): 211–21.

5. Matthew Paris, *Historia anglorum*, ed. Frederic Madden, Rolls Series 44 (London: Longman's, Green, Reader, and Dyer, 1866): 188–89. For Matthew Paris's dates and reliability see Antonia Gransden, *Historical Writing in England*, vol. 1, *C. 550 to 1307* (London: Routledge and Kegan Paul, 1974), 356–79.

6. See my "Intercession and the High-Medieval Queen: The *Esther* Topos," *Power of the Weak?: Women and Power in the Middle Ages*, annual conference of the Centre for Medieval Studies, University of Toronto, February 1990.

7. Francis Lancelott's *The Queens of England and their Times*, 2 vols. (New York: Appleton, 1890–94), can only be termed historical fiction and Mary Howitt's *Biographical Sketches of the Queens of Great Britain from the Norman Conquest to the Reign of Victoria* (London: Bohn, 1851), though more firmly grounded in the literary sources, is flawed by the author's tendency to accept every chronicler as completely reliable in all details. Elsie Thornton Cook's *Her Majesty: The Romance of the Queens of England, 1066–1910* (New York: Dutton, 1927; reprint, New York, 1970), while published in the twentieth century, retains a Victorian outlook. A notable exception to the general trend to see Matilda as an unhappy nonentity occurs in Agnes Strickland, *Lives of the Queens of England from the Norman Conquest from the Official Records and other Private and Public Documents* (London: Bell, 1889), 1:72–111.

8. I handle the problems concerning the marriage in the second chapter of my doctoral dissertation, " 'Another Esther in Our Times': Matilda II and the Formation of a Queenly Ideal in Anglo-Norman England (Scotland)," University of California Santa Barbara, 1992. The two most complete twelfth-century accounts are by Eadmer of Canterbury, *Eadmeri Historia novorum in Anglia*, ed. Martin Rule, Rolls Series 81 (London: Longman, 1884; Reprint, 1964), 121–27; and Hermann of Tournai, *Liber de restauratione abbatiae S. Martini Tornacensis, Monumenta Germaniae Historica Scriptores* 14 (Hannover: Hahn, 1956): 281–82.

9. William of Malmesbury, *De gestis regum Anglorum*, ed. William Stubbs, Rolls Series 90 (London: Eyre and Spottiswoode, 1887–89), 2:494–95. Unless otherwise noted, all translations are my own.

10. For Anselm's letter of reprimand see *S. Anselmi Cantuariensis archiepiscopi opera omnia*, ed. Francis S. Schmitt (1946–61; Reprint Stuttgart: Fromann, 1968), 5 : 284–85 (epistola #346). Matilda's most consistent patronage was of the Augustinian canons but she also favored Benedictine houses, particularly those whose abbots had personal ties to the royal circle, including members of Matilda's natal family. See John Compton Dickinson, *The Origins of the Austin Canons and Their Introduction into England* (London: Society for the Preservation of Christian Knowledge, 1950), 97–113. See also Christopher Brooke and Gillian Keir, *London, 800–1216: The Shaping of a City* (Berkeley and Los Angeles: University of California Press, 1975), 97–100, 314–23; and Huneycutt, "Another Esther," chap. 4.

11. See Ewald Könsgen "Zwei unbekannte Briefe zu den *Gesta regum* de Wilhelm von Malmesbury," *Deutsches Archiv für Erforschunges des Mittelalters* 31 (1975): 204–14; and Rodney Thomson, "William of Malmesbury as Historian and Man of Letters," *Journal of Ecclesiastical History* 29 (1978): 387–413.

12. William of Malmesbury, *De gestis regum Anglorum*, 2: 494–95.

13. Matilda's dower has proven impossible to reconstruct because of the lack of reliable documentation, but the evidence that does exist shows that she controlled some lands in the north of England, large portions of the city of London, parts of the county of Rutland, the city of Exeter, as well as some of the other areas controlled by her Anglo-Saxon predecessors. Her monastic holdings included the abbeys of Malmesbury, Waltham, and Barking. See "Another Esther," chap. 3.

14. Matilda's governmental activity has been the focus of much of the recent historiographical discussion of her reign. See, among others, Hollister, *Monarchy, Magnates and Institutions*, 229–30, 233–34; Francis West, *The Justiciarship in England* (Cambridge: Cambridge University Press, 1966), 14–15; Henry Gerald Richardson, *The Governance of Mediaeval England from the Conquest to Magna Carta* (Edinburgh: University of Edinburgh Press, 1963), 162–65; Edward J. Kealey, *Roger of Salisbury, Viceroy of England* (Berkeley and Los Angeles: University of California Press, 1972), 31–33 and Lois L. Huneycutt, "Images of Queenship in the High Middle Ages," *Haskins Society Journal: Studies in Medieval History* 1 (1989): 65.

15. Of the twenty-three charters issued by the queen in which the place of issue can be identified, nine, or just over a third, were issued from Westminster. William was also correct when describing the living conditions at Westminster. Westminster Palace, rebuilt by William Rufus in the final years of his reign, was one of the largest and most magnificent in contemporary Europe. See Thomas Beaumont James, *The Palaces of Medieval England c. 1050–1550: Royalty, Nobility, the Episcopate and Their Residences from Edward the Confessor to Henry VIII* (London: Batesford, 1990), 35–37, as well as Howard Montagu Colvin, R. A. Brown, and A. J. Taylor, eds., *The History of the King's Works* (Oxford: Oxford University Press, 1963–73), 1 : 45.

16. For Holy Trinity Aldgate, see the plans reconstructed from archaeological information in W. R. Lethaby, "The Priory of Holy Trinity, or Christ Church, Aldgate," *Home Counties Magazine* 2 : 5 (January 1900): 45–53. The only indication of the style

of Saint Giles comes from a drawing by Matthew Paris in the autograph manuscript of his *Chronica majora* (Cambridge, Corpus Christi College MS 16–26). The drawing, captioned "Memoriale Matildis reginae scilicet hospitale Sancti Egidii quod est Londoniae," is reproduced in Suzanne Lewis, *The Art of Matthew Paris in the Chronica Majora* (Berkeley and Los Angeles: University of California Press, 1987), fig. 47, p. 445. See also Rotha Mary Clay, *The Medieval Hospitals of England* (London: Methuen, 1909), 71.

17. For the rebuilding of Waltham see Rosalind Ransford, ed., *The Early Charters of the Augustinian Canons of Waltham Abbey, Essex 1062–1230* (Woodbridge, England: Boydell, 1989), xxiv; for the queen's association with Abingdon see Joseph Stevenson, ed. *Chronicon monasterii de Abingdon*, Rolls Series 2 (London: Longman, Brown, Green, Longmans, and Roberts, 1858), 2:49–52, 2:88–89, 2:97–100, 2:106–7, 2:109–11, 2:116–17, 2:287–89. Hereafter cited as *Abingdon Chronicle*. The primary source for the queen's interest in Merton Priory is the foundation history (London College of Arms MS. Arundel 28), which has never been printed in full. Some of the relevant sections are printed in M. L. Colker, ed., "Latin Texts Concerning Gilbert, Founder of Merton Priory," *Studia Monastica* 12 (1970): 241–72. For Selby Abbey, see J. T. Fowler, ed., *The Coucher Book of Selby*, (Durham, England: Yorkshire Archaeological Society and Topographical Association, 1891–93), 1:25, entry 23; for the rebuilding see T. S. R. Boase, *English Art, 1100–1216* (Oxford: Clarendon, 1953), 23. Matilda gave land to Tynemouth priory, a dependent of Saint Albans and was present at Saint Albans for the 1116 consecration of the newly rebuilt church. See Thomas Walsingham, *Gesta abbatum monasterii Sancti Albani*, ed. Henry Thomas Riley, Rolls Series 28, pt. 4 (London: Longmans, Green, 1867), 1:70–71.

18. The nineteenth-century collaborators Owen Manning and William Bray repeated a seventeenth-century account claiming that Matilda built a bridge on the London-Portsmouth road, in the Surrey village of Cobham, after one of her ladies drowned while trying to ford the river during a flood. That the queen built the bridge is well attested in the place names of the area, but there is no surviving documentation of the explanation that the project was inspired by a drowning. The story appears to have first been reported in a lost 1239 *inspeximus* into the upkeep of the bridge. See Owen Manning and William Bray, *The History and Antiquities of the County of Surrey*, 3 vols. (London: White, 1809), 2:732. The *inspeximus* in question was on a roll of 23 Henry III, which was reported lost in 1780. See also *Victoria History of the County of Surrey*, ed. H. E. Malden (Westminster: Constable, 1902–12), 3:442. For the bridges linking London and Essex see *The Victoria History of the County of Essex*, ed. W. R. Powell, et al. (London: Constable and St. Catherine's; Oxford, England: Oxford University Press, 1903–78), 6:44–45, 6:59–60, 6:90.

19. See Gilbert Torry, *The Book of Queenhithe: The History of a Harbour and the City Ward* (Buckingham: Barracuda, 1979), 14–17, 35. Also, Ernest L. Sabine, "Latrines and Cesspools of Mediaeval London," *Speculum* 9 (1934): 303–21. The records of a fourteenth-century lawsuit contain a good description of the toilet complex at Queen-

hithe as it then existed. See Henry Thomas Riley, ed., *Munimenta Gildhallae Londoniensis: Liber albus, Liber custumarum, et Liber Horn*, Roll Series 120 (London: Longman, Brown, Green, Longmans, and Roberts, 1859), vol. 2, pt. 1, pp. cxii; and "Liber albus," Ibid., vol. 3, pp. 445–49.

20. Gundulph served as Archbishop Anselm's deputy while Anselm was out of the country. The *Vita Gundulphi* speaks, not implausibly, of a special fondness between the young queen and the elderly bishop. See Rodney Thomson, ed., *Vita Gundulphi: The Life of Gundulph, Bishop of Rochester* (Toronto: Pontifical Institute of Medieval Studies, 1977), sec. 37, p. 61; see also R. A. L. Smith, "The Place of Gundulph in the Anglo-Norman Church," *English Historical Review* 58 (1943): 257–72; and Marylou Ruud, "Monks in the World: The Case of Gundulph of Rochester," *Anglo-Norman Studies* 11 (1989): 245–60. Faritius, a monk of Malmesbury, became abbot of Abingdon and served as a physician to both Henry and Matilda. He was a consultant to Matilda during her pregnancies. When Henry tried to have him appointed archbishop of Canterbury in 1116, the Norman churchmen united to resist the appointment, claiming that a man who had formerly spent his time "smelling women's urine" was unfit for episcopal duties. See William of Malmesbury, *Gesta pontificum Anglorum*, ed. N. E. S. A. Hamilton, Rolls Series 52 (London: Longman, 1870): 125–26; Eadmer of Canterbury, *Eadmeri Historia novorum*, 222–23, and the *Abingdon Chronicle* 2: 287. Discussed in David Knowles, *The Monastic Order in England: A History of its Development from the Times of St Dunston to the Fourth Lateran Council, 943–1216*, 2d edition (Cambridge: Cambridge University Press, 1966), 180–81; Denis Bethell, "English Black Monks and Episcopal Elections in the 1120s," *English Historical Review* 84 (1969): 673–98; and Martin Brett, *The English Church under Henry I* (Oxford: Oxford University Press, 1975), 73.

21. See Charles Reginald Dodwell, *Anglo-Saxon Art: A New Perspective* (Ithaca, N.Y.: Cornell University Press, 1982), 216–17.

22. William of Poitiers speaks of hordes of precious gold and silver candlesticks, goblets, crucifixes, and other objects that William the Conqueror brought back with him into Normandy. His claims are made plausible by comparing the delight of the Normans with the anguish of Anglo-Saxon chroniclers who complained bitterly about the despoiling of their churches. See Raymonde Foreville, ed., *Histoire de Guillaume le Conquérant* (Paris: Belles Lettres, 1952), 224–26, 256. For the quality of and demand for English needlework, see A. G. Christie, *English Medieval Embroidery* (Oxford: Clarendon, 1938).

23. Ivo of Chartres, "Epistolae," in J. P. Migne, ed. *Patrologia cursus completus, series latina*, 221 vols. (Paris, 1844–64), 139, cols. 125–26, ep. 107; hereafter cited as *PL*.

24. Therese Latzke, "Der Topos Mantelgedicht," *Mittellateinisches Jahrbuch* 6 (1970): 109–31.

25. Eugène de Lépinois and Lucien Merlet, eds. *Cartulaire de Notre Dame de Chartres* (Chartres: Garnier, 1862–65), 3:204. For the possible gift to Westminster, see

John Flete, *The History of Westminster Abbey*, ed. J. Armitage Robinson (Cambridge: Cambridge University Press, 1909), 72.

26. *PL* 162, cols. 125–26, ep. 107.

27. *PL* 162, cols. 148–49, ep. 142.

28. The gift to Hildebert is mentioned in *PL* 171, cols. 160–62.

29. Bernard of Clairvaux, "Apologia ad Guillelmum, Santi Theodorici abbatem," *PL* 182, col. 915. See also Joan Evans, *Monastic Life at Cluny, 910–1157* (Oxford: Oxford University Press, 1931; reprint, Hamden, Conn.: Archon, 1968), 94; and Frank Barlow, *The English Church, 1066–1154* (London: Longman's, 1979), 185 n. 35.

30. For a discussion of medieval ideas of the female relationship to food and the provisioning of food, see Caroline Walker Bynum, *Holy Feast, Holy Fast: The Religious Significance of Food to Medieval Women* (Berkeley and Los Angeles: University of California Press, 1987), esp. 76–112, 277–96.

31. *PL* 162, cols. 148–49, ep. 142.

32. *PL* 171, cols. 160–61. Hildebert's conception of the female as an active participant in the priestly function is explored in Deborah McBride, "The Bishop and the Court: A Look at the Exchanges Between Hildebert Of Lavardin and the Courtly Personages with Whom He Corresponded," Seminar paper, University of California, Santa Barbara, March 1991. I am grateful to Ms. McBride for sharing her unpublished work with me.

33. For an overview of the chronology of the decline in women's access to power and authority in the feudal world, see Jo Ann McNamara and Suzanne Wemple, "The Power of Women through the Family in Medieval Europe, 500–1000" (1981; Reprinted in *Women and Power in the Middle Ages*, eds. Mary Erler and Maryanne Kowaleski [Athens: University of Georgia Press, 1988]: 83–102); but see also my "Images of Queenship" as well as Marjorie M. Chibnall, "Women in Orderic Vitalis," *Haskins Society Journal: Studies in Medieval History* 2 (1990): 105–21.

34. *PL* 171, cols. 289–90.

35. André Boutemy, ed. "Notice sur le recueil poétique du Manuscrit Cotton Vitellius A xii du British Museum," *Latomus* 1 (1937), 304–5. See Elisabeth van Houts, "Latin Poetry as a Source for Anglo-Norman History: The *Carmen de Hastingae Proelio*," *Journal of Medieval History* 15 (1989): 39–62.

36. Benedeit, *St Brendan*, lines 2–6. For the Anglo-Norman *Voyage of St Brendan* and its patronage, see first the excellent critical edition of Edwin G. R. Waters (Oxford: Clarendon, 1928), hereafter *St Brendan*. Citations to the poem are to this edition. Waters, after some hesitation in which he admitted Matilda's possible patronage, opted in favor of Henry's second wife, Adeliza of Louvain. Subsequent arguments in favor of Matilda's patronage include Robert L. Ritchie, "The Date of the 'Voyage of St Brendan,'" *Medium Aevum* 19 (1950): 64–66; and Legge, *Anglo-Norman Literature and Its Background*, 9. See also John Fox, *A Literary History of France*, vol. 1, *The Middle Ages* (London: Bowes, 1974), 34–42. Fox (36) accepts Matilda as the poem's patron as well as Ritchie's dating to ca. 1106.

37. [Turgot?], "The Life of St Margaret of Scotland," in *Acta sanctorum quotquot toto orbe coluntur vel a catholicis scriptoribus celebrantur*, vol. 1, ed. by Jean Bolland, Godfrey Henschenius, Daniel Papenbroch, et al. (1658; reprint, Paris: Palme, 1863–1910), pars. 10–16. For a discussion of the context and dating of the *vita*, see also Lois L. Huneycutt, "The Idea of the Perfect Princess: The *Life of Saint Margaret* in the Reign of Matilda II, 1100–1118," *Anglo-Norman Studies* 12 (1989): 81–97.

38. *PL* 171, col. 1660.

39. For Marbod's poem, see *PL* 171, col. 1660. Discussed in Elizabeth Salter, *English and International: Studies in the Literature, Art, and Patronage of Medieval England*, ed. Derek Pearsall and Nicolette Zeeman (Cambridge, England: Cambridge University Press, 1988), 12–13; as well as Annette Georgi, *Das lateinische und deutsche Preisgedicht des Mittelalters in der Nachfolge der genus demonstrativum* (Berlin: Schmidt, 1969), 75–88.

40. *PL* 171, col. 154.

41. *Life of St Margaret*, pars. 18–20, 10–11.

42. Ibid., par. 12.

43. Elisabeth van Houts collected nine poems written for Matilda during her lifetime or as epitaphs, all but one refer to her lineage. See van Houts, "Latin Poetry and the Anglo-Norman Court," 51. The quotation comes from one of the anonymous poems in Cotton Vitellius A xii. See Boutemy, "Notice sur le recueil poétique," 7 n. 10.

44. *Life of St Margaret*, pars. 1–6.

45. Janet L. Nelson, "Perceptions du pouvoir chez les historiennes a du haut moyen age," in Michel Rouche and Jean Heuclin, eds., *La femme au moyen age* (Maubeuge: Touzot, 1990), 76–77. See also Elisabeth van Houts, "Women and the Writing of History in the Early Middle Ages: The Case of Abbess Matilda of Essen and Aethelweard," *Early Medieval Europe* 1 (1992): 53–68. The most authoritative statements on the patterns of kinship recognition in medieval society are still to be found in Georges Duby, *The Chivalrous Society*, trans. Cynthia Postan (Berkeley and Los Angeles: University of California Press, 1977).

46. The charters that record Matilda's many gifts to religious houses show that the gifts were almost as often made for her parents and siblings as for the souls of herself, her husband, and her children. Of the thirty-one charters known to have been issued by the queen, only two have survived in the original. These two have clauses naming the souls who are to benefit from her gifts, as do six of the charters that have survived in cartulary copies. Of these eight, one mentions her father only; three mention the welfare of Henry, herself, and their children; and two are for the souls of Henry, Matilda, and both of their parents. The two originals have the most elaborate beneficiary clauses, which suggests that many clauses were abbreviated or deleted in the cartulary copies. See Huneycutt, "Another Esther," app. 1.

47. Marjorie Chibnall, *The Empress Matilda: Queen Consort, Queen Mother, and Lady of the English* (Oxford: Blackwell, 1991), 18–44, discusses the importance of the marriage.

48. Several chroniclers reporting the marriage hint of a long courtship. William of Malmesbury says that Henry's friends, chiefly the bishops of the kingdom, persuaded him to marry, and that he chose the daughter of the king of the Scots, "to whom he had long been attached" (*De gestis regum Anglorum*, 2:495). Orderic Vital reports that Henry, "appreciating the high birth of the maiden whose perfection of character he had long adored, chose her as his bride" (*The Ecclesiastical History of Orderic Vitalis*, ed. Marjorie Chibnall (Oxford: Clarendon, 1972–80), 5:300–301. Eadmer's account emphasizes that Matilda was free to marry by declaring that "long after she discarded the veil, the king fell in love with her" (*Eadmeri Historia novorum*, 127).

49. Eadmer, *Eadmeri Historia novorum*, 121.

50. For the deathbed prophecy see Frank Barlow, ed., *Vita Ædwardi Regis: The Life of King Edward Who Rests at Westminster* (London: Nelson, 1962), 75–76. For commentary and interpretation see Robert L. G. Ritchie, *The Normans in Scotland* (Edinburgh: University of Edinburgh Press, 1954), 110–11; and Frank Barlow, *Edward the Confessor* (Berkeley and Los Angeles: University of California Press, 1970), 247–49.

51. Thomson, "William of Malmesbury," discusses the commission and speculates on the circumstances of the production of the *Gesta regum*.

52. See Jill Tattersall, "Expedition, Exploration and Odyssey: Extended Voyage Themes and Their Treatment in Some Early French Texts," in *Studies in Medieval French Language and Literature Presented to Brian Woledge in Honour of his 80th Birthday*, ed. Sally Burch North (Geneva: Droz, 1988); and Robin F. Jones, "The Precocity of Anglo-Norman and the *Voyage of St Brendan*," in *The Nature of Medieval Narrative*, ed. Minnette Grunmann-Gaudet and Robin F. Jones (Lexington: French Forum, 1980): 145–58, esp. 155–56.

53. Benedeit, *St Brendan*, lines 2–6, and also Ritchie, "Date of St. Brendan," 64–66.

54. See R. N. Illingworth, "The Structure of the Anglo-Norman *Voyage of St. Brendan*," *Medium Ævum* 55 (1986): 217–29, esp. 227; also Robin F. Jones, "The Mechanics of Meaning in the Anglo-Norman *Voyage of Saint Brendan*," *Romanic Review* 71 (1980): 105–13; and M. Burrell, "Narrative Structures in *Le voyage de Saint Brendan*," *Parergon* 17 (1977): 3–9.

55. Fox, *Literary History of France*, 35–36.

56. See Martin Biddle, "Seasonal Festivals and Residence: Winchester, Westminster, and Gloucester in the Tenth Through Twelfth Centuries," *Anglo-Norman Studies* 8 (1986): 51–72, esp. app. C for the schedule of Henry's festivals.

57. William of Malmesbury, *De gestis regum Anglorum*, 2:495.

58. Adelard wrote of having played before the queen and some French students in the year before he wrote *De eodem et diversa*. Precise dating of the treatise has proven impossible, but internal evidence places it to the period between 1105 and 1116. But even though Adelard's treatise dates to the reign of Queen Matilda, it is possible that Adelard was referring to Bertrada of Montfort, queen consort and later widow of Philip I of France. There was no queen consort in France between 1108 and 1115, but, if the treatise were written after the death of Philip I, Adelard could still have been

referring to Bertrada as the queen mother. However, because of Matilda's known love for exotic music and because of Adelard's later documented ties to the Anglo-Norman court, it is also possible that he was referring to Queen Matilda. See Adelard of Bath, "Des Adelard von Bath Traktat *De eodem et diversa* zum ersten Male hersausgegeben und historisch-kritisch untersucht," ed. Hans Wilner. *Beiträge zur Geschichte der Philosophie des Mittelalters* 4 (1903): 1–112, at 25–26. Discussed by Lawrence Wright, "The Role of Musicians at Court in Twelfth-Century Britain," in *Art and Patronage in the English Romanesque*, ed. Sarah Macready and F. H. Thompson (London: Society of Antiquaries, 1986), 97–106. The bishop to whom the treatise is dedicated, William of Syracuse, does not appear in surviving documents as bishop until 1112, but that reference implies that he had been in office for some time. His predecessor had died in 1104. Lynn Thorndike, in *A History of Magic and Experimental Science* (New York: Macmillan, 1923–58), 2:44–45, believed the queen in question to be Matilda, but Charles Homer Haskins, in *Studies in the History of Mediaeval Science* (Cambridge, Mass.: Harvard University Press, 1927), 20–22, was skeptical.

59. John Southworth, *The English Medieval Minstrel* (Woodbridge, England: Boydell, 1989), 39. A thirteenth-century inquest reveals that William received a grant of four and a half bovates of land at Wiston during the reign of Henry I and paid only sixteen pence a year in rent, although the land was assessed at ten shillings.

60. Ibid., 39–40. An alternative version of the story places Rahere's conversion to the time of the White Ship disaster (1120), but if he had indeed been a canon at Saint Paul's before the shipwreck, the first explanation seems the likelier.

61. Ibid., 39. See also David C. Douglas, "The Song of Roland and the Norman Conquest of England," *French Studies* 14 (1960): 99–116.

62. Goscelin was still active in 1107, albeit very old. See Barlow, *Vita Ædwardi Regis*, 91–111.

63. Orderic Vital, *Ecclesiastical History*, 5:296.

Of Queens, Courts, and Books: Reflections on the Literary Patronage of Thirteenth-Century Plantagenet Queens

✴ ✴ ✴ JOHN CARMI PARSONS

        The importance of aristocratic patronage to the growth of vernacular literatures in the medieval period is no more open to dispute than is the dominant role women played in that process.[1] Surveys of medieval book owners and dedicatees have repeatedly confirmed noblewomen's role as disseminators of vernacular literary culture, most especially the international brides whose migrations were critical to the transmission of many works.[2] Such surveys, however, fail to support discussions that seek to penetrate beyond the limits established by ownership and dedications. Authorities worthy of credit warn that evidence for ownership proves only the fact of possession and cannot justify assumptions about owners' literacy or literary interests; the value of dedications as proof of patrons' literary purposes is lessened by the realization that writers seeking employment or reward could pen more than one such address per work. Secure conclusions about medieval patrons' literary endeavors require proof that owners ordered or acquired works other than those received through dedication, legacy, or gift, some evidence for the circumstances in which volumes were ordered or purchased and, ideally, for the process of creation. It was perhaps with such considerations in mind that Vivian Galbraith threatened to reduce medieval noblewomen's interest in books to the merely decorative by implying that for them, literacy was a salon refinement comparable to the sketchbook or the piano in Victorian times.[3] But while the kind of evidence required to sustain discussion of an individual patron's activities is rare, it does exist, as in the case of the Countess Mahaut of Artois (d. 1329). This article examines surviving evidence for the literary interests of Eleanor of Provence (d. 1291) and Eleanor of Castile (d. 1290), successive queens of England in the thirteenth century, whose careers offer examples of the problems posed by the lack of such evidence as well as the inferences that can be drawn from reliable source material for medieval noblewomen's literary patronage.[4]

Though we may confidently dismiss the legend that the twelve-year-old Eleanor of Provence first attracted Henry III's notice by composing a romance of some twelve thousand lines and seeing to it that he got a copy, there may be a grain of truth to popular accounts of her childhood as a long courtly idyll in the south.[5] Her 1236 marriage coupled her with a king whose cultural activities, chiefly artistic and architectural, were almost exclusively bound up with his vigorous promotion of the cult of Edward the Confessor as a royal tutelary. Henry was no bibliophile, but despite the exalted atmosphere that must have been created by his reliance on rituals connected with the Confessor's cult, his courtiers loved poetry and song, and the few volumes the king and his wife are known to have possessed do suggest a shared taste for courtly literature.[6] Henry owned an unidentified "great book of romance," and Eleanor's copy of the *Roman de Guillaume le Conquerant* came to their grandson Edward of Caernarvon in 1298; in 1250, she borrowed the *Geste d'Antioc* from the master of the Temple and soon had scenes from it painted in her chambers. She is also known to have purchased "romances," but it is unclear whether these were composed at her commission or merely copied for her.[7] The vernacular works known to have been created for Henry III and his circle were of a devotional nature, mostly saints' lives in verse.[8] Two of these were dedicated to his queen: a life of Saint Edward, most likely written by Matthew Paris around 1245, when Henry began to reconstruct Westminster Abbey,[9] and John de Hoveden's *Rossignos*, composed after Henry's death in November 1272 but before his son Edward I returned to England from his Crusade in August 1274.[10]

This is just the kind of evidence that might mean everything or nothing. The wall paintings suggest that Eleanor of Provence appreciated literature as entertainment or because it had potential for her decorating schemes. Perhaps she was drawn to the *Geste d'Antioc* in 1250 because Henry had just taken the cross, or because her sister Margaret was then on Crusade with her husband, Louis IX of France. Her copy of *Guillaume le Conquerant* and the life of Saint Edward hint at an interest in dynastic matters consistent with Henry's cult of Saint Edward. But as no proof exists of her personal interests or her reasons for acquiring these works, or (if this was the case) for commissioning them, it is unwise for the moment to say more than what is outlined above.

The situation is quite different in the case of the woman who married the future Edward I in 1254. Daughter of Ferdinand III of Castile and half-sister of Alphonso X, Eleanor of Castile passed her formative years at what was then the most aggressively literary court in Europe. Her youth thus exposed her to a lively program of vernacular literary endeavor, as her father promoted moral reform through education and encouraged administrative use of the vernacular, and as Alphonso sponsored vernacular translations, chronicles, law codes, and other writings in which he explored widely ranging ideas on history, kingship, and law, in the process creating Castilian prose. The differing attitudes toward literary production at the Castilian and English courts were not the only contrast Eleanor encountered upon her transfer to England. Henry III's lofty view of his kingship, and the elaborate rites with which he surrounded himself, would have been alien to her. The chivalric ethos of the Castilian court, so far from exalting kingship, affirmed its unity with the kingdom in upholding the military values of a society geared to recovering Christian lands from Muslim control. The Castilian monarchy, moreover, boasted neither ancestral saints nor heroes and knew little of royal anointings; as Alphonso X thus scorned the idea of regal thaumaturgic powers, it is regrettable that we have no evidence for Eleanor's reaction to the spectacle of her father-in-law (and later her husband) touching for the King's Evil.[11] International royal brides often had to assimilate such contrasts, and for such women to establish themselves as effective presences implied not merely passive compliance with new customs, but thoughtful and practical integration. The capacity to do so was an important key to their success, and much of the meaning of this article will revolve around these challenges and how royal women met them.[12]

The records of Eleanor of Castile's life show her to have been a highly cultivated woman whose adjustment to life in England did not include rejection of the literary traditions of her youth. That her interests were inspired by her years in Castile is suggested by evidence that she exchanged works with her brother, including Alphonso's 1264 French version of the Arabic *Ladder of Mohammed*, perhaps a manuscript of his vast law code the *Siete partidas*, and *Meliadus*, an Arthurian romance written to Edward I's commission in 1273, which likely reached Castile during Alphonso's reign and influenced the composition of *Tristán de Leonis*, the earliest surviving Castilian romance on Arthurian themes.[13] These, again, are only tokens of ownership, but more immediate evidence for Eleanor's continuing interests is found in her wardrobe records, which prove that she maintained the only personal scriptorium documented at a northern European court at this period.[14] In the last five years of her life, this workshop was staffed by a *pictor*, Godfrey, and a *scriptor*, Roger, whom the accounts explicitly distinguish from her administrative *clerici*. Provision of clothing and other needs, and construction of a chamber for the scribes at Westminster in 1289,[15] prove they were her householders, not temporary hirees, though others were retained for particular jobs—for example, the Richard du Marche who illuminated a psalter for Eleanor in 1289–90.[16]

Godfrey and Roger purchased the materials they used—vellum, ink, quills, pigments, gold leaf, glue, and mucilage—all "for the queen's books,"[17] but the wardrobe rarely identified those who bought parchment "for the wardrobe and the queen's letters."[18] The regularity of these purchases, and the scattered locations where they were made, prove that these workers traveled with the queen, as far afield as Aquitaine between 1286 and 1289, steadily copying and illuminating, and boards purchased for binding imply a full range of book-producing activity.[19] That Godfrey and Roger produced books, not letters or accounts, is put beyond doubt by a January 1288 purchase of vellum "to write the life of Blessed Thomas" and in May 1288 a purchase of parchment for covering lives of Saint Thomas and Saint Edward. When illuminated letters were required in 1289, moreover, Godfrey did not work on them: two temporary workers were hired.[20]

The three manuscripts that have been linked to Eleanor—the Trinity and Douce Apocalypses and the Cambridge life of Saint Edward—date from the 1250s and 1260s, well before Eleanor's scriptorium is documented, and in any event they did not come from a single workshop.[21] Two manuscripts were undertaken in the mid-1280s for the intended marriage of Eleanor's son Alphonso to a daughter of the count of Holland: the "Bird" Psalter, possibly produced at Gloucester or Winchcombe, and the unfinished "Alphonso" Psalter, perhaps a product of the London Dominican priory. A Dominican patron, Eleanor founded the London priory, but despite traces of her personal tastes in the Bird Psalter's avian decorations and the Alphonso Psalter's hunting scenes, neither volume can be linked to her.[22] There are, then, no claimants to represent the products of her workshop, nor does the evidence suggest that its work was widely known. A manuscript of *Escanor*, an Arthurian work dedicated to Eleanor in the early 1280s, possibly reached Edward's cousins in Savoy but did not certainly come from her scriptorium, nor can it be shown that Eleanor circulated manuscripts beyond her immediate circle. Her books were most probably among the unspecified personal effects she is known to have bequeathed to her daughters, whose marriages presumably scattered the volumes in England and abroad—but only after Eleanor's death disbanded her workshop.[23] This profile suggests that her workers produced saints' lives or the "romances," also noted in her accounts, which she certainly carried about with her, and the more elaborate volumes with commemorative functions, such as the psalters and apocalypses, were the work of others.[24] Such a hypothesis is borne out by the psalter illuminated by du Marche in 1289–90, and by evidence that some of Eleanor's religious books were purchased: a *portiferium* in 1278, or the psalter and seven primers she bought at Cambridge in 1289.[25]

Surviving manuscripts or no, the existence of this scriptorium can be attributed exclusively to Eleanor's interests: no such office is known under Henry III, and after Eleanor died in 1290, Edward I pensioned off her staff.[26] That the workshop existed at all thus shows that Eleanor's literary endeavors were an important part of her life, and the advantages to her were many; because Eleanor of Provence purchased her romances outside the court, her choice of works might have been restricted to those professional scribes had available to copy, but Eleanor of Castile's scriptorium freed her from dependence on outside workers and permitted her to direct her scribe to copy whatever attracted her notice. Of course, evidence for the existence of a personal scriptorium is not the only means of demonstrating the distinction between the ownership of books and the deliberate acquisition or commissioning of a work for a specific purpose: books could also be acquired by purchase, loan, or commission. Her workshop notwithstanding, Eleanor did purchase some of her books and is known to have borrowed others.[27] (Contemporary volumes with Edward's arms, which perhaps belonged to him in her lifetime, may have been known to her as well,[28] and surviving works associated with her suggest familiarity with other works she is not known to have possessed: the "great book" Edward provided as the basis for *Meliadus* was either *Palamedes* or the prose *Tristan*, and *Escanor* describes paintings of the Troy cycle.[29]) As noted above, however, solid evidence for the circumstances of the purchase or loan of a book is needed before anything substantive can be said about an owner's purpose in buying a particular work, a borrower's desire in requesting it, or a patron's intention in commissioning it. Such information is lacking for Eleanor of Provence's purchases but does exist for some of the works Eleanor of Castile acquired or commissioned apart from the products of her workshop. In fact, not one of the works associated with Eleanor of Castile's patronage can be shown to have been produced by her scriptorium, but the indications of her sustained literary interests provided by the evidence for her workshop strongly imply that those interests are also reflected in works she is known to have commissioned or otherwise acquired. The rest of this article will concentrate on these, seeking any patterns among them and the contexts in which they were acquired or ordered.

Two works reliably attributed to Eleanor's patronage illustrate what is meant here. The first, an Anglo-Norman version of Vegetius's *De re militari*, the medieval bible of chivalry, was prepared for Edward by Eleanor's clerk mr Richard, probably while they were at Acre in 1271–72.[30] The second dates from the 1280s, when the queen asked Archbishop John Pecham for an explication of pseudo-Dionysius's *De celesti hierarchia*; the primate replied with his only vernacular theological work, really a sermon in letter form, in which Pecham took the original tack of comparing the hierarchy to the ranks of the king's officials—just that earthly example to which a woman of Eleanor's rank might be expected to respond most readily.[31] The Vegetius translation, commissioned for her husband while he was actively campaigning, suggests that there were close links between Eleanor's literary activity and events in her life; their immediacy is indeed strengthened by mr Richard's personalization of the text for Edward by adding to it a brief reference to a skirmish Edward had won at Kenilworth shortly before his victory at Evesham, in August 1265. That the queen sought written authority for her own instruction is shown by Pecham's treatise, which also suggests that her desire to know (in Dominica Legge's words) "what [angels] were for . . . and why the Pseudo-Dionysius had written about them" was aroused by current learned discussion. The *Hierarchia* had been retranslated with a fresh commentary by Robert Grosseteste between 1235 and 1243, and as Legge remarks regarding Pecham's treatise, its themes were likely "in the air" in Eleanor's day.[32] An active patron of the universities, the queen associated with men of learning and appointed them to high office in her administration; in 1290 she contacted an Oxford master about one of her books, and her promotion of formal learning—perhaps another legacy of her early years—could have exposed her to discussion of pseudo-Dionysius's work.[33] It is not unlikely that so vigorous a supporter of the Preachers, herself perhaps taught by the friars in her childhood, sought informed understanding of church doctrine; that mendicant influences indeed shaped Eleanor's pious practices is further implied by her books of hours and rosaries, and Pecham's *Jerarchie* makes it appear very much as though the intellectual energy evident in her literary pursuits carried over to her religious practices as well.[34]

Translation and treatise together also show that for Eleanor, as for her father and brother, the use of the vernacular ensured wider accessibility to knowledge—not surprising for a woman at any time during the medieval period, nor especially so at a time when in England, Anglo-Norman was fast rising to challenge Latin as a language of both culture and administration.[35] These works, created at Eleanor's commission, further witness a shift away from the devotional verse works written for Henry III and Eleanor of Provence, and toward instructive works in prose, the idiom of law and history current at the Castilian court of Eleanor's youth.[36] Her liking for focused vernacular literary expression reveals her interests to have been more than the diversion Galbraith implied, and her purposeful relationship with works she commissioned or acquired makes the uses of her patronage a pertinent field of enquiry.

This leads to discussion of a work acquired just after Eleanor succeeded her mother in 1279 as countess of Ponthieu in Picardy. The existence of this work is known only from a Ponthevin account noting payment authorized by the queen "pour un romanz de Isembart," written, illuminated, and bound in Ponthieu in 1280. The significance of this vanished romance revolves around the figure of Isembart, first found in the early *chanson de geste* now known as *Gormond et Isembard*, which developed from traditions that long flourished in Ponthieu, originating with a Norman invasion routed by Louis III in 881 at Saucourt in that county. The *geste* depicted Isembart only as a noble who rebelled against the French king and allied with the Norman leader Gormond, but as chroniclers assimilated the *geste* as fact, Isembart inevitably acquired an identity. In the twelfth century Geoffrey of Monmouth's rather garbled version of the tale made Isembart into a nephew of the French king, and in the thirteenth Aubri of Troisfontaines and Philippe Mouskès described him as the son of Count Guérin of Ponthieu, heir to a vast principality near Amiens, who was alienated from his loving royal uncle by the counsel of jealous enemies at court.[37]

It is hardly necessary to remark the close connection here again evident between life and literary activity. Eleanor's interest in Isembart shortly after she succeeded in Ponthieu implies that she saw him as an ancestor, or at least a predecessor, who required some respectable literary credentials. But the work has wider implications suggested by the fact that Eleanor's romance almost certainly embodied her response to the thirteenth-century chroniclers' version of Isembart's career, not to the *geste*, which did not identify Isembart as a count of Ponthieu. As the unlocalized noble of the *geste*, Isembart would have held no meaning for the new countess of Ponthieu, and even if her "romanz de Isembart" was merely a copy of the *geste*, her interest was most probably attracted by the chroniclers' elaborated accounts of Isembart as heir to the county. (That her romance was a new work and not a copy of the *geste*, however, is indicated by its evident emphasis on Eleanor's "ancestor" Isembart: the *geste* was known as *Gormond*, the name of its main protagonist.[38])

Although it is unclear exactly how or when Eleanor encountered the chronicle reports of Isembart's career, the strong indications that she was acquainted with historical writings add another dimension to her patronage and require some attention to the ways in which she evolved familiarity with the works of chroniclers. That the queen was possessed of a well-developed historical consciousness is not impossible; there was an ardent interest in historical writing at the Castilian court of her youth, and as was often the case with international brides, Eleanor perhaps carried a national chronicle to her new home in 1255—in her case the Latin history completed by her father's chancellor in 1243.[39] Her role intersects usefully here with ideas by Martin Hume and Lucy Keeler on thirteenth-century Anglo-Castilian cross-fertilization in historical writing, and with what Antonia Gransden has called a "literary interest in history at [Edward I's] court," manifested in his reign in the "official" Westminster continuation of the *Flores historiarum*. Gransden compares this to the *Grandes chroniques de France*, but the *Flores* continuation also echoes Alphonso X's dictum that royal chronicles should be written by observers near the court.[40] That Eleanor's Isembart romance found its point of departure in the chroniclers' accounts of "Count Isembart" may, then, mark her exploitation of another asset she brought from Castile to England (and it should be borne in mind that the chronicles that made Isembart the heir to Ponthieu were written neither in Castile nor in England, but in France).

The cross-cultural influences behind Eleanor's romance, and its links to the works of chroniclers, were perhaps not restricted to the Castile-England axis in the queen's background. If her Castilian youth did equip her to deal knowledgeably with chronicles, certain literary and political traditions in her mother's family hint that her ability to integrate such influences in or through the written word had led her to cultivate "Count Isembart" as an ancestor and a type for the counts of Ponthieu with an eye to legitimizing a political agenda for her new inheritance.[41] Gabrielle Spiegel has seen the early-thirteenth-century wave of vernacular translations of the *Pseudo-Turpin Chronicle* among Franco-Flemish magnates as embodying opposition to Philip Augustus's expansion of Capetian authority into the great fiefs of northwestern France—including Ponthieu. Spiegel emphasizes as "anti-Capetian in motive" the importance the noble sponsors of these translations attached to their (in one case fictional) descents from Charlemagne, whose idealized presence in *Pseudo-Turpin* "made him an apt figure for the esthetic correction of the present on the basis of what the past had been . . . . an anti-type of the increasingly assertive French monarchy under Philip Augustus." As Spiegel summarizes, "*Pseudo-Turpin* served as a mediated criticism of Capetian kingship by a group of Flemish aristocrats acutely aware of the challenges to their own independence posed by the revival of royal power . . . [and] functioned . . . as a historiography of resistance, verbalizing hostility to the monarchy in the guise of a . . . fantasy masquerading as historical fact concerning a glorious, collective past which, by the genetic logic of historical consciousness then current, was potentially present in each succeeding generation of noble heirs."

It cannot be proved that Eleanor knew *Pseudo-Turpin*, but it is not impossible that her Isembart romance was partly inspired by political considerations very similar to those Spiegel attributes to the noble sponsors of the *Pseudo-Turpin* translations. There seems a palpable, if inverted, connection between the vast domains with which the thirteenth-century French chroniclers endowed Isembart, and the loss of three Ponthevin *baillages* in 1225 as the cost of reconciliation with the Capetians after Eleanor's maternal grandfather joined the coalition of northwestern French nobles defeated by Philip Augustus at Bouvines. Perhaps not entirely coincidentally, that grandfather was Simon of Dammartin, a brother of that Count Renaud of Boulogne who was among Philip's most prominent opponents and was also one of those who sponsored a *Pseudo-Turpin* translation.[42] Whether or not Eleanor was aware of this link to those translations and the opposition to Capetian authority they embodied, it may not be going too far to see her Isembart romance in much the same light; "Count Isembart," his vast estates vouched for by French chroniclers, might have functioned as an evocation of the past glory of the counts of Ponthieu, which his noble "descendants" and heirs Eleanor and Edward I would now revive and defend. Their policies in Ponthieu would suggest as much: using English wealth to restore that diminished comital demesne while carefully avoiding any opportunity for the French crown to intrude itself into Ponthevin affairs.[43] While proposing an idealized image for the counts of Ponthieu, then, Eleanor's romance could also define or prescribe her role as countess. (And if—as is not unlikely—the lost work developed the chronicler's idea that Isembart was alienated from his royal uncle by jealous enemies, it might also have implied an excuse for Count Simon's treason.)

Did Eleanor accomplish anything similar in England? That Isembart, an ancestral figure verified by chroniclers, could have been promoted by Eleanor to support her activity in Ponthieu does recall Noel Denholm-Young's idea that she encouraged, indeed reawakened, Plantagenet interest in Arthuriana.[44] And it is true that Edward I manipulated the Arthurian image for his own political purposes—significantly, in the present context, as a means to assert himself as the legitimate successor to, and reviver of, the Arthurian imperium.[45] But reassessment of Edward's supposedly consuming interest in Arthur is compelled by Michael Prestwich's cogent arguments that any such Arthurian cult is more imagined than real. Rejecting the idea that Edward put himself forward as a new Arthur, Prestwich emphasizes that the king embraced a more eclectic range of models than implied by earlier studies.[46] The secular and chivalric ethos Eleanor experienced at the Castilian court not improbably led her to encourage Edward's predilection for knightly endeavors in a general way—as suggested by the Vegetius translation—but the indications of her interest in Arthur are really no more plentiful than are Edward's. She may have sent a manuscript of *Meliadus* to Castile, and one of *Escanor* to Savoy, but is otherwise known only as the dedicatee of *Escanor*, written by one Girard of Amiens between 1279 and 1282; and though Girard probably wrote the work during a stay at the English court and certainly deployed the common device that Eleanor proposed *Escanor*'s subject, there is no proof that the queen commissioned the romance.[47]

Although Eleanor's Arthurian sponsorship thus lacks verification, Paul Binski preserves the idea of a certain cultural relationship between husband and wife, noting that virtually all the books recorded in Edward's family were owned by or originated with Eleanor, and discreetly hinting at her husband's "suggestibility."[48] Beryl Smalley helpfully puts Edward's Arthurian interest in a broader context by remarking that the accomplishments of Edward's reign restored the idea of an heroic age, allowing his deeds to be seen in the same light as romances of chivalry. In this atmosphere comparisons between Edward and Arthur were common, but he was also compared to Alexander, to the English Athelstan, Edgar, and Richard I, and to Judas Maccabee; although he never forgot the Confessor's cult, Edward himself seems to have favored Maccabee, and quite certainly Britain's ancient imperial past had a strong hold on him.[49] The diversity evident here was much greater than what would be implied by Edward's supposed Arthurian cult and contrasts sharply with Henry III's fixation on the Confessor. It also reflects the newly cosmopolitan interest in history at the Edwardian court. As Edward broadened the historical focus of his kingship, so literary production at his court turned away from the devotional verse works produced for the circle of Henry III and Eleanor of Provence, instead favoring romance and instructive prose, marked by strong overtones of secular history—and (as Binski implies) virtually all that is known of this production points to Eleanor's promotion. Although there exists no evidence that she sponsored a literary work for England comparable to her Isembart romance for Ponthieu, it appears nonetheless that the queen's influence did have an impact on Edward's court, perhaps even upon the public face of his reign.

In the broader context of the role Eleanor's literary activity played in her career as a matrimonial and cultural ambassador, her Isembart romance functions most strikingly as evidence for her capacity for assimilation. Her early years in Castile would not have exposed her to a royal ancestral cult; in promoting a work on a Ponthevin ancestral figure who was all but certainly identified from French chronicles, she thus turned her ability to exploit the written word, a resource developed in her youth, to a purpose alien to that early experience, and there is reason to think that her literary habits were what nourished the sophistication and flexibility that allowed her to absorb the novelty. Upon arrival in England, Eleanor was given, or obtained, a copy of the life of Edward the Confessor Matthew Paris had dedicated to Eleanor of Provence; the work was probably meant to introduce Edward's bride to the cult Henry III so urgently valued,[50] and it was very likely through this work that Eleanor of Castile first digested the idea of an ancestral saint. Literature may have helped many royal women in the process of cultural assimilation; when Eleanor's daughter Margaret married the duke of Brabant's son in 1290, for example, a vernacular chronicle was written there to teach her the language and history of her new home.[51] It cannot be shown that all international wives received or promoted works to reflect the changes and transitions that typified their lives, but the influences that appear to have underlain Eleanor of Castile's Isembart romance make it clear that she dealt with such passages not by passively accepting the new customs she encountered in England, but by seizing upon and actively deploying them.

The historical and ancestral focus of her patronage, moreover, gave important new overtones to roles assumed by royal women in previous centuries. Eleanor concerned herself more intently with the secular past than with the awesome realm of saintly royal dead, but her actions do recall that Henry I's wife Edith-Matilda encouraged creation of the *vita* of her mother, Margaret of Scotland. Though evidence is lacking for Eleanor of Provence's purposes in acquiring her copy of *Guillaume le Conquerant*, it is tempting to see the work as further evidence of queens' dynastic concerns; the same can be said of the life of Edward the Confessor owned by both Eleanors, and Eleanor of Castile's Isembart romance carries this dynastic preoccupation a step further. The preservation of the past through commemoration of ancestors was an important duty of royal women in earlier centuries, but as religious services became the exclusive sphere of male ecclesiastics, these women evolved other ways to memorialize the lineage: the church alone had the power to canonize ancestors, but a historically minded literary queen could virtually create them, shaping the past to afford the royal lineage the legitimizing bulwark of antiquity—a significant accession to the ruling line's symbolic capital.[52] In this regard it may be noted that despite evidence for literary activity in the Ponthevin comital entourage under Eleanor's grandmother Marie Talvas

(d. 1250),[53] there is no proof that earlier counts of Ponthieu exploited the Isembart connection. Eleanor's romance thus introduced to her French maternal inheritance elements of the ancestral cult she encountered in England, bolstered by an historical awareness characteristic of the Castilian court.

International royal brides' literary endeavors should, then, be seen as more than mere proof of cultural activity. They are also revelations of the unique multicultural perspectives open to these women, a resource that could be developed on many levels.[54] A queen, for example, emerged as the natural instructor for a new generation of diplomatic brides. Eleanor of Castile's daughters were well educated and of a literary turn—friars of her favored Dominican order lived with her children and probably taught them; her eldest daughter, Eleanor, was certainly literate, and the fourth, Mary, a Benedictine nun, probably commissioned and certainly was the dedicatee of a vernacular prose chronicle by the Dominican friar Nicholas Trevet.[55] But a queen's training of her daughters had ramifications that led far beyond the purely domestic, for their preparation could subtly color matrimonial diplomacy: Henry II's daughters, for example, carried Geoffrey of Monmouth's chronicle to Germany, Castile, and Sicily to introduce the British legends to those territories and tout the glories of English kingship.[56]

A queen's control of her daughters' education, moreover, obligated the king toward her, adding to her influence and giving her a voice in the girls' future, as when Eleanor successfully objected to a daughter's marriage at too early an age in 1282.[57] This was not power in the sense of controlling the actions of others (although few queens could safely ignore the need or the opportunity to develop that capacity); it was rather what is implied by Carolyn Heilbrun's definition of power as "the ability to take one's place in whatever discourse is essential to action and the right to have one's part matter."[58] Eleanor of Castile's example shows that such power was linked to the perspectives open to international wives, to their ability to absorb and manipulate the cultural contrasts to which their careers exposed them. The attentive nourishing of such capacities was one way in which royal wives could legitimize their access to practical wisdom and the authority to enforce it (in Paul Strohm's words) and thereby strengthen their hand in other areas, as for example the queen's socially prescribed mediation with the king. Her intercession was an established means of royal communication with the realm, its very informality an invitation to the queen to bolster it by whatever means she might dispose, including the aura of experience and wisdom she could cultivate through literary endeavor; skillfully manipulated, mediation allowed a royal consort to move from the margins to the center of power.[59]

The importance to medieval noblewomen of their endeavors in the creation of vernacular literature is obscured by the tendency to explain them by saying that women's use of the vernacular reflects their exclusion from formal Latin education, or that in sponsoring literary creation they showed themselves to be masters of the feminine arts of peace, not the male technology of war. The former clearly implies the untenable position that vernacular culture was a poor second to Latin culture in the evolution of medieval civilization; the latter smacks of a modern distinction between public and private. As with the intercession that allowed queens to traverse official boundaries, it is hard to spot in a royal woman's literary activity exactly where the limits may fall between the public and private spheres.[60] Such limits are generally more fluid than may appear at first glance, and ironically interpenetration was favored by the marginalized status of medieval women of rank: unfettered by institutionalized powerlessness, they were free to adopt informal and unofficial methods readily accessible to manipulation and experimentation. Working from the margins and interstices, these international women breached cultural boundaries through just this kind of maneuvering.[61]

The general observations offered here about such women's strategies as patrons would, therefore, in all likelihood apply for the many noblewomen and queens whose activities are unknown to us only because relevant evidence has perished, remains undiscovered, or needs to be reconsidered. That the lives and literary activity of many of Eleanor's colleagues (including Eleanor of Provence) cannot be as closely documented as hers, however, is no reason to think her case unique or her methods startlingly original: as the challenges she faced were common to most royal wives, her strategies were most probably similar to those adopted by a host of diplomatic brides. The ideas evolved here from examination of Eleanor of Castile's patronage might, for example, justify a brief reconsideration of one of the works associated with Eleanor of Provence, as suggested by the Isembart romance's association with Eleanor of Castile's accession in Ponthieu. This was one of those times of dynastic transition or anomaly—regencies, minorities, kings' absences—with which queens are especially identified. A like relationship can be observed for John de Hoveden's *Rossignos*, dedicated to the widowed Eleanor of Provence after Henry III's death in November 1272 and before Edward I's return to England in August 1274, a royal absence unprecedented at a time of dynastic transition. The range of historical, and especially chivalric, figures who appear in *Rossignos*, its devotional nature notwithstanding, anticipates that shift away from the religious works produced at Henry III's court to the new historical and chivalric sensibilities manifest under Edward I. When he wrote *Rossignos*,

Hoveden was either already in the dowager's service, hoping for a position with her, or was perhaps seeking to enlist her influence so he might obtain one with the new king. The possibilities would exist, then, that the royal widow indicated to Hoveden the desirability of a work forecasting what many must have known would be the tone of her son's reign, so very different from that of Henry III's reign; or that Hoveden saw her as the royal wife and mother who embodied a certain continuity between the reigns—to whom he might fittingly dedicate a work that spanned the differences between them.[62]

Whether she actively inspired *Rossignos* or passively received it, it is striking that so markedly transitional a work was dedicated to a dowager queen at such a time. As Eleanor of Castile would later order her Isembart romance upon her accession in Ponthieu, perhaps to define her regime there, a work associated with her mother-in-law may have been elicited by an earlier moment of dynastic transition. Literary works are also connected with other similar moments that had a direct impact upon royal women—marriage, for example, as witness Eleanor of Castile's copy of the life of Saint Edward and the chronicle written for her daughter's arrival in Brabant. The products of medieval royal women's patronage might profitably be reexamined with an eye to their possible common origins in, and relationships to, crises, passages, or anomalies. It was at these moments that such women were the more easily able to extend their influence into the political arena, and through literary or artistic patronage that they could inscribe themselves in political discourse. That medieval queens' patronage could be underlain by such widely pervasive factors common to the lives of the vast majority of them argues for a broader examination of their patronage to identify similar factors and the related uses to which they turned the literary or artistic works they sponsored.

This is precisely what the unusually ample source material in Eleanor of Castile's case does reveal—the mechanics whereby a woman's ability to deploy the written word could invest her actions with greater consequence.[63] As has been seen here, the influence a royal consort thus established could extend her reach into arenas she could not otherwise readily enter; the formation of female networks that relied on the transmission of books, the education of children, marriage, and patronage, perpetuated such influence by re-creating the unofficial systems through which those on the margins operate.[64] It is surely no more appropriate to describe the results as the " 'secondary gains' of devious dominance"[65] than it is to accept silently Galbraith's comparison of medieval noblewomen's literacy to Victorian parlor graces. Few women of rank could have afforded to regard such accomplishments quite so lightly.

NOTES

1. My thanks to Germaine Warkentin, to Elizabeth A. R. Brown for cautionary words, to Margaret Howell for valuable references, to Brian Stock for advice and encouragement, to Barbara Sargent-Baur for the opportunity to present an early version of this material at the Fifth Pennsylvania Symposium, University of Pittsburgh (October 1991), to Janet Nelson for many valuable suggestions, and to June Hall McCash for her invitation to publish this article. Any flaws and oversights are mine.

Unless otherwise stated all manuscripts are London, Public Record Office (E 101 equals Exchequer Accounts, various; S.C. 1 equals Ancient Correspondence; S.C. 6 equals Ministers' Accounts; C 47 equals Chancery miscellany; JUST 1 equals Justices Itinerant).

2. Herbert Grundmann, "Die Frauen und die Literatur im Mittelalter: Ein Beitrag zur Frage nach der Entstehung des Schrifttums in der Volkssprache," *Archiv für Kulturgeschichte* 26, no. 2 (1935): 129–61; reprinted in *Ausgewählte Aufsätze*, MGH 25, 1–3 (Stuttgart: Hiersmann, 1976–78), 3:67–95. See also Rita Lejeune, "La femme dans les littératures française et occitane du XIᵉ au XIIIᵉ siècle," in *La femme dans les civilisations des Xᵉ–XIIIᵉ siècles: Actes du colloque tenu à Poitiers les 23–25 Septembre 1976* (Poitiers: Centre d'Etudes de civilisation médiévale, Université de Poitiers, 1976) published in *Cahiers de civilisation médiévale* 20 (1977): 201–16; Joan M. Ferrante, "The Education of Women in the Middle Ages in Theory, Fact, and Fantasy," in *Beyond Their Sex: Learned Women of the European Past*, ed. Patricia H. Labalme (New York: New York University Press, 1980; paperback ed. 1984), 9–42; Susan Groag Bell, "Medieval Women Book Owners: Arbiters of Lay Piety and Ambassadors of Culture," in *Women and Power in the Middle Ages*, ed. Mary Erler and Maryanne Kowaleski (Athens: University of Georgia Press, 1988), 149–87.

3. Erich Auerbach, *Literary Language and Its Public in Late Latin Antiquity and in the Middle Ages*, trans. Ralph Manheim (New York: Pantheon, 1965), 290–94; Henry John Chaytor, *From Script to Print* (Cambridge: Cambridge University Press, 1950), 83–84; Malcolm B. Parkes, "The Literacy of the Laity," in *Literature and Western Civilization: The Medieval World*, ed. David Daiches and Anthony Thorlby (London: Aldus, 1973), 555–56; C. P. Wormald, "The Uses of Literacy in Anglo-Saxon England and Its Neighbors," *Transactions of the Royal Historical Society*, 5th ser., 27 (1977), 96; M. T. Clanchy, *From Memory to Written Record: England, 1066–1307* (Cambridge: Harvard University Press, 1979; reprint, London: Fontana, 1983), 175–85; V. H. Galbraith, "The Literacy of the Medieval English Kings," *Proceedings of the British Academy*, 21 (1935): 215.

4. On Mahaut, Jules Marie Richard, "Les livres de Mahaut, Comtesse d'Artois et de Bourgogne," *Revue des questions historiques* 40 (1886): 135–41; on the two Eleanors, Mary Dominica Legge, *Anglo-Norman Literature and Its Background* (Oxford: Clarendon, 1963), 364.

5. Agnes Strickland, *Lives of the Queens of England*, 2nd ed. (London: Hurst and

Blackett, 1851; reissued 1854), 2:356–417; Martha Biles, "The Indomitable Belle: Eleanor of Provence, Queen of England," in *Seven Studies in Medieval English History and Other Historical Essays Presented to Harold S. Snellgrove,* ed. Richard H. Bowers (Jackson: University Press of Mississippi, 1983), 113–31; Gerard Sivéry, *Marguerite de Provence: Une reine au temps des cathédrales* (Paris: Fayard, 1987), 11–26. Margaret Howell of Oxford, who is preparing a study of Eleanor's life, notes that her legendary authorship of "Blandin de Cournouailles" is still credited (e.g., Nicholas Orme, *From Childhood to Chivalry: The Education of the English Kings and Aristocracy, 1066–1530* [New York: Methuen, 1984], 162).

6. M. T. Clanchy, *England and Its Rulers, 1066–1272* (Totowa, N.J.: Barnes and Noble, 1983), 280–83; R. Kent Lancaster, "Artists, Suppliers, and Clerks: The Human Factors in the Art Patronage of King Henry III," *Journal of the Warburg and Courtauld Institutes* 35 (1972): 105–6; Paul Binski, "Reflections on *La estoire de Saint Ædward le Rei:* Hagiography and Kingship," *Journal of Medieval History* 16 (1990): 333–50. On Henry's disinterest in books, Nigel J. Morgan, *Early Gothic Manuscripts, 1190–1285: A Survey of Manuscripts Illuminated in the British Isles* (London: Oxford University Press, 1982-1988), 2:11; for his courtiers, Thomas Arnold, ed., *Memorials of St. Edmund's Abbey,* Rolls Series 96 (London, 1890–96), 2:137.

7. Hilda Johnstone, *Edward of Carnarvon* (Manchester: Manchester University Press, 1946), 18; *Calendar of Liberate Rolls,* 1:288; *Calendar of Close Rolls 1247–1251,* 283; Howard Montagu Colvin, R. A. Brown, and A. J. Taylor, eds., *History of the King's Works* (Oxford: Oxford University Press, 1963–73), 129, 502, 760, 914, 916. Howell has kindly provided references from Eleanor's wardrobe accounts showing that in 1252–53 she paid thirty-five shillings "for a romance made by the hand of William Paris' at Oxford," thirteen and a half pence "for binding a certain romance of the queen's" (the same book?), and ten shillings "for a romance bought of Peter the Parisian" (E 101/349/18, 19). The "Trinity" Apocalypse, once associated with Eleanor of Provence, is now thought to have belonged to her daughter-in-law, but she has been linked to a psalter now in the Metropolitan Museum, New York. I must thank Suzanne Lewis for a copy of her paper "The Trinity Apocalypse and Eleanor of Castile," read at a 1990 Oxford symposium, "The History of the Book" (cf. Morgan, *Early Gothic Manuscripts,* 4:73–76). Harvey Stahl has described the Metropolitan Museum Psalter in correspondence. On reading the psalter at court, Henry Richards Luard, ed., *Flores historiarum per Matthaeum Westmonasteriensem collecti,* Rolls Series, no. 95 (London, 1890), 2:228.

8. Elizabeth Salter, *English and International: Studies in the Literature, Art, and Patronage of Medieval England,* eds. Derek Pearsall and Nicolette Zeeman (Cambridge: Cambridge University Press, 1988), 88–92; Josiah Cox Russell, "Master Henry of Avranches as an International Poet," *Speculum* 3 (1928): 34–63, and Josiah Cox Russell with J. P. Hieronimus, eds., *The Shorter Latin Poems of Master Henry of Avranches Relating to England* (Cambridge, Mass.: Medieval Academy of America, 1935), esp.

18–22, 137–42; Arnold, *Memorials of St. Edmund's Abbey*, 2:137; Richard Vaughan, *Matthew Paris* (Cambridge: Cambridge University Press, 1958), 168–81.

9. Henry Richards Luard, ed., *Lives of Edward the Confessor*, Rolls Series 3 (London: Longman, Brown, Green, Longmans, and Roberts, 1858), 25–157; Kathryn Young Wallace, *"La estoire de Seint Aedward le Rei" Attributed to Matthew Paris* (London: Anglo-Norman Text Society, 1983). See also Binski, "Reflections on *La estoire de Saint Ædward le Rei*," 333–50.

10. On *Rossignos* see Frederic James Edward Raby, *Poems of John of Hoveden*, Surtees Society 154 (Durham: Andrews, 1939); Louise W. Stone, "Jean de Howden, poète anglo-normand du XIIIᵉ siècle," *Romania* 69 (1946–47): 496–519; Legge, *Anglo-Norman Literature and Its Background*, 232–35; Juliet Vale, *Edward III and Chivalry: Chivalric Society and Its Context, 1270–1350* (Woodbridge, England: Boydell, 1982), 20–21. The work is discussed further below.

11. For Eleanor, John Carmi Parsons, *The Court and Household of Eleanor of Castile in 1290* (Toronto: Pontifical Institute of Mediaeval Studies, 1977) and "Eleanor of Castile: Legend and Reality Through Seven Centuries," in *Eleanor of Castile, 1290–1990: Essays to Commemorate the 700th Anniversary of Her Death, 28 November 1290*, ed. David Parsons (Stamford, England: Watkins in association with the University of Leicester Department of Adult Education, 1991). See also Evelyn Stefanos Procter, *Alfonso X of Castile: Patron of Learning* (Oxford: Clarendon, 1951; reprint, Westport, Conn: Greenwood Press, 1980); Antonio Ballesteros Beretta, *Alfonso X, el Sabio* (Barcelona: Salvat, 1963), 297–313; John Esten Keller, *Alfonso X, el Sabio* (New York: Twayne, 1967); Julio Gonzalez, *Reinado y diplomas de Fernando III* (Córdoba: Monte de Piedad y Caja de Ahorros de Córdoba, 1980–86), 1:11–22; J. N. Hillgarth, *The Spanish Kingdoms 1250–1516* (Oxford: Clarendon, 1976), 1:215–21; Robert I. Burns, ed., *Emperor of Culture: Alfonso X the Learned of Castile and His Thirteenth-Century Renaissance* (Philadelphia: University of Pennsylvania Press, 1990); A. J. Cardeñas, "If Not Alphonso X, Then Who?," *Manuscripta* 34 (1990): 201. On ritual context, T. F. Ruiz, "Une monarchie sans sacre: La monarchie castillane du Bas Moyen Age," *Annales ESC* 3 (1984): 429–53, trans. as "Unsacred Monarchy: The Kings of Castile in the Late Middle Ages," in *Rites of Power: Symbolism, Ritual and Politics Since the Middle Ages*, ed. Sean Wilentz (Philadelphia: University of Pennsylvania Press, 1985), 109–44; Frank Barlow, "The King's Evil," *English Historical Review* 95 (1980): 3–27; Michael Prestwich, *Edward I* (Berkeley and Los Angeles: University of California Press, 1988), 113.

12. Cf. János M. Bak, "Roles and Functions of Queens in Árpadian and Angevin Hungary, ca 1000–1386," and Inge Skovgaard-Petersen with Nanna Damsholt, "Queenship in Medieval Denmark," in *Medieval Queenship*, ed. John Carmi Parsons (New York: St. Martin's, 1993), respectively, 13–24, 25–42. See also Louise Fradenburg, "Rethinking Queenship," introduction to *Women and Sovereignty* (Edinburgh: Edinburgh University Press, 1992), 5.

13. On *The Ladder of Mahomet*, Procter, *Alfonso X of Castile*, 16–19; Keller, *Alfonso X*, 150–52; Alice E. Lasater, *Spain to England: A Comparative Study of Arabic, European, and English Literature of the Middle Ages* (Jackson: University Press of Mississippi, 1974), 32. The text is ed. Enrico Cerulli, *Il "Libro della scala" e la questione delle fonti arabo-spagnole della "Divina Commedia"* (Vatican City: Bibliotheca Apostolica Vaticana, 1949), and José Muñoz Sendino, *La escala de Mahoma* (Madrid: Ministerio de asuntos exteriores, Dirección general de relaciones culturales, 1949). A manuscript of the first portion of the *Partidas*, certainly a product of Alphonso X's scriptorium in the 1260s, may have reached England in that decade, but its provenance is admittedly unknown (London, British Library, Add. 20787); see J. Homer Herriott, "A Thirteenth-Century Manuscript of the *Primera Partida*," *Speculum* 13 (1938): 278–94; Procter, *Alfonso X of Castile*, 113. On *Meliadus*, William James Entwistle, *The Arthurian Legend in the Literatures of the Spanish Peninsula* (New York: Dutton, 1925), 109, 113; María Rosa Lida de Malkiel, "Arthurian Literature in Spain and Portugal," in *Arthurian Literature in the Middle Ages: A Collaborative History*, ed. Roger Sherman Loomis (Oxford: Clarendon, 1959), 406–7.

14. Possibly in emulation of Alphonso X (Ballesteros Beretta, *Alfonso X, el Sabio*, 297–313). See Beriah Botfield and T. Turner, eds., *Manners and Household Expenses of England in the Thirteenth and Fifteenth Centuries* (London: Nicol, 1841), 103, 104, 139; Benjamin Byerly and Catherine Ridder Byerly, eds., *Records of the Wardrobe and Household, 1285–1286* (London: H. M. Stationery Office, 1977), no. 2368, and *Records of the Wardrobe and Household, 1286–1289* (London: H. M. Stationery Office, 1986), nos. 208, 1676, 3207, 3210, 3213–14, 3217, 3220, 3223–24, 3226–27, 3234, 3236, 3238, 3239–40, 3246; Parsons, *Court and Household*, 13–14. Elfrida Saunders, *English Illumination* (1933; reprint, New York: Hacker, 1969), 67, misread *Close Rolls 1247–1251*, 521, and concluded Henry III had a writing office under Ralph Dunion, *custos librorum*; but Dunion was really a clerk of the king's children (*liberorum*) (Thomas F. Tout, *Chapters in the Administrative History of Medieval England* [Manchester: Manchester University Press, 1920–33], index p. 6:255, s.v. "Dunion, Ralph"). Robert Branner, *Manuscript Painting in Paris During the Reign of St. Louis: A Study of Styles* (Berkeley and Los Angeles: University of California Press, 1977), 3–7, finds no scriptorium at Louis's court.

15. Byerly and Byerly, *Records 1286–1289*, nos. 3207, 3210, 3214, 3220, 3223, 3227, 3234, 3246; Parsons, *Court and Household*, 64, 70, 81, 82, 95, 97, 102, 126, 128, 132; a *scriptor* Philip occ. 1290 (Parsons, *Court and Household*, 96), and for John de Stella and Hugh de Hibernia see nn. 16, 26. Construction of the chamber in December 1289 is recorded in C 47/4/5 fol. 2v.

16. Richard had thirty shillings, Hil. term 1290, "pro seruicio suo dum stetit in obsequio Regine" (S.C. 6/1089/25 m. 4) and was paid in 1292 for the psalter and boards to bind it (Botfield and Turner, *Manners*, 103). John de Stella occ. as her *scriptor*, September 1285–December 1288 (Byerly and Byerly, *Records 1285–1286*, no. 2368; *Records 1286–1289*, no. 2096).

17. Byerly and Byerly, *Records 1286–1289*, nos. 3208, 3210, 3217, 3228, 3236, 3240; Parsons, *Court and Household*, 84, 86, 87 bis, 92, 95, 97, 101, 102, 104, 107–8, 110, 118, 131.

18. Byerly and Byerly, *Records 1286–1289*, nos. 3208, 3210, 3217, 3225 (a damaged entry), 3234; Parsons, *Court and Household*, 73, 80, 82, 83, 87, 88, 105, 108, 117, 132. A buyer of wardrobe parchment is named only in Byerly and Byerly, no. 3221; parchment was purchased anonymously for both wardrobe and books, and ink for both by the scribe Roger (nos. 3236, 3239); Parsons, *Court and Household*, 79, shows ink purchased anonymously for both.

19. The purchases at various locations are remarked by Morgan, *Early Gothic Manuscripts*, 4:35 n. 22. For repairs, Byerly and Byerly, *Records 1286–1289*, no. 3217. For boards see n. 15; Eleanor's goldsmith Adam paid two shillings "pro tablettis ad libros . . . liberatis Regine" (E 101/684/13, fragment s.d.), and in 1291 purchased "tabliaus a liure" at Paris for her daughter Eleanor (E 101/684/56/2 m. 1; on young Eleanor see below). Jeweled bindings and silver ornaments for her books are also noted (John Carmi Parsons, "The Beginnings of English Administration in Ponthieu: An Unnoticed Document of 1280," *Mediaeval Studies* 50 [1988]: 397; Byerly and Byerly, *Records 1285–1286*, no. 385, *Records 1286–1289*, no. 3225; Parsons, *Court and Household*, 90).

20. It is unclear whether the life of Saint Thomas was a new work or recopied (Byerly and Byerly, *Records 1286–1289*, no. 3208, where the original is damaged and the name of the purchaser cannot be deciphered); for the lives bound in 1288, no. 3217, and for the hired painters, no. 3238.

21. M. R. James, *The Apocalypse in Latin and French (Bodleian, MS Douce 180)* (London: Roxburghe Club, 1922); Saunders, *English Illumination*, 84, 88–89; Otto Pächt and J. J. G. Alexander, *Illuminated Manuscripts in the Bodleian Library, Oxford* (Oxford: Clarendon, 1966–73), vol. 3, no. 469, pls. 43–45; J. J. G. Alexander and Paul Binski, eds., *Age of Chivalry: Art in Plantagenet England, 1200–1400* (London: Royal Academy of Arts in association with Weidenfeld and Nicolson, 1987), no. 351 and 133, 143, 152, 156, 341; Morgan, *Early Gothic Manuscripts*, vol. 2, no. 153. For the Trinity Apocalypse, see n. 6. The Cambridge Life of Edward the Confessor (EE.iii.59, Cambridge University Library) is discussed in M. R. James, ed. and trans., *La estoire de seint Ædward le rei*, Roxburghe Club Edition (Oxford: Oxford University Press, 1920); see also Morgan, *Early Gothic Manuscripts*, no. 123, and Binski, "Reflections on *La estoire de Saint Ædward le Rei*."

22. On the "Bird" Psalter (Cambridge, Fitzwilliam Museum 2–1954), see Lucy Freeman Sandler, *Gothic Manuscripts, 1285–1385: A Survey of Manuscripts Illuminated in the British Isles* (London: Miller, 1986; New York: Oxford University Press, 1986), vol. 2, no. 10; Francis Wormald and Phyllis M. Giles, *A Descriptive Catalogue of the Additional Illuminated Manuscripts in the Fitzwilliam Museum Acquired between 1895 and 1979* (Cambridge: Cambridge University Press, 1982), 2:475–79. On the "Alphonso" Psalter (London, British Library, Add. 24686), Sandler, *Gothic Manu-*

scripts, vol. 2, no. 1; Peter Brieger, *English Art, 1216–1307* (Oxford: Oxford University Press, 1957), 4:223–24; Alexander and Binski, *Age of Chivalry,* no. 357. Eleanor's hunting and aviaries are discussed in my forthcoming study of her life. W. B. Yapp, "The Birds of English Medieval Manuscripts," *Journal of Medieval History* 5 (1979): 343, sees an interest in natural history among thirteenth-century patrons and doubts if "artists would make the lavish use that they did of birds in [the] Alphonso [psalter] . . . unless the patron who commissioned the book requested it"; cf. G. E. Hutchinson, "Attitudes Toward Nature in Medieval England: The Alphonso and Bird Psalters," *Isis* 65 (1974): 5–37.

23. For the Savoy MS, Gerard J. Brault, "Les manuscrits des oeuvres de Girart d'Amiens," *Romania* 80 (1959): 433–66; Henri Michelant, ed., *Der Roman von Escanor, von Gerard von Amiens* (Tübingen, 1886) is discussed further below. On Eleanor's legacies to her daughters, Parsons, *Court and Household,* 134; cf. Hutchinson, "Attitudes Towards Nature," 29–33. Edward II possessed two works associated with his mother, the Castilian chronicle she perhaps brought to England in 1255 and the version of Vegetius she commissioned for Edward I in 1271–72, the latter probably a later copy made for their son's knighting in 1306 (see 6, 9–10).

24. Byerly and Byerly, *Records 1286–1289,* no. 3217, misreads "remanentes" for the correct "romancias" in E 101/352/11 m. 2, and fails to remark a considerable patch of damaged parchment before "libros Regine," which in the MS is actually on the next line down; for "romances" in the queen's baggage in 1290, Parsons, *Court and Household,* 90.

25. C 47/4/1 fol. 12r; Parsons, *Court and Household,* 63–64. It is unknown how Eleanor acquired her books of hours (Botfield and Turner, *Manners,* 136).

26. On the lack of such an office under Henry III, see nn. 6, 13. In 1300 Edward I sought a corrody at Chertsey Abbey for Eleanor's *scriptor* Hugh de Hibernia (for whom see Botfield and Turner, *Manners,* 104); S.C. 1/16/29 is the abbot's refusal, quoting in full Edward's request of 13 April 1300.

27. For purchases, Parsons, *Court and Household,* 66–67, 87. Eleanor's letter to the abbot of Cerne thanks him for sending her a book "sicut petivimus" (JUST 1/542 m. 7d, dated at Exeter, 1 January s.a.; she was at Cerne 6 December 1285 and at Exeter 1 January 1286 [Byerly and Byerly, *Records 1285–1286,* nos. 1977, 1992]). The book lent her was perhaps the Anglo-Norman chess treatise written at Cerne in the late thirteenth century (R. Eales, "The Game of Chess: An Aspect of Medieval Knightly Culture," in *The Ideals and Practice of Medieval Knighthood, I: Papers from the First and Second Strawberry Hill Conferences,* ed. Christopher Harper, Bill Harvey, and Ruth Harvey [Woodbridge, Eng.: Boydell, 1986], 28).

28. I owe to Alison Stones references to a manuscript of Brunetto Latini's *Livre dou Tresor* (Paris, Bibliothèque nationale, fr. 571), and a prose *Lancelot* (London, British Library, Royal 19 C 4). Books noted in Edward's wardrobe inventories after Eleanor's death included "a book of chronicles," his mother's *Roman de Guillaume le Conquerant* (later given to his son as above, 176), the Rutilius treatise (see n. 30), a book of "organ

chants," the *Gesta Tancredi*, and two others "of a religious character" (Mary Anne Everett Green, *Lives of the Princesses of England from the Norman Conquest* [London: Colburn, 1849–55], 2:284).

29. For *Meliadus*, James Douglas Bruce, *The Evolution of Arthurian Romance from the Beginnings Down to the Year 1300*, 2d ed. (Baltimore: Johns Hopkins University Press; Göttingen: Vandenhoeck and Ruprecht, 1928), 26–28; and Cedric E. Pickford, "Miscellaneous French Prose Romances," in Loomis, *Arthurian Literature in the Middle Ages*, 350–52. On the wall paintings, see Michelant, *Der Roman von Escanor*, lines 15597–15746; Colvin, *King's Works*, 129, 502, 760, 914, 916.

30. Lewis Thorpe, "Mastre Richard, a Thirteenth-Century Translator of the 'De Re Militari' of Vegetius," *Scriptorium* 6 (1952): 39–50; and "Mastre Richard at the Skirmish of Kenilworth?" *Scriptorium* 7 (1953): 262–65 (cf. Prestwich, *Edward I*, 50); Giles and Wormald, *Descriptive Catalogue*, 1:82–84. Morgan, *Early Gothic Manuscripts*, vol. 2, no. 150, thinks the version dates from the late 1260s, but cf. Jaroslav Folda, *Crusader Manuscript Illumination at Saint-Jean-d'Acre, 1275–1291* (Princeton: Princeton University Press, 1976), 16–17, 129–30, 199. Legge may be right in thinking the extant MS, probably of the early fourteenth century, was prepared for Edward of Caernarvon's knighting in 1306 ("The Lord Edward's Vegetius," *Scriptorium* 7 [1953]: 262–65); certainly he owned a copy in the 1320s (Vale, *Edward III and Chivalry*, 49–50). The extant manuscript's pasted-in miniature of a naval engagement, which Folda connects to the Acre school of illuminators, could have been taken from the MS prepared there in 1271–72. On medieval respect for Vegetius, Maurice H. Keen, *Chivalry* (New Haven, Conn.: Yale University Press, 1984), 111–12. Edward I owned a copy of Rutilius's *De re rustica*, but no translation is recorded (M. Green, *Princesses*, 2:284).

31. Mary Dominica Legge, "John Pecham's *Jerarchie*," *Medium Aevum* 19 (1942): 77–84, entirely supersedes A. Rosin, "Die 'Hierarchie' des John Peckham, historisch interpretiert," *Zeitschrift für Romanische Philologie* 2 (1932): 583–614 (unknown to Legge); Legge, *Anglo-Norman in the Cloisters: The Influence of the Orders upon Anglo-Norman Literature* (Edinburgh: Edinburgh University Press, 1950), 81–82, and *Anglo-Norman Literature and Its Background* (Oxford: Clarendon, 1963), 225–26; Decima L. Douie, *Archbishop Pecham* (Oxford: Clarendon, 1952), 52.

32. Legge, *Anglo-Norman in the Cloisters*, 81–82; Ruth Barbour, "A Manuscript of Pseudo-Dionysius Areopagita Copied for Robert Grosseteste," *Bodleian Library Record* 6 (1958): 401–16; Richard William Southern, *Robert Grosseteste: The Growth of an English Mind in Medieval Europe* (Oxford: Clarendon; New York: Oxford University Press, 1986), 200–203.

33. Botfield and Turner, *Manners*, 96, 103, 107–8, 135–36; Strickland Gibson, ed., *Statuta antiqua Universitatis Oxoniensis* (Oxford: Clarendon, 1931), 13, 16; M. B. Hackett, *The Original Statutes of Cambridge University* (Cambridge: Cambridge University Press, 1970), 233; T. H. Aston, and Rosamond Faith, "The Endowments of the University and Colleges to circa 1348," in *The History of the University of Oxford, Vol. 1: The Early Oxford Schools*, ed. J. I. Catto (Oxford: Clarendon, 1984), 276, 278, 283.

For the 1290 letter, Parsons, *Court and Household*, 94 (it cannot be proved that the master Richard de Cumbe of 1290 is the Richard who translated Vegetius in 1271–72). In 1277 she appointed as her wardrobe keeper mister Geoffrey de Aspale, an Oxford man who commented on most of Aristotle's scientific works (Alfred B. Emden, *A Bibliographical Register of the University of Oxford* [Oxford: Clarendon, 1957–59], 1:60–61; E. Macrae, "Geoffrey of Aspall's Commentaries on Aristotle," *Medieval and Renaissance Studies* 6 [1968]: 94–134; *CPR 1281–1292*, 229 [cf. Parsons, *Court and Household*, 75]).

34. On Eleanor's relations with the Dominicans and her books of hours and rosaries as indicating mendicant influence in her religious life, John Carmi Parsons, "Piety, Power, and the Reputations of Two Thirteenth-Century English Queens," vol. 1 of *Queens, Regents and Potentates, Women of Power*, ed. Theresa M. Vann (Cambridge, Eng.: Academia, 1993). On books of hours, above, n. 25, and for rosaries, Parsons, *Court and Household*, 106. For the friars' role in educating her children, below.

35. For Ferdinand III and Alphonso X, above; Bell, "Medieval Women Book Owners," 149–50; Clanchy, *From Memory to Written Record*, 154; W. Rothwell, "The Role of French in Thirteenth-Century England," *Bulletin of the John Rylands Library* 58 (1976): 462–66.

36. This shift was not, of course, exclusive to the court (Legge, *Anglo-Norman in the Cloisters*, 121; Emile J. Arnould, *Le manuel des Péchés: Étude religieuse anglo-normande (XIIIᵉ siècle)* [Paris: Droz, 1940], 1–13; M. Thomas, "Une compilation anglo-normande de la fin du XIIIᵉ siècle: 'La vie de gent de religion,'" in vol. 2 of *Recueil de travaux offerts à M. Clovis Brunel* [Paris: Société de l'École des Chartes, 1955], 2:586–98).

37. J. C. Parsons, "Beginnings of English Administration in Ponthieu," 376, 395, 398, with authorities cited; Paul Scheffer-Boichorst, ed., *Chronica Albrici monachi Trium Fontium a monacho novi monasterii Hoiensis interpolata*, MGH SS no. 23 (Hanover, 1874), 743–44 ("Hic enim per adulatorum indigna consilia regis avunculi, quam non meruerat, incurrisset offensam"). On romance as historical source, Richard Firth Green, *Poets and Princepleasers: Literature and the English Court in the Late Middle Ages* (Toronto: University of Toronto Press, 1980), 136–37.

38. Giraldus Cambrensis, *De principis instructione*, in *Opera omnia*, ed. J. S. Brewer, Rolls Series 21 (London: Longman, 1861–91), 8:258.

39. O'Callaghan, *A History of Medieval Spain*, 515. For an English chronicle carried abroad by Henry II's daughters, below. The work Eleanor seems to have taken to England was Rodrigo Ximénez de Rada's *De rebus Hispaniae libri IX*, ed. Francisco Lorenzana, in *Roderici Toletani Opera*, vol. 22, *Textos Medievales* (Madrid, 1793; reprint, Valencia, 1970), the only Castilian narrative that mentions her birth; for the copy owned by her son, Francis Palgrave, *The Antient Kalendars and Inventories of the Treasury of His Majesty's Exchequer*, Record Commission (London: Eyre and Spottiswoode, 1836), 1:106.

40. Martin Andrew Sharp Hume, *Spanish Influence on English Literature* (London: Nash, 1905; Reprint New York: Haskell House, 1964), 63–67; Laura Keeler, *Geoffrey*

de Monmouth and the Late Latin Chroniclers (Berkeley and Los Angeles: University of California Press, 1946), 57–58, noting Eleanor's marriage to Edward I (at 55 n. 26); Antonia Gransden, "The Continuation of the *Flores Historiarum* from 1265 to 1327," *Mediaeval Studies* 36 (1974): 491, *Historical Writing in England, C. 550 to C. 1307* (London: Routledge and Kegan Paul, 1974), 1:441–43, and "Propaganda in English Mediaeval Historiography," *Journal of Medieval History* 1 (1975): 363. On Alphonso X, Keeler, *Geoffrey de Monmouth*, 57–58.

41. On typology in medieval historical writing, Gabrielle Spiegel, "Political Utility in Medieval Historiography: A Sketch," *History and Theory* 14 (1975): 320–21. Diana B. Tyson, "Patronage of French Vernacular History Writers in the Twelfth and Thirteenth Centuries," *Romania* 100 (1979): 220–21, identifies few female patrons of historical writing in that period and suggests that Frenchwomen's interest in the subject, if any, did not extend to patronage.

42. Ian Short, *The Anglo-Norman Pseudo-Turpin Chronicle of William de Braine* (Oxford: Oxford University Press, 1973), 2; Gabrielle Spiegel, "*Pseudo-Turpin*, the Crisis of the Aristocracy, and the Beginnings of Vernacular Historiography in France," *Journal of Medieval History* 12 (1986): 207–23 (the passages quoted at 216). On legitimation of political activity by exploitation of historical traditions, Laurent Theis, "Dagobert, Saint-Denis, et la royauté française au moyen âge," in *Le métier d'historien au Moyen Age: Etudes sur l'historiographie médiévale*, ed. Bernard Guénée (Paris: Centre de recherches sur l'histoire de l'occident médiéval, 1977), 28. On the 1225 surrender, Parsons, "Beginnings of English Administration in Ponthieu," 392; Hilda Johnstone, "The County of Ponthieu, 1279–1307," *English Historical Review* 29 (1914): 438–39.

43. Parsons, "Beginnings of English Administration in Ponthieu," 394–96.

44. Noel Denholm-Young, *History and Heraldry, 1254 to 1310: A Study of the Historical Value of the Rolls of Arms* (Oxford: Clarendon, 1965), 47. Her southern origins led some to ask how she could have known the matter of Britain, but they are answered by the copy of Geoffrey of Monmouth taken to Castile in 1170 by her Plantagenet great-grandmother, a daughter of Henry II (Michelant, *Der Roman von Escanor*, vi; and Karl Julius Holzknecht, *Literary Patronage in the Middle Ages* [Philadelphia: Collegiate, 1923], 93; cf. Entwistle, *Arthurian Legend*, 33–35, 47–50, 119–22, and Lida de Malkiel, "Arthurian Literature in Spain and Portugal," 406–7).

45. John Carmi Parsons, "The Second Exhumation of King Arthur's Remains at Glastonbury, 19 April 1278," *Arthurian Literature* 12 (1992): 173–77. See also Peter Johanek, "König Arthur und die Plantagenets: Über den Zusammenhang von Historiographie und höfischer Epik in mittelalterlicher Propaganda," *Frühmittelalterliche Studien* 21 (1987): 346–89, esp. 364–66.

46. Roger Sherman Loomis, "Edward I, Arthurian Enthusiast," *Speculum* 28 (1953): 114–24, and "Arthurian Influence on Sport and Spectacle," in *Arthurian Literature in the Middle Ages*, 558–59; but cf. Prestwich, *Edward I*, 120–22.

47. Each of Girard's three known works is dedicated to a different royal patron (the

others were Philip IV of France and Charles of Anjou); it would seem that he sought employ from each in turn but never obtained it, a result perhaps to be attributed to the poor quality of his works. See Robert Bossuat, Louis Pichard, and Guy Raynaud de Lage, *Dictionnaire des lettres françaises: Le Moyen Age* (Paris: Fayard, 1974), 321–22; the text is Michelant, *Der Roman von Escanor*. On the Savoy MS, see Brault, "Manuscrits de Girart d'Amiens," and "Arthurian Heraldry and the Date of *Escanor*," *Bulletin bibliographique de la Société Internationale Arthurienne* 11 (1959): 81–88. Probably Eleanor met Girard when in France to claim Ponthieu in 1279; *Escanor*'s familiarity with English geography and life at the English court suggests that he spent some time there. *Escanor* notes at lines 24434–35 Guinevere's squire "Martin d'Espaigne," whom Michelant (644n) thought was modeled on one of Eleanor's servants—perhaps her squire Martin Ferrandi (Byerly and Byerly, *Records 1285–1286*, nos. 809, 845–46, and *Records 1286–1289*, nos. 112, 188, 744, 1652, 1767, 3217–18, 3224, 3238, 3242; Parsons, *Court and Household*, 69, 76, 77).

48. Binski, Paul, *The Painted Chamber at Westminster* (London: Society of Antiquaries of London, 1986; distributed by Thames and Hudson), 101. Werner L. Gundersheimer, "Women, Learning, and Power: Eleanora of Aragon and the Court of Ferrara," in Labalme, *Beyond their Sex*, 43–65, esp. 55, posits a like affinity between the learned Duchess Eleanora and her "astute and competent but somewhat lazy" husband. Edward I was in no sense "lazy," but clearly his interests did not include literature (Prestwich, *Edward I*, 108–22).

49. Prestwich, *Edward I*, 117–22; Beryl Smalley, *English Friars and Antiquity in the Early Fourteenth Century* (Oxford: Blackwell, 1960), 10–12. For examples, "The Praise of the Young Edward," in *Political Songs of England*, ed. C. T. Wright (London: Nichols for the Camden Society, 1839), 128–32; *Commendatio lamentabilis in transitu magni regis Edwardi*, in *Chronicles of the Reigns of Edward I and Edward II*, ed. W. Stubbs, Roll Series 76 (London: Longman, 1882–83), 2:8, 2:11, 2:14–15; Binski, *Painted Chamber*, 97. At least one writer gave Edward's arms to Arthur (Gerard J. Brault, *Early Blazon: Heraldic Terminology in the Twelfth and Thirteenth Centuries with Specific Reference to Arthurian Literature* (Oxford: Clarendon, 1972), 21–22.

50. Binski, "Reflections on *La estoire de Seint Aedward le rei*," 339–40; Ruiz, "Unsacred Monarchy," 126. On the extant manuscript, perhaps Eleanor's presentation copy (1255), see references in nn. 8, 9, and 21.

51. M. Green, *Live of the Princesses*, 2:376–78; Vale, *Edward III and Chivalry*, 22.

52. Pauline Stafford, *Queens, Concubines, and Dowagers: The King's Wife in the Early Middle Ages* (Athens: University of Georgia Press, 1983), 120–21, 124; Gerd Althoff, *Adels- und Königs-familien im Spiegel ihrer Memorialüberlieferung: Studien zum Totengedenken der Billunger und Ottonen* (Munich: Fink, 1964), 163–70, 196–200, 238–39; Derek Baker, " 'A Nursery of Saints': St Margaret of Scotland Reconsidered," in *Medieval Women: Essays Presented to Rosalind M. T. Hill on the Occasion of Her Seventieth Birthday*, ed. Derek Baker, Studies in Church History, Subsidia 1 (Oxford: Blackwell for the Ecclesiastical History Society, 1978) 124–25; Lois L. Huneycutt,

"The Idea of the Perfect Princess: *The Life of Saint Margaret* in the Reign of Matilda II, 1100–1118," *Anglo-Norman Studies* 12 (1989): 81–97. On the links between noblewomen's commemoration of ancestral dead and their interest in historical writing, see Elisabeth van Houts, "Women and the Writing of History in the Early Middle Ages: The Case of Abbess Matilda of Essen and Aethelweard," *Early Medieval Europe* 1 (1992): 53–68, esp. 54–55, 57–59.

53. Gerbert de Montreuil produced several works for Marie between 1225 and 1237 (Bossuat, Picard, and Reynaud de Lage, *Dictionnaire des lettres françaises*, 308, 660; Rita Lejeune, "La femme dans les littératures," 207). Given its familiarity with marriages in the houses of Pontieu and Dammartin, the romance known as *La fille du comte de Pontieu* was perhaps written for one of those families; the text is edited by Clovis Felix Brunel (Paris: Champion, 1923), who suggests a date late in the reign of Philip Augustus (1180–1223)—thus in the lifetime of Marie, who married Simon of Dammartin between 1208 and 1210 (Brunel, *Recueil des actes des comtes de Pontieu (1026–1279)* [Paris, 1930], vii–viii and no. 188; J.-B. Teulet, ed., *Layettes du Trésor des Chartes,* [Paris, 1863–1909], vol. 1, no. 854; Leopold Delisle, ed., *Cartulaire normand de Philippe-Auguste, Louis VIII, Saint-Louis et Philippe-le-Hardi* [1852; Reprint, Geneva: Mégoriotis: 1978], no. 168). Eleanor's mother (Marie's daughter) lived in Ponthieu as a widow and perhaps possessed a French prose *Tristan* written by a Norman scribe and illuminated by a Spaniard (Paris, Bibliothèque nationale, fr. 750; see Roger Sherman Loomis, *Arthurian Legends in Medieval Art* [London: Oxford University Press, 1938], 92, figs. 210–12).

54. Gerda Lerner, *The Creation of Patriarchy* (New York and Oxford: Oxford University Press, 1986), 48.

55. For young Eleanor's literacy, Byerly and Byerly, *Records 1285–1286*, no. 403 (cf. Galbraith, "Literacy of the Medieval English Kings," 215); the friars were in the children's household in 1289–90 (C 47/4/5 fols. 13r, 29r). Mary likely requested Trevet's chronicle and gave him information. The work contains a great deal of detailed Plantagenet family lore otherwise unrecorded; Trevet, prior of the London Dominicans and an internationally renowned scholar, had no need to court Mary's patronage with an unsolicited work. See R. J. Dean, "Nicholas Trevet, Historian," in *Medieval Learning and Literature: Essays Presented to Richard William Hunt*, ed. J. J. G. Alexander, M. T. Gibson (Oxford: Clarendon, 1976), 339–49; Gransden, *Historical Writing in England*, 1:501–7. A text based on a sampling of manuscripts was prepared by A. Rutherford, "The Anglo-Norman Chronicle of Nicholas Trivet" (Ph.D. diss., University of London, 1932) (I owe this reference to Frank Mantello).

56. Rita Lejeune, "Rôle littéraire de la famille d'Aliénor d'Aquitaine," *Cahiers de civilisation médiévale* 1 (1958): 319–37, is reliable on Monmouth's transmission by Henry's daughters, though some of Lejeune's work must be handled with caution (cf. Elizabeth A. R. Brown, "Eleanor of Aquitaine: Parent, Queen, and Duchess," in *Eleanor of Aquitaine: Patron and Politician*, ed. William W. Kibler [Austin: University of Texas Press, 1976], with review by John C. Moore, *Speculum* 53 [1978]: 148–49). Further

examples are cited in John Carmi Parsons, "Mothers, Daughters, Marriage, Power: Some Plantagenet Evidence, 1150–1500," in Parsons, *Medieval Queenship*, 63–78.

57. Francisque Michel and Charles Bémont, eds., *Rôles gascons, 1242–1307* (Paris, 1896–1906), vol. 2, no. 597; cf. John Carmi Parsons, "The Year of Eleanor of Castile's Birth and Her Children by Edward I," *Mediaeval Studies*, 46 (1984): 260. This incident is discussed at greater length in Parsons, "Mothers, Daughters, Marriage, and Power," 63–78.

58. Carolyn G. Heilbrun, *Writing a Woman's Life* (New York: Norton, 1988), 18 (I owe this reference to Germaine Warkentin).

59. Lois M. Huneycutt, "Intercession and the High-Medieval Queen: The *Esther* Topos," and John Carmi Parsons, "The Queen's Intercession in Thirteenth-Century England," in *Power of the Weak*, ed. S. B. MacLean and J. Carpenter (Urbana: University of Illinois Press, in press); Paul Strohm, "Queens as Intercessors," in *Hochon's Arrow: The Social Imagination of Fourteenth-Century Texts* (Princeton: Princeton University Press, 1992), 95–120. Cf. remarks on literary noblewomen's relationships with their husbands, above and n. 48.

60. Michelle Zimbalist Rosaldo, "Woman, Culture and Society: A Theoretical Overview," in *Woman, Culture and Society*, eds. Michelle Zimbalist Rosaldo and Louise Lamphere (Stanford: Stanford University Press, 1974), 17–42. The "public-private" distinction for queenly power is questioned in Fradenburg, "Rethinking Queenship," 5–6, and in John Carmi Parsons, "Family, Sex, and Power: The Rhythms of Medieval Queenship," introduction to *Medieval Queenship*, 9–10; cf. Erler and Kowaleski, *Women and Power*, 4–5.

61. E.g., G.-H. Allard, ed., *Aspects de la marginalité au moyen âge* (Montreal: L'Aurore, 1975); Michel Mollat, *Les pauvres au Moyen Age* (Brussels: Complexe, 1978); Bronislaw Geremek, *The Margins of Society in Late Medieval Paris*, trans. Jean Birrell (Cambridge: Cambridge University Press, 1987); Michael M. Sheehan, ed., *Aging and the Aged in Medieval Europe* (Toronto: Pontifical Institute of Mediaeval Studies, 1990); Fradenburg, "Rethinking Queenship." Sharon Kettering, "The Patronage Power of Early Modern French Noblewomen," *Historical Journal* 32 (1989): 817–41, treats women's patronage in a more overtly political context than the present article, but shows that institutionalized powerlessness often concealed the influence women exerted through unofficial means.

62. Queens' associations with "times out of joint" are stressed by Fradenburg, "Rethinking Queenship," 7. *Rossignos* alludes to Judas Maccabee, Hector, Troilus, Caesar, Charlemagne, Godfrey of Bouillon, Bohemund of Antioch, Tancred of Sicily, Gawain, Lancelot, Yvain, Perceval, Roland, Alexander, and Arthur. Though the earliest evidence that Hoveden was Eleanor of Provence's clerk postdates *Rossignos*, it is rarely if ever possible to pinpoint the moment at which a clerk entered royal service, and it is not unlikely that he was already in her employ in 1272–74 (see references in n. 10). Other examples of works associated with royal women at times of transition are not

lacking. Perhaps the best known are the eleventh-century Latin *Encomium Emmae Reginae* and *Vita Aedwardi Regis* (Pauline Stafford, "The Portrayal of Royal Women in England, Ninth-Eleventh Centuries," in Parsons, ed., *Medieval Queenship*, 163–65). Elizabeth McCartney has studied works dedicated to Louise of Savoy, mother of Francis I of France, after she was named her son's guardian and tutor while he was heir to the throne in the last years of the ailing and sonless Louis XII, and when Louise acted as regent while Francis was absent on his Italian campaigns and as Charles V's prisoner. It is unclear if Louise ordered these works, but it is significant that they were addressed to her at such times ("The King's Mother and Royal Prerogative in Early Sixteenth-Century France," in Parsons, *Medieval Queenship*, 115–41). In a paper read at the Twenty-Sixth International Congress on Medieval Studies, Western Michigan University, May 1991, Richard Schneider of York University discussed manuscripts commissioned by Isabella of France for Edward III in the period between Edward II's deposition in January 1327 and her own downfall in October 1330.

63. For another example, see Janet L. Nelson, "Gender and Genre in Women Historians of the Early Middle Ages," in *L'historiographie médiévale en Europe*, ed. Jean-Philippe Genet (Paris: Editions du centre nationale de la recherche scientifique, 1991), 149–63.

64. Parsons, "Mothers, Daughters, Marriage, and Power"; Bell, "Medieval Women Book Owners," esp. 158–67; Barbara A. Hanawalt, "Lady Honor Lisle's Networks of Influence," in Erler and Kowaleski, *Women and Power in the Middle Ages*, 188–212.

65. Erik H. Erikson, "Womanhood and the Inner Space," in *Identity, Youth, and Crisis* (New York: Norton, 1968), 261–94, quoted by Gundersheimer, "Women, Learning and Power," 51, where Eleanora of Ferrara's literary endeavors are adduced in opposition to Erikson's position.

Piety, Politics, and Power: The Patronage of Leonor of England and Her Daughters Berenguela of León and Blanche of Castile

✳ ✳ ✳ Miriam Shadis

The royal women of medieval France and Castile used patronage as a way to cultivate political power and authority.[1] Diffusing the boundaries between the public and the private, they developed patronage projects with the specific goals of building and reinforcing their own power and that of their family or lineage.[2] As a way to cultivate power, the goals (if not the outcome) of women's patronage were perhaps not different from men's, but the choices women made did differ from those of their male counterparts. The women in this study follow generally matrilineal preferences, influencing generations of daughters and granddaughters. In examining royal women's practice of patronage at the courts of France and Castile-León, I will begin with the influence of Eleanor of Aquitaine and her daughter Leonor of England, and then emphasize the work and interests of two of Leonor's daughters, the royal sisters Berenguela of León (1180–1246) and Blanche of Castile (1188–1252).[3]

These women's patronage put resources and attention into producing their families (both past and future) as powerful institutions, at the same time making the family a significant place for mothers. Their efforts parallel an earlier development in history writing, wherein the writing of genealogy became an important tool in constructing agnatic *lignage* at the same time that genealogy reaffirmed the same *lignage*.[4] In the study presented here, women used their patronage to affirm the power of their lineage and to place themselves squarely within that lineage. As women they biologically complicated the male, linear history used in standard medieval genealogical narrative. Eleanor, Leonor, Berenguela, and Blanche built and maintained necropolises as a way to perpetuate their own personal influence indefinitely, gaining power for themselves as well as for their families. The establishment of such burial places for themselves and their families would remind all who saw them—especially future members of their family—of the elements of their lineage and family structure, and power. The iconography surrounding such monu- . ments to the dead (and the dead themselves, literally) is, as we shall see, a very important part of how this power would be represented.

Although Eleanor of Aquitaine has been generally mythologized as a great patron, there has been some debate regarding her actual interest in such matters. Elizabeth A. R. Brown has argued that she is more appropriately understood as a politician with little interest in patronage.[5] This seems an unnecessary distinction—even Brown recognizes that Eleanor's temper and ideas were much influenced by her cultural milieu, which included flourishing ateliers as well as a sophisticated, artistically stimulated court life, dependent upon ducal patronage. One of the underlying arguments of this essay is that it is unnecessary to conceive of the patron and the politician as two separate entities: that the goals of patronage and politicking were to establish self and family—as well as to please God. We see this in the life of Eleanor's daughter Leonor of England, queen of Castile, and even more clearly in Eleanor's granddaughters Berenguela and Blanche. Eleanor of Aquitaine clearly influenced the preferences of her daughter Leonor and thus her granddaughters. Generally these women reiterated their connections to their natal families, or they bolstered the prestige of their own children. Interestingly, there is not a great deal of focus on their marital families, although in the case of the women discussed here, that may well be due to their particular marital circumstances.[6]

The institution most clearly associated with Eleanor of Aquitaine is that of Fontevrault, the female Benedictine abbey in Poitou where Eleanor spent much of her time and to which she ultimately retired from court life. She had also chosen Fontevrault as a burial site for herself, her husband Henry II, and her son Richard the Lion-Hearted. It has been suggested, moreover, that Eleanor's younger children, Leonor, Joanna, and John, spent much of their time as children at this abbey while their mother conducted her glittering court at Poitiers.[7] Certainly a link can be drawn between Fontevrault and Leonor of England's future activity as a patron in Castile. Fontevrault was remembered by Leonor and her husband Alfonso VIII[8] and seems to have served as a model for Leonor's main act of patronage: the female Cistercian abbey of Las Huelgas in Burgos, the construction of which began around the year 1188.[9]

Imitating the use of Fontevrault as a family burial site, Las Huelgas was founded specifically as a necropolis for the royalty of Castile. An important difference, however, was manifested in the choice of the Cistercian order. On the face of it, the Castilian monarchs' patronage of the Cistercian order seems unremarkable—the Cistercians had, by the late twelfth century, reached the height of their popularity.[10] The insistence of Leonor and her husband that the abbey be both Cistercian and female bears further investigation, however, especially with regard to the institutionally ambivalent position of the Cistercians concerning women in their order and the continued patronage of female Cistercians by their daughters Berenguela and Blanche. Perhaps "the problem of Cistercian women" made the order a good choice for Alfonso and Leonor. By establishing a convent whose constituents would be on the fringes of the institution, they as patrons would have more influence in the operation of the sacred space. This would in the long run be important as the role of the abbey in the life (and deaths) of the royal family developed.

The late twelfth and early thirteenth centuries were characterized, as far as the Cistercian order was concerned, by an increase both in the number of women seeking to join the order and in resistance to them on the part of the male-oriented institution.[11] In this period women who sought entry to the order posed a serious problem to the men who ran it. While the Cistercians could do nothing about women who desired to imitate their life, they actively discouraged the formal association of women with their order. This did not stop certain female foundations from identifying themselves as Cistercian.[12] What could the male Cistercians do about women who wished to adopt their way of life, or about powerful kings and queens who chose to found Cistercian convents? It appears that on this account the order had to deal with the pope as well, to whom many would-be Cistercians and patrons appealed.[13] Cistercian resistance to women grew, despite, or perhaps because of, increasing numbers of women who wished to either join or patronize the order. A 1228 statute declared that women might form independent houses associated with the order, but that the order itself would assume no responsibility for them.[14] Ultimately the nuns at Las Huelgas seemed to turn this institutional problem to their advantage; the mechanisms by which they did so are key to understanding the importance such female institutions had for their founders, especially as extensions of personal and family power.

The foundation charter reveals nothing about the rationale for creating a women's house at Las Huelgas.[15] Perhaps the simplest explanation for this insistence that Las Huelgas be female would be the connection between Leonor of England and her mother's favored institution, Fontevrault. At Fontevrault the abbess was to "have and maintain the power of ruling the church of Fonte-vrault and all the places belonging to that church, and they are to obey her. They are to revere her as their spiritual mother, and all the affairs of the church, spiritual as well as secular, are to remain in her hands, or to be given to whomever she assigns, just as she decides."[16] The founder of Fontevrault, Robert of Arbrissel, intentionally curtailed the possibility that men could have authority or control over the abbess, although the abbey still depended upon the male members of their extended community for sacerdotal functions.[17] By insisting that Las Huelgas be female, and that its abbess enjoy the highest authority known for an abbess in Europe, Alfonso and Leonor followed the model of Fontevrault set up by Robert of Arbrissel. The inspiration of Fonte-vrault for the foundation of Las Huelgas further reinforces the influence of family (or, more precisely, mother) in determining this act of patronage.

Las Huelgas has long been celebrated for the special powers believed to have been held by the abbess, not only in terms of her association with secu-lar power, but also in terms of sacred practice.[18] Whatever special powers the abbess might have held (for example, hearing the nuns' confessions and preaching homilies), these were not endowed either in the original royal and papal charters, nor in subsequent articulations of the abbey's rights and privi-leges.[19] Confusion about the monastery's precise status may stem from the position of Las Huelgas as both female and Cistercian—independent from episcopal supervision and most tithes, yet subject to men (local clerics and bishops) for its spiritual needs.[20]

The historian Amancio Rodríguez points to other possible origins for these extraordinary powers attributed to the abbess. The first, he believes, is a mis-reading on the part of historians of a bull of Clement III, dated 2 January 1188, which outlined the general rights and liberties of the abbey and declared spe-cifically that no bishop should cause either directly or indirectly a sentence to be promulgated against the abbey or its nuns.[21] Rodríguez points out that this bull seemed to put the abbey under the direct protection of the pope and to free the nuns from all but self-censorship, but did not endow the abbess her-self with any particular rights or privileges.[22] A second bull of 12 May 1188 further asserted the independence of the abbess from any synod, foreign con-vent, or intervention from any quarter in terms of the institutional operation of the abbey.[23] These are institutional liberties, but they do not reveal any spiritual privileges.

Rodríguez argues that the promise of protection by the pope did not ex-pressly release Las Huelgas from obedience to the local bishop (of Burgos) but was rather a pro forma expression of support usually given to new foundations by the apostolic see, and though it may have limited the power of the order in some regards vis-à-vis the abbey, it did not signify a complete exemption.[24] However, exemption from the authority of the direction of the bishop of Burgos (who of course represented the papacy) for all intents and purposes left Las Huelgas to operate on its own judgment, if only because communications with Rome were so difficult.

Furthermore, in 1187 the Chapter General of Cîteaux, at the request of Alfonso VIII and various abbesses in Castile, designated Las Huelgas as the head abbey over all female Cistercian abbeys in Castile and León, with the right to call a chapter general within its own walls, requiring that the other Cistercian abbesses present themselves to the abbess of Las Huelgas. In this respect the abbess of Las Huelgas emulated the head of the entire Cistercian order—truly a unique position, even if not endowed with sacerdotal privileges.[25] The first chapter meeting convened at Las Huelgas on 27 April 1189; after initial meetings, however, no documents recording chapter meetings appear to survive, nor is it easy to say when the chapters ceased to meet. Rodríguez suggests that with the coming of royal princesses to Las Huelgas in the late 1220s, the nature of the abbey's authority changed, and it was no longer necessary to assert primacy through chapter meetings.[26]

Although no specific evidence indicates that the abbess of Las Huelgas actually carried out sacerdotal duties, evidence does exist that at least by 1210 she was perceived to be doing so. A letter dated 11 December 1210, from Pope Innocent III to Abbot Gui of Morimond, Bishop Adamo of Palencia, and Bishop Garsía of Burgos condemned generally the abuses of abbesses in the dioceses of Palencia and Burgos, abuses that included preaching homilies, hearing confessions, and blessing novices. Innocent goes on to explain that this behavior is particularly unacceptable because the abbesses are women, for, as he puts it, even though Mary was more perfect and of greater dignity than the apostles, it was to them, and not to her, that the keys to the kingdom of heaven were given.[27] Rodríguez theorizes that such abuses might have come about because, despite increasing attention to and articulation of canon law, the situation in Castile (distance from Rome and Clairvaux, efforts of the reconquest, internal warfare, lack of communication, and a generally fractured society), coupled with necessity and royal protection, may have "permitted" an abbess occasionally to act outside of her ecclesiastical jurisdiction. Once this had happened, these practices were quickly naturalized into her routine with little or no second thought. What Rodríguez attributes to the "ignorance" of the abbesses with respect to the legitimacy of women and priestly prerogative may well have been willful opportunism. It is difficult to believe that the abbess of such a central, royal institution would have been ignorant of the privileges of gender within the church.[28]

Second, the institutional relationship of the Cistercian order to the royal house of Castile might explain Leonor and Alfonso's insistence that Las Huelgas be female. Male institutions were generally independent of secular authority, and were exempt from royal and clerical taxes, as well as from episcopal visitation.[29] Leonor and Alfonso exempted Las Huelgas from most royal and clerical taxes and supported its independence from episcopal authority, perhaps in an attempt to equalize the nuns' position within the Cistercian order.[30] The institutionally ambivalent position of women in the Cistercian order, however, allowed Alfonso and Leonor to exert some authority vis-à-vis that order. Leonor and Alfonso may have seen female institutions as sites upon which to exert more power as patrons in offering special protection to these women (or insisting upon it from the pope). The status of the abbess, at least in regard to the other abbeys of Castile and León, was a direct result of the patrons' influence and not only reflected their own royal power but also reflected sacred power back upon them. Thus they could more directly control the outcome of their giving, and their status as patrons was enhanced.[31]

At Las Huelgas the cooperative activity between royal women and the abbess (generally not a royal person but always of noble status) was very important.[32] Las Huelgas provided an arena for women to exercise both power and authority, both internally, as abbesses and nuns, and externally, as royal patrons. From the second decade of the thirteenth century on, Las Huelgas seems to have been governed in a cooperative manner by both a religious authority (the abbess) and a secular authority (a female member of the royal family). These princesses and queens played an important role in securing certain rights and privileges for the monastery in the "outside" world, by serving as liaisons between the monastery and the royal court, and as guarantors for those wishing to patronize the abbey, assuring that the wishes of the donor would be carried out.

The first abbess of Las Huelgas, Doña Misol, was selected by Alfonso VIII and Leonor from the Abbey of Tulebras in Navarre. She was followed by Sancha García, who was abbess from 1207 until 1229–30. The Abbess Sancha appears one last time in November of 1230,[33] but from that date until October of 1232 there is no mention of a specific abbess. From 1230 to 1240 the abbess herself does not appear very often by name in the sources, suggesting that she was not a very significant character, that there was no effective abbess, or simply that in that period her role as liaison to the outside world was changing. In 1229, or during the 1230s, a younger daughter of the founders entered the abbey. Leonor, whose marriage to Jaime I of Aragon was annulled in 1229, took the veil and remained at Las Huelgas until her death in 1244. Sometime before 1230 the Infanta Constanza, also a daughter of the founders and sister of Berenguela and Blanche, joined the convent, along with Constanza, the daughter of Berenguela and Alfonso IX of León.[34] Rodríguez thinks that perhaps the elder Constanza ruled the abbey without actual election as abbess. Part of the evidence for this is a 1232 document in which the infanta mandated that her chaplain, Don Fernando, assess and record the entire holdings of the abbey, with no mention of the abbess.[35] Throughout 1230, however, there appears frequently a Frey Martín or Frey Domingo acting in the name of the abbess (without identifying her) or in the name of the abbey—in other words, these documents are not being issued by the abbess herself. Frey Martín or the prioress (and future abbess) Inés Lainez act in her stead, and donations are addressed to the abbey as a whole, and even more interestingly, to the infantas. In February of 1231 Fernando III confirmed an earlier donation of Alfonso VIII, to "the abbey Santa Maria Regalis and her nuns, [and] _____, her current abbess," leaving a blank space where the abbess's name ought to have appeared.[36] In October 1232 the abbess María Pérez de Guzmán appears, acting consistently in concert with the infantas. She appears infrequently, however—and not at all between May 1236 and September 1238 (and in 1238 only once).[37] Finally in September 1240 the prioress Inés Lainez is first mentioned as abbess. She is a much more consistent presence, although the presence of the infantas and practice of lay brothers representing the abbey continue unabated.

Around 1241 Fernando III's daughter the Infanta Berenguela, aged ten or eleven, entered Las Huelgas. As early as 1245 this princess was making her presence felt in an agreement between one patron, Doña Elvira, and her son Gonzalo Moriel, who addressed the infanta as their "lady," or *señora*.[38] By April of 1246, at the latest, it appears that she had taken the veil.[39] Although the Infanta Berenguela became a nun, she retained her position of authority vis-à-vis the convent and her royal family. The abbesses, first Doña Inés and then, after 1253, Doña Elvira Fernández, acted with her consent, and she retained her own *merino*—a court official who served a king, or in this case the princess, in a judicial capacity, particularly in relation to the estates of that person.[40] After Fernando III's death in 1252, Berenguela's presence was noted by her brother Alfonso X. In a gift of February 1255, for example, he recognized his sister as the "lady and head of the monastery."[41] In the same document we see the original purpose of the abbey bear fruit, the necropolis fulfilling its function (as a reminder of family power) as Alfonso X contended that his gift was intended "to do good and to show mercy to the abbess and to the convent of this same place and for the souls of the very noble and honorable king Don Alfonso, my grandfather, who built the above named monastery, and of his wife the queen Doña Leonor and of the queen Doña Berenguela, my grandmother and of the queen Doña Beatrice my mother, and of the others *of my lineage* who are buried here."[42] In 1255 also Berenguela sealed a charter with her own seal, after that of the abbess Elvira, "so that this deed will be even more firm and more stable, I, the Infanta Doña Berenguela, place my seal on this charter."[43] Although Alfonso X referred to his sister as the head of the abbey, and future papal correspondence was addressed to her as such, as late as 1262 she had not yet become abbess.[44] It is not clear that she ever did so, which raises a very interesting and complicated question that can be applied to all the royal women who entered this abbey: Why would the patrons of the abbey not ensure that a member of their family held the most powerful position in that abbey? I suspect that there is a great deal more work to be done regarding the status and freedom of monastic women with regard to their royal sponsors. Perhaps it was most beneficial for the abbey to have an abbess who would not be connected to the royal family, yet to have on hand a powerful member of the family (such as Constanza or Berenguela) would surely be an asset. Regardless, we see in the Infanta Berenguela's life the height of the development between a type of cogovernance between the abbess and her royal charge.

The Infanta Berenguela's entry into the abbey in 1241 is presumed to have been the decision of her grandmother and namesake, Queen Berenguela of León. Rodríguez assumes that it was around 1244 that Queen Berenguela retired to the abbey. It is not clear whether she actually entered the Cistercian order, but the *Kalendarium vetus* of Las Huelgas, which records her death in November 1246, makes no mention of it, and therefore it would seem that she did not.[45] Even before Berenguela's permanent arrival at the monastery, she was credited with influencing much or most of her family's important donations to and decisions regarding Las Huelgas (including her granddaughter's oblation).[46]

Queen Berenguela herself acted as a representative of the abbey in 1243, perhaps even before her retirement there. In February of that year the noblewoman Mayor Ordóñez requested upon her deathbed that she be buried in the monastery, in return for which she would donate an estate in Cabia and a mule worth fifty *maravedís;* she asked particularly for the "mercy of the queen doña Berenguela." Mayor noted that she was putting "everything in the power of the Queen Doña Berenguela and of the abbess Doña Inés." She also asked that Berenguela assure that all of her debts be paid out of her inheritance (and that her relatives not be allowed to interfere).⁴⁷ Here Berenguela acted in reverse of her sister and granddaughter; they represented the interests of the abbey to the outside world, whereas she represented the interests of Mayor to the abbey. Queen Berenguela here serves not simply as a liaison but truly as a patron, protecting the wishes of a loyal noble and ensuring as a result that the abbey would benefit.

The explicit motivation for the endowment of female institutions such as Fontevrault, Las Huelgas, and later, Blanche's abbeys of Maubuisson and Lys was their dual purpose as both a retreat and final resting place.⁴⁸ This was complicated by the fact that the Cistercians restricted burial within their monasteries. Throughout the twelfth and into the thirteenth century, abbots were reprimanded by the Chapter General for burying secular people by methods contrary to the Cistercian rule.⁴⁹ Not until 1227 did Pope Gregory IX consent that founders of the monasteries and the faithful who wished to be (except excommunicants and usurers) might be interred in Cistercian monasteries.⁵⁰ In the interim, despite this prohibition, Alfonso VIII and Leonor made clear their intention to be buried along with other family members in their Cistercian project. Interestingly, no reprimands regarding secular burial were handed down by the Chapter General to Cistercian abbesses. Given the nuns' ambivalent relationship with the order, this is not particularly surprising, but it may give us another clue to the reasons a female foundation would be attractive to patrons such as Leonor and her daughters.⁵¹ These burial sites, really a type of royal pantheon, were specifically entrusted to the care of women. The practice of women caring for the dead has yet to be fully explored, but I offer it here as evidence to support my thesis that these women were interested in constructing their own power as well as that of their families.⁵²

The royal family of Castile continued to patronize a great many churches, cathedrals and monastic foundations. One other Cistercian monastery stands out, however, as it reflects both physically and philosophically the goals of Berenguela and her family. The male institution of Matallana, founded between 1173 and 1175, became the site of a tremendous building project taken on by Berenguela and her daughter-in-law, Beatrice of Swabia.⁵³

It seems probable that a provisional church was built or the renovation of an old one served the Cistercian monks who were first installed at the monastery of Matallana.⁵⁴ However, not long after her marriage to Fernando, Beatrice of Swabia began the construction of a massive abbey church, possibly at her mother-in-law's prompting.⁵⁵ The new church at Matallana, built between 1224 and 1234, followed the plan of that of Las Huelgas, with the exception of massive pillars needed to support the much larger building.[56] It seems very likely that Beatrice (and Berenguela, who continued the project when her daughter-in-law died) can be credited with the choice of Las Huelgas as a model for the new church, which not only reflected the physical plan of Las Huelgas but was also established to house the remains of the royal family.[57] Although Las Huelgas continued as the institution of choice in this regard, it is believed that members of the family of Alfonso de Molina (Berenguela's second son) were buried at Matallana. The tombs that remain belong to the Meneses family, the family of Alfonso's third wife, Mayor Alfonso de Meneses, and appear to date from the end of the thirteenth century. Certainly the nature of Las Huelgas as a royal pantheon influenced the construction of sepulchres there.[58] The lack of physical remains prevents further speculation concerning the royal agenda for this abbey.

Although considered to be of French Gothic provenance, the architectural histories of Las Huelgas and Matallana are not related to those of the foundations of Blanche of Castile, other than in terms of a general disregard for Cistercian prohibitions against grandeur, layered upon a Cistercian Gothic plan. It is possible to argue that the French royal tradition of burying their dead at Saint Denis influenced Blanche more than her Castilian heritage in her establishment of two female Cistercian abbeys, Notre-Dame la Royale (known as Maubuisson) and Notre-Dame du Lys, which were intended as familial burial places. However, given the existence of Saint Denis, well established for the same purpose as Las Huelgas, it is interesting that Blanche set out to establish her own personal version of a legacy of family power which, more than any other establishment in France, reflects her personal heritage originating in Fontevrault and Las Huelgas.

The abbey of Maubuisson was begun around the year 1236—at least part of the buildings were finished by 1241, when Blanche established a charter for the monastery, in which she declared that it had been founded as an abbey for female Cistercians, in memory of her father and mother and husband (Louis VIII)—and that it was to be called Notre-Dame la Royale.[59] The church was completed and dedicated 26 June 1244 by the bishop of Paris and submitted to the order general in September 1244. The first abbess, Guillemette, was selected from another royal foundation, Saint Antoine of Paris. The second abbess was Blanche de Brienne, Blanche's great-niece and a granddaughter of Berenguela; thereafter, most abbesses were of noble, old families.

Using Maubuisson, art historian Terryl Kinder argues that Blanche "played a role in determining the architectural style of the buildings with which she was closely affiliated."[60] Regarding Blanche's choice of the Cistercian order, along with the order's severe architectural style, she says "the austere Cistercian spirituality seems to have coincided with (or perhaps helped to form?) her strong sense of ethics, for Blanche's subsequent patronage and involvement with the Order reflect more than pious convention."[61] I argue for a different basis for those ethics. It is tempting, but really too difficult, to assess much about Blanche's character or particular spiritual disposition from these foundations. Rather, it seems that the same motivations that applied to her parents' construction of Las Huelgas might apply in Blanche's case, perhaps in an even more powerful way: a generation later, Blanche continued to assert her power as a patron of female Cistercians, particularly through the establishment of royal burial sites, which proclaim that power to posterity. After the dedication of the church in 1244, Blanche asked the Cistercian order to protect Maubuisson and regard it as a daughter abbey, as Alfonso VIII and Leonor had done with Las Huelgas.[62]

Blanche chose, at the end of her life, to adopt the Cistercian habit and to be buried at Maubuisson.[63] The abbey became a royal necropolis as more members of the royal family were buried there over time, including Jean de Brienne (Berenguela of León's grandson), the entrails of Blanche's son Alphonse of Poitiers, and other family members and grandchildren of Louis (including the entrails of Charles le Bel and Jeanne d'Evreux in 1370).[64]

The circumstances surrounding the foundation of Notre-Dame du Lys are more obscure. There is evidence that the abbey existed (at least in some form) by 1244, but typically the foundation charter is dated a few years later, in June of 1248, and comes directly from Louis IX, without mention of Blanche.[65] However, one month later Louis gave a right of use to the abbey. In this document Louis attributes the construction of the abbey to Blanche; in contemporary documents and chronicles, one or the other or both are variously given credit for the foundation of the monastery. Gronier-Prieur, who has done the most careful research regarding this foundation, feels that Louis should be credited with putting up the finances for construction of the abbey, but that it was Blanche's inspiration. After the construction of Maubuisson, it seems that Blanche could not afford another major foundation.[66] Lys was located near Melun, which had been traditionally a domain of dowager queens and had served as a favorite royal residence. Being within the royal domain, the abbey received special privileges and liberties pertaining to the Cistercians, which limited the power of the local archbishop (of Sens) over it.[67]

While Blanche did not choose Lys as the site of her final retreat and resting place, she did not neglect the abbey in the matter of a personal legacy. At the consecration of the abbey church of Lys in 1253, her heart was enshrined in an elaborate tomb at Notre-Dame du Lys.[68] This endowment established Lys as well as Maubuisson as a center for the articulation of personal piety and authority for future members of the royal family, who continued to use the abbey as a center for prayer and burial.[69] Blanche's burial at both places emphasizes their special importance to her—and reiterates to us the significance of caring for the dead to these women.

All of these monasteries expressed a particular relationship of the queens to the church and to their families. Different acts of patronage, however, offer different versions of family and female authority. Berenguela and Blanche patronized the Cistercian order particularly as acts of filial devotion and in an effort to establish and reinforce the continuity of their families' authority and power. Because religious patronage was integral to the image of a powerful, influential ruler as an expression of wealth, Christian legitimacy, and control, patronage of the Cistercian order seems completely ordinary. However, Berenguela and Blanche's continued patronage of this particularly masculine order seems to represent a clear expression of female domination or control in a male arena. In Christian Spain, Cistercians were indispensable in the rehabilitation of lands and communities across depopulated territory, but foundations like Las Huelgas (although possessed of powerful seigneuries) hardly contribute to the practical efforts of the Cistercian monks in the reaffirmation of Christian society at large. They do, however, contribute to the reaffirmation of these women's royal authority. In this regard the use of female monastic foundations as burial places and family retreats is an extremely important and deliberate element. Berenguela's and Blanche's special patronage of women in an order resistant to them does not indicate any feminist sensibilities on their part, but rather an effort to identify themselves with the power of the order, as well as their personal ability to control their endowments. Ultimately, these expressions of power were directed at their own families, their noble cohort, and the institutions of the church.

Other forms of patronage, however, expressed different versions of Berenguela's and Blanche's power, and to different audiences, although often with the same goal of establishing the power and authority of family and self. Blanche and Berenguela further explored the potential of their own patronage through their involvement with the thirteenth-century constructions of the cathedrals of Burgos and Toledo and reconstruction of the cathedral of León in Spain and of Chartres in France.[70] Cathedrals served as a different kind of forum for these women to express their power: they were open to all members of society, and their very size, as well as their windows, portals, tympana, and liturgical treasures provided countless lessons to all who passed by.

The Gothic reconstruction of the cathedral of León was begun during the reign of Alfonso IX of León, Berenguela's husband, probably at about the same time of their marriage (1198–1204), and continued throughout the reign of Fernando III and his son, Alfonso X. Berenguela's known interest in the rebuilding of the city walls and the construction of a royal palace[71] suggest that it was Berenguela, and not her husband, who sponsored this work on the cathedral.[72] The Gothic campaigns of the Cathedrals of Burgos and Toledo, begun in 1222 and 1226 respectively, were certain to come under the watchful eye of Queen Berenguela, whose son Fernando, though a primary patron of these buildings, was often absent throughout their construction.[73] The family's special relationship to the Cathedral of Toledo (which was also the seat of the primate of Spain) was emphasized by a gift of the archbishop of Toledo, Rodrigo Ximénez de Rada, who endowed fifteen chapels, one in particular for "the lord king Fernando and his mother doña Berenguela."[74] Although it seems fairly normal that the archbishop would remember his most important patron, the king, the fact that he includes the king's mother in this gift stresses her importance to the archbishop and the cathedral, as well as to the kingdom at large.

We can be a great deal more specific about Blanche of Castile's involvement with the thirteenth-century reconstruction of Notre-Dame de Chartres. The French royal family had sponsored much of the rebuilding of the cathedral after the ruinous fire of 1195, and so the immense rebuilding project was a part of Blanche's life from the time of her marriage to Prince Louis in 1200. An early donation to the cathedral attributed to Blanche is a simple grisaille window dedicated to the Virgin, located in the central apsidal chapel. After she assumed the regency for her son Louis IX, the height of her power is reflected in the glass of some of the most famous windows in France—the north transept window cycle. The political significance of these windows to Blanche's power will be discussed below.

Nearly all of these projects were dedicated to the Virgin Mary, reflecting the temper of the times, as well as a predilection for the Cistercians.[75] However, for Berenguela and Blanche personally, patronage of such projects also indicates an appropriation of Mary's patronage that any royal mother might desire. They take Mary, a queenly mother, as their patron and thus imply that they are like her. It is Mary's *queenly* status that is associated with these women and their endowments. The official name of Maubuisson, for example, was Notre-Dame la Royale. The official name of Las Huelgas was Santa Maria Regalis: essentially the same name; certainly the same patron, Mary the Royal Queen of Heaven. Blanche and Berenguela's identification with the Blessed Virgin Mary was part of their iconographic and ideological environment and culture, but they chose to exploit this association, and to do so *politically*. The way in which these women used the iconography of the Virgin Mary to support their own positions is particular to their use of authority. Out of what may become countless examples of the use of Marian iconography in women's artistic patronage, let me offer two: one, the tomb of Berenguela at the monastery of Las Huelgas, and the other, Blanche's windows at the Cathedral of Chartres.

Berenguela of León apparently left clear instructions that her tomb, unlike those of her siblings and parents, was to be plain, without adornment. It is accepted by historians such as Florez and Rodríguez that Berenguela's testament specified that her sepulcher be plain and humble.[76] In fact, two contemporary tombs at the monastery of Las Huelgas have been attributed to Berenguela. One is completely plain, bereft even of paint; the other is adorned with elaborately carved scenes from the life of the Virgin, culminating in the coronation of the Virgin in heaven by her son, Jesus.[77] This coronation provides a nice reversal of the actual abdication on Berenguela's part to her son, Fernando: an abdication that in fact gave her as much power as if she had herself been crowned by him.[78] The explanation for the two tombs is this: Berenguela's namesake granddaughter (the nun Berenguela) apparently commissioned an elaborate tomb for her grandmother, presumably the one into which Queen Berenguela's remains were translated in 1251. This infanta furthermore petitioned Pope Innocent IV for an indulgence for all those who assisted with the translation ceremony, which he granted.[79] Upon the infanta's death in 1288 or 1289, however, the nuns of Las Huelgas, deciding to respect the wishes of the queen, reburied her and then entombed the younger Berenguela in the decorated sepulcher. There is no (discovered) written evidence that can corroborate which tomb actually contained which woman: furthermore, evidence of polychromy on other uncarved tombs suggests that the original tomb may not have been plain either.[80]

I am interested here in the way in which the images on the carved tomb were intended to evoke the memory of Queen Berenguela: she is clearly associated in the mind of her granddaughter with the Virgin, particularly with Mary in her role as royal mother. The power of family and Marian devotion expresses itself in the sculptural program on Berenguela's sepulcher in Las Huelgas. Although Berenguela herself did not commission this work, the image of the Queen of Heaven receiving her rightful crown, commissioned by Berenguela's granddaughter, surely reinforces as well as historicizes the legitimacy of Berenguela's claims to and use of power.

We see a similar use of religious, royal, and familial iconography when we examine Blanche's windows at the Cathedral of Notre-Dame de Chartres. Here Blanche announces her authority with no trace of Cistercian reticence. The windows that she endowed are magnificently rich in color, size, and symbolism, and reflect the culmination of Blanche's own power and authority. The rose window in the north transept (built around 1230) depicts the Virgin enthroned with her son, surrounded by various prophets and the emblems of Blanche's power: the fleur-de-lys of France and the castles of Castile (which stress both her associations with her powerful natal family and her role as queen of France). Beneath the window rise up lancets, containing Saint Anne with Mary and Old Testament kings (secular authority) and prophets (sacred legitimacy). The authority of the royal mother radiating over the north transept is echoed in the lancet showing Saint Anne, the mother of Mary. The motif of maternal authority stands in sharp contrast with the Christ of the south-transept rose window, emphasizing the male authority of the enthroned. The window had been endowed a decade earlier by none other than Blanche's rival the comte de Dreux, Pierre Mauclerc.[81]

Blanche's window can be seen as a response to Mauclerc. They used the cathedral as an arena in which to continue their battle begun over the regency of France in 1226, and their glorious donations as explicit exhibitions of their power. Blanche sought religious justification for her secular authority and power through her donations to the beautiful building and through identification of herself with the Royal Mother of Heaven. She reaffirmed her secular, worldly power as well, not only for her contemporaries but also to remind the future of the strength of her family. Clearly, she saw herself, through her association with Mary and her patronage of these windows, as a source of power and authority for French royalty.[82]

Blanche and Berenguela's patronage of religious institutions, inasmuch as those institutions served to articulate personal power and family authority and stability, can be seen as part of a larger development wherein we observe the process of state building (establishing the authority of the monarchy) working against the pressures of feudal fracturing. Further examination of the purpose of women's patronage within the dynamic of the struggle for power in the broader political arena may lead us to a new, more subtle understanding of the evolution of the thirteenth-century model of government. Berenguela's patronage of the Cistercian-based military orders such as Calatrava and Uclés gave her direct involvement in enabling the Christian conquest of Iberia, which was in part an effort to establish Spanish royal identity. Her commission of Lucas de Túy's *Crónica de España* gives us a beautiful example of yet another type of patronage and its relationship to the growth of the monarchy.

Lucas tells us that the "very wise and very glorious queen of 'Las Españas,' doña Berenguela . . . commanded me to write these books . . . concerning the history of the Spanish kings."[83] The written histories of thirteenth-century Spain were part of a grand effort of the kings and their clerical supporters to historicize and authenticate their power.[84] Berenguela's appropriation of this mode should be seen as an effort on her part to "set the record straight"—as well as to assert her own authority to do so.

Through this varied patronage we see women such as Eleanor of Aquitaine, Leonor of England, Berenguela, and Blanche asserting for themselves a certain amount of power and authority. They instructed their sons and daughters as well as their grandchildren in the discourses of power, gender, authority, and piety. Their patronage of monastic institutions reveals their family's influence on their religious preferences, but also the role that women such as Blanche and Berenguela played in their families in terms of their attention to their lineage through the care of the dead. Furthermore, these women clearly saw themselves as important elements in that lineage and strove to represent their importance to the world through the visual and physical results of their patronage, calling attention to their royal motherhood, explicitly in association with the Virgin Mary. Finally, and most important, their patronage of the regular and secular church, and of the writing of history, reveals their strategies for ensuring the power of their families and the foundation of hereditary monarchy.

NOTES

1. The essays in Mary Erler and Maryanne Kowaleski, eds. *Women and Power in the Middle Ages* (Athens: University of Georgia Press, 1988), discuss how women succeeded in garnering power for themselves in a variety of ways. The editors' introduction provides a particularly helpful discussion of the distinctions between power and authority.

2. In her study of the patronage of the abbey La Trinité in the Vendôme, France, Penelope Johnson suggests that Agnes of Burgundy's personal patronage of La Trinité reflects the type of power available to her, as opposed to her husband's (Geoffrey Martel, count of Anjou) official patronage, but that nonetheless, such patronage was a way of demonstrating her power, even within the marriage itself. See Penelope D. Johnson, *Prayer, Patronage, and Power: The Abbey of La Trinité, Vendôme, 1032–1187* (New York: New York University Press, 1981), especially 11–13.

3. For more on the relationships between the mothers and daughters of this family (including some discussion of their patronage), see John Carmi Parsons, "Mothers,

Daughters, Marriage, and Power: Some Plantagenet Evidence, 1150–1500," in *Medieval Queenship*, ed. John Carmi Parsons (New York: St. Martin's, 1993), 63–78.

4. This eleventh- and twelfth-century movement has been identified by historian Gabrielle Spiegel. Spiegel's remarks concerning the grounding of history in biology are particularly important here—human procreation, mapped out by genealogy, becomes an agent of historical change. A genealogy also articulates a specific place in the political world for the family described by it. See Gabrielle M. Spiegel, "Genealogy: Form and Function in Medieval Historical Narrative," *History and Theory* 22 (1983): 43–53; and "History, Historicism, and the Social Logic of the Text," *Speculum* 65 (1990): 59–86. My dissertation, "Motherhood, Lineage, and Royal Power in Medieval Castile and France: Berenguela of León (1180–1246) and Blanche of Castile (1188–1252)" (Ph.D. diss., Duke University, 1994), examines the variety of ways in which medieval royal mothers worked to affirm their dynasties and their own powerful positions within those dynasties.

5. Elizabeth A. R. Brown, "Eleanor of Aquitaine: Parent, Queen, and Duchess," in *Eleanor of Aquitaine: Patron and Politician*, ed. William W. Kibler (Austin: University of Texas Press, 1976).

6. Eleanor of Aquitaine's relationship with her husband, Henry II, was fraught with jealousy and competition—it may have been a personal coup for her to outlive her husband and see him buried in her favorite establishment. Her daughter Leonor of England seems to have had a very happy, stable relationship with her husband, Alfonso VIII of Castile; nonetheless her patronage looks both backward to her mother's activity and forward to that of her children. Berenguela's marriage to Alfonso IX of León was short-lived (1198–1204) and seems not to have served as inspiration for her patronage. Although Blanche of Castile was happily married to Louis VIII of France for twenty-six years, her major acts of patronage all occurred after his death and, like her mother's, looked backward to her natal family and forward to her children's futures for their inspiration.

7. Amy Kelly, *Eleanor of Aquitaine and the Four Kings*, (Cambridge, Mass.: Harvard University Press, 1958), 328.

8. On 30 June 1190, for example, Alfonso and Leonor conceded an annual rent of one hundred *aureos* from Magán (near Toledo) to Fontevrault, for the soul of Henry II Plantagenet. Julio Gonzalez, *El reino de Castilla en la epoca de Alfonso VIII: Documentos* (Madrid: Escuela de estudios medievales, 1960), v.3, no. 551 (hereafter *Documentos*).

9. The construction of the abbey continued through the thirteenth century, but negotiations regarding the foundation of the abbey had commenced at the latest by 1187, when the actual foundation charter is dated. See below, in text. Both the historian-archbishop Rodrigo Ximénez de Rada and Alfonso X (the Wise) assert that it was at Leonor's insistence that she and her husband began Las Huelgas. Rodrigo Ximénez de Rada, *Historia de rebus hispanie*, ed. Juan Fernández Valverde (Turnholti: Brepols, 1987), libro 8, cap. 33. Alfonso X, *Primera crónica general de España*, ed. Ramón Menéndez-Pidal (Madrid: Gredos, 1955), cap. 1006.

10. The historians Lizoain and García argue that Alfonso was interested in the expansion of the Cistercian order and that their "guaranteed piety"—as opposed to the dubious spiritual efficacy of wealthy, independent Cluniacs (whom Alfonso and Leonor also patronized, to be sure)—was appropriate to the establishment of a pantheon. Throughout his life Alfonso patronized a variety of male Cistercian monasteries, and actually turned over at least five previously Benedictine monasteries to be reformed by the Cistercians. In 1175 Valbení was turned over to the Cistercian order, followed by Valbuena in 1176, San Cebrían de Montes de Oca in 1189, Ovila in 1191, and Gumiel in 1194 (*Documentos*, v. 2, no. 236; v. 3, nos. 531, 572, and 628, and p. 813). The Cistercian monasteries of Sacramenia, Herrera, Bonaval, Matallana, Bujedo, and Monsalud also received his attention. See also Vicente Angel Alvarez Palenzuela, *Monasterios cistercienses en Castilla, siglos XII–XIII* (Valladolid: Universidad de Valladolid, 1975) esp. chap. 3, "La fundacion de monasterios cistercienses en Castilla." In regard to the establishment of Las Huelgas as a female house, Lizoain and García take an even more pragmatic—and thoroughly unexamined—view; Las Huelgas was founded for women as a place to protect unmarried daughters, to provide a quiet haven from the bustling, sometimes uncomfortable life of the itinerant court, as well as to enable female vocation. José Manuel Lizoain Garrido and Juan José García, *El monasterio de las Huelgas: Historia de un señorio cisterciense burgales, siglos XII y XIII* (Burgos: Garrido Garrido, 1988), 15–16.

11. See Sally Thompson, "The Problem of the Cistercian Nuns in the Twelfth and Early Thirteenth Centuries," in *Medieval Women: Essays Presented to Rosalind M. T. Hill on the Occasion of Her Seventieth Birthday*, ed. Derek Baker, Studies in Church History, Subsidia 1 (Oxford, Eng.: Blackwell for the Ecclesiastical History Society, 1978), 227–52; and Simone Roisin, "L'efflorescence cistercienne et le courant féminin de piété au XIIIe siècle," *Revue d'histoire ecclésiastique* 39 (1943): 342–78.

12. In 1184 Pope Lucius III imposed stricter enclosure for Cistercian nuns, which caused a greater problem for the men of the order, because they were then burdened with any business the nuns might carry out in the world at large. Louis J. Lekai, *The Cistercians: Ideals and Reality* (Kent, Ohio: Kent State University Press, 1977), 351. Nevertheless, it seems as if the nuns generally disregarded this imposition, for in 1213 the Chapter General itself declared that all nuns should be cloistered. *Statuta capitulorum generalium ordinis cisterciensis*, ed. D. Josephus-Maria Canivez (Louvain: Bureau de la Revue, 1933–41), 1213, cap. 3 (hereafter *Statuta*). This was followed in 1220 by a resolution prohibiting the further incorporation of convents (this resolution was repeated in 1225 and 1228, suggesting its ineffectiveness; *Statuta* 1220, cap. 4; 1225, cap. 7; 1228, cap 16).

13. In 1222 the order appealed to the pope not to interfere in these matters (*Statuta* 1222, cap. 30). Not until 1251 did Innocent IV allow that the Cistercian order could ignore future papal briefs concerning the incorporation of women into the order, but by this date the presence of women in the order was well established. Lekai, *The Cistercians*, 349–52.

14. *Statuta* 1228, cap. 16.

15. *Documentos*, no. 472, 1 June 1187 Burgos. "Inter cetera monasteria que ad honorem Dei et obsequium edificantur, magnum meritum obtinet apud Deum monasterium dicatis feminis constructum." See also *Documentación del Monasterio de Las Huelgas (1116–1230)*, ed. José Manuel Lizoain Garrido, Fuentes Medievales Castellano-Leonesas, vol. 30, no. 11 (Burgos: Garrido Garrido, 1985) (hereafter *Documentación*).

16. Rule 2 of Fontevrault, cited by Penny Shine Gold, *The Lady and the Virgin: Image, Attitude, and Experience in Twelfth-Century France* (Chicago: University of Chicago Press, 1985), 99.

17. Ibid., 112–13.

18. See for example, S. Thompson, "Problem of the Cistercian Nuns," 238; Margaret Wade Labarge cites the proverb that if the pope could marry, the only woman eligible would be the abbess of Las Huelgas (*A Small Sound of the Trumpet: Women in Medieval Life* [Boston: Beacon, 1986], 33, 107). On the historiography of Las Huelgas, Lizoain and García note: "Idénticos razos incorporan las crónicas históricas de carácter general y particular que se realizaron con posteriordad, en especial durante todo el siglo XVII y la primera mitad del XVIII, cuya única novedad venía representada por la sistemática alusión a la jurisdicción eclesiástica de la abadesa." Lizoain and García, *El Monasterio de Las Huelgas*, 26, and introduction.

19. Research thus far has not revealed any direct evidence of the abbesses' carrying on so boldly.

20. Lekai, *The Cistercians*, 65–70.

21. *Documentación*, no. 21.

22. Amancio Rodríguez López, *El Real Monasterio de las Huelgas y el Hospital del Rey* (Burgos: Centro Católico, 1907), 1:41. Rodríguez takes it for granted that the abbess did in fact cross sacramental boundaries.

23. *Documentación*, no. 22. The bull asserts that the abbey owes nothing to the bishops except "the obedience which is owed"—that it is entitled to all of the privileges of its order and that especially no bishop may interfere with the election of the abbess.

24. Rodríguez López, *El Real Monasterio*, 43–44.

25. *Documentación*, nos. 13, 16. This new status met with some resistance on the part of abbeys that already owed other allegiances, or were older and more established than the upstart royal project, but after a second appeal on the part of Alfonso VIII to the Chapter General of 1188, there was general acquiescence. *Documentación*, no. 19. This status is not discussed in the foundation charter, although clearly the issue was presented to the Chapter General in the same year. I doubt that Leonor and Alfonso could have mandated such status in their original "gift" to the Cistercian order.

26. Rodríguez López, *El Real Monasterio*, 69.

27. *Documentación*, no. 104. "Nova quedam sunt auribus intimata, quod abbatisse, videlicet, in Burgensi et Palentina diocesibus constitute moniales proprias benedicunt, ipsarumque confessiones in criminibus audiunt, et legentes evangelium presumunt

publice predicare." Although the pope's letter suggests other abbesses besides that of Las Huelgas acting in this way, historians generally attribute this problem to Las Huelgas alone. Thus far I have found one other instance of papal censure of abbesses appropriating priestly prerogative, when in 1241 a Cistercian abbess in León was accused of veiling nuns (and in the presence of King Fernando and Queen Berenguela!): "Praeclarissimo religiosi viri sanctissimi de se demisse sentientis facinori arrogantissimae monialis insanam temeritatem, quae velandarum virginum auctoritatem, episcopi adscriptam sacris canonibus, muliebri superbia arrogavit, subjicere visum est, cum ad posteritatis documentum usus esse posuit." *Annales eccleasistici*, ed. Augustino Theiner (Vatican City, 1870), vol. 21, 1241, cap. 56.

28. Rodríguez López, *El Real Monasterio*, 186.

29. Such exemptions were not "givens" for female foundations, whose institutional relationship to the order was uncertain. See P. Gold, *The Lady and the Virgin*, 86.

30. As they did most Cistercian foundations? Alfonso and Leonor's 1203 gift to the monastery of Herrera is addressed to the Cistercian abbot Arnaldo and suggests that the Cistercian order should be freed from all tributes normally paid by all monasteries in the realm. "Facio cartam donacionis . . . et vobis domino Arnauldo, eiusdem instanti abbati, vestrisque successoribus, *et omnibus monachis ibidem sub regula Cisterciensis ordinis* Deo servientibus, presentibus et futuris perhenniter duraturam" (*Documentos*, no. 740; emphasis added).

31. S. Thompson suggests that Alfonso be credited for influencing the broader incorporation of women into the Cistercian order because of Las Huelgas ("Problem of the Cistercian Nuns," 237).

32. The fact that the abbess was not a royal woman is curious and needs to be considered as a by-product of the complexity of patronage. Initially, of course, the founders needed experienced nuns to run their abbey. Initially, as well, the founders needed to choose women who would be acceptable to the order they wished to patronize, and were perhaps limited in the choice of any relatives who might be appropriate. However, this poses a problem, as royal women such as Leonor disburse power to other women who are not members of the family or lineage they seek to exalt. This seeming inconsistency might be explained by a closer examination of the relationship between the abbess and her patron. Such a choice may reflect the limits of the abbess's power, perhaps set by the patron, who also thus defines her own power.

33. *Documentación*, no. 252.

34. Thus, Berenguela and Blanche had two sisters and one daughter (Blanche's niece) in residence at the abbey throughout the 1230s and 1240s. Documents from December 1222 mention Don Fernando, chaplain of the infantas, acting for the abbess of Las Huelgas (*Documentación*, nos. 180, 181, 182). In April 1227 a donation to Las Huelgas is recorded as being given to "the monastery of Las Huelgas of Burgos, and to the infantas, and to the abbess" (*Documentación*, no. 208). In 1229 the abbess Sancha acted "with the infantas and with all our convent" (*Documentación*, no. 235).

35. Rodríguez López, *El Real Monasterio*, 131–32; also *Documentación*, no. 269. Rodríguez also discusses bulls of Pope Gregory IX directed at the abbess of Las Huelgas without actually naming her: see *Documentación*, nos. 280, 281, 282, and 284.

36. *Documentación*, no. 260.

37. Ibid., no. 310.

38. Ibid., no. 354.

39. Ibid., nos. 365, 366, and 367; Innocent IV refers to Berenguela as having "assumed the clothes of religion."

40. Ibid., no. 418.

41. Ibid., no. 480. The exact phrase is "sennora e mayor del monasterio."

42. Ibid., no. 480; emphasis added.

43. Ibid., no. 482. Also, on 27 November 1257 the infanta took steps to ensure the integrity of Las Huelgas as an elite and viable institution, in order "to honor her grandparents who established the monastery and chose to be buried there, and to honor all the kings and queens and others of their lineage who are buried there." She established that there should always be in residence one hundred nuns of noble origin; forty girls, also of noble origin, who might grow up to be nuns in the convent; and forty lay women, to serve the nuns. (Ibid., no. 501.)

44. A privilege of Pope Alexander IV to the nuns of Las Huelgas allowing them to use special outerwear (although this was contrary to the Rule of Saint Benedict) was addressed to Berenguela and refers to the convent as "hers," at the same time acknowledging the presence of an abbess (without naming her). 6 August 1259, Ibid., no. 509. Unfortunately, the publication of documents relevant to Las Huelgas has been completed only up until the year 1262, at which time we see Berenguela still acting in concert with the abbess, at this date a Doña Eva. At the end of her life, the infanta may have become abbess of Las Huelgas (as some historians have assumed). Her brother's *Primera crónica* says simply that she entered the convent as a virgin and was consecrated to God by her parents (cap. 1036).

45. "VI Idus Novembris obiit Novilisima et Venerabilis Berengaria, Regina Castellae et Leonis, filia Aldefonsi, illustrisimi Regis Castellae, Era MCCLXXXIV, Kalendarium vetus Burgense," cited in Rodríguez López, *El Real Monasterio*, 140.

46. Rodríguez López cites her eulogy in the *Primera crónica* in this regard, but his reference is to a general discussion of her influence and importance, and not in regard to Las Huelgas specifically (Alfonso X, *Primera crónica*, cap. 1073). Rodríguez López, *El Real Monasterio*, 140–41.

47. *Documentación*, no. 337. 26 February 1243.

48. Were they family or female retreats? The name of Las Huelgas may suggest a family home: *huelga* coming from *holgar*, meaning "hearth." The royal family spent a great deal of time in Burgos, but the problem of cloistered nuns would indicate that only female members of the family, if any, actually resided on the convent premises when they came to town. Later, in the fourteenth century, a tower was constructed at the convent for use as a residence for the entire royal family.

49. As late as 1222, the chapter noted once again that "the old customs would be observed concerning the burial of founders" (*Statuta*, cap. 9). This allowed the burial of founders only, prohibiting the burial of nonreligious people in the monastery—such as children, other relatives, or even other patrons. See *Statuta* 1157, cap. 63.

50. *Documentación*, no. 215.

51. At any rate, an architectural solution to this prohibition was found: raised tombs were used. These aboveground sepulchres, removed from contact with hallowed ground by stone pedestals carved as lions, met the letter of the law. María Jesus Gomez Barcena, *Escultura gótica funeraria en Burgos* ([Burgos]: Diputacíon provincial de Burgos, 1988), 194.

52. This is admittedly problematic: obviously great male institutions (such as the abbey of Saint Denis in France) were established as necropolises. The foundations under discussion here were intended to house the remains of all members of the family, male and female, but the question of why they were given to the care of women persists—the patrons' insistence upon female foundations cannot be divorced from their intention to use the institutions as necropolises.

53. There had been a Benedictine monastery at that site since the late tenth century. On 10 November 1173 Alfonso VIII made a gift to Tello Perez and his wife, Gontrada, of an estate which had previously belonged to the Hospital of Jerusalem (*Documentos*, no. 190). In December of 1175 Alfonso confirmed Tello and Gontrada's gift of the same property (Matallana) to the Cistercian order (*Documentos*, no. 240).

54. Francisco Antón y Casaseca, *Monasterios medievales de la provincia de Valladolid* (Valladolid: Librería Santarén, 1942), 173.

55. A 1255 privilege of Alfonso X confirming earlier privileges to the monastery mentions Beatrice as the main patron of the abbey church. Luis Fernández Martín, "Colección diplomatica del monasterio de Santa María de Matallana." *Hispania sacra* 25 (1972): 412. A Cistercian statute from the Chapter General of 1217 indicates an early interest that Berenguela took in this monastery, when she obtained an excuse for the abbot regarding attendance at the Chapter General (*Statuta* 1217, cap. 33). With the construction of the abbey church we see Beatrice quickly incorporated into the patronage projects of her *marital* family—by her mother-in-law, who continued thus to promote the interests of her *natal* family and personal lineage. This is further evidence of Berenguela's influence—in fact it is her son (Alfonso de Molina) and his family who are buried at Matallana. Beatrice herself was buried at Las Huelgas, until Alfonso X had his mother's remains translated to Seville.

56. Antón y Casaseca, *Monasterios medievales*, 172; the abbey church became a ruin in 1848, due to weak walls, insufficiently buttressed for their size. Fernández Martín, "Colección diplomatica," 385. Fernández cites the seventeenth-century scholar Angel Manrique, who wrote of the then extant abbey that "there is no church more elegant and sumptuous in Castile. Certainly it is among the most important in Spain, inferior to none, with the exception of a few cathedrals" ("Colección diplomatica," 393).

57. Chueca Goitia dates the construction of the church at Las Huelgas between the

years 1225 and 1250, along with the chapter hall and the cloister (Fernando Chueca Goitia, *Historia de la arquitectura española: Edad antigua y edad media* (Madrid: Dossat, 1965), 321. There seems to be a consensus among historians regarding these dates, but it makes the question of influence upon Matallana problematic, as the construction of the two churches conceivably took place at the same time. One might assume that the plan for Las Huelgas was well in place by the time construction actually began.

A commemorative stone originally set above a door in the church states "Anno Millesimo Ducentesimo Vigesimoctavo Regina Beatrix Bonae Memoriae Coepit Aedificare Ecclesiam Hanc, et Obiit Aera Millesima Ducentesima Septuagesima Tertia, Et Ex Tunc Regina Berengaria Coepit Ecclesiam Fabricare. Abbas Aegidius" (cited in Antón y Casaseca, *Monasterios medievales*, 172).

58. By the time of the construction of Matallana's abbey church, Cistercian restrictions had become artistic custom: the tombs at Matallana were also freestanding, aboveground, and resting on lions. Unlike the tombs at Las Huelgas (but similar to those at the Cathedral of Burgos), carved figures of the deceased decorate the tops of these sepulchres. Antón y Casaseca, *Monasterios medievales*, 193.

59. *Gallia Christiana* (Paris, 1744), "Instrumenta," in vol. 7, no. 138. In 1237 Blanche had petitioned the Cistercian Chapter General for permission to bring nuns to an abbey that she had begun to build; this was certainly Maubuisson (*Statuta* 1237, cap. 27). See also Jean LeBeuf, *Histoire de la ville de tout le diocèse de Paris* (Paris: Féchoz et Letouzey, 1883–93), 118.

60. Terryl N. Kinder, "Blanche of Castile and the Cistercians," *Commentarii Cistercienses* 27, nos. 3 and 4 (1976): 161. Kinder argues that Maubuisson followed a more traditionally Cistercian architectural plan than was usual for female institutions. She connects this to Blanche's commitment to the principles of the order and her relationship to its "highest authorities" (183).

61. Ibid., 162. In 1222, before the statute against women entering the order was enacted, Blanche had been associated in prayers with the order. *Layettes du trésor des Chartes*, ed. Alexandre Teulet (Paris, 1863–1909).

62. Kinder, "Blanche of Castile," 167.

63. Matthew Paris noted Blanche's death in his *English History*, trans. J. A. Giles (London: Bohn, 1852–54): "Seeing that death was near at hand, she left orders for her body to be buried at a nunnery at Pontoise, which she had founded and built in great magnificence; indeed, prior to her death she became a professed nun, and took the veil, over which was placed the crown, and she also wore the robes of a queen, and in this manner dressed she was buried becomingly." (3:7) The Cistercian Chapter General of 1253 also noted her passing and established an anniversary to be celebrated for her (*Statuta*, 1253, cap. 6). See also LeBeuf, *Histoire*, 120.

64. LeBeuf, *Histoire*, 120–21. After the French Revolution, Blanche's tomb was moved to Saint-Denis, where it is evidently in the north transept. Kinder, "Blanche of Castile," 167, n. 28.

65. Armande Gronier-Prieur, *L'abbaye Notre Dame du Lys à Dammarie-les-Lys*

(Verneuil-l'Etang, France: Amis des monuments et des sites de Seine-et-Marne, 1971), 21. Gronier-Prieur's work, published by the Monuments historiques de Seine-et-Marne after her death, does not include the original notes and citations, although many documents are cited in the text. The original manuscript with the notes and archival references may be consulted at the Departmental Archives of Seine-et-Marne.

66. Ibid., 21–23. The first abbess of Lys, Alix de Vienne, came from Maubuisson.

67. Ibid., 55.

68. The tomb of Blanche's heart was described by Sébastien Rouilliard in the seventeenth century: "Ce coeur est soubs une tombe de marbre soutenue de quatre piliers: et au-dessus est la statue de cette Royne très illustre" (cited by Gronier-Prieur, L'abbaye Notre-Dame, 147).

69. Ibid., 25. The division of Blanche's body between her two favorite foundations adds a new dimension to the problem of these patrons' attempts to affirm their lineage and family future, since it would seem to signify a kind of fracturing of the source of that lineage (the mother herself). However, the patron's purpose behind foundation is reiterated by this act of disarticulation—the emphasis becomes on the roles of the nuns themselves in caring for the dead—and the patron's love for a particular convent. That this was effective as part of a greater program to establish lineage is borne out by future generations' continued use of both Maubuisson and Lys for the same purpose.

70. The discussion that follows represents an initial exploration of how such activity is an important dimension of women's patronage, but in-depth research awaits before specific conclusions can be drawn.

71. The putative remains of which lie just down the street from the cathedral, in the playground of the Colegio de Santa Teresa. Clearly such secular construction would be an expression of power and would fall under the rubric of patronage.

72. Lucas de Túy, Crónica de España, ed. Julio Puyol y Alonso (Madrid: Tipografía de la "Revista de archivos, bibliotécas y museos," 1926); "Queen Berenguela built a royal palace from stone and lime in León near the monastery of St. Isidore, and she likewise restored the towers of León which the barbarian king Almanzor had destroyed. This most serene queen was eager to adorn the monastery of the blessed Isidore, and the rest of the principal churches of the kingdom with gold, silver, precious stones" (cap. 93, p. 411). Careful examination of all documentation relevant to the Gothic campaign of the Cathedral of León under Berenguela's husband, Alfonso IX, needs to be carried out before we can assert that Alfonso IX acted alone.

73. Fernando III relied heavily on his mother in carrying out all of his kingly endeavors. In 1217, upon the death of her brother, Enrique I, Berenguela had become the rightful heir to the throne of Castile. After some negotiation, she abdicated to her seventeen year old son, Fernando. Despite this abdication, and Fernando's authentic assumption of royal power, Berenguela continued throughout her life to enable her son's rule, by arranging his marriages, sending him supplies while he was on crusade (and governing Castile-León while he was absent), and even negotiating for him the kingdom of León. I argue in my dissertation that this abdication in fact gave her as

much power (and more security) than if she had tried to keep the throne for herself.

74. Madrid, Archivo Histórico National Codice 987B, Liber Priv. Tolet. Eccl. fol. 30r–fol. 30v. 1238.

75. Regarding new foundations, the Cistercian *Capitula* presented to Pope Calixtus II in 1119 states: "It has been decreed that all our monasteries must be dedicated to the Queen of Heaven and Earth" (chap. 9, "The Founding of New Abbeys") in Lekai, *The Cistercians*, app. 1, p. 448.

76. The evidence for this is mainly the assertions of the nuns at Las Huelgas contemporary to these authors. For example, see Rodríguez López, "In the same nave and a little further on [from another tomb] is found the sepulcher of the Queen Doña Berenguela, without any adornment by the express will of herself, according to what the Community has told us" (*El Real Monasterio*, 268). P. Enrique Florez, *Memorias de las reinas catolicas de España* (1761; reprint, Madrid: Aguilar, 1945), 1:600.

77. One could argue that these scenes depict the early life of Christ; however the allusions to the relationship between mother and son are too important to be overlooked, and the fact that the scenes arrive at the heavenly coronation of the Virgin, (and not Calvary or the Resurrection, for example) persuades me that these scenes are intended to reflect the life of the royal mother. These scenes include the Annunciation, the Visitation, the Birth of Christ, the angels greeting the shepherds, the Adoration of the Magi, the Massacre of the Innocents, the Presentation in the Temple, and the Flight into Egypt. For a full description of this tomb, see Gomez Barcena, *Escultura gótica funeraria*, 196–97.

78. See n. 73 above.

79. The pope then granted an indulgence of forty days for this, as well as for those who visited the sepulchre during the next ten years, and those who prayed the Our Father for her soul were to receive another ten days. In 1253 Innocent extended this indulgence to all penitents who visited the tombs of any person buried at the abbey on their anniversary. Rodríguez López, *El Real Monasterio*, 141–42.

80. Rodríguez López cites as proof for this switch the opening of the tombs in 1844 and finding in the more elaborate tomb an "uncorrupted cadaver, dressed in the Cistercian habit" (Ibid., 169). Only the younger Berenguela is actually known to have become a nun; the uncorrupted corpse is offered as proof of identification because of the younger woman's generally recognized sanctity. The tombs have not remained undisturbed, and a large number of them have no iconographic clues as to the identity of the remains intended for them. The tomb attributed to Fernando la Cerda (late thirteenth century) is without sculpture but retains painted decoration. Other notables such as Enrique I have plain tombs: as he was not a religious, and he was a king, it seems probable that eventually his tomb would be decorated somehow. Considering this, why wouldn't Berenguela's tomb have been painted, however simply? In terms of iconography and personal expression, then, the fact that her tomb is undecorated literally signifies nothing. In fact, Rodríguez López recites a list of tombs without adornment, making his certainty regarding identification of the interred and

any possibility of such identification all the more improbable. He notes that three Constanzas (Queen Berenguela's sister, daughter, and granddaughter) and Isabel of Molina (another granddaughter) among others were all interred in tombs without adornment (264).

81. See Painter's felicitous description of Peter's donation in *The Scourge of the Clergy: Peter of Dreux, Duke of Brittany* (Baltimore: Johns Hopkins University Press, 1937), 30–31. Regarding the relationship between Blanche and Peter's donations, Painter says: "Peter's donation as a whole rivals if it does not actually outshine that of the royal family. His gift honors Christ, the King—theirs only His Virgin Mother. The ducal house of Brittany was to reign in the southern sunlight while their Capetian rivals were left on the bleak northern side. Peter's gift to Chartres was conceived on the scale of his ambition rather than on that of his actual position in the feudal world" (31).

82. Chartres also displays Blanche's connections with her extended family. Next to Blanche's early grisaille donation depicting the Virgin is a window depicting Saint James of Compostela. It is possible that this window was chosen in reference to Blanche and her heritage, particularly as it stands so close to her own donation. Saint James was the nephew of the Virgin whose window he stands next to: perhaps this window is an explicit reference to Blanche's own nephew, Fernando III, as the words "rex castelle" appear on it. Regardless of whether the donor was an anonymous friend, Fernando, or Blanche herself, the reference to the powerful crusading kingdom of Blanche's origin must be interpreted as a reference to Blanche's own personal power.

83. Lucas de Túy, *Crónica de España*, 3.

84. Besides Berenguela's commissioning of the *Crónica de España*, there was the very important *De rebus Hispanie*, written by the courtier and archbishop of Toledo de Rada for Fernando III, and the *Primera crónica*, compiled under the supervision of Alfonso X.

Patterns of Women's Literary Patronage: England, 1200–ca. 1475

✖ ✖ ✖ KAREN K. JAMBECK

In her classic study *English and International: Studies in the Literature, Art, and Patronage of Medieval England,* Elizabeth Salter writes of "the silences" that "seem to surround and isolate" many writings of the Middle Ages. She provocatively suggests that for "the attentive ear" the apparent silences "are filled with an active world." In that study Salter filled in many conspicuous silences, perhaps most notably in the area of literary patronage.[1] Subsequent investigations of book ownership and patronage have helped to eliminate still more of these gaps in our knowledge of medieval writings, readers, and manuscript culture.[2] In England from the thirteenth to the late fifteenth century, for instance, the literary patronage of at least thirty women, excluding queens, has been recognized.[3] The discovery of these individuals is indeed significant, as are concomitant findings that situate these patrons within marriage alliances, broad family galaxies, and social and geographic contexts. One promising line of inquiry, however, has remained largely neglected: the relationships and linkages among medieval women involved in literary patronage.[4] To elucidate these relationships, this essay traces patterns of women's literary patronage that emerge in England over a period of almost three hundred years. Examining writings assigned to their patronage in concert with their life records, this study explores connections among women who have been identified as medieval patrons. It argues that patronage was one way in which these women defined themselves, for by supporting literary works of social and moral significance they were able to preserve documents embodying values and ideals they deemed important, and to pass on these values, particularly along cognatic (as opposed to agnatic) lines.

The writing supported by these women reveals significant information about them and their world. Less eclectic than it first appears, this aggregation of some thirty works includes a collection of sermons (Gospels with accompanying homilies or expositions), a meditation on the vanity of this world, a manuscript compilation comprising a treatise entitled *How to Learn to Die* and two exempla, an exposition on the Mass, a poem based upon a biblical passage, six devotional works focusing on the Virgin Mary, a poem on the passion of Christ, ten saints' lives, a chronicle, a historical or family romance, a Christianized classical romance, a translation of Boethius's *Consolation of Philosophy*, a treatise on the French language, a treatise on estate management, some lyric poems, and a translation of Christine de Pizan's *Epistle of Othea*. (A complete list of works and dedications appears at the end of this essay.) Marked by their devotional and religious nature, their didacticism, and their seriousness, these works are, for the most part, vernacular translations of religious, moral, or instructional writings infused with an edifying purpose.[5]

Although this assortment of texts corresponds closely to the readings recommended especially for women in the fourth century by Saint Jerome and later by Christine de Pizan,[6] these works share other important attributes. Most, for instance, depict exemplary women, the prime example being the Virgin Mary, "the paragon of religious virtue and the ideal feminine type."[7] The same may be said, of course, about the saints' lives that make up at least a third of the writings commissioned by these patrons. First among them is the popular medieval saint Mary Magdalen, known as a model of the penitent sinner and a woman who had attained special status. Throughout the Middle Ages writers stress Mary Magdalen's unqualified devotion to Jesus as well as his special love for her. The first to see the resurrected Christ, she was "ranked with the apostles of the church" and was believed to hold an exalted place among women.[8] These are the attitudes reflected in Osbern Bokenham's *Life of Mary Magdalen*. Explaining the genesis of this work, Bokenham recalls that Isabel Bourchier, countess of Eu, had requested him to write about Mary Magdalen, the "apostyllesse" of the apostles, for whom she has long had "of pure affeccyoun . . . a synguler deuocyoun" (lines 5065–68),[9] going on to elucidate the saint's special rank:

> Pryuylegyd was þis blyssyd Mayre
> Wyth synguler chershyng of hyr loue, Messye,
> Both in hys lyuyng & in hys passyoun."
> (lines 5727–29)

Also included in this grouping of commissioned saints' lives are Saint Katherine, Saint Margaret, Saint Agatha, and Saint Dorothy,[10] who withstand the forces of society and of evil to uphold their beliefs, rejecting the expectations of marriage, family, and society, and refusing to submit to any but a transcendent authority.[11]

Represented here too are wives and mothers who incorporated traditional feminine roles and behaviors of maternal nurturance and guidance into their spiritual life. Saint Anne's faith led to her becoming the mother and earthly moral guide of the Virgin Mary and matriarch of a human family that paralleled the Holy Trinity.[12] Another of these saints, the virtuous Elizabeth of Hungary, nurtured her immediate family and carried out extensive philanthropies while she was married to the wealthy and powerful Landgrave, prince of Thuringa, to whom she bore three children. Upon her husband's death she devoted herself to a life of chastity, piety, and charitable works, thereby gaining great honor in this world and the next.[13] These accounts honor wives and mothers who rise to spiritual heights because of their exemplary virtue and faith, and who are revered by men and women alike. Exhibiting self-knowledge, self-respect, and courage, these saints serve as exemplars of both Christian and womanly ideals.[14] Functioning as models of Christian heroism, all of these female saints can be characterized by Sheila Delany's observations concerning the protagonists of Bokenham's *Legendys:* they are "powerful, articulate women who are indubitably worthy to do God's work."[15]

Worthy matrons also figure prominently in the lives of the three male saints who are part of this group. Perhaps the best known of these matrons is Monica, the mother of Saint Augustine. A pious and determined woman, Monica, who profoundly influenced her son, was herself revered as a saint, particularly from the twelfth century onward. Similarly, the mother of Saint Edmund of Abingdon, Mabel Rich, also an important spiritual guide for her son, was so highly esteemed in thirteenth-century England that a cult grew up around her, rivaling that of the saint himself. Saint Jerome's life, too, intertwines with the lives of notable women, particularly Paula and Eustochium, his spiritual and intellectual companions and cofounders of religious houses.[16] So great was Paula's reputation that since ancient times she has been recognized with a feast day.[17] These examples of Paula and Eustochium, Mabel Rich, and Monica clearly illustrate Rosemary Ruether's observation that stories of "Mothers of the Church" are often embedded in stories by and about men.[18]

The theme of estimable feminine character is not restricted to the commissioned saints' lives. Even Lydgate's *Epistle to Sibille,* a verse paraphrase of Proverbs 31:10–31, praises the virtuous woman:

But a woman provident in dede,
I mene suche one þat prudent is and wyse,

þe whiche of Herte þe lorde above doþe drede,
Sheo worþy is to haue ful gret pryce.
                    (lines 120–23)[19]

Similar virtue is exemplified in secular narratives like Lydgate's *Guy of Warwick*, which depicts the legendary Warwick antecedents. Thus, while the "notable, ffamous, worthy knyght," Guy, combats the Danes, his wife, Felice, the "example of trouthe and womanhede" (in some versions of the tale she is also known for her "science"), provides alms for the poor and, from all indications, oversees both her family and her lands in her husband's absence. Upon Guy's death his "hooly wyf" arranges a model Christian burial for him and, after putting her worldly and spiritual affairs in order, bequeaths the earldom of Warwick to her son.[20] So, too, in John Metham's *Amoryus and Cleopes*, a Christianized allegorical romance depicting a knight who "dyd many wurthy dedys be the help off a lady," the redoubtable and intelligent Lady Cleopes helps Amoryus not only to overcome the dragon but also to establish himself firmly in both the secular and spiritual domains.[21]

In light of such insistence on womanly virtues, Hoccleve's manuscript collection (Durham University Library, MS Cosin. V.III.9), dedicated to the countess of Westmorland,[22] offers additional insights into an author's attention to a feminine audience. Consisting of an introductory "Complaint," a framing dialogue, a treatise called "How to Learn to Die," and translations of two exempla from the *Gesta Romanorum*, the collection contains a dialogue in which Hoccleve announces his plan to translate some works, "in honour and preysynge" of women (especially in light of any offense the author's *Epistle to Cupid* might have caused). Hoccleve's first selection is a tale from the "Romayn deedis" in "honour and plesance of yow, my ladyes" (lines 820–22).[23] This first exemplum, an analogue of the Constance tale entitled "Jereslaus's Wife," recounts the vicissitudes endured by an empress who, through virtue and strength of character, surmounts her misfortunes and, unlike many of her counterparts, successfully brings her enemies to justice.[24] The second exemplum, "The Tale of Jonathas," relates the experiences of a young man who, after succumbing to temptation, eventually finds his way. It is Jonathas's mother who provides the thematic and structural focus for the narrative; in both tales, as Mary Pryor demonstrates, Hoccleve modifies his sources in order to place positive emphasis on women.[25]

The centerpiece of Hoccleve's manuscript, "How to Learn to Die," is an English adaptation of portions of Heinrich Suso's treatise *Horologium Sapientiae* (ca. 1334). As in the case of Guischart de Beauliu's *Sermon*, "How to Learn to Die" stresses avoiding the viciousness and vanity of this world in order to be prepared for death and ultimately for God's grace:[26]

> To lerne for to die / is to han ay
> Bothe herte and soule / redy to hens to go
> . . . whan deeth cometh.
> (lines 50–52)

The main concern of the treatise is to keep the soul

> fro perisshynge
> By souffrance of greet labour and travaill
> And exercyse of vertuous lyuynge.
> (lines 793–95)

As in Walton's translation of the *Consolation of Philosophy*, where Boethius is guided by the allegorical Dame Sapience, Hoccleve's Sapientia instructs her disciple, explaining how to learn to die, how to live, how to receive her (i.e., eternal wisdom), and how to "loue" and "honure" her (lines 22–28).[27]

Such affirmations of womanhood culminate in Stephen Scrope's translation of Christine de Pizan's *Epistle of Othea*. A feminized retelling of classical myths and legends, the *Epistle* defines women's contributions and illuminates their roles both as virtuous models and "as teachers and arbiters of culture."[28] In this epistolary treatise Othea addresses the Trojan prince Hector, instructing him on living well and pointing out "how prudence and wisdome be moderis and conditoures of all virtues (section 1).[29] In her allegorical narrative, Christine de Pizan underscores the wisdom and abilities of female characters drawn from classical legend and myth.[30] But esteem is not limited to goddesses; mortal women, too, have wisdom and strength of character, and they too deserve honor and recognition. The worthy Pantaselle (section 15) and Andromatha, for instance, stand as examples of wise women whose "advice" and "counsel" should be welcomed (section 88). Recounting in a final narrative how a Cumean sibyl led Caesar Augustus to truth, Othea once again indirectly urges the knight to listen to the counsel of a wise woman,[31] thus reinforcing one of the work's central themes. In this context the central character, Othea, serves as a unifying force, for, as Charity Cannon Willard has observed, she is "the goddess of Prudence and the personification of feminine wisdom."[32]

This insistence on feminine ideals, however, constitutes only a portion of the information that these works have to offer. Repeatedly, the writers represented here indicate that a patron has actively sought out a particular work. The fullest extant account is provided by Osbern Bokenham, who recounts how the countess of Eu commissioned a life of Mary Magdalen. Describing her abiding devotion to the saint, the countess expresses her wish for an English version of the life of the "Blyssyd Mary mawdelyn":

> To han maad, & for my sake
> If ye lykyd þe labour to take,
> & for reuerence of hyr, I wold you preye.
> (5065–75)[33]

Such commissions suggest that these works have much to tell us about the patrons' thoughts and concerns.

Particularly in their illustration of values and virtues, these writings limn principles of feminine honor—both private and public—principles resembling those codified by Christine de Pizan in *A Medieval Woman's Mirror of Honor: The Treasury of the City of Ladies*.[34] These values resonate within the context of individual patron's lives and link generations of patrons along matrilineal lines.

The following family profiles focus on connections among medieval patrons, centering primarily on four families—those of Elizabeth Berkeley, countess of Warwick; Blanche, duchess of Lancaster; Joan FitzAlan, countess of Hereford; and Joan Beaufort, countess of Westmorland.

Born to wealth and education, Elizabeth Berkeley (d. 1422) was the only child and sole heir of Thomas Lord Berkeley (d. 1417) and Margaret (d. 1391/92), daughter and heir of Warin, Lord Lisle. That education was valued in Elizabeth's family is evidenced by her father's patronage of John of Trevisa's translations. And Elizabeth, too, is responsible for a translation that suggests the level of both her literacy and literary taste. In 1410, she commissioned John Walton's translation of Boethius's *De consolatione philosophiae*; its dedication includes an acrostic of her name and his:

> . . . in reuerence of your worthynesse
> Madame thys work at your instance
> I have begonne after my symplenesse
> In wyl to do yow seruyce and plesance.[35]

With her marriage to Richard Beauchamp, earl of Warwick and count of Aumale (d. 1439), Elizabeth became countess of Warwick; additionally, she was in her own right baroness of Lisle and baroness of Teyes.[36]

All evidence suggests that Elizabeth Berkeley led an eventful life. Her claim to the Berkeley inheritance marks the beginning of the Great Berkeley Law-suit, which began in 1417 and continued for almost two centuries. Although Elizabeth was Thomas's heir, her cousin James Berkeley, the eldest male in the collateral line, obtained the Castle of Berkeley on the basis of an entailment; from that point the struggle for the inheritance began. In one petition to the king's council, Elizabeth complained that James Berkeley employed armed men to prevent her from entering her manor. While conducting her legal struggles, she seems to have led an often peripatetic existence, which involved traveling with an entourage of thirty to sixty people. C. D. Ross infers from records of extended visits by clerics that she enjoyed their company. In the midst of such activity, her surviving household account book indicates an orderly and efficient household.[37]

Elizabeth's eldest daughter, Margaret Beauchamp (d. 1467/68), was also a patron of letters. The second wife of John Talbot, first earl of Shrewsbury (who was slain in France in 1453),[38] she was, upon her marriage in 1425, "joint heiress presumptive" of the powerful earl of Warwick. Along with her husband, Margaret is associated with the *Talbot Hours* (Cambridge, Fitzwilliam Museum, MSS. 40–1950 and 41–1950), the former containing Lydgate's prayer to Alban (fols. 132–35).[39] In addition, the dedicatory note of Lydgate's *Guy of Warwick* specifies that the poet composed this English "tale" about the legendary progenitor of the Beauchamps at the request of Margaret, countess of Shrewsbury.[40]

Although scholars have suggested that she commissioned *Guy of Warwick* for her father, Margaret may well have had other motives in selecting this account of her noble forebears the valorous Guy and the virtuous Felice.[41] In this "family romance," it is through his well-born wife, Felice, that Guy becomes earl of Warwick, and through Felice her son Reynbourne will gain the title after her death (line 558–59):[42]

> The stok descendyng of antyquyte
> To Guy his ffader be tytle of mariage,
> Affter whos deth, of lawe and equyte,
> Reynborne to entre in-to his herytage.
> (stanza 71, lines 561–64)

As noted earlier, the issue of inheritance and title from mother to daughter and then mother to son dated from Elizabeth Berkeley's pursuit of her inheritance after her father's death, in 1417. When Elizabeth died in 1422, Margaret took up the battle for the Berkeley estates against her cousin James, ostensibly to provide her son John, the future Lord Lisle and the eldest son of his father's second marriage to Margaret, with an inheritance. This strategy was particularly significant because the bulk of Talbot's estate was destined for his son by his first marriage. Although a temporary reconciliation occurred just before James's death in 1463, shortly thereafter James's son William Berkeley "petitioned the Crown" against the claims of Margaret (then a widow since 1453). After her son's death in 1453, Margaret served as the guardian of her grandson Thomas, whose rights she fought to preserve. The contest for the Berkeley inheritance continued throughout the remainder of Margaret's life and was resolved only when, shortly after her death in 1467/68, her grandson and heir, Thomas Talbot, viscount of Lisle, challenged William Berkeley and was killed by the latter in a duel.[43]

Although less is known about the literary activities of Blanche of Lancaster (d. 1369) and her daughter Philippa (d. 1415), the fact that their names appear in contemporary poems leads to their inclusion here. Daughter and coheir of Henry Grosmont, duke of Lancaster, and his wife, Isabel Beaumont,[44] Blanche belonged to a family in which education seems to have been the norm; as an act of penance, for instance, her father composed a devotional treatise entitled *Le livre des seyntz medicines* and an account of the laws of war, the latter now lost.[45] Despite a 1347 agreement calling for the marriage of Blanche and John Segrave, she remained single until she was eighteen, when she married John of Gaunt (d. 1399), the son of Edward III and Philippa of Hainault. During their ten years of married life, John spent significant periods of time in campaigns abroad; nevertheless, Blanche bore him five children. Her inheritance of the vast Lancaster fortunes upon the deaths of her father (1361) and her sister, Maud (1362),[46] brought John the title of duke of Lancaster and made him one of the wealthiest men of the realm.[47]

Although Blanche was no more than twenty-eight when she succumbed to the plague, Froissart lauds her, ostensibly as a patron, in his *Le joli buisson de jonece,* and some of his poems may have been directed to her.[48] Both John of Gaunt and Blanche of Lancaster have been traditionally linked to Geoffrey Chaucer, whose *Book of the Duchess* supposedly commemorates her untimely death. According to the Speght edition, moreover, Blanche was the patron of Geoffrey Chaucer's ABC poem (also known as *La priere Nostre Dame*). Deriving from a prayer in Deguileville's *Pèlerinage de la vie humaine,*[49] the ABC poem consists of alphabetically ordered stanzas addressed to the Virgin Mary. Such poems, as Susan Bell has observed, were used not only for private devotions, but also for teaching children reading and moral and religious values, and it is not unlikely that Blanche may have put her ABC to similar uses.[50]

As for Blanche's daughter, Philippa of Lancaster is named by Eustache

Deschamps in one of his *balades*. Since Deschamps addresses the *balade* to "Phelippe," who resides "en Lancastre," scholars generally contend that the poem was composed before 1386, when Philippa, then aged twenty-seven, accompanied her father abroad in his attempt to gain the crown of Castile, and certainly before Philippa married John I of Portugal in 1387.[51] Unlike the pious English verses associated with her mother, the French poem of Deschamps celebrates secular love, honoring Philippa as a partisan of the Order of the Flower:

> Pour ce que j'ay oy parler en France
> De deux ordres en l'amoureuse loy,
> Que dames ont chascune en defferance,
> L'une fueille et l'autre fleur,
>
> . . . .
>
> A droit jugier je me tien a la flour.
> (lines 1–10)[52]

Whether or not Deschamps sent this poem unbidden, to address her in this manner tacitly acknowledges Philippa's capacity for literary patronage.

Another paradigm of literary patronage in medieval England consists of family constellations comprising grandmothers, mothers, and daughters. One such family originates with Joan FitzAlan (d. 1419), whose parents were the powerful Richard FitzAlan, earl of Arundel (d. 1375/76), and his second wife, Eleanor (d. 1372). In 1359 Joan married Humphrey de Bohun, earl of Hereford, Essex, and Northampton (d. 1372/73), who was a bibliophile of some note.[53] For almost half a century after the death of her husband, the last male in the Bohun line, Joan, dowager countess of Hereford, "held, in addition to her dower, a substantial amount of property enfeoffed by her husband to trustees." Her administrative abilities were notable, and some of her surviving letters suggest that she was an active participant in the affairs of her estates.[54]

As a widow Joan was a great benefactor to Walden Abbey. It is also during this period that Hoccleve dedicated to her the "Complaint of the Virgin," a translation of one of the poems in *Pèlerinage de l'âme*, part of Deguileville's trilogy, to which the *Pèlerinage de la vie humaine* also belonged. Indeed, M. C. Seymour speculates that Hoccleve may have translated all fourteen Deguileville poems, and perhaps the entire *Pèlerinage de l'âme*,[55] for Joan Fitz-Alan, countess of Hereford. Although any direct connection would be difficult to prove, it is worth noting that the earlier-mentioned poem derived from Deguileville's *Pèlerinage de la vie humaine*, Chaucer's ABC, or *Prière de Nostre Dame* appears to have been composed for Blanche of Lancaster, Joan FitzAlan's cousin.[56] Of related interest here, too, is the suggestion that Joan may have been the owner of the Symeon manuscript (London, British Library, MS Add. 22283), which contains "religious and moralistic verse and prose."[57]

Joan FitzAlan's two daughters, Mary de Bohun (d. 1394) and Eleanor de Bohun (d. 1399), and her granddaughter Anne Stafford, have also been recognized as book owners and literary patrons. Despite her marriage in 1380/81 to Henry of Bolingbroke, Mary de Bohun is included here because she was never queen, dying in childbirth before Henry IV's coronation in 1399.[58] She was the owner of a French *Lancelot* (London, British Library, Royal MSS 20.D.iii and iv) and some psalters; two of the latter had been begun for her father, who died when Mary was about four, but were completed for her. Subsequently, when Mary's daughter Philippa went to Denmark to marry King Erik, she took with her a psalter containing a miniature of her mother.[59]

Coheir of the Bohun fortune and wife of Thomas Woodstock, duke of Gloucester (d. 1397), Joan FitzAlan's daughter Eleanor de Bohun may have commissioned at least one of the Bohun manuscripts (Edinburgh, National Library of Scotland, MS Adv. 18.6.5).[60] Additionally, she bequeathed a remarkable number of books in her will. To her daughter Isabella, a nun in the Minories in London, she left a half dozen religious books, among them a French Bible, "un livre de decretales en Francois," and "un livre 'de vitis patrum.'" To her daughter Joanna she willed a psalter and "autres devocions," and to her eldest daughter, Anne of Woodstock, a collection of saints' lives: "un livre beal & bien enluminee de legenda aurea en Frauncois."[61]

Not only did Anne of Woodstock (d. 1438) receive her mother's *Legenda aurea*, she was the sole heir of Thomas of Woodstock, and she inherited Eleanor of Bohun's vast estates and, eventually, those of her grandmother Joan FitzAlan, dowager countess of Hereford, as well.[62] A woman of both rank and means in her own right, Anne married three times. Her first two husbands were Thomas, earl of Stafford (d. 1392), and later, Thomas's brother and heir, Edmund Stafford, earl of Stafford and subsequently of Buckingham (d. 1403); to the latter she bore two daughters, Anne and Philippa. After Edmund Stafford's death at the Battle of Shrewsbury, Anne married again (about 1419), this time William Bourchier (d. 1426), with whom she had five children. (A son from this marriage, William Bourchier, would eventually become the husband of Isabel, the well-known patron of Osbern Bokenham.)[63] Surviving her last husband by a dozen years, Anne was "perhaps the wealthiest woman in England," controlling over half of the Stafford inheritance (her dowers from her two marriages to the Stafford brothers) and her mother's half of the Bohun inheritance, along with some additional inheritances. The dowager countess's estates, moreover, were run with great effectiveness, and her benefactions include gifts to the Priory of Llanthony and the College of Pleshey.[64] Styling herself "Anne countesse of Stafford, Bockingh' Herford' and Northampton, and lady of Breknoc" (all the titles but Buckingham deriving from her mother's family), she declares in her will that she made her testament "in English tonge, for my most profit, redyng, and understandyng in yis wise."[65] Anne Stafford's will and her correspondence with the prior of Llanthony, Carole Rawcliffe concludes, "show her to be a serious and well-educated woman."[66] It is Anne, countess of Stafford, who commissioned Lydgate to "compile and make" the "Invocation to Saint Anne" and a life of Saint Anne, though only the "Invocation" survives.[67] That the saint is matron, mother, and recognized matriarch may well have heightened the work's significance for the countess of Stafford, for whom matrilineal connections were of great importance.

So strong is the tradition of patronage in Joan FitzAlan's family, patronage continues into the fourth generation with her great-granddaughter Anne Stafford (d. 1432). Daughter of Anne of Woodstock and Edmund, earl of Stafford (heirs to the Stafford estates and much of the Bohun fortune), Anne married twice. In 1415 she wed Edmund Mortimer, earl of March (d. 1424/25), who was recognized by Richard II's followers as the legitimate heir to the crown but who chose instead to support Henry V. One token of the couple's social status is their participation in the coronation of Henry V's queen, Katherine of Valois, in 1421. Four years later, however, Edmund, earl of March, died of the plague, and Anne was permitted her dower only by promising not to marry without license.[68] To Anne, countess of March, Lydgate dedicates his *Legend of St. Margaret*,[69] explaining that "my lady March" commanded him to consult the French and Latin versions of the saint's life and "therof make a compylacyoun" (lines 70–74). In this work Lydgate's narrative emphasizes not only the saint's honor and Christian heroism, but also her rank, and he calls attention to her high birth by having Margaret communicate the information in her own words:

> Touchynge my linage, by successyoun
> My blode conveied is fro grete noblesse.
> (lines 155–56)

At the end of the narrative, the poet begins his envoy with the following address:

> Noble princesses and ladyes of estate,
> And gentilwomen lower of degre,

Lefte vp your hertes, calle to your aduocate
Seynt Margarete, gemme of chastite.

(lines 519–22)

Well aware of his patron's standing, Lydgate stresses the parallels between
the aristocratic saint and his noble audience, the countess and her retinue,
including family and friends.[70]

Fourth among the families of patrons considered here is that of Joan Beaufort (d. 1440) and her descendants. The illegitimate daughter of Katherine
Swynford (1350–1403)[71] and John of Gaunt (d. 1398/99), Joan was sister to
John Beaufort, earl of Somerset, and to Cardinal Beaufort; in addition, she was
half-sister to Philippa of Lancaster and Henry IV.[72] In the year following the
death of her first husband, Sir Robert Ferrers (d. 1396), Joan married Ralph
Neville, earl of Westmorland (d. 1425), a trusted retainer of John of Gaunt;
that same year she and her brothers were legitimated. Because Ralph Neville's
marriage to Joan opened great opportunities to him, the couple prospered, and
many of their fourteen children married into wealthy and prestigious families.

After the earl of Westmorland's death in 1425, Joan Beaufort lived as a
widow for fifteen years,[73] and it is from this period that the documents relating
to her literary activities date. The first is a letter in which she requests that the
two books she has lent to the king—*The Chronicle of Jerusalem* and *The Voyage
of Godfrey of Bouillon*—be returned to her.[74] She has also been identified as
the owner of Nicholas Love's English translation of the pseudo-Bonaventuran
Meditationes vitae Christi and the *Speculum vitae*, also in English (MS e. Mus.
35, Bodleian Library, Oxford). She is also the dedicatee of Hoccleve's manuscript compilation (Durham University Library, MS Cosin. V. III. 9).[75]

Two of Joan of Beaufort's daughters also manifest their mother's affinity
for books. The first is Cecily Neville (1415–95), who at the age of nine married Richard, duke of York, son of Richard, earl of Cambridge, and Anne
Mortimer, both descendants of Edward III. Richard of York was one of the
greatest landholders of his time, and his marriage to Cecily Neville brought
him invaluable family and political connections. Traveling with her husband,
who served as the king's lieutenant, Cecily gave birth to at least eight children in England, Rouen, and Dublin. Later, when the duke of York was forced
into exile because of his political activities, Cecily was placed in the custody
of her sister Anne Neville, duchess of Buckingham. For thirty-five years after
her husband's death in 1460, Cecily lived off her dower lands as a widow, actively directing her household and her estates and devoting attention to her
grandchildren.[76]

Despite the fact that no surviving works have been traced to her patronage,[77] Cecily Neville's conduct and her preferences in reading materials are germane to this study. In his well-known analysis of the household ordinance of Cecily, duchess of York, C. A. J. Armstrong summarizes her daily activities, shedding light on her habits and tastes: these included reciting "the matins of the day," reading aloud at dinner devotional works like Bonaventure's *Life of Christ* or a saint's life from the *Golden Legend*, tending to the business of her estates and household, and discussing at supper the earlier readings. The duchess's interests were reflected not only in her books but also in her tapestries, which depicted Christ's Passion, the lives of Mary Magdalen and other saints, and the Wheel of Fortune.[78] Also worth noting is that in her will Cecily Neville bequeathed a significant number of books, especially service books (for example, missals, antiphonaries, graduals) and devotional works, including a breviary destined for Lady Margaret Beaufort. To one of her granddaughters, Brigitte, she left a *Legenda aurea*, a life of Saint Katherine of Sienna, and "a boke of Saint Matilde"; she bequeathed "a portuous with claspes silver and gilte covered with purple velvet" to her "doughter Cecill"; in addition, to her granddaughter Anne de la Pole, prioress of Syon, she left an English book of Bonaventure and Hilton, and "a boke of the Revelacions of Saint Burgitte."[79] Whether or not Cecily commissioned any of these works remains an open question. Nonetheless, family connections link her closely to this network of patrons: her mother, Joan Beaufort; her daughter Margaret of York;[80] her sister-in-law and Osbern Bokenham's sponsor, Isabel Bourchier; and her sister Anne, duchess of Buckingham.

Anne Neville (d. 1480), the fourth-born daughter of Joan Beaufort and Ralph Neville, has also received increasing attention as a connoisseur of books and a literary patron. Her marriage (about 1424) allied her to one of the richest men in fifteenth-century Europe, Humphrey Stafford, earl of Stafford (d. 1460), who was created duke of Buckingham in 1444. In the course of her marriage, Anne gave birth to five daughters and seven sons. Approximately seven years after her husband was slain at the Battle of Northampton, Anne Neville married (ca. 1467) Walter Blount, first baron Mountjoy (d. 1474).[81] During the last years of her life, Anne, who had skillfully controlled all the Stafford estates until her son came of age, continued her able administration of a substantial portion of the lands that had come to her via her jointure, as her extant day books illustrate. Surviving documents record her twenty-three attempts to recover debts as well as her suit against the king, who had "claimed the wardship of one of her vassals."[82]

As dowager duchess, Anne Neville Stafford was in a position to enjoy her penchant for books. In addition to the works listed as bequests in her testament—a French book of Epistles and Gospels, a "primer with clasps of silver gilt covered with purple velvet," a French book entitled *Lucum*, and an English *Legenda sanctorum*—she appears also to have possessed Cambridge, Corpus Christi College, MS 61, which contains the famous "Troilus Frontispiece" portrait.[83] Anne has also been identified as the "Duches of Bokyngham," the "ryght hyghe and myghty pryncesse," to whom was dedicated *The Nightingale* (ca. 1444). Once attributed to John Lydgate, the poem bears a relationship to the *Philomena*, which in vernacular form had attracted the patronage of Eleanor of Provence in the previous century.[84] In this allegorical commemoration of Christ's Passion, a nightingale (representing the feminized human soul) sings at each of the canonical hours and then expires. In the prologue of *The Nightingale*, the poet sends his "lityll quayere" to find a place "amonge [the duchess's] bokys" so "hyre peple" may hear it and understand the song's spiritual sense (lines 1–16). The poet's suggestion that this religiously inspired and morally edifying work be read aloud to those around the duchess offers an instructive parallel to the practice of Anne's sister, Cecily, who, in addition to whatever contact she may normally have had with her sister, spent considerable time in Anne's protective custody.[85]

Like Anne Neville, countess of Stafford and duchess of Buckingham, her daughter Anne Stafford (d. 1472) has also been identified as the sponsor of a literary work, thereby extending the tradition of patronage into the third generation in Joan Beaufort's family. As the daughter of the duke and duchess of Buckingham, Anne Stafford ranked high among the aristocrats of her time. One index of her status is the proposed marriage alliance (ca. 1450) between one of Buckingham's daughters, most probably Anne, and the dauphin, who would later become Louis XI of France.[86] Whatever unions may have been considered, Anne married twice. Her first husband, Aubrey de Vere, whom she wed about 1460, was the son and heir apparent of John de Vere, earl of Oxford (d. 1462), and Elizabeth Howard de Vere, countess of Oxford (d. 1475). This is the Elizabeth de Vere to whom Osbern Bokenham dedicated his *Life of St. Elizabeth*, and it seems likely that Anne Stafford de Vere would probably have been cognizant of her mother-in-law's patronage as well as that of her own mother. Early in 1462 Anne's husband and her father-in-law were tried for treason and executed. That same year the young, childless widow Anne received confirmation of her jointure of nine de Vere manors;[87] shortly thereafter she married Sir Reynold (also referred to as Thomas) Cobham of Sterborough (d. 1471), who had succeeded to his family's estates about 1460.[88]

Anne Stafford de Vere, Carl Bühler argues, is most probably the "hye princesse" to whom Stephen Scrope dedicated his translation of Christine de

Pizan's *Epistle of Othea* (Pierpont Morgan Library, MS 775) between 1440 and 1459.[89] Approximately two and a half decades before Scrope translated the *Epistle*, Hoccleve, stating his intent to write "in honur and plesance of yow ladyes," had produced for Joan Beaufort, countess of Westmorland, a work that depicts women and their concerns positively and responsibly. In his envoy the poet commended the work to his patron:

Go, smal book / to the noble excellence
Of my lady / of Westmerland / and seye,
Hir humble seruant / with al reuerence
Him recommandith vnto hir nobleye;
And byseeche hire / on my behalue & preye,
Thee to receyue for hire owne right;
And looke thow / in al manere weye
To plese hir wommanhede / do thy might
    Humble seruant
    To your gracious
    noblesse
    T: Hoccleue.[90]

That Joan of Beaufort's granddaughter, Anne Stafford de Vere, would support the translation of Christine de Pizan's *Epistle of Othea*, which also addresses the concerns of thoughtful women in the Middle Ages, makes eminent sense.

Tracing the continuity of medieval literary patronage in direct lines from mother to daughter is but one of the avenues requiring further exploration. Other cognatic family relationships also merit examination: for example, connections among sisters, aunts and nieces, and cousins. The patrons of Matthew Paris, a chronicler at the Benedictine Abbey of Saint Albans, offer an intriguing example. Among Matthew Paris's works is a "Vie de Saint Edmond" for Isabel de Warenne, countess of Arundel (d. 1282). Her parents were the magnate William de Warenne and his wife, Maud, a coheir of William and Isabel Marshal (earl and countess of Pembroke), and she was the wife of Hugh de Albini, earl of Sussex and Arundel (d. 1243). For almost forty years after his death, Isabel lived a widow, overseeing her secular affairs, contributing to a cell at Saint Albans, and founding a convent church at Marram. She also traveled to Pontigny to visit the shrine of Edmund of Abingdon, where she persuaded officials to allow women "to enter the Cistercian community for the purposes of seeking the saint's blessing."[91]

But the countess of Arundel was only one of Matthew Paris's patrons. In his notes on the flyleaf of Trinity College, MS E. 1. 40 (which contains the

"Vie de Seint Auban"), Matthew Paris sketches the plan for an illustrated book for the countess of Winchester.[92] If Paris is referring here to Eleanor, countess of Winchester (d. 1274), it is noteworthy that she was a first cousin of Isabel de Warenne (d. 1282), the patron of Matthew's "Vie de Saint Edmond."[93] The two countesses were the daughters of sisters, Sibyl and Maud Marshal, the wives of William de Ferrers, earl of Derby (d. 1254), and William de Warenne, earl of Surrey (d. 1240), respectively. (Sibyl and Maud were, moreover, daughters and coheirs of William Marshal [d. 1219] and Isabel Fitz-Gilbert [d. 1220], earl and countess of Pembroke.)[94] Given this kinship, yet another reader and potential patron of Matthew Paris has relevance here: the countess of Cornwall, named in the famous note (also in Trinity College, MS E. 1. 40) recording the lending of manuscripts.[95] This countess of Cornwall has usually been identified as Sanchia of Provence, Richard of Cornwall's third wife and the sister of Queen Eleanor of Provence, herself a patron of Matthew Paris's *Estoire de Seint Ædward le Rei*.[96] However, the time period encompassing Matthew Paris's literary activity also includes the later years of yet another countess of Cornwall: Richard of Cornwall's first wife was Isabel Marshal (d. 1240), sister of the abovementioned Sibyl and Maud and, therefore, aunt of both Isabel, countess of Arundel, and Eleanor, countess of Winchester.[97] Such connections may be more common than previously recognized, as the translations of poems from Deguileville's *Pèlerinage* for Blanche of Lancaster and her cousin Joan FitzAlan also suggest.

Clarifying women's roles in literary patronage will also illuminate broader literary networks. One case calling for further research is that of Alice Chaucer (d. 1475), the only daughter and heir of Thomas Chaucer and Maud Burghersh, younger daughter and coheir of Sir John Burghersh and Ismania Hanham. An heiress in her own right, Alice married at least twice, first Thomas Montagu, earl of Salisbury (d. 1428), and second William, earl and later duke of Suffolk (d. 1450).[98] As a consequence of her own inheritance and later her dowers and jointure, Alice not only enjoyed affluence and high position during marriage but lived as a wealthy and esteemed widow for a quarter of a century, directing the "powerful maintenance of her estate"; making benefactions to religious, charitable, and educational institutions; conducting litigation; and negotiating a marriage alliance between her only son, John de la Pole, and Elizabeth, the daughter of the duke of York.[99]

From her earliest days Alice would have been exposed to literature in the manor at Ewelme, where her father, Thomas Chaucer (d. 1434),[100] received aristocratic guests, many with a literary bent. It has frequently been suggested that this is the context in which she first became acquainted with Lydgate, who dedicated his *Virtues of the Mass* to her.[101] Moreover, two of Alice Chaucer's husbands are known as men of letters. Thomas Montagu, earl of Salisbury (d. 1428) was himself a poet, a friend of Christine de Pizan, and a patron of Lydgate; similarly, William de la Pole, earl and later duke of Suffolk (d. 1450), was also noted for his literary inclinations and is reputed to have written several poems to his wife.[102] Several of Alice's letters survive, including one in which she expresses concern for her books. Yet even though it has been intimated that Alice Chaucer took part in her husbands' literary pursuits, she has received scant attention.[103]

The same holds true for Alice's mother, Maud Burghersh (d. 1436/37), the coheir of Sir John Burghersh, Lord Kerdeston. It has been noted that Maud brought Thomas Chaucer not only Ewelme but substantial land holdings. She appears to have been an able woman, increasing her properties in Oxford, Cambridge, Essex, Hampshire, and Suffolk not only as a result of her thrice-widowed mother's death (1420) but also through subsequent negotiations with her only sister, Margaret.[104] Apart from this, however, the records remain virtually silent. Derek Pearsall has speculated that Lydgate may have intended his "Balade at the Departing" and his "My Lady Dere" as companion pieces, one for Thomas Chaucer and one for his wife.[105] And one has to wonder what role Maud played in the literary activities of her husband and her only daughter.

As the preceding examples illustrate, these individuals belonged to a class of women whose role in building the economic and political strength of the medieval nobility has been well established. Along with their status came great responsibility, guiding an often numerous family as well as directing a large household.[106] Another significant factor is that the majority are related matrilineally. And a third shared characteristic is that most lived as widows for a considerable time.

This last factor merits further discussion. One aspect of medieval widowhood in England was that as *femme sole*, a woman enjoyed special legal status. Whereas a "wife's legal personality," according to common law, "was merged in that of her husband," with the consequence that she was "no longer a legal entity," the widow who elected "to remain in *pura vidua etate sua* finally gained legal recognition," and she could "exercise exclusive control over and full responsibility for land."[107] Moreover, as a widow, a woman who had married well or had married two or three times could gain control of any estates that she had inherited from her family, and the dowers or jointures that came to her upon the death of her husband or husbands besides; in addition, she might gain control of her son's estates until he came of age. In situations "where the dowager was herself an heiress, and therefore had both an inheritance and a dower, she might achieve control of a very large estate for a long time." [108] Widows, though not widowers, as Kate Mertes has demonstrated, commonly headed households, and these women were not merely titular heads of household. In such situations many medieval women demonstrated marked administrative ability in overseeing their households and their lands: "their accounts are among the best kept and preserved and their establishments among the most economical and orderly." [109] In addition to having control over her estates, the widow, perhaps for the first time, gained independence and exercised control in her life. And from the time of the Magna Carta, if she "chose to live as a widow neither king nor suitor could stop her from doing so." [110] This freedom, commingled with life experience, undoubtedly led the women mentioned above to an increased self-awareness, and evidence of their literary patronage, as well as of their benefactions, corresponds largely to the time of their widowhood. And from our latter-day perspective, one of the great advantages is that the widow is visible. [111]

One of the implications of such findings is that these women of achievement would seem to have learned the lesson of success from their mothers or mother figures. The repetitions of accomplishment from mother to daughter certainly suggest that line of transmission. Rowena Archer contends that "the least traceable but probably the most important single preparation for the future [managing large estates] was the expertise acquired through parental example by simply being, in early life, in the midst of routine estate management." [112] Certainly women learned in this way, but, in addition to lived example, these women found other means of passing on their values. Of interest in this regard are two treatises—one on estate management and one on the French vocabulary required of a landholder—that were dedicated to Margaret Lacy, countess of Lincoln, and Denise Munchensy respectively. [113] Whether any of these individuals recorded her personal ideas in writing is not known, for apart from a few official letters like those of Joan FitzAlan and Alice Chaucer, their own writings seem not to have survived. These women succeeded, however, in communicating—and still communicate—their thoughts through the works they commissioned, preserving writings that reflect feminine capability and self-worth.

The values exhibited in the lives of the patrons parallel those inscribed in the writings they sponsored. The dual record of the literary works they supported in conjunction with information that can be gleaned about their lives demonstrates that these women were capable, serious-minded, and self-aware. The patterns of patronage that emerge here indicate that they success-

fully transmitted values and attitudes—among them the tradition of patronage itself—to subsequent generations, especially to matrilineal descendants:
daughters, nieces, and granddaughters.[114] In the absence of the women's own
words, these writings give eloquent testimony to their high consciousness and
moral purpose. Their literary patronage, albeit on the margins of a discourse
they could not directly control,[115] establishes their participation in that discourse, and the writings sponsored by these women constitute an enduring
legacy. By remaining alert to women's roles and relationships in the context
of literary patronage, we will discover the sounds of a very active world that
has lain silent far too long.

Words and Dedications

WORK AND AUTHOR	DEDICATION
La Vie de Saint Edmond, Matthew Paris (ca. 1250)	"la cuntesse de Arundel et d'Essexe, dame Ysabelle"[116]
Sermon, Guischart de Beauliu (ca. 1200)	"ma dame Dionise"[117]
Reules Seynt Robert, Robert Grosseteste (1240–42)	"la contesse de Nichole"[118]
Miroir ou les évangiles des domnées, Robert de Greatham (ca. 1240–50)	"Dame Aline"[119]
Traité, Walter Bibbesworth (ca. 1240–50)	"ma dame Dyonise de Mountechensi"[120]
Chronicle, Nicholas Trevet (ca. 1327–29)	"ma dame Marie"[121]
"ABC" or "La Priere de Nostre Dame," Geoffrey Chaucer (mid-14th century)	[Blanche of Lancaster][122]
"Balade," Eustache Deschamps (ca. 1380)	"Phelippe"[123]
"Complaint of the Virgin," Thomas Hoccleve (before 1405)	"ma dame de Hereford"[124]
Boethius, *De consolatione philosophiae*, trans. John Walton (1410)	"Elisabet Berkeley"[125]
"Balade to Edward Duke of York," Thomas Hoccleve (1411)	"my gracious lord of York . . . worthy prince Edward" and "the noble princesse and lady deere"[126]

Legend of St. Margaret, John Lydgate (1415–26)	"My lady March" [127]
Durham, MS Cosin V. III. 9, Thomas Hoccleve (after 1422)	"my lady of Westmerland" [128]
"Invocation to St Anne" [and perhaps a life of Saint Anne], John Lydgate (1427–30)	"my Ladie Anne Countasse of Stafford" [129]
The Virtues of the Mass, John Lydgate (1427–30)	"Countesse de Suthefolchia" [130]
Fyfftene Ioyes of Oure Lady, John Lydgate (ca. 1427–30)	"the worshipfull Pryncesse Isabelle nowe Countasse of Warr' lady Despenser" [131]
Guy of Warwick, John Lydgate (ca. 1427–30)	"Margarite Countas of Shrowesbury Ladye Talbot Fournyual and Lisle" [132]
"Epistel to Sibille," John Lydgate (1427–50)	"Cybille" [133]
"A Tretise for Lauandres," John Lydgate (1427–50)	[Sibyl Boys of Holme Hale] [134]
The Nightingale [once attributed to John Lydgate] (ca. 1444)	"Duches of Bokyngham." [135]
Life of St. Dorothy, Osbern Bokenham (before 1445)	"Ioon Hunt . . . and Isabel, hys wyf " [136]
Life of Mary Magdalen, Osbern Bokenham (ca. 1445)	"þe lady Bowsere . . . the countesse of Hu" [137]
Life of St. Katherine, Osbern Bokenham (1446–47)	"Kateryne Howard" and "Kateryne Denstoun" [138]
Life of St. Anne, Osbern Bokenham (before 1445)	"Kateryne Denston" [139]
Life of St. Elizabeth, Osbern Bokenham (ca. 1445)	"Elyzabeth Ver" [140]
Life of St. Agatha, Osbern Bokenham (1445–47)	"Agas Fleg" [141]
Life of Saint Jerome (ca. 1429)	"þe hygh pryncesse Margarete duchesse of Clarence" [142]
S. Hieronymous [Life of Saint Jerome], anonymous (early 15th century)	"Right nobill and worthy lady" [143]
Life of St. Augustine, John Capgrave (ca. 1450)	"a noble creatur, a gentill woman" [144]

Amoryus and Cleopes, John Metham (ca. 1448)   "The knyght, Mylys Stapylton and his lady" [145]

Christine de Pizan, *Epistle of Othea,* trans.   "hye princesse" [146]
Stephen Scrope (ca. 1440–59)

NOTES

1. Elizabeth Salter, *English and International: Studies in the Literature, Art and Patronage of Medieval England,* ed. Derek Pearsall and Nicolette Zeeman (Cambridge, Eng.: Cambridge University Press, 1988), 3.

2. Susan Groag Bell, "Medieval Women Book Owners: Arbiters of Lay Piety and Ambassadors of Culture," in *Women and Power in the Middle Ages,* ed. Mary Erler and Maryanne Kowaleski (Athens: University of Georgia Press, 1988), 149–87; Joel T. Rosenthal, "Aristocratic Cultural Patronage and Book Bequests, 1350–1500," *Bulletin of the John Rylands University Library of Manchester* 64 (1982): 522–48; Susan Hagen Cavanaugh, "A Study of Books Privately Owned in England, 1300–1450" (Ph.D. diss., University of Pennsylvania, 1980).

3. The literary patronage of queens has received extensive treatment in both individual studies and broader investigations. See, for example, Marlijne Hemelaar, "Ex Libris Adelizae, Eleanorae et aliarum: The Queens of England, Literary Patronage, and Book Ownership, 1066–1509" (Thesis, University of Leiden, 1992); Karl Julius Holzknecht, *Literary Patronage in the Middle Ages* (Philadelphia: Collegiate, 1923); Rita Lejeune, "Rôle littéraire d'Aliénor d'Aquitaine et de sa famille," *Cultura Neolatina* 14 (1954): 5–57; and Salter, *English and International.* In the present essay I adopt Holzknecht's definition of literary patronage: "employment of favor, protection, and influential support to advance the interests of art. . . . [However,] patronage may omit the subsidy and may be simply an encouraging interest in letters extended by a person superior in wealth or position to an author with or without donatives of money or honors." Thus patronage "need not always imply financial support and may be only the encouragement of a connoisseur's interest and approval" (*Literary Patronage,* 4). See also Samuel Moore, "General Aspects of Patronage in the Middle Ages," *Library,* 3d ser., 4 (1913): 369–92, and "Patrons of Letters in Norfolk and Suffolk, c. 1450," *PMLA* 27 (1912): 186–207 and 28 (1913): 79–105.

4. If we accept John Benton's contention that the keys to self awareness from the twelfth century on are "Mother Church" and "biological mothers," there is great need to investigate the ways in which women taught and influenced others as well as the channels by which they transmitted ideas and values ("Consciousness of Self and Perceptions of Individuality," in *Renaissance and Renewal in the Twelfth Century,*

ed. Robert L. Benson and Giles Constable [Cambridge: Harvard University Press, 1982], 294).

5. On women's increasing roles in providing religious and moral background for families and households see Bell, "Medieval Women Book Owners," 149–87; Sharon Farmer, "Persuasive Voices: Clerical Images of Medieval Wives," *Speculum* 61 (1986): 517–43; and David Herlihy, *Medieval Households* (Cambridge, Mass.: Harvard University Press, 1985), 115–26. On women's reading and education, see Joan M. Ferrante, "The Education of Women in the Middle Ages in Theory, Fact, and Fantasy," in *Beyond Their Sex: Learned Women of the European Past*, ed. Patricia H. Labalme (New York: New York University Press, 1980), 9–42; and Chiara Frugoni, "The Imagined Woman," in *A History of Women in the West: II. Silences of the Middle Ages*, ed. Christiane Klapisch-Zuber (Cambridge: Belknap Press of Harvard University Press, 1992), 397.

6. Regarding the education of young Paula, the daughter of Toxotius and the granddaughter of Paula, Jerome writes, "Instead of jewels or silk let her love the manuscripts of the Holy Scriptures. . . . Let her learn the Psalter first, . . . then let her learn lessons of life in the Proverbs of Solomon . . . Ecclesiastes, Job . . . [and] the Gospels. . . . Let her grandmother take her [young Paula] on her lap and repeat to her grandchild the lessons she once taught her daughter" (*Select Letters of St. Jerome*, trans. F. A. Wright [Cambridge, Mass.: Harvard University Press, 1933], 364–67). Similarly, Christine de Pizan's Prudence recommends, "The lady willingly will read books inculcating good habits, as well as studying on occasion devotional books. She will disdain volumes describing dishonest habits or vice never allowing them in her household. She will not permit them in the presence of any daughter, relative, or lady-in-waiting." Christine also recommends saints' lives and cites Proverbs 31:10–31 (*A Medieval Woman's Mirror of Honor. The Treasury of the City of Ladies*, trans. Charity Cannon Willard [Tenafly, N.J.: Bard Hall, and Persea, 1989], 93, 174).

7. See, for example, Marina Warner, *Alone of All Her Sex: The Myth and Cult of the Virgin Mary* (New York: Random House/ Vintage Books, 1976), 81–223. Eleanor McLaughlin also observes that "medieval spirituality was populated with female figures: the saints, the Queen of Saints, Mary," and "even God himself was as really our mother as He is our Father." Pointing to the important role of female saints, the Virgin Mother, and Mary Magdalen, McLaughlin argues that respect for women coexisted with "the contrasting androcentrism, even misogyny of the theological tradition" ("Women, Power, and the Pursuit of Holiness in Medieval Christianity," in *Women of Spirit: Female Leadership in the Jewish and Christian Traditions*, ed. Rosemary Ruether and Eleanor McLaughlin [New York: Simon and Schuster, 1979], 125).

8. The first to see the resurrected Christ, she was "ranked with the apostles of the church" and was believed to hold an exalted place among women. Given her role as the first messenger of the salvation attached to the Resurrection, she was particularly emblematic of God's mercy to women (Helen Meredith Garth, *Saint Mary Magdalene in Mediaeval Literature* [Baltimore: Johns Hopkins University Press, 1950], 80–99).

See also Christine de Pizan, who, in her City of Ladies, places Mary Magdalen second after the Virgin Mary. (*The Book of the City of Ladies*, trans. Earl Jeffrey Richards [New York: Persea, 1982], 80, 219).

9. The line numbers correspond to Osbern Bokenham, *Legendys of Hooly Wummen*, ed. Mary S. Serjeantson, Early English Text Society, O.S. 206 (London: Oxford University Press, 1938), 136–74.

10. Katherine refuses marriage with the emperor Maxence because she is the bride of Christ. After she eloquently defends her position and deters the emperor, he arranges a debate between her and fifty of his best trained "clerkys." Katherine, who has been trained in the seven liberal arts, adroitly silences them, speaking "wythowte rhethoryk, in wurdys bare / or agumentatyf dysceptacyoun" (lines 6762–63). See Bokenham, *Legendys of Hooly Wummen*, 172–201. Margaret, too, refuses an unwanted marriage with her abductor Olibrius and overcomes the assaults of Satan in the form of both a "felle dragoun" and the "lykenesse of a man" (Henry Noble Mac-Cracken, ed., *The Minor Poems of John Lydgate*, Early English Text Society, O.S. 192 [London: Oxford University Press, 1934], 1:173–92). Having vowed her virginity to Christ, Agatha prevails despite an attempted seduction by the consul Quincyan and subsequent torture (Bokenham, *Legendys of Hooly Wummen*, 227–43). Dorothy resists marriage with the prefect Fabricius, her exemplary virtue and courage serving to edify even the taunting young pronotary Theophilus (ibid. 130–36). The legend of yet another saint appears in Robert de Greatham's *Miroir ou évangile des domnées*: Thaïs achieves a thoroughgoing repentance which gains her Heaven (Marion Y. H. Aitken, ed., *Etude sur "Le miroir ou les évangiles des domnées" de Robert de Gretham* [Paris: Champion, 1922], 170–74).

11. Rosemary Ruether, while acknowledging the negative side of asceticism, points out its positive aspect for women: "In its rejection of marriage and motherhood as the Christian norm, asceticism paradoxically suggested that women might now be liberated" from their traditionally defined roles ("Mothers of the Church," in *Women of Spirit*, 72). So, too, Diane Bornstein observes in regard to Christine de Pizan's praise of chastity and virginity, virgins and chaste women can transcend the limiting functions (like sex and childbearing) assigned them traditionally by society (Bornstein, ed., "Introduction," *Ideals for Women in the Works of Christine de Pizan*, Medieval and Renaissance Monograph Series, no. 1 [Detroit: Michigan Consortium for Medieval and Early Modern Studies, 1981], 7).

12. Bokenham, *Legendys of Hooly Wummen*, 38–58. Bokenham also refers readers to Lydgate's book of "owre ladyes lyf" (lines 2005–7). In the visual arts of the Middle Ages, Sheingorn points out, the Virgin Mary and the baby Jesus are frequently depicted together with Saint Anne. Such representations "emphasize these [maternal] aspects of women's behavior in the late Middle Ages. Christ owed his physical body, the Incarnation itself, to his maternal ancestors, and a glorification of his body implied a glorification of all aspects of maternal parenting" ("Appropriating the Holy Kinship: Gender and Family History," in Kathleen Ashley and Pamela Sheingorn, *Interpreting*

Cultural Symbols: Saint Anne in Late Medieval Society (Athens: University of Georgia Press, 1990), 176–78). In this connection, too, Bell has noted that in medieval iconography Saint Anne was frequently depicted teaching the young Virgin Mary to read ("Medieval Women Book Owners," 173).

13. Bokenham, *Legendys of Hooly Wummen*, 257–88. See also David Hugh Farmer, ed., *Oxford Dictionary of Saints*, 2d ed. (Oxford: Oxford University Press, 1987), 139.

14. Herlihy notes that in the Middle Ages "the mother played a far more active role and enjoyed higher prestige and stature than we have hitherto recognized" (*Medieval Households*, 124). Christine Reno goes further still, arguing that saints like these have risen above traditional gender roles to attain respect, power, and esteem ("Virginity as Ideal in Christine de Pizan's *Cité des Dames*," in *Ideals for Women*, ed. Bornstein, 69–90). Citing Jerome's *Commentary on the Epistle to the Ephesians*, Thomas Heffernen argues that celibacy allowed a woman, "for the very first time, to rise above her traditional status and become like a man" (*Sacred Biography. Saints and Their Biographers in the Middle Ages* [New York: Oxford University Press, 1988], 242, 259).

15. *A Legend of Holy Women: A Translation of Osbern Bokenham's Legends of Holy Women*, trans. Sheila Delany (Notre Dame, Ind.: Notre Dame University Press, 1992), xxx.

16. In *John Capgrave's Lives of St Augustine and St Gilbert of Sempringham and a Sermon*, ed. J. J. Munro, Early English Text Society, O.S. 140 (London: Kegan Paul, Trench, Trübner, 1910), Monica appears in chapters 2–24. As the "patron of mothers," Monica's feast day is the day before that of Saint Augustine, her son (Michael Walsh, ed., *Butler's Lives of Patron Saints*, rev. ed. [New York: Harper & Row, 1987], 345–48). On Mabel Rich and Paula, see A. T. Baker, ed., "La Vie de Saint Edmond, Archevêque de Cantorbéry," *Romania* 55 (1929): 333–34, 345–46; C. H. Lawrence, *St. Edmund of Abingdon: A Study in Hagiography and History* (Oxford: Clarendon, 1960), 68; Carl Horstmann, "Prosalegenden," *Anglia* 3 (1880): 332; and Ferdinand Cavallera, *Saint Jérôme: Sa vie et son oeuvre*, 2 vols. (Paris: Champion, 1922), 84–120, 166–89. Note too that it is Jerome who sets forth a program for the education of women. See, for instance, F. A. Wright, *Select Letters of St. Jerome*, 364–67, 466–69.

17. Farmer, *Oxford Dictionary of Saints*, 341–42.

18. Ruether, "Mothers of the Church," 76.

19. MacCracken, *Minor Poems of Lydgate*, 1:14–18. Christine de Pizan observes: "we can repeat the Book of Solomon's praise for the wise woman" (*Mirror of Honor*, 174). Note also that in the last half of the twelfth century Sanson de Nantuil translated part of the book of Proverbs at the request of a woman named Aëliz de Cundé (Claire Isoz, ed., *Proverbes de Salemon by Sanson de Nantuil* (London: Anglo-Norman Text Society, 1988), 1:6.

20. MacCracken, *Minor Poems of Lydgate*, 2:523–38.

21. Proffering vital information, Cleopes counsels, "Wele, . . . vndyr this forme than do ryght thus, / As I schal teche yow, and for no fere yt forgete; / For yff ye do, ye schal ther yowre lyffe lete (lines 1307–9; *The Works of John of Metham Including*

"The Romance of Amorys and Cleopes," ed. Hardin Craig, Early English Text Society, O.S. 132 [London: Kegan Paul, Trench, Trübner, 1916], viii–ix; 1–81). Amoryus, in his turn, willingly accepts her wise instruction. Additionally, this poem develops the theme of the young couple's maturing love; having begun in the temple of Venus, their mutual affection is transformed into a profound, virtuous bond following their symbolic death, rebirth, and conversion to Christianity. After a long, fruitful life the couple die and are buried together.

22. Frederick James Furnivall and I. Gollancz, Hoccleve's Works: The Minor Poems, rev. Jerome Mitchell and A.I. Doyle, Early English Text Society, E.S. 61 and 73; reprinted in 1 vol. (London: Oxford University Press, 1970), xxv. Unless otherwise noted, the line numbers are based on Furnivall and Gollancz's edition. See also Mary Ruth Pryor, ed., "Thomas Hoccleve's Series: An Edition of Manuscript Durham Cosin V III 9" (Ph.D. diss., University of California, Los Angeles, 1968).

23. In this connection, Hoccleve also alludes to Duke Humphrey as a potential patron (Prior, "Thomas Hoccleve's Series," 225–40).

24. Furnivall and Gollancz, Hoccleve's Minor Poems, 140–78.

25. Pryor, "Thomas Hoccleve's Series," 101–12, 241–92.

26. Interestingly, Guischart's Sermon refers to the Virgin Mary as "la reine des ciels ki en (sun) cors lout porte" (line 1613), and specifically includes "dames" and "puceles" in the salvational scheme (1. 1871; Le Sermon de Guischart de Beauliu, ed. Arvid Gabrielson [Uppsala: A.-B. Akademiska, 1909]).

27. Pryor, "Thomas Hoccleve's Series," 86–88. Such feminized allegorical characters, Joan Ferrante has argued, figure prominently in the literature of the Middle Ages, and their presence reflects several important principles: "the need for the female as well as the male in the order of things; the identification of the female with good qualities, with the higher parts of human nature; and the presentation of women not only as forces of evil, seducing man into sin, but also as forces for good leading him upwards to virtue" (Woman As Image in Medieval Literature from the Twelfth Century to Dante [New York: Columbia University Press, 1975; reprint Durham, N.C.: Labyrinth, 1985], 64).

28. Diane Bornstein, "Self-Consciousness and Self Concepts in the Work of Christine de Pizan," in Ideals for Women, 19.

29. Epistle of Othea, trans. Stephen Scrope, ed. Curt F. Bühler, Early English Text Society 264 (Oxford: Oxford University Press, 1970), 8. Subsequent references to Scropes's translation are based upon this edition; section numbers appear in the text between parentheses.

30. Ceres, who "fonde the crafte to ere lande," represents generosity (section 24). The young gentlewoman, Io, who "fonde many maneres of lettres," embodies love of learning (section 29). And Minerva, a "ladi of grete connynge," established "the crafte to make armure," signifying faith and virtue, which are "delyuered to the good knyghte be his moder" (section 13). Christine, as Diane Bornstein has noted, "argues for the

real importance of women as an uplifting, civilizing influence" ("Self-Consciousness," 19–20).

31. Christine's interpretation of this allegory drives the point home: "There where Othea seiþ þat she hath writen to him an hundrith auctorites and þat Augustus lerned of a womman is to vnderstand þat good wordis & good techingis is to preise, of what persoone þat seith it" (section 100). See Jane Chance's introduction to *Christine de Pizan's "Letter of Othea to Hector"* (Newburyport, Mass.: Focus Information Group, 1990), 32.

32. "Be Othea we schal understaunde the vertu of prudence and of wisedome" (7–8). See also Charity Cannon Willard, *Christine de Pizan: Her Life and Works* (New York: Persea, 1984), 94.

33. Bokenham, *Legendys of Hooly Wummen*, 139.

34. Christine de Pizan discusses at length the qualities associated with true honor: among the virtues she extols are faith, humility, charity, wisdom, prudence, constancy, courage, discretion, and sobriety or moderation (*Mirror of Honor*, 83–117).

35. For the acrostic the editor cites the 1525 printed edition (Boethius, *Boethius: De consolatione philosophiae*, trans. John Walton, ed. Mark Science, Early English Text Society, O.S. 170 [London: Oxford University Press, 1927], xliii–xlvi).

36. George Edward Cokayne, *The Complete Peerage of England, Scotland, Ireland, Great Britain and the United Kingdom Extant, Extinct, or Dormant*, new ed., rev. Vicary Gibbs et al., (London: Saint Catherine, 1910–1959), 2:131–32; 8:54; 12.2:381–82. Hereafter cited as *CP*.

37. C. D. Ross, "The Household Accounts of Elizabeth Berkeley, Countess of Warwick, 1420–1," *Transactions of the Bristol and Gloucestershire Archaeological Society* 70 (1952): 81–105; Thomas Dudley Fosbroke, *Abstracts and Extracts of Smyth's "Lives of the Berkeleys"* (London: Nichols, 1821), 143–55; Alexandra Sinclair, "The Great Berkeley Law-Suit Revisited 1417–39," *Southern History* 9 (1987): 34–50.

38. *CP* 11:698–705. See also A. J. Pollard, *John Talbot and the War in France 1427–1453* (London: Royal Historical Society, 1983), 8.

39. Derek Pearsall, *John Lydgate* (London: Routledge and Kegan Paul, 1970), 284, 291 n. 45. On the dedication page, in addition to illustrations of Saint George and John Talbot are those described as Saint Margaret and Margaret Beauchamp. See Francis Wormald and Phyllis M. Giles, *A Descriptive Catalogue of the Additional Illuminated Manuscripts in the Fitzwilliam Museum Acquired between 1895–1979* [Cambridge: Cambridge University Press, 1982], 441–53.

40. MacCracken, *Minor Poems of Lydgate*, 2:516.

41. Walter F. Schirmer, *John Lydgate: A Study in the Culture of the Fifteenth Century*, trans. A. E. Keep (Berkeley and Los Angeles: University of California Press, 1961), 93–94. Note also that Isabel Despenser (d. 1439), Richard Beauchamp's second wife, and stepmother of Margaret, commissioned Lydgate to translate the *Fifteen Joys of Mary*. Pearsall points out the connection between Beauchamp's second wife and his

daughter (71). The possibility that either the stepmother or stepdaughter (Margaret being slightly older) might have influenced the other's patronage cannot be ruled out.

42. After his marriage to Elizabeth Berkeley, Richard Beauchamp styled himself "comes de Warrewyk et de Aumale, seigneur L'Isle et capitayne de Rouen" (*CP* 8:54).

43. Pollard, *John Talbot*, 131–32; *CP* 2:131–33, 8:54–59.

44. Unfortunately, little is known about Blanche's mother, Isabel. It is perhaps significant, however, that she was the daughter of Henry, first Lord Beaumont (the French partisan of Edward I), and Alice Comyn, daughter and coheir of Sir Alexander Comyn (*CP* 7:409, 2:375).

45. Emile J. Arnould, ed., *Le livre de seyntz medicines: The Unpublished Devotional Treatise of Henry of Lancaster*, Anglo-Norman Text Society (Oxford: Blackwell, 1940). In addition, it is from Henry's sister Isabel, at the time a nun at Amesbury, that Henry V purchased a romance (Juliet Vale, *Edward III and Chivalry: Chivalric Society and Its Context, 1270–1350*, [Woodbridge, England: Boydell, 1982], 51).

46. Popular opinion held that Maud had been poisoned at the behest of her brother-in-law so that the Lancaster inheritance "might be reunited" (under John's control). See *CP* 7:410; and Robert Somerville, *The History of the Duchy of Lancaster, 1265–1603*, vol. 1 (London: The Chancellor and the Council of the Duchy of Lancaster, 1953) 1:67–68.

47. Blanche's children were born between 1360 and 1368: Philippa, John, Elizabeth, Henry (later to become Henry IV of England), and Edmund. See Norman W. Webster, *Blanche of Lancaster* (Driffield, England: Halstead, 1990), 43; and Marjorie Anderson, "Blanche Duchess of Lancaster," *Modern Philology* 45 (1947): 152–59. It is worth noting that of Blanche's three children who survived past infancy, two (Henry and Phillipa) would exhibit marked literary affinities. For Henry's activities, see Cavanaugh, "Books Privately Owned," 408–11.

48. After paying tribute to his benefactor Philippa of Hainaut, who died a month earlier than Blanche, the French poet extols the duchess of Lancaster:

Ossi sa fille de Lancastre—
Haro! mettés moi un emplastre
Sur le coer! car quant m'en souvient,
Certes souspirer me couvient,
Tant sui plains de merancolie
Elle morut jone et jolie,
Environ de .XXII. ans,
Gaie, lie, frisce, esbatans,
Douce, simple, d'umle samblance
La tres bonne dame eut nom Blance.
J'ai trop perdu en ces .II. dames,
J'en tors mes poins, j'en bach mes pames.

(lines 241–52)

Jean Froissart, *Le joli buisson de jonece,* ed. Anthime Fourrier (Geneva: Droz, 1975), 55.

49. Larry D. Benson, ed., *The Riverside Chaucer,* 3d ed. (Boston: Houghton Mifflin, 1987), 633. See also, George B. Pace, "Speght's Chaucer and MS. GG.4.27," *Studies in Bibliography* 21 (1968): 225–35. Jeanne Krochalis indicates that the ABC was for Anne of Bohemia, wife of Richard II; however, she does not offer supporting evidence ("The Books and Reading of Henry V and His Circle," *Chaucer Review* 23 [1988]: 50–77).

50. Bell, "Medieval Women Bookowners," 163. Blanche's son, Henry IV (d. 1413), was also known for his appreciation of books and learning. See, for example, James Westfall Thompson, *The Medieval Library* (Chicago: University of Chicago Press, 1939), 401. Henry was perhaps also encouraged by his wife, Mary de Bohun, daughter of Hoccleve's patron Joan FitzAlan (*CP* 6:477).

51. George L. Kittredge, "Chaucer and Some of His Friends," *Modern Philology* 1 (1903): 4–5. Among Philippa's surviving correspondence are two letters, one to Richard II and one to Thomas Archbishop of Canterbury. (Mary Dominica Legge, ed., *Anglo-Norman Letters and Petitions from All Souls MS. 182,* Anglo-Norman Text Society [Oxford: Blackwell, 1941], 347–48, 73–74).

52. Eustache Deschamps, *Oeuvres complètes,* ed. H.E. de Queux Saint-Hilaire and Gaston Raynaud, Société des anciens textes français (Paris: Firmin Didot, 1884), 4:259–61. Two other *balades* and a *roundel* by Deschamps may also have connections with Philippa (257–58, 261–64). See also Kittredge, "Chaucer and Some of His Friends," 3–5; and *CP* 7:415. On the Order of the Flower and the Leaf, see Kittredge, "Chaucer and Some of His Friends," 1–3.

53. *CP* 6:473–74, 1:243–44. On Humphrey's literary holdings, see Cavanaugh, "Books Privately Owned," 108–9.

54. Since Humphrey left no male heir, his estate was divided among Joan, his widow, and their daughters Eleanor and Mary (George A. Holmes, *The Estates of the Higher Nobility in Fourteenth-Century England* [Cambridge: Cambridge University Press, 1957], 24–25; *CP* 6:474). See also Legge, *Anglo-Norman Letters,* 388, 399–400, 416–17.

55. Fourteen poems from Deguileville are incorporated into a 1413 prose translation of the *Pèlerinage de l'âme.* These poems, usually attributed to Hoccleve, appear in Frederick James Furnivall, ed., *Hoccleve's Works: The Regement of Princes and Fourteen Minor Poems,* Early English Text Society, E.S. 72 (London: Kegan Paul, Trench, Trübner, 1897). See also M.C. Seymour, *Selections from Hoccleve* (Oxford: Clarendon, 1981), xiv–xv; and *CP* 6:474.

56. Joan FitzAlan's mother, Eleanor, the second wife of Richard FitzAlan, earl of Arundel (d. 1375/76), was sister of Blanche's father, Henry Grosmont; thus, Joan and Blanche were the granddaughters of Henry, earl of Lancaster, and Maude, daughter and heiress of Sir Patrick Chaworth (*CP* 1:244).

57. A. J. Doyle, "English Books in and out of Court from Edward III to Henry VII," in *English Court Culture in the Later Middle Ages,* ed. V. J. Scattergood and J. W. Sherborne (New York: St. Martin's, 1983), 168. Notably, after Joan's death her grand-

son Henry V purchased books from her estate (Cavanaugh, "Books Privately Owned," 346).

58. *CP* 6:477; 728. Before she died at twenty-four, Mary bore at least six children, in addition to Henry of Monmouth (later Henry V).

59. See Krochalis, "Books of Henry V," 54; Eric Millar and Montague Rhodes James, *The Bohun Manuscripts: A Group of Five Manuscripts Executed in England About 1370 for Members of the Family* (Oxford: Roxburghe Club, 1936); Cavanaugh, "Books Privately Owned," 111–12. Philippa also received from the royal surgeon, John Arderne, an illustrated manual in Latin (Krochalis, "Books of Henry V," 54, 71 n. 23). In this connection, it is possible that Joan FitzAlan may have had a continuing influence on her grandchildren, even after Mary's death. She wrote at least one letter (possibly to Hugh Waterton) expressing concern for her grandchildren and mentioning Philippa by name (Legge, *Anglo-Norman Letters*, 399–400). Of note here, too, are Nicholas Orme's observations that Katherine Waterton was the *maîtresse* of Philippa, daughter of Mary de Bohun and Henry Bolingbroke, and that ABC books were purchased for Philippa, aged three, and Blanche, aged five (Nicholas Orme, *From Childhood to Chivalry: The Education of the English Kings and Aristocracy, 1066–1530* [New York: Methuen, 1984], 26, nn. 127, 158).

60. Thomas of Woodstock's father, Edward III, arranged the marriage between his son and the Bohun heiress Eleanor. According to one account Thomas tried to induce his minor sister-in-law, Mary, to enter the convent, hoping to secure her share of the Bohun inheritance as well as Eleanor's; however, John of Gaunt "rescued" her from the castle of Pleshey and arranged for her marriage to his son Henry of Derby (later to become Henry IV). See Holmes, *Estates of the Higher Nobility*, 24–25; and *CP* 6:474–77, 5:727–28. On the extensive list of books seized from Pleshey castle upon the arrest of Thomas of Woodstock, it should be noted that Pleshey constituted part of the Bohun inheritance, and that there is a question about how many of these volumes came to him through his wife. See also Cavanaugh, "Books Privately Owned," 111, 842–51; and Krochalis, "Books of Henry V," 51–52; Millar and James, *Bohun Manuscripts*, 3.

61. See also the books bequeathed to Eleanor's son Humphrey: "un Cronike de Fraunce en Frauncois"; a "regimine principum"; "un livre de vices et de vertues"; and a rhymed "historie de chivaler a cigne" (John Nichols, ed., *A Collection of All the Wills Now Known To Be Extant of the Kings and Queens of England, Princes and Princesses of Wales, and Every Branch of the Blood Royal, from the Reign of William the Conqueror to That of Henry the Seventh Exclusive* [London: Nichols, 1780], 181–83). Scattergood identifies the books as "a two-volume Bible in French, a book of decretals also in French, Comestor's *Biblia Scholastica*, the *Vitae patrum* by Jerome and John Cassian, Gregory's *Cura Pastoralis*, four psalters . . . a [Golden Legend], a book of vices and virtues," and in addition to the French romance of the *Chivaler a Cigne* were "a chronicle of France in French, and a version of Egidus's *De Regimine Principum*. Scattergood goes on to observe that most of these works are in French, or possibly

Latin, but not in English ("Literary Culture at the Court of Richard II," in *English Court Culture*, 35).

62. Holmes, *Estates of the Higher Nobility*, 25. Carole Rawcliffe, *The Staffords, Earls of Stafford and Dukes of Buckingham, 1394–1521* (Cambridge: Cambridge University Press, 1978), 12–17.

63. *CP* 12.1:181, 5:176–78. Isabel Bourchier's family background, which is indeed notable, exceeds the scope of the present essay. She and her brother, Richard of York, were the offspring of Richard of Conisburgh, earl of Cambridge (executed 1415), and Anne Mortimer, daughter of Roger Mortimer, earl of March, and Eleanor Holland. On her mother's side, Isabel is descended from Elizabeth, countess of Ulster (d. 1363), wife of Lionel, duke of Clarence. The countess of Ulster, whose accounts indicate that the young Chaucer served in her household, was a granddaughter of the Clare heiress and founder of Clare College, Elizabeth de Burgh (d. 1360), herself a noted bibliophile. Elizabeth de Burgh's mother was the formidable Joan of Acre (d. ca. 1307), daughter of Edward I and Eleanor of Castile, and sister of Mary (d. 1332), the nun of Amesbury who commissioned Trevet's *Chronicle*. See *CP* 5:138; 12.2:905; 3:244–45; 5:708–10.

64. Rawcliffe, *The Staffords*, 12–18, 84, 105; Rowena E. Archer, " 'How ladies . . . who live on their manors ought to manage their households and estates': Women as Landholders and Administrators in the Later Middle Ages," in *Woman Is a Worthy Wight: Women in English Society, c. 1200–1500*, ed. P. J. P. Goldberg (Gloucester, England, and Wolfeboro Falls, N.H.: Sutton, 1992), 172; Kate Mertes, *The English Noble Household, 1250–1600* (Oxford: Blackwell, 1988), 210; Bonnie S. Anderson and Judith P. Zinsser, *A History of Their Own* (New York: Harper and Row, 1988), 1:328.

65. J. Nichols, *Collection of Wills*, 278.

66. Rawcliffe, *The Staffords*, 95.

67. MacCracken, *Minor Poems of Lydgate*, 1:130–32. See also Schirmer, *John Lydgate*, 190.

68. *CP* 8:452–53. Shortly thereafter she married John Holland, earl of Huntingdon (d. 1447), with whom she had at least one son. See *CP* 5:208–12, 8:453.

69. MacCracken, *Minor Poems of Lydgate*, 1:173–92.

70. Of some relevance here is the fact that Joan FitzAlan was the maternal aunt of the patron of Symon Winter's *Life of St. Jerome* (New Haven, Yale Beinecke Library, MS. 317), Margaret Holland, Duchess of Clarence (d. 1439), Margaret's mother being Alice FitzAlan (d. 1415), the daughter of Richard FitzAlan (d. 1375/76) and Eleanor (d. 1372/73). Margaret's father was Thomas Holland, earl of Kent (d. 1350) (*CP* 7:156). Perhaps significantly, Margaret also lived a long and active widowhood, during which time she made many benefactions to Syon, including a Bible (George R. Keiser, "Patronage and Piety in Fifteenth-Century England: Margaret, Duchess of Clarence, Symon Wynter, and Beinecke MS 317," *Yale University Library Gazette* 60, nos. 1 and 2 [1985]: 32–46; and Cavanaugh, "Books Privately Owned," 562.)

71. Katherine Roet Swynford was the daughter of Sir Payne Roet, who had come

to England with Queen Philippa of Hainaut. She served as governess to the daughters of John of Gaunt and Blanche of Lancaster. (For a discussion of the role of the *maîtresse* in aristocratic families, see Nicholas Orme, "The Education of the Courtier," in *The English Court in the Later Middle Ages*, ed. V. J. Scattergood and J. W. Sherborne [London: Duckworth, 1983] 71–72). Despite a general lack of information concerning Katherine Swynford, it is likely that she had some education and that she may well have exercised some influence on the literary sensibilities of her daughter, Joan Beaufort, and perhaps on her charge, Philippa of Lancaster. Katherine, who, as the third wife of John of Gaunt, became duchess of Lancaster, was, of course, the sister of Philippa Roet Chaucer, the wife of the poet.

72. Joan was also the aunt of Henry V, John duke of Bedford, and Humphrey duke of Gloucester. For reference to Jacqueline de Hainault, once married to Humphrey, see Eleanor Prescott Hammond, "Lydgate and the Duchess of Gloucester," *Anglia* 27 (1904): 381–98.

73. *CP* 12.2:547.

74. Thomas Rymer, *Foedera, conventiones litterae, et cujuscunque generis acta publica*, 2d ed. (London: Tonson, 1727), 10:317.

75. Furnivall and Gollancz, *Hoccleve's Works*, xxv. Unless otherwise noted, the line numbers are based on this edition. Note too that Hoccleve's *How to Learn to Die* was dedicated separately to Humphrey duke of Gloucester, whereas the complete Durham Cosin manuscript was dedicated to his aunt Joan, countess of Westmorland. See also Pryor, "Thomas Hoccleve's Series," 64–69; H. C. Schultz, "Thomas Hoccleve, Scribe," *Speculum* 12 (1937): 71, 73; Cavanaugh, "Books Privately Owned," 606; J. Thompson, *The Medieval Library*, 402.

76. Charles Ross, *Richard III* (Berkeley and Los Angeles: University of California Press, 1981), 3–5. See also *CP* 12.2:909.

77. John Hardyng, in rededicating his *Chronicle* to Richard of York, recommends the work to Cecily and their children. See Orme, *From Childhood to Chivalry*, 161; and John Hardyng, *Chronicle*, ed. Henry Ellis (London: 1812), 23.

78. C. A. J. Armstrong, "The Piety of Cicely, Duchess of York: A Study in Late Medieval Culture," in *For Hillaire Belloc: Essays in Honor of His 71st Birthday*, ed. Douglas Woodruff (New York: Sheed and Ward, 1942), 68–91; John Nichols, ed., *Collection of Ordinances and Regulations for the Government of the Royal Household* (London: Society of Antiquaries, 1790), 37–39.

79. John Gough Nichols and John Bruce, eds., *Wills from Doctors' Commons*, (Westminster: Nichols for the Camden Society, 1863), 2–3. On the identification of these works, see Hemelaar's listing: the *Revelations of Saint Bridget of Sweden*; the *Life of St. Katherine of Siena*; the *Life of St. Mathilda*, an English translation of Mathilda of Hackeborn's *Liber specialis gratie*, also known as the Book of Saint Maud or the Book of Ghostly Grace; *De infantia salvatoris*; the *Golden Legend*; and a volume containing Walter Hilton's *On Contemplative and Active Life* and the pseudo-Bonaventuran *Mirrour of the Blessed Lyf of Jesu Christ*, by Nicholas Love, prior of the Carthusian Mount

Grace in Yorkshire (*Ex libris Adelizae*, 73). This last item echoes with the Love translation of the *Meditatione vitae Christi* thought to be owned by Cecily's mother, Joan Beaufort.

80. As duchess of Burgundy, Margaret of York commissioned several religious books. Caxton recognizes her as the patron of his *Recuyell of the Historyes of Troyes*, published in Bruges in 1475/76. Although her patronage is connected with Burgundy, her tastes are said to have been cultivated in England under the supervision of her mother, Cecily. See, for example, the introduction and appendix of Thomas Kren, ed., *Margaret of York, Simon Marmion, and the Visions of Tondal: Papers Delivered at a Symposium Organized by the Department of Manuscripts of the J. Paul Getty Museum in Collaboration with the Huntingdon Library and Art Collections, June 21–24, 1990* (Malibu, Calif.: J. Paul Getty Museum, 1992), 257–63; Muriel Hughes, "Margaret of York, Duchess of Burgundy, Diplomat, Patroness, Bibliophile, and Benefactress," *Private Library*, 3d ser., 7 (1984): 3–17; "The Library of Margaret of York, Duchess of Burgundy," *Private Library*, 3d ser., 7 (1984): 53–78; and Joel T. Rosenthal, "Aristocratic Cultural Patronage and Book Bequests, 1350–1500," *Bulletin of the John Rylands University Library of Manchester* 64 (1982): 541, 544.

81. CP 2:388–89. Anne Neville was therefore the daughter-in-law of Anne of Woodstock, countess of Stafford (d. 1438) and sister-in-law of Anne, countess of March (d. 1429/32), both patrons of Lydgate.

82. Kate Mertes, *English Noble Household*, 210. Recorded in surviving documents are her twenty-three attempts to recover debts through litigation (Rawcliffe, *The Staffords*, 54, 179). See also Bonnie S. Anderson and Judith P. Zinsser, *A History of Their Own* (New York: Harper and Row, 1988), 1:328.

83. Nicholas Harris Nicolas, ed., *Testamenta Vetusta*, (London: Nichols, 1826), 356–57. The books cited were bequeathed to her daughter-in-law Lady Margaret Beaufort (daughter of the second duke of Somerset), who would become the matriarch of the Tudor line and a patron in her own right. See Rawcliffe, *The Staffords*, 96; and Anne Crawford, "The Piety of Late Medieval Queens," in *The Church in Pre-Reformation Society: Essays in Honour of F. R. H. Du Boulay*, ed. Caroline M. Barron and Christopher Harper-Bill (Woodbridge, Eng.: Boydell, 1985), 54–55. See Margaret Galway, "The 'Troilus' Frontispiece," *Modern Language Review* 44 (1949): 161.

84. John Lydgate, *Lydgate's Minor Poems: The Two Nightingale Poems*, ed. Otto Glauning, Early English Text Society, E.S. 80 (London: Kegan Paul, Trench, Trübner, 1900) xxxiv–xxxix; Mary Dominica Legge, *Anglo-Norman Literature and Its Background* (Oxford: Clarendon, 1963), 233; MacCracken, *Minor Poems of Lydgate*, 1:xxxiii; Pearsall, *John Lydgate*, 267–68. Note, however, that the question of Lydgate's canon is an open one. See Stephen R. Reimer, "The Lydgate Canon: A Project Description," *Literary and Linguistic Computing* 5 (1990): 248–49. The line numbers are from Glauning's edition. On the *Philomena*, see Legge, *Anglo-Norman Literature*, 233; Lydgate, *Lydgate's Minor Poems*, xxxviii–xxxix.

85. In this work the poet also alludes to the death of the duke of Warwick (Henry

Beauchamp [d. 1444/45]), son of Richard Beauchamp, earl of Warwick (d. 1439). Glauning points out that Henry Beauchamp was "brother-in-law to Richard Nevil [the king maker], who married Anne, Henry's sister and heiress" (Glauning, *Lydgate's Minor Poems*, xxxvi–xxxvii). Henry Beauchamp, it should be noted, was also the husband of Anne Neville's niece Cecily, daughter of Anne's brother Richard Neville and Alice Montagu, earl and countess of Salisbury (*CP* 11:398).

86. Gaston du Fresne de Beaucourt, *Histoire de Charles VII* (Paris: Picard, 1890), 5:137. See also, *Dictionary of National Biography*, ed. Leslie Stephen and Sidney Lee (Oxford: Oxford University Press, 1885–90), 18:861.

87. *CP* 10:238–39. Elizabeth Howard was the heir (in her own right) of John Howard, duke of Norfolk; after John de Vere's death she was the dowager countess with her one-third interest in the earl of Oxford's estates. Like Saint Elizabeth, who was driven from the court by her brother-in-law after the death of her husband, the widowed Elizabeth de Vere was divested of her lands between 1473 and 1475 (*CP* 10:238–39). See also M. A. Hicks, "The Last Days of the Countess of Oxford," *English Historical Review* 103 (1988): 76–95; and Anne Crawford, "Victims of Attainder: The Howard and de Vere Women in the Late Fifteenth Century," in *Medieval Women in Southern England* (Reading, Eng.: University of Reading, 1989), 62.

88. *CP* 10:239, 3:354.

89. In his introduction (xix–xx) to Scrope's translation, Bühler mentions two less probable candidates as dedicatee of the *Epistle of Othea*: the first is Anne Stafford de Vere's mother, Anne Neville, duchess of Buckingham. The second is Anne Beauchamp (d. 1492), wife of Richard Neville, earl of Warwick. Anne Beauchamp was the daughter of Richard Beauchamp, thirteenth earl of Warwick, and his second wife, Isabel Despenser (*CP* 12.2:382, 392), who was the patron of Lydgate's *Fifteen Joys of Our Lady*. Both these women would also fit the suggested paradigm of literary patronage.

90. Furnivall and Gollancz, *Hoccleve's Minor Poems*, 242.

91. A. T. Baker, "Saints' Lives Written in Anglo-French: Their Historical, Social, and Literary Importance," *Transactions of the Royal Society of the United Kingdom* n.s., 4 (1924): 145; *CP* 1:238–39.

92. The note reads: "In the countess of Winchester's book let there be a pair of images on each page, thus: . . ." (James's translation). The book either was never completed or was lost. See *Illustrations to the Life of St. Alban in Trinity College Dublin MS E. 1. 40*, ed. W. R. L. Lowe and E. F. Jacob. (Oxford: Clarendon Press, 1924), 16. See also Richard Vaughan, *Matthew Paris* (Cambridge: Cambridge University Press, 1958), 170–71.

93. Eleanor was the third wife of Roger de Quincy, earl of Winchester (d. 1264). The earl's second wife was Maud or Matilda de Bohun (d. 1252) (*CP* 12.2:753–54). See A. Baker, "La Vie de Saint Edmond," 338–39.

94. *CP* 12.1:501–2; *CP* 10:358–64.

95. James translates the note as follows: "G. send, please, to the lady countess of Arundel, Isabel, that she is to send you the book about Saint Thomas the Martyr

and Saint Edward which I translated and illustrated and which the lady countess of Cornwall may keep until Whitsuntide" (*Estoire de Seint Ædward le rei*, 21).

96. *La Estoire de seint Ædward le Rei. Attributed to Matthew Paris*, Kathryn Young Wallace (London: Anglo-Norman Text Society, 1983), xvi. See also *La Estoire de seint Ædward le rei*, ed. Montague Rhodes James. Roxburghe Club Edition (Oxford: Oxford University Press, 1920), 25.

97. *CP* 3:431. An area that merits further study is the ancestry of Isabel, countess of Arundel, and Eleanor, countess of Winchester. Their maternal line is particularly notable. Their grandmother was Isabel, countess of Pembroke, who was sister and heir of Gilbert de Strigoil and who married William Marshal (d. 1219) (*CP* 10:358). Their great-great-grandmother, Isabel Beaumont (wife of Gilbert FitzGilbert de Clare [d. ca. 1148]), was the daughter and heir of Robert de Beaumont, earl of Leicester (d. 1118), a magnate noted in his time for his education (*CP* 10:351). See also Michael Altschul, *A Baronial Family in Medieval England: The Clares, 1217–1314* (Baltimore: Johns Hopkins University Press, 1965), 21; and David Crouch, *The Beaumont Twins: The Roots and Branches of Power in the Twelfth Century* (Cambridge: Cambridge University Press, 1986), 207–11.

98. Ismania was married first to Sir John de Ralegh; second to Maud's father, John de Burghersh (d. 1391); and third to Lawrence Berkerolles (*CP* 7:199). Alice was also married or engaged to Sir John Philip (d. 1415). See, for example, Carol A. Metcalfe, "Alice Chaucer, Duchess of Suffolk, c. 1404–1475" (Ph.D. diss., University of Keele, 1970), 14–15; *CP* 12.1:447.

99. Archer, "How ladies," 154–55; Metcalfe, "Alice Chaucer," 50–58; *CP* 12.1:448–50.

100. Thomas's parents, Geoffrey Chaucer and Philippa Roet Chaucer, both died before Alice Chaucer was born in 1404/5.

101. Moore, "Patrons of Letters (I)," 201–4. Alice is also purported to be the recipient of a rhymed acronym by Thomas Pycard. See MS. Additional 16165, f. 248; and Seymour, *Selections from Hoccleve*, 127.

102. Twenty poems in the Bodleian Fairfax manuscript are ascribed to William de la Pole, who knew Charles d'Orléans. See Metcalfe, "Alice Chaucer," 55; Martin B. Ruud, *Thomas Chaucer* (Minneapolis: University of Minnesota Press, 1926), 87, 88; Schirmer, *John Lydgate*, 61, 121, 252; *CP* 11:393–95, 12.1:443–48.

103. Bodleian MSS DD Ewelme, a.7, A 46, A 47, A 48. Among the books she mentions are "a frensh boke of the *Citee de Dames*" (perhaps Christine de Pizan's *Livre de la Citee des Dames*); *Les quatre fils Aymon*; a French book of the tales of philosophers; a Latin book on the moral instruction of a prince; and a book in English of a pilgrimage (possibly John Lydgate's *Pilgrimage of the World*). See Archer, "How ladies," 156, 176 n. 35, 176–77 nn. 45, 46 Metcalfe, "Alice Chaucer," 57. See also Pearsall, *John Lydgate*, 162–63, 173.

104. Metcalfe, "Alice Chaucer," 1; Ruud, *Thomas Chaucer*, 2–3; *CP* 7:193–99.

105. Pearsall, *John Lydgate*, 162.

106. See, for example, G. A. Holmes, who stresses "the importance of female succession in medieval landownership" (*Estates of the Higher Nobility*, 10). On the activities and responsibilities of medieval noblewomen, see Margaret Wade Labarge, *A Baronial Household of the Thirteenth Century* (New York: Barnes and Noble, 1965); Diane Bornstein, "The Ideal of the Lady of the Manor," in *Ideals for Women*, 117–28; and Christine de Pizan, *Mirror of Honor*, 81–147.

107. Archer, "How ladies," 162. See also Caroline M. Barron, "The 'Golden Age' of Women in London," in *Medieval Women in Southern England*, eds. Keith Bate, Anne Curry, Christopher Hardman, and Peter Noble (Reading, Eng.: University of Reading, 1989), 35. See also Ruth Kittel, "Women Under the Law in Medieval England, 1066–1485," in *The Women of England from Anglo-Saxon Times to the Present: Interpretive Bibliographical Essays*, ed. Barbara Kanner (Hamden, Conn.: Archon, 1979), 124–37.

108. Increasingly popular from the mid-thirteenth century on, jointures, which were essentially "joint tenancy in survivorship by a landholder and his wife" and which increased the widow's security, were usually part of the marriage contract negotiations (Chris Given-Wilson, *The English Nobility in the Late Middle Ages* [London: Routledge and Kegan Paul, 1987], 139–40). See also May McKisack, *The Fourteenth Century, 1307–1399* (Oxford: Clarendon, 1956), 261; and Doris Mary Stenton, *The English Woman in History* (London: Allen and Unwin, 1957), 35. Holmes also points out that not only were heiresses important in marriage alliances but they sometimes "managed to control an inheritance" over a long period of time, as did Elizabeth de Burgh, the great Clare heiress (*Estates of the Higher Nobility*, 10).

109. Mertes, *English Noble Household*, 54. See also Archer, "How ladies," 149–81.

110. For a French parallel, see Christine de Pizan, *Mirror of Honor* (200–201). See also Stenton, *English Woman*, 54–55; Barron "Golden Age of Women," 35–37.

111. Archer points out a woman may have conducted herself similarly during her married life, whether husbands were present or absent, as she did as a widow, but when she is a married woman whose legal identity is submerged in her husband's, we tend to lose sight of her (Archer, "How ladies," 162).

112. Ibid., 152.

113. Between 1240 and 1242 Robert Grosseteste dedicated his *Reules Seynt Robert* to the recently widowed countess of Lincoln, Margaret Lacy (d. 1266), daughter and heir of Robert de Quincy (d. 1217) and his wife, Hawise (the coheir of Ranulf earl of Chester). Both the countess of Lincoln and her daughter Maud led active lives as widows, though no literary patronage has been linked to the name of the latter (*CP* 7:679–80; Altschul, *Baronial Family*, 36–37). The second is a treatise composed for Lady Denise, or Dionysia, Munchensy by Walter Bibbesworth. Rothwell observes that "Bibbesworth was able to take for granted . . . an elementary knowledge of grammar and basic everyday terminology. What his English patroness needed, in order to make her children competent users of French, was the specialized vocabulary which they would have to master for the running of their estates once they had come of age" (W. Rothwell, "A Mis-judged Author and a Mis-Used Text: Walter de Bibbesworth and

his 'Tretiz,' " *Modern Language Review* 77 [1982]: 282). Denise Munchensy (d. 1304), the daughter and heir of Nicholas de Anesty (*CP* 9:421), married three times (Walter Langton [d. 1234]; Warin de Munchensy [d. 1255]; and Robert Butyller [d. ca. 1272]) (*CP* 9:421–22). After the death of her third husband she remained a widow for more than two decades, administering her estates, serving as custodian and executor of her son's estate, pursuing litigation as guardian of her granddaughter's inheritance, and founding Waterbeach Abbey for Minoresses (*CP* 9:421–24). See also Albert C. Baugh, "The Date of Walter of Bibbesworth's Traité," in *Festschrift für Walther Fischer* (Heidelberg: Winter, 1959), 30; and Michael Hicks, "The English Minoresses and Their Early Benefactors," in *Monastic Studies: The Continuity of Tradition,* ed. Judith Loades (Bangor, Wales: Gwynedd, 1990), 158. On the numerous parallels between the advice offered by the *Reules Seynt Robert* and that offered by Christine de Pizan, see Archer, "How ladies," 157.

114. One striking example of the transmission of such a work is the *Life of Saint Anne,* which Osbern Bokenham wrote for Katherine Clopton Denston in honor of her young daughter Anne (Bokenham, *Legendys of Hooly Wummen,* 57–58, lines 2092–98).

115. Margaret Patterson Hannay's observations about women in Tudor England have some resonance here: "Confined to certain areas of discourse, they speak through religious writing and translation. . . . Although these English women were relegated to the margins of discourse—to patronage, translation, dedications of translations, epitaphs, letters, and private devotional meditations—they did find their own words through the proclamations of the word of God" (*Silent but for the Word: Tudor Women as Patrons, Translators, and Writers of Religious Works* [Kent, Ohio: Kent State University Press, 1985], 14).

116. Isabel de Warenne, countess of Arundel (d. 1282). This name and those in subsequent notes represent the most widely accepted identification of dedicatees. On Isabel de Warenne, see A. Baker, "La vie de saint Edmond," 332–81. A second saint's life, the Latin *Life of Richard de Wyche,* composed by Ralph Bocking about 1270, is also associated with Isabel countess of Arundel and with Archbishop Kilwardby (Legge, *Anglo-Norman Literature,* 270).

117. Lady Dionysia Hacon (d. ca. 1200). Gabrielson, *Sermon de Guischart de Beauliu,* 58. See also Legge, *Anglo-Norman Literature,* 138.

118. Margaret Lacy, countess of Lincoln (d. 1266). *Walter of Henley's Husbandry Together with an Anonymous Husbandry, Seneschaucie, and Robert Grosseteste's Rules,* ed. and trans. Elizabeth Lamond (London: Longmans, Green, 1890), xlii, 123–50. See also Dorothea Ochinsky, *Walter of Henley and Other Treatises on Estate Management and Accounting* (Oxford: Clarendon, 1971), 388–407.

119. Aline or Elena Zouche (d. 1296), daughter of Robert de Quincy and wife of Alan Zouche. K. V. Sinclair, "The Anglo-Norman Patrons of Robert the Chaplain and Robert of Greatham," *Forum for Modern Language Studies* 28 (1992): 200–203. This identification by Sinclair supersedes the earlier one: Aline or Eleanor Monfort (dates

uncertain). Aitken, *Etude sur "Le miroir."* See also Margaret Deanesly, *The Lollard Bible and Other Medieval Biblical Versions* (Cambridge: Cambridge University Press, 1920; reprint 1966), 149.

120. Dionysia Munchensy (d. 1304). *Le traité de Walter de Bibbesworth sur la langue française,* ed. Annie Owen (Paris: Presses Universitaires de France, 1929), 43. On the identification of Dionysia Munchensy, see Baugh, "Date of Bibbesworth's *Traité*," 21–33.

121. Mary (d. 1332), the daughter of Edward I and Eleanor of Castile. Although she accompanied her grandmother, Eleanor of Provence, to Amesbury, and became a nun, Mary is included here because of her apparent worldliness and her family connections. Legge, *Anglo-Norman Literature,* 299–302.

122. Blanche of Lancaster (d. 1369). Benson, *The Riverside Chaucer,* 637–40, 1076. See also Pace, "Speght's Chaucer," 225–35; and *CP* 7:415.

123. Philippa of Lancaster (d. 1415). Deschamps, *Oeuvres complètes,* 4:259–61, 10:220.

124. Joan FitzAlan, countess of Hereford (d. 1419). Furnivall and Gollancz, *Hoccleve's Minor Poems,* 1–8. See also, Seymour, *Selections from Hoccleve,* 1–7, 103.

125. Elizabeth Berkeley (d. 1422). Walton, *Boethius,* xlv–xlvi.

126. The duke and duchess of York, Edward (d. 1415) and Philippe de Mohun (d. 1431). Furnivall and Gollancz, *Hoccleve's Minor Poems,* 49–51. See also Seymour, *Selections from Hoccleve,* 55–56, 126. According to Seymour (126), the *Balade* is an envoy which would have been appended to a presentation copy of *Regiment of Princes.*

127. Anne Stafford, countess of March (d. 1432). MacCracken, *Minor Poems of Lydgate,* 1:173–92. See also Schirmer, *John Lydgate,* 154–55; and Pearsall, *John Lydgate,* 168.

128. Joan Beaufort, countess of Westmorland (d. 1440). Furnivall and Gollancz, *Hoccleve's Minor Poems,* xxv, 95–242. See also Pryor, "Thomas Hoccleve's Series," 68.

129. Anne of Woodstock, countess of Stafford (d. 1438). MacCracken, *Minor Poems of Lydgate,* 1:130–33. See also Schirmer, *John Lydgate,* 155.

130. Alice Chaucer, countess of Suffolk (d. 1475). MacCracken, *Minor Poems of Lydgate,* 1:87–115. See also Schirmer, *Lydgate,* 61; and Pearsall, *John Lydgate,* 162.

131. Isabel Despenser, countess of Warwick (d. 1439). MacCracken, *Minor Poems of Lydgate,* 1:260–67; Schirmer, *John Lydgate,* 194; Pearsall, *John Lydgate,* 168.

132. Margaret Beauchamp Talbot, countess of Shrewsbury (d. 1467). MacCracken, *Minor Poems of Lydgate,* 2:516–38; Schirmer, *John Lydgate,* 94.

133. Lady Sibyl Boys of Holme Hale, widow of Roger Boys (d. 1421). MacCracken, *Minor Poems of Lydgate,* 1:14–18; Pearsall, *John Lydgate,* 73.

134. MacCracken, *Minor Poems of Lydgate,* 1:xix, 2:723; Schirmer, *John Lydgate,* 110–11; Pearsall, *John Lydgate,* 73.

135. Anne Neville, countess of Stafford and duchess of Buckingham (d. 1480). Glauning, *Lydgate's Minor Poems,* 1–15.

136. John and Isabel Hunt (not as yet satisfactorily identified). Bokenham, *Legendys of Hooly Wummen*, 130–36. See also Delany, *A Legend of Holy Women*, 205.

137. Isabel Bourchier, countess of Eu (d. 1484). Bokenham, *Legendys of Hooly Wummen*, 136–72; Moore, "Patrons of Letters (II)," 87–89.

138. Katherine Moleyns Howard (d. 1465) and Katherine Clopton Denston (d. after 1445). Bokenham, *Legendys of Hooly Wummen*, 172–201; Moore, "Patrons of Letters (II)," 85.

139. Katherine Clopton Denston. In the epilogue Bokenham mentions Katherine and her husband, John Denston, along with their daughter Anne (Bokenham, *Legendys of Hooly Wummen*, 38–58). See also Moore, "Patrons of Letters (II)," 84; and Gail McMurray Gibson, "Saint Anne and the Religion of Childbed," in *Interpreting Cultural Symbols: Saint Anne In Late Medieval Society*, ed. Kathleen Ashley and Pamela Sheingorn (Athens: University of Georgia Press, 1990), 95–110.

140. Elizabeth Howard de Vere, countess of Oxford (d. 1475). Bokenham, *Legendys of Hooly Wummen*, 257–89. See also Moore, "Patrons of Letters (II)," 86.

141. Agatha Flegg (d. after 1446). Bokenham, *Legendys of Hooly Wummen*, 225–43; Moore, "Patrons of Letters (II)" 91–92.

142. Margaret Holland, duchess of Clarence (d. 1439/40). Keiser, "Patronage and Piety," 32–46. The *Life of St. Jerome* is preserved in four fifteenth-century manuscripts (including the following entry, the anonymous Saint Hieronymus): Yale MS 317, which includes the version dedicated to Margaret, duchess of Clarence, Cambridge Saint John's College MS N.17, London, Lambeth Palace MSS 72 and 732 (cf. following note). See also Barbara Shaillor, *Catalogue of Medieval and Renaissance Manuscripts in the Beinecke Rare Book and Manuscript Room, Yale University* (Binghamton, N.Y.: Medieval & Renaissance Texts & Studies, 1982), 2, 120. On the multiplicity of manuscripts, Keiser points out the prologue on fol. 5r: "that hit sholde lyke your ladyship first to rede hit & to do copye hit for yourself, & syth to lete *oper* rede hit & copye hit, who so wyll" (41).

143. Patron unidentified. Horstmann, "Prosalegenden," 328–60. Contained in London, Lambeth Palace MS 432. See preceding note.

144. Patron unidentified. Munro, *John Capgrave's Lives*, 1–60.

145. Sir Miles Stapleton of Ingham (d. 1466) and Catherine de la Pole Stapleton (d. after 1466), daughter and heir of Sir Thomas de la Pole. Craig, *Works of John of Metham*, viii–ix; 1–81. See also Frederick James Furnivall, ed., *Political, Religious, and Love Poems*, Early English Text Society, 15 (London: Kegan Paul, Trench, Trübner, 1866, re-edited 1903), 301–8; and Moore, "Patrons of Letters (I)," 197–201.

146. Anne Stafford de Vere (d. 1472). Scrope, *Epistle of Othea*, xix–xxi.

Elizabeth de Burgh: Connoisseur and Patron

✖ ✖ ✖ Frances A. Underhill

King Edward III stimulated a great outpouring of cultural spectacles, especially in his conscious promotion of chivalric themes. Tournaments and royal processions incorporated dazzling pageantry and Arthurian allusions designed to popularize his French military activities and to enhance devotion to the crown.[1] The wealthiest of magnates could not match the splendor of Edward's regal environment, but his example set standards of taste and fashion.[2] The royal themes designed to undergird the king's statecraft and military adventures had a decidedly masculine cast. A woman, especially one of independent means and important connections, might emulate the richness of costume, jewelry, and costly furnishings. However, since females were precluded from service to the state and its military endeavors, they could be rather creative in their cultural expressions even while adhering to the aesthetic norms of their society.

Elizabeth de Burgh, lady of Clare, exemplifies the possibilities of female cultural leadership and patronage. Her family background included royal and comital ancestors; her landed wealth and independent status as a widow gave her freedom in pursuing her own patterns of cultural involvement. Her father was Gilbert de Clare, earl of Gloucester and the wealthiest of the English magnates before his death. Princess Joan, daughter of King Edward I, was Elizabeth's mother. When Elizabeth's brother, the heir to the great Clare fortune, was killed in 1314, Elizabeth and her sisters divided the estates equally, making each a wealthy heiress. In addition, Elizabeth had dower and jointure lands from each of her three marriages. Sometime after the death of her last husband in 1322, she took a vow of chastity that protected her from more marital adventures and ensured that she could direct her life and patronage without a husband's supervision. Married women lost legal control of their properties during periods of marriage, a problem no longer of concern to Elizabeth. Since Elizabeth lived until 1360, she had ample time and treasure to indulge her own aesthetic pleasures and the promotion of artistic and intellectual achievements of others.

The most important fourteenth-century arts often are classified today as minor arts: embroidery, goldsmiths' works, illuminated manuscripts, carvings in ivory and jewelry. All of these qualified as major artistic endeavors in the Middle Ages and ones most likely to be patronized by the laity. Laypeople contributed money to the grander sculptural and building programs of cathedrals and churches, but the resident clergy tended to control overall design. In a few instances, when a lord or lady founded and funded a whole friary, chantry, or college, they exercised the dominant control as they did when erecting their own domestic structures. Elizabeth de Burgh loved and purchased all the so-called minor arts; contributed funds to major ecclesiastical projects; founded and built two friaries, a chantry, several chapels, and a college; added to three of her principal residences; and built a house in London. Beyond that, she enjoyed music, bought books, and interacted with some of the prominent intellectuals of her day. Her patronage was broadly conceived, touching the heart of fourteenth-century culture and art.

Our knowledge of Elizabeth comes from the various printed English royal calendars, from her will and her statutes for Clare College, Cambridge University, her greatest foundation.[3] An important collection of her household accounts exists in the Public Record Office (London).[4] They were intended to serve immediate domestic purposes rather than the interest of future historians, so frequently they fail to inform on the most interesting topics. The run is incomplete, so that not all of the various types of accounts remain for each year of Elizabeth's tenure as lady of Clare. With all these caveats, the accounts offer insights into the daily life, the purchases of luxury goods, the building programs, and the patronage projects of this outstanding woman.

Unfortunately, the artifacts and structures on which she expended so much care and capital are more ruinous. Only fragments of her two major religious foundations remain, with her castles in barely better condition. Her gifts of books and buildings to Clare College were destroyed. The sumptuous ecclesiastical vestments and communion plate failed to escape the wanton destruction of the sixteenth and seventeenth centuries.[5] In spite of these problems, we can see the spirit of her patronage and her love of beauty if not the objects on which her concern was lavished.

The nobility of fourteenth-century England enjoyed a style of living that emphasized the dominance of the head of the household and created a carefully delineated sense of hierarchy among the staff, from counselor down to scullery pages. The lord, or in this case lady, sat in a great thronelike chair (Elizabeth's was called a *cathedra*), presiding over the lesser folk at meals, where one's status determined the quality and quantity of one's refreshment. Each member of the vast household played a role in this domestic theater.

The role-playing and theatricality were emphasized by the custom of annual clothing distribution or livery by the head of the household. Although livery distributions occurred in all royal, noble, and gentry households, personal tastes prevailed. For example, in Edward III's livery of 1360, all the royal family wore garments of mabryn, with subtle differences in gold ribbon or furs to distinguish status within the group. The massed effect of the royal family at Christmas services would have impressed onlookers by its cohesiveness and elegance.[6] Elizabeth opted for more surprise and variety in her liveries. Usually the different ranks within the household were clothed alike, with theatrical effect coming from the medley of colors, often in combinations that moderns would find clashing rather than complementary.[7] One year the clerks and young women wore brown, the squires a combination of azure blue material and striped stuff, and the more important servants had outfits that combined wool medley and tan striped cloth. The grooms received costumes of red and tawny; the pages wore red and green. The little clerks were dressed in green, and the manorial officials were given red-striped outfits.[8] Furs and silver fringe decorated the costumes of the more exalted staff, with fewer decorations and furs at the lower levels.[9]

The amounts and types of material for Elizabeth's own garments are enumerated, but little is mentioned about decoration. The most specific description comes from her will, where she left her daughter a shawl with tawny background embroidered with parrots and cockerels. Her peacock mantle also suggests embroidery rather than colorful woven cloth. Most of the lady's beds had coverlets of fur and expensive cloth, but one set of green coverlets had borders with "powders of Huan," which is embroidery work.[10] She transferred her hangings from one residence to another when she moved and put up special decorative banners for Corpus Christi day.[11] These hangings probably were painted with religious themes, similar to those of Queen Isabella.[12] Elizabeth owned two suspended carriages or chariots, which typically were painted in gilt and favorite colors, covered with a canopy of the finest materials and furnished with embroidered cushions.[13]

One of the most dramatic rites in noble households was the Mass, celebrated in private chapels. Elizabeth created an ambience of visual delights, with the richly decorated altar, the beautiful altar goods, and the stunning clerical vestments, some covered with the exquisite *opus anglicanum* embroidery. Her will and the one surviving goldsmith's account from 1332–33 allow us to glimpse the altar equipment and the vestments.[14] She maintained several goldsmiths on her personal staff as well as buying in London. For example, Elizabeth's servants purchased finished items for her, such as a pax for fifty shillings.[15] She ordered six images that year, but she hired John de Markeby to come from London to Clare to fashion the sculptures where she could watch the artist in action and perhaps direct him a bit. The images cost fourteen pounds thirteen shillings fourpence; the expenses of John's travel, meal allowance, and materials raised the cost to over fifty pounds. Elizabeth must have been pleased, for she gave John a gift of twenty shillings when the work was completed. It is possible that the images were to form the visual focus for a complex retable, for carpenters' wages for making a "table" are interspersed with John de Markeby's fees. The subjects portrayed in these images are not mentioned, but nearly thirty years later two images were bequeathed in her will: one a silver-gilt image of the Blessed Virgin and the other a gold image of John the Baptist "standing in the desert." These last were probably products of other years, but they suggest the types of art she favored. The Clare goldsmiths concentrated on domestic plate and jewelry in 1332–33. The enameler, who was hired at three shillings per week, stayed for twenty-eight weeks and produced religious items as well as personal ones.

Over the years, the lady of Clare patronized goldsmiths who left her with a great inventory of ecclesiastical plate to disperse in her last testament: chalices, holy-water pots, sprinklers, censers, boxes "for the body of our Lord," cruets, and a candleholder. She also spent heavily on items for her table, objects made of silver, silver-gilt, gold, and semiprecious stones.[16] Joel Rosenthal gently chides the nobility for the loving detail with which they enumerated their silver services, but these were works of art, not the expendable dishes "garni" that were purchased by the hundreds.[17] Nor did Elizabeth hoard all her art works but gave them to friends and staff members during her lifetime. For example, her resident goldsmiths made a silver platter weighing 104 shillings two pence half-penny for Gilbert Cordail, the keeper of her wardrobe; a silver pot for Robert de Stalynton, the receiver of Clare; and a gold ring for the earl of Hereford.[18] Otherwise, her testament gives only a partial picture of Elizabeth's patronage of the goldsmiths' art.

She employed several goldsmiths who resided in the Clare Castle precincts, probably between 1326 and 1341. The core of this group included Thomas Aurifaber, Robert of Tewksbury, William atte Hall, and Robert Aurifaber.[19]

Usually these men resided at Clare, but occasionally they traveled to other sites when Elizabeth so directed. Thomas Aurifaber worked at Angleseye in the 1330s when Elizabeth was occupied in founding a chantry there.[20] In 1334 the lady's goldsmiths spent thirty-three days in Walsingham, perhaps creating the beautiful works noted by the canons on another occasion.[21]

Sometime between 1341 and 1343, the department seems to have closed down, for none of these men appear on the 1343 livery list.[22] There were good reasons for Elizabeth and the goldsmiths to terminate the arrangement. The men traveled away from Clare often, for the necessary silver, gold, wire, enamels, and professional equipment that were available in urban centers but not the small market town of Clare. The smiths may have resented the additional chores of buying lampreys or other foodstuffs for the household in the course of their journeys, although in the household it was even common for priests to buy fish or pigs or grain when it was deemed convenient. The formation of prestigious gilds or companies in London probably enticed provincial goldsmiths to the city, and customers could find a broad spectrum of precious goods there. Elizabeth had never relied solely on her departmental goldsmiths, so eliminating the office may have appealed to her as well as suiting the artists. She continued to maintain some artists in her household, if names can be trusted: Robert the Illuminator, Robert le Peintor, and Thomas le Purtreour.[23]

When Elizabeth purchased artistic works, they often had a religious use. In 1337, when her niece Margaret Despenser, a nun, died, a scene of the Four Evangelists painted on buckram was bought for her sepulchre, as were wax images. These latter usually appealed to poorer folk, who offered the wax castings of saints at their favorite shrines or altars.[24] The lady invested more in the tomb of her half-brother Edward Monthermer at Clare Friary. He died in 1339, but work on his memorial continued still in 1352.[25] Perhaps the tomb was made of a harder stone than the alabaster that was just becoming fashionable in the 1330s, and that was easier to carve.[26] As Elizabeth neared death herself, she sent a staff member to examine the sepulchre of Queen Isabella, probably because she contemplated beginning work on her own.[27] Incidentally, Isabella's tomb featured her effigy, carved in alabaster by a female London artist.[28] Elizabeth succeeded in erecting a memorable tomb for herself, worthy of explicit imitation later in the century by John Hastings, earl of Pembroke.[29] Unfortunately, neither Elizabeth's tomb in the Minories church nor the Hastings tomb survives.[30]

Religious themes dominated medieval art forms, so Elizabeth's collection conformed to the prevailing tastes. We do not know the extent of her possessions, but some descriptions of the works occur in her will. She donated a gold footed cup for the "body of our Lord" to the king's college at Windsor, including three little silver-gilt angels that accented its purpose. The Black Prince received a golden tabernacle with an image of the Virgin, two little carved angels of gold, and a large silver and enamel cross flanked by the statues of Mary and John. The duke of Lancaster was left a piece of the True Cross enclosed in a framed cross with a gold and enamel case. Elizabeth's granddaughter inherited a tableau of the Annunciation. The London Minoresses were granted a crystal reliquary, and two other reliquaries went to Tewksbury, a kind of Clare mausoleum.[31]

Enameled works and ivories were purchased or produced for Elizabeth. Joan Evans suggests that the ivories depicting the Annunciation and the Epiphany currently in the Clare College collection were donated by the lady.[32] She lavished much of her money on elaborate ecclesiastical vestments.[33] Some may have featured costly silk materials rather than added decorations, and others were splendid in their famed *opus anglicanum* embroidery.[34] John de Lenne, one of Elizabeth's executors, received a habit of silk checkered with silver-gilt, which he later donated to Clare College.[35] The vestment given to the Minoresses was decorated with a thousand pearls, a rather typical addition to embroidered goods.[36] The cope bequeathed to Anglesey Priory had three silver crests on its red taffeta cloth of gold. More elaborate ecclesiastical vestments went to Hereford Cathedral and Clare College. The cathedral's cope was of samite, encrusted with pearls and embroidered with images and archangels.[37] Clare College received several vestments for specific seasons of the church calendar, but the most impressive were the red silk outfit embroidered with images in gold and the black and tan vestment with flowers and arabesques.[38] These English embroideries were great art, prized throughout Europe for their extraordinary technique and design.[39]

Possibly some of the embroidery issued from the women's atelier at Clare Castle, for one year the purchases included embroidery thread, fine linen suitable for backing, expensive silk material, and two cloths of gold.[40] The bulk was probably purchased, much from Thomas Cheiner, who is identified as an embroiderer by Christie.[41] I think it more likely that Cheiner operated a London workshop specializing in *opus anglicanum*, for Elizabeth purchased silver buttons from him, which suggests a broader range of inventory.[42] Moreover, Elizabeth awarded Cheiner with livery as a squire in 1343, where his name appears in the run of merchants so honored by the lady of Clare.[43] Fourteenth-century *opus anglicanum* often was produced in embroidery workshops, where the designs were planned and then executed by both women and men. One pattern book survives from the period with motifs that suggest its use by both embroiderers and painters of retables and pictures.[44] The vestments, surplices, and the embroidery on Elizabeth's personal bed coverings and clothing show a continuing patronage of this spectacular English art form.

Elizabeth loved jewelry, often gold rings with precious stones. She bequeathed the finest of these to intimate friends: a gold ring with a ruby to the Black Prince, and two gold rings to Mary de Sancto Paulo, the countess of Pembroke. One was set with a diamond and the other with a sapphire; the gold cross that the countess received also had a sapphire.[45] The goldsmith account from 1332–33 indicates that twelve rings were purchased or fashioned locally in that accounting year, as well as brooches, clasps, belts, and a coronet for the lady's daughter.[46] In 1351–52, Elizabeth purchased silk belts decorated with silver or enamel, gold chains enameled in red, and a gold chain incorporating pearls and diamonds in its design.[47]

A more utilitarian type of art is found in the personal seals of the Crown, institutions, and private individuals. Legal documents required authentication, which was accomplished by sealing the documents with wax on which the proper seal was stamped. Because forgers commonly sought to duplicate seals, it was important to make them real works of art and difficult to copy. The great institutions and personages preferred that seals be fabricated from silver, with finely detailed carvings.

At least two seals of Elizabeth survive, carved with references to the heraldic arms of her three husbands and those of her grandfather King Edward I and her grandmother Eleanor of Castile, along with the chevrons of Clare.[48] In 1359 she presented her foundation of Clare Hall a more elaborately designed seal, which depicts the lady of Clare giving the master and scholars the statutes by which they will be governed. She holds a book in one hand and the statutes in the other. Above her in triple-canopied niches are representations of Mary and the infant Jesus, John the Baptist with the *agnus dei,* and Saint John the Divine with his symbolic devices of an eagle and a palm branch. The shields of Edward I and Eleanor of Castile flank the canopy; Elizabeth's shield is below the figural work.[49] Because the seal measures only two and a half by one and five-eighths inches, it required a true artist in metalwork, capable of intricate workmanship and possessing a sure sense of design.

Great art accompanied the lady of Clare throughout her day. We know less of her patronage of music, although she delighted in musical works. Specific minstrels appear in her younger days: Perot Tromper in 1320, and Patrick Vidulator, Adam Harper, Martin Trumper, Richard Vidulator, and W. Taborer, whom she hired to accompany her son at his knighting ceremony.[50] Queen Philippa knew of her fondness for song and lent her John the

Harper for the celebration of Candlemas in 1352.[51] Perhaps the lady employed professional musicians on her staff after 1330, but Roger Citoler is the only name that seems to fit a musical category. However, Elizabeth loved her organ, which was transported from residence to residence and occasionally lent but always reclaimed in time for major holidays. Perhaps Roger Citoler played the instrument, for once he was dispatched to fetch it and on another occasion he was summoned to the castle for Ascension Day.[52]

Many fourteenth-century nobles supported choirs of boys or men, but the Clare accounts never mention such a group. Only one hint makes such a choir seem likely: gifts for the participants in the "boy-bishop" ceremonies in December 1351.[53] Normally this pleasant charade centered on the choir, where the choirboys elected one of their members to lead the procession on the eve of Holy Innocents Day and to pretend to high ecclesiastical dignity for the following twenty-four hours.[54] Perhaps her assemblage of "little clerks" was a choir that produced this semicomic drama.

Elizabeth did not patronize music in the same way that she supported the visual arts. She enjoyed good singing, however, and prescribed that the young poor boys attending Clare College should be "instructed in singing, grammar and logic."[55] She dictated the nature of the church services for the college, with the Sunday and holiday masses to be celebrated "with notes, and then we enjoin all the fellows and boys to attend, sing and help." The anniversaries of her death were to be observed with "the *placebo* and the *dirige*, as well as the mass with notes."[56] Her own service books were "well-noted," so presumably she could read music.[57] All these show a love of religious music but give no indication that she routinely supported composers or professional musicians.[58]

Fourteenth-century nobles were literate in French and knew some formal Latin as well.[59] Many enjoyed reading and began to amass personal libraries. Elizabeth may have become a collector early in her life, but the first documented example of her book buying came in 1324, when she hired a scribe to copy the *Vitae patrum*, at a cost of eight shillings, room, and meals at table.[60] Her vein of serious reading continued in February 1327, when she borrowed three books on surgery from the royal collection; she also borrowed four romances that same day.[61] Unfortunately, the household rolls mention book buying only incidentally. By the early fourteenth century stationer shops existed in London, and Elizabeth did procure books in that city.[62] She sent seven horses to transport her book purchases home in 1350–51.[63] The next year she commissioned the copying of a book, buying three dozen pieces of vellum and vermilion for the project.[64] We learn of other book purchases because she bought silver or decorated book covers to be added locally.[65]

Elizabeth's will reveals something of her library. She left two antiphoners and two other service books to Peter de Ereswell, a member of her staff. The bulk of the collection went to Clare College: two antiphoners, two missals, a book of legends, a Bible, a book of decretals compiled by Hugh de Vercelli, another pair of decretals, the legends of the saints, a book of questions, and Archbishop Bradwardine's *De causa Dei contra Pelagianos*.[66] The list indicates a preference for serious titles; no romances are included, although the book of legends could have fit this category. The antiphoners and "well-noted" missal speak to her piety and love of music. The Bible could have been in either French or Latin, as wealthy families in England could purchase French translations by the fourteenth century.[67] Most noble libraries included a copy of the legends of the saints. The decretal volumes expound on canon law, and the book of questions and the Bradwardine book are theological in content. The volume by Bradwardine, a major medieval thinker, shows the depth of Elizabeth's intellectual interests and concerns for her spiritual health. Bradwardine (d. 1349) was responding to theologians, such as Ockham, who seemed to exalt man at the expense of God through the operation of free will. Bradwardine exalted God's grace and denied that people have freedom to act independently in a moral fashion without divine participation. The book figured in the contemporary theological debates on the relationship of faith and reason, and it championed faith against the challenges of skepticism.[68] Elizabeth's library demonstrates her very broad interests in scripture, hagiography, canon law, and theological works. Her books in Latin raise the question of her ability to read that language. She had time to study Latin and a continuing supply of clerics within her household to serve as teachers. We do not know if she had the inclination to read Latin texts on her own or if she was content to have them read and translated for her by men on her clerical staff.[69]

Besides providing broad intellectual themes, some of these volumes must have delighted the eye. The greatest illuminated manuscripts of the period were produced for East Anglian patrons and in the East Anglian style typified by "its freshness, its earthiness . . . its fine colour."[70] Elizabeth paid a Franciscan of Cambridge to illuminate a book for her in 1351; that same year she purchased other illuminated works.[71] Robert the Illuminator was employed in her household for at least five years and probably longer.[72] Matthew Scriptor and Walter Scriptoris appear in the rolls in 1326 and 1349–50 respectively, but they probably handled only routine scribal chores rather than fine illumination.[73]

The book that Elizabeth sent her daughter for her purification after childbirth must have been an extraordinary example of illumination, for it cost thirty-six pounds.[74] The service book given to King Edward III for his Windsor chapel surely was illuminated as well.[75] The law book donated to Richard de Plessy need not have been, for it seems to be a book for his studies.[76]

The paucity of information on her purchases of books masks the extent of the lady's interest in her library, her reading program, and her love of learning. For a laywoman, she maintained wide contacts with some leading fourteenth-century intellectuals and writers. Between 1326 and 1330, Friar Richard de Conyngton visited Clare at Elizabeth's behest on several occasions. Conyngton, a Franciscan, was once provincial minister of his order in England and another writer who attacked Ockham. His writing focused primarily, however, on the controversy over poverty that split the order in the early part of the century.[77] The issue of poverty also tied in with the controversy setting the friars against the secular and monastic clergy, who feared the friars' appropriation of fees for confessions and burials. Conyngton retired to the Cambridge friary, and it was from there that Elizabeth summoned him to Clare.[78] Naturally, the household accounts present only the costs of his escort, not the content of conversations.

Similar lacunae attach to Elizabeth's relationships with other scholars, but many were associated with Cambridge University. Walter de Bykerton was a Franciscan master at Cambridge who probably preached in her chapel in 1351 and who received two gifts of six shillings eight pence from her.[79] Master John de Stratton visited Elizabeth with great regularity and at her request.[80] She was always generous with him, as a gift of twenty shillings in 1351 illustrates.[81] Robert Godewyk studied at Cambridge before taking his doctorate in theology at Oxford. He became provincial prior of the Augustinian friars and presumably visited Elizabeth more than the rolls show because of the easy proximity of Clare Castle and Clare Friary.[82] He too received a gift from the lady: twenty shillings in 1352.[83] William Tychemersch, who was summoned to Elizabeth in London, was a former provincial minister of the Franciscans, with a doctorate in theology.[84] Master Walter de Thaxted, who farmed the rectory at Great Bardfield near her Bardfield residence, was a master at Clare College from 1326 to 1342.[85] Robert Spaulding, a fellow at Clare College in 1330, never appeared in the extant accounts, but Elizabeth went to great pains to ensure him a pension in 1355. Her original chantry endowment at Anglesey Priory paid for two priests. Under a new grant made in 1355, Elizabeth added a small amount to the priory's income and dropped the stipulation for two priests. In lieu of one of these chantry chaplains, Anglesey was to provide Robert Spaulding with an annual pension of one hundred shillings.[86] Other university men who appear in the rolls probably represented concerns for the administration of Clare Hall. Cambridge University had suffered greatly from the Black Death, so it is not surprising to see Elizabeth's concerns for her college intensify in the decade of the 1350s.[87]

Elizabeth employed at least two clerics with university degrees in important positions in her household, including them in the intimacy of her *familia*.[88] Robert de Stalynton, who received his master's degree from Cambridge, served for many years on the lady's staff as receiver of Clare and as clerk of her chamber. He was mentioned in the rolls as early as 1334, but his position was clearer by 1336, when he received wages from the household of one shilling a day.[89] In 1338 he became rector of Litlington, presented by University Hall, the floundering antecedent of Clare College.[90] Elizabeth's influence probably was critical in the appointment, for she assumed patronage of the hall that year. Stalynton continued to serve the lady of Clare at least through 1351–52.[91] Master Thomas de Friskeneye, an Oxford man, presided at Elizabeth's manorial court sessions in Clopton and Walsingham in 1351–52. He was another recipient of gifts, receiving ten shillings that year.[92] The king commissioned him to survey Clare College in 1353.[93]

There is no evidence that these scholars formed any sort of intellectual circle. However, two other friends of the lady were associated with William Bateman, bishop of Norwich and founder of Trinity College at Cambridge. Both John Paschal and Simon Sudbury belonged to his episcopal household before progressing to higher office.[94] John Paschal, a Carmelite friar, Cambridge graduate, and bishop of Llandaff, corresponded with Elizabeth and visited her in both England and Wales.[95] Paschal had a good reputation as a diocesan and an even better one as a writer and preacher.[96] During the height of the Black Death, Bishop Paschal was one of the few visitors to the lady, presumably offering spiritual comfort. Elizabeth recognized academic potential in younger men as well. She brought young Master Simon Sudbury into her *familia* and gave him a generous gift of ten pounds ten shillings in 1351–52.[97] Sudbury studied at Paris, receiving the doctorate in canon law there before becoming archbishop of Canterbury. For Elizabeth he was a neighbor and the son of one of her liveried squires and favorite merchants, Nigel Thebaud of Sudbury. She enjoyed promoting the education of local youths, although Sudbury achieved higher ecclesiastical rank than her other protégés.[98]

Master Simon Bredon was a priest, but his academic specialty was medicine. He joined Elizabeth's household from 1357 to 1359, probably to treat her rather than engage in intellectual discourse with her.[99] He wrote one book on medicine, which has been described as "excruciatingly dull and devoid of interest" but with the acknowledgment that "his contemporaries held him in high esteem." He wrote thirteen other books, mainly on astronomy and mathematics.[100]

The lady of Clare appreciated learning and went beyond exchanges with educated men to found a hall or college at Cambridge University. Technically Richard Badew founded University Hall, but when he was short of funds, he resigned his rights in 1338 to Elizabeth de Burgh, and she became the official foundress of Clare College.[101] Actually, her financial aid had begun two years earlier, and her patronage continued for the rest of her life, as she provided the college with endowments that brought in a comfortable sixty pounds annually.[102] She received a papal license to build a chapel for the college in 1348, but probably had constructed some housing for the fellows and students in earlier years.[103]

Elizabeth eagerly embraced her new hall, even though the process of foundation was lengthy and expensive.[104] She explicitly stated her motives for the foundation in the 1359 statutes. Naturally she wanted prayers for her soul after death, the primary goal of all medieval donations.[105] She mandated that the anniversaries of her death were to be observed by a mass, but she wanted more regular prayers. Each day after dinner, the scholars were to remember her: "May the life of Elizabeth de Burgh our foundress, by the grace of God, be directed to salvation"; after her death they were to pray "May the soul of Elizabeth de Burgh, our foundress, and the souls of all faithful departed, by God's mercy, rest in peace."[106]

In all of this, the lady of Clare followed the conventions of the day. She reflected another typical outlook when she acknowledged that her property was "given to us by God" and that some part of that wealth should be directed to his glory.[107] Elizabeth moved beyond these usual noble objectives in her foundation by embracing the idea of education benefiting the community. By the fifteenth century this motive was more common as the prestige of learning grew, but in the fourteenth century the nobility found other channels for their generosity. The only two colleges founded by noble donors in the period owed their existence to women: Elizabeth and her best friend, Mary de Sancto Paulo, who established Pembroke College, perhaps imitating Elizabeth's initiative. Few noble sons attended university unless destined for the church, and afterward even those practiced "minimal or even niggardly benefaction" to the schools.[108] Otherwise, educational donations excited few nobles. Elizabeth pioneered a new form of lay generosity, opening an area for donations formerly the province of royalty or clerics.

Love of learning motivated Elizabeth's patronage of education. In her preamble to the statutes for Clare College, she spoke eloquently of the "sweetness" of learning, a telling phrase in a time when sugar was rare and expensive. She wanted knowledge, "that pearl of science," to be extended by her scholars to "give light to them that walk in dark paths of ignorance." [109] Again the language is significant, as she recalled the beauty of pearls she used elsewhere and applied that aesthethic idea to learning. The idea of light had theological overtones, but light had a personal importance to this woman who routinely furnished twenty pounds of candles for the chapel at Candlemas.

The statutes call for community benefits rather than career enhancement for individuals. She wanted to "promote the advancement of divine worship, the welfare of the state, and the extension of these sciences," by concentrating on the study of theology and the arts. All the personnel associated with the foundation were male; there is no evidence that she ever contemplated sponsorship of any educational establishment for women. Church law and societal norms stood in the way, even for so adventuresome a patroness.

Clare College stands as Elizabeth's greatest and most lasting act of patronage, but she supported education in less dramatic ways as well. She donated oak trees for the repair of King's College, Cambridge. [110] She sent two young boys to Oxford in 1331, paying the salary of their master and expending seventeen pounds eight shillings two pence farthing on their total expenses. [111] Two relatives of her staff were given educational opportunities at her expense. Hugh de Colyngham studied at King's Bench, and Thomas Marshal matriculated at Cambridge. [112] The son of her chariot driver received his fees for the little school in Clare. [113] Some of these last "scholarships" may have lacked real altruism, for the lady needed skilled staff for legal and administrative work and probably found supporting local talent a reasonable method to accomplish that end.

The nobility of England favored building enterprises, both as charities and for enhancing their domestic quarters, ventures that Elizabeth engaged in over the years. She paid for a license to endow the prior and convent of Ely with a lifetime interest in some of her property, just at the time when their great octagon tower was being constructed. [114] Her testamentary bequest to Walsingham Priory allowed the canons to embark on additions to their church. [115] Walsingham had received earlier donations, as had the Greyfriars Church in London. [116] The lady partially financed a transept at the parish church in neighboring Thaxted and joined her friend Lady Wake in benefiting the poor Franciscan friary at Ware. [117] All these were worthy enterprises, but Elizabeth liked to put her own stamp on her benefactions in ways not possible in these churches.

The Augustinian friary at Clare offered more possibilities, because it was a family foundation, a near neighbor, and the site of her mother's tomb. A fifteenth-century poem called "The Dialogue at the Grave" credited Elizabeth with great generosity: "Dortour, chapiter hous, and fraitour which she made out of the grounde, both planncher and wall. And who the Rofe? —She alone did al."[118] She may also have contributed to the friars' new church, dedicated in 1338.[119]

A struggling house of Augustinian canons at Anglesey provided another opportunity to show generosity while keeping some measure of personal control. The Clares had long been associated with the priory, and Elizabeth was its patron. The proximity of Anglesey to Cambridge and the fact that the prior owned a house in that town may have been useful to Elizabeth during the early years of her collegiate foundation.[120] She endowed the house generously, founded a chantry there, and built a chapel to house it.[121] Elizabeth also built a domestic range for herself at Anglesey, using it often as a convenient pied-à-terre for her visits to Mary de Sancto Paulo at the Denney or Waterbeach convents or Mary's residences in the area.[122]

Elizabeth founded and built two new friaries, at Ballinrobe in Ireland and Walsingham in Norfolk. The Irish house has almost totally disappeared, but it was an important house in its size and impact on western Ireland.[123] Probably Elizabeth initiated this foundation as a gift of thanksgiving for the birth of her son in 1312. The canons of Walsingham Priory strongly opposed her project of founding a Franciscan house near theirs. Walsingham was a major pilgrimage shrine, and the canons feared a loss in revenue from Franciscan competition. They phrased their appeal to Elizabeth in arguments that had pitted monks against friars for more than fifty years, suggesting that they expected Elizabeth to be familiar with the controversy. The lady of Clare perservered in her objectives and founded a friary in the town in 1347.[124] Her actions sprang from a long devotion to the Franciscans and from her desire to provide a hostel for poorer pilgrims who sought the benefit of the Marian relics. The friars received small bits of property and presumably funds with which to build their house, church, and hostel.[125] In the end Elizabeth managed to keep the good will of both the canons and the friars.

The lady contributed substantially to ecclesiastical institutions while also building for her own comfort. She constructed a chapel and a range of domestic buildings at Usk Castle in Wales[126] and made extensive renovations at her Bardfield manor and at Clare Castle.[127] The rolls record the names of thirty-seven of her workmen at Clare and Bardfield. Most may have enjoyed good reputations locally, but three of the men have merited inclusion in Harvey's book on medieval architects: Richard atte Cherche, Roger Stephen, and John Cressing. The first two were masons, the last a carpenter.[128] In the medieval period masons and carpenters drew and executed the building plans, qualifying them as architects. Elizabeth was not the only patron of these men, but their employment at Clare shows that she recognized talent and utilized it.

Her favorite architect was Richard Felsted, whom she employed at projects for nearly thirty years.[129] Felsted first appeared in the Clare accounts in 1326, when he received a gift of one hundred shillings.[130] He had just completed construction at Hanley, a royal castle, where he was described as "master of the said works."[131] His groom was at Clare in 1334, suggesting that his master was involved in some project for Elizabeth. In 1336–37, the lady sent for Felsted, used him in some capacity in Cambridge, and purchased iron for his needs.[132] Contacts continued in 1338–39 and the next year he again visited Elizabeth.[133] In 1342 Felsted and Richard atte Cherche worked together in London, so one can assume that Felsted recommended Cherche for Elizabeth's later renovations at Clare Castle. The lady awarded Felsted livery as a squire in 1343; the earl of Lancaster followed suit in 1347, after Felsted built additions to Kenilworth Castle.[134] In 1350 she began contemplating building a house in London, adjacent to the convent of the London Minoresses. She hired Richard Felsted for the work, which progressed through 1351–52.[135] Except for the London house, the accounts fail to identify which of Elizabeth's building projects Felsted supervised. During the 1330s, when contact between them was frequent, the lady built at Anglesey and Cambridge. Felsted's employment by Elizabeth's dear friend, the earl of Lancaster, suggests that she recommended him highly, though his reputation alone was sufficient for regular assignments. Of all the artists and architects appearing in the accounts, Elizabeth patronized Felsted over the longest period of time. She found in him those qualities of aesthetic creativity and superior craftsmanship that she supported in other arts.

The lady's patronage focused broadly across the spectrum of literary, academic, and artistic endeavors. Although she cannot be identified with promoting many specific artists, authors, or architects, her love of beauty and her ability to purchase the finest works stimulated artistic production. Her greatest role as patron was in education, where her foundation endured and benefited scholars well past her own life span. Perhaps only Mary de Sancto Paulo demonstrated a similar pattern of benefactions, and she too was a wealthy widow. Amassing beautiful objects of art and building in a grand manner appealed to most of the English nobility, but few other women had the independent wealth of these two and the freedom to indulge personal tastes rather than familial or spousal ends. Noblemen acquired ecclesiastical treasures and enhanced their libraries and choirs, but most had the additional expense of knightly entourages, less necessary for Mary and Elizabeth. Men tended to follow the exciting themes of military valor and chivalric enterprise that dominated much of England's cultural history during Edward III's reign. Elizabeth's patronage demonstrates that other creative impulses prevailed as well.

NOTES

1. Interesting studies of fourteenth-century royal culture include Juliet Vale, *Edward III and Chivalry: Chivalric Society and Its Context, 1270–1350* (Woodbridge, Eng.: Boydell, 1982); Stella Mary Newton, *Fashion in the Age of the Black Prince* (Totowa, N.J.: Rowman and Littlefield, 1980); and V. J. Scattergood, and J. W. Sherborne, eds., *English Court Culture in the Later Middle Ages* (New York: St. Martin's, 1983).

2. Differences between royal and magnate possessions may be seen in the inventory that Queen Isabella brought to England for her marriage to Edward II; Walter E. Rhodes, "The Inventory of Jewels and the Wardrobe of Queen Isabella," *English Historical Review* 12 (1897): 518–21.

3. Her will is found in John Nichols, *A Collection of All the Wills Now Known to Be Extant of the Kings and Queens of England, Princes and Princesses of Wales, and Every Branch of the Royal Blood, from the Reign of William the Conqueror to that of Henry the Seventh Exclusive* (London: Nichols, 1780; reprint, AMS Press, 1969); her statutes in an English version in James Heywood, *Early Cambridge University and College Statutes* (London: Bohn, 1855).

4. E101 series: Exchequer, King's Remembrancer: Various Accounts.

5. Marion Campbell, "Metalwork in England, c. 1200–1400" in *Age of Chivalry: Art in Plantagenet England, 1200–1400*, ed. J. J. G. Alexander and Paul Binski (London: Royal Academy of Arts, 1987), 162–63, notes that "of precious metal items intended for ecclesiastical use not a single cross, candlestick, shrine, reliquary, monstrance or jeweled mitre is left." Survival of domestic plate is infrequent, for unfashionable pieces routinely were melted down for new items or to meet financial exigencies.

6. Newton, *Fashion*, 65–66.

7. Elizabeth may have been a bit old-fashioned in her outlook. The vivid colors that were fashionable in the 1340s were more subdued in later years. See Newton, *Fashion*, 64.

8. E101/94/2.

9. For livery descriptions see E101/94/9, 92/9, 94/1, 94/2.

10. J. Nichols, *Collection of Wills*, 30, 35. "Powdered" refers to an embroidery technique used for background; I have not found a reference to "Huan."

11. E101/91/29, 93/17.

12. Isabella's wallhangings featured the Nativity and the Apocalypse. See Joan Evans, *English Art, 1307–1461* (Oxford: Clarendon, 1949), 137–38.

13. Marjorie Boyer, "Medieval Suspended Carriages," *Speculum* 34 (1959): 360–61, argues that by the fourteenth century, suspended carriages provided a fairly comfortable means of travel for noblewomen. These "chariots" had decorated wooden sides and arches covered with fine material. French fashion decreed that the great noblewoman have two such vehicles, one for herself and one for her women. Elizabeth met the French standard.

14. The goldsmith's account is E101/91/30. The material on Elizabeth's chapel equipment, plate, and jewelry is drawn from this account or from J. Nichols, *Collection of Wills*, unless otherwise noted.

15. When an item is said to cost fifty shillings, that is approximately what it weighed if it were made of silver, with reasonable adjustments for the art work. Elizabeth purchased gold, usually at a rate of ten pence of gold costing ten shillings of silver. This conversion rate is fairly standard in the 1332–33 account.

16. Her will enumerated some 28 items from her chapel and over 250 silver or silver-gilt pieces from her dinnerware collection. Other items, such as bells or candlesticks, could have been used either in the chapel or in her hall.

17. Joel T. Rosenthal, *The Purchase of Paradise* (London: Routledge and Kegan Paul, 1972), 91.

18. E101/91/30.

19. References to these goldsmiths are found in E101/91/12, 91/15, 91/25, 92/2, 95/10, 91/27, 92/3, 95/2, 92/9, 92/13, 92/14. In 1332–33, a goldsmith from Bury Saint Edmunds named Robert was on a sort of retainer fee; see E101/91/30.

20. E101/91/25 recorded four trips in 1330–31; 92/2 mentioned one trip in 1334.

21. E101/92/2. At least one of the goldsmiths may have returned in 1338–39: E101/92/9. In a letter protesting Elizabeth's plans for a Franciscan house in Walsingham, the prior and canons of the great Augustinian house there recalled Elizabeth's previous gifts to them of precious jewels: James Lee-Warner, "Petition of the Prior and Canons of Walsingham, Norfolk, to Elizabeth, Lady of Clare," *Archaeological Journal* 26 (1869): 170.

22. The livery list has over two hundred persons receiving clothes that year. See E101/92/23.

23. The first two are on the 1343 livery list; the last in her will.

24. See Heather Swanson, *Medieval Artisans* (Oxford: Blackwell, 1989), 99. The wax images found at Exeter Cathedral often have strings attached which indicate that they were to be hung, most likely on the railing surrounding the tombs. See U. M. Radford, "The Wax Images Found at Exeter Cathedral," *Antiquaries Journal* 29 (1949): 164.

25. E101/93/12.

26. Evans, *English Art*, 153.

27. See E101/94/2 for the visit.

28. F. D. Blackley, "Isabella of France, Queen of England, 1308–1358 and the Late Medieval Cult of the Dead," *Canadian Journal of History* 15 (1980): 28–30.

29. J. Nichols, *Collection of Wills*, 92–94.

30. The Minories church was destroyed, but a statue of a female has recently been recovered from the site. It could have been donated by the lady of Clare but did not form part of her sepulchre, for it seems to be a niche figure. See Alexander and Binski, *Age of Chivalry*, 390–91, for a description and photograph.

31. J. Nichols, *Collection of Wills*, 35–37.

32. Evans, *English Art*, 192.

33. She bequeathed thirty-six cloths of gold to religious groups in her will. Cloth of gold normally refers to woven cloth with gold thread forming the warp and silken thread the weft; occasionally it may be cloth where gold embroidery is liberally applied.

34. J. Nichols, *Collection of Wills*, 25–26. Camoka was a woven gold patterned silk that was used in several of the vestments.

35. Alfred B. Emden, *A Biographical Register of the University of Cambridge to 1500* (Cambridge: Cambridge University Press, 1963), 363.

36. Donald King, "Embroidery and Textiles," in Alexander and Binski, *Age of Chivalry*, 161. Newton, *Fashion*, 22, notes that in 1342–43, large pearls sold for threepence each and small ones for a halfpence.

37. Hereford Cathedral. Dean and Chapter Archives, #4625.

38. J. Nichols, *Collection of Wills*, 31–32.

39. A. G. Christie, *English Medieval Embroidery* (Oxford: Clarendon, 1938), 1–4.

40. E101/93/12.

41. Christie, *English Medieval Embroidery*, 36.

42. E101/93/12.

43. E101/92/23. An Alice Cheyner received livery as a damoiselle that same year, so it is tempting to see her as Thomas's daughter and identify her as the Alice Aurifrigeria noted as an important embroiderer in Christie, *English Medieval Embroidery*, 35.

44. Evans, *English Art*, 19–20; and D. King, "Embroidery and Textiles," 161.

45. J. Nichols, *Collection of Wills*, 37.

46. E101/91/30.

47. E101/93/12.

48. Mansfield D. Forbes, ed., *Clare College, 1326–1926* (Cambridge: Cambridge University Press, 1928), 1:12, n. 2.

49. Forbes, *Clare College*, 1:13.

50. E101/94/10, 91/18.

51. E101/93/12.

52. E101/92/11, 92/13.

53. E101/93/12.

54. M. N. Maltman, "Boy-Bishop," *New Catholic Encyclopedia*, 2:741; Shulamith Shahar, *Childhood in the Middle Ages* (London: Routledge, 1990), 179–82.

55. Heywood, *Early Cambridge Statutes*, 138.

56. *Ibid.*, 139.

57. J. Nichols, *Collection of Wills*, 31.

58. Queen Philippa was a true patron, commissioning Jean de la Mote to write memorial poems for her father, which were apparently set to music, as Jean is identified as a minstrel. See Nigel Wilkins, "Music and Poetry at Court: England and France in the Late Middle Ages," in Scattergood and Sherborne, *Court Culture*, 191–92, for reference to Jean.

59. M. T. Clanchy, *From Memory to Written Record: England, 1066–1307* (Cambridge, Mass.: Harvard University Press, 1979), 196; Nicholas Orme, "The Education of the Courtier" in Scattergood and Sherborne, *Court Culture*, 80.

60. James Westfall Thompson, *The Medieval Library* (Chicago: University of Chicago Press, 1939; reprint, New York: Hafner, 1967), 645.

61. Vale, *Edward III and Chivalry*, 169.

62. E101/92/27, 93/8.

63. E101/93/8.

64. E101/93/12. The household purchased vermilion, materials for ink, and "colors" in other years, but these may have been used for other purposes than bookmaking: 92/3, 95/2, 92/12.

65. E101/93/12.

66. J. Nichols, *Collection of Wills*, 25, 31; R. W. Hunt, "Medieval Inventories of Clare College Library," *Transactions of the Cambridge Bibliographic Society* 1 (1950): 124n.

67. *Cambridge History of the Bible*, ed. G. W. H. Lampe (Cambridge: Cambridge University Press, 1969), 1:448, 451; Nicholas Harris Nicolas, ed. *Testamenta Vetusta* (London: Nichols, 1826), 1:xxvii.

68. Gordon Leff, "Thomas Bradwardine's *De Causa Dei*," *Journal of Ecclesiastical History* 7 (1956): 21–29; David Knowles, *The Religious Orders in England* (Cambridge: Cambridge University Press, 1957), 2:74–89. Leff, 22, notes that Bradwardine's contemporaries dubbed him "Doctor Profundis."

69. John de Lenne, a trusted clerical counselor, might be a likely candidate for either teaching or translating for her. He possessed a copy of *De regimine principum*, presumably that of Giles of Rome, which dealt with education and which he bequeathed to Clare College; see Emden, *Biographical Register of Cambridge*, 363.

70. J. J. G. Alexander, "Painting and Manuscript Illumination for Royal Patrons in the Later Middle Ages," in Scattergood and Sherborne, *Court Culture*, 161; Margaret Rickert, *Painting in Britain in the Middle Ages* (Baltimore: Penguin, 1954), 160.

71. E101/93/12.

72. E101/92/9, 92/23.

73. E101/91/12, 93/6.

74. E101/91/25.

75. Vale, *Edward III and Chivalry*, 53.

76. E101/91/12.

77. Alfred B. Emden, *A Biographical Register of the University of Oxford* (Oxford: Clarendon, 1957–59), 1:477.

78. E101/91/12, 91/25.

79. E101/93/12; John H. R. Moorman, *The Grey Friars in Cambridge, 1225–1538* (Cambridge: Cambridge University Press, 1952), 159–60.

80. Emden, *Biographical Register of Cambridge,* 562; E101/94/2, 93/8, 93/18.

81. E101/93/12.

82. Emden, *Biographical Register of Oxford,* 2:780; E101/95/8.

83. E101/93/12.

84. Emden, *Biographical Register of Cambridge,* 588; E101/94/2.

85. E101/95/8; Emden, *Biographical Register of Cambridge,* 580; William John Harrison, *Notes on the Masters, Fellows, Scholars, and Exhibitioners of Clare College* (Cambridge: Printed for the College, 1953), 3.

86. Edward Hailstone, Jr., *The History and Antiquities of the Parish of Bottisham and the Priory of Anglesey* (Cambridge, Eng.: Cambridge Antiquarian Society, 1873), 261–62; Harrison, *Notes,* 22–23.

87. Master John de Harleton, who was fetched "on the lady's business" in 1358–59, was probably a fellow of Clare Hall: E101/94/2 and Emden, *Biographical Register of Cambridge,* 287. Master Ralph de Kerdington was Master of Clare College in the 1350s: E101/93/19 and Emden, *Biographical Register of Cambridge,* 336.

88. A third cleric, Henry de Motelot, a priest in Elizabeth's household, claimed to be a fellow at Clare College, but no documents authenticate this: E101/92/12; Emden, *Biographical Register of Cambridge,* 415; Harrison, *Notes,* 22–23.

89. E101/92/2, 95/2.

90. Emden, *Biographical Register of Cambridge,* 548.

91. E101/93/12, when he received a gift of sixty shillings.

92. E101/95/7, 93/10, 93/12.

93. Emden, *Biographical Register of Oxford,* 2:729–30.

94. J. R. L. Highfield, "The English Hierarchy in the Reign of Edward III," *Transactions of the Royal Historical Society* 6 (1956): 129.

95. E101/93/2, 94/7, 93/12.

96. *Dictionary of National Biography,* 15:434, lists six titles attributed to him; John le Neve, *Fasti Ecclesiae Anglicanae* (London: Institute for Historical Research, 1962), 9:21.

97. E101/93/10, 93/12.

98. Le Neve, *Fasti Ecclesiae Anglicanae* 1:95, 2:34, 3:17, 4:4.

99. E101/94/1.

100. Charles H. Talbot, *Medicine in Medieval England* (New York: American Elsevier, 1967), 198–200; Emden, *Biographical Register of Oxford,* 1:257–58.

101. Albert C. Chibnall, *Richard de Badew and the University of Cambridge* (Cambridge: Cambridge University Press, 1963), 31.

102. *Calendar Patent Rolls, 1334–38*, 237; Chibnall, *Richard de Badew*, 40–41. He estimates that the King's Hall, a royal foundation, was endowed for an income of about £103 each year.

103. *Calendar of Entries in the Papal Registers Relating to Great Britain and Ireland* (London: H.M. Stationery Office, 1897), 3:269.

104. E. F. Jacob, "Founders and Foundations in the Later Middle Ages," *Bulletin of Historical Research* 35 (1962): 33.

105. J. A. F. Thomson, "Piety and Charity in Late Medieval London," *Journal of Ecclesiastical History* 16 (1965): 194. Most of Rosenthal, *Purchase of Paradise*, is based on this thesis.

106. Heywood, *Early Cambridge Statutes*, 139, 141.

107. Ibid., 114; Thomson, "Piety and Charity," 195.

108. Joel T. Rosenthal, "The Universities and the English Nobility," *History of Education Quarterly* 9 (1969): 431.

109. All quotations from the preamble are found in Heywood, *Early Cambridge Statutes*, 113–14.

110. *Calendar of Close Rolls, 1339–41*, 82–83.

111. E101/91/27.

112. E101/91/27, 92/4, 92/9, 92/11.

113. E101/459/24.

114. *Calendar of Patent Rolls, 1327–30*, 61.

115. Charles Green and A. B. Whittingham, "Excavations at Walsingham Priory, Norfolk, 1961," *Archaeological Journal* 125 (1968): 273.

116. Warner, "Petition of the Prior and Canons," 167–69; Edward Hutton, *The Franciscans in England, 1224–1538* (London: Constable, 1926), 166.

117. John Hough, *Essex Churches* (Woodbridge, Eng.: Boydell, 1983), 151; Roy Midmer, *English Mediaeval Monasteries, 1066–1540* (Athens: University of Georgia Press, 1979), 319.

118. Katherine Weston Barnardiston, *Clare Priory: Seven Centuries of a Suffolk House* (Cambridge, Eng.: Heffer, 1962), 67; Nikolaus Pevsner, *Suffolk* (Harmondsworth, Eng.: Penguin, 1961), 149, agrees, adding a vaulted chamber to the lady's list. Barnardiston thinks the chamber may have been the library or infirmary (19). The poem was written by Osbern Buckenham or Bokenham, who was a friar at the priory in the fifteenth century: *The Cartulary of the Augustinian Friars of Clare*, ed. Christopher Harper-Bill (Woodbridge, Eng.: Boydell, 1991), no. 189n.

119. Francis Roth, *The English Austin Friars, 1249–1538* (New York: Augustinian Historical Institute, 1966), 1:261.

120. Miri Rubin, *Charity and Community in Medieval Cambridge* (Cambridge: Cambridge University Press, 1987), 109.

121. *Calendar of Patent Rolls, 1330–34*, 39, 159, and *1334–38*, 90; Hailstone, *History and Antiquities*, 162–70, describes the ruins of the priory.

122. Building expenses are in E101/92/12; visits in many rolls, including E101/92/4, 92/7, 92/9, 92/13, 92/24.

123. F. X. Martin, "The Augustinian Friaries of Pre-Reformation Ireland" *Augustiniana* 6 (1956): 361–62.

124. "Petition," 167–69; E101/92/30, 95/8.

125. See Alan R. Martin, *Franciscan Architecture in England* (Manchester: Manchester University Press, 1937), 129–37, for details on the remains of the friary.

126. J. K. Knight, "Usk Castle and Its Affinities," in *Ancient Monuments and Their Interpretation: Essays Presented to A. J. Taylor*, ed. M. R. Apted, R. Gilyard-Beer, and A. D. Saunders (London and Chichester: Phillimore, 1977), 147–48.

127. E101/458/4, 459/24, 459/25, 459/26.

128. John Harvey, *English Mediaeval Architects*, Rev. ed. (Gloucester: Alan Sutton, 1987), 52, 75, 283.

129. The rolls refer to this man as either Richard Felsted or Richard Carpenter even in instances where the description of the work in progress shows that a single individual was meant. Harvey, *English Mediaeval Architects*, 107, provides his biography.

130. E101/91/12.

131. R. Allen Brown, H. M. Colvin, and A. J. Taylor, *The History of the King's Work* (London: H. M. Stationery Office, 1963), 2:668–69.

132. E101/92/2, 92/4, 92/5, 95/2.

133. E101/92/9, 92/11.

134. E101/92/23; Harvey, *English Mediaeval Architects*, 107.

135. The location of Elizabeth's house is described in Gerald A. Hodgett, *The Cartulary of Holy Trinity, Aldgate* (London: London Record Society, 1971), 188.

Some Norfolk Women and Their Books, ca. 1390–1440

Ralph Hanna III

Any discussion of women and patronage must necessarily recognize a serious paradox or fissure at its center. Inherent in this conventional designation for the support or sustenance of artistic activity are double implications that would seem at the outset particularly disabling in any discussion concerning a female agent. To the extent that such a study should strive to provide a liberatory narrative, a discussion of women's power to direct their lives, the student must also recognize disquieting implications inherent in the problem. It is possible that women may, at best, achieve power only at second hand and only at the expense of other groups perhaps more marginalized than they themselves. Moreover, such power may be achieved only fitfully.

For the word *patronage,* when conjoined with the activities or behavior of women, overtly marks such behavior by gender and by class. Moreover, such marking has typified most treatments of women as book patrons ever since Susan Groag Bell's fine pioneering effort in the field.[1] Although the gender and class implications inherent in studies of book patronage may be distinguished, fundamental to an interest in these activities by women has always been what is conventionally called "the immasculation of the feminine subject." First of all, the term *patron* defines a role clearly masculine: the word is, after all, a derivative of the Latin root *patr-,* "father." Insofar as literary patronage forms a desideratum, then, a woman patron claims for herself a masculine position, and may engage in an activity merely imitative and/or appropriative of already extant male efforts. She may remain always a shadow second, an attenuated version of a more fully fledged masculine realm of activity. Thus

Bell, for example, though correctly insisting upon the utterly central maternal role in education at home, does not insist strenuously enough that such a role was usually gender-distinguished and centered upon the full education of daughters *only*. And she fails to remind us that sons were typically removed from such maternal tutelage at age six to be given separate masculine training, the "initiation rite" which would integrate them into male/Latinate culture.[2]

Secondly, the title *patron* necessarily implies a notion of social subservience. At the least problematized,[3] patronage presupposes an exchange between a superior and employee, rewarded or protected for her efforts, artistic or otherwise. In this interchange between master and servant, the term *patronage* at least initially privileges the position occupied by those with the power to command (and to pay).[4] Their inspiration, in many cases their conceptions and specifications, and their cash generate the social relationship. And given the artifacts customarily discussed in patronage studies, the exchange that forms patronage does not reflect simply relative social power/powerlessness: women patrons are very apt to represent classes uniquely privileged, not infrequently magnatial but seldom below the urban *patri*ciate. Thus, women patrons tend to be the socially powerful, women who can act independently only because of the achieved success of their consort or male parent. Moreover, the artifacts that draw them to our attention will always be formed within dominant social notions of artistic output: they will tend, as the innumerable books of hours to which Bell directs our attention indicate, toward high art productions.

I want to open out the topic "women and book patronage" by writing about women's activities with books in an arena removed from an aristocratic siting, both its social expropriations and its High Art emphases. Such a move will allow me to foreground the category "gender" as it effects book use. And as a corollary, I want to examine what I call "activities with books"—not necessarily the originary gesture of commissioned authorship (which seems to me frequently bound up with clandestine patriarchal metaphors; cf. Chaucer, "the father of English poetry").

I thus address the topic by looking at a range of women's activities with books over about a fifty-year period in Norfolk. All four women I discuss are engaged in literary and literate culture; they all foster book production and book use and are committed to the propagation of religious works. My exemplary women are all involved in religious argument and controversy: their book activities depend upon a desire to spread the faith as they see it, a specific doctrinal awareness. All then operate within a certain measured selflessness, a subjugation to an eternal ideology.

My examples consist of two pairs of figures. In each case one of the pair has a well-documented career, and I extrapolate to suggest that the material experience of the second woman was similar. Further, my examples are deliberately selective and deliberately skewed: ample material on what is conventionally considered patronage by female members of the urban upper classes, gentry, and nobility/royalty of East Anglia has long been available.[5] But much less formalized (and inherently more problematic) efforts go on at other social sites and are no less worthy of consideration. Yet at the same time that my narrative records moments of liberation and triumph, I have to acknowledge its faultedness as well. In the instances I survey, women are reabsorbed into male culture, and their experiences with books, however powerful, are impromptu and always subject to difficult negotiation.

I thus begin my discussion of women's activities with books at a village level. Evidence for book involvement concerning two peasant women, Margery Baxter of Martham and Avis Mone of Loddon, comes from the 1428–31 trial register of Bishop Alnwick of Norwich.[6] We know the activities of both these women because they belonged to a heterodox community, one apparently most powerful in a series of scattered Norfolk villages. But although isolated locales, these hamlets formed a literary community that extended well beyond county boundaries and was linked by textual exchanges, often over surprising distances.

Baxter and Mone came to Alnwick's attention because they were Lollards, followers of the sect's apostle to Norfolk, William White, who was executed in 1428. And given the academic roots of this heresy and its insistence upon the validating power of the Gospel text, Lollard communities were perforce book-bound. As the Norwich register indicates, the construction of a literary community involved access to scriptural texts (and perhaps to others as well), a formalized model of book use involving "schools," and a gender-neutral sense of who was an acceptable reader, and thus student, of scripture.[7]

The trial records, of which Baxter's is the most extensive—indeed it takes the form of a lengthy narrative—indicate protracted involvement of women within the Lollard textual community. Such involvement is at least initially secondary, but ultimately might involve a highly tactile form of book use. The specific references to texts in the Norfolk documents are all to volumes imported to the countryside by men: William White, who had earlier taught in Kent, brought his books to instruct others; Baxter and her husband learned their doctrine from Nicholas Belward of South Elem, who had gone to London to purchase a Lollard New Testament.[8]

However, given the surreptitious nature of heterodox commitment, the physical texts were not themselves simply male property. Both missionaries and books, in the context of persecution, had to be hidden somewhere. And women participated in both activities integral to the preservation of a textual community. Thus, among the charges against Baxter was her hiding William White within her household. Mone, whose house was the fixed site of an ongoing Lollard "school," appears to have sheltered a considerably wider range of malefactors, real or imagined; Foxe, for example, reports that "White and his wife had their chief abode" with the Mones. And Baxter, according to the record, also transported White's books, from a cache in Yarmouth the ten miles to one in her home village, Martham. Similarly, Baxter's husband claimed that Mone's daughter, as well as her servant John Pert, could read English—in the context, as we will see, a sign that they could function as direct disseminators of heretical doctrine.[9]

Such details, of course, show one perhaps unsurprising similarity between this peasant reading community and the magnatial ones customarily the subject of patronage studies. In both instances, the fundamental literary unit was the household. In their home the Mones ran a formal school with an extensive clientele; Baxter sheltered both the arch-heresiarch of East Anglia and presumably his books in hers. Moreover, much book use (along with other heretical activity) was absolutely household-bound. Reading and discussing religious topics went on in comfortably domestic surroundings; indeed, much of the trial description lacks totally that demarcated performative setting which typifies many representations of medieval aristocratic book use.[10] Baxter's husband read to her at night in her (bed)room; she discussed Lollard ideas with three other women before a fireplace while they sewed. And the ultimate example of the bishop's intrusive surveillance involved a serving girl's curious inspection of a covered pot on the fire in Baxter's house (which revealed that she, in keeping with Lollard doctrine, intended to eat meat on a fasting day). Book use thus represented one extension of a trusted domestic community. And in fact the powerful evocations of household values—the conjugal chamber, the hospitable hearth, the communion of the dinner table, cooperative labor[11]—are inextricably bound with the contents of those books that constituted heterodox belief. Before Baxter and her husband slept together at night, they shared the comfort of the Gospels and some mutual discussion of their meaning.

However, both Baxter and Mone's involvement with books remained in one sense secondary. Neither woman appears to have been literate in either the medieval Latinate sense or in our own. They were not ocular readers but aural ones, dependent on someone else's reading to access the text.[12] Thus, although physically proximate to the volumes that inspired their faith and, on at least some occasions, apparently responsible for the very safety of such volumes, they were forced to rely upon males for any understanding of the books' contents. Whatever their importance to constructing the situation in which books might be read, these women could not perform that reading on their own. As in the magnatial situation, access to writing came through the ears, through public or quasi-public reading.

Although such dependency seems to reinscribe the rule of patriarchy, in which women are always secondary,[13] in this specific Lollard community this situation does not appear an unmitigated debility. In fact, Baxter quite overtly (and Mone by Baxter's report) used their secondary status to develop what may be construed a more powerful model of book dispersal than men, dependent on a written text, might conceive. From the trial records, purely aural access to the book did not form simply a passive activity, hearing a voice drone on. Rather, both Baxter and Mone had developed mechanisms for absorbing what they had heard, for processing and comprehending written ideas in a mode analogous to what their male lectors did through the eye. Moreover, because they knew that, unlike those who read to them, they could not return to the volumes for consultation on various points, they processed the texts with an eye to memorial use. They absorbed texts in the interest of possible oral performance, whether as internal meditation or overtly vocal teaching. In so doing, they became in fact the book (or the usable portions thereof): they rendered the physical volume in some measure superfluous and incorporated it within themselves. They embodied texts and transported them in their corporeal persons, gave to them a life beyond mere vellum, and thus attained a flexibility (if not perhaps what masculine scholars might consider an accuracy) of use that their male correligionists might not have achieved.[14]

Such an embodiment of the book forms nearly the entirety of the bishop's complaint against Baxter. For the whole charge against her reflects a single occasion of proselytizing: Baxter allegedly attempted, at very great length and with great thoroughness, given the range of Lollard doctrine, to convince another woman (who reported her) of the truth of heterodoxy. Moreover, in the course of this conversation, it becomes evident that Baxter did not view this oral missionary activity as an isolated event: she mentions an earlier effort at converting a Carmelite friar from Yarmouth, in this case by using the standard métier of Lollardy, the explanation of Gospel passages in the vernacular.

Whatever one is to think of the degree of coercion and editing that lies behind Joan Clifland's charges against Baxter, a variety of quite idiosyncratic views characterizes the report. These, I suggest, whatever editing produced the register, represent material traces of Baxter's beliefs. And they all indicate that Baxter was not just a woman deprived of her subjectivity and merely a vocal vehicle for truths of male origin. For in addition to such transmittal of male texts, her idiosyncracies suggest that she had formulated for herself a version of Lollardy that privileged both the mechanism by which she had attained this belief system and the way she disseminated it, the female body as evangelical vehicle. Ultimately, Baxter patronized books by living them and dispersing them through her living example.[15]

Consider Baxter's most sweeping demonstration to Clifland of a basic Lollard tenet, that the crucifixes in churches simply form examples of those "graven images" prohibited in the first commandment. She says, "If you should wish to see the true cross of Christ I wish to show it to you here in your own house," and the account continues: "And this witness asserted that she willingly wanted to see the true cross of Christ. And the foresaid Margery said, 'see,' and then she stretched out her arms, saying to this witness, 'This is the true cross of Christ, and you ought and may see and adore this cross every day here in your own house, and you labor in vain so long as you go to churches to adore or pray to any images or dead crosses.'"[16] This claim, that the physical person of the truly believing Christian in fact embodies the true mechanism of salvation, reflects the two poles of Baxter's ecclesiology.[17] On the one hand, she rejects conventional Catholic Christianity as "heresies and idolatries" or "false mawmentryes and lawes": in the latter formulation canonical legislation governing belief is merely one subset of a broader *mawmentrye*, worship of a dead idol, conciliar or papal opinion, not of a divine presence. And she makes a similarly physicalized and embodied claim for what constitutes the true church: "Every man and woman who are of the same opinion as she are good priests, and . . . holy church only exists in the places where all those of her sect live [and not in churches or among ordained priests]."[18] Baxter tropes upon this presence of Holy Church, the physically localizable household as "the body of the faithful"; she feels an imperative to carry this localizable presence in her body—just as she physically carried White's books—so as to spread it into new locales, new household communities.

Baxter's sheer ingenuity and the quality of her daring as a person in contact with books can be overestimated, however. For ultimately she became reabsorbed into one or another form of masculinized book culture. Most obviously, we know Baxter only through the male record of an ecclesiastical inquiry (the final abjuration originally taken down by John Exeter, clerk and notary; Tanner, *Trials*, 41). This court forced her to recant her views and subjected her book/body to public humiliation and discipline—at least six public scourgings in her smock before her entire village community. And inferential evidence, which I have discussed elsewhere,[19] survives to indicate that her very physical survival to become what she might have considered a defaced text may have been dependent upon husbandly—and not just ecclesiastical—coercion. The record indicates that both William Baxter alias Wright and Margery Baxter survived their inquisition by fingering coreligionists for the bishop; in this process, so far as it is reconstructible, William appears far more active than Margery, and, just possibly, he obliterated the book that he had helped create through a turncoat assertion of conjugal power.

The village heterodoxy of Baxter and Mone appears considerably removed from the traditions of mystical theology. But analogies will emerge through a comparison of the activities with books of these two aurally literate Lollards and the most famous Norfolk religious women of the later Middle Ages, the anchoress Julian of Norwich and Margery Kempe of King's Lynn.[20] As in the case of Baxter and Mone, there is an interesting disproportion of available evidence: like Baxter's trial record, Kempe's *Book* provides an extensive narrative account and admits of protracted analysis. In contrast, Julian's life always and only comprised the sixteen revelations she received 13 May 1373 and her protracted meditations upon their meaning.

Like Baxter and Mone, Kempe and Julian's religious activity was initially stimulated through contact with texts read by males. Kempe's account is filled with narratives of spiritual direction: she refers on several occasions to "comownyng in scriptur whech sche lernyd in sermonys & be comownyng wyth clerkys" (29/30–32, cf. 144/5–7). Oral public instruction, the sermon, for her alternates with private consultations with several well-disposed male figures:[21] such consultation, although it includes so sacramental an activity as private confession (cf. Archbishop Arundel's approbation of this special devotion at 36/18–27), extends through spiritual conversations to hearing books read aloud. Like Baxter and Mone, she is provided by her chosen male supporters with those texts that shape her religious being.

At least in the shorter version of her *Showings*, Julian similarly identifies the origins of her visionary/meditative existence. She was inspired with a longing for three wounds by a text she learned through a sermon: "I harde a man telle of halye kyrke of the storye of saynte Cecylle" (204/46–47). Scholars have usually viewed Julian's textual activity as a progressive depersonalization in the interests of authorizing her text, and Julian deletes the comment in her later, longer version.[22]

Kempe refers on four occasions (39/19–26, 143/20–29, 152/32–154/14, 165/37–166/11) to a relatively narrow range of texts that stand in a reciprocal relationship to her activity with books.[23] In addition to the Bible and some form of commentary on it (143/23–27; cf. 97/33–35 and 235/35–38 for her recirculating such heard experiences), she persistently identifies as books she heard read (note the insistence of 39/23, 25) a "book of St. Bride," the pseudo-Bonaventuran *Stimulus amoris*, Rolle's *Incendium amoris*, and "Hylton." This last, presumably Walter Hilton's *Scala*, would have been the only one of these works that would certainly have been English: Kempe's aural reading experience necessarily relied upon a clerical support staff because, whatever the form of her English literacy, she shows no evidence of Latin competence.[24]

Julian's learning and literacy have always been perceived differently. Her editors claim that she was "a great scholar" who pillaged a monastic (presumably, given the sources they associate with her, Carthusian) library and reabsorbed its materials into her experience. But in this claim Colledge and Walsh, quite contemptuously, I think, seek to eradicate any possibility that Julian could respond with originality to her personal experience. And they ignore the very few bits of overt evidence in the text, for example, 222/41–42 (short version only) "I am a womann, *leued*, febille, and freylle;" 285/2 (long version) "a symple creature vnlettyrde" (although this last might refer only to her state at the time of the revelations). If we take these statements at face value, Julian may well have benefited through something like the same "communing" Kempe describes more explicitly.

Such male reading figures create for Kempe an extended clerical household that resembles those domestic groups that fostered Baxter and Mone. Not simply her exceptional interest in devotion but her social status obviously allowed her such an extradomestic outlet: as a member of the Lynn patriciate, she might coerce a special notice denied others.[25] Given Kempe's interest in holy virginity, usually found incongruous by her interlocutors, this redefinition may be connected with a variety of efforts at reformulating household situations: thus her biological family, including the fourteen children she bore, appears in her text primarily through her negotiations to free her body from the sexuality of her husband, John Kempe (the famous 23/9–25/27). Kempe seeks a denatured family, one thoroughly spiritualized, in keeping with her efforts to enact a holy life: her instructors' readings convey, just as William Baxter's did to his wife, the theoretical underpinnings of such a life devoted to holy love.

The original experience enshrined in Julian's *Showings* is equally familial. Her actual deathbed vision involves her mother (234/29) and thus, inferentially, the household community (another reference removed in the longer version). But when Julian meditates on her experience, it takes place, increasingly in the longer version, in the depersonalized textual world in which she speaks, not for herself, but for all Christians.

In contrast, Kempe, like Baxter, actively absorbs her texts and seeks to re-enact them. So successful is she in this pursuit that she displaces their status as the sources that have in fact constituted her holy acts: early on, Jesus iden-tifies Saint Bridget of Sweden, author/subject of one of Kempe's favorite and most mentioned books, not as a paradigm to be imitated but as a similar whom she has already surpassed (47/26–35; and cf. 95/10–37).[26] And the two latest appearances in her account of the reading lists—now bolstered by the lives of Saint Mary of Oignes and Elizabeth of Hungary—have much the same flavor: the texts now appear not as sources but as verifications of the holiness of Kempe's own enactments. She so thoroughly embodies the holy living she feels herself instructed to achieve that the texts now are primarily valuable as indicating to others that behavior apparently unique to her has received ca-nonical approbation elsewhere and thus stands beyond reproach. Rather than the creation of texts she has inveigled others into reading to her, she stands as a figure who thoroughly enacts an ideal: the texts simply confirm the value inherent in her enactment.

Yet textual absorption and its physical enactment, in teaching others, as Baxter and Mone did, for example,[27] do not exhaust Kempe's embodiment of the texts she heard. For in addition to her surrogate familial community of readers/counselors, as several critics have noted, Kempe in her visions also participates in a second textually based surrogate household, the Holy Family.[28] This family is textualized because Kempe certainly derived it from a book her clerics read her, although a book which may be completely sup-pressed in her account, the pseudo-Bonaventuran *Meditationes vitae Christi*.[29] This font of affective piety, with its encouragement of an active sensory co-participation in Gospel history, animates much of Kempe's visionary contact with divinity. But the shape of Kempe's *Book* indicates that such textualized intrusion of the biblical household into her consciousness was an insufficiently powerful achievement.

For just as Kempe's invocation of surrogate households displaces from her account any literal domestic community, she equally displaces anything re-sembling her normal life as a prominent citizen and businesswoman of Lynn.[30] Instead, the literary genre with which Kempe's account most nearly accords is the pilgrimage narrative: rather than experience the gospel textually, through either biblical narrative or Bonaventuran meditation, she seeks (and has the money to afford) the actual tactile experience of the gospel, to visit the Pal-estinian holy sites. And there she achieves the full bodily expression of her sanctity, her love for Jesus: at Calvary (68/12–29), she is seized with those fallings and bellowings that form her most distinctive (and externally horrifying) form of holy expression. At this point Kempe's bodily absorption and enactment of the holy texts that informed her becomes total (and unlike Baxter's "crucifixion," totally involuntary): visibly—and disquietingly—she becomes the holy women at Calvary, lives the *Meditationes* in her flesh.

Insofar as her text provides information, Julian's experience appears equally text-centered and embodied. Although Julian mentions the preacher's Saint Cecilia in the context of her third gift, a desired three wounds, the other gifts she prays for join a Cecilia-like bodily experience with what she initially poses as a Kempe-like coparticipation in the Passion. The second gift Julian seeks, a "sicknes . . . so hard as to the death" (287/1), replicates the story of Cecilia's wounding, her three days mortally stricken yet spiritually purified, drained of earthly concerns. Similarly, although she expects to recover (see 287/28–33, more explicit in the longer version), Julian wishes to experience palpably the edge of death, to achieve a salvific purgation, by Jesus' merciful acceptance of her imitative bodily suffering.

Only once this experience is underway (292/43–293/52) does Julian pray for the second gift she has long desired—like Kempe, to join the Bonaventuran Marys in their compassion for Jesus' visible suffering. Although Julian vacillates as to whether such an experience involves "bodely sight" (286/12) or merely compassion (292/48–293/50), she is clearly stimulated by her Cecilian corporeal suffering: like the saint's, it mirrors Jesus's suffering sacrifice for humanity. And, just as with Kempe's involuntary bellowings, divine grace responds to deep physically expressed yet text-inspired longing: Jesus rewards Julian to an extent she has not dared to hope—she receives the sequence of bodily sights which make her book.

Kempe's activity with books (and inferentially, what we are allowed to know of Julian's) complicatedly reflects situations analogous to those of Baxter and Mone. All depend upon literate male figures for their access to the texts they desire; all know these texts only through situations of oral reading performed by males and, in Kempe's case specifically, involving at least a measure of impromptu oral translation from Latin. And all prove extraordinarily receptive to information taken in through the ear: the texts become physically reformed in their bodies and can be immediately accessed for the instruction of others, the expansion of their originally familial textual community.[31]

But at the end of Baxter's career, she was reabsorbed and reappropriated by male book culture: in the process, the physical book of her body was expunged. Kempe's life (and inferentially Julian's) involves considerably more complicated gestures of reappropriation, in Kempe's case associated with her refusal of silence: leaving a written record, producing a book that would have a greater permanence than that corporeal experience it would chronicle, required further direct dealings with male literates. For whether or not Kempe could read English, the text contains no evidence that she could write it.

In Kempe's *Book* writing initially appears as a male imperative. Early in her public career as holy woman, she relates, she was in fact beseiged both with requests that she provide a written account of herself and with offers to produce such an account: "Summe of these worthy & worshepful clerkys tokyn it in perel of her sowle and as þei wold answer to God þat þis creatur was inspyred wyth þe Holy Gost and bodyn hyr þat sche schuld don hem wryten & makyn a booke of hyr felyngys & hir reuelacyons. Sum proferyd hir to wrytyn hyr felyngys wyth her owne handys" (3/20–26).[32] For these male interlocutors, the text they seek would not simply communicate Kempe's value but in some measure validate it, place it in the fixed graphemic form in which it could be subject to traditional testing. But at this point Kempe, guided by her divine friend/husband/interlocutor Jesus, feels no such angst for permanent scrutiny:[33] under divine tutelage she can resist the lures of record, can choose to continuously enact her revelation in her body.

Only twenty years later, Kempe's account runs, does Jesus actually instruct her to find a writer who will receive her dictated account of her living. And at this point the tables are turned: rather than willing aid in her book-producing project, Kempe encounters resistance to getting her life written. Her final tribulation is thus to endure this refusal of aid. But at this point in her career, book production has become charged in a way it has not before: at issue in the dictation of the book is no longer simply the matter of accurate record. The amanuensis Kempe seeks cannot be a mere transcriptional notary but must offer something more. Writers now refuse their services to Kempe because they share the socially prevalent suspicious reading of her sanctity; the appropriate writer must demonstrate a "credens" (4/3–4, 55/21) in those feelings which Kempe has enacted. Hence, as Lochrie points out,[34] the original text, apparently copied by Kempe's expatriate son, is not "Lynn-legible" but a mass of strange continental letter forms and spellings (4/14–18): it *is* in fact the text of belief, but not a text open to any of the dubious potential scribes available to Kempe in her hometown. Thus, to produce the *Book*, Kempe must coopt her chosen scribe, force him to undergo a conversion experience, to learn to read with *credens*, "belief"; only then will he be capable of (and agree to) decipherment of the extant script. And only then can she offer those corrections (see 5/10–12) that will form the appropriate text useful for public consumption.

But such a gesture at commanding book production involves further perils of male reappropriation. For having received the text, the male amaneunsis can make it into the vehicle of his own "credens," can replace Kempe's faith in her visionary life with his own. And such reappropriation goes on within the text itself. At the head of book 2, the scribe explicitly announces that his "credens" in Kempe's holiness enables him to offer a sequel based not on those internal feelings that Kempe has always enacted, but on her more factitious reports of events and his external observation: "Afftyr þat . . . þe preiste of whom is befornwretyn had copijd þe same tretys aftyr hys sympyl cunnyng, he held it expedient to honowr of þe blisful Trinite þat hys holy werkys xulde be notifyid & declaryd to þe pepil, whan it plesyd hym, to þe worschip of hys holy name. And þan he gan to writyn . . . sweche grace as owr Lord wrowt in hys sympyl creatur ʒerys þat sche leuyd aftyr, not alle but summe of hem aftyr hyr owyn tunge" (221/1–12). And such an external view of the holy woman bodily enacting the strength of her faith becomes even more attenuated in the *Book*'s final chapter, in which Kempe's experience is routinized into a simple guide to prayer (248/1–254/3).[35]

But this scribal enthusiasm for the book, the belief that the male writer can form, through his "credens," a guide to Kempe's generally inexpressible bodily experience, does not end the range of male appropriations to which Kempe (and Julian as well) have been subjected. For our knowledge of both women's texts is entirely dependent upon their absorption within male reading communities. In Kempe's case the surviving medieval copy, British Library, MS Add. 61823, looks to have been taken directly by an apparently male scribe named Salthouse from the scribal holograph Kempe had overseen; after a time when it may have been owned by a Cambridgeshire vicar, it passed into the library of the Charterhouse at Mount Grace (N. Yks.).[36] And there the book received annotations that assimilate Kempe's spiritual behavior to that practiced by two of the house's most famous late-fifteenth-century figures, Richard Methley and John Norton.[37] In such usage Kempe's *Book* loses touch with the performative space of both experience and composition and becomes, like most medieval books, simply a volume for private consultation.

The emergence of Julian's experience from body to book was similar to Kempe's. Her actual textual production was delayed for twenty years (see 520/86), in this case, not because of divine prohibition of script, but because of a deep desire to comprehend fully the merciful meaning of her visions.

We might, thus, imagine Julian engaged for a protracted period in a by now familiar pattern—using memory to dilate upon and to articulate fully a bodily textual experience in the absence of written record. Although *The Showings* carefully occludes, save for a possible reference to dictation (666/4–7),[38] the process by which these meditations entered writing, the transmission of the finished work once again involved reappropriation by male organizations. We know the shorter version of Julian's text only through a book, British Library, MS Add. 37790, which, on the basis of James Greenhalgh's monogram, certainly belonged to another Carthusian house, perhaps that at Sheen. The longer version survives only in late continental copies (and Serenus Cressy's print): although at least one of these was copied by recusant Benedictine nuns, the most likely vehicle for Julian's dispersal is through their male spiritual directors, perhaps preeminently Augustine Baker.[39] Both books, Kempe's and Julian's, could achieve their circulation only through a reliance on male-sponsored networks of book production, in both cases those associated not with the free life of the spirit chronicled in the texts themselves but with organized religious institutions.

At the end of an excellent study of medieval literacy, Margaret Aston directs attention to Henry VIII's 1543 restrictions on Bible reading. For Henry, "the lower sort . . . women, artificers, apprentices, journeymen, serving-men of the degree of yeoman or under, husbandmen, labourers" are to be denied access to Scripture.[40] This late example should serve as a pregnant reminder that the possibility of acquiring, using, and disseminating books remained subject, well into the Renaissance, to gender distinctions that (at least in Henry's legal language) were also deeply implicated in class structure. In such situations women's effort to fulfill their literary interests, especially sophisticated religious interests (rather than the simple desire to receive a splash service-book produced according to narrowly standardized specifications), can involve extraordinary difficulties. Such textual efforts and desires require acts of extraordinary and inventive negotiation. They produce modes of book acquisition, of use, of appropriation, and of directed re-publication quite different from those familiar within High Art literate culture; and these modes appear the more inventive in precise proportion to the degree to which such a desire to enter literate culture encounters resistance. Moreover, such invention testifies to the very fragility of women's attempts to fulfill themselves in and through the written word. And ultimately such efforts, whatever their inventiveness, seem never to forestall male reappropriation, retextualization, of flexible and intriguing female experiences with books. In fact, my survey of several Norfolk women would suggest that the most successful female appropriations and recirculations of texts will always escape us, will have been those experiences which remained pure textual embodiment and resisted precisely that male re-textualizing through which we know Baxter and Kempe most directly. The only other alternative to such textual embodiment against the odds would seem that silence which shrouds the apparently analogous experiences of Avis Mone and Julian of Norwich.[41]

NOTES

1. Susan Groag Bell, "Medieval Women Book Owners: Arbiters of Lay Piety and Ambassadors of Culture," in *Women and Power in the Middle Ages,* ed. Mary Erler and Maryanne Kowaleski (Athens: University of Georgia Press, 1988), 149–87.

2. See Bell, "Medieval Women Book Owners," 148–51; Walter J. Ong, "Latin Language Study as a Renaissance Puberty Rite," *Studies in Philology* 56 (1959): 103–24; and Nicholas Orme, *From Childhood to Chivalry: The Education of the English Kings and Aristocracy, 1066–1530* (New York: Methuen, 1984), 16–28.

3. Although I suggest some such qualifications in "Sir Thomas Berkeley and His Patronage," *Speculum* 64 (1989): 878–916, and in "Producing Manuscripts and Editions," in *Crux and Controversy in Middle English Textual Criticism,* ed. Charlotte Brewer and Alastair Minnis (Cambridge, Eng.: Boydell, 1992), 109–30, esp. 112–19.

4. Cf. the dramatic representation in John Trevisa's "Dialogus" and "Epistola," in *Medieval English Studies Presented to George Kane,* ed. Edward Donald Kennedy, Ronald Waldron, and Joseph S. Wittig (Wolfeboro, N.H.: Brewer, 1988), 285–99.

5. See Samuel Moore, "Patrons of Letters in Norfolk and Suffolk, c. 1450," *PMLA* 27 (1912): 186–207 and 28 (1913): 79–105.

6. See Norman P. Tanner, *Heresy Trials in the Diocese of Norwich, 1428–31,* Camden Society, 4th ser., 20 (London: Royal Historical Society, 1977), esp. 41–51 (Baxter) and 138–44 (Mone). See also Margaret Aston's review, "William White's Lollard Followers," in her *Lollards and Reformers: Images and Literacy in Late Medieval Religion* (London: Hambledon, 1984): 70–100. Mone's confession, with elaborate annotations, some silently referring to Baxter, also appears in Anne Hudson, *Selections from English Wycliffite Writings* (Cambridge: Cambridge University Press, 1978), 34–37. I have also discussed Baxter in "The Difficulty of Ricardian Prose Translation: The Case of the Lollards," *Modern Language Quarterly* 51 (1990): 319–40.

7. For Lollard "schools," see Anne Hudson, *The Premature Reformation: Wycliffite Texts and Lollard History* (Oxford: Clarendon, 1988), esp. 174–94.

8. For White's books, see Tanner, *Trials,* 41. For Belward, a member of a family widely implicated in spreading Lollard ideas, cf. Baxter's husband's testimony, including the assertion that Belward taught them both "and wrought with them continually

by the space of one year, and studied diligently upon the New Testament" (John Foxe, *The Acts and Monuments*, 4th ed., ed. Josiah Pratt [London: Religious Tract Society, 1887], 3:597); and cf. Tanner, *Trials*, 47; Margaret Aston, "Lollardy and Literacy," *History* 62 (1977): 347–71, reprinted in *Lollards and Reformers*, 193–217. White's servant Alice was either a reader or a book conveyer: Hugh Pie, a priest associated with the Mones, willed her a New Testament (at the time in the keeping of a man from Colchester, in Essex); see Foxe, *Acts*, 3:597.

9. See Foxe, *Acts*, 3:591, 597. Baxter reported that "the wife of Thomas Mone is the woman most intimate with and wisest in the teaching of William White" ["uxor Thome Mone est secretissima et sapientissima mulier in doctrina W. White"]; see Tanner, *Trials*, 47.

10. For example, the famous *Troilus* frontispiece, in Cambridge, Corpus Christi College, MS. 61; the described reading of a romance of Thebes at Chaucer, *Troilus and Criseyde* 2. 81–108; the evocation of postprandial literary recitation at a great feast in *Wars of Alexander* 1–14.

11. The sewing before the fire involves Baxter and her associates in a trade gender-marked, perhaps even some let-out piecework associated with woolens.

12. This important category, the aural literate, is a discovery insisted upon by Susan Schibanoff; see her "Taking the Gold Out of Egypt: The Art of Reading as a Woman," in *Gender and Reading: Essays on Readers, Texts and Contexts*, ed. Elizabeth A. Flynn and Patrocinio P. Schweickart, (Baltimore: Johns Hopkins University Press, 1986), 83–106, esp. 87–90. See further M. Aston, "Lollardy and Literacy" and "Devotional Literacy," reprinted in *Lollards and Reformers*, 101–33. Avis Mone affixed her seal to the (unique among Norfolk defendants) English list of charges that she recanted (but she signed only with a cross): this would seem to indicate that she possessed at least "business reading literacy," the ability to ascertain the accuracy of contracts.

13. Cf. Chaucer's Wife of Bath's Prologue, where the Wife memorially recreates vast stretches of her husband's "Book of Wikked Wyves"—again a text she knows from domestic nighttime readings. Yet like the women I describe, she achieves a personalized manipulative use of the book—broadly, to embarrass her various male interlocutors.

14. Claire Cross, " 'Great Reasoners in Scripture': The Activities of Women Lollards, 1380–1530," *Studies in Church History*, subsidia 1 (1978): 359–80, cites several late examples of woman Bible memorizers (in these cases, probably as full substitutes for vellum volumes).

15. In contrast, Mone, widely implicated as a "wise woman," never requires narrative description in the register.

16. " 'Si vos affectatis videre veram crucem Christi ego volo monstrare eam tibi hic in domo tua propria.' Et ista iurata asseruit se libenter videre velle veram crucem Christi. Et prefata Margeria dixit, 'vide,' et tunc extendebat brachia sua in longum, dicens isti iurate, 'hec est vera crux Christi, et istam crucem tu debes et potes videre et adorare omni die hic in domo tua propria, et adeo tu in vanum laboras quando vadis ad

ecclesias ad adorandas sive orandas aliquas ymagines vel cruces mortuas' "; see Tanner, *Trials*, 44.

17. Other examples of such an embodied belief would include Baxter's contentions that baptism occurs in utero, that consent in mutual love (clearly nonverbal) constitutes matrimony, and that she possesses a "carta" of salvation in her womb (this last a topic now being investigated by Rita Copeland and Steven Justice).

18. For the phrases I cite, see Tanner, *Trials*, 45; and for the longer quotation, 49: "Omnis homo et omnis mulier qui sunt de opinione eiusdem Margerie sunt boni sacerdotes, et . . . sancta Ecclesia et tantum in locis habitacionum omnium existencium de secta sua." Other Norfolk defendants also attacked what they called "material churches," i.e., those representing idolatrous papal authority and not true divinity; see, e.g., 58, 61, 67, 73.

19. See Hanna, "Difficulty," 337–38 n. 31.

20. All my citations (hereafter cited by page and line numbers in the text) are from the standard editions: Julian of Norwich, *A Book of Showings to the Anchoress Julian of Norwich*, ed. Edmund Colledge and James Walsh (Toronto: Pontifical Institute, 1978); Margery Kempe, *The Book of Margery Kempe*, ed. Sanford Brown Meech and Hope Emily Allen, Early English Text Society, O.S., 212 (London: Oxford University Press, 1940).

21. At 142/14–21, Kempe finds sermons less fulfilling than these private consultations. Perhaps the most important of her teachers—others include a Dominican hermit of Lynn, Robert Spryngold (her confessor), and Richard of Caister (vicar of Saint Stephen's, Norwich)—is Alan of Lynn OCarm; for his first validation of Kempe's works, see 22/11–22. And he is apt to have introduced her to the spiritual library I discuss in the next paragraph but one; see Alfred B. Emden, *A Biographical Register of the University of Cambridge to 1500* (Cambridge: Cambridge University Press, 1963), 381–82, for his prodigious literary activity, most especially construction of contents tables and indices to several of Kempe's sources.

22. For a familiar explanation of this reference, see Chaucer, Second Nun's Tale, 523–46. On Julian's self-authorization, see Barry Windeatt's pioneering study, "Julian of Norwich and Her Audience," *Review of English Studies* 28 (1977): 1–17; and, most recently, Lynn Staley Johnson, "The Trope of the Scribe and the Question of Literary Authority in the Works of Julian of Norwich and Margery Kempe," *Speculum* 66 (1991): 820–38, esp. 830–33.

23. For extensive discussion see Karma Lochrie's fine study, *Margery Kempe and Translations of the Flesh* (Philadelphia: University of Pennsylvania Press, 1991), 114–20.

24. The most flagrant example of not understanding Latin occurs at 112/34–113/10. But Kempe's degree of literacy is probably minimalized in the text for purely strategic reasons, as indicating yet another form of God's special grace. Certainly, as an urban aristocratic businesswoman, one would expect her to have been able to read, at

the very least, contracts; and 218/7, noted by Lochrie, *Translations*, 126, suggests she can read. Whether she was also a writing literate, however, would have been another question altogether (see below, esp. n. 32). For my discussion of Julian in the next paragraph, see Colledge and Walsh, *Showings*, 41–47; my citation appears on 198.

25. Cf. her insistence upon her social status, the daughter of a man five times mayor of Lynn, at 9/20–25 and 111/25–32.

26. The second passage occurs during Kempe's stay in Rome, where she revises her relationship to other, more noxious predecessors; see Karma Lochrie, "The Book of Margery Kempe: The Marginal Woman's Search for Literary Authority," *Journal of Medieval and Renaissance Studies* 16 (1986): 33–55, esp. 51–52.

27. And as Julian apparently did as well—including counseling Kempe; see *Book* 42/7–43/20.

28. For other discussions, see Clarissa W. Atkinson, *Mystic and Pilgrim: The Book and World of Margery Kempe* (Ithaca, N.Y.: Cornell University Press, 1983); Gail McMurray Gibson, *The Theatre of Devotion: East Anglican Drama and Society in the Late Middle Ages* (Chicago: University of Chicago Press, 1989), 47–65; and David Aers, *Community, Gender, and Individual Identity: English Writing, 1360–1430* (London: Routledge, 1988), 103–4.

29. Cf. "Boneventur" (143/28) for the single possible reference (although even here perhaps a genitive modifying the following title). Nicholas Love's English translation could have been available to Kempe, although it is unlikely to have been so at the time of the main events described in bk. 1, ca. 1412–14.

30. The most pregnant example is Kempe's 1438 admission into the oligarchic guild that essentially governed Lynn, printed *Book*, 358–59. One might see the representation as in fact intertextually inspired, because as Wayne Shumaker pointed out long ago ("Alison in Wander-Land: A Study in Chaucer's Mind and Literary Method," *Journal of English Literary History* 18 [1951]: 86–87), the General Prologue portrait of the Wife of Bath would suggest that pilgrimage was the central feature of her life; but her Prologue emphasizes the misogyny inherent in everyday bourgeois existence.

31. Perhaps the clearest example in Kempe's *Book* occurs at 115/4–20, what sounds a very canned catechetical statement of eucharistic orthodoxy designed either to confute Lollards or to prevent her from being confused with a Lollard enthusiast like Baxter (see Tanner, *Trials*, 45, for Baxter's "panis materialis").

32. I think L. Johnson, "Scribe," 834, misreads the second of these sentences, where the second *hyr* means "her," i.e., Kempe's, the third *her* means "their." "Proferyd" must mean "offered," and presumably contrasts (as polite, rather than constraining) with the *bodyn* "commanded" of the preceding sentence. Cf. also 45/16–19, where Jesus assumes that Kempe will have a letter written for her, not do it herself (although this may simply reflect his class assumptions about patrician behavior).

33. Cf. Lochrie, "Marginal," 55, on Kempe's alienation from her own written record; and the similar view of the socially reabsorbed Kempe argued by Aers, *Community*, 108–16.

34. "Marginal," 36–37.

35. One might compare the apothegmatic presentation, the only form in which Kempe was available from the sixteenth century until the rediscovery of her book in 1934, in De Worde's and Pepwell's prints; see *Book*, 353–57, and Lochrie, *Translations*, 220–26.

36. See *Book*, xxxii–xlv. The scribal note at 38/4 and signs of textual disruption in the several subsequent chapters suggest that some leaves of the exemplar had become disordered. The disruptions here, conjoined with the detail at 5/30, are probably sufficient to allow reconstruction of the form of the original ms.

37. See Lochrie, *Translations*, 206–20, who uses this material to routinize Kempe's behavior, without altogether exploring the potential gender issues involved.

38. Cited in L. Johnson, "Scribe," 830, 832.

39. See Colledge and Walsh, *Showings*, 1–18.

40. M. Aston, "Lollardy and Literacy," 368–69.

41. I am grateful to Beth Robertson and Kandi K. Leonard for encouragement and a wealth of constructive suggestions about this paper.

The Patronage of Isabel of Portugal

✴ ✴ ✴ CHARITY CANNON WILLARD

The importance of the literary and artistic patronage of Philip the Good, duke of Burgundy, during the middle years of the fifteenth century is well known. At the same time, it should be recognized that this flowering of the arts could not have been achieved without the help of those surrounding him, although their collaboration is all too often overlooked. This is especially true of the remarkable woman who was his third duchess. Isabel of Portugal, whom he married in 1430, is all too frequently forgotten, although it was on the occasion of their marriage, celebrated in Bruges, that Philip created his Order of the Golden Fleece and adopted as his motto "Altre n'auray" [I Will Have No Other]. In the catalog of the exhibition organized in Bruges in 1962 to celebrate the order's long history, Isabel was merely mentioned in passing. It was only in 1991 that an exhibition at the Belgian Royal Library was devoted to her important contribution to her adopted country.[1]

It is undeniably true that for a number of years this duchess supported her husband's literacy and artistic, as well as his political, programs with intelligence and devotion. Among her accomplishments was bringing about the liberation of René d'Anjou, held captive in Dijon by Philip for some years after the Battle of Bugnéville, as well as negotiating freedom for Charles d'Orléans, the king of England's prisoner for twenty-five years after the French defeat at Agincourt.[2] A handsome copy of René d'Anjou's pious *Mortifiement de vaine plaisance* bearing Isabel's coat of arms and her motto "Tant que vivray" [As Long As I Live] (Brussels Royal Library MS 10308) recalls the first accomplishment, whereas the second is recorded in the Ballade 88 by Charles d'Orléans, where he says:

Et sans plus despendre langage
A cours mots, plaise vous penser
Que vous laisse mon coeur en gage
Pour tousjours, sans jamais faulser.
Si me vueillez recommander
A ma cousine; car croyés
Que en vous deux, tant que vivrés,
J'ai mise toute ma fiance;
Et vostre party loyaument
Tendray, sans faire changement,
De cueur, de corps et de puissance![3]

[And without wasting more language, in brief words, may it please you to think that I leave you my heart in forfeit, forever, without evasion ever. So please commend me to my cousin, for believe me that in you two, as long as you shall live, I have placed all my confidence. And your cause with loyalty I will support, without any change of heart, of body, or of strength.]

Further evidence of her involvement in literary concerns is to be found in a poem added to one manuscript of Martin LeFranc's *Champion des Dames* (Paris, Bibliothèque nationale, MS fr. 12476) bearing the curious title "Complainte du livre du Champion des Dames a Maistre Martin LeFranc son acteur."[4] This poem reveals that the author is disappointed that his longer poem has not been well received by the duke of Burgundy, to whom he had presented a copy. It is understandable that the duke might not, indeed, have been pleased, for instance, by the laudatory passage devoted to the feats of Joan of Arc, who had, after all, been captured by the Burgundians before being handed over to the English army. It would appear, however, that the poet had been led to believe that the situation might be remedied by the intercession of one of the Burgundian courtiers, Jean de Créquy, sometimes referred to as a "literary advisor" to the duke, and by the support of the Duchess Isabel, of whom he writes:

Mais toy, qui hautement te clames
Et partout te faiz appeller
Le loial *Champion des Dames,*
Comment oses tu reculer
Du palais ou l'on voit voler
Blancs atours comme clerz heaumes?

En plus seur lieu ne poez aler
Alasses ore en cent reaumes.

Mesmement ou est la duchesse
Du sang de Portugal semee,
De vertu et d'onneur princesse
En terre et en chiel amée,
Tu ne doibs craindre la honée
De ceulx qui de ton cas se galent,
Car elle veult que renommée
Soit donnée a ceulx qui le valent.

[But you, who loudly proclaim and have yourself called the loyal Champion of Ladies, how do you dare withdraw from the palace where one sees flying white headdresses like knightly helmets? You could not find a better spot if you were to go to a hundred realms.

Right there is the duchess born of Portuguese blood, princess of virtue and honor beloved on earth and in heaven. You should not fear the taunts of those who dishonor your cause, for she wishes for renown to be conferred on those who merit it.]

There is no doubt that Isabel was a cultivated princess. The daughter of Portugal's King João I, she was also the granddaughter of England's John of Gaunt through her mother, Philippa of Lancaster. Thus Henry V and his brothers were her cousins and the influential cardinal of Winchester, with whom she negotiated the release of Charles d'Orléans, her uncle. The children produced by the Portuguese-English marriage were called by the Portuguese poet, Luis Camões, the *ínclita geracão* [the illustrious generation]. The oldest son, Duarte, who followed his father as king of Portugal, collected an impressive library and was author of a moral work entitled *The Loyal Counsellor*. The second son, Pedro, who traveled across Europe, visiting Flanders in 1428, collaborated with his confessor in writing a *Book of Benefits,* based on Seneca but including quotations from numerous other classical authors.[5] Henry the Navigator is the best known of these brothers, but there were also João, the master of the Order of Santiago, whose granddaughter would be Queen Isabel of Spain, and Fernando, the Martyr of Fez, the inspiration for Calderón de la Barca's drama *The Perfect Prince.* It was an ambitious, talented, and energetic family, and Isabel was not unworthy of them.

Although Isabel never saw her native land after her marriage in northern Europe, she kept in constant touch with her family. Unfortunately, as time

passed her brothers were plagued with a variety of misfortunes. After the failure of a Portuguese effort to take possession of the Moroccan city of Tangiers,
led by Henry the Navigator in 1437, Fernando was given over as a hostage to
protect the retreat of the Portuguese army, although this was done with the
understanding that he could be ransomed by the return of Ceuta, captured
by the Portuguese in 1415. Unfortunately the country could not agree on the
course to follow. Money was offered for Fernando's release, but to no avail,
and there was considerable resistence to the idea of giving up Ceuta. Duarte,
by now king, was particularly upset by the dilemma, to the point where he
died in 1438, leaving behind a son too young to reign. Fernando was left to
die a martyr's death in a Moroccan prison in Fez in 1443.

The youth of Duarte's heir brought about a power struggle between his
widow and Pedro. Although the queen died in 1445, at about the time that
her son Afonso reached the age to rule and was married to Pedro's daughter,
Isabel, a new rift developed between uncle and nephew fomented by Pedro's
bastard brother, the count of Barcelos. This led to the outbreak of civil war,
resulting in Pedro's death in battle in 1449.

The duke and duchess of Burgundy immediately sent an ambassador to
Portugal to protest these events, rescuing three of Pedro's children who were
endangered by his enemies and offering a safe haven to some of his followers.

It has been suggested[6] that likenesses of Philip and Isabel can be identified among the mourners of a celebrated tapestry representing the Justice
of Trajan and Herkenbald woven at about this time and now in the Historical Museum of Berne in Switzerland. This tapestry is known to have been
inspired by the scenes of Justice painted by Rogier Van der Weyden in the
Town Hall of Brussels but destroyed in the bombardment of the city in 1695.
They were, however, described and admired by visiting painters and chroniclers from about 1441 onward. It is not certain that the figures in question
were present in the original paintings, but the tapestry could well have been
woven during the years when the Portuguese were divided over the fate of
Dom Fernando, the idea represented by the Justice of Trajan being that justice
must supersede family bonds. Pedro, in his book *The Virtuous Benefactor*, had
insisted that one's country should come before family ties.[7]

Further creditability is given to this identification by the representation
of the duke and duchess, along with other members of their entourage, in a
painting representing the Marriage at Cana, the central panel of a tryptich
showing the Miracles of Christ, attributed to the Master of the Legend of
Saint Catherine, now in Melbourne, Australia.[8]

There is little evidence that Isabel arrived at the Burgundian court with an extensive library of her own. Later inventories refer to two books of hours, one in Portuguese and the other in Latin and Portuguese. More notable is a reference to the "Livre de Duarte," suggesting that Isabel was interested in disseminating her brother's ideas beyond the borders of Portugal. Likewise significant is an entry in the official household accounts a short time after her arrival for the rebinding and regilding of the pages of eight volumes in the ducal library.[9] There is also an interesting reference to four volumes bearing the notation "acheté du gouverneur de Lille." Between 1435 and 1459 the governor of Lille was Baudoin d'Oignies, who was also Isabel's maître d'hôtel.[10] These volumes included Raoul de Presles's translation of Saint Augustine's *City of God*, which takes on a special interest in view of the fact that Isabel's father had a special admiration for Saint Augustine's writings, and both Duarte and Pedro owned and read them.[11]

Another book from this group is even more significant. This was Christine de Pizan's *Livre des Trois Vertus*, a copy of which the duchess sent to her niece Isabel, queen of Portugal. The first half of the book is devoted to the duties of a successful queen, and Isabel may well have felt that her niece had need of guidance. In any case, the young queen had the book translated into Portuguese. It was among the first books published in Portugal, in 1518, under the patronage of Queen Leonor, widow of Isabel's son, João II.[12]

Isabel of Portugal's influence is sometimes difficult to trace, because it was carried on quietly, or even anonymously, but it seems probable that a manuscript now in the library of Evora, the city where she was born and which was long a favorite residence of the royal court, came from her. This is a volume of religious poems, some of them attributable to Jean Miélot, a translator and editor from Lille, who produced a number of manuscripts for the duke and duchess.[13]

A more significant instance of Isabel's contribution to the transmission of a spiritual text to Portugal, however, is her role in the first Portuguese translation of the *Imitation de Jésus-Christ* by Thomas à Kempis. Wishing to establish a memorial to her brother Fernando in Lisbon, she invited to Bruges Brother João Alvaro, the chaplain who had remained with Fernando during his years of imprisonment in Morocco and after his death had managed to smuggle the prince's entrails back to Portugal for interment in the royal chapel at Batalha. He was later the spiritual director of all the monasteries in the bishopric of Porto, where he became interested in monastic reform. It was in 1468 that he sent to Portugal his translation of the first book of the *Imitation*. Soon afterward, he left Bruges for Rome, where, with Isabel's help, he was able to obtain papal authorization for the reforms he wanted to initiate as well as to found a memorial chapel for Fernando in the Church of Saint Anthony of Padua in Lisbon.

As it turned out, the most significant aspect of this mission was the introduction of Thomas à Kempis to the Iberian Penisula, where it had a significant influence on the spirituality of Saint Theresa of Avila, among others.[14]

Isabel's influence on translation, however, was not limited to French into Portuguese, for she was also involved in the French translation of the *Triunfo de las doñas*, written by the Galician Juan Rodriguez de la Cámera. This translation was made at the request of Vasco Quemada de Villalobos, one of Duarte's companions who had found refuge at the Burgundian court. The translator was Fernando de Lucena, another Portuguese refugee, who served Isabel as one of her secretaries.[15] Rodriguez de la Cámera's book had been written as a reply to Boccaccio's slander of women in *Il Corbaccio*. A letter appended to one manuscript of the translation (Brussels, Bibliothèque Royale, MS 2027) makes it clear that the translation was intended to counteract the influence exercised at court by certain courtiers, "compaignons de cabaret," whose comments about women offended the sober Portuguese exile. This complaint takes on special interest when considered in the light of the tales attributed to Burgundian noblemen in the *Cent nouvelles nouvelles* inspired in large measure by Boccaccio's *Decameron*. A copy of Fernando de Lucena's translation was presented to Duke Philip in a manuscript dated 1460.[16]

Fernando de Lucena has sometimes been confused with Vasco de Lucena, another Portuguese exile at the Burgundian court, who is remembered for his French translation of the *Histoire d'Alexandre* by Quintus Curtius and also Xenephon's *Traité des faiz et hautes promesses de Cyrus*.[17]

Isabel's personal taste in books, however, seems to have centered on spiritual texts. This is evident, for instance, from two manuscripts copied for her by another secretary, Jacotín de Ramecourt (now Lille, Bibliothèque municipale, MS 124; and Paris, Bibliothèque nationale, MS fr. 917). These manuscripts are similar in appearance, both resembling the books copied in Lille during the middle years of the fifteenth century. The Paris manuscript has one illustration, a watercolor of modest quality recalling the illustration in a copy of Heinrich Suso's *Horloge de Sapience* (Brussels, Bibliothèque Royale, MS 10981), also written on paper and produced in Jean Miélot's workshop in 1448.

The Lille manuscript copied by Jacotín de Ramecourt includes three texts. The first, incorrectly catalogued as a translation of Pope Innocent III's *De miseria conditionis humanae*, is in fact Jean Miélot's translation of a treatise known as *Le miroir de l'âme pecheresse*, sometimes attributed to Denis the Carthusian but probably the work of his contemporary Jacques de Gruytrobe, who was undoubtedly influenced by Innocent III. The second text is made up of extracts from Jean Gerson's *Mendacité spirituelle*, a dialogue between man and his soul, and the third is the *Dialogus* of Saint Bonaventure, also known as the *Soliloquium*, or *Imago mundi*. It is introduced with the title: "Comment on doit querir humilité."

As for the *Vie de Saint Bernard*, Isabel undoubtedly became acquainted with the saint's birthplace, the Château de Fontaine, during periods she spent in Dijon, especially in 1433–34, but the relationship between Saint Bernard's monastery of Clairvaux and Portugal was long-standing. The important Portuguese monastery of Alcobaça was established by monks from Clairvaux in 1152.[18]

An examination of additions to the ducal library suggests that Isabel might have had something to do with a group of manuscripts acquired around 1456. These are simple in style and with a minimum of ornamentation, similar to the manuscripts from Lille. They scarcely seem to represent the duke's usual taste, nor indeed his interests at the time. These manuscripts include Miélot's translation of Denis de Ryckel's *Quatre dernières choses* (Brussels, Bibliothèque Royale, Ms. 11, 129) and Miélot's *Moralités et traités de la science de bien mourir* (Paris, Bibliothèque nationale, Ms. fr. 124410). There were also new copies of the *Miroir de la salvation humaine* by Vincent de Beauvais (now Glasgow University Library Ms. T.2.18) and the Pseudo-Bonaventure's *Aquillon de l'amour divin*, translated by the Franciscan Jean de Brixay. This last is of particular interest, as a miniature shows the volume being presented to a lady in the court dress of that period.[19]

On the other hand, there was a new wave of spiritual texts in the 1460s, corresponding to the period when the duke's health had failed. These are all handsome manuscripts, copied by David Aubert and illustrated by Loyset Liédet in Bruges, where the duke was living at the time of his illness. The contrast between the two groups would seem to be significant.[20]

Spiritual concerns, along with devotion to her family, appear to have dictated Isabel's artistic patronage both in Portugal and in Northern Europe.

Her father, João I, had founded the royal chapel in Batalha Monastery, north of Lisbon, to commemorate his victory, with English help, over the Spanish at Aljubarrota in 1387. All the family, with the exception of Isabel, would be buried there, but her interest in her father's foundation would continue after her departure from Portugal, as the record of gifts she sent to it makes evident. She was granted special permission by succeeding kings to send works of art from Flanders for the decoration of the chapel where her brothers are memorialized by life-sized effigies surrounding the parents in the center.[21]

In view of these effigies, it is not surprising to find Isabel representing the duke in commissioning a magnificent tomb for his ancestor, Louis de Mâle, count of Flanders, in the Church of Saint Pierre in Lille. As this prince, who had died in 1384, had passed on his heritage to the Valois dukes of Burgundy, he was an important ancestor. Family tombs for the first two dukes were already in progress at the Chartreuse de Champmol, on the outskirts of Dijon, and in 1453 it was decided to provide a suitable tomb for Louis de Mâle, along with his wife and his daughter, Margaret of Flanders, Philip's grandmother, who had preferred to be buried in her own territories rather than with her husband, Philip the Bold, in Champmol. In order to carry out this project, Isabel negotiated with the Brussels coppersmith Jacques de Gerynes to provide the three figures on the stone base, which was ordered from the nearby quarries of Antoing. Around this foundation there was to be an inscription in brass letters; beneath this was to be fashioned of brass an arcade where in twenty-four niches were to be placed small statues of the duke's descendants. It is evident that the intention was not only to honor the ancestors but to call attention to the importance of the family as a whole.

The resulting tomb was so impressive that it was imitated for Philip's great-aunt, the duchess Jeanne of Brabant, through whom the province of Brabant had been added to the Burgundian realms. This was carried out by Jacques de Gerynes in the Church of the Carmes in Brussels. The model also served for the tomb of Isabel's daughter-in-law, Isabel of Bourbon, in the Cathedral of Antwerp, although this was not completed until 1476, when neither Philip nor Isabel, nor indeed Jacques de Gerynes, was among the living. Today it is not possible to decide from which of these tombs come ten statuettes of family members still preserved in Amsterdam's Rijksmuseum, but they give some idea of the charm of all three.[22]

Considerably less well known is the small copper effigy of a Portuguese prince in a chapel of the Cathedral of Braga. This was also commissioned by Isabel, presumably at the workshop of Jacques de Gerynes, and sent to Portugal as a memorial to her brother Afonso, who had died in Braga in 1400 at the age of ten.[23]

A better-known example of Isabel's patronage is her contribution to the magnificent tomb of her nephew Jaime, cardinal of Portugal, in the Basilica of San Miniato al Monte, near Florence. Jaime was one of the sons of her favorite brother, Pedro, one of the nephews sheltered at the Burgundian court after Pedro's death. In view of Jaime's inclination to a religious life, Isabel arranged to have him named to some benefices in Flanders and later sent to Rome, where, at the age of twenty, he was named archbishop of Lisbon, triumphing over one of his father's political enemies. In spite of his youth he played a part in one important international affair. In 1455 he was named by Pope Nicholas V as an executor of the bull intended to determine for Spain and Portugal rights of conquest in lands that were already being discovered beyond the European continent. Unfortunately he died three years later while on a mission to Florence, and there he was buried on land the Portuguese royal family had already acquired from Florentine merchants. The tomb, a masterpiece of Renaissance art, was the work of a talented group of Florentine artists. Although Isabel was not involved in the design of the tomb, her interest and her financial support made her one of its principal patrons.[24]

Along with preserving the memory of her family, Isabel showed a comparable concern for the spiritual welfare of the living. Even before leaving Portugal she had been a patron of the Convent of Penha Longa, near the royal palace of Cintra.[25] One of her first philanthropies after her marriage involved the Saint Jacques Hospital in Lille. In an agreement with the city, she took charge of the reconstruction of a building which had long been used to lodge pilgrims on their way to Santiago de Compostela. Isabel added to the structure a maternity hospital for poor women. In 1437 she ordered a window for it where she was to be shown kneeling before the hospital's patron saint in the company of the duke and their four-year-old son, Charles.[26]

In 1451 she acquired further land in Lille, some of which had earned a bad reputation because of some public baths. She founded in their place a convent of Gray Sisters. Two years later she helped this community adopt the rule of the Poor Clares. It should be noted that since the days of Queen Isabel of Aragon in the early fourteenth century, there had been a special relationship between these Franciscans and the Portuguese royal family. The Duchess Isabel's interest and patronage must surely have contributed to the growth of this order in northern France and the Netherlands during the fifteenth century.[27]

Her interest in the reforms of Saint Clare is likewise recorded in 1445, when an effort was being made to found a Clarist convent in the saint's native town of Corbie. Although the monks of the ancient abbey in the town opposed this, Isabel was able to obtain a special papal bull and she even asked the future Louis XI to try to soften the monks' opposition. In spite of the dauphin's evident lack of interest, the new convent was founded in time for the saint to be buried there in 1447.[28]

Isabel should also be remembered for her role in the foundation of a community of Brigittine nuns in Termonde. She had given evidence of her interest in the Swedish Saint Birgitta in 1438, when the ducal accounts record her payment for translation of the saint's *Revelations* and her *Rule*.[29]

The Carthusians, especially favored by the duke's family, also attracted her interest. Shortly after the birth of her son, Charles, in Dijon on 11 November 1433, she made a donation to the Chartreuse of Champmol. This gift was commemorated by a copper plaque that, although destroyed in 1792, can be reconstructed from records preserved in Dijon's Archives de la Côte d'Or.[30]

In 1438 Isabel established a foundation at the Chartreuse du Val-Sainte-Marguerite in Basel, at the time when an important ecclesiastical council was taking place there, in which Burgundy was playing an important role. The copper plaque commemorating this donation is still preserved in the Historical Museum of Basel, showing the ducal family attended by their patron saints, kneeling in prayer. The accompanying Latin inscription records Isabel's endowment of two anniversary masses and of two monks to celebrate daily masses for the salvation of Philip and Charles as well as for her own. Prayers were also to be offered for her parents, the king and queen of Portugal.[31]

There were still other foundations: one at the Chartreuse du Val Saint-Esprit at Gosny, near Bethune in Picardy, where she was to be temporarily buried after her death until her remains could be transported, with those of the duke, to the Chartreuse of Champmol. A similar foundation, also with a plaque, was made for the Chartreuse de Mont-Renaud, near Noyon.[32] These plaques were the sort of metalwork done in Tournai, Ghent, and Bruges, all noted for this craft during the Middle Ages. It seems probable that the furnishings for the chapels mentioned in connection with these donations were also of metal made by the duchy's craftsmen.[33]

Donor's portraits in a different medium generally resembled those on the plaques. These offer the best available likenesses of Isabel in view of the loss of Jan Van Eyck's two official portraits painted during the marriage negotiations in Portugal.[34] The most interesting of these portraits was the one formerly to be found in the small church near the former Chartreuse de Gosnay, with which Isabel had extensive relations over a considerable period of time. This portrait is now preserved in the Museum of Arras. There Isabel is to be seen accompanied by her patron saint, Elizabeth of Hungary. As is the case elsewhere, her coat of arms is shown encircled and accompanied by her motto "Tant que vivray."[35]

A nineteenth-century sketch in Lisbon's Museum of Ancient Art preserves the record of another lost painting, this one attributed to Rogier Van der

Weyden, originally sent by Isabel to Batalha Abbey. The copy was made by Domingos Antonio de Sequeira, during a visit to the abbey in the early years of the nineteenth century.[36]

Even in view of this extensive activity as patron throughout much of her life as duchess of Burgundy, probably the most interesting period of her life comprised the final years when she retired from court life to devote herself to meditation and charitable works at her Château de la Motte-aux-Bois in the Forest of Nieppe, not far from Lille. It was there, in fact, that she sponsored the translations already mentioned and also the manuscript of the *Life of Saint Bernard*.

Various explanations have been proposed by northern historians for this retreat: disapproval of Philip's well-known philandering, a quarrel between Philip and their son Charles; but the most significant possibility is that this sort of withdrawal was not uncommon in the Portuguese royal family—from Isabel's ancestor Queen Isabel of Aragon, an unofficial saint, to her descendant the Emperor Charles V of the Holy Roman Empire, who was also king of Spain. Whatever the reason, she chose to lead a life of piety, although she did not fail to appear at court again on such occasions as the christening of her granddaughter, Mary, in 1457, or to look after her husband during his final illness in 1467, or to receive Margaret of York when she arrived for her marriage to Charles in 1468.

Already in 1454 she had founded a community of Gray Sisters near the château. In addition to the hospital for old women already established in the château, she added a hospital nearby, where she herself helped to care for the ill.[37] In the course of her contacts with the Chartreuse of Gosnay she embroidered with her own hands a chasuble for their chapel. What is particularly important, however, is that all this was combined with her patronage of writers.

With regard to Vasco de Lucena's translation, the *Faictz et gestes d'Alexandre le Grand*, it should be noted that, although Alexander the Great had long been considered a hero at the Burgundian court, Vasco de Lucena's version, based on the Latin biography written by Quintus Curtius, arrived by way of Italy through the Italian translation made in 1438 by Pier Candido Decembri. In the prologue to his French translation, Vasco de Lucena points out, in dedicating the work to Charles the Bold, that he considered the historical Alexander preferable to the legendary one as an example of virtue for the young duke. Having a great concern for the authenticity of his sources, he made use of Plutarch's life of Alexander to reconstruct chapters missing from his principal source. He probably knew Plutarch through the Latin translation made by Guarino da Verona. For the *Cyropedia* he used Poggio's Latin translation, undertaken at the suggestion of Pope Nicholas V. Thus he was among the first intellectuals in northern Europe to profit from Italian humanistic efforts to make Greek literature better known.[38]

Similar humanistic interests in the group assembled by Isabel at La Motte-aux-Bois are to be noted in a manuscript preserved in the Municipal Library of Arras, a copy of Petrarch's *De remediis*, *De otio*, and *De vita solitaria* in the original Latin bearing the mention that it was copied at the Château de Nieppe in 1469.[39]

A final example of her contribution to the cause of humanism is to be seen by the fact that it was Isabel who paid for Robert Gaguin's first studies in Paris. The son of a poor family in the region, Gaguin may have attracted Isabel's particular attention because he was born the same year as her son Charles. She probably knew him first as a student in the Préavin monastery near her château where Trinitarian brothers devoted themselves to the education of poor children. In 1457, however, he was able to go to the University of Paris, where he remained to play a significant role in humanistic circles. Associated with the early printing ventures of Guillaume Fichet, his own literary productions included a new translation of Caesar's *Commentaries* and of Livy's *Third Decade*. His *Compendium de origine et gestis francorum* (1495) represents one of the first attempts in France to make use of methods derived from the great historians of antiquity. He also distinguished himself in the church and in diplomacy as well as in literature. As general of the Trinitarian order he went to the Iberian Peninsula to assist in the recovery of Christian captives from infidel hands.

In 1467 he returned to La Motte-aux-Bois, at Isabel's request, to translate into Latin the epitaph prepared for Duke Philip's tomb. Unfortunately the text of the Latin life he wrote of the duchess after her death has disappeared. The *Vitae Elizabeth, comitissae Flandriae, filiae Joannis nominis premi Lusitaniae regis* existed as late as the seventeenth century at the Préavin Trinitarian monastery near La Motte-aux-Bois, although a document from there may preserve a partial translation. The text of the Latin epitaph for her tomb composed by Vasco de Lucena has been preserved, but the tomb in the Chartreuse de Champmol, like the Latin biography, disappeared during the French Revolution.[40]

Nevertheless, Isabel's example as noblewoman and patron was not lost. Her daughter-in-law, Margaret of York was a worthy successor, remembered especially for her patronage of William Caxton's early printing ventures. Equally important both as political figure and patron was her great-granddaughter,

Margaret of Austria, followed in the next generation by Marie of Hungary, both of whom governed the Netherlands for their nephew and brother, Emperor Charles V. In writing the history of women, the contributions of such as these should not be forgotten.

NOTES

1. *La Toison d'Or: Cinq siècles d'art et d'histoire.* Catalog of an exhibition organized by the Ministère de l'education nationale and the City of Bruges, Musée Communal des Beaux Arts, 14 July–30 September 1962 (Tielt, Belgium: Lannoo, 1962); *Isabelle de Portugal, Duchesse de Bourgogne,* exposition Bibliothèque Royale Albert Ier, 5 octobre–23 novembre 1991 (Brussels: Bibliothèque Royale, 1991).

2. Pierre Champion, *Vie de Charles d'Orléans* (Paris: Champion, 1910), 272–311.

3. Charles d'Orléans, *Poésies,* ed. Pierre Champion (Paris: Champion, 1966), 1:141.

4. Paris, Bibliothèque Nationale Ms. fr. 12470, fol. 150; Gaston Paris, "Un poème inédit de Martin LeFranc," *Romania* 16 (1887): 436–37.

5. Alvaro J. da Costa Pimpão, *Historia da literatura Portuguesa: Idade Media* (Lisbon: Atlântida, 1959), 191–217.

6. André de Mandach, "A la découverte du code secret d'une tapisserie du XVe siècle: La justice de Trajan et d'Archambault de Bourbon," *Trésors du Musée d'histoire de Berne* (Annecy, 1976).

7. See Rodriguez Lapa, *Dom Duarte e os Prosadored da Casa de Aviz* (Lisbon: Gráfica Lisbonenses, 1940), 56.

8. M. Conway and Semour de Ricci, "A Flemish Triptych for Melbourne," *Burlington Magazine* 40 (1922): 163–71; *Isabelle de Portugal, Duchesse de Bourgogne,* 149–51.

9. Georges Doutrepont, *La littérature française à la cour des ducs de Bourgogne* (Paris: Champion, 1909), 127–28.

10. Ibid., 136, 208–9, 293. For Baudoin d'Oignies as Isabel of Portugal's maître d'hôtel: Lille, Archives du Nord, B 3373, nos. 115, 154. Hereafter referred to as ADN.

11. Mario Martins, *Estudos da literatura medieval* (1956; reprint, Lisbon: Verbo, 1969), 465–66.

12. Charity Cannon Willard, "A Portuguese Translation of Christine de Pisan's *Livre des Trois Vertus,*" *PMLA* 78 (1963): 459–64.

13. Evora, Biblioteca Pública Ms. CXXIV/ 2–9. Louis Mourin, "Poésies religieuses françaises inconnues dans des manuscrits de Bruxelles et d'Evora," *Scriptorium* 3 (1949): 218–29; Paul Perdizet, "Jean Miélot, l'un des traducteurs de Philippe le Bon," *Revue de l'histoire littéraire de la France* 14 (1907): 472–82.

14. Costa Pimpão, *Historia da literatura Portuguesa*, 291–94; Martins, *Estudos da literatura medieval*, chap. 8, "A versão portuguesa da 'Vita Christi' e seus problemas."

15. Charity Cannon Willard, "Isabel of Portugal and the French Translation of the 'Triunfo de las Doñas,'" *Revue belge de philologie et d'histoire* 43 (1965): 961–69.

16. Brussels, Royal Library Ms. 10778.

17. Danielle Gallet-Guerne, *Vasque de Lucène et la Cyropédie à la cour de Bourgogne (1470)* (Geneva: Droz, 1974), 3–21.

18. G. Ferreira Borges, "Saint Bernard et le Portugal: L'histoire et la légende," in *Mélanges Saint Bernard*, XXIVᵉ Congrès de l'Association bourguignonne des sociétés savantes (Dijon: Marilier, 1953), 134–50.

19. Doutrepont, *Littérature française à la cour des ducs de Bourgogne*, 213–19.

20. *La miniature flamande: Le mécénat de Philippe le Bon*, exposition organisée à l'occasion du 400ᵉ anniversaire de la fondation de la Bibliothèque Royale de Philippe II le 12 avril 1559 (Brussels: Bibliothèque Royale, 1959), 99–165.

21. Francisco de Sousa Viterbo, "D. Isabel de Portugal, duquesa de Borgonha," *Archivo histórico portuguéz* 3 (1905): 88.

22. Richard Vaughan, *Philip the Good* (London: Longmans, Green, 1970), 153–54; ADN B 3375/113512; *Flanders in the Fifteenth Century*, catalogue of the exposition "Masterpieces of Flemish Art: Van Eyck to Bosch," October–December 1960, organized by the Detroit Institute of Arts and the City of Bruges (Detroit and Brussels: Institute of Arts and Centre National de Recherches Primitifs Flamands, 1960), 264–67.

23. *Les guides bleues: Portugal, Madère-Açores*, ed. Magdelaine Traisot (Paris: Hachette, 1957), 242.

24. Frederick Hartt, Gino Corti, and Clarence Kennedy, *The Chapel of the Cardinal of Portugal (1434–1459) at San Miniato in Florence* (Philadelphia: University of Pennsylvania Press, 1964).

25. Francisco de Sousa Viterbo, *D. Isabel de Portugal, duquesa da Borgonha: Notas documentães para a sua biographia et para a historia das relações entre Portugal et a corte de Borgonha* (Lisbon: Off. Typ., 1905), 29.

26. ADN B 1962; Louis Trenard, ed., *Histoire de Lille*, Publications de la Faculté des lettres et sciences humaines de Lille (Lille: Giard, 1970), 1:283.

27. Louis Dancoisne, *Histoire du couvent des Pauvres Clares de Lille* (Lille: Danel, 1868), 15.

28. E. Sainte-Marie Perrin, *La belle vie de Sainte Colette de Corbie, 1381–1447* (Paris: Plon-Nourrit 1921); Pierre André Pidoux de Maduère, *Sainte Colette* (Paris: Gabalda, 1924).

29. ADN 163, fol. 234v.

30. Pierre Quarré, *Plaques de fondation d'Isabelle de Portugal, duchesse de Bourgogne, aux Chartreuse de Bâle et de Champmol-les-Dijon* (Basel: Historisches Museum, 1960), 30.

31. Ibid., 29.

32. Ibid., 32, 34–36.

33. Jean Squilbecke, "Le travail de métal à Bruxelles," in *Bruxelles au XVe siècle* (Brussels: Editions de la Librairie encyclodédique, 1953), 262–71.

34. Solomon Reinach, "Un portrait d'Isabelle de Portugal, 1429," *Revue archéologique* 5 (1922): 174.

35. Auguste Charles Menche de Loisne, "Les tableaux de l'église d'Hesdigneul-les-Béthune," *Bulletin archéologigue du Comité des travaux historiques* (1901): 48–57.

36. José de Figueiredo, "Un panneau inconnu de Rogier van der Weyden," *Boletím de arte e arqueologia* 1 (1921): 91–94.

37. The inventory of this hospital, made shortly after her death, has been published by Amaury de la Grange from ADN B 3515, no. 123.955, in the *Annales du Comité Flamand de France* 58 (1935): 419–29.

38. Robert Bossuat, "Les sources du Quinte-Curse de Vasque de Lucène," *Mélanges dédiés à la mémoire de Félix Grat*, ed. Emile A. van Moé, Jeanne Vieillard, and Pierre Marot (Paris: Pecqueur-Grat, 1946–49), 1:347–52; Gallet-Guerne, *Vasque de Lucène*, 57–67.

39. Elizabeth Pellegrin, *Manuscrits de Pétrarque dans les bibliothèques de France*, Censimento dei Codici Petrarcheschi (Padua: Antenore, 1966), 2:97–98.

40. Robert Bossuat, "Traductions françaises des 'Commentaires de César' à la fin du XVe siècle," *Bibliothèque d'humanisme et renaissance* 4 (1944): 346–54; Robert Gaguin, *Roberti Gaguini epistole et oratione*, ed. Louis Thuasne, Bibliothèque littéraire de la renaissance, vols. 2–3 (Paris: Bouillon, 1903–1904), 1:7n; Charity Cannon Willard, "Isabel of Portugal, Patroness of Humanism?" in *Miscellanea di studi e ricerche sul Quattrocentro francese*, ed. Franco Simone (Turin: Giappichelli, 1967), 519–44.

The catalog of the Brussels exposition attributes the biography to Vasco de Lucena. A passage from the translation is preserved in ADN, Fonds Godefroy, B 16,600, but there is no record of his having written such a life, whereas Gaguin's authorship is documented. The epitaph is to be found in Malines, Groot Seminarie Ms. 17, fol. 526v.

Bibliography

ABBREVIATIONS FREQUENTLY CITED

EETS   Early English Text Society
     O.S.   Original Series
     E.S.   Extra Series

MGH   *Monumenta Germaniae Historica*
     AA   *Auctores antiquissimi*
     SRM   *Scriptores rerum Merovingicarum*
     SS   *Scriptores*

PL   *Patrologiae cursus completus, series Latina,* ed. J. P. Migne. Paris: Migne, 1844–64.

RS   Rolls Series (Rerum Britannicarum medii aevi scriptores)

Abelard, Peter. *Petri Abaelardi opera.* Edited by Victor Cousin. Paris: Imprimerie Royale, 1849.

Adam de Perseigne. *Lettres.* Edited by Jean Bouvet. Paris: Cerf, 1960.

Adams, Monni. *Designs for Living: Symbolic Communication in African Art.* Cambridge: Carpenter Center for the Visual Arts in cooperation with the Peabody Museum of Archeology and Ethnology, Harvard University, 1982.

Adelard of Bath. "Des Adelard von Bath Traktat *De eodem et diversa* zum ersten Male hersausgegeben und historisch-kritisch untersucht." Edited by Hans Wilner. *Beiträge zur Geschichte der Philosophie des Mittelalters* 4 (1903): 1–112.

Aers, David. *Community, Gender, and Individual Identity: English Writing, 1360–1430.* London: Routledge, 1988.

Affeldt, Werner, et al., eds. *Frauen im Frühmittelalter: Eine ausgewählte kommentierte Bibliographie.* Frankfurt am Main: Lang, 1990.

Aitken, Marion Y. H., ed. *Etude sur "Le miroir ou les évangiles des domnées" de Robert de Gretham.* Paris: Champion, 1922.

Alexander, J. J. G. "Painting and Manuscript Illumination for Royal Patrons in the Later Middle Ages." In *English Court Culture in the Later Middle Ages,* edited by V. J. Scattergood and J. W. Sherborne. New York: St. Martin's, 1983.

Alexander, J. J. G., and P. Binski, eds. *Age of Chivalry: Art in Plantagenet England, 1200–1400.* London: Royal Academy of Arts in association with Weidenfeld and Nicolson, 1987.

Alfonso X. *Primera crónica general de España.* Edited by Ramón Menéndez-Pidal. Madrid: Gredos, 1955.

Alford, John A., ed. *A Companion to Piers Plowman.* Berkeley and Los Angeles: University of California Press, 1988.

Allard, G.-H., ed. *Aspects de la marginalité au Moyen Age.* Montreal: L'Aurore, 1975.

Allen, Prudence. *The Concept of Woman: The Aristotelian Revolution, 750 BC–AD 1250.* Montreal: Eden, 1985.

Althoff, Gerard. *Adels- und Königs-familien im Spiegel ihrer Memorialüberlieferung: Studien zum Totengedenken der Billunger und Ottonen.* Munich: Fink, 1964.

Altschul, Michael. *A Baronial Family in Medieval England: The Clares, 1217–1314.* Baltimore: Johns Hopkins University Press, 1965.

Alvarez Palenzuela, Vincente Angel. *Monasterios cistercienses en Castilla, siglos XII–XIII.* Valladolid: Universidad de Valladolid, 1975.

Ambrose. *De obitu Theodosii.* Edited by Otto Faller. In *Corpus scriptorum ecclesiasticorum Latinorum,* vol. 73. Vienna: Hoelder-Pichler-Tempsky, 1955.

Analecta Franciscana. Vol. 3. Edited by Bernardo A. Bessa. Florence: Collegio St. Bonaventura, 1897.

Anderson, Bonnie S., and Judith P. Zinsser. *A History of Their Own.* New York: Harper and Row, 1988.

Anderson, Marjorie. "Blanche Duchess of Lancaster." *Modern Philology* 45 (1947): 152–59.

Andreas Capellanus. *The Art of Courtly Love.* Edited and translated by John J. Parry. New York: Columbia University Press, 1941.

Andreescu-Treadgold, Irina, and Warren Treadgold. "Dates and Identities in the Imperial Panels in San Vitale." *Byzantine Studies Conference Abstract of Papers* 16 (1990): 52–54.

The Anglo-Saxon Chronicle. Translated and edited by G. N. Garmonsway. London: Dent, 1954.

Annales ecclesiastici. Edited by Augustino Theiner. Vatican City, 1870.

Anselm of Canterbury. *S. Anselmi Cantuariensis archiepiscopi opera omnia.* Edited by Francis S. Schmitt. 1946–61. Reprint, Stuttgart: Fromann, 1968.

Antón y Casaseca, Francisco. *Monasterios medievales de la provincia de Valladolid.* Valladolid: Librería Santarén, 1942.

Appel, Carl, ed. *Bernard von Ventadour: Seine Lieder.* Halle: Niemeyer, 1915.

Arbois de Jubainville, Henri de. *Histoire des ducs et des comtes de Champagne*. Paris: Durand, 1859–67.

Archer, Rowena E. " 'How ladies . . . who live on their manors ought to manage their households and estates': Women as Landholders and Administrators in the Later Middle Ages." In *Woman Is a Worthy Wight: Women in English Society, c. 1200–1500*, edited by P. J. P. Goldberg. Gloucester, Eng., and Wolfeboro Falls, N.H.: Sutton, 1992.

Armstrong, C. A. J. "The Piety of Cicely, Duchess of York: A Study in Late Medieval Culture." In *For Hillaire Belloc: Essays in Honor of His 71st Birthday*, edited by Douglas Woodruff. New York: Sheed and Ward, 1942.

Armstrong, Regis J., and Ignatius C. Brady, trans. *Francis and Clare: The Complete Works*. New York: Paulist, 1982.

Arnold, Thomas, ed. *Memorials of St Edmund's Abbey*. RS 96. London, 1890–96.

Arnould, Emile J. *Le manuel des Péchés: Etude religieuse anglo-normande (XIIIe siècle)*. Paris: Droz, 1940.

——— , ed. *Le livre de seyntz medicines: The Unpublished Devotional Treatise of Henry of Lancaster*. Anglo-Norman Text Society. Oxford: Blackwell, 1940.

Arts Council of Great Britain. *English Romanesque Art, 1066–1200*. Exhibition Catalog, Hayward Gallery. London: Weidenfeld and Nicolson, 1984.

Ashley, Kathleen, and Pamela Sheingorn. *Interpreting Cultural Symbols: Saint Anne in Late Medieval Society*. Athens: University of Georgia Press, 1990.

Aston, Margaret. "Lollardy and Literacy." *History* 62 (1977): 347–71. Reprinted in *Lollards and Reformers: Images and Literacy in Late Medieval Religion*. London: Hambledon, 1984.

——— . "William White's Lollard Followers." In her *Lollards and Reformers: Images and Literacy in Late Medieval Religion*. London: Hambledon, 1984.

Aston, T. H., and Rosamond Faith. "The Endowments of the University and Colleges to circa 1348." In *The History of the University of Oxford, The Early Oxford Schools*, edited by J. I. Catto. Vol. 1. Oxford: Clarendon, 1984.

Atkinson, Clarissa W. *Mystic and Pilgrim: The Book and World of Margery Kempe*. Ithaca, N.Y.: Cornell University Press, 1983.

Aubert, Marcel, Louis Grodecki, Jean Lafond, and Jean Verrier. *Les vitraux de Notre-Dame et de la Sainte-Chapelle de Paris (Corpus vitrearum Medii Aevi, France I)*. Paris: Nouvelles editions latines, 1959.

Auerbach, Erich. *Literary Language and Its Public in Late Latin Antiquity in the Middle Ages*. Translated by Ralph Manheim. New York: Pantheon, 1965.

Auracher, Theodor. "Der sogenannte poitevinische Pseudo-Turpin." *Zeitschrift für romanische Philologie* 1 (1877): 259–336.

Avril, François. "L'atelier du Psautier d'Ingeburge: Problèmes de localisation et de datation." In *Hommage à Hubert Landais*. Paris: Blanchard, 1987.

Backes, Martina. *Das literarische Leben am kurpfälzischen Hof zu Heidelberg im 15. Jahrhundert*. Tübingen: Niemeyer, 1992.

Backhouse, Janet, D. H. Turner, and Leslie Weber. *The Golden Age of Anglo-Saxon Art, 966–1066*. Bloomington: Indiana University Press, 1984.

Bainton, Roland H. *Women of the Reformation in France and England*. Minneapolis: Augsburg, 1973. Reprint, Boston: Beacon, 1975.

Baird, Joseph L., and John R. Kane, eds. *La querelle de la rose: Letters and Documents*. Chapel Hill: University of North Carolina Department of Romance Languages, 1978; distributed by University of North Carolina Press.

Bak, János M. "Roles and Functions of Queens in Arpadian and Angevin Hungary, *ca* 1000–1386." In *Medieval Queenship*, edited by John Carmi Parsons. New York: St. Martin's, 1993.

Baker, A. T. "Saints' Lives Written in Anglo-French: Their Historical, Social, and Literary Importance." *Transactions of the Royal Society of the United Kingdom*, n.s., 4 (1924).

———, ed. "La Vie de Saint Edmond, Archevêque de Cantorbéry." *Romania* 55 (1929): 332–81.

Baker, Derek, ed. *Medieval Women: Essays Presented to Rosalind M. T. Hill on the Occasion of Her Seventieth Birthday*. Studies in Church History, Subsidia 1. Oxford: Blackwell for the Ecclesiastical History Society, 1978.

———. " 'A Nursery of Saints': St Margaret of Scotland Reconsidered." In *Medieval Women: Essays Presented to Rosalind M. T. Hill on the Occasion of Her Seventieth Birthday*, edited by Derek Baker. Studies in Church History, Subsidia 1. Oxford: Blackwell for the Ecclesiastical History Society, 1978.

Ballesteros Beretta, Antonio. *Alfonso X, el Sabio*. Barcelona: Salvat, 1963.

Barbour, Ruth. "A Manuscript of Pseudo-Dionysius Areopagita Copied for Robert Grosseteste." *Bodleian Library Record* 6 (1958): 401–16.

Barilli, Renato. *Rhetoric*. Translated by Giuliana Menozzi. Minneapolis: University of Minnesota Press, 1989.

Barlow, Frank. *Edward the Confessor*. Berkeley and Los Angeles: University of California Press, 1970.

———. *The English Church, 1066–1154*. London: Longman's, 1979.

———. "The King's Evil." *English Historical Review* 95 (1980): 3–27.

———, ed. *Vita Ædwardi Regis: The Life of King Edward Who Rests at Westminster*. London: Nelson, 1962.

Barnardiston, Katherine Weston. *Clare Priory: Seven Centuries of a Suffolk House*. Cambridge, England: Heffer, 1962.

Barron, Caroline M. "The 'Golden Age' of Women in London." In *Medieval Women in Southern England*, edited by Keith Bate, Anne Curry, Christopher Hardeman, and Peter Noble. Reading, Eng.: University of Reading, 1989.

Baron, Françoise. "Les sculpteurs de Mahaut, comtesse d'Artois et de Bourgogne (1302–1329)." *Positions des thèses et des mémoires des élèves de l'Ecole du Louvre, 1953–1959*. Paris: Musées de France, 1959.

Bartlett, Anne Clarke. "Miraculous Literacy and Textual Community in Hildegard of Bingen's 'Scivias.'" *Mystics Quarterly* 18 (1992): 43–55.

Bataille, Georges. "The Notion of Expenditure." In *Visions of Excess: Selected Writings, 1927–1939*, edited by Allan Stoekl. Translated by Allan Stoekl, Carl R. Lovitts, and Donald M. Leslie, Jr. Minneapolis: University of Minnesota Press, 1985.

Bate, Keith. "La littérature latine d'imagination à la cour d'Henri II d'Angleterre." *Cahiers de civilisation médiévale* 34 (1991): 3–26.

Baudri de Bourgeuil. *Les oeuvres poétiques de Baudri de Bourgeuil.* Edited by Phyllis Abraham. 1926. Reprint, Paris: Slatkine, 1974.

Baugh, Albert C. "The Date of Walter of Bibbesworth's Traité." In *Festschrift für Walther Fischer.* Heidelberg: Winter, 1959.

Beaven, Marilyn, Elizabeth Pastan, and Madeline H. Caviness. "The Gothic Window from Soissons: A Reconsideration." In *Fenway Court, 1983.* Boston: Gardner Museum, 1983.

Beck, Hans-Georg. *Kaiserin Theodora und Prokop: Der Historiker und sein Opfer.* Munich: Piper, 1986.

Becker, Philipp August. "Von den Erzählern neben und nach Chrestien de Troyes." *Zeitschrift für romanische Philologie* 56 (1936): 241–76.

Beckwith, John. *Early Medieval Art: Carolingian, Ottonian, Romanesque.* New York: Oxford University Press, 1975.

Bede. *Venerabilis Baedae opera historica.* Edited by Charles Plummer. Oxford: Clarendon, 1896.

Bedos-Rezak, Brigitte. "Medieval Women in French Sigillographic Sources." In *Medieval Women and the Sources of Medieval History*, edited by Joel T. Rosenthal. Athens: University of Georgia Press, 1990.

Beech, George T. "The Eleanor of Aquitaine Vase, William IX of Aquitaine, and Muslim Spain." *Gesta* 32 (1993): 3–10.

Bell, Susan Groag. "Medieval Women Book Owners: Arbiters of Lay Piety and Ambassadors of Culture." *Signs* 7 (1982): 742–68. Reprinted in *Women and Power in the Middle Ages*, edited by Mary Erler and Maryanne Kowaleski. Athens: University of Georgia Press, 1988, and also in *Sisters and Workers in the Middle Ages.* Edited by Judith M. Bennett, Elizabeth A. Clark, Jean F. O'Barr, B. Anne Vilevi, and Sarah Westphal-Wihl. Chicago: University of Chicago Press, 1989.

Bell, Susan Groag, and J.-M. Richard. "Une petite nièce de Saint Louis, Mahaut, comtesse d'Artois et de Bourgogne (1302–1329)." *Positions des thèses et des mémoires des élèves de l'Ecole du Louvre, 1953–1959.* Edité sous la direction des Musées de France. Paris, 1959.

Benedeit. *The Anglo-Norman Voyage of the St Brendan.* Edited by Edwin G. R. Waters. Oxford: Clarendon, 1928.

Bennert, Uwe. "Art et propagande politique sous Philippe IV le Bel: Le cycle des rois de France dans la Grand'salle du palais de la cité." *Revue de l'art* 97 (1992): 46–59.

Bennett, Adelaide H. "A Book Designed for a Noblewoman: An Illustrated *Manuel des Péchés* of the Thirteenth Century." In *Medieval Book Production: Assessing the Evidence*, edited by Linda L. Brownrigg. Los Altos Hills, Calif.: Anderson-Lovelace, 1990.

Benson, Larry D., ed. *The Riverside Chaucer.* 3d ed. Boston: Houghton Mifflin, 1987.

Benton, John F. "Consciousness of Self and Perceptions of Individuality." In *Renaissance and Renewal in the Twelfth Century*, edited by Robert L. Benson and Giles Constable. Cambridge: Harvard University Press, 1982.

———. "The Court of Champagne as a Literary Center." *Speculum* 36 (1961): 551–91.

Bergert, Fritz. *Die von den Trobadors genannten oder gefeierten Damen: Beihefte zur Zeitschrift für romanische Philologie.* Halle: Niemeyer, 1913.

Bergolte, M. "Die Rolle des Stifters bei der Grundung mittelalterlicher Universitäten, erörtert am Beispiel Freiburgs und Basels." *Basler Zeitschrift für Geschichte und Altertumskunde* 85 (1985): 85–119.

Berman, Constance. "Women as Donors and Patrons to Southern French Monasteries in the Twelfth and Thirteenth Centuries." In *The Worlds of Medieval Women: Creativity, Influence, and Imagination*, edited by Constance H. Berman, Charles W. Connell, and Judith Rice Rothschild. Morgantown: West Virginia University Press, 1985.

Bernard of Clairvaux. "Apologia ad Guillelmum, Santi Theodorici abbatem." In PL, vol. 182, cols. 895–919.

Bethell, Denis. "English Black Monks and Episcopal Elections in the 1120s." *English Historical Review* 84 (1969): 673–98.

Bezzola, Reto R. *Les origines et la formation de la littérature courtoise en Occident, 500–1200.* Paris: Champion, 1944, 1960, 1963.

Biddle, Martin. "Seasonal Festivals and Residence: Winchester, Westminster, and Gloucester in the Tenth Through Twelfth Centuries." *Anglo-Norman Studies* 8 (1986): 51–72.

Biles, Martha. "The Indomitable Belle: Eleanor of Provence, Queen of England." In *Seven Studies in Medieval English History and Other Historical Essays Presented to Harold S. Snellgrove*, edited by Richard H. Bowers. Jackson: University Press of Mississippi, 1983.

Binski, Paul. *The Painted Chamber at Westminster.* London: Society of Antiquaries of London, 1986; distributed by Thames and Hudson.

———. "Reflections on *La estoire de Saint Ædward le Rei*: Hagiography and Kingship." *Journal of Medieval History* 16 (1990): 333–50.

Bischoff, Bernhard. "Literarisches und künstlerisches Leben in St. Emmeram während des frühen und hohen Mittelalters." *Studien und Mitteilungen zur Geschichte des Benediktiner Ordens* 51 (1933): 106–10.

Blackley, F. D. "Isabella of France, Queen of England, 1308–1358 and the Late Medieval Cult of the Dead." *Canadian Journal of History* 15 (1980): 23–47.

Blair, Peter Hunter. *An Introduction to Anglo-Saxon England*. Cambridge: Cambridge University Press, 1956.

Blake, Norman Francis. *William Caxton and His World*. London: Deutsch, 1969.

Blakeslee, Merritt R. "Apostrophe, Dialogue, and the Generic Conventions of the Troubadour *Canso*." In *The Spirit of the Court: Selected Proceedings of the Fourth Congress of the International Courtly Literature Society*, edited by Glyn S. Burgess and Robert A. Taylor. Cambridge: Brewer, 1985.

Bloch, R. Howard. *Etymologies and Genealogies: A Literary Anthropology of the French Middle Ages*. Chicago: University of Chicago Press, 1983.

Boase, T. S. R. *English Art, 1100–1216*. Oxford: Clarendon, 1953.

Böckeler, Maura. *Hildegard of Bingen, Wisse di Wege, Scivias*. Berlin: Sankt Augustinus, 1928.

Boethius. *Boethius: De consolatione philosophie*. Translated by John Walton. Edited by Mark Science. EETS, O.S. 170. London: Oxford University Press, 1927.

Boinet, Amédée. *La cathédrale de Bourges*. Paris: Laurens, 1952.

Boitneau, Pierre. "L'histoire de France en français de Charlemagne à Phillippe-Auguste." *Romania* 90 (1969): 79–99.

Bokenham, Osbern. *A Legend of Holy Women: A Translation of Osbern Bokenham's Legends of Holy Women*. Translated by Sheila Delany. Notre Dame, Ind.: University of Notre Dame Press, 1992.

———. *Legendys of Hooly Wummen*. Edited by Mary S. Serjeantson. Early English Text Society, O.S. 206. London: Oxford University Press, 1938.

Borland, C. R., and R. L. G. Ritchie. "Fragment d'une traduction française en vers de la *Chronique en prose* de Guillaume le Breton." *Romania* 42 (1913): 1–22.

Bornstein, Diane, ed. *Ideals for Women in the Works of Christine de Pizan*. Medieval and Renaissance Monograph Series, no. 1. Detroit: Michigan Consortium for Medieval and Early Modern Studies, 1981.

———. *The Lady in the Tower: Medieval Courtesy Literature for Women*. Hamden, Conn.: Archon, 1983.

———. "Self-Consciousness and Self Concepts in the Work of Christine de Pizan." In *Ideals for Women in the Works of Christine de Pizan*, edited by Diane Bornstein. Medieval and Renaissance Monograph Series, no. 1. Detroit: Michigan Consortium for Medieval and Early Modern Studies, 1981.

Bossuat, Robert. *Le Moyen Age*. Paris: Del Duca–De Gigord, 1955.

———. "Les sources du Quinte-Curse de Vasque de Lucène." In *Mélanges dédiés à la mémoire de Félix Grat*, edited by Émile-A. van Moé, Jeanne Vieillard, and Pierre Marot. Paris: Pecqueur-Grat, 1946–49. 1:347–52.

———. "Traductions françaises des 'Commentaires de César' à la fin du XVe siècle." *Bibliothèque d'humanisme et renaissance* 4 (1944): 346–54.

Bossuat, Robert, Louis Pichard, and Guy Raynaud de Lage. *Dictionnaire des lettres françaises: Le Moyen Age*. Published under the direction of Georges Grente, assisted by Albert Pauphilet, Louis Pichard, and Robert Barroux. Paris: Fayard, 1974.

Botfield, Beriah, and T. Turner, eds. *Manners and Household Expenses of England in the Thirteenth and Fifteenth Centuries*. London: Nicol, 1841.

Boutemy, André, ed. "Notice sur le recueil poétique de Manuscrit Cotton Vitellius A xii, du British Museum." *Latomus* 1 (1937): 278–313; reprinted in vol. 23 (1964): 296–313.

Boutière, Jean, and A.-H. Schutz. *Biographies des troubadours*. 1950. Reprint, New York: Franklin, 1972.

Boyer, Marjorie. "Medieval Suspended Carriages." *Speculum* 34 (1959): 359–66.

Bradshaw, Gillian. *The Bearkeeper's Daughter*. Boston: Houghton Mifflin, 1987.

Brahney, Kathleen. "When *Silence* Was Golden: Female Personae in the *Roman de Silence*." In *The Spirit of the Court: Selected Proceedings of the Fourth Congress of the International Courtly Literature Society,* edited by Glyn S. Burgess and Robert A. Taylor. Cambridge: Brewer, 1985.

Branca, Vittore. *Boccaccio: The Man and His Works*. Translated by Richard Monges. New York: New York University Press, 1976.

Branner, Robert. *Manuscript Painting in Paris During the Reign of St. Louis: A Study of Styles*. Berkeley and Los Angeles: University of California Press, 1977.

———. *St. Louis and the Court Style in Gothic Architecture*. London: Zwemmer, 1965.

Brault, Gerard J. "Arthurian Heraldry and the Date of Escanor." *Bulletin bibliographique de la Société Internationale Arthurienne* 11 (1959): 81–88.

———. *Early Blazon: Heraldic Terminology in the Twelfth and Thirteenth Centuries with Specific References to Arthurian Literature*. Oxford: Clarendon, 1972.

———. "Les manuscrits des oeuvres de Girart d'Amiens" *Romania* 80 (1959): 433–66.

Breckenridge, James D. *Age of Spirituality*. Edited by Kurt Weitzmann. New York: Metropolitan Museum of Art, 1978.

Brenk, Beat. "Bildprogrammatik und Geschichtsverständnis der Kapetinger im Querhaus der Kathedrale von Chartres." *Arte medievale*, 2d ser., 5 (1991): 71–96.

Brett, Martin. *The English Church Under Henry I*. Oxford: Oxford University Press, 1975.

Brieger, Peter. *English Art, 1216–1307*. Oxford: Oxford University Press, 1957.

Brilliant, Richard. *Portraiture*. Cambridge: Harvard University Press, 1991.

Brooke, Christopher, and Gillian Keir. *London, 800–1216: The Shaping of a City*. Berkeley and Los Angeles: University of California Press, 1975.

Broomfield, F., ed. *Thomae de Chobhem summa Confessorum*. Louvain: Nauwelaerts, 1968.

Brown, Elizabeth A. R. "Eleanor of Aquitaine: Parent, Queen, and Duchess." In *Eleanor of Aquitaine: Patron and Politician*, edited by William W. Kibler. Austin: University of Texas Press, 1976.

Brown, Peter. *The Body and Society: Men, Women, and Sexual Renunciation in Early Christianity*. New York: Columbia University Press, 1988.

Brown, R. Allen, H. M. Colvin, and A. J. Taylor. *The History of the King's Work.* London: H. M. Stationery Office, 1963.

Bruce, James Douglas. *The Evolution of Arthurian Romance from the Beginnings Down to the Year 1300.* 2d ed. Baltimore: Johns Hopkins University Press; Göttingen: Vandenhoeck and Ruprecht, 1928.

Brunel, Clovis Félix, ed. *La fille du comte de Ponthieu.* Paris: Champion, 1923.

———. *Recueil des actes des comtes de Pontieu (1026–1279).* Paris: Imprimerie Nationale, 1930.

Bruzelius, Caroline A., Constance H. Berman, eds. "Monastic Architecture for Women." *Gesta* 31, no. 2 (1992): 73–134.

Büchler, Alfred. "Zu den Psalmillustrationen der Haseloff-Schule II. Psalter mit eklektischen Programmen." *Zeitschrift für Kunstgeschichte* 54 (1991): 75–90.

Buetter, Brigitte. "Profane Illuminations, Secular Illusions: Manuscripts in Late Medieval Courtly Society." *Art Bulletin* 74 (1992): 75–90.

Bullington, Rachel. *The "Alexis" in the Saint Albans Psalter: A Look into the Heart of the Matter.* Garland Studies in Medieval Literature 4. New York: Garland, 1991.

Bulst, Walther. "Liebesbriefgedichte Marbods." In *Liber floridus: Mittellateinische Studien Paul Lehmann Gewidmet,* edited by Bernhard Bischoff and Suso Brechter. St. Ottilien: Eos, 1950.

Bur, Michel. "Les comtes de Champagne et la 'Normanitas': Sémiologie d'un tombeau." *Proceedings of the Battle Conference on Anglo-Norman Studies* 3 (1980): 22–32, 202–3.

Burns, Robert I., ed. *Emperor of Culture: Alfonso X the Learned of Castile and His Thirteenth-Century Renaissance.* Philadelphia: University of Pennsylvania Press, 1990.

Burrell, M. "Narrative Structures in *Le voyage de Saint Brendan.*" *Parergon* 17 (1977): 3–9.

Bury, J. B. *History of the Later Roman Empire.* Vol. 2. 1923. Reprint, New York: Dover, 1958.

Buschinger, Danielle, and Wolfgang Spiewok, eds. *Le mécénat de la cour de Brunswick: Actes d'un colloque organisé dans le cadre du 7ème Congrès triennal de la Société pour l'étude de la littérature courtoise (1992) à l'Université du Massachusetts, Amherst (USA). Wodan: Greifwalder Beirrtäge zum Mittelalter,* vol. 24, ser. 3. *Tagunsbände und Sammelschriften,* vol. 11. Greifswald: Reineke, 1993.

Busquet, Raoul. *Etudes sur l'ancienne Provence.* Paris: Champion, 1930.

Byerly, Benjamin, and Catherine Ridder Byerly, eds. *Records of the Wardrobe and Household, 1285–1286.* London: H. M. Stationery Office, 1977.

———. *Records of the Wardrobe and Household, 1286–1289.* London: H. M. Stationery Office, 1986.

Bynum, Caroline Walker. *Holy Feast, Holy Fast: The Religious Significance of Food to Medieval Women.* Berkeley and Los Angeles: University of California Press, 1987.

Calendar of Entries in the Papal Registers Relating to Great Britain and Ireland. London: H. M. Stationery Office, 1897.

Cambridge History of the Bible. Edited by G. W. H. Lampe. Cambridge: Cambridge University Press, 1969.

Cameron, Alan. "The Empress and the Poet: Paganism and Politics at the Court of Theodosius II." *Yale Classical Studies* 27 (1982): 217–90.

Cameron, Alan, and Jacqueline Long. *Barbarians and Politics at the Court of Arcadius.* Berkeley and Los Angeles: University of California Press, 1993.

Cameron, Averil. *Procopius and the Sixth Century.* Berkeley and Los Angeles: University of California Press, 1985.

Campbell, Alistair, ed. *Encomium Emmae Reginae.* London: Royal Historical Society, 1949.

Campbell, Marion. "Metalwork in England, c. 1200–1400." In *Age of Chivalry: Art in Plantagenet England, 1200–1400,* edited by J. J. G. Alexander and Paul Binski. London: Royal Academy of Arts, 1987.

Campbell, Miles W. "Emma, Reine d'Angleterre, mère denaturée ou femme vindicative?" In *Annales de Normandie* 23 (1973): 97–114.

Camus, Marie-Thérèse. "La reconstruction de Saint-Hilaire-le-Grand de Poitiers à l'époque romane: La marche des travaux." *Cahiers de civilisation médiévale* 25 (1982): 101–20.

Camuzat, Nicolas. *Promptuarium sacrum antiquitatum Tricassinae diocesis.* Troyes: Moreau, 1610.

Capgrave, John. *John Capgrave's Lives of St Augustine and St Gilbert of Sempringham, and a Sermon.* Edited by J. J. Munro. EETS, O.S. 140. London: Kegan Paul, Trench, Trübner, 1910.

Cardeñas, A. J. "If Not Alphonso X, Then Who? In Search of a Sponsor for a Copy of the *Libro de las animalias que caçan.*" Abstract of a paper given at the Seventeenth Saint Louis Conference of Manuscript Studies. *Manuscripta* 34 (1990): 201.

Cartellieri, Alexander. *Philipp II August, König von Frankreich.* Vol. 1. Leipzig: Dyksche, 1899–1900.

The Cartulary of the Augustinian Friars of Clare. Edited by Christopher Harper-Bill. Woodbridge, Eng.: Boydell, 1991.

Cartwright, Julia. *Isabella d'Este.* London: Murray, 1903. Reprint New York: Dutton, 1923.

Cavallera, Ferdinand. *Saint Jérôme: Sa vie et son oeuvre.* 2 vols. Paris: Champion, 1922.

Cavanaugh, Susan Hagen. "A Study of Books Privately Owned in England, 1300–1450." Ph.D. diss., University of Pennsylvania, 1980.

Caviness, Madeline H. "(En)gendering Marginalia in Books for Men and Women." *A Conference on Medieval Archaeology in Europe: Art and Symbolism: Pre-Printed Papers,* no. 7. York, 1993.

———. "Gender Symbolism and Text Image Relationships: Hildegard of Bingen's

Scivias." In *Medieval Translation Theory and Practice,* edited by Jeanette Beer. Kalamazoo, Mich.: Center for Medieval Studies, in press.

————. "Images of Divine Order and the Third Mode of Seeing." *Gesta* 22 (1983): 99–120.

————. "Patron or Matron? A Capetian Bride and a *Vade Mecum* for Her Marriage Bed." *Speculum* (special issue, *Studying Medieval Women: Sex, Gender, Feminism,* edited by Nancy F. Partner) 68 no. 2 (1993): 333–62.

————. "The Rationalization of Sight *and* the Authority of Visions? A Feminist (Re)vision." *Museu Nacional d'Art de Catalunya Bulletin,* in press.

————. "Saint-Yved of Braine: The Primary Sources for Dating the Gothic Church." *Speculum* 59 (1984): 526–41.

————. "'The Simple Perception of Matter' and the Representation of Narrative, ca. 1180–1280." *Gesta* 30 (1991): 48–64. [Revision to be published as "The Rationalization of Sight *and* the Authority of Visions? A Feminist (Re)vision." *Museu Nacional d'Art de Catalunya Bulletin,* in press.]

————. "Suger's Glass at Saint-Denis: The State of Research." In *Abbot Suger and Saint Denis: A Symposium,* edited by Paula Gerson. New York: Metropolitan Museum of Art, 1986.

————. *The Sumptuous Arts at the Royal Abbeys of Reims and Braine.* Princeton: Princeton University Press, 1990.

Cerulli, Enrico, ed. *Il "Libro della scala" e la questione delle fonti arabo-spagnole della "Divina commedia."* Vatican City: Bibliotheca Apostolica Vaticana, 1949.

Chabaneau, Camille. "Poésies inédites des troubadours du Périgord." *Revue des langues romanes* 25 (1884): 209–38.

Chambers, David, comp. *Patrons and Artists in the Italian Renaissance.* London: Macmillan, 1970.

Champion, Pierre. *La librairie de Charles d'Orléans.* Paris: Champion, 1910.

————. *Vie de Charles d'Orléans.* Paris: Champion, 1910.

Chance, Jane, ed. *Christine de Pizan's "Letter of Othea to Hector."* Newburyport, Mass.: Focus Information Group, 1990.

Charles d'Orléans. *Poésies.* Edited by Pierre Champion. Paris: Champion, 1966.

Chaytor, Henry John. *From Script to Print.* Cambridge: Cambridge University Press, 1950.

Chibnall, Marjorie M. *Anglo-Norman England, 1066–1166.* Oxford: Blackwell, 1986.

————. *The Empress Matilda: Queen Consort, Queen Mother, and Lady of the English.* Oxford: Blackwell, 1991.

————. "Women in Orderic Vitalis." *Haskins Society Journal: Studies in Medieval History* 2 (1990): 105–21.

Chinball, Albert C. *Richard de Badew and the University of Cambridge.* Cambridge: Cambridge University Press, 1963.

Chrétien de Troyes. *Le Chevalier de la Charrete.* Edited by Mario Roques. Paris: Champion, 1958.

————. *Erec et Enide.* Edited by Mario Roques. Paris: Champion, 1981.

Christie, A. G. *English Medieval Embroidery.* Oxford: Clarendon, 1938.

Christine de Pizan. *The Book of the City of Ladies.* Translated by Earl Jeffrey Richards. New York: Persea, 1982.

————. *The Epistle of Othea.* Translated by Stephen Scrope and edited by Curt F. Bühler. EETS, O.S. 264. Oxford: Oxford University Press, 1970.

————. *A Medieval Woman's Mirror of Honor: The Treasury of the City of Ladies.* Translated by Charity Cannon Willard. Tenafly, N.J.: Bard Hall; New York: Persea, 1989.

————. *Oeuvres poétiques de Christine de Pisan.* Edited by Maurice Roy. Paris: Fimin Didot, 1886–96.

Chronicon Æthelweardi, The Chronicle of Æthelweard. Edited and translated by Alistair Campbell. London: Nelson, 1962.

Chueca Goitia, Fernando. *Historia de la arquitectura española: Edad antiqua y edad media.* Madrid: Dossat, 1965.

Claassens, Geert. "Die scone die mi peisen doet . . . De vrouw als opdrachtgeefster van middeleeuwse literatuur." *Tydschrift voor vronwenstudies* 3 (1982): 325–46.

Clanchy, M. T. *England and Its Rulers, 1066–1272.* Totowa, N.J.: Barnes and Noble, 1983.

————. *From Memory to Written Record: England, 1066–1307.* Cambridge: Harvard University Press, 1979; London: Fontana, 1983.

Clark, Elizabeth A. *Jerome, Chrysostom, and Friends: Essays and Translations.* New York: Miller, 1979.

Clay, Rotha. *The Hermits and Anchorites of England.* London: Methuen, 1914.

————. *The Medieval Hospitals of England.* London: Methuen, 1909.

Cokayne, George Edward. *The Complete Peerage of England, Scotland, Ireland, and Great Britain and the United Kingdom Extant, Extinct, or Dormant.* New ed., revised by Vicary Gibbs et al. London: Saint Catherine, 1910–59.

Colby, Alice M. *The Portrait in Twelfth-Century French Literature: An Example of the Stylistic Originality of Chrétien de Troyes.* Geneva: Droz, 1965.

Colker, M. L., ed. "Latin Texts Concerning Gilbert, Founder of Merton Priory." *Studia Monastica* 12 (1970): 241–72.

Colledge, Edmund, and James Walsh, eds. *A Book of Showings to the Anchoress Julian of Norwich.* Toronto: Pontifical Institute, 1978.

Collinson, Patrick. "The Role of Women in the English Reformation Illustrated by the Life and Friendships of Anne Locke." *Studies in Church History* 2 (1965): 258–72.

Colvin, Howard Montagu, R. A. Brown, and A. J. Taylor, eds. *History of the King's Works.* Oxford: Oxford University Press, 1963–73.

Conway, M., and Semour de Ricci. "A Flemish Triptych for Melbourne." *Burlington Magazine* 40 (1922): 163–71.

Cook, Elsie Thornton. *Her Majesty: The Romance of the Queens of England, 1066–1910.* New York: Dutton, 1927.

Cosman, Madeleine Pelner. "Christine de Pizan's Well-Tempered Feminism." Introduction to *A Medieval Woman's Mirror of Honor: The Treasury of the City of Ladies.* Translated by Charity Cannon Willard. Tenafly, N.J.: Bard Hall; New York: Persea, 1989.

Costa Pimpão, Alvaro J. da. *Historia da literatura Portuguesa: Idade Media.* Lisbon: Atlântida, 1959.

Coudanne, Louise. "Baudonivie, Moniale de Sainte-Croix et biographe de Sainte Radegonde." In *Etudes merovingiennes: Actes des journées de Poitiers 1er–3 mai 1953.* Paris: Picard, 1953.

Courbet, Patrick. "L'autel portatif de la comtesse Gertrude de Brunswick (vers 1040): Tradition royale de Bourgogne et conscience aristocratique dans l'Empire des Saliens." *Cahiers de civilisation médiévale* 34 (1991): 97–120.

Coussemaker, Charles Edmond Henri de. *Oeuvres complètes d'Adam de la Halle.* Paris: Durand and Pedone-Lauriel, 1872.

Crane, Susan. *Insular Romance: Politics, Faith, and Culture in Anglo-Norman and Middle English Literature.* Berkeley and Los Angeles: University of California Press, 1986.

Crawford, Anne. "The Piety of Late Medieval Queens." In *The Church in Pre-Reformation Society: Essays in Honour of F. R. H. Du Boulay,* edited by Caroline M. Barron and Christopher Harper-Bill. Woodbridge, England: Boydell, 1985.

———. "Victims of Attainder: The Howard and de Vere Women in the Late Fifteenth Century." In *Medieval Women in Southern England.* Reading, England: University of Reading, 1989.

Cross, Claire. "'Great Reasoners in Scripture': The Activities of Women Lollards, 1380–1530." *Studies in Church History,* subsidia 1 (1978): 359–80.

Cross, Tom Peete, and William A. Nitze. *Lancelot and Guenevere: A Study on the Origins of Courtly Love.* New York: Phaeton, 1970.

Crouch, David. *The Beaumont Twins: The Roots and Branches of Power in the Twelfth Century.* Cambridge: Cambridge University Press, 1986.

Curnow, Maureen Lois Cheney. "*Le livre de la cité des dames:* A Critical Edition." Ph.D. diss., Vanderbilt University, 1975.

Curtius, Ernst Robert. *European Literature and the Latin Middle Ages.* Translated by Willard R. Trask. New York: Bollingen Foundation, 1953. Reprint, New York: Harper and Row, 1963.

Dancoisne, Louis. *Histoire du couvent des Pauvres Clares de Lille, 1453–1792.* Lille: Danel, 1868.

David, C. W. "The Claim of Henry I to Be Called Learned." In *Anniversary Essays in Medieval History by Students of Charles Homer Haskins.* Edited by Charles Holt Taylor. Boston: Houghton Mifflin, 1929.

Davis, Natalie. *Society and Culture in Early Modern France: Eight Essays.* Stanford, Calif.: Stanford University Press, 1975.

Dean, R. J. "Nicholas Trevet, Historian." In *Medieval Learning and Literature: Essays*

Presented to Richard William Hunt, edited by J. J. G. Alexander and M. T. Gibson. 1966. Reprint, Oxford: Clarendon, 1976.

Deanesly, Margaret. *The Lollard Bible and Other Medieval Biblical Versions.* Cambridge: Cambridge University Press, 1920.

DeGanck, Roger, trans. *The Life of Beatrice of Nazareth.* Kalamazoo, Mich.: Cistercian, 1991.

Deker-Hauff, Hansmartin. *Die Chronik der Grafen von Zimmern.* Konstanz: Thorbecke, 1964–72.

Delany, Sheila, trans. *A Legend of Holy Women.* Notre Dame, Ind.: Notre Dame University Press, 1993.

Delbrück, Richard. "Porträts byzantinischer Kaiserinnen." *Mitteilungen des kaiserlich deutschen archäologischen Instituts, Römische Abteilung* 28 (1913): 310–52.

Delisle, Léopold. *Le cabinet des manuscrits de la Bibliothèque impériale.* Vol. 1. Paris: Imprimerie Impériale, 1868.

——— . *Recueil des historiens des Gaules et de la France.* Paris: Palme, 1896–1904.

——— , ed. *Cartulaire normand de Philippe-Auguste, Louis VIII, Saint-Louis et Philippe-le-Hardi.* 1852. Reprint, Geneva: Mégariotis, 1978.

Del Monte, Alberto, ed. *Peire d'Alvernha: Liriche, filologia romanze.* Turin: Loetscher-Chiantore, 1955.

Demosthenes. *De corona.* Translated by Charles Anthony Vince and James Herbert Vince. Loeb Classical Library. Cambridge: Harvard University Press, 1926.

Denholm-Young, Noel. *History and Heraldry, 1254 to 1310: A Study of the Historical Value of the Rolls of Arms.* Oxford: Clarendon, 1965.

Dept, Gaston G. *Les influences anglaise et française dans le comté de Flandre au début du XIIIe siècle.* Paris: Champion, 1928.

Deschamps, Eustache. *Oeuvres complètes.* Edited by H. E. de Queux de Saint-Hilaire and Gaston Raynaud. Société des anciens textes français. Paris: Firmin Didot, 1878–1903.

Dethan, Georges. *Gaston d'Orléans, conspirateur et prince charmant.* Paris: Berger-Levrault, 1959.

Deuchler, Florens. *Der Ingeborgpsalter.* Berlin: de Gruyter, 1967.

de Vries, Dini Hogenelst en Saskia. "Die scone die mi peisen doet . . . De vrouw als opdrachtgeefster van middeleeuwse literatuur." *Tijdschrift voor vrouwenstudies* 3 (1982): 325–46.

Dhuoda. *Manuel pour mon fils.* Edited by Pierre Riché. Paris: Cerf, 1975.

Dickinson, John Compton. *An Ecclesiastical History of England: The Later Middle Ages.* New York: Barnes and Noble, 1979.

——— . *The Origins of the Austin Canons and Their Introduction into England.* London: Society for the Preservation of Christian Knowledge, 1950.

Diehl, Charles. *Byzantine Empresses.* Translated by Harold Bell and Theresa de Kerpely. New York: Knopf, 1963.

——— . *Théodora: Impératrice de Byzance.* Paris: Rey, 1904.

Dodwell, Charles Reginald. *Anglo-Saxon Art: A New Perspective.* Ithaca, N.Y.: Cornell University Press, 1982.

————. *Painting in Europe, 800–1200.* Harmondsworth, England: Penguin, 1971.

Donizo. *Vita Mathildis.* Edited by Luigi Simeoni. Bologna: Zanichelli, 1930–34.

Dorian, Frederick. *Commitment to Culture: Art Patronage in Europe, Its Significance for America.* Pittsburgh: University of Pittsburgh Press, 1964.

Douglas, David C. "The Song of Roland and the Norman Conquest of England." *French Studies* 14 (1960): 99–116.

Douie, Decima L. *Archbishop Pecham.* Oxford: Clarendon, 1952.

Doutrepont, Georges. *La littérature française à la cour des ducs de Bourgogne.* Paris: Champion, 1909.

Downey, Glanville. *Ancient Antioch.* Princeton: Princeton University Press, 1963.

————. "Notes on Procopius, *De Aedificiis* Book I." In vol. 2 of *Studies Presented to David Moore Robinson on His Seventieth Birthday,* edited by George E. Mylonas and Doris Raymond. St. Louis: Washington University Press, 1953.

————. "Procopius on Antioch: A Study of Method in the *De Aedificiis. Byzantion* 14 (1939): 361–78.

Doyle, A. J. "English Books in and out of Court from Edward III to Henry VII." In *English Court Culture in the Later Middle Ages,* edited by V. J. Scattergood and J. W. Sherborne. New York: St. Martin's, 1983.

Duby, Georges. *The Chivalrous Society.* Translated by Cynthia Postan. Berkeley and Los Angeles: University of California Press, 1977.

Dunn, Charles W. *The Foundling and the Werewolf: A Literary-Historical Study of "Guillaume de Palerne."* Toronto: University of Toronto Press, 1960.

Duvernoy, Emile. *Le duc de Lorraine Mathieu 1er (1139–76).* Paris: Picard, 1904.

Eadmer of Canterbury. *Eadmeri Historia novorum in Anglia.* Edited by Martin Rule. RS 81. London: Longman, 1884. Reprint, 1964.

Eales, R. "The Game of Chess: An Aspect of Medieval Knightly Culture." In *The Ideals and Practice of Medieval Knighthood, I: Papers from the First and Second Strawberry Hill Conferences,* edited by Christopher Harper, Bill Harvey, and Ruth Harvey. Woodbridge, England: Boydell, 1986.

Effenberger, Arne, and Hans-Georg Severin. *Das Museum für Spätantike und Byzantinische Kunst: Staatliche Museen zu Berlin.* Mainz am Rhein: Von Zabern, 1992.

Emden, Alfred B. *A Biographical Register of the University of Cambridge to 1500.* [*BRUC*] Cambridge: Cambridge University Press, 1963.

————. *A Bibliographical Register of the University of Oxford.* Oxford: Clarendon, 1957–59.

Ennen, Edith. *The Medieval Woman.* Translated by Edmund Jephcott. Oxford: Oxford University Press, 1989.

————. "Zur Städtepolitik der Eleonore von Aquitanien." In *Civitatum Communitas: Festschrift für Heinz Stoob zum 65. Geburtstag,* edited by H. Jäger, F. Petri, and H. Quirin. Cologne: Böhlau, 1984.

Ennodius. *Magni Felicis Ennodii opera omnia*. Edited by William Hartel. Corpus scriptorum ecclesiasticorum, vol. 6. Vienna: Geroldi, 1882.

Ensslin, W. "Pulcheriaz." *Paulys Real-Encyclopädie der classischen Altertumswissenschaft* 23 (Stuttgart: Metzler, 1959), 1954–63.

Entwistle, William James. *The Arthurian Legend in the Literatures of the Spanish Peninsula*. New York: Dutton, 1925.

Epistolae Karolini Aevi. Edited by Ernst Dümmler. MGH. Berlin: Weidmann, 1895, 1898–99. Reprint, Munich: MGH, 1978.

Epistolae Merovingici et Karolini Aevi. Vol. 6, *Sancti Bonifacii et Lulli epistolae*. MGH. Societas Aperiendis Fontibus Rerum Germanicarum Medii Aevi. Berlin: Weidmann, 1892.

Le epistole metriche di Baldericus Burguliensis. Edited by M. Teresa Razzoli. Milan: SAEDA, 1936.

Erikson, Erik H. "Womanhood and the Inner Space." In *Identity, Youth, and Crisis*. New York: Norton, 1968.

Erlande-Brandenburg, Alain. *Gothic Art*. Translated by I. Mark Paris. New York: Abrams, 1989.

Erler, Mary, and Maryanne Kowaleski, eds. *Women and Power in the Middle Ages*. Athens: University of Georgia Press, 1988.

Estow, Clara. "Widows in the Chronicles of Late Medieval Castile." In *Upon My Husband's Death: Widows in the Literature and Histories of Medieval Europe*, edited by Louise Mirrer. Ann Arbor: University of Michigan Press, 1992.

Eudociae Augustae, Procli Lycii, Claudianus. Edited by Arthur Ludwich. Bibliotheca scriptorum Graecorum et Romanorum. Leipzig: Teubner, 1897.

Eusebius. *Vita Constantini*. Edited by Friedhelm Winkelmann. *Griechischen Christlichen Schriftsteller der ersten Jahrhunderts*. Berlin: Akademie, 1975.

Evans, Joan. *English Art, 1307–1461*. Oxford: Clarendon, 1949.

———. *Monastic Life at Cluny, 910–1157*. Oxford: Oxford University Press, 1931. Reprint, Hamden, Conn.: Archon, 1968.

Facinger, Marion F. "A Study of Medieval Queenship: Capetian France, 987–1237." *Studies in Medieval and Renaissance History* 5 (1968): 1–47.

Fairweather, Janet. "Fiction in the Biographies of Ancient Writers." *Ancient Society* 5 (1974): 231–75.

Farley, Mary Ann, and Francis Wormald. "Three Related English Romanesque Manuscripts." *Art Bulletin* 22 (1940): 157–61.

Farmer, David Hugh, ed. *Oxford Dictionary of Saints*. 2d ed. Oxford: Oxford University Press, 1987.

Farmer, Sharon. "Persuasive Voices: Clerical Images of Medieval Wives." *Speculum* 61 (1986): 517–43.

Fassbinder, Marie. *Die Selige Agnes von Prag*. Werl: Dietrich-Coelde, 1957. Translated into French by G. Daubié as *Princesse et moniale Agnès de Bohème, amie de Sainte Claire*. Paris: Editions franciscaines, 1962.

La Femme au moyen âge. Edited by Michel Rouche and Jean Heuclin. Sous la haute présidence de Georges Duby. Maubeuge: Jean Touzot, 1990.

Fenlon, Iain. *Music and Patronage in Sixteenth-Century Mantua.* Cambridge: Cambridge University Press, 1980.

Fernández Martín, Luis. "Colección diplomatica del monasterio de Santa María de Matallana." *Hispania sacra* 25 (1972): 391–435.

Fernández Valverde, Juan, ed. *Historia de rebus Hispanie.* Turnholti: Brepols, 1987.

Ferrante, Joan M. "The Education of Women in the Middle Ages in Theory, Fact, and Fantasy." In *Beyond Their Sex: Learned Women of the European Past,* edited by Patricia H. Labalme. New York: New York University Press, 1980; paperback ed. 1984.

———. *The Political Vision of the Divine Comedy.* Princeton: Princeton University Press, 1984.

———. "Whose Voice? The Influence of Women Patrons on Courtly Romances." In *Literary Aspects of Courtly Culture. Selected Papers from the Seventh Triennial Congress of the International Courtly Literature Society, University of Massachusetts, Amherst, USA, 27 July–August 1992,* edited by Donald Maddox and Sara Sturm-Maddox. Cambridge, England: Brewer, 1994.

———. *Woman as Image in Medieval Literature, from the Twelfth Century to Dante.* New York: Columbia University Press, 1975. Reprint, Durham, N.C.: Labyrinth, 1985.

Ferreira Borges, G. "Saint Bernard et le Portugal: L'histoire et la légende." In *Mélanges Saint Bernard.* XXIVe Congrès de l'Association Bourguignonne des Sociétés Savantes. Dijon: Marilier, 1953.

Field, Hugh, ed. *Ramon Vidal de Besalú: Obra poètica.* Vol. 2. Barcelona: Curial, 1991.

Fiero, Gloria K. "The *Dits:* The Historical Context." In *Three Medieval Views of Women,* edited and translated by Gloria K. Fiero, Wendy Pfeffer, and Mathé Allain. New Haven: Yale University Press, 1989.

Figueiredo, José de. "Un panneau inconnu de Rogier van der Weyden." *Boletim de arte e arqueologia* 1 (1921): 91–94.

Fish, Stanley. "There's No Such Thing as Free Speech, and It's a Good Thing Too." *Boston Review* 17, no. 1 (February 1992): 3–4, 23–26.

Flanders in the Fifteenth Century. Catalogue of the Exposition "Masterpieces of Flemish Art: Van Eyck to Bosch," October–December 1960, organized by the Detroit Institute of Arts and the City of Bruges. Detroit and Brussels: Institute of Arts and Centre National de Recherches Primitifs Flamands, 1960.

Flax, Jane. "Do Feminists Need Marxism?" In *Building Feminist Theory,* edited by the *Quest* staff. New York: Longman, 1981.

Flete, John. *The History of Westminster Abbey.* Edited by J. Armitage Robinson. Cambridge: Cambridge University Press, 1909.

Florez, P. Enrique. *Memorias de las reinas catolicas de España.* Vol. 1. 1761. Reprint, Madrid: Aguilar, 1945.

Foerster, Wendelin, ed. *Der Karrenritter und das Wilhelmsleben*. Halle: Niemeyer, 1899.

Folda, Jaroslav. *Crusader Manuscript Illumination at Saint-Jean-d'Acre, 1275–1291*. Princeton: Princeton University Press, 1976.

Folet, N. *Hôpitaux lillois disparus*. Lille, 1899.

Forbes, Mansfield D., ed. *Clare College, 1326–1926*. Cambridge: Cambridge University Press, 1928.

Foreville, Raymonde, ed. *Histoire de Guillaume le Conquérant*. Paris: Belles Lettres, 1952.

Fortunatus, Venantius. *De vita Sanctae Radegundis*. In *De vita Sanctae Radegundis libri duo*. Edited by B. Krusch. MGH, SRM 2. Hannover, 1889.

———. *Venanti Fortunati carmina*. Edited by Friedrich Leo. MGH AA vol. 4. part 1. Berlin, 1881.

———. *Venanti Honori Clemenentiani Fortunati presbyteri Italici opera poetica*. Edited by Friedrich Leo. MGH AA vol. 4. part 1. Berlin, 1881.

Fosbroke, Thomas Dudley. *Abstracts and Extracts of Smyth's "Lives of the Berkeleys."* London: Nichols, 1821.

Foss, Michael. *The Age of Patronage; The Arts in England, 1660–1750*. Ithaca, N.Y.: Cornell University Press, 1972.

Fourquin, Guy. *Lordship and Feudalism in the Middle Ages*. Translated by Iris and A. L. Lytton Sells. New York: Pica, 1976.

Fourrier, Anthime. *Le courant réaliste dans le roman courtois en France au Moyen Age*. Vol. 1, *Les débuts (XIIe siècle)*. Paris: Nizet, 1960.

Fowler, J. T., ed. *The Coucher Book of Selby*. Durham, England: Yorkshire Archaeological Society and Topographical Association, 1891–93.

Fowler, Kenneth. *The King's Lieutenant: Henry of Grosmont, First Duke of Lancaster, 1310–1361*. London: Elek, 1969.

Fox, John. *A Literary History of France*. Vol. 1, *The Middle Ages*. London: Bowes, 1974.

Fox, Matthew. *Illuminations of Hildegard of Bingen*. Santa Fe: Bear, 1985.

Foxe, John. *The Acts and Monuments*. 4th ed. Edited by Josiah Pratt. London: Religious Tract Society, 1887.

Fradenburg, Louise. *Women and Sovereignty*. Edinburgh: Edinburgh University Press, 1992.

Frank, Francine, and Frank Anshen. *Language and the Sexes*. Albany: State University of New York, 1983.

Frappier, Jean. "Sur un procès fait à l'amour courtois." *Romania* 93 (1972): 145–93.

Freeman, Michelle. "Marie de France's Poetics of Silence: The Implications for a Feminine *Translatio*." *PMLA* 100 (1984): 860–83.

———. "The Power of Sisterhood: Marie de France's 'Le Fresne.'" *French Forum* 12 (January 1987): 5–26.

Fresne de Beaucourt, Gaston du. *Histoire de Charles VII*. Paris: Picard, 1881–91.

Froissart, Jean. *Oeuvres de Froissart: Chroniques.* Edited by Kervyn de Lettenhove. Brussels: Devaux, 1867.

———. *The Chronicles of Jean Froissart in Lord Berners' Translation.* Edited by Gillian Anderson and William Anderson. Carbondale: Southern Illinois University Press, 1963.

———. *Le joli buisson de jonece.* Edited by Anthime Fourrier. Geneva: Droz, 1975.

Frugoni, Chiara. "L'iconographie de la femme au cours des Xe–XIIe siècles." In *La femme dans les civilisations des Xe–XIIIe siècles: Actes du colloque tenu à Poitiers les 23–25 septembre 1976.* Poitiers: Centre d'études supérieures de la civilisation médiévale, 1977. Published in *Cahiers de civilisation médiévale* 20 (1977): 177–88.

———. "The Imagined Woman." In *A History of Women in the West: II. Silences of the Middle Ages,* edited by Christiane Klapisch-Zuber. Cambridge: Belknap Press of Harvard University Press, 1992.

Furnivall, Frederick James, ed. *Hoccleve's Works: The Regement of Princes and Fourteen Minor Poems.* EETS, E.S. 72. London: Kegan Paul, Trench, Trübner, 1897.

———, ed. *Political, Religious, and Love Poems.* EETS, O.S. 15. London: Kegan Paul, Trench, Trübner, 1866. Reprint, 1903.

Furnivall, Frederick James, and I. Gollancz. *Hoccleve's Works: The Minor Poems,* revised by Jerome Mitchell and A. I. Doyle. EETS, E.S. 61, 73. Reprint in 1 vol., London: Oxford University Press, 1970.

Gaborit-Chopin, Danielle. In *Le trésor de Saint-Denis.* Exhibition, Musée du Louvre 12 March–17 June. Paris: Réunion des musées nationaux, 1991.

Gabriel, Astrik L. *The Educational Ideas of Vincent of Beauvais.* Notre Dame, Ind.: University of Notre Dame Press, 1962.

Gaguin, Robert. *Roberti Gaguini epistole et oratione.* Edited by Louis Thuasne. Bibliothèque littéraire de la renaissance, vols. 2–3. Paris: Bouillon, 1903–4.

Gaimar, Geoffrey. *The Anglo-Norman Metrical Chronicles of Geoffrey Gaimar.* Edited by Thomas Wright. 1850. Reprint, New York: Franklin, 1976.

Galbraith, V. H. "The Literacy of the Medieval English Kings." *Proceedings of the British Academy* 21 (1935): 201–38.

Gallet-Guerne, Danielle. *Vasque de Lucène et la Cyropédie à la cour de Bourgogne (1470).* Geneva: Droz, 1974.

Galway, Margaret, "The 'Troilus' Frontispiece." *Modern Language Review* 44 (1949): 161–77.

Garth, Helen Meredith. *Saint Mary Magdalene in Mediaeval Literature.* Baltimore: Johns Hopkins University Press, 1950.

George, Judith W. *Venantius Fortunatus: A Latin Poet of Merovingian Gaul.* Oxford: Clarendon, 1992.

Georgi, Annette. *Das lateinische und deutsche Preisgedicht des Mittelalters in der Nachfolge der genus demonstrativum.* Berlin: Erich Schmidt, 1969.

Geremek, Bronislaw. *The Margins of Society in Late Medieval Paris.* Translated by Jean Birrell. Cambridge: Cambridge University Press, 1987.

Gibbon, Edward. *The Decline and Fall of the Roman Empire.* 3 vols. Reprint, New York: Modern Library, [1923].

Gibson, Gail McMurray. "Saint Anne and the Religion of Childbed." In *Interpreting Cultural Symbols: Saint Anne in Late Medieval Society,* edited by Kathleen Ashley and Pamela Sheingorn. Athens: University of Georgia Press, 1990.

———. *The Theater of Devotion: East Anglican Drama and Society in the Late Middle Ages.* Chicago: University of Chicago Press, 1989.

Gibson, Strickland, ed. *Statuta antiqua Universitatis Oxoniensis.* Oxford: Clarendon, 1931.

Gilday, Rosi. "The Women Patrons of Neri di Bicci," Paper presented at the Twenty-eighth International Congress on Medieval Studies, Kalamazoo, Mich., May 1993.

Gies, Frances, and Joseph Gies. *Women in the Middle Ages.* New York: Crowell, 1978.

Giraldus Cambrensis. *De principis instructione.* In *Opera omnia,* edited by J. S. Brewer. Rolls Series 21. London: Longman, 1861–91.

Giraut de Bornelh. *Sämtlich Lieder des Trobadors Giraut de Bornelh.* Edited by Adolf Kolsen. Vol. 1. Halle: Niemeyer, 1910.

Given-Wilson, Chris. *The English Nobility in the Late Middle Ages.* London: Routledge and Kegan Paul, 1987.

Glauning, Otto, ed. *Lydgate's Minor Poems: The Two Nightingale Poems.* EETS, E.S. 80. London: Kegan Paul, Trench, Trübner, 1900.

Godefroy-Ménilgaise, Denys Charles. "Mahaut comtesse d'Artois." *Mémoires de la Société des Antiquaires de France* 28 (1865): 181–230.

Gold, Barbara K., ed. *Literary and Artistic Patronage in Ancient Rome.* Austin: University of Texas Press, 1982.

Gold, Penny Shine. *The Lady and the Virgin: Image, Attitude, and Experience in Twelfth-Century France.* Chicago: University of Chicago Press, 1985.

Goldbacher, Alois. *Sancti Augustini epistolae.* Corpus Scriptorum Ecclesiasticorum Latinorum, no. 57. Vienna: Tempsky, 1911.

Goldschmidt, A. *Der Albanipsalter in Hildesheim.* Berlin: Siemens, 1895.

Gomez Barcena, María Jesus. *Escultura gótica funeraria en Burgos.* [Burgos]: Diputacíon provincial de Burgos, 1988.

Gonzales, Julio. *El reino de Castilla en la epoca de Alfonso VIII: Documentos.* Madrid: Escuela de estudios medievales, 1960.

———. *Reinado y diplomas de Fernando III.* 3 vols. Córdoba: Monte de Piedad y Caja de Ahorros de Córdoba, 1980–86.

Gössmann, Elisabeth. "Hildegard of Bingen" in *Medieval, Renaissance and Enlightenment Women Philosophers.* Vol. 2 of *A History of Women Philosophers.* Edited by Mary Ellen Waithe. Dondrecht, Netherlands, and Boston: Kluwer, 1989.

———. "The Image of the Human Being According to Scholastic Theology and the Reaction of Contemporary Women." *Ultimate Reality and Meaning* 11 (1988): 183–95.

Grabar, André. "Quel est le sens de l'offrande de Justinien et de Théodora sur les mosaïques de Saint-Vital?" *Felix Ravenna* 81 (1960): 63–77.

Grange, Amaury de la. Hospital Inventory from ADN B3515, no. 123.955. *Annales du Comité Flamand de France* 58 (1935): 419–29.

Gransden, Antonia. "The Continuation of the *Flores Historiarum* from 1265 to 1327." *Mediaeval Studies* 36 (1974): 472–92.

——. *Historical Writing in England.* Vol. 1, *C. 550 to c. 1307.* London: Routledge and Kegan Paul, 1974.

——. "Propaganda in English Mediaeval Historiography." *Journal of Medieval History* 1 (1975): 363–81.

Graves, Robert. *But It Still Goes On: An Accumulation.* London: Cape, 1930.

Greek Anthology. Vol. 1. Translated by W. R. Paton. Loeb Classical Library. Cambridge: Harvard University Press, 1916.

Green, Charles, and A. B. Whittingham. "Excavations at Walsingham Priory, Norfolk, 1961." *Archaeological Journal* 125 (1968): 273.

Green, Mary Anne Everett. *Lives of the Princesses of England from the Norman Conquest.* London: Colburn, 1849–55.

Green, Richard Firth. *Poets and Princepleasers: Literature and the English Court in the Late Middle Ages.* Toronto: University of Toronto Press, 1980.

Greenhill, Eleanor S. "Eleanor, Abbot Suger, and Saint-Denis." In *Eleanor of Aquitaine: Patron and Politician,* edited by William K. Kibler. Austin: University of Texas Press, 1976.

Gregory of Tours. *History of the Franks.* Translated by Lewis Thorpe. New York: Penguin, 1974.

——. *Liber in gloria Confessorum.* 106. Edited by W. Arndt and B. Krusch. MGH, SRM. I/II. Hanover, Germany: Hanian, 1884–85.

Grimm, Reinhold R. *Schöpfung und Sündenfall in der altfranzösischen Genesisdichtung des Evrat.* Bern: Lang, 1976.

Grodecki, Louis. *Le vitrail roman.* Fribourg: office du livre, 1977.

Gronier-Prieur, Armande. *L'abbaye Notre Dame du Lys à Dammarie-les-Lys.* Verneuil-l'Etang, France: Amis des monuments et des sites de Seine-et-Marne, 1971.

Grundmann, H. "Die Frauen und die Literatur im Mittelalter: Ein Beitrag zur Frage nach der Entstehung des Schrifttums in der Volkssprache." *Archiv für Kulturgeschichte* 26, no. 2 (1935): 129–61. Reprinted in *Ausgewählte Aufsätze.* MGH 25, 1–3. Stuttgart: Hiersmann, 1976–78.

Guiart, Guillaume. *La branche des royaux lignages: Chronique métrique de Giuillaume Guiart.* Edited by J.-A. Buchon. Paris: Verdière, 1828.

Les guides bleues: Portugal. Madère Açores. Edited by Magdelaine Traisot. Paris: Hachette, 1957.

Guillaume de Poitiers. *Histoire de Guillaume le Conquérant.* Edited and translated by Raymonde Foreville. Paris: Société d'édition "Les belles lettres," 1952.

Guischart de Beauliu, *Le Sermon de Guischart de Beauliu*, ed. Arvid Gabrielson. Uppsala: A.-B. Akademiska, 1909.

Gundersheimer, Werner L. "Women, Learning, and Power: Eleanora of Aragon and the Court of Ferrara." In *Beyond Their Sex: Learned Women of the European Past*, edited by Patricia H. Labalme. New York: New York University Press, 1980.

Guy, Henri. *Essai sur la vie et les oeuvres littéraires du trouvère Adam de le Halle*. Paris: Hachette, 1898.

Hackett, M. B. *The Original Statutes of Cambridge University*. Cambridge: Cambridge University Press, 1970.

Hadju, Robert. "The Position of Noblewomen in the Pays des Coutumes, 1100–1300." *Journal of Family History* 5 (1980): 122–44.

Haight, Anne Lyon, ed. *Hroswitha of Gandersheim*. New York: Hroswitha Club, 1965.

Hailstone, Edward, Jr. *The History and Antiquities of the Parish of Bottisham and the Priory of Anglesey*. Cambridge, England: Cambridge Antiquarian Society, 1873.

Hall, G., ed. *"Li Rommans de Troies:* A Translation by Jean de Flixecourt." Ph.D. diss., University of London, 1951.

Hallam, Elizabeth M. *Capetian France, 987–1328*. London: Longman, 1980.

Hamburger, Jeffrey F. "Art Enclosure and the *Cura Monialium:* Prolegomena in the Guise of a Postscript." *Gesta* 31, no. 2 (1992): 108–34.

Hammond, Eleanor Prescott. "Lydgate and the Duchess of Gloucester." *Anglia* 27 (1904): 381–98.

Hanawalt, Barbara A. "Lady Honor Lisle's Networks of Influence." In *Women and Power in the Middle Ages*, edited by Mary Erler and Maryanne Kowaleski. Athens: University of Georgia Press, 1988.

Hanna, Ralph. "The Difficulty of Ricardian Prose Translation: The Case of the Lollards." *Modern Language Quarterly* 51 (1990): 319–40.

———. "Producing Manuscripts and Editions." In *Crux and Controversy in Middle English Textual Criticism*, edited by Charlotte Brewer and Alastair Minnis. Cambridge, England: Boydell, 1992.

———. "Sir Thomas Berkeley and His Patronage." *Speculum* 64 (1989): 878–916.

———. "Some Commonplaces of Late Medieval Patience Discussions: An Introduction." In *The Triumph of Patience: Medieval and Renaissance Studies*, edited by Gerald J. Schiffhorst. Orlando: University Presses of Florida, 1978.

Hannay, Margaret Patterson, ed. *Silent but for the Word: Tudor Women as Patrons, Translators, and Writers of Religious Works*. Kent, Ohio: Kent State University Press, 1985.

Hardyng, John. *Chronicle*. Edited by Henry Ellis. London, 1812.

Harrison, Martin. *A Temple for Byzantium*. Austin: University of Texas Press, 1989.

Harrison, William John. *Notes on the Masters, Fellows, Scholars, and Exhibitions of Clare College*. Cambridge: Printed for the College, 1953.

Harrsen, Meta. "The Countess Judith of Flanders and the Library at Weingarten Abbey." *Papers of the Bibliographic Society of America* 24, pts. 1 and 2 (1930): 1–13.

Hartt, Frederick, Gino Corti, and Clarence Kennedy. *The Chapel of the Cardinal of Portugal (1434–1459) at San Miniato in Florence*. Philadelphia: University of Pennsylvania Press, 1964.

Harvey, John. *English Mediaeval Architects*. Rev. ed. Gloucester: Alan Sutton, 1987.

Harvey, Susan Ashbrook. *Asceticism and Society in Crisis: John of Ephesus and the Lives of the Ancient Saints*. Berkeley and Los Angeles: University of California Press, 1990.

Haskell, Francis. *Patrons and Painters: A Study in the Relations Between Italian Art and Society in the Age of the Baroque*. New York: Harper and Row, 1971.

Haskins, Charles Homer. "Henry II as a Patron of Literature." In *Essays in Medieval History Presented to Thomas Frederick Tout*, edited by A. G. Little and F. M. Powicke. Manchester: Printed for the subscribers n.p., 1925.

——— . *Studies in the History of Mediaeval Science*. 2d edition. Cambridge: Harvard University Press, 1927.

Heffernan, Thomas. *Sacred Biography: Saints and Their Biographers in the Middle Ages*. New York: Oxford University Press, 1988.

Heilbrun, Carolyn G. *Writing a Woman's Life*. New York: Norton, 1988.

Heisner, B. "Marie de Medici: Self-Promotion Through Art." *Feminist Art Journal* 6 (1977): 21–26.

Hemelaar, Marlijne. "Ex Libris Adelizae, Eleanorae et aliarum: The Queens of England, Literary Patronage, and Book Ownership, 1066–1509." Thesis, University of Leiden, 1992.

Henderson, Jane Frances Anne. "A Critical Edition of Evrat's Genesis: Creation to the Flood." Ph.D. diss., University of Toronto, 1977.

Henry, A., ed. "Le Roman du Hem." In *Travaux de la Faculté de Philosophie et Lettres de l'Université de Bruxelles*, vol. 3. Paris: Les belles lettres, 1938.

Hentsch, Alice A. *De la littérature didactique au Moyen Age s'adressant spécialement aux femmes*. 1903. Reprint, Geneva: Slatkine, 1975.

Herlihy, David. "Land, Family, and Women in Continental Europe, 701–1200." In *Women in Medieval Society*, edited by Susan Mosher Stuard. Philadelphia: University of Pennsylvania Press, 1976.

——— . *Medieval Households*. Cambridge: Harvard University Press, 1985.

——— . *Opera Muliebria: Women and Work in Medieval Europe*. New York: McGraw-Hill, 1990.

Hermann of Tournai. *Liber de restauratione abbatiae S. Martini Tornacensis*. MGH SS 14 (Hannover: Hahn 1956).

Hermogenes. *On Types of Style*. Translated by Cecil W. Wooten. Chapel Hill: University of North Carolina Press, 1987.

Herrad of Landsberg. *Hortus deliciarum*. Edited by Rosalie Green, Michael Evans, C. Bischoff, and M. Curschmann. London: Warburg Institute, 1979.

——— . *Hortus deliciarum (Garden of Delights)*. Commentary and notes by A. Straub and G. Keller; edited and translated by Aristide D. Caratzas. New Rochelle, N.Y.: Caratzas, 1977.

Herrin, Judith. "The Byzantine Secrets of Procopius." *History Today* 38 (1988): 36–42.

Herriott, J. Homer. "A Thirteenth-Century Manuscript of the *Primera Partida*." *Speculum* 13 (1938): 278–94.

Heywood, James. *Early Cambridge University and College Statutes*. London: Bohn, 1855.

Hicks, M. A. "The Last Days of the Countess of Oxford." *English Historical Review* 103 (1988): 76–95.

Hicks, Michael. "The English Minoresses and Their Early Benefactors." In *Monastic Studies: The Continuity of Tradition*, edited by Judith Loades. Bangor, Wales: Gwynedd, 1990.

Highfield, J. R. L. "The English Hierarchy in the Reign of Edward III." *Transactions of the Royal Historical Society* 6 (1956): 115–38.

Hildebert of Lavardin. *Carmina minora*. Edited by A. Brian Scott. Leipzig: Teubner, 1969.

———. *Opera omnia*. In PL, vol. 162. Paris, 1854.

Hillgarth, J. N. *The Spanish Kingdoms, 1250–1516*, 2 vols. Oxford: Clarendon, 1976–78.

Hirschfeld, Yizhar. *Judean Desert Monasteries in the Byzantine Period*. New Haven, Conn.: Yale University Press, 1992.

Histoire litteraire de la France, ouvrage commencé par des religieux bénédictins de la congrégation de Saint-Maur et continué par des membres de l'Institut des inscriptions et belles lettres. Paris: Imprimerié Nationale, 1733–1898.

Historiae ecclesiasticae, vol. 2. Edited by Auguste Leprevost. Paris: Renouard, 1840.

Historiae patriae monumenta, ed. Caroli Alberti. Augustae Taurinorun: Regio typographeo, 1836.

Hodgett, Gerald A. *The Cartulary of Holy Trinity, Aldgate*. London: London Record Society, 1971.

Hoff, Ursula, and Martin Davis. "Les primitifs flamands." In *The National Gallery of Victoria, Melbourne*. Brussels: Centre national de recherches Primitifs Flamands, 1971.

Holdsworth, Christopher J. "Christina of Markyate." In *Medieval Women: Essays Presented to Rosalind M. T. Hill on the Occasion of Her Seventieth Birthday*, edited by Derek Baker. Studies in Church History, Subsidia 1. Oxford: Blackwell for the Ecclesiastical History Society, 1978.

Holländer, Hans. *Early Medieval Art*. New York: Universe, 1974.

Hollister, C. Warren. *Monarchy, Magnates and Institutions in the Anglo-Norman World*. London: Hambledon, 1986.

Holmes, George A. *The Estates of the Higher Nobility in Fourteenth-Century England*. Cambridge: Cambridge University Press, 1957.

Holmes, Urban Tigner. "The Anglo-Norman Rhymed Chronicle." In *Linguistic and*

Literary Studies in Honor of Helmut A. Hatzfeld, edited by Alessandro S. Crisafulli. Washington: Catholic University of America Press, 1964.

Holum, Kenneth G. *Theodosian Empresses: Women and Imperial Dominion in Late Antiquity.* Berkeley and Los Angeles: University of California Press, 1982.

Holzknecht, Karl Julius. *Literary Patronage in the Middle Ages.* Philadelphia: Collegiate, 1923.

Horstmann, Carl. "Prosalegenden." *Anglia* 3 (1880): 293–360.

Hough, John. *Essex Churches.* Woodbridge, England: Boydell, 1983.

Howitt, Mary. *Biographical Sketches of the Queens of Great Britain from the Norman Conquest to the Reign of Victoria.* London: Bohn, 1851.

Hrotsvit. *Hrotsvithae opera.* Edited by Helene Homeyer. Paderborn: Schöningh, 1970.

———. *Hrotsvithae opera.* Edited by Karl Strecker. Leipzig: Teubner, 1906.

———. *Hrosvithae liber tertius.* Text with translation by Mary Berardine Bergman. Covington, Ky.: Sisters of Saint Benedict, 1943.

Hudson, Anne. *The Premature Reformation: Wycliffite Texts and Lollard History.* Oxford: Clarendon, 1988.

———. *Selections from English Wycliffite Writings.* Cambridge: Cambridge University Press, 1978.

Huemer, Johann. "Zur Geschichte der mittellateinischen Dichtung: Arnulfi delicie cleri." *Romanische Forschungen* 2 (1886): 211–46.

Hughes, Muriel. "Margaret of York, Duchess of Burgundy, Diplomat, Patroness, Bibliophile, and Benefactress." *Private Library,* 3d ser., 7 (1984): 3–17.

———. "The Library of Margaret of York, Duchess of Burgundy." *Private Library,* 3d ser., 7 (1984): 53–78.

Hume, Martin Andrew Sharp. *Spanish Influence on English Literature.* London: Nash, 1905. Reprint, New York: Haskell House, 1964.

Huneycutt, Lois L. "'Another Esther in Our Times': Matilda II and the Formation of a Queenly Ideal in Anglo-Norman England (Scotland)." Ph.D. diss., University of California, Santa Barbara, 1992.

———. "The Idea of the Perfect Princess: *The Life of Saint Margaret* in the Reign of Matilda II, 1100–1118." *Anglo-Norman Studies* 12 (1989): 81–97.

———. "Images of Queenship in the High Middle Ages." *Haskins Society Journal: Studies in Medieval History* 1 (1989): 61–71.

———. "Intercession and the High-Medieval Queen: The *Esther* Topos." Paper presented at "Power of the Weak? Women and Power in the Middle Ages," annual conference of the Centre for Mediaeval Studies, University of Toronto, February 1990.

———. "Medieval Queenship." *History Today* 39 (1989): 16–22.

Hunt, E. D. *Holy Land Pilgrimage in the Later Roman Empire, A.D. 312–460.* New York: Oxford University Press, 1982.

Hunt, R. W. "Medieval Inventories of Clare College Library." *Transactions of the Cambridge Bibliographic Society* 1 (1950): 105–125.

Huot, Sylvia. "Visualization and Memory: The Illustration of Troubadour Lyric in a Thirteenth-Century Manuscript." *Gesta* 31, no. 1 (1992): 3–14.

Hutchinson, G. E. "Attitudes Toward Nature in Medieval England: The Alphonso and Bird Psalters." *Isis* 65 (1974): 5–37.

Hutton, Edward. *The Franciscans in England, 1224–1538.* London: Constable, 1926.

Huynes, Jean. *Histoire générale de l'abbaye du Mont Saint-Michel.* Edited by Eugène de Robillard de Beaurepaire. Rouen: A. Le Brument, 1872–73.

Illich, Ivan. *In the Vineyard of the Text: A Commentary to Hugh's "Didascalicon."* Chicago: University of Chicago Press, 1993.

Illingworth, R. N. "The Structure of the Anglo-Norman *Voyage of St Brendan* by Benedeit." *Medium Aevum* 55 (1986): 217–29.

Irigarey, Luce. *Speculum de l'autre femme.* Paris: Minuit, 1974.

Isabelle de Portugal. Duchesse de Bourgogne. Exposition Bibliothèque Royale Albert Ier, 5 octobre–23 novembre 1991. Brussels: Bibliothèque Royale, 1991.

Isoz, Claire, ed. *Proverbes de Salemon by Sanson de Nantuil.* London: Anglo-Norman Text Society, 1988.

Ivo of Chartres. "Epistolae." In PL, vol. 162: 11–290.

Jacob, E. F. "Founders and Foundations in the Later Middle Ages." *Bulletin of Historical Research* 35 (1962): 33.

James, M. R., ed. and trans. *La estoire de seint Ædward le rei.* Roxburghe Club Edition. Oxford: Oxford University Press, 1920.

———. *The Apocalypse in Latin and French (Bodleian, MS Douce 180).* London: Roxburghe Club, 1922.

James, Thomas Beaumont. *The Palaces of Medieval England c. 1050–1550: Royalty, Nobility, the Episcopate and Their Residences from Edward the Confessor to Henry VIII.* London: Batesford, 1990.

Jenkins, T. Atkinson. "*Eructavit:* An Old French Metrical Paraphrase of Psalm XLIV." *Gesellschaft für romanische Literatur* 20. Dresden, 1909.

Jerome. *Sancti Eusebii Hieronymi epistulae.* Edited by Isidorus Hilberg. 1910. Reprint, New York: Johnson, 1970.

———. *Select Letters of St. Jerome.* Loeb Classical Library, translated by F. A. Wright. Cambridge: Harvard University Press, 1933.

Johanek, Peter. "König Arthur und die Plantagenets: Über den Zusammenhang von Historiographie und höfischer Epik in mittelalterlichen Propaganda," *Frühmittelalterliche Studien* 21 (1987): 346–89.

John, Helen. "Hildegard of Bingen: A New Medieval Philosopher?" *Hypatia* 7 (1992): 115–23.

John of Ephesus. *Lives of the Eastern Saints.* Edited and translated by E. W. Brooks. In *Patrologia Orientalis* vol. 18, fasc. 4. Paris: Firmin-Didot, 1924.

John of Lydus. *De magistratibus.* In *John Lydus and the Roman Past,* by Michael Maas. New York: Routledge, 1992.

John the Poor. *De contemplatione.* Edited by F. Richter. In *Archiv für Kunde österreicher Geschichtsquellen* 3 (1849).

Johnson, Lynn Stanley. "The Trope of the Scribe and the Question of Literary Authority in the Works of Julian of Norwich and Margery Kempe." *Speculum* 66 (1991): 820–38.

Johnson, Penelope D. *Equal in Monastic Profession: Religious Women in Medieval France*. Chicago: University of Chicago Press, 1991.

———. *Prayer, Patronage, and Power: The Abbey of La Trinité, Vendôme, 1032–1187*. New York: New York University Press, 1981.

Johnstone, Hilda. *Edward of Carnarvon*. Manchester: Manchester University Press, 1946.

———. "The County of Ponthieu, 1279–1307." *English Historical Review* 29 (1914): 435–52.

Jones, Robin F. "The Mechanics of Meaning in the Anglo-Norman *Voyage of Saint Brendan*." *Romanic Review* 71 (1980): 105–13.

———. "The Precocity of Anglo-Norman and the *Voyage of St Brendan*." In *The Nature of Medieval Narrative*, edited by Minnette Grunmann-Gaudet and Robin F. Jones. Lexington, Ky.: French Forum, 1980.

Jordan, Alyce A. "The Crafting of a King: Politics and Poetics in the Old Testament Windows of the Sainte Chapelle in Paris." Paper presented at the joint meeting of the Medieval Academy of America and the Medieval Association of the Pacific, Tucson, 1993.

Jordan, Karl. *Henry the Lion: A Biography*. Translated by P. S. Falla. Oxford: Clarendon, 1986.

Jourdain, Charles. "Mémoires sur l'éducation des femmes au Moyen Age." *Mémoires de l'Institut national de France, Académie des inscriptions et belles lettres* 28 (1874): 79–133.

Julian of Norwich. *A Book of Showings to the Anchoress Julian of Norwich*. Edited by Edmund Colledge and James Walsh. Toronto: Pontifical Institute, 1978.

Kauffmann, Claus Michael. *Romanesque Manuscripts, 1066–1190: A Survey of Manuscripts Illuminated in the British Isles*. London: Miller, 1975.

Kealey, Edward J. *Roger of Salisbury, Viceroy of England*. Berkeley and Los Angeles: University of California Press, 1972.

Keeler, Laura. *Geoffrey de Monmouth and the Late Latin Chroniclers*. Berkeley and Los Angeles: University of California Press, 1946.

Keen, Maurice H. *Chivalry*. New Haven, Conn.: Yale University Press, 1984.

Keiser, George R. "Patronage and Piety in Fifteenth-Century England: Margaret, Duchess of Clarence, Symon Wynter, and Beinecke MS 317." *Yale University Library Gazette* 60, nos. 1 and 2 (1985): 32–46.

Keller, Hans-Erich. "Literary Patronage in the Time of Philip Augustus." In *The Spirit of the Court: Selected Proceedings of the Fourth Congress of the International Courtly Literature Society*, edited by Glyn S. Burgess and Robert A. Taylor. Cambridge, England: Brewer, 1985.

Keller, John Esten. *Alfonso X, el Sabio*. New York: Twayne, 1967.

Kellogg, Judith. *Medieval Artistry and Exchange: Economic Institutions, Society, and Literary Form in Old French Narrative.* New York: Lang, 1989.

Kelly, Amy. *Eleanor of Aquitaine and the Four Kings.* Cambridge: Harvard University Press, 1958.

Kelly, Douglas. *The Art of Medieval French Romance.* Madison: University of Wisconsin Press, 1992.

Kelly, Henry Ansgar. "Gaston Paris's Courteous and Horsely Love." In *The Spirit of the Court: Selected Proceedings of the Fourth Congress of the International Courtly Literature Society,* edited by Glyn S. Burgess and Robert A. Taylor. Cambridge: Brewer, 1985.

Kelly, Joan. "Early Feminist Theory and the Querelle des Femmes, 1400–1789." In *Women, History, and Theory: The Essays of Joan Kelly.* Chicago: University of Chicago Press, 1984.

Kelly-Gadol, Joan. "Did Women Have a Renaissance?" In *Becoming Visible: Women in European History,* edited by Renate Bridenthal and Claudia Koonz. Boston: Houghton Mifflin, 1977.

Kempe, Margery. *The Book of Margery Kempe,* edited by Sanford Brown Meech and Hope Emily Allen. EETS, O.S. 212. London: Oxford University Press, 1940.

Kettering, Sharon. "The Patronage Power of Early Modern French Noblewomen." *Historical Journal* 32 (1989): 817–41.

———. *Patrons, Brokers, and Clients in Seventeenth-Century France.* New York: Oxford University Press, 1976.

Kibler, William W., ed. *Eleanor of Aquitaine: Patron and Politician.* Austin: University of Texas Press, 1976.

Kimmelman, Michael. "Havemeyer Collection: Magic at the Met Museum." *New York Times,* 26 March 1933, sec. C1, p. 30.

Kinder, Terryl N. "Blanche of Castile and the Cistercians." *Commentarii Cistercienses* 27, nos. 3 and 4 (1976): 161–88.

King, Catherine. "Medieval and Renaissance Matrons, Italian-Style." *Zeitschrift für Kunstgeschichte* 55 (1992): 372–93.

King, Donald. "Embroidery and Textiles." In *Age of Chivalry: Art in Plantagenet England, 1200–1400,* edited by J. J. G. Alexander and Paul Binski. London: Royal Academy of Arts in association with Weidenfeld and Nicolson, 1987.

Kittel, Ruth. "Women Under the Law in Medieval England, 1066–1485." In *The Women of England from Anglo-Saxon Times to the Present: Interpretive Bibliographical Essays,* edited by Barbara Kanner. Hamden, Conn.: Archon, 1979.

Kittredge, George L. "Chaucer and Some of His Friends." *Modern Philology* 1 (1903): 1–18.

Klapisch-Zuber, Christiane, ed. *Silences of the Middle Ages.* Vol. 2 of *A History of Women in the West.* General editors, Georges Duby and Michelle Perrot. Cambridge: Belknap Press of Harvard University Press, 1992.

Knight, J. K. "Usk Castle and Its Affinities." In *Ancient Monuments and Their Inter-*

pretation: Essays Presented to A. J. Taylor, edited by M. R. Apted, R. Gilyard-Beer, and A. D. Saunders. London and Chichester: Phillimore, 1977.

Knowles, David. *The Monastic Order in England, A History of Its Development from the Times of St Dunstan to the Fourth Lateran Council, 940–1216.* 2d ed. Cambridge: Cambridge University Press, 1966.

———. *The Religious Orders in England.* Cambridge: Cambridge University Press, 1957.

Könsgen, Ewald. "Zwei unbekannte Briefe zu den *Gesta regum* de Wilhelm von Malmesbury." *Deutsches Archiv für Erforschunges des Mittelalters* 31 (1975): 204–14.

Kornbluth, Genevra. "The Susanna Crystal of Lothar II: Chastity, the Church, and Royal Justice." *Gesta* 31 (1992): 25–39.

Körner, Sten. *The Battle of Hastings, England, and Europe, 1035–1066.* Lund: Gleerup, 1964.

Krautheimer, Richard. "Again Saints Sergius and Bacchus." *Jahrbuch der Österreichischen Byzantinistik* 23 (1974): 251–53.

Kren, Thomas, ed. *Margaret of York, Simon Marmion, and the Visions of Tondal: Papers Delivered at a Symposium Organized by the Department of Manuscripts of the J. Paul Getty Museum in Collaboration with the Huntingdon Library and Art Collections, June 21–24, 1990.* Malibu, Calif.: J. Paul Getty Museum, 1992.

Krochalis, Jeanne. "The Books and Reading of Henry V and His Circle." *Chaucer Review* 23, no. 1 (1988): 50–77.

Krueger, Roberta L. "Misogyny, Manipulation, and the Female Reader in Hue de Rotelande's *Ipomedon.*" In *Courtly Literature: Culture and Context. Selected Papers from the 5th Triennal Congress of the International Courtly Literature Society, Dalfsen, The Netherlands, 9–16 August, 1986,* edited by Keith Busby and Erik Kooper. Philadelphia: Benjamins, 1990.

———. *Women Readers and the Ideology of Gender in Old French Verse Romance.* Cambridge: Cambridge University Press, 1993.

Kylie, Edward, trans. *The English Correspondence of Saint Boniface.* New York: Cooper Square, 1966.

Kyriakis, Michael J. "The University: Origin and Early Phases in Constantinople." *Byzantion* 41 (1971): 161–82.

Labalme, Patricia H., ed. *Beyond Their Sex: Learned Women of the European Past.* New York: New York University Press, 1980.

Labarge, Margaret Wade. *A Small Sound of the Trumpet: Women in Medieval Life.* Boston: Beacon, 1986.

———. *A Baronial Household of the Thirteenth Century.* New York: Barnes and Noble, 1965.

Lage, G. Raynaud de. "Les 'romans antiques' dans l'histoire ancienne jusqu'à César." *Le moyen âge* 63 (1957): 267–309.

Lamb, Mary Ellen. "The Countess of Pembroke and the Art of Dying." In *Women in the Middle Ages and Renaissance: Literary and Historical Perspectives,* edited by Mary Beth Rose. Syracuse, N.Y.: Syracuse University Press, 1986.

Lamond, Elizabeth, ed. and trans. *Walter of Henley's Husbandry Together with an Anonymous Husbandry, Seneschaucie, and Robert Grosseteste's Rules.* London: Longmans, Green, 1890.

Lancaster, R. Kent. "Artists, Suppliers, and Clerks: The Human Factors in the Art Patronage of King Henry III." *Journal of the Warburg and Courtauld Institutes* 35 (1972): 81–107.

Lancelott, Francis. *The Queens of England and Their Times.* 2 vols. New York: Appleton, 1890–94.

[Langland, William.] *Piers the Plowman: A Critical Edition of the A-Version.* Edited by Thomas A. Knott and David C. Fowler. Baltimore: Johns Hopkins University Press, 1952.

———. *Piers Plowman, the B. Version. Will's Visions of Piers Plowman, Do-Well, Do-Better, and Do Best.* Edited by George Kane and E. Talbot Donaldson. London: Athlone Press, University of London, 1975.

Lapa, Rodriguez. *Dom Duarte e os Prosadored da Casa de Aviz.* Lisbon: Gráfica Lisbonenses, 1940.

Lasater, Alice E. *Spain to England: A Comparative Study of Arabic, European, and English Literature of the Middle Ages.* Jackson: University Press of Mississippi, 1974.

Latzke, Therese. "Der Topos Mantelgedicht." *Mittellateinisches Jahrbuch* 6 (1970): 109–31.

Lawless, George. *Augustine of Hippo and His Monastic Rule.* Oxford: Clarendon, 1987.

Lawrence, C. H. *St. Edmund of Abingdon: A Study in Hagiography and History.* Oxford: Clarendon, 1960.

Layettes du trésor des chartes. Edited by Alexandre Teulet, Joseph de Laborde, Elie Burger, and H. François Delaborde, 5 vols. Paris, 1863–1909. Reprint, Nendeln, Liechtenstein: Kraus, 1977.

Lazar, Moshé. "Cupid, the Lady, and the Poet: Modes of Love at Eleanor of Aquitaine's Court." In *Eleanor of Aquitaine: Patron and Politician,* edited by William W. Kibler. Austin: University of Texas Press, 1976.

LeBeuf, Jean. *Histoire de la ville de tout le diocèse de Paris.* Paris: Féchoz et Letovzey, 1883–93.

Leclercq, Jean. "Les relations entre Venance Fortunat et Sainte Radegonde." In *La riche personnalité de Sainte Radegonde.* Poitiers: Comité du XIVe centenaire, 1988.

Lee-Warner, James. "Petition of the Prior and Canons of Walsingham, Norfolk, to Elizabeth, Lady of Clare." *Archaeological Journal* 26 (1869): 166–73.

Lefèvre, Yves. "Autres romans du XIIe siècle." *Grundriss der romanischen Literaturen des Mittelalters,* vol. 4, pt. 1. Heidelberg, 1978.

Leff, Gordon. "Thomas Bradwardine's *De Causa Dei.*" *Journal of Ecclesiastical History* 7 (1956): 21–29.

Legge, Mary Dominica. *Anglo-Norman in the Cloisters: The Influence of the Orders upon Anglo-Norman Literature.* Edinburgh: Edinburgh University Press, 1950.

―――. *Anglo-Norman Letters and Petitions from All Souls MS. 182.* Anglo-Norman Text Society. Oxford: Blackwell, 1941.

―――. *Anglo-Norman Literature and Its Background.* Oxford: Clarendon, 1963.

―――. "L'influence littéraire de la cour d'Henri Beauclerc." In *Mélanges offerts à Rita Lejeune.* Gembloux, Belgium: Duculot, 1969. Vol. 1, 679–87.

―――. "The Influence of Patronage on Form in Medieval French Literature." In *Stil- und Formprobleme in der Literatur,* edited by Paul Böckmann. Heidelberg: Winter, 1959.

―――. "John Pecham's *Jerarchie.*" *Medium Aevum* 19 (1942): 77–84.

―――. "La littérature anglo-normande au temps d'Aliénor d'Aquitaine." *Cahiers de civilisation médiévale* 29 (1986): 113–18.

―――. "The Lord Edward's Vegetius." *Scriptorium* 7 (1953): 262–65.

―――. "Les origines de l'anglo-normand littéraire." *Revue de linguistique romane* 31 (1967): 44–54.

Le Glay, Edward. *Histoire de Jeanne de Constantinople, Comtesse de Flandre et de Hainaut.* Lille: Vanackere, 1841.

Lehugeur, Paul. *Histoire de Philippe le Long, roi de France, 1316–1322.* Paris: Hachette, 1897.

Lejeune, Rita. "La femme dans les littératures française et occitane du XIe au XIIIe siècles." In *La femme dans les civilisations des Xe–XIIIe siècles: Actes du colloque tenu à Poitiers les 23–25 septembre 1976.* Poitiers: Centre d'etudes supérieures de civilisation médiévale, Université de Poitiers, 1976. Published in *Cahiers de civilisation médiévale* 20 (1977): 201–16.

―――. "Rôle littéraire d'Aliénor d'Aquitaine et de sa famille." *Cultura Neolatina* 14 (1954): 5–57.

―――. "Rôle littéraire de la famille d'Aliénor d'Aquitaine." *Cahiers de civilisation médiévale* 1 (1958): 319–37.

Lekai, Louis J. *The Cistercians: Ideals and Reality.* Kent, Ohio: Kent State University Press, 1977.

Lemerle, Paul. *Byzantine Humanism: The First Phase.* Translated by Helen Linday and Ann Moffat. Canberra: Australian Association of Byzantine Studies, 1986.

le Neve, John. *Fasti Ecclesiae Anglicanae.* London: Institute for Historical Research, 1962.

Lépinois, Eugène de, and Lucien Merlet, eds. *Cartulaire de Notre Dame de Chartres.* Chartres: Garnier, 1862–65.

Lerner, Gerda. *The Creation of Patriarchy.* New York and Oxford: Oxford University Press, 1986.

Lethaby, W. R. "The Priory of Holy Trinity, or Christ Church, Aldgate." *Home Counties Magazine* 2, no. 5 (January 1900): 45–53.

Lewis, Suzanne. "The Apocalypse of Isabella of France." *Art Bulletin* 72 (1990): 224–60.

————. *The Art of Matthew Paris in the Chronica Majora*. Berkeley and Los Angeles: University of California Press, 1987.

————. "The Trinity Apocalypse and Eleanor of Castille." Paper presented at the 1990 Oxford Symposium, "The History of the Book."

Lida de Malkiel, María Rosa. "Arthurian Literature in Spain and Portugal." In *Arthurian Literature in the Middle Ages: A Collaborative History*, edited by Roger Sherman Loomis. Oxford: Clarendon 1959.

"Livre noir de la cathédrale de Coutances." In *Gallia Christiana*. Paris: Ex Typographia Regia, 1716–1865. 11, inst. col. 218.

Lizoain, Garrido, José Manuel, ed. *Documentación del Monasterio de Las Huelgas (1116–1230)* Fuentes Medievales Castellano-Leonesas, vol. 30. Burgos: Garrido Garrido, 1985.

Lizoain, Garrido, José Manuel, and Juan José García. *El monasterio de las Huelgas: Historia de un señorío cisterciense burgales, siglos XII y XIII*. Burgos: Garrido Garrido, 1988.

Lochrie, Karma. "*The Book of Margery Kempe*: The Marginal Woman's Search for Literary Authority." *Journal of Medieval and Renaissance Studies* 16 (1986): 33–55.

————. *Margery Kempe and Translations of the Flesh*. Philadelphia: University of Pennsylvania Press, 1991.

Loisne, Auguste Charles Menche de. "Les tableaux de l'église d'Hesdigneul-les-Béthune." *Bulletin archéologique du Comité des travaux historiques* (1901): 48–57.

Loomis, Roger Sherman. "Arthurian Influence on Sport and Spectacle." In *Arthurian Literature in the Middle Ages: A Collaborative History*. Oxford: Clarendon, 1959.

————. *Arthurian Legends in Medieval Art*. London: Oxford University Press, 1938.

————. "Edward I, Arthurian Enthusiast." *Speculum* 28 (1953): 114–24.

LoPrete, Kimberly A. "The Anglo-Norman Card of Adela of Blois." *Albion* 22, no. 4 (1990): 569–89.

————. "Exemplary Women Rulers in Hugh of Fleury's *Historia Ecclesiastica* Written for Adela of Blois." Paper presented to the Medieval Academy, March 1992.

————. "The Latin Literacy of Adela of Blois." Paper presented at the International Congress of Medieval Studies, Kalamazoo, Mich. May 1991.

Luard, Henry Richards, ed. *Lives of Edward the Confessor*. RS 3. London: Longman, Brown, Green, Longmans, and Roberts, 1858.

————, ed. *Flores historiarum per Matthaeum Westmonasteriensem collecti*. RS 95. London, 1890.

Lucas, Angela M. *Women in the Middle Ages: Religion, Marriage, and Letters*. New York: St. Martin's, 1983.

Lucas de Túy. *Crónica de España*. Edited by Julio Puyol y Alonso. Madrid: Tipografía de la "Revista de archivos, bibliotécas y museos," 1926.

Ludwich, Arthur, ed. *Eudociae Augustae.* Bibliotheca scriptorum Graecorum et Romanorum Teubneriana. Leipzig: Teubner, 1897.

Lueke, Janemarie. "The Unique Experience of Anglo-Saxon Nuns." In *Medieval Religious Women*, vol. 2, *Peaceweavers*, edited by Lillian T. Shank and John A. Nichols. Kalamazoo, Mich.: Cistercian, 1987.

Luscombe, David Edward. *The School of Peter Abelard.* Cambridge: Cambridge University Press, 1969.

Luttrell, Claude. *The Creation of the First Arthurian Romance.* Evanston, Ill.: Northwestern University Press, 1974.

Lytle, Guy Finch, and Stephen Orgel, eds. *Patronage in the Renaissance.* Princeton: Princeton University Press, 1981.

MacBain, William. "Some Religious and Secular Uses of the Vocabulary of *Fin'Amor* in the Early Decades of the Northern French Narrative Poem." *French Forum* 13, no. 3 (1988): 261–76.

MacCracken, Henry Noble, ed. *The Minor Poems of John Lydgate.* EETS, O.S. 192. London: Oxford University Press, 1934.

Macrae, E. "Geoffrey of Aspall's Commentaries on Aristotle." *Medieval and Renaissance Studies* 6 (1968): 94–134.

McBride, Deborah. "The Bishop and the Court: A Look at the Exchanges Between Hildebert of Lavardin and the Courtly Personages with Whom He Corresponded." Seminar paper, University of California, Santa Barbara, March 1991.

McCartney, Elizabeth. "The King's Mother and Royal Prerogative in Early Sixteenth-Century France." In *Medieval Queenship*, edited by John Carmi Parsons. New York: St. Martin's, 1993.

McCash, June Hall. "Marie de Champagne and Eleanor of Aquitaine: A Relationship Reexamined." *Speculum* 54 (1979): 698–711.

————. "Marie de Champagne's 'Cuer d'ome et cors de fame': Aspects of Feminism and Misogyny in the Twelfth Century." *The Spirit of the Court: Selected Proceedings of the Fourth Congress of the International Courtly Literature Society, Toronto, 1983*, edited by Glyn S. Burgess and Robert A. Taylor. Cambridge: Brewer, 1985.

————. "Mutual Love as a Medieval Ideal." In *Courtly Literature: Culture and Context: Selected Papers from the Fifth Triennial Congress of the International Courtly Literature Society, Dalfsen, The Netherlands, 9–16 August 1986*, edited by Keith Busby and Erik Kooper. Philadelphia: Brewer, 1990.

McKisack, May. *The Fourteenth Century, 1307–1399.* Oxford: Clarendon, 1956.

McLaughlin, Eleanor. "Women, Power, and the Pursuit of Holiness in Medieval Christianity." In *Women of Spirit: Female Leadership in the Jewish and Christian Traditions*, edited by Rosemary Ruether and Eleanor McLaughlin. New York: Simon and Schuster, 1979.

McLaughlin, T. P., ed. "Abelard's Rule for Religious Women." *Medieval Studies* 18 (1956): 241–92.

McNamara, Jo Ann. "Hagiography and Nunneries in Merovingian Gaul." In *Women of the Medieval World,* edited by Julius Kirshner and Suzanne F. Wemple. Oxford: Blackwell, 1985.

McNamara, Jo Ann, and Suzanne Wemple. "The Power of Women Through the Family in Medieval Europe, 500–1100." In *Women and Power in the Middle Ages,* edited by Mary Erler and Maryanne Kowaleski. Athens: University of Georgia Press, 1988.

Maddox, Donald, and Sara Sturm-Maddox. *Literary Aspects of Courtly Culture: Selected Papers from the Seventh Triennial Congress of the International Courtly Literature Society, University of Massachusetts, Amherst, USA, 27 July–1 August 1992.* Cambridge, England: Brewer, 1994.

Malalas, John. *The Chronicle of John Malalas.* Translated by Elizabeth Jeffreys, Michael Jeffreys, and Roger Scott. Melbourne: Australian Association for Byzantine Studies, 1986.

Mallet, C. E. "The Empress Theodora." *English Historical Review* 2 (1887): 1–20.

Mallet, Jacques. "Modalités du mécénat des comtes et comtesses d'Anjou au XIe siècle." In *Artistes, artisans, et production artistique au Moyen Age,* vol. 2, *Commande et travail,* edited by Xavier Barral I Altet. Paris: Picard, 1987.

Maltman, M. N. "Boy-Bishop." *New Catholic Encyclopedia,* 2:741.

Mandach, André de. "A la découverte du code secret d'une tapisserie du XVe siècle: La justice de Trajan et d'Archambault de Bourbon." In *Trésors du Musée d'histoire de Berne.* Annecy, 1976.

———. *Chronique dite saintongeaise: Texte franco-occitan inédit "Lee." A la découverte d'une chronique gasconne du XIIIe siècle et de sa poitevinisation.* Tübingen: Niemeyer, 1970.

———. "Naissance et développement de la chanson de geste en Europe." In *Chronique de Turpin,* vol. 2. Geneva: Droz, 1963.

Mango, Cyril. "The Church of Saints Sergius and Bacchus at Constantinople and the Alleged Tradition of Octagonal Palatine Churches." *Jahrbuch der Österreichischen Byzantinistik* 21 (1972): 189–94.

———. "The Church of Sts. Sergius and Bacchus Once Again." *Byzantinische Zeitschrift* 68 (1975): 385–92.

Mango, Cyril, and Ihor Sevčenko. "Remains of the Church of Saint Polyeuktos at Constantinople." *Dumbarton Oaks Papers* 15 (1961): 243–47.

Manning, Owen, and William Bray. *The History and Antiquities of the County of Surrey.* 3 vols. London: White, 1809.

Marbod of Rennes. *Opera omnia.* In PL, vol. 171. Paris, 1893.

Marrow, Deborah. *The Art Patronage of Maria de' Medici.* Ann Arbor: UMI Research Press, 1982.

Martin, Alan R. *Franciscan Architecture in England.* Manchester: Manchester University Press, 1937.

Martin, F. X. "The Augustinian Friaries of Pre-Reformation Ireland." *Augustiniana* 6 (1956): 361–62.

Martin, Henry. *Les miniaturistes français.* Paris: Leclerc, 1906.

Martins, Mario. *Estudos da literatura medieval.* 1956. Reprint, Lisbon: Verbo, 1969.

Mathews, Thomas F. "Architecture et liturgie dans les premières églises palatiales de Constantinople." *Revue de l'art* 24 (1974): 22–29.

Meiss, Millard. *French Painting in the Time of Jean de Berry.* London: Phaidon, 1967.

Menander. *Menander Rhetor.* Translated and edited by D. A. Russell and N. G. Wilson. Oxford: Oxford University Press, 1981.

Mertes, Kate. *The English Noble Household, 1250–1600.* Oxford: Blackwell, 1988.

Metcalfe, Carol A. "Alice Chaucer, Duchess of Suffolk, c. 1404–1475." Ph.D. diss., University of Keele, 1970.

Metham, John. *The Works of John of Metham Including "The Romance of Amoryus and Cleopes."* Edited by Hardin Craig. EETS, O.S. 132. London: Kegan Paul, Trench, Trübner, 1916.

Meyer, Paul, ed. *L'histoire de Guillaume le Maréchal.* Paris: Renouard, 1891–1901.

———. "Les premières compilations françaises d'histoire ancienne." *Romania* 14 (1885): 1–81.

———. "Prologue en vers français d'une histoire perdue de Philippe Auguste." *Romania* 6 (1877): 494–98.

Micha, Alexandre. "Chrétien de Troyes." *Grundriss der romanischen Literaturen des Mittelalters.* Vol. 4, pt. 1. Heidelberg: Winter, 1978.

Michel, Francisque, and Charles Bémont, eds. *Rôles gascons, 1242–1307.* Paris, 1896–1906.

Michelant, Henri, ed. *Der Roman von Escanor, von Gerard von Amiens.* Tübingen, 1886.

———. *"Guillaume de Palerne" publié d'après le manuscrit de la Bibliothèque de l'Arsenal à Paris.* Paris: Firmin-Didot, 1876.

Midmer, Roy. *English Mediaeval Monasteries, 1066–1540.* Athens: University of Georgia Press, 1979.

Millar, Eric, and Montague Rhodes James. *The Bohun Manuscripts: A Group of Five Manuscripts Executed in England About 1370 for Members of the Family.* Oxford: Roxburghe Club, 1936.

Miner, Dorothy. *Anastaise and Her Sisters: Women Artists of the Middle Ages.* Baltimore: Walters Art Gallery, 1974.

La miniature flamande: Le mécenat de Philippe le Bon. Exposition organisée à l'occasion du 400e anniversaire de la fondation de la Bibliothèque Royale de Philippe II le 12 avril 1559. Brussels: Bibliothèque Royale, 1959.

"Les miniatures du 'Scivias' de Sainte Hildegarde, conservées à la Bibliothèque de Wiesbaden." In *Académie des inscriptions et belles lettres: Monuments et mémoires.* Vol. 18. Paris: Leroux, 1911.

Mirrer, Louise, ed. *Upon My Husband's Death: Widows in the Literature and Histories of Medieval Europe.* Ann Arbor: University of Michigan Press, 1992.

Mitchell, Linda E. "Noble Widowhood in the Thirteenth Century: Three Generations of Mortimer Widows, 1246–1334." In *Upon My Husband's Death: Widows in the*

Literature and Histories of Medieval Europe, edited by Louise Mirrer. Ann Arbor: University of Michigan Press, 1992.

Mollat, Michel. *Les pauvres au Moyen Age*. Brussels: Complexe, 1978.

Molinier, Emile, and Auguste Longnon, eds. *Obituaires de la province de Sens*. Vol. 2, *Diocèse de Chartres*. Paris: Imprimerie nationale, 1906.

Moore, John C. Review of *Eleanor of Aquitaine: Patron and Politician*, edited by William W. Kibler. *Speculum* 53 (1978): 148–49.

Moore, Samuel. "General Aspects of Patronage in the Middle Ages." *Library*, 3d ser., 4 (1913): 369–92.

———. "Patrons of Letters in Norfolk and Suffolk, c. 1450." *PMLA* 27 (1912): 186–207; 28 (1913): 79–105.

Moorman, John H. R. *The Grey Friars in Cambridge, 1225–1538*. Cambridge: Cambridge University Press, 1952.

Morgan, Nigel J. *Early Gothic Manuscripts, 1190–1285: A Survey of Manuscripts Illuminated in the British Isles*. London: Oxford University Press, 1982–88.

Mourin, Louis. "Poésies religieuses françaises inconnues dans des manuscrits de Bruxelles et d'Evora." *Scriptorium* 3 (1949): 218–29.

Muckle, J. T., ed. "Abelard's Letter of Consolation to a Friend and Letters 1–7." *Medieval Studies* 12 (1950): 163–213.

———. "The Letter of Heloise on Religious Life and Abelard's First Reply." *Mediaeval Studies* 17 (1955): 240–81.

———. "The Personal Letters Between Abelard and Heloise." *Mediaeval Studies* 15 (1953): 47–94.

Muñoz Sendino, José. *La escala de Mahoma*. Madrid: Ministerio de asuntos exteriores, Dirección general de relaciones culturales, 1949.

Muratova, Xenia. "Bestiaries: An Aspect of Medieval Patronage." In *Art and Patronage in the English Romanesque*, edited by Sarah Macready and F. H. Thompson. Society of Antiquaries of London, Occasional Paper, n.s., 8. London: Burlington House, 1986.

Musset, Lucien. "Le mécénat des princes normands au XIe siècle." In *Artistes, artisans, et production artistique au Moyen Age*, vol. 2, *Commande et travail*, edited by Xavier Barral I Altet. Paris: Picard, 1987.

Musto, Ronald G. "Queen Sancia and the Spiritual Franciscans." In *Women of the Medieval World*, edited by Julius Kirschner and Suzanne F. Wemple. Oxford: Blackwell, 1985.

Mütherich, Florentine, and Karl Dachs, eds. *Regensburger Buchmalerei von frühkarolingischer Zeit bis zum Ausgang des Mittelalters*. Austellung der Bayerischen Staatsbibliothek München und der Museen der Stadt Regensburg. Munich: Prestel, 1987.

Myers, Bernard S., and Trewin Copplestone, eds. *Art Treasures in France: Monuments, Masterpieces, Commissions, and Collections*. New York: McGraw-Hill, 1969.

Naber, Antoinette. "Les goûts littéraires d'un bibliophile de la cour de Bourgogne." In *Courtly Literature: Culture and Context: Selected Papers from the 5th Triennial Congress of the International Courtly Literature Society, Dalfsen, The Netherlands, 9–*

16 August, 1986, edited by Keith Busby and Erik Kooper. Philadelphia: Benjamins, 1990.

Nelson, Janet L. "Gender and Genre in Women Historians of the Early Middle Ages." In *L'historiographie médiévale en Europe,* edited by Jean-Philippe Genet. Paris: Editions du Centre national de la recherche scientifique, 1991.

———. "Perceptions du pouvoir chez les historiennes a du haut moyen âge." In *La femme au moyen âge,* edited by Michel Rouche and Jean Heuclin. Maubeuge: Touzot, 1990.

Newman, Barbara. "Divine Power Made Perfect in Weakness: St. Hildegard on the Frail Sex." In *Medieval Religious Women.* Vol. 2 of *Peaceweavers,* edited by John A. Nichols and Lillian Thomas Shank. Kalamazoo, Mich.: Cistercian, 1987.

———. "Flaws in the Golden Bowl: Gender and Spiritual Formation in the Twelfth Century." *Traditio* 45 (1989–90): 111–46.

———. *Sister of Wisdom: St. Hildegard's Theology of the Feminine.* Berkeley and Los Angeles: University of California Press, 1987.

Newton, Stella Mary. *Fashion in the Age of the Black Prince.* Totowa, N.J.: Rowman and Littlefield, 1980.

Nicolas, Nicholas Harris, ed. *Testamenta Vetusta.* London: Nichols, 1826.

Nichols, John. *A Collection of All the Wills Now Known to Be Extant of the Kings and Queens of England, Princes and Princesses of Wales, and Every Branch of the Blood Royal, from the Reign of William the Conqueror to that of Henry the Seventh Exclusive.* London: Nichols, 1780.

———, ed. *Collection of Ordinances and Regulations for the Government of the Royal Household.* London: Society of Antiquaries, 1790.

Nichols, John Gough, and John Bruce, eds. *Wills from Doctors' Commons.* Westminster: Nichols for the Camden Society, 1863.

Nichols, Stephen G., Jr., John A. Galm, and A. Bartlett Giamatti, with Roger J. Porter, Seth L. Wolitz, and Claudette M. Charbonneau, eds. *The Songs of Bernart de Ventadorn.* Rev. ed. Chapel Hill: University of North Carolina Press, 1965.

Nicholson, Derek E. T., ed. *The Poems of the Troubadour Peire Rogier.* Manchester: Manchester University Press, 1976.

Nicholson, Joan, "Feminae Gloriosae: Women in the Age of Bede." In *Medieval Women,* edited by Derek Baker. Oxford: Blackwell, 1978.

Nilgen, Ursula. "Psalter der Christina von Markyate (sogenannter Albani-Psalter)." In *Der Schatz von St. Godehard.* Exhibition catalog. Hildesheim: Diözesan-Museum, 1988.

Nochlin, Linda. "Why Are There No Great Women Artists?" In *Women in Sexist Society: Studies in Power and Powerlessness,* edited by Vivian Gornick and Barbara Moran. New York: Basil, 1971. Reprinted in *Art and Sexual Politics,* edited by Thomas B. Hess and Elizabeth C. Baker. New York: Macmillan, 1971.

Nye, Andrea. "A Woman's Thought or a Man's Discipline? The Letters of Abelard and Heloise." *Hypatia* 7 (1992): 1–22.

O'Brien, Mary. *Politics of Reproduction.* Boston: Routledge and Kegan Paul, 1981.

Ochinsky, Dorothea. *Walter of Henley and Other Treatises on Estate Management and Accounting.* Oxford: Clarendon, 1971.

O'Callaghan, Joseph F. *A History of Medieval Spain.* Ithaca: Cornell University Press, 1975.

Ong, Walter J. "Latin Language Study as a Renaissance Puberty Rite." *Studies in Philology* 56 (1959): 103–24.

Openshaw, Kathleen M. "Weapons in the Daily Battle: Images of the Conquest of Evil in the Early Medieval Psalter." *Art Bulletin* 75 (1993): 17–38.

Orderic Vital. *The Ecclesiastical History of Orderic Vitalis.* Edited and translated by Marjorie Chibnall. Oxford: Clarendon, 1969–80.

———. *Historiae ecclesiasticae.* Edited by Auguste Le Prévost. Paris: Renouard, 1838–55.

Origen. *On First Principles.* Text and translation by G. W. Butterworth. New York: Harper and Row, 1966.

Orme, Nicholas. *From Childhood to Chivalry: The Education of the English Kings and Aristocracy, 1066–1530.* New York: Methuen, 1984.

———. "The Education of the Courtier." In *The English Court in the Later Middle Ages,* edited by V. J. Scattergood and J. W. Sherborne. London: Duckworth, 1983.

Ormont, H. "Anonyme, auteur du 'Livre de la Tresoye,' de l'abbaye d'Origny." in *Histoire littéraire de la France,* 35: 640–41. Paris: Imprimerie Nationale, 1921.

Ortner, Sherry B., and Harriet Whitehead, eds. *Sexual Meanings: The Cultural Construction of Gender and Sexuality.* Cambridge: Cambridge University Press, 1981.

Oschinsky, Dorothea. *Walter of Henley and Other Treatises on Estate Management and Accounting.* Oxford: Clarendon, 1971.

Owen, Annie. *Le traité de Walter de Bibbesworth sur la langue française.* Paris: Presses Universitaires de France, 1929.

Pace, George B. "Speght's Chaucer and MS. GG.4.27." *Studies in Bibliography* 21 (1968): 225–35.

Pächt, Otto, and J. J. G. Alexander. *Illuminated Manuscripts in the Bodleian Library, Oxford.* Oxford: Clarendon, 1966–73.

Pächt, Otto, C. R. Dodwell, and Francis Wormald. *The St Albans Psalter (Albani Psalter).* London: Warburg Institute, 1960.

Painter, Sidney. *The Scourge of the Clergy: Peter of Dreux, Duke of Brittany.* Baltimore: Johns Hopkins University Press, 1937.

Palgrave, Francis. *The Antient Kalendars and Inventories of the Treasury of His Majesty's Exchequer.* Record Commission. London: Eyre and Spottiswoode, 1836.

Paris, Gaston. *Esquisse historique de la littérature française au Moyen Age.* Paris: Colin, 1907.

———. "Etudes sur les romans de la Table ronde." *Romania* 10 (1881): 465–96; 12 (1883): 459–534.

———. *La littérature française au Moyen Age.* 1914. Reprint, New York: AMS, 1975.

———. *Manuel d'ancien-français: La littérature au Moyen Age, XIe–XIVe siècles.* Paris, 1888.

———. "Un poème inédit de Martin LeFranc." *Romania* 16 (1887): 383–437.

———. *La poésie du Moyen Age: Leçons et lectures.* Paris: Hachette, 1885–95.

———. "La vie de saint Edmond, archevêque de Cantorbéry. Edited by A. T. Baker. *Romania* 55 (1929): 332–81.

Paris, Matthew. *English History From the Year 1235 to 1273.* Translated by J. A. Giles. London: Bohn, 1852–54.

———. *Historia Anglorum.* Edited by Frederic Madden. RS 44. London: Longmans, Green, Reader, and Dyer, 1866–69.

Paris, Paulin. "Livres de Jehanne d'Evreux." *Bulletin du Bibliophile* (1838): 492–94.

———. *Nouvelle étude sur la Chanson d'Antioche.* Paris: Techener, 1878.

Parkes, Malcolm B. "The Literacy of the Laity." In *Literature and Western Civilization: The Medieval World,* edited by David Daiches and Anthony Thorlby. London: Aldus, 1973.

Parsons, John Carmi. "The Beginnings of English Administration in Ponthieu: An Unnoticed Document of 1280." *Mediaeval Studies* 50 (1988): 371–403.

———. *The Court and Household of Eleanor of Castile in 1290.* Toronto: Pontifical Institute of Mediaeval Studies, 1977.

———. "Eleanor of Castile: Legend and Reality Through Seven Centuries." In *Eleanor of Castile, 1290–1990: Essays to Commemorate the 700th Anniversary of Her Death, 28 November 1290,* edited by David Parsons. Stamford, England: Watkins in association with the University of Leicester Department of Adult Education, 1991.

———. "Family, Sex, and Power: The Rhythms of Medieval Queenship." In *Medieval Queenship,* edited by John Carmi Parsons. New York: St. Martin's, 1993.

———. "Mothers, Daughters, Marriage, and Power: Some Plantagenet Evidence, 1150–1500. In *Medieval Queenship,* edited by John Carmi Parsons. New York: St. Martin's, 1993.

———. "Piety, Power, and the Reputations of Two Thirteenth-Century English Queens." In *Queens, Regents and Potentates,* vol. 1 of *Women of Power.* Edited by Theresa M. Vann. Cambridge, England: Academia, 1993.

———. "The Queen's Intercession in Thirteenth-Century England." In *Power of the Weak,* edited by S. B. MacLean and J. Carpenter. Urbana: University of Illinois Press, in press.

———. "The Second Exhumation of King Arthur's Remains at Glastonbury, 19 April 1278." *Arthurian Literature* 12 (1992): 173–77.

———. "The Year of Eleanor of Castile's Birth and Her Children by Edward I." *Mediaeval Studies* 46 (1984): 245–65.

———, ed. *Medieval Queenship.* New York: St. Martin's, 1993.

Parsons, Sister Wilfrid, trans. *Saint Augustine: Letters.* New York: Fathers of the Church, 1951–56.

Paul the Deacon, *Pauli Diaconi historia Romana.* Edited by Amedeo Crivellucci. Rome: Tipografia del Senato, 1914.

Pearsall, Derek. *John Lydgate.* London: Routledge and Kegan Paul, 1970.

Peire d'Auvergne. *Peire d'Auvergne: Die Lieder.* Edited by Rudolph Zenker. 1900. Reprint, Geneva: Slatkine, 1977.

Pellegrin, Elizabeth. *Manuscrits de Pétrarque dans les bibliothèques de France.* Censimento dei Codici Petrarcheschi, no. 2. Padua: Antenore, 1966.

Perdizet, Paul. "Jean Miélot, l'un des traducteurs de Philippe le Bon." *Revue de l'histoire littéraire de la France* 14 (1907): 472–82.

Perrin, E. Sainte-Marie. *La belle vie de Sainte Colette de Corbie, 1381–1447.* Paris: Plon-Nourrit, 1921.

Perrot, Françoise. "Le vitrail, la croisade, et la Champagne: Réflexion sur les fenêtres hautes du choeur à la cathédrale de Chartres." In *Les champenois et la croisade: Actes des quatrièmes journées remoises, 27–28 novembre, 1987,* edited by Yvonne Bellanger and Danielle Quéruel. Paris: Amateurs de Livres, 1989.

Petit-Dutaillis, Charles. "Fragment de l'histoire de Philippe Auguste roi de France: Chronique en français des années 1214–1216." *Bibliothèque de l'Ecole des Chartres* 87 (1926): 98–141.

Petot, Pierre, and André Vandenbossche. "Le statut de la femme dans les pays coutumiers français du XIIIe au XVIIe siècle." In *La femme: Recueils de la Société Jean Bodin pour l'histoire comparative des institutions,* vol. 12. Brussels: De Boeck, 1952–62.

Petrarch, Francesco. *De remediis utriusque fortunae.* Translated by Peter Stahel and Georg Spalatin. Augsburg: Heinrich Steiner, 1532. Reprint, Leipzig: Manfred Lemmer, 1984.

Pevsner, Nikolaus. *Suffolk.* Harmondsworth, England: Penguin, 1961.

Pickford, Cedric E. "Miscellaneous French Prose Romances." In *Arthurian Literature in the Middle Ages,* edited by Roger Sherman Loomis. Oxford: Clarendon, 1959.

Pidoux de Maduère, Pierre André. *Sainte Colette.* Paris: Gabalda, 1924.

Pietropaolo, Domenico. "Literary Taste at the Court of the Last Medici." In *The Spirit of the Court: Selected Proceedings of the Fourth Congress of the International Courtly Literature Society, Toronto 1983,* edited by Glyn S. Burgess and Robert A. Taylor. Cambridge, England: Brewer, 1985.

Piramus, Denis. *La "Vie seint Edmund le rei": Poème anglo-normand du XIIe siècle.* Edited by Hilding Kjellmann. 1935. Reprint, Geneva: Slatkine, 1974.

Plato. *Phaedrus.* Translated by R. Hackforth. Indianapolis: Bobbs Merrill, 1952.

Plummer, John, ed. *The Hours of Catherine of Cleves.* New York: Braziller, 1966.

Pollard, A. J. *John Talbot and the War in France, 1427–1453.* London: Royal Historical Society, 1983.

Poole, Austin Lane. *From Domesday Book to Magna Carta, 1087–1216.* 2d ed. Oxford: Clarendon, 1955.

Prestwich, Michael. *Edward I.* Berkeley and Los Angeles: University of California Press, 1988.

Previté-Orton, C. W. *The Shorter Cambridge Medieval History.* Cambridge: Cambridge University Press, 1953.

Procopius. *Anecdota*. Translated by Henry Bronson Dewing. Loeb Classical Library. Cambridge: Harvard University Press, 1935.

———. *Buildings*. Translated by Henry Bronson Dewing. Loeb Classical Library. Cambridge: Harvard University Press, 1940.

Procter, Evelyn Stefanos. *Alfonso X of Castile: Patron of Learning*. Oxford: Clarendon, 1951. Reprint, Westport, Conn.: Greenwood Press, 1980.

Pryor, Mary Ruth, ed. "Thomas Hoccleve's Series: An Edition of Manuscript Durham Cosin V III 9." Ph.D. diss., University of California, Los Angeles, 1968.

Quarré, Pierre. *Plaques de fondation d'Isabelle de Portugal, duchesse de Bourgogne, aux Chartreuse de Bâle et de Champol-les-Dijon*. Basel: Historisches Museum, 1960.

Quentin-Bauchart, Ernest. *Les femmes bibliophiles de France*. Paris: Morgand, 1886.

Raby, Frederic James Edward. *A History of Christian Latin Poetry*. Oxford: Clarendon, 1927.

———. *Poems of John of Hoveden*. Surtees Society 154. Durham: Andrews, 1939.

Radford, U. M. "The Wax Images Found at Exeter Cathedral." *Antiquaries Journal* 29 (1949): 164–68.

Radice, Betty, trans. *The Letters of Abelard and Heloise*. Harmondsworth, England: Penguin, 1974.

Randall, Lillian M. C. *Medieval and Renaissance Manuscripts in the Walters Art Gallery*. Vol. 1, *France, 875–1240*. Baltimore: Johns Hopkins University Press, 1989.

Ransford, Rosalind, ed. *The Early Charters of the Augustinian Canons of Waltham Abbey, Essex 1062–1230*. Woodbridge, England: Boydell, 1989.

Rawcliffe, Carole. *The Staffords, Earls of Stafford and Dukes of Buckingham, 1394–1521*. Cambridge: Cambridge University Press, 1978.

Reimer, Stephen R. "The Lydgate Canon: A Project Description." *Literary and Linguistic Computing* 5, no. 3 (1990): 248–49.

Reinach, Solomon. "Un portrait d'Isabelle de Portugal, 1429." *Revue archéologique* 5 (1922): 174.

Reindel, Kurt. *Die Briefe der deutschen Kaiserzeit*, 4 vols. *Die Briefe des Petrus Damiani* (Munich: MGH 1983–1988, 1989).

Recueil des historiens des Gaules et de la France. Paris: Aux dépens des librairies associés, 1738–1919.

Reno, Christine, "Virginity as Ideal in Christine de Pizan's *Cité des Dames*." In *Ideals for Women in the Works of Christine de Pizan*, edited by Diane Bornstein. Detroit: Michigan Consortium for Medieval and Early Modern Studies, 1981.

Rhodes, Walter E. "The Inventory of Jewels and the Wardrobe of Queen Isabella." *English Historical Review* 12 (1897): 517–21.

Richard, Alfred. *Histoire des comtes de Poitou, 778–1204* Vol. 2. Paris: Picard, 1903.

Richard, Jules Marie. "Les livres de Mahaut, Comtesse d'Artois et de Bourgogne." *Revue des questions historiques* 40 (1886): 135–41.

———. *Une petite-nièce de Saint Louis, Mahaut, comtesse d'Artois et de Bourgogne (1302–1329)*. Paris: Champion, 1887.

Richardson, Henry Gerald. *The Governance of Mediaeval England from the Conquest to Magna Carta.* Edinburgh: University of Edinburgh Press, 1963.

――――. "The Letters and Charters of Eleanor of Aquitaine." *English Historical Review* 74 (1959): 193–213.

Rickert, Margaret. *Painting in Britain in the Middle Ages.* Baltimore: Penguin, 1954.

Riley, Henry Thomas, ed. *Munimenta Gildhallae Londoniensis: Liber albus, Liber custumarum, et Liber Horn.* RS 120. London: Longman, Brown, Green, Longmans, and Roberts, 1859.

Ritchie, R. L. G. "The Date of the *Voyage of St Brendan.*" *Medium Aevum* 19 (1950): 64–66.

――――. *The Normans in Scotland.* Edinburgh: University of Edinburgh Press, 1954.

Rodríguez López, Amancio. *El Real Monasterio de las Huelgas y el Hospital del Rey.* Vol. 1. Burgos: Centro Catolico, 1907.

Roelker, Nancy L. "The Role of Noblewomen in the French Reformation." *Archive for Reformation History* 63, no. 2 (1972): 168–95.

Rogers, Nicholas. "The Original Owner of the Fitzwarin Psalter." *Antiquaries Journal* 59 (1989): 257–60.

Roisin, Simone. "L'efflorescence cistercienne et le courant féminin de piété au XIIIe siècle." *Revue d'histoire ecclésiastique* 39 (1943): 342–78.

Rooses, Max. "Les contrats passés entre Rubens et Marie de Medicis concernant les deux galéries du Luxembourg." *Bulletin-Rubens* 5 (1910): 216–20.

Rosaldo, Michelle Zimbalist. "Woman, Culture and Society: A Theoretical Overview." In *Woman, Culture and Society,* edited by Michelle Zimbalist Rosaldo and Louise Lamphere. Stanford: Stanford University Press, 1974.

Rose, Mary Beth, ed. *Women in the Middle Ages and Renaissance: Literary and Historical Perspectives.* Syracuse, N.Y.: Syracuse University Press, 1986.

Rosenthal, Joel T. "Aristocratic Cultural Patronage and Book Bequests, 1350–1500." *Bulletin of the John Rylands University Library of Manchester* 64 (1982): 522–48.

――――. *Medieval Women and the Sources of Medieval History.* Athens: University of Georgia Press, 1990.

――――. *The Purchase of Paradise.* London: Routledge and Kegan Paul, 1972.

――――. "The Universities and the English Nobility." *History of Education Quarterly* 9 (1969): 415–37.

Rosin, A. "Die 'Hierarchie' des John Peckham, historisch interpretiert." *Zeitschrift für Romanische Philologie* 2 (1932): 583–614.

Ross, Charles. *Richard III.* Berkeley and Los Angeles: University of California Press, 1981.

Ross, C. D. "The Household Accounts of Elizabeth Berkeley, Countess of Warwick, 1420–1." *Transactions of the Bristol and Gloucestershire Archaeological Society* 70 (1952): 81–105.

Roth, Francis. *The English Austin Friars, 1249–1538.* New York: Augustinian Historical Institute, 1966.

Rotha, Mary Clay, *The Medieval Hospitals of England.* London: n.p., 1909.

Rothwell, W. "A Mis-judged Author and a Mis-used Text: Walter de Bibbesworth and his 'Tretiz.'" *Modern Language Review* 77 (1982): 282–93.

——. "The Role of French in Thirteenth-Century England." *Bulletin of the John Rylands Library* 58 (1976): 462–66.

Rubin, Miri. *Charity and Community in Medieval Cambridge.* Cambridge: Cambridge University Press, 1987.

Ruether, Rosemary. "Mothers of the Church." In *Women of Spirit: Female Leadership in the Jewish and Christian Traditions,* edited by Rosemary Ruether and Eleanor McLaughlin. New York: Simon and Shuster, 1979.

Ruiz, T. F. "Une monarchie sans sacre: La monarchie castillane du Bas Moyen Age." *Annales ESC* 3 (1984): 429–53.

——. "Unsacred Monarchy: The Kings of Castile in the Late Middle Ages." (Translation of "Une monarchie sans sacre.") In *Rites of Power: Symbolism, Ritual and Politics Since the Middle Ages,* edited by Sean Wilentz. Philadelphia: University of Pennsylvania Press, 1985.

Russell, Josiah Cox. "Master Henry of Avranches as an International Poet." *Speculum* 3 (1928): 34–63.

Russell, Josiah Cox, and Hieronimus, J. P., eds. *The Shorter Latin Poems of Master Henry of Avranches Relating to England.* Cambridge, Mass.: Medieval Academy of America, 1935.

Rutherford, A. "The Anglo-Norman Chronicle of Nicholas Trivet." Ph.D. diss., University of London, 1932.

Ruud, Martin B. *Thomas Chaucer.* Minneapolis: University of Minnesota Press, 1926.

Ruud, Marylou. "Monks in the World: The Case of Gundulph of Rochester." *Anglo-Norman Studies* 11 (1989): 245–60.

Rymer, Thomas. *Foedera, conventiones litterae, et cujuscunque generis acta publica.* 2d ed. London: Tonson, 1727.

Sabine, Ernest L. "Latrines and Cesspools of Mediaeval London." *Speculum* 9 (1934): 303–21.

Salter, Elizabeth. *English and International: Studies in the Literature, Art, and Patronage of Medieval England.* Edited by Derek Pearsall and Nicolette Zeeman. Cambridge: Cambridge University Press, 1988.

Sande, Siri. "Zur Porträtplastik des sechsten nachchristlichen Jahrhunderts." *Acta ad archaeologiam et artium historiam pertinentia* 6 (1975): 65–106.

Sandler, Lucy Freeman. *Gothic Manuscripts, 1285–1385: A Survey of Manuscripts Illuminated in the British Isles.* London: Miller; New York: Oxford University Press, 1986.

Sankovitch, Tilde. "Lombarda's Reluctant Mirror: Speculum of Another Poet." In *The Voice of the Trobairitz: Perspectives on the Women Troubadours,* edited by William D. Paden. Philadelphia: University of Pennsylvania Press, 1989.

Santi, Bruno. *Le ricordanze di Neri di Bicci, 10 marzo 1453–24 aprile 1475.* Pisa: Marlin, 1976.

Sauerländer, Willibald. *Gothic Sculpture in France, 1140–1270.* New York: Abrams, 1972.

Saunders, Elfrida. *English Illumination.* 1933. Reprint, New York: Hacker, 1969.

Saward, Susan. *The Golden Age of Maria de' Medici.* Ann Arbor: University of Michigan Press, 1982.

Scase, Wendy. *Piers Plowman and the New Anticlericalism.* Cambridge: Cambridge University Press, 1989.

Scattergood, V. J., and J. W. Sherborne, eds. *English Court Culture in the Later Middle Ages.* London: Duckworth, 1983.

Schaus, Margaret, and Susan Mosher Stuard. "Citizens of No Mean City: Medieval Women's History." *Choice* 30 (December 1992): 583–95.

Scheffer-Boichorst, Paul, ed. *Chronica Albrici monachi Trium Fontium a monacho novi monasterii Hoiensis interpolata.* MGH SS, no. 23. Hanover, 1874.

Scheler, Auguste, ed. *Dits de Watriquez de Couvin.* Brussels: Devaux, 1868.

———, ed. *Dits et contes de Baudouin de Conde et de son fils Jean de Conde.* Brussels: Devaux, 1866–67.

Schibanoff, Susan. "Taking the Gold Out of Egypt: The Art of Reading as a Woman." In *Gender and Reading: Essays on Readers, Texts and Contexts,* edited by Elizabeth A. Flynn and Patrocinio P. Schweickart. Baltimore: Johns Hopkins University Press, 1986.

Schirmer, Walter F. *John Lydgate: A Study in the Culture of the Fifteenth Century.* Translated by A. E. Keep. Berkeley and Los Angeles: University of California Press, 1961.

Schirmer, Walter F., and Ulrich Broich. *Studien zum literarischen Patronatim England des 12. Jahrhunderts.* Cologne: Westdeutscher, 1962.

Schleif, Corine. "Hands That Appoint, Anoint, and Ally: Late Medieval Donor Strategies for Appropriating Approbation Through Painting." *Art History* 16 (1993): 1–32.

———. "The Man on the Right and the Woman on the Left: Place and Displacement in Sacred Iconography and Donor Imagery." Unpublished paper.

Schulenberg, Jane. "Saints' Lives as a Source for the History of Women, 500–1100." In *Medieval Women and the Sources of Medieval History,* edited by Joel T. Rosenthal. Athens: University of Georgia Press, 1990.

Schultz, H. C. "Thomas Hoccleve, Scribe." *Speculum* 12 (1937): 71–81.

Schultz-[Goya], Oskar. *Die provenzalischen Dichterinnen.* Leipzig: Fock, 1888.

Scott, A. B., ed. *Carmina minora.* Leipzig: Teubner, 1969.

Scrope, Stephen, trans. *Epistle of Othea.* Edited by Curt F. Bühler. EETS 264. Oxford: Oxford University Press, 1970.

Sedulius Scotus. *Seduli Scotti carmina quadraginta ex codice Bruxellensi.* Edited by Ernst Dümmler. Halis: Formis Hendeliis, 1869.

Seton, Walter W. *Some New Sources for the Life of Blessed Agnes of Bohemia.* Aberdeen: Aberdeen University Press, 1915.

Seymour, M. C. *Selections from Hoccleve*. Oxford: Clarendon, 1981.

Shadis, Miriam. "Motherhood, Lineage, and Royal Power in Medieval Castile and France: Berenguela of Léon (1180–1246) and Blanche of Castile (1188–1252)." Ph.D. diss., Duke University, 1994.

Shahîd, Irfan. "Procopius and Arethas." *Byzantinische Zeitschrift* 50 (1957): 39–67.

Shahar, Shulamith. *Childhood in the Middle Ages*. London: Routledge, 1990.

Shaillor, Barbara. *Catalogue of Medieval and Renaissance Manuscripts in the Beinecke Rare Book Room and Manuscript Room, Yale University*. Binghamton, N.Y.: Medieval and Renaissance Texts and Studies, 1982.

Sheehan, Michael M., ed. *Aging and the Aged in Medieval Europe. Selected Papers from the Annual Conference of the Centre for Medieval Studies, University of Toronto, Held 25–26 February and 11–12 November 1983*. Toronto: Pontifical Institute of Mediaeval Studies, 1990.

Sheingorn, Pamela. "Appropriating the Holy Kinship: Gender and Family History." In *Interpreting Cultural Symbols: Saint Anne in Late Medieval Society*, edited by Kathleen Ashley and Pamela Sheingorn. Athens: University of Georgia Press, 1990.

———. "The Medieval Feminist Art History Project." *Medieval Feminist Newsletter* 12 (1991): 5–10.

———. "'The Wise Mother': The Image of St. Anne Teaching the Virgin Mary." *Gesta* 32 (1993): 69–80.

Short, Ian. *The Anglo-Norman Pseudo-Turpin Chronicle of William de Braine*. Oxford: Oxford University Press, 1973.

Shumaker, Wayne. "Alison in Wander-Land: A Study in Chaucer's Mind and Literacy Method." *Journal of English Literary History* 18 (1951): 77–89.

Sinclair, Alexandra. "The Great Berkeley Law-Suit Revisited, 1417–39." *Southern History* 9 (1987): 34–50.

Sinclair, K. V. "The Anglo-Norman Patrons of Robert the Chaplain and Robert of Greatham." *Forum for Modern Language Studies* 28 (1992): 193–208.

Sivéry, Gérard. *Marguerite de Provence: Une reine au temps des cathédrales*. Paris: Fayard, 1987.

Skovgaard-Petersen, Inge, with Nanna Damsholt. "Queenship in Medieval Denmark." In *Medieval Queenship*, edited by John Carmi Parsons. New York: St. Martin's, 1993.

Smalley, Beryl. *English Friars and Antiquity in the Early Fourteenth Century*. Oxford: Blackwell, 1960.

———. *The Study of the Bible in the Middle Ages*. 1952. Reprint, Notre Dame, Ind.: Notre Dame University Press, 1964.

Smith, R. A. L. "The Place of Gundulph in the Anglo-Norman Church." *English Historical Review* 58 (1943): 257–72.

Somerville, Robert. *The History of the Duchy of Lancaster*. Vol. 1, *1265–1603*. London: The Chancellor and the Council of the Duchy of Lancaster, 1953.

Sousa Viterbo, Francisco de. *D. Isabel de Portugal, duquesa da Borgonha: Notas documentães para a sua biographia et para a historia das relaçoes entre Portugal et a corte de Borgonha.* Lisbon: Off. Typ., 1905.

―――. "D. Isabel de Portugal, duquesa de Borgonha." *Archivo histórico portuguéz* 3 (1905): 81–106.

Southern, Richard William. *Robert Grosseteste: The Growth of an English Mind in Medieval Europe.* Oxford: Clarendon; New York: Oxford University Press, 1986.

Southworth, John. *The English Medieval Minstrel.* Woodbridge, England: Boydell, 1989.

Sozomen. *Ecclesiastical History.* Translated by Edward Walford. London: Bohn, 1855.

Spiegel, Gabrielle. "Genealogy: Form and Function in Medieval Historical Narrative." *History and Theory* 22 (1983): 43–53.

―――. "History, Historicism, and the Social Logic of the Text." *Speculum* 65 (1990): 59–86.

―――. "Political Utility in Medieval Historiography: A Sketch." *History and Theory* 14 (1975): 320–31.

―――. "*Pseudo-Turpin,* the Crisis of the Aristocracy, and the Beginnings of Vernacular Historiography in France." *Journal of Medieval History* 12 (1986): 207–23.

―――. *Romancing the Past: The Rise of Vernacular Prose Historiography in Thirteenth-Century France.* Berkeley and Los Angeles: University of California Press, 1993.

Squilbecke, Jean. "Le travail de métal à Bruxelles." In *Bruxelles au XVe siècle.* Brussels: Editions de la Librairie encyclopédique, 1953.

Stafford, Pauline. *Queens, Concubines, and Dowagers. The King's Wife in the Early Middle Ages.* Athens: University of Georgia Press, 1983.

―――. "The Portrayal of Royal Women in England, Ninth–Eleventh Centuries." In *Medieval Queenship,* edited by John Carmi Parsons. New York: St. Martin's, 1993.

Stanger, Mary D. "Literary Patronage at the Medieval Court of Flanders." *French Studies* 11 (1957): 214–29.

Statuta capitulorum generalium Ordinis Cisterciensis. Edited by D. Josephus-Maria Canivez. Louvain: Bureau de la Revue, 1933–41.

Steiner, Arpad. *Vincent of Beauvais, "De Eruditone Filiorum Nobilium."* Cambridge: Harvard University Press, 1938.

Stenton, Doris Mary. *The English Woman in History.* London: Allen and Unwin, 1957.

Stephen, Leslie, and Sidney Lee, eds. *Dictionary of National Biography.* Oxford: Oxford University Press, 1885–90.

Stevenson, Joseph, ed. *Chronicon monasterii de Abingdon.* RS 2. London: Longman, Brown, Green, Longmans, and Roberts, 1858.

Stone, Louise W. "Jean de Howden, poète anglo-normand du XIIIe siècle." *Romania* 69 (1946–47): 496–519.

Stones, Alison. Review of *Early Gothic Manuscripts, 1250–1285,* vol. 2, *A Survey of Manuscripts Illustrated in the British Isles,* by Nigel Morgan. *Speculum* 68 (1993): 213–16.

Stričević, Djordje. "The Iconography of the Compositions Containing Imperial Portraits in San Vitale." *Starinar* 9–10 (1958–59): 67–76.

———. "Sur le problème de l'iconographie des mosaïques impériales de Saint-Vital." *Felix Ravenna* 85 (1962): 80–100.

Strickland, Agnes. *Lives of the Queens of England,* 2d ed. London: Hurst and Blackett, 1851. Reissued 1854.

———. *Lives of the Queens of England from the Norman Conquest from the Official Records and Other Private and Public Documents.* London: Bell, 1889; Philadelphia: Barrie, 1902.

Strohm, Paul. *Hochon's Arrow: The Social Imagination of Fourteenth-Century Texts.* Princeton: Princeton University Press, 1992.

Stubbs, William, ed. *Chronicles of the Reigns of Edward I and Edward II.* 2 vols. RS 76. London: Longman, 1882–83.

Swanson, Heather. *Medieval Artisans.* Oxford: Blackwell, 1989.

Talbot, Charles H. *The Life of Christina of Markyate.* Oxford: Clarendon, 1959.

———. *Medicine in Medieval England.* New York: American Elsevier, 1967.

Tanner, Norman P. *Heresy Trials in the Diocese of Norwich, 1428–31.* Camden Society, 4th ser., 20. London: Royal Historical Society, 1977.

Tattersall, Jill. "Expedition, Exploration, and Odyssey: Extended Voyage Themes and Their Treatment in Some Early French Texts." In *Studies in Medieval French Language and Literature Presented to Brian Woledge in Honour of his 80th Birthday,* edited by Sally Burch North. Geneva: Droz, 1988.

Taylor, Michael D. "The Pentecost at Vézelay." *Gesta* 19 (1980): 9–15.

Temple, Elzbieta. *Anglo-Saxon Manuscripts, 900–1066.* London: Miller, 1976.

Teulet, Alexandre, ed. *Layettes du trésor des Chartes.* Paris, 1863–1909.

Theis, Laurent. "Dagobert, Saint-Denis, et la royauté français au moyen âge." In *Le métier d'historien au Moyen Age: Etudes sur l'historiographie médiévale,* edited by Bernard Guénée. Paris: Centre de recherches sur l'histoire de l'occident médiéval, 1977.

Thibaut, Francisque. *Marguerite d'Autriche et Jehan Lemaire de Belges.* Paris: Leroux, 1888.

Thibout, Marc. "Chronique: Peinture murale." *Bulletin monumental* 125 (1967): 95–96.

Thiébaux, Marcelle. *The Writings of Medieval Women.* New York: Garland, 1987.

Thomas, Marcel. "Une compilation anglo-normande de la fin du XIIIe siècle: 'La vie de gent de religion.'" In vol. 2 of *Recueil de travaux offerts à M. Clovis Brunel.* Paris: Société de l'École des Chartes, 1955.

Thompson, James Westfall. *The Literacy of the Laity in the Middle Ages.* New York: Franklin, 1963.

———. *The Medieval Library.* Chicago: University of Chicago Press, 1939. Reprint, New York: Hafner, 1967.

Thompson, Sally. "The Problem of the Cistercian Nuns in the Twelfth and Early Thirteenth Centuries." In *Medieval Women: Essays Presented to Rosalind M. T. Hill on the Occasion of Her Seventieth Birthday,* edited by Derek Baker. Studies in Church History, Subsidia 1. Oxford: Blackwell for the Ecclesiastical History Society, 1978.

———. "Why English Nunneries Had No History: A Study in the Problems of the English Nunneries Founded After the Conquest." In *Distant Echoes,* edited by John A. Nichols and Lillian Thomas Shank. Kalamazoo, Mich.: Cistercian, 1984.

Thomson, J. A. F. "Piety and Charity in Late Medieval London." *Journal of Ecclesiastical History* 16 (1965): 178–95.

Thomson, Rodney, ed. *Vita Gundulphi. The Life of Gundulf, Bishop of Rochester.* Toronto: Pontifical Institute of Medieval Studies, 1977.

———. "William of Malmesbury as Historian and Man of Letters." *Journal of Ecclesiastical History* 29 (1978): 387–413.

Thorndike, Lynn. *A History of Magic and Experimental Science.* New York: Macmillan, 1923–58.

Thorpe, Lewis. "Mastre Richard, a Thirteenth-Century Translator of the 'De Re Militari' of Vegetius." *Scriptorium* 6 (1952): 39–50.

———. "Mastre Richard at the Skirmish of Kenilworth?" *Scriptorium* 7 (1953): 262–65.

La Toison d'Or: Cinq siècles d'art et d'histoire. Catalog of an exhibition organized by the Ministère de l'education national and the City of Bruges, Musée Communal des Beaux Arts, 14 July–30 September 1962. Tielt, Belgium: Lannoo, 1962.

Torry, Gilbert. *The Book of Queenhithe: The History of a Harbour and the City Ward.* Buckingham: Barracuda, 1979.

Tout, Thomas F. *Chapters in the Administrative History of Medieval England.* Manchester: Manchester University Press, 1920–33.

Trenard, Louis, ed. *Histoire de Lille.* Publications de la Faculté des lettres et sciences humaines de Lille. Lille: Giard, 1970.

Le Trésor de Saint-Denis. Exhibition catalog, Musée du Louvre 12 March–17 June 1991. Paris: Réunion des musées nationaux, 1991.

Trevisa, John. "Dialogus." In *Medieval English Studies Presented to George Kane,* edited by Edward Donald Kennedy, Ronald Waldron, and Joseph S. Wittig. Wolfeboro, N.H.: Brewer, 1988.

———. "Epistola." In *Medieval English Studies Presented to George Kane,* edited by Edward Donald Kennedy, Ronald Waldron, and Joseph S. Wittig. Wolfeboro, N.H.: Brewer, 1988.

Trevor-Roper, Hugh Redwald. *Princes and Artists: Patronage and Ideology at Four Habsburg Courts, 1517–1633.* New York: Harper and Row, 1976.

[Turgot?]. "The Life of St Margaret of Scotland." In *Acta sanctorum quotquot toto orbe coluntur vel a catholicis scriptoribus celebrantur,* vol. 1, edited by Jean Bolland, Godfrey Henschenius, Danial Papenbroch, et al. Brussels and Antwerp: Joannem Mevrsium, 1658. Reprint, Paris: Palme, 1863–1910.

Tyson, Diana B. "Patronage of French Vernacular History Writers in the Twelfth and Thirteenth Centuries." *Romania* 100 (1979): 180–222.

Vale, Juliet. *Edward III and Chivalry: Chivalric Society and Its Context, 1270–1350.* Woodbridge, England: Boydell, 1982.

Vandercook, John W. *Empress of the Dusk: A Life of Theodora of Byzantium.* New York: Reynal and Hitchcock, 1940.

van Houts, Elisabeth. "Latin Poetry as a Source for Anglo-Norman History: The *Carmen de Hastingae Proelio.*" *Journal of Medieval History* 15 (1989): 39–62.

———. "Women and the Writing of History in the Early Middle Ages: The Case of Abbess Matilda of Essen and Aethelweard." *Early Medieval Europe* 1 (1992): 53–68.

Vasconcellos, Antonio Garcia Ribeiro de. *Evolução do culto de Doña Isabel de Aragão.* Coimbra: Imprensa de Universidade, 1894.

Vaughan, Richard. *Matthew Paris.* Cambridge: Cambridge University Press, 1958.

———. *Philip the Good.* London: Longmans, Green, 1970.

Verlaguet, P.-A. *Cartulaire de l'abbaye de Silvanès.* Rodez: Carrere, 1910.

Viard, Jules, ed. *Les grandes chroniques de France.* Paris: Société de l'histoire de France, 1920–54.

Vic, Claude de, and Joseph Vaissète. *Histoire générale de Languedoc.* Vol. 6. Toulouse: Privat, 1872.

Victoria History of the County of Essex. Edited by W. R. Powell et al. London: Constable and St. Catherine's; Oxford: Oxford University Press, 1903–78.

Victoria History of the County of Surrey. Edited by H. E. Malden. Westminster: Constable, 1902–12.

Vincent de Beauvais. *De eruditione filiorum nobilium.* Edited by Arpad Steiner. Cambridge, Mass.: Mediaeval Academy of America, 1938.

———. "Speculum historiale." Baltimore, Walters Art Gallery, MS 140.

Viriville, Vallet de. "La bibliothèque d'Isabeau de Bavière." *Bulletin du bibliophile* 14 (1858): 663–87.

Vita Ædwardi Regis qui apud Westmonasterium requiescit. In *Lives of Edward the Confessor,* edited by Henry R. Luard. RS 3. London: Longman, Brown, Green, Longmans, and Roberts, 1858.

Vita Sancti Simeonis comitis Crespeiensis. In PL, vol. 156, col. 1222, charte 14.

Von Simson, Otto G. *Sacred Fortress: Byzantine Art and Statecraft in Ravenna.* 1948. Reprint, Princeton: Princeton University Press, 1987.

Wadding, Luke. *Annales minorum.* Edited by J. M. Fonesca. 1731. Reprint, Florence: Claras Aquas (Quaracchi), 1932.

Wailly, Natilis de. *Récits d'un ménéstrel de Reims au treizième siècle.* Paris: Renouard, 1876.

Waithe, Mary Ellen, ed. *Medieval, Renaissance, and Enlightenment Women Philosophers.* Vol. 2 of *A History of Women Philosophers,* Dordrecht, Netherlands and Boston: Nijhoff/Kluver, 1987.

Walker, Sue Sheridan, ed. *Wife and Widow in Medieval England.* Ann Arbor: University of Michigan Press, 1993.

Wallace, Kathryn Young. *"La estoire de Seint Ædward le Rei" Attributed to Matthew Paris.* London: Anglo-Norman Text Society, 1983.

Walpole, Ronald N. "Charlemagne's Journey to the East: The French Translation of the Legend by Pierre of Beauvais." *University of California Publications in Semetic Philology* 11 (1951): 433–56.

———. *Philip Mouskes and the Pseudo-Turpin Chronicle.* Berkeley and Los Angeles: University of California Press, 1947.

Walsh, Michael, ed. *Butler's Lives of Patron Saints.* Rev. ed. New York: Harper and Row, 1987.

Walsingham, Thomas. *Gesta abbatum monasterii Sancti Albani.* Edited by Henry Thomas Riley. RS 28, pt. 4. London: Longmans, Green, 1867.

Walters, Lori J. "Jeanne and Marguerite de Flandre as Female Patrons." *Dalhousie French Studies* 28 (1994): 15–27.

Ward, Elizabeth. "Caesar's Wife: The Career of the Empress Judith, 819–29." In *Charlemagne's Heir: New Perspectives on the Reign of Louis the Pious, 814–40,* edited by Peter Godman and Roger Collins. Oxford: Clarendon, 1990.

Ward, Jennifer C. *English Noblewomen in the Later Middle Ages.* London: Longman, 1992.

Warner, Marina. *Alone of All Her Sex: The Myth and Cult of the Virgin Mary.* London: Wiedenfeld and Nicolson, 1976; paperback ed. New York: Random House/ Vintage, 1976.

Warren, Ann K. "The Nun as Anchoress: England, 1100–1500." In *Distant Echoes,* edited by John A. Nichols and Lillian Thomas Shank. Kalamazoo, Mich.: Cistercian, 1984.

Wattenbach, Wilhelm. "Lateinische Gedichte aus Frankreich in elften Jahrhundert." *Sitzungsberichte der Akademie der Wissenschaften.* Berlin, 1891.

Webster, Norman W. *Blanche of Lancaster.* Driffield, England: Halstead, 1990.

Weitzmann, Kurt. *Late Antique and Early Christian Book Illumination.* New York: Braziller, 1977.

Wellman, Paul I. *The Female: A Novel of Another Time.* New York: Doubleday, 1953.

Wemple, Suzanne. "S. Salvatore/S. Giulia: A Case Study in the Endowment and Patronage of a Major Female Monastery in Northern Italy." In *Women of the Medieval World: Essays in Honor of John H. Mundy,* edited by Julius Kirshner and Suzanne F. Wemple. Oxford: Blackwell, 1985.

———. *Women in Frankish Society.* Philadelphia: University of Pennsylvania Press, 1981.

West, Francis. *The Justiciarship in England.* Cambridge: Cambridge University Press, 1966.

Wilkins, Nigel. "Music and Poetry at Court: England and France in the Late Middle Ages." In *English Court Culture in the Later Middle Ages,* edited by V. J. Scattergood and J. W. Sherborne. New York: St. Martin's, 1983.

Willard, Charity Cannon. *Christine de Pizan: Her Life and Works.* New York: Persea, 1984.

———. "Isabel of Portugal and the French Translation of the 'Triunfo de las Doñas.'" *Revue belge de philologie et d'histoire* 43 (1965): 961–69.

————. "Isabel of Portugal, Patroness of Humanism?" In *Miscellanea di studi e ricerche sul Quattrocentro francese*, edited by Franco Simone. Turin: Giappichelli, 1967.

————. "Jean de Werchin, Seneschal de Hainaut: Reader and Writer of Courtly Literature." In *Courtly Literature: Culture and Context: Selected papers from the 5th Triennial Congress of the International Courtly Literature Society, Dalfsen, The Netherlands, 9–16 August 1986*, edited by Keith Busby and Erik Kooper. Philadelphia: Benjamins, 1990.

————. "A Portuguese Translation of Christine de Pisan's *Livre des Trois Vertus*." *PMLA* 78 (1963): 459–64.

William of Malmesbury. *De gestis regum Anglorum*. Edited by William Stubbs. RS 90. London: Eyre and Spottiswoode, 1887–89.

————. *Gesta pontificum Anglorum*. Edited by N. E. S. A. Hamilton. RS 52. London: Longman, 1870.

William of Poitiers. *Histoire de Guillaume le Conquerant*. Edited and translated into French by Raymonde Foreville. Paris: Société d'édition des belles-lettres, 1952.

Williamson, Joan B. "Phillipe de Mezière's Book for Married Ladies: A Book from the Entourage of the Court of Charles VI." In *The Spirit of the Court: Selected Proceedings of the Fourth Congress of the International Courtly Literature Society, Toronto 1983*, edited by Glyn S. Burgess and Robert A. Taylor. Cambridge: Brewer, 1985.

Wilmart, André. "Eve et Goscelin." *Revue bénédictine* 46 (1934): 414–38; 50 (1938): 42–83.

Wilson, Katharina. *Hrotsvit of Gandersheim: The Ethics of Authorial Stance*. Leiden: Brill, 1988.

Windeatt, Barry. "Julian of Norwich and Her Audience." *Review of English Studies* 28 (1977): 1–17.

Woledge, Brian. *Bibliographie des romans et nouvelles en prose française antérieurs à 1500*. Geneva: Droz, 1975.

Woledge, Brian, and H. P. Clive. *Répertoire des plus anciens textes en prose française depuis 842 jusqu'aux premières années du XIIIe siècle*. Geneva: Droz, 1964.

Wormald, C. P. "The Uses of Literacy in Anglo-Saxon England and Its Neighbors." *Transactions of the Royal Historical Society*, 5th ser., 27 (1977): 95–114.

Wormald, Francis, and Phyllis Giles. *A Descriptive Catalogue of the Additional Illuminated Manuscripts in the Fitzwilliam Museum Acquired Between 1895 and 1979*. Cambridge: Cambridge University Press, 1982.

Wright, Lawrence. "The Role of Musicians at Court in Twelfth-Century Britain." In *Art and Patronage in the English Romanesque*, edited by Sarah Macready and F. H. Thompson. London: Society of Antiquaries of London, 1986.

Wright, Thomas, ed. *The Anglo-Latin Satirical Poets and Epigrammitists of the Twelfth Century*. London: Longman, 1872.

————. *Political Songs of England*. London: Nichols for the Camden Society, 1839.

Ximénez de Rada, Rodrigo. *De rebus Hispaniae libri IX*. Edited by Francisco Lorenzana. In *Roderici Toletanti Opera*, vol. 22, *Textos Medievales*. Madrid, 1793; Reprint, Valencia, 1970.

————. *Historia de rebus hispanie.* Edited by Juan Fernández Valverde. Turnholti: Brepols, 1987.

Yapp, W. B. "The Birds of English Medieval Manuscripts." *Journal of Medieval History* 5 (1979): 315–49.

The Year 1200: A Centennial Exhibition. New York: Metropolitan Museum of Art, 1970.

Zumthor, Paul. *Essai de poétique médiévale.* Paris: Seuil, 1972.

————. *Histoire littéraire de la France médiévale, VIe–XIVe siècles.* Paris: Presses universitaires de France, 1954.

Contributors

MADELINE H. CAVINESS is Mary Richardson Professor and a professor of art history at Tufts University. She is a fellow and recent past president of the Medieval Academy of America as well as president of the Corpus Vitrearum. Her publications include *The Early Stained Glass of Canterbury Cathedral, ca. 1175–1220*, which was awarded the John Nicholas Brown Prize of the Medieval Academy of America in 1981; *The Windows of Christ Church Cathedral, Canterbury*; and *Sumptuous Arts at the Royal Abbeys in Reims and Braine*, which was awarded the Charles Homer Haskins Medal of the Medieval Academy in 1993.

JOAN M. FERRANTE is a professor of English and comparative literature at Columbia University. She is a fellow of the Medieval Academy and the president of the Dante Society. She is the author or editor of numerous books and articles, including *Woman as Image in Medieval Literature, The Political Vision of the Divine Comedy*, and a translation (with Robert Hanning) of *The Lais of Marie de France*. She is currently preparing a volume on women of letters in the Middle Ages.

RALPH HANNA III is a professor of English at the University of California, Riverside. His interest in the interface of literacies in late medieval England has led him to concentrate on William Langland, alliterative poetry, and prose translation from 1370–1413. He has published extensively on the medieval transmission and reception of literary texts.

LOIS L. HUNEYCUTT is an assistant professor of history at California State University, Hayward. She has written a number of articles on medieval women and is currently preparing an edition of *The Life of St. Margaret of Scotland*.

KAREN K. JAMBECK is a professor of English at Western Connecticut State University. She has published articles reflecting research interests that range from cognitive theory to Chaucer. Her most recent publications have focused on Marie de France, and she is currently preparing a critical edition of Marie's *Fables*.

JUNE HALL MCCASH is a professor of French at Middle Tennessee State University. Her publications include *Love's Fools: Troilus, Aucassin, and Calisto and the Parody of the Courtly Lover* as well as articles that have appeared in such journals as *Speculum*

373

and *Medievalia et Humanistica*. She is co-author of *The Jekyll Island Club: Southern Haven for America's Millionaires* and president of the International Courtly Literature Society, North American Branch. She is currently working on a study of the *Lais* of Marie de France.

ANNE L. McCLANAN is a doctoral candidate with a concentration in Byzantine Art in the Department of Fine Arts of Harvard University. She has contributed to the *Dictionary of Art* and *Byzantine Churches of Sardis,* based on archeological research in Turkey and Jordon.

STEPHEN G. NICHOLS is the James M. Beall Professor of French at Johns Hopkins University. He is a fellow of the Medieval Academy whose numerous publications include *The Visual Text: Word and Image in a Manuscript Culture* and *Romanesque Signs: Early Medieval Narrative and Iconography,* which was awarded the James Russell Lowell Prize for best book by the Modern Language Association in 1984.

JOHN CARMI PARSONS is a senior fellow at the Centre for Renaissance and Reformation Studies at the University of Toronto. Among his publications are *The Court and Household of Eleanor of Castile in 1290* and *Medieval Queenship.* He has recently completed a study of Eleanor of Castile, wife of Henry I of England.

MIRIAM SHADIS has taught courses in women's history and medieval history at Duke University, the University of North Carolina, and North Carolina State University. She is currently on a post-doctoral appointment at Villanova University.

CHARITY CANNON WILLARD is Professor Emerita of Ladycliffe College. She has published numerous works on Christine de Pizan, whose *Selected Writings* she has recently edited. She has translated and published *Christine de Pizan: Her Life and Works, A Medieval Woman's Mirror of Honor: The Treasury of the City of Ladies,* and edited (with Eric Hicks) a French edition entitled *Le Livre des Trois Vertus de Christine de Pizan.* She is currently preparing a biography of Isabel of Portugal.

FRANCES A. UNDERHILL is Professor Emerita at the University of Richmond. She has published articles on Elizabeth de Burgh and Clare College, Mary de Sancto Paulo, and on the use of household accounts in studying medieval history. She is currently preparing a biography on Elizabeth de Burgh, Lady of Clare.

Index

Abelard, Peter, 27, 111; letters to Héloïse, 80–81, 100 (n. 22), 146 (n. 23); *Problemata*, 80–81

Abingdon Abbey, 125, 158, 169 (n. 17)

Abingdon Chronicle, 124, 169 (n. 17)

Acciaiuoli, Andrea (countess of Altaville), 28

Acciaiuoli, Niccolò, 28

Adam, 193 (n. 19). *See also* Goldsmiths

Adam (abbot of Perseigne), writings of, 20; for Agnes, 79; for Blanche (countess of Champagne), 79, 100 (n. 19); for countess of Chartres, 79

Adamo (bishop of Palencia), 206

Adela (countess of Blois), 3, 35 (n. 4), 83, 86, 95, 102 (nn. 34, 35), 104 (nn. 49, 51). *See also* Baudri of Bourgeuil; Hildebert of Lavardin (bishop of Le Mans); Hugh of Fleury

Adelaide (sister of Otto III), 124

Adelard of Bath, 165; *De eodem et diversa*, 173–74 (n. 58)

Adelchis (son of Desiderius and Ansa), 22

Adelheid (2d wife of Otto I), 89–90, 93, 104 (n. 47)

Adeliza of Louvain, 4–5, 26, 166–67 (n. 3), 171 (n. 36)

Adelpurga (duchess of Benevento), 87, 102 (n. 38). *See also* Paul the Deacon

Adenet le Roi: *Cleomadés*, 23–24

Aeda (mother of Oda of Saxony), 8, 90–91

Aelfgifu of Northumbria, 41 (n. 66), 125–27, 131

Aëliz de Cundé, 251 (n. 19)

Aelred de Rievaulx, 27; *De institutione inclusarum*, 100 (n. 19)

Aeneas, 87

Aethelred II, the Unready, 16–17, 41 (n. 66), 103 (n. 42), 125, 127

Aethelweard: *Chronicle*, 102 (n. 37), 103 (n. 41); written for Matilda (abbess of Essen), 102 (n. 37)

Agatha, Saint, 229, 250 (n. 10). *See also* Bokenham, Osbern; Saints' lives

Agency, female, 6, 288

Agnes (mother of Emperor Henry IV), 93

Agnes. *See* Adam (abbot of Perseigne)

Agnes (abbess of Sainte-Croix), 12, 39 (n. 39), 82, 101 (n. 26). *See also* Fortunatus, Venantius

Agnes. *See* Baudri de Bourgeuil; Hildebert of Lavardin (bishop of Le Mans)

Agnes of Braine (countess of Bar), 131–33, 136

Agnes of Burgundy, 31, 217 (n. 2)

Agnes of Poitou (wife of Emperor Henry III), 15

Agnes of Prague, 22, 45 (n. 90), 45–46 (n. 91)

Aiden (monk), 27

Alan of Lynn OCarm, 303 (n. 21)

Albert of Fructuaria, 15

Albina. *See* Augustine, Saint
Alcobaça, monastery of, 312
Alcuin, writings of, 77–78, 99 (nn. 13, 14); for Gisla, 77, 81; for Gundrada, 77, 99 (nn. 13, 14); for Rotruda, 77, 81
Aldhelm, 98 (n. 11)
Alexander, 95, 184, 200 (n. 62), 316
Alexander IV (pope), 222 (n. 44)
Alexis, Saint, 108, 112
Alfonso de Molina, 223 (n. 55)
Alfonso of Portugal: death of, 309, 313
Alfonso VIII (king of Castile), 15–16, 135, 203–12 passim, 218 (nn. 6, 8), 219 (n. 10), 220 (n. 25), 223 (n. 53)
Alfonso IX (king of León), 214, 218 (n. 6), 221 (n. 30), 225 (n. 72)
Alfonso X, the Wise (king of Castile and León), 182, 208–9, 218 (n. 9), 223 (n. 55); *Ladder of Mohammed*, 177; *Primera crónica*, 222 (n. 46), 227 (n. 84); scriptorium, 192 (n. 13); *Siete partidas*, 177
Alfred (son of Aethelred and Emma), 41 (n. 66), 92, 127
Algasia. *See* Jerome, Saint
Alice de Curcy, 26
Aline (patron of Robert de Greatham), 24
Alix de Blois, 23
Alix de Vienne (abbess of Lys), 225 (n. 66)
Allegory, xvi–xviii, 118–21, 252 (n. 27)
Almanzor (king of barbarians), 225 (n. 72)
Alnwick (bishop of Norwich), 290
Alphonse I of Toulouse, 7
Alphonse VIII. *See* Alfonso VIII (king of Castile)
Alphonse IX. *See* Alfonso IX (king of León)
Alphonse of Poitiers, 212

Alphonso X. *See* Alfonso X, the Wise (king of Castile and León)
Alvaro, João, 310
Amalsuntha (daughter of Theodoric), 88
Amazons, 95–96
Ambrose, Saint (bishop of Milan), 74–77, 80, 98 (n. 10); *De obitu Theodosii*, 68 (n. 3); letters to Marcellina, 76, 96
Amiens, 181
Anastaise, 32. *See also* Illuminators
Andreas Capellanus, 37 (n. 23)
Andromatha, 232
Angleseye, 270, 280; priory at, 271, 275, 279
Anglo-Saxon Chronicle, 127
Anicia Juliana, 51, 53–54, 66
Anicius Olybrius, 53
Anne (countess of March), 259 (n. 81)
Anne, Saint, 130, 138, 142, 216, 230, 250–51 (n. 12), 263 (n. 114)
Anne de la Pole (prioress of Syon), 240
Anne of Bohemia, 255 (n. 49)
Anne of Brittany, 31; daughter of, 22
Anne of France, 31
Anne of Woodstock (countess of Stafford), 237–38, 247, 259 (n. 81), 264 (n. 129); patronage of Lydgate, 238, 259 (n. 81)
Ansa (queen of the Lombards), 22, 45 (n. 89)
Anselberga (abbess of Saint Salvatore), 45 (n. 89)
Anselm, Saint (archbishop of Canterbury), 157, 161, 164, 167 (n. 3), 168 (n. 10); writings for Adela, 101 (n. 31), 104 (n. 48)
Anselm (bishop of Lucca), 94, 97 (n. 1)
Antioch, 61
Antwerp, 21; Cathedral of, 313
Aquileia, 88
Arcadius, 65
Architects, 279; architectural patronage,

16, 159, 170, 287 (n. 129), 278–80
Arderne, John (surgeon), 256 (n. 59)
Arethas (king of the Ghassanids), 62
Aristotle, 98 (n. 6), 115, 196 (n. 33)
Arnaldo (abbot of Herrera), 221 (n. 30)
Arnaut Daniel, xv
Arnulf: Delicie cleri, 15
Arras: Museum of, 315; Municipal
    Library of, 317
Athelstan, 184
Arthur (king of England), 198 (n. 49),
    200 (n. 62); interest in Arthuriana,
    183–84, 266. See also Edward I (king
    of England)
Arthurian literature, 26, 33, 177–79,
    183–85, 266; dissemination of,
    15–16, 186
Arundel, archbishop, 294
Athaulf (king of the Goths), 88
Aubert, David, 312
Aubrey de Vere, 241
Aubri of Troisfontaines, 181
Augustine, Saint, 74–80 passim, 230,
    251 (n. 16); The City of God, 76, 79,
    98 (n. 8), 310; Confessions, 79; letters
    of, 75, 76
Augustinians, 168 (n. 10), 278–79;
    Augustinian Rule, 75
Aurifaber, Robert, 269
Aurifaber, Thomas, 269–70
Aurifrigeria, Alice, 283 (n. 43)
Austin (canon of Wigmore), 27
Author portraits, 115
Aymeri II of Narbonne, 7
Azalaïs de Porcairagues, 8, 32, 37
    (n. 23)

Badew, Richard, 277
Baker, Augustine, 300
Ballinrobe (Ireland), friary at, 279
Balthard, 101 (n. 27)

Barcelos, count of, 309
Bardfield manor, 275, 279
Bardone, 94
Barking, Abbey of, 27, 48 (n. 113), 168
    (n. 13); nuns of, 98 (n. 11)
Basileía (imperial dominion), 51–52,
    59, 67
Batalha: royal chapel at, 310; abbey at,
    312, 316
Bateman, William (bishop of Norwich),
    276
Battles: Agincourt, 306; Aljubarrota,
    312; Bouvines, 183; Bugnéville, 306;
    Northampton, 240; Shrewsbury, 237;
    Tinchebrai, 164
Baudoin d'Oignies, 310, 318
Baudonivia (nun of Sainte-Croix), 35
    (n. 5); De vita Sanctae Radegundis, 12
Baudouin VIII of Flanders, 26
Baudri of Bourgeuil, 35 (n. 4), 81, 83–
    86, 102 (n. 35); epitaph for Benedicta,
    79; poems exchanged with
    Constantina, 84–85, 102 (n. 34).
    Poems for: Adela of Blois, 83, 86, 102
    (nn. 34, 35); Agnes, 84; Beatrice, 84;
    Cecilia, 84; Emma, 84; Muriel, 84
Baxter, Margery, 290–305 passim
Baxter, William, 294, 301 (n. 8)
Beatrice, 84
Beatrice (marchioness of Tuscany, wife
    of Boniface II), 92–93; rule of, 93
Beatrice (of Dante's Commedia), xvi,
    xviii
Beatrice of Nazareth, 21, 35 (n. 5)
Beatrice of Swabia, 210–11
Beatrix of Tuscia, 150 (n. 67)
Beauchamp, Anne, 260 (n. 89)
Beauchamp, Henry (duke of Warwick),
    260 (n. 85)
Beauchamp, John (Lord Lisle), 234
Beauchamp, Margaret (countess of
    Shrewsbury), 247, 253 (nn. 39, 41),

Beauchamp, Margaret (*continued*)
264 (n. 132); patronage of John
Lydgate, 234

Beauchamp, Richard (earl of Warwick),
233, 253 (n. 41), 254 (n. 42), 260
(nn. 85, 89)

Beaufort, Joan (countess of
Westmorland), 233, 239–42, 247,
257–58 (nn. 71, 72), 259 (n. 79), 264
(n. 128)

Beaufort, John (earl of Somerset), 239

Beaufort, Henry (cardinal), 239

Beaufort, Margaret, 32, 240, 259 (n. 83)

Beaumont, Isabel (duchess of
Lancaster), 235, 254 (n. 44), 261
(n. 97)

Becket, Thomas, Saint (archbishop of
Canterbury), 128, 178, 193 (n. 20),
261 (n. 95)

Bede, 13, 164

Belgian Royal Library, 306

Belleville Breviary, 153 (n. 97)

Belmain, Jean (bishop of Poitiers), 129

Belmeis, Richard (bishop of London),
165

Belward, Nicholas, 290, 301 (n. 8)

Benedeit l'apostoïle: *Voyage of Saint
Brendan*, 25, 162, 164–65, 171 (n. 36)

Benedicta, 79

Benedictines, 12–13, 108, 168 (n.10),
300; abbeys and, 12, 13, 203, 219
(n. 10), 223 (n. 53)

Benedictine Rule, 80

Berengar, 89

Berenguela of León (daughter of
Alfonso VIII of Castile and Leonor of
England), 202–4, 208–11 passim,
213–17, 218 (n. 6), 221 (nn. 27, 34),
222 (n. 44), 223 (n. 55), 225–27
passim; patronage of Las Huelgas,
202–27 passim; patronage of Lucas de
Túy, 216–17

Berenguela of León (daughter of
Fernando III of León and Castile, nun
at Las Huelgas), 208–9, 215

Bergyth, 101 (n. 27)

Berkeley, Elizabeth (countess of
Warwick), 233–34, 246, 254 (n. 42),
264 (n. 125)

Berkeley, James, 234–35

Berkeley, Margaret, 233–35

Berkeley, Thomas, 233

Berkeley, William, 235

Berkerolles, Lawrence, 261 (n. 98)

Bernard, Jeanne, 13

Bernard de Ventadorn, 8, 37 (n. 23)

Bernard of Anduze, 37 (n. 20)

Bernard of Clairvaux, Saint, 160;
writings for Sophia, 100 (n. 19)

Bertrada of Montfort, 173–74 (n. 58)

Bestiaries, 26

Bibbesworth, Walter, 262–63 (n. 113);
Traité, 246

Bible, 78, 80, 256–57 (n. 61), 274, 295,
300, 302 (n. 14)

Bible moralisée, 136

Birgitta, Saint. *See* Bridget, Saint (of
Sweeden)

Black Death, 276; plague, 235

Black Prince, 271

Blanche. *See* Damian, Peter

Blanche (duchess of Lancaster), 233,
235, 243, 246, 254 (nn. 44, 48), 255
(n. 50), 256 (n. 56), 258 (n. 71);
children of, 254 (n. 47); patronage of
Jean Froissart, 235–36

Blanche de Brienne (abbess of
Maubuisson), 211

Blanche de Navarre (countess of
Champagne), 9, 17–18, 24, 43
(n. 73), 79, 100 (n. 19), 143

Blanche of Castile, 135–38, 152 (n. 88),
202–3, 208, 211–17, 218 (n. 6), 221
(n. 34), 224 (nn. 59, 60, 61), 224

(n. 64), 225 (nn. 65, 68); association with Virgin Mary, 214–17; burial of body at Pontoise, 213, 224 (n. 63), 225 (n. 69); burial of heart at Notre-Dame du Lys, 213, 225 (nn. 68, 69); children of, 22; patronage of Chartres, 214–16, 227 (n. 82)

Blandin de Cournouailles, 190 (n. 5)

Blount, Walter, 240

Boccaccio, 27, 29; *De mulieribus claris*, 27–29; *Il Corbaccio*, 311; *Decameron*, 311

Bocking, Ralph: *Life of Richard de Wyche*, 263 (n. 116). See also Saints' lives

Boethius, xvi–xviii, 79; *De consolatione philosophiæ*, xvi, xviii, 21, 229, 232, 246

Bohemund of Antioch, 200 (n. 62)

Bokenham, Osbern, 229–30, 232, 237, 250 (n. 12), 265 (n. 139), 286 (n. 118); *Legendys of Hooly Wummen*, 230, 250 (n. 10); *Life of Mary Magdalen*, 229, 247; *Life of St. Agatha*, 229, 247; *Life of St. Anne*, 247, 263 (n. 114); *Life of St. Dorothy*, 229, 247; *Life of St. Elizabeth*, 241, 247; *Life of St. Katherine*, 229, 247; *Life of Saint Margaret*, 229

Bolingbroke, Henry, 256 (n. 59)

Bonaventure, Saint, 304; *Dialogus*, 312; *Life of Christ*, 240

Boniface, Saint, 82; letter exchanges with: Bugga, 77; letter exchanges with Abbess Eadburg, 77; account of Abbess Hildelida, 77

Boniface II of Tuscany, 92–93

Books: aural reading of, 290–301 passim; embodiment of, 290–301 passim; ownership of, 106, 142, 179, 228; production of, xii–xiii, 289, 298–300

Books of hours, 10, 21, 23, 32, 194 (n. 25), 196 (n. 34), 289, 310; hours of Jeanne d'Evreux, 140, 142; hours of Jeanne II de Navarre, 140–42

Bourchier, Isabel (countess of Eu), 233, 247, 257 (n. 63), 264 (n. 137); patronage of Osbern Bokenham, 229, 237, 240

Bourchier, William (father), 237

Bourchier, William (son), 237

Bourges, cathedral of, 138–40

Bourgot le Noir, 32. See also Illuminators

Bouton of Corbeveau: *Miroir des dames*, 28. See also *Speculum Dominarum*

Boys, Roger, 264 (n. 133)

Boys, Sibyl, of Holme Hale, 247, 264 (n. 133)

Bradwardine, Thomas (archbishop), 274

Braga, Cathedral of, 313

Bredon, Simon, 276

Bridget, Saint (of Sweden), 295; *Revelations*, 240, 258–59 (n. 79), 315; *Rule*, 315

Brigitte (granddaughter of Cecily Neville), 240

Brigittine nuns, 315

Bruges, 306, 310, 312, 315

Brunetto Latini: *Livre dou Tresor*, 194 (n. 28)

Bugga, 92–93

Burghersh, John (Lord Kerdston), 243–44, 261 (n. 98)

Burghersh, Margaret, 244

Burghersh, Maud, 243–44

Burgos, 203, 213, 222 (n. 48); bishop of, 206; cathedral of, 213–14

Butyller, Robert, 263 (n. 113)

Byzantine Empire, x, 50, 53, 61, 66

Caedmon, 13, 27, 47 (n. 112)

Caesar Augustus, 232

Caesaria (sister of Caesarius of Arles), 98 (n. 10)

Caesarius of Arles, 98 (n. 10)

Calatrava, 216

Calderón de la Barca, 308

Calixtus II (pope), 226 (n. 75)

Cambridge, 244, 279–80; Cambridge University, 275–78

Camões, Luis, 308

Canossa, 93–95

Canterbury Cathedral, 129, 131

Capetians, 127, 133, 135, 151 (n. 79), 182–83, 227 (n. 81)

Capgrave, John, 247

Carmes, Church of the (Brussels), 313

Carpenter, Richard. See Felsted, Richard

Carthusians, 315

Cassian, John, 256–57 (n. 61)

Cassiodorus, 79

Catherine, Saint. See Katherine, Saint

Catherine of Cleves, 21

Cato, 85

Caxton, William, 49 (n. 132), 317; Recuyell of the Historyes of Troyes, 33, 259 (n. 80).

Cécile (abbess of Caen), 35 (n. 4), 42 (n. 68), 83, 102 (n. 33). See also Baudri of Bourgeuil; Hildebert of Lavardin (bishop of Le Mans)

Cecilia, Saint, 13, 145 (n. 11), 294, 297

Cent nouvelles nouvelles, 311

Ceres, 252 (n. 30)

Cerne (abbot of), 194 (n. 25)

Cesara (queen of Persia), 88

Ceuta, 309

Champmol, Chartreuse de, 313, 315, 317

Chansons de geste, 23–24, 165, 181

Charlemagne, 26, 77, 96, 99 (n. 13), 102 (n. 38), 182, 200 (n. 62)

Charles d'Orléans, 261 (n. 102), 306, 308

Charles of Anjou, 198 (n. 47)

Charles of Burgundy, 315–16

Charles the Bold, 316

Charles IV, le Bel (king of France), 28, 140, 143, 212

Charles V, le Sage (king of France), 28, 49 (n. 130)

Charles V (Roman emperor, king of Spain), 201 (n. 62), 316, 318

Charles VIII (king of France), 31

Charter House at Mount Grace, 258–59 (n. 79), 229

Chartres, Notre-Dame de, 42 (n. 68), 138, 140, 159, 213–16, 227 (nn. 81, 82)

Chaucer, Geoffrey, 261 (n. 100), 302 (n. 10), 303 (n. 22); Book of the Duchess, 235; La priere Nostre Dame (ABC poem), 235–36, 246; Second Nun's Tale, 303 (n. 22); Troilus and Criseyde, 302 (n. 10)

Chaucer, Alice (countess of Suffolk), 243–45, 247, 261 (nn. 98, 100, 101), 264 (n. 130)

Chaucer, Philippa Roet, 258 (n. 71), 261 (n. 100)

Chaucer, Thomas, 243–44, 261 (n. 100)

Chaworth, Patrick, 255 (n. 56)

Cheiner, Thomas (embroiderer), 271

Chertsey Abbey, 194 (n. 26)

Cheyner, Alice, 283 (n. 43)

Chivaler a Cigne, 256–57 (n. 61)

Chrétien de Troyes, 15, 18; Le Chevalier de la charrete, xiii–xiv, 102 (n. 36); Erec et Enide, 4; Cligès, 25; Perceval, 25

Christ. See Jesus Christ

Christina of Markyate, 108–13 passim, 145 (n. 11); Psalter of, 107, 108–12 passim, 118, 133, 142. See also Psalters

Christine (abbess of Gandesheim), 38 (n. 28), 91

Christine de Pizan, 6, 29–34, 49
    (n. 132), 232–33, 249–53 passim,
    262–63 (n. 113); *Enseignements
    moraux*, 23; *Epistle of Othea*, 229,
    232, 241–42, 247, 260 (n. 89); *Livre
    de la cité des dames*, 30, 261 (n. 103);
    Portuguese translation of *Tresor*, 310;
    role in the Quarrel of the Rose, 34, 49
    (n. 135); *Trésor de la cité des dames ou
    Livre des trois vertus*, 31, 49 (n. 126),
    233, 261 (n. 103), 310; *See also*
    Scrope, Stephen
Christ's College, Cambridge, 32
Chronicle of Jerusalem, 239
Chronicles, 5, 26, 182–88 passim, 196
    (n. 39), 199 (n. 55), 239. See also
    Pseudo-Turpin Chronicle; Trevet,
    Nicolas
Chrysostom, 80
Cicero, 85
Cintra: royal palace at, 314
Cistercians, 9, 20, 210–14, 216, 219
    (nn. 10), 220 (n. 25), 223 (n. 55), 224
    (nn. 58, 60, 63), 226 (nn. 75, 76, 80);
    attitudes toward women, 204, 213,
    219 (n. 13); Cistercian abbesses, 206;
    Cistercian nuns, 219 (n. 12); female
    abbeys, 204
Citoler, Roger, 273
Clairvaux, monastery of, 100, 160, 206,
    312
Clare, 270; Clare Castle, 269–70, 275,
    279–80
Clare College, Cambridge, 271, 274–77,
    284 (n. 69), 285 (nn. 87, 88);
    founding of, 267, 277
Clare Friary, 270, 275, 278
Clare Hall, 272, 276, 285 (n. 87)
Clare of Assisi, Saint, 314; rule of, 22,
    45–46 (n. 91)
Clemence of Barking, 48 (n. 113)
Clemence of Hungary (wife of Louix X,
    le Hutin), 153 (n. 99)

Clement III, 205
Cleomadés. See Adenet le Roi
Cleveland, Museum of, 17
Clifland, Joan: charges against Margery
    Baxter, 292
Clopton, 276
Cluny, 42 (n. 68), 160; Cluniacs, 219
    (n. 10)
Cnut (king of England and Denmark),
    16, 41 (n. 66), 91–92, 124–27
Cobham, Reynold, of Sterborough, 241
College of Navarre, 32
Comestor, Peter, 256–57 (n. 61)
Comyn, Alexander, 254 (n. 44)
Comyn, Alice, 254 (n. 44)
Conrad (son of Henry IV), 94
Conrad II (emperor of Salian
    dynasty), 14
Constantina. *See* Baudri of Bourgeuil
Constantine Porphyrogenito (Byzantine
    emperor), 64
Constantine the Great, 50
Constantine VI, 96
Constantinople, 51, 53, 58–61,
    64–65, 88
Constanza of Castile (daughter of
    Alfonso VIII and Leonor of England),
    208, 227 (n. 80)
Constanza of León (daughter of
    Berenguela and Alfonso IX of León),
    208–9, 227 (n. 80)
Coorland, Gautier (architect), 16. *See
    also* Architects
Coppersmiths, 313
Corbie, 314
Cordail, Gilbert (wardrobe keeper), 269
Coutances, cathedral of, 42 (n. 68)
Cressing, John, 279. *See also* Architects
Cressy, Serenus, 300
Creusa (wife of Aeneas), 87
Crónica de España. See Lucas de Túy
Curtius, Quintus, 311, 316
Cyrus, 95

Cysoing, abbey of, 133

Damasus (pope), 98 (n. 5)
Damian, Peter, letters of: to Blanch,
    78–79; to Agnes of Poitou, 15
Dancers, 23
Dante, xv–xvi, 33, 104 (n. 46)
Debora (biblical figure), 75, 94, 96
De infantia salvatoris, 258 (n. 79)
Decembri, Pier Candido, 316; De
    regimine principum, 284 (n. 69)
Dedications, 2–3, 35 (n. 2), 73, 175
Dedimia (abbess of Sainte-Croix), 12
Deguileville, Guillaume, 235–36;
    Pèlerinage de l'âme, 255 (n. 55);
    Pèlerinage de la vie humaine, 235,
    243; Hoccleve's translation of
    Pèlerinage de l'âme, 255 (n. 55)
Delilah (biblical figure), 142
Demetrias (granddaughter of Proba), 76
Denis de Ryckel, 312
Denis Piramus, 24
Denis the Carthusian, 311
Denney, convent at, 279
Denston, Anne, 263 (n. 114), 265
    (n. 139)
Denston, John, 265 (n. 139)
Denston, Katherine Clopton, 247, 263
    (n. 114), 265 (nn. 138, 139)
Deschamps, Eustache, 235–36, 255
    (n. 52); "Balade," 246; dedication to
    Philippa of Lancaster, 246
Desiderius (king of the Lombards), 22,
    45 (n. 89), 87, 102 (n. 38)
Despenser, Isabel (countess of
    Warwick), 247, 253 (n. 41), 260
    (n. 89), 264 (n. 131); patronage of
    John Lydgate, 260 (n. 89)
Despenser, Margaret, 270
Dhuoda (duchess of Septimania), 14
Digna, 88
Dijon, 306, 312–13, 315

Dominica (empress), 87
Domingo, Frey, 208
Domingos Antonio de Sequeira, 316
Dominicans, xi, 178, 186, 196 (n. 34)
Donizo (monk of Canossa), 92–95, 104
    (n. 47); Vita Mathildis, 97 (n. 1),
    102–3 (n. 38). See also Matilda of
    Tuscany
Donor portraits, 35 (n. 2), 62–64, 107,
    113, 120, 124, 147 (n. 29), 315
Dorothy, Saint, 229, 250 (n. 10)
Douce Apocalypse, 178
Duarte (king of Portugal, son of João I),
    308–10; The Loyal Counsellor, 308
Dunion, Ralph, 192 (n. 14)
Durand de Champagne, 28
Durham, cathedral of, 158

Eadburg (abbess), 77, 82
Eadmer of Canterbury, 167 (n. 8), 173
    (n. 48)
Edith (wife of Otto I), 89
Edith-Matilda. See Mathilda of Scotland
    (wife of Henry I of England)
Edith of Wessex (wife of Edward the
    Confessor), 102 (n. 37)
Edmund (earl of Stafford and
    Buckingham), 237–38
Edmund Ironside, 103 (n. 42)
Edmund of Abingdon, Saint, 230, 242
Education: as background to patronage,
    14–15, 233–35; cathedral schools,
    124; education of women, 46 (n. 92),
    163, 186, 249 (nn. 5, 6); women's
    role in, 22–23, 186, 188, 248 (n. 4),
    280, 289
Edward (duke of York), 264 (n. 126)
Edward of Caernarvon, 176, 195 (n. 30)
Edward I (king of England), 176–80,
    182–84, 187, 194 (n. 23), 195 (n. 30),
    197 (n. 40), 198 (n. 48), 254 (n. 44),

257 (n. 63), 266, 272; interest in
Arthuriana, 183–84
Edward II (king of England), 194
(n. 23), 201 (n. 62), 281 (n. 2)
Edward III (king of England), xvi, 5, 201
(n. 62), 235, 239, 256 (n. 60), 268,
275, 281; interest in Arthuriana, 266
Edward IV (king of England), 32
Edward the Confessor, Saint, 17, 48
(n. 113), 92, 102 (n. 37), 104 (n. 45),
127, 149 (n. 53), 163–64, 178, 188;
cult of, 176, 184–85. See also Paris,
Mattew; Vita Aedwardi Regis
Egbert II, 17
Egidus, 256–57 (n. 61)
Eibingen, monastery of, 147 (n. 31)
Eilhart von Oberg, 15, 40 (n. 59)
Eleanor (countess of Winchester), 243,
260 (nn. 92, 93), 261 (n. 97). See
also Paris, Matthew
Eleanor (daughter of Eleanor of Castile),
193 (n. 19)
Eleanor de Bohun, 237, 256 (nn. 60, 61)
Eleanor of Aquitaine, 6–8, 15, 33, 36–37
(n. 18), 127–31, 135, 149 (n. 58), 150
(nn. 61, 67), 202–3, 217, 218 (n. 6)
Eleanor of Castile (queen of England),
176–201 passim; 257 (n. 63), 272;
exchange of works with Alfonso X of
Castile and León, 177; scriptorium,
178–79
Eleanor of England. See Leonor of
England (queen of Castile)
Eleanora of Ferrara, 201 (n. 65)
Eleanor of Provence (queen of England),
176, 179–80, 184–85, 187, 200
(n. 62), 241, 243, 264 (n. 121)
Eleanor of Saint-Quentin, 138
Elisabeth of Schönau, 12, 100 (n. 19)
Elizabeth (countess of Ulster), 257
(n. 63)
Elizabeth (wife of Edward IV), 32

Elizabeth de Burgh (lady of Clare), 262
(n. 106); family background, 257
(n. 63); foundation of Clare College,
32; patronage, 266–87 passim; vow
of chastity, 266
Elizabeth of Hungary, Saint, 230, 260
(n. 87), 296. See also Bokenham,
Osbern; Saints' lives
Elizabeth de Vere, 241, 247, 265
(n. 140), 260 (n. 87)
Elizabeth of York, 243
Elvira, Doña (patron of Las Huelgas),
208
Ely Abbey, 278; church of, 124
Embroidery, 271, 283 (n. 43). See also
Needlework
Emma, 84–85. See also Baudri of
Bourgeuil
Emma Aelfgifu. See Emma of
Normandy (queen of England)
Emma of Normandy (queen of
England), 10, 16, 41 (n. 66), 42
(n. 68), 91–92, 124–28
Encomium Emmae Reginae, 16, 41
(n. 66), 127, 201 (n. 62). See also
Emma of Normandy (queen of
England)
Enfances Ogier, 23
Ennodius, writings of: for Euprepia, 82;
for Firminia, 100 (n. 24)
Enrique I of Castile, 225 (n. 73), 226
(n. 80)
Erik (king of Denmark), 237
Ermengard (Roman empress, wife of
Lothar I), 78, 83, 99 (n. 15), 101
(n. 29)
Ermengarde de Narbonne, 7–8, 16, 23,
37 (nn. 19, 20, 23, 24)
Ermold, 102 (n. 37)
Eructavit cor meum, 20
Escanor, 178–79, 184, 198 (n. 47)
Espec, Walter, 5

Esther (biblical queen), 78, 94, 96, 99
    (n. 15), 101 (n. 29)
Etienne de Blois, 3, 43–44 (nn. 69,
    73), 95
Eudokia Augusta, 51–54, 61, 68 (n. 14)
Eudoxia (wife of Arcadius), 65
Euphemia (Byzantine empress), 60, 71
    (n. 62)
Euprepia, 82, 100 (n. 24)
Eusebius, 51, 68 (n. 3), 79
Eustochium, 79, 230. *See also* Jerome,
    Saint
Eutropius, 87
Eva, Doña (abbess of Las Huelgas), 222
    (n. 44)
Eve (biblical figure), 115, 140, 142
Eve (nun at Wilton and Saint Laurent),
    79, 99–100 (n. 18). *See also* Goscelin
    of Saint Bertin (monk of Canterbury)
Evora, 310
Evrat (clerk at Saint-Etienne of
    Troyes), 19
Ewelme, manor of, 243–44
Exeter, 127, 168 (n. 13); cathedral at,
    282 (n. 24)

Fabiola. *See* Jerome, Saint
Fabricius, 250 (n. 10)
Faritius (abbot of Abingdon, physician),
    159, 170 (n. 20)
Felice (wife of Guy of Warwick), 231,
    234
Felsted, Richard, 287 (n. 129). *See also*
    Architects
Ferdinand III of Castile. *See*
    Fernando III (king of León and
    Castile)
Fernández, Elvira, 208–9
Fernando (chaplain of Constanza), 208,
    221 (n. 34)
Fernando, Martyr of Fez, 308–11
    passim
Fernando de Lucena, 311

Fernando la Cerda, 226 (n. 80)
Fernando III (king of León and Castile),
    177, 208, 215, 221 (n. 27), 225
    (n. 73), 227 (nn. 82, 84)
Ferrers, Robert, 239
Fichet, Guillaume, 317
Fille du comte de Pontieu, 199 (n. 53)
Fin'amor (fine amor), 15
Firminia. *See* Ennodius
FitzAlan, Alice, 257–58 (n. 70)
FitzAlan, Eleanor, 236, 255 (n. 56), 257
    (n. 70)
FitzAlan, Joan (countess of Hereford),
    233, 236–38, 243–46, 255 (n. 50), 255
    (n. 57), 256 (n. 59), 264 (n. 124);
    daughter of, 255 (n. 54), 257 (n. 70)
FitzAlan, Richard (earl of Arundel),
    236, 255 (n. 56), 257–58 (n. 70)
Fitzgerold, Warin, 26
Fitzgilbert, Constance, 4
FitzGilbert, Isabel, 242–43, 261 (n. 97)
FitzGilbert de Clare, Gilbert, 261
    (n. 97)
Flavia Flaccilla, 51–52
Flavius Anicius Olybrius, 53
Flegg, Agatha, 247, 265 (n. 141)
Flores historiarum, 182
Fontaine, château of, 312
Fontevrault, abbey of, 36 (n. 18), 130,
    203–5, 210, 218 (n. 8)
Fortunatus, Venantius, 39 (n. 39), 84;
    De Vita Sanctae Radegundis, 11;
    poems for Radegund, 82; poems for
    Agnes, 82, 101 (n. 26)
Franciscans, 9, 13, 28, 275, 278, 312,
    314
Francis I (king of France), 201 (n. 62)
Francis of Assisi, 9, 46 (n. 91)
Freculf: *Chronicon*, 102 (n. 37);
    dedication to Empress Judith, 102
    (n. 37); writing for female
    patrons, 96
Frederick Barbarossa, 17

Froissart, Jean, xvi, 5; *Le joli buisson de jonece*, 235, 254–55 (n. 48)

Fulbert (bishop of Chartres), 113

Fulgerius (chaplain to the convent at Nazareth), 18

Furia. *See* Jerome, Saint

Gabriel, 142

Gaguin, Robert, 317

Gaimar, Geoffrey, 4–5, 36 (n. 11); *Estoire des Engleis*, 5, 26

Galla Placidia, 65, 88

Gandersheim, convent of, 8, 38 (n. 28), 124

García, Sancha (abbess of Las Huelgas), 207

Garsía (bishop of Burgos), 206

Gawain, 200 (n. 62)

Geoffrey de Aspale, 196 (n. 33)

Geoffrey Gaimar. *See* Gaimar, Geoffrey

Geoffrey Martel (count of Anjou), 217 (n. 2)

Geoffrey of Monmouth, 181, 186, 197 (n. 44), 199 (n. 56)

Geoffrey of Vendôme, 100 (n. 18)

Gerberga I (abbess of Gandersheim), 38 (n. 28), 90

Gerberga II (abbess of Gandersheim), 12, 88, 90. *See also* Hrotsvit of Gandersheim

Gerbert de Montreuil, 199 (n. 53)

Gerson, Jean, 312

Gertrude of Brunswick, 9, 17–18

Geruchia. *See* Jerome, Saint

Gesta Romanorum, 231

Gesta Tancredi, 195 (n. 28)

Geste d'Antioc, 176

Ghent, 315

Gilbert de Clare (earl of Gloucester), 266

Gilbert de Strigoil, 261 (n. 97)

Giles of Rome, 284 (n. 69)

Giotto, 38 (n. 31)

Girard of Amiens, 184, 197–98 (n. 47). See also *Escanor*

Giraut de Bornelh, 8, 37 (n. 23)

Gisela (wife of Emperor Conrad II), 14–15

Gisla. *See* Alcuin, writings of

Godewyk, Robert, 275

Godfrey (*pictor*), 178–79

Godfrey of Bouillon, 200 (n. 62)

Godwinson, Tostig (earl of Northumbria), 124

Golden Legend. See Legenda aurea

Goldsmiths, 193 (n. 19), 267, 269–72, 282 (nn. 14, 19, 21)

Gonnor (wife of Richard II of Normandy), 42 (n. 68)

Gonzalo Moriel, 208

Gormond et Isembard, 181–82, 184, 186–87

Goscelin of Saint Bertin (monk of Canterbury), 165, 174 (n. 62); *Liber confortatorius*, 79; writings for Eve (nun of Wilton and recluse of Angers), 79

Gosnay, Chartreuse de, 315–16

Grandes chroniques de France, 182

Gray Sisters, 314

Greenhalgh, James, 300

Gregory (abbot of Saint-Albans), 108

Gregory VII (pope), 93

Gregory IX (pope), 210, 222 (n. 35)

Gregory of Nyssa, 51

Gregory of Tours, 12

Gregory the Great, Saint (pope), 104 (nn. 48, 52), 115, 117 (fig. 10); *Cura pastoralis*, 256–57 (n. 61)

Greyfriars Church (London), 278

Grimbald (physician), 159

Grosmont, Henry (duke of Lancaster), 235, 255 (n. 56)

Grosmont, Isabel, 254 (n. 45)

Grosseteste, Robert, 180; *Reules Seynt Robert*, 246, 262–63 (n. 113);

Grosseteste, Robert (*continued*)
  translation and commentary of
  Pseudo-Dionysus's *De celesti
  hierarchia*, 180
Guarino da Verona, 317
Guérin of Ponthieu, 181
Guibert of Parma (bishop), 94
Guilbert de Clare (earl of Gloucester),
  266
Guillaume de Palerne, 47 (n. 107)
Guillaume le Conquerant, 176, 194
  (n. 28)
Guillemette (abbess of Maubuisson),
  211
Guinevere, 198 (n. 47)
Gui of Morimond (abbot), 206
Guiraut de Calanso, 16
Guischart de Beauliu: *Sermon*, 231, 246,
  252 (n. 26)
Gundrada (granddaughter of
  Charlemagne). *See* Alcuin,
  writings of
Gundulph of Rochester, 159, 170
  (n. 20). *See also* Architects
Guy (earl of Warwick), 231, 234

Hacon, Dionysia, 246, 263 (n. 117)
Hadju, Robert, 9
Hagia Irene, church of, 56
Hagia Sophia, church of, 54, 58–59
Hala, Edessene monk, 58
Haman, 94
Hanhan, Ismania, 243, 261 (n. 98)
Hanley Castle, construction of, 280
Hardyng, John, 258 (n. 77)
Harold (king of Anglo-Saxon England),
  158
Harold Harefoot, 16, 41 (n. 66), 92, 104
  (n. 45)
Harper, Adam, 272
Harthacnut, 16–17, 41 (n. 66), 92, 104
  (n. 45)

Hartwic (abbot of Saint Emmeram), 113
Haserensis, 15
Hastings, John (earl of Pembroke), 270
Hathumoda (abbess of Gandersheim),
  38 (n. 28), 90
Hawise de Quincy, 262 (n. 113)
Hector of Troy, 200 (n. 62), 232
Hedwig of Silesia, 8–9, 22
Hedybia. *See* Jerome, Saint
Helena (mother of Constantine the
  Great), 51–52, 67, 96
Héloïse, 27, 100 (n. 22); letters to
  Abelard, 80, 124; *Problemata*, 80–81
Heluis d'Ecouffans, 13
Henri I, le Libéral (count of
  Champagne), 18
Henri II (count of Champagne), 18, 36
  (n. 18), 44 (n. 76)
Henry (lord of Beaumont), 254 (n. 44)
Henry (earl of Lancaster), 255 (n. 56)
Henry de Motelot, 285 (n. 88)
Henry III (Roman emperor), 14–15
Henry IV (Roman emperor), 17, 93–94
Henry V (Roman emperor), 94, 163
Henry of Bolingbroke. *See* Henry IV
  (king of England)
Henry I of Silesia, 8–9
Henry the Fowler (king of
  Germany), 89
Henry the Lion of Saxony, 15, 17, 40
  (n. 59)
Henry the Navigator, 308–9
Henry the Young (king of England),
  129
Henry I (king of England), 25–26, 42
  (n. 69), 43 (n. 73), 155, 157–58, 161–
  66 passim, 172 (n. 46), 173 (n. 48),
  185
Henry II (king of England), 24, 36
  (n. 18), 43 (nn. 69, 73), 95, 127–29,
  149 (n. 58), 186, 196 (n. 39), 197
  (n. 44), 199 (n. 56), 218 (nn. 6, 8)
Henry III (king of England), 176–77,

179–80, 184–85, 187–88, 192 (n. 14), 194 (n. 23)

Henry IV (king of England), 237, 239, 254 (nn. 45, 47), 255 (n. 50)

Henry V (king of England), 238, 256 (nn. 57, 58), 258 (n. 72), 308

Henry VI (king of England), 32

Henry VII (king of England), 32

Henry VIII (king of England), 300

Hercules, 95

Hereford, cathedral at, 271

Herrad of Landsberg (abbess of Hohenburg), 130; *Hortus deliciarum*, 35 (n. 5), 113, 117–123 passim

Herrara, monastery of, 221 (n. 30)

Herveus (recluse), 99 (n. 18)

Hilarius, 100 (n. 18)

Hild (abbess of Whitby), 12, 27

Hildebert of Lavardin (bishop of Le Mans), 81, 83–84, 101 (n. 32), 102 (n. 33), 160–62; letters and poems to Cecilia, 83; letters and poems to Muriel, 83; poems in praise of Adela of Blois, 83

Hildegard of Bingen, 12, 39 (n. 45), 100 (n. 19), 113–14, 118, 127, 143; *Scivias*, 113, 115, 117, 120 (fig. 13), 147 (n. 31)

Hildeli (abbess of the Abbey of Barking), 27

Hildelida, Abbess, 77, 82

Hilton, Walter, 240; *On Contemplative and Active Life*, 259 (n. 79); *Scala*, 295

Historical Narrative, 86–97 passim, 102 (n. 37), 182, 197 (n. 41). *See also* Chronicles

Hoccleve, Thomas, 239, 242, 246–47, 255 (n. 50); "Balade to Edward Duke of York," 246; "Complaint of the Virgin," 236, 246; *Epistle to Cupid*, 231; "How to Learn to Die," 229, 231–32, 258 (n. 75); "Jereslaus's

Wife," 231; *Regement of Princes*, 255 (n. 55), 264 (n. 126); "The Tale of Jonathas," 231; translations from the *Gesta Romanorum*, 231; translations from *Pèlerinage de l'âme*, 236

Hohenberg, abbey of, 35 (n. 5), 117, 122 (fig. 15), 123 (fig. 16)

Holland, Eleanor, 257 (n. 63)

Holland, John, 257 (n. 68)

Holland, Margaret (duchess of Clarence), 247, 257 (n. 70), 265 (n. 142)

Holland, Thomas (earl of Kent), 257 (n. 70)

Holofernes, 87, 94

Holy Trinity Aldgate, 158, 168 (n. 16)

Homer, 85

Homerocentones, 52

Horace, 79

Hormisdas Palace (Constantinople), 57–59

Hortus deliciarum. See Herrad of Landsberg (abbess of Hohanburg)

Hospitalers, Order of, xi

Howard, Elizabeth de Vere (countess of Oxford), 241, 247, 265 (n. 140), 260 (n. 87)

Howard, John (duke of Norfolk), 260 (n. 87)

Howard, Katherine Moleyns, 247, 265 (n. 139)

Hrabanus Maurus, 101 (n. 29). Commentaries of: dedicated to Empress Ermengard, 99 (n. 15); dedicated to Empress Judith, 78

Hrotsvit of Gandersheim, 88–90, 104 (n. 47); *Gesta Ottonis*, 12, 88, 103 (n. 41); *Primordia coenobii Gandeshemensis*, 8, 90

Hugh de Albini (earl of Sussex and Arundel), 242

Hugh de Colyngham, 278

Hugh de Hibernia (*scriptor*), 194 (n. 26)

Hugh de Vercelli, 274

Hugh of Flavigny, 104 (n. 48)

Hugh of Fleury, 3, 95–96, 104 (n. 52); dedication to Matilda of Tuscany, 104 (n. 49); *Historia ecclesiastica*, 86, 95, 104 (n. 49); dedication to Adela of Blois, 86, 104 (n. 49); *Modernorum regum Francorum liber*, 104 (n. 49)

Hugh of Saint Victor, xii

Hugh IV (count of Saint-Pol), 47 (n. 107)

Hugot, Jean, 18, 43 (n. 73)

Hugues de Sainte-Marie. *See* Hugh of Fleury

Humanism, 317

Humphrey (duke of Gloucester), 258 (nn. 72, 75)

Humphrey de Bohun (earl of Hereford, Essex, and Northampton), 236, 255 (n. 54), 256 (n. 61)

Hunt, Isabel, 247, 265 (n. 136)

Hunt, John, 247, 265 (n. 136)

Illuminators, 32, 140, 153 (n.97), 178–80, 192 (n. 16), 270; patronage of manuscript illumination, 267, 274–75

Ingeborg of Denmark (wife of Philip Augustus), 133–35

Ingeborg Psalter, 116 (fig. 8), 133–35. *See also* Psalters

Ingelram, 104 (n. 50)

Innocent III (pope), 206, 311–12; *De miseria conditionis humanae*, 311

Innocent IV (pope), 215, 219 (n. 13), 226 (n. 79)

Irene (empress of Rome, mother of Constantine VI), 96

Isabeau of Bavaria, 31

Isabel (daughter of Pedro of Portugal), 309

Isabel de Warenne (countess of Arundel), 242–43, 246, 261 (nn. 95, 97), 263 (n. 116); patronage of Matthew Paris, 242, 246

Isabella d'Este, 33, 36 (n. 15)

Isabella of France (wife of Edward II), 201 (n. 62), 270, 281 (n. 2)

Isabelle de Coucy, 131

Isabel of Aragon, 314, 316

Isabel of Bourbon, 313

Isabel of Molina, 227 (n. 80)

Isabel of Portugal (duchess of Burgundy), 306–20 passim; marriage of, 306; motto, 306

Isabel of Spain, 308

Isembart, romance of, 181–88 passim. *See also* Eleanor of Castile (queen of England)

Italica. *See* Augustine, Saint

Ivo, bishop of Chartres, 159–61

J. Pierpont Morgan Library (New York), xvi, 22, 136

Jacotín de Ramecourt, 311

Jacqueline de Hainault, 258 (n. 72)

Jacques de Gerynes (coppersmith), 313

Jacques de Gruytrobe, 311

Jahel, 94

Jaime (archbishop of Lisbon), 313–14

Jaime I of Aragon, 208

James, Saint, 227 (n. 82)

Jean, duc de Berry, 49 (n. 130)

Jean d'Arras, 46 (n. 100)

Jean de Brienne, 212

Jean de Brixay, 312

Jean de Castel, 23

Jean de Créquy, 307

Jean de Joinville. *See* Joinville, Jean de

Jean de la Mote (minstrel), 284 (n. 58)

Jean de Meun, xvi–xvii

Jean de Vignay, xiii, xvii–xviii; translation of Vincent de Beauvais's *Speculum historiale*, xi, xiv

Jean le Noir, 32. *See also* Illuminators

Jeanne de la Poterne the Younger, 13

Jeanne d'Evreux, 28, 140, 142, 153
(n. 99), 212

Jeanne de Navarre, xvi, xviii, 28, 32, 48
(nn. 117, 118)

Jeanne II de Navarre, 136, 140–42. *See
also* Psalters

Jeanne of Auvergne (duchess of
Berry), 31

Jeanne of Brabant, 313

Jeanne of Burgundy, xi–xii, xvii–xviii

Jeanne of Flanders, 21

Jean Sans Peur, 49 (n. 126)

Jerome, Saint, 33, 46 (n. 92), 74–75, 77,
79–81, 97 (n. 4), 98 (nn. 5, 6), 99
(n. 13), 103 (n. 39), 104 (n. 52), 229–
30, 256 (n. 61); *Commentary on the
Epistle of the Ephesians, Vitae patrum*,
256–57 (n. 61). Writings for:
Algasia, 75; Celantia, 98 (nn. 5, 6);
Demetrias, 98 (n. 6); Eustochium, 75,
98 (n. 6); Fabiola, 75; Furia, 98
(n. 6); Geruchia, 98 (n. 6); Hedybia,
75, 98 (nn. 5, 6); Laeta, 98 (n. 6);
Marcella, 74–75, 81, 98 (nn. 5, 6);
Paula, 75, 98 (n. 5), 249 (n. 6); Paula
(granddaughter of Paula), 75, 249
(n. 6); Principia, 75; Salina, 98 (n. 6)

Jerusalem, 52, 74–75, 117, 165, 223
(n. 53)

Jesse Tree. *See* Tree of Jesse

Jesus Christ, xvi, 70 (n. 44), 78, 81, 90,
94, 108, 111–13, 120, 129, 131, 133,
135–36, 142, 151 (n. 79), 161, 215,
216, 226 (n. 77), 227 (n. 81), 229,
240–41, 250 (n. 12), 272, 293,
297–98, 309

Jewelry, 267, 272, 282 (n. 21)

Jiménez de Rada, Rodrigo. *See* Ximénez
de Rada, Rodrigo (archbishop of
Toledo)

Joan (countess of Westmorland), 258
(n. 75)

Joan (princess, daughter of Edward I),
266

Joanna (daughter of Eleanor de Bohun),
237

Joanna of England, 203

Joan of Acre, 257 (n. 63)

Joan of Arc, 307

João (master of the Order of Santiago),
308

João I (king of Portugal), 31, 236, 308,
312

João II (king of Portugal), 310

John (duke of Bedford), 258 (n. 72)

John (king of England), 18, 150 (n. 61),
203

John de Harleton, 285 (n. 87)

John de Hoveden, 176, 187–88, 200
(n. 62)

John de la Pole, 243

John de Lenne, 284 (n. 69)

John de Markeby (sculptor), 269

John de Ralegh, 261 (n. 98)

John de Stratton, 275

John de Vere (earl of Oxford), 241, 260
(n. 87)

John of Ephesus, 57–60

John of Gaunt (duke of Lancaster), 235,
239, 256 (n. 60), 258 (n. 71), 308

John of Hephaestu, 58

John of Lydus, 60

John of Oberg, 40 (n. 59)

John of Trevisa, 233

John the Baptist, 8, 90, 272

John the Cappodocian, 60

John the Evangelist, 78, 118, 272

John I of Portugal, 31, 236, 308, 312

John the Harper, 272–73

John the Poor (abbot of Fécamp), 15

Joinville, Jean de, xv, xvi, xviii; *Histoire
de Saint Louis*, xv–xvi

Jongleurs, 4, 23
Judas Maccabee, 184, 200 (n. 62)
Judith (biblical heroine), 78, 87, 94, 96, 103 (n. 39), 118
Judith (countess of Flanders), 21, 124–25
Judith of Bavaria (wife of Louis the Pious), 83, 99, 101 (n. 28). See also Hrabanus Maurus
Juliana (mother of Demetrias). See Augustine, Saint
Julian Argentarius, 63
Julian of Norwich, 294–301 passim, 303 (n. 22); The Showings, 294–95, 300
Justina (the Arian), 96
Justine I (Byzantine emperor), 53–54, 60–61, 71 (n. 62)
Justinian (Byzantine emperor), 50, 54, 56–57, 59–61, 63–64, 66, 70–71 (n. 58), 71 (n. 78), 88

Katherine, Saint, 229, 309. See also Bokenham, Osbern; Saints' lives
Katherine of Siena, Saint, 240, 258–59 (n. 79)
Katherine of Valois, 238
Kempe, John, 295
Kempe, Margery, 294–305 passim; The Book of Margery Kempe, 295, 298–99, 303 (nn. 21, 24), 304 (nn. 26, 27, 29, 30, 31, 32, 33), 305 (nn. 35, 37)
Kenilworth, 180; castle at, 280
Kent, 290
Kilwardby (archbishop), 263 (n. 116)
King's College, Cambridge, 278
King's Evil, 177
King's Hall, 286 (n. 102)
King's Lynn, 294–96, 303 (n. 21), 304 (nn. 25, 30)
Konrad: Rolandslied, 15, 40–41 (n. 59)

La Trinité, abbey of (Caen), 35 (n. 4), 42 (n. 68), 217 (n. 2)

Lacy, Margaret (countess of Lincoln), 245–46, 262 (n. 113), 263 (n. 118)
Ladder of Mohammed. See Alfonso X, the Wise (king of Castile and León)
Laeta. See Jerome, Saint
Lainez, Inés (abbess of Las Huelgas), 208–9
Lais, 24
Lambert of Saint Omer, 114
Lancelot (prose), 194 (n. 28), 237
Langton, Walter, 263 (n. 113)
Las Huelgas: abbess of, 206–9, 219 (n. 10), 220 (nn. 18, 22, 23), 222 (nn. 35, 44); abbey of, 203–15 passim, 221 (nn. 27, 34), 222 (nn. 43, 44), 223 (n. 55), 224 (nn. 57, 58), 226 (n. 76); name of, 221 (nn. 27, 32), 222 (n. 48)
Latin: Latinate culture, 187, 289, 291; use of, xiv–xvii, 26–27, 36 (n. 11), 40 (n. 57), 47 (n. 111), 74, 80, 86, 100 (n. 22), 115, 124, 180, 182, 272, 274, 295, 297, 303, 310, 315, 316–17
Laurette d'Alsace, 26
Lavinia (wife of Aeneas), 87
Le Mans, cathedral of, 160
LeFranc, Martin, 307
Legenda aurea, 237, 240, 256–57 (n. 61), 259 (n. 79)
Legenda sanctorum, 241
Legend of Saint Margaret, 238–39. See also Lydgate, John; Saints' lives
LeHarpur, William, 165, 174 (n. 59)
León, cathedral of, 213–14, 225 (n. 72)
Leonor of Castile (daughter of Alfonso VIII and Leonor of England), 208
Leonor of England (queen of Castile), 15–16, 41 (nn. 60, 61), 135, 202–27 passim
Leonor of Portugal: patronage of Christine de Pizan's work, 31, 310
Letters to women, 73–81 passim

Liber de divinorum operum, 115
Liber floridus, 114
Liber vitae, 125
Liédet, Loyset, 312
Life of Edward the Confessor. See *Vita Aedwardi Regis*
Life of Mary Magdalen, 229, 240. *See also* Bokenham, Osbern; Saints' lives
Life of Richard de Wyche, 263 (n. 116). *See also* Saints' lives
Life of Saint Agatha, 247. *See also* Bokenham, Osbern; Saints' lives
Life of Saint Alexis, 108. *See also* Saints' lives
Life of Saint Anne, 247, 263 (n. 114). *See also* Bokenham, Osbern; Saints' lives
Life of Saint Augustine, 247. *See also* Saints' lives
Life of Saint Dorothy, 247. *See also* Bokenham, Osbern; Saints' lives
Life of Saint Elizabeth, 241, 247. *See also* Bokenham, Osbern; Saints' lives
Life of Saint Jerome, 247. *See also* Saints' lives
Life of Saint Katherine, 229. *See also* Bokenham, Osbern; Saints' lives
Life of Saint Katherine of Siena, 240, 247. *See also* Saints' lives
Life of Saint Margaret of Scotland, 18, 163, 185, 240. *See also* Saints' lives
Life of Saint Mathilda, 258–59 (n. 79). *See also* Saints' lives
Lille, 310, 312, 314
Lionel (duke of Clarence), 257 (n. 63)
Literacy: aural, 302 (n. 12); of men, 14–15, 40 (n. 57); of women, 14–15, 94, 106, 131, 142, 157, 167 (n. 4), 175, 199 (n. 55), 289, 291, 295, 298, 300, 303–4 (n. 24)
Liudgard (daughter of Otto I), 89
Liudulf (duke of Saxony, son of Otto I), 8, 38 (n. 28), 89–90

Liutgard (queen of France), 90
Liutprand, 102
Livre des seyntz medicines, 235
Llanthony, priory of, 238
Lollards, 290–93, 301 (n. 8), 304 (n. 31)
London, 158, 168 (n. 13), 169 (n. 18), 267, 275, 280, 290
Longchamp, abbey of, 13
Lothar (king of Italy), 89
Lothar Crystal, 151 (n. 78)
Lothar I, 83
Lothar (king of Italy), 89
Louis de Mâle (count of Flanders), 313
Louis I (the Pious), 83
Louis III (king of France), 181
Louis VII (king of France), 37 (n. 19), 44 (n. 76), 127–28, 131
Louis VIII (king of France), 133, 212
Louis IX, Saint (king of France), xi–xii, xvi, 133, 135–36, 138, 152 (n. 88), 176, 214
Louis X, le Hutin (king of France), 143, 153 (n. 99)
Louis XI (king of France), 31, 241, 314
Louis XII (king of France), 31, 201 (n. 62)
Louise of Savoy, 31, 201 (n. 62)
Louvre, 142
Love, Nicholas, 258 (n. 79), 304 (n. 29)
Lucas de Túy, 216–17; *Crónica de España,* 216, 227 (n. 84)
Lucius III (pope), 219 (n. 12)
Lucretia, rape of, 87
Lucum, 241
Lull, bishop of Mainz, 82
Lydgate, John, 230–31, 241, 243–44, 250 (n. 12), 259 (n. 84); "Balade at the Departing," 244; "Epistle to Sibille," 230, 247; *Fifteen Ioyes of Oure Lady,* 260 (n. 89), 247; *Guy of Warwick,* 231, 234, 247; "Invocation to Saint Anne," 247; *Legend of St. Margaret,* 238–39, 247; "My Lady

Lydgate, John (*continued*)
Dere," 244; *The Nightingale* (possible attribution), 247; *Pilgrimage of the World*, 261–62 (n. 103); "A Tretise for Lauandres," 247; *The Virtues of the Mass*, 244, 247
Lyric poetry, 7–8, 23, 81–86 passim, 229–65 passim
Lys, abbey of (Notre-Dame du Lys), 210–12, 225 (nn. 66, 69)

Macrobius, 80
Magna Carta, 245
Mahaut (countess of Artois), 21, 143, 176
Malalas, John, 52, 60–62; *Chronicle*, 51, 60–61
Malcolm Canmore, 15, 40 (n. 57), 156
Malcolm III (king of Scotland), 15, 40 (n. 57), 156
Malmesbury (abbey of), 168 (n. 13)
Manutio, Aldo, 33. *See also* Caxton, William; Fichet, Guillaume
Marbod of Rennes, 101 (n. 32), 162
Marcella. *See* Jerome, Saint
Marcellina. *See* Ambrose, Saint (bishop of Milan)
Marcia (painter), 29
Mare (holy man), 58
Margaret (daughter of Eleanor of Castile), 185
Margaret of Anjou (queen of England), 32
Margaret of Austria, 31, 318
Margaret of Flanders, 313
Margaret of Provence, 176; children of, 22, 136
Margaret of Scotland, Saint, 15, 18, 156, 162, 163, 185, 229, 238–39, 240, 250 (n. 10), 253 (n. 39). *See also* Bokenham, Osbern; Lydgate, John; Saints' lives

Margaret of York (duchess of Burgundy), 156, 162, 185, 316–17; patron of Caxton's *Recuyell of the Historyes of Troyes*, 33, 259 (n. 80)
Marguerite de Bourgogne (wife of Louis X), 31, 49 (n. 126), 143
Marguerite de Navarre, 28
Marguerite de Provence (wife of Louis IX), 176; children of, 22, 136
Marguerite of Bavaria, 31, 49 (n. 126)
María Pérez de Guzmán (abbess of Las Huelgas), 208
Marie de Berry, 31
Marie de Bourbon, 31
Marie de Brabant, 23, 46 (n. 100)
Marie de Champagne, 18–21, 23, 26, 44 (n. 76), 100 (n. 19); patronage of Chrétien de Troyes, xiii–xiv, 15, 18–19
Marie de France, 24
Marie of Hungary, 318
Marie Talvas, 185, 199 (n. 53)
Markyate, priory of, 107, 112
Marshal, Isabel (daughter of Isabel FitzGilbert Marshal), 243
Marshal, Isabel FitzGilbert (countess of Pembroke), 242–43, 261 (n. 97)
Marshal, Maud, 243
Marshal, Sibyl, 243
Marshal, Thomas, 278
Marshal, William (earl of Pembroke), 242–43, 261 (n. 97)
Martha (biblical figure), 94
Martin, Saint, 13
Martín, Frey, 208
Martin Ferrandi (squire), 198 (n. 47)
Mary (nun of Amesbury, daughter of Edward I and Eleanor of Castile), 246, 257 (n. 63), 264 (n. 121)
Mary, Virgin, 21, 45 (n. 86), 52, 111, 113, 115, 117–18, 120, 130–31, 133, 138, 140, 142, 146 (n. 23), 206, 214–

17, 227 (nn. 81, 82), 229, 230, 235, 249 (n. 7), 250 (n. 8), 250–51 (n. 12), 252 (n. 26), 272, 279, 297

Mary (sister of Lazarus), 94

Mary de Bohun, 237, 255 (n. 50), 256 (nn. 58, 59)

Mary de Sancto Paulo (countess of Pembroke), 277, 279–81

Mary Magdalen, 21, 111–12, 124, 133, 136, 146 (n. 23), 229, 233, 240, 249 (n. 7), 249–50 (n. 8), 297. *See also* Bokenham, Osbern; *Life of Mary Magdalen*; Saints' lives

Mary of Oignes, Saint, 296

Matallana: abbey of, 210, 219 (n. 10), 223 (n. 55), 224 (nn. 57, 58); church of, 210–11

Mathilda (sister of Otto II), 124

Mathilda of Hackeborn, 258–59 (n. 79)

Mathilde (abbess of Quedlinburg). *See* Widukind of Corvey

Matilda (abbess of Essen), 102 (n. 37). *See also* Aethelweard

Matilda (daughter of Henry I of England), 42–43 (n. 69), 43 (n. 73), 94

Matilda (Maud) de Bohun, 261 (n. 93)

Matilda (wife of Henry the Fowler), 89

Matilda, (wife of William the Conqueror), 42 (n. 68)

Matilda of Courtenai (countess of Nevers), 138–39

Matilda of Flanders, 35 (n. 4)

Matilda of Saxony (wife of Henry the Lion), 15, 40 (n. 59)

Matilda of Scotland (wife of Henry I of England), 15, 20, 25, 42 (n. 68), 44 (n. 81), 155–74 passim, 185; building projects, 158; literary patronage, 18, 161–66 passim; patronage of music, 165; patronage of needlework and metalwork, 159

Matilda of Tuscany, 92–95; patron of Donizo, 92, 97 (n. 1), 104 (nn. 46, 48, 49)

Matrilineal paradigms, 14, 40 (n. 51), 129, 202, 228, 233, 238, 244, 246; other female cognatic relations, 242

Maubuisson, abbey of (Notre-Dame la Royale), 210–12, 214, 224 (nn. 59, 60), 225 (nn. 66, 69)

Maud de Lacy (wife of Richard, earl of Gloucester), 150 (n. 70)

Maud of Lancaster, 235, 254 (n. 46), 256 (n. 56)

Maud de Warenne, 242

Maxence (emperor), 250 (n. 10)

Maximian, 71 (n. 78)

McNamara, Jo Ann, 11

Mechtild von der Pfalz, 49 (n. 131)

Melania (wife of Pinian). *See* Augustine, Saint

Meliadus, 177, 179, 184

Menander, 56, 69 (n. 34), 71 (n. 59)

Meneses, Alfondo de, 211

Merton Priory, 158, 169 (n. 17)

Metalwork, patronage of, 159, 166, 315

Metham, John: *Amoryus and Cleopes*, 231, 248, 251–52 (n. 21)

Miélot, Jean, 310–12; *Moralités et traités de la science de bien mourir*, 312; translations of Denis de Ryckel's *Quatre dernières choses*, 312; translations of *Le miroir de l'âme pecheresse*, 311

Milan, 76–77

Minerva, 252 (n. 30)

Miroir des dames. See Speculum dominarum

Misol, Doña (abbess of Las Huelgas), 207

Mone, Avis, 290–92, 294, 296–97, 301, 302 (nn. 9, 12, 15)

Mone, Thomas, 302 (n. 9)

Monica (mother of Saint Augustine), 230, 251 (n. 16)

Monophysites, 57–59, 67, 70 (n. 58)

Montagu, Alice (countess of Salisbury), 260 (n. 85)

Montagu, Thomas (earl of Salisbury), 243–44

Monthermer, Edward, 238, 270

Mont-Renaud, Chartreuse de (Noyon), 315

Mont Saint-Michel, 42 (n. 68)

Mortimer, Anne, 239, 257 (n. 63)

Mortimer, Edmund (earl of March), 238

Mortimer, Roger (earl of March), 257 (n. 63)

Motte-aux-Bois, Château de la (Lille), 316–17

Mouskès, Philippe, 181

Munchensy, Denise (or Dionysia), 245–46, 262–63 (n. 113), 264 (n. 120)

Muriel (nun). *See* Baudri of Bourgeuil; Hildebert of Lavardin (bishop of Le Mans)

Museum of Ancient Art (Lisbon), 315

Music, women's patronage of, 1, 23, 165, 174 (nn. 59, 60), 272–73, 284 (n. 58)

Mutual love, 159, 303 (n. 17)

Narbonne, 15, 37 (n. 23). *See also* Ermengarde de Narbonne

Nazareth, abbess of, 21

Needlework, 42 (n. 68), 83, 170 (n. 22), 283 (n. 43), 271, 281; liturgical vestments, 159–60, 267, 271, 316; women's patronage of, 124, 159–60, 166, 267–69, 271–72, 283 (n. 33), 316

Neri di Bicci: *Ricordanze*, 13, 36 (n. 15), 40 (n. 50)

Neville, Anne (countess of Stafford, duchess of Buckingham), 239–41,

247, 259 (n. 81), 260 (nn. 85, 89), 264 (n. 135)

Neville, Cecily (duchess of York), 239–40, 258 (n. 77), 259 (nn. 79, 80)

Neville, Ralph (earl of Westmoreland), 239–40

Neville, Richard (earl of Warwick and Salisbury), 260 (nn. 85, 89)

Nicholas de Anesty, 263 (n. 113)

Nicolas de Senlis, 26, 46 (n. 103)

Nicholas V (pope), 314, 317

Nieppe, forest of (Lille), 316; château of, 317

Nike Riots, 56

Nilgen, Ursula, 108

Norfolk, 290, 294, 302 (n. 12), 303 (n. 18)

Norwich, 290

Notker, 14

Notre-Dame de Chartres. *See* Chartres, Notre-Dame de

Notre-Dame du Lys, 210–12, 225 (nn. 66, 69)

Notre-Dame la Royale, 210–12, 214, 224 (nn. 59, 60), 225 (nn. 66, 69)

Nun of Barking, 48 (n. 113)

Nuns, patronage of, 10–13, 35 (n. 5), 113–24 passim

Oceanus, 74–75

Ockham, 274–75

Oda (wife of Liudulf of Saxony), 8, 38 (n. 28), 90–91

Odilia, Saint, 120

Olibrius, 250 (n. 10)

Orderic Vital (monk of Saint Evroul), 35 (n. 4), 166, 173 (n. 48)

Order of the Golden Fleece, 306

Ordóñez, Mayor, 209

Origen, 74–75, 80; *Homilies on the Song of Songs*, 98 (n. 5)

Orme, Nicholas, 256 (n. 59)
Orkneyinga Saga, 8, 37 (n. 24)
Orosius, 79, 87
Otto I (emperor), 88–90, 102 (n. 37), 104 (n. 47)
Otto II (emperor), 88, 90
Ovid, 153 (n. 99); *Ars amatoria*, 80
Oxford, 244; Oxford University, 275–76

Pacilla (wife of Theodosius), 96
Palamedes, 179
Pammachus, 74–75
Pantaselle, 232
Paraclete, 27
Paris, Matthew, 156, 224 (n. 63); *Chronica majora*, 135, 169 (n. 16); *Estoire de Seint Ædward le Rei*, 176, 185, 243; "Vie de Saint Auban," 243; "Vie de Saint Edmond," 242–43, 246
Paris, William, 190 (n. 7)
Partonopeu de Blois, 23
Paschal, John (bishop of Llandaff), 276
Paschal II (pope), 161, 167 (n. 3)
Patronage: as collaborative effort with artist, xiii–xiv, 3, 5, 18–19, 73–97 passim; definition of, 4, 35 (n. 5), 248 (n. 3), 289; evidence of, 2, 175–76; familial expectation for, 14–16; importance of, 1–2; masculine root of, 288; matrilineal paradigms of, 14, 202, 228, 233; modes of payment, 4–5, 12, 269–77 passim; corporate, 12, 35 (n. 5); of holy women, 10–13, 35 (n. 5), 113–24 passim; of married women, 7–9, 13–14, 23, 38 (n. 27); of single women, 13; of widows, 7, 9–10, 13; of the Virgin Mary, 34, 214–17; of women artists, 32, 270; reasons for, 14–25, 33; and assertion of power, 1–2, 17, 20; concerns for women, 11, 18–19, 27, 33–34, 60; dynastic reasons for, 17, 176, 185, 199 (n. 52), 202–27 passim, 234; educational purposes, 22–23, 25, 33; personal reasons for, 18, 25, 33; political reasons for, 16–18, 25, 33, 73, 200 (n. 61), 202, 216–17, 288; religious, 8–9, 20–23, 33, 42 (n. 68), 45 (n. 89), 96, 213, 269–71; and social responsibility, 16, 23–25, 33
Paul, Saint, 146 (n. 23)
Paula, 79, 230, 249 (n. 6). See also Jerome, Saint
Paula (daughter of Eustochium), 249 (n. 6). See also Jerome, Saint
Paulina. See Augustine, Saint
Paul the Deacon, 96, 102 (n. 38); *Historia Romana*, 87; dedication to Adelpurga, 87
Peaceweavers, 165
Pecham, John (archbishop), 180
Pedro of Portugal, 308–10, 313; *Book of Benefits*, 308; *The Virtuous Benefactor*, 309
Peire d'Alvernhe, 8, 37 (n. 23)
Peire Rogier, 7, 15, 41 (n. 60)
Pelagius, 76
Pembroke College, 277
Penha Longa, convent of, 314
Penthesilea, 95
Perceval, 25, 200 (n. 62)
Perez, Gondrada, 223 (n. 53)
Perez, Tello, 223 (n. 53)
Pert, John, 291
Peter of Dreux, 227 (n. 81)
Peter of Lara, 37 (n. 20)
Peter the Deacon, 115, 117 (fig. 10)
Peter the Parisian, 190 (n. 7)
Petrarch, 33, 317
Petronilla (nun at Saint Laurent), 99 (n. 18)

Philanthropia, 51, 54, 56, 62, 66

Philip, John, 261 (n. 98)

Philip Augustus, 18, 44 (n. 76), 133, 182–83

Philippa (wife of Erik of Denmark), 237, 256 (n. 59)

Philippa of Hainaut, xvi, xviii, 5, 36 (n. 14), 235, 254 (n. 47), 258 (n. 71), 284 (n. 58)

Philippa of Lancaster, 235–36, 239, 246, 254 (n. 47), 255 (nn. 51, 52), 264 (n. 123), 308

Philippe de Mohun, 264 (n. 126)

Philippe de Thaon, 26

Philip I (king of France), 173 (n. 58)

Philip III, the Bold (king of France), 313

Philip IV, the Fair (king of France), xvi–xviii, 28, 153 (n. 99), 198 (n. 47)

Philippe V, le Long (king of France), 143

Philip the Good (duke of Burgundy), 306–7, 309–11, 315–17

Philomena, 241

Pie, Hugh, 302 (n. 8)

Pierre Mauclerc (comte de Dreux), 216

Piers Plowman, 138

Placidia the Younger, 53–54

Plato, 69 (n. 32), 120

Pleshey: castle of, 256 (n. 60); College of, 238

Pliny, 33

Plutarch, 316

Poggio, 317

Poitiers, 11, 128, 203; cathedral of, 128–29

Ponthieu, 181, 183–88 passim, 198 (n. 47), 199 (n. 53)

Pontigny, 242

Pontoise, abbey at, 224 (n. 63)

Poor Clares, 22, 314

Porto, bishopric of, 310

Praxedes, 94

Préavin Trinitarian monastery, 317

Premonstratensians, 131

Primera crónica. See Alfonso X, the Wise (king of Castile and León)

Principia. See Jerome, Saint

Printers, 33, 317. *See also* Caxton, William

Proba, 76. *See also* Augustine, Saint

Procopius, 54–67 passim; *Anecdota*, 50, 55–57, 60, 62, 67 (n. 2), 70 (n. 42); *Buildings*, 50, 56–59, 61, 67–68 (n. 2); *Wars*, 61, 68 (n. 2)

Procula (wife of Pilate), 120

Prophet Isaiah, Church of the, 53

Prostitutes: as patrons, 140

Prudentius (bishop of Troyes), 99 (n. 13)

Psalters, 16, 130–31, 145 (nn. 15, 16), 190 (n. 7), 192 (n. 16), 237; "Alphonso" Psalter, 178, 193–94 (n. 22); "Bird" Psalter, 178, 193 (n. 22); of Blanche of Castile, 22–23, 133; of Christina of Markyate (also known as Saint Albans Psalter), 107, 108–12 passim, 133, 142; of Eleanor of Castile, 178–79; Ingeborg Psalter, 116 (fig. 8); of Isabeau of Bavaria, 23; of Jeanne II de Navarre, 136, 141 (fig. 29); of Saint Louis, 136; Shaftesbury Psalter, 113

Pseudo-Bonaventure: *Aquillon de l'amour divin*, 312; *Meditationes vitae Christi*, 239, 296–97; *Mirrour of the Blessed Lyf of Jesu Christ*, 258 (n. 79), 304 (n. 29); *Stimulus amoris*, 295

Pseudo-Dionysius, 180

Pseudo-Kodinos, 64

Pseudo-Turpin Chronicle, 26, 46 (n. 103), 47 (n. 107), 182–83

Psychomachaea, 118

Pucelle, Jean. *See* Illuminators
Pulcheria, 52, 56
Pycard, Thomas, 261 (n. 101)

Quarrel of the Rose, 34, 49 (n. 135)
Quatre fils aymon, Les, 261–62 (n. 103)
Quedlinberg, 124
Queens' College, Cambridge, 32
Quemada de Villalobos, Vasco, 311
Querelle des femmes, 34

Radegund, Saint (queen of France), 11–
    12, 22, 35 (n. 5), 39 (n. 39), 82. *See
    also* Fortunatus, Venantius
Rahere (minstrel and canon of Saint
    Paul's), 165, 174 (n. 60)
Raimbaut d'Aurenga, 16, 40 (n. 60)
Ralph de Kerdington, 285 (n. 87)
Ramón Vidal de Besalú, 41 (n. 61)
Rangerius, 97 (n. 1); *Liber de anulo et
    baculo*, 94
Ranulf (earl of Chester), 262 (n. 113)
Raoul de Presles, 310
Raymond of Toulouse, 7
Regiment of Princes, 264 (n. 126)
Renaud (count of Boulogne), 183
René d'Anjou, 306
Revelations of Saint Bridget of Sweden.
    See Bridget, Saint (of Sweeden)
Reynbourne (earl of Warwick), 234
Rich, Mabel, 230
Richard (duke of York), 239, 257
    (n. 63), 258 (n. 77)
Richard (earl of Gloucester), 150 (n. 70)
Richard atte Cherche, 279–80. *See also*
    Architects
Richard de Conyngton, 275
Richard de Cumbe, 196 (n. 33)
Richard de Plessy, 275
Richard du Marche, 178–80, 192
    (n. 16). *See also* Eleanor of Castile

(queen of England); Illuminators
Richard I, the Lion-Hearted (king of
    England), 26, 43 (n. 73), 129, 203
Richard II (king of England), 238, 255
    (n. 49), 255 (nn. 49, 51)
Richard of Caister, 303 (n. 21)
Richard of Conisburgh (earl of
    Cambridge), 239, 257 (n. 63)
Richard of Cornwall, 243
Richard I of Normandy, 16
Richard II of Normandy, 16, 42 (n. 68),
    125
Rievaulx, Abbey of, 5
Rijksmuseum (Amsterdam), 313
Rilinda (abbess), 120, 123 (fig. 16)
Robert (archbishop of Rouen), 120
Robert de Beaumont (earl of Leicester),
    261 (n. 97)
Robert de Greatham, 24; *Miroir ou Les
    évangiles des domnées*, 246, 250
    (n. 10)
Robert de Quincy, 262 (n. 113)
Robert de Stalynton, 269, 276
Robert le Peintor, 270
Robert of Anjou (king of Naples), 28
Robert of Arbrissel, 205
Robert of Bury Saint Edmunds
    (goldsmith), 282 (n. 19)
Robert of Tewksbury (goldsmith), 269
Robert I (count of Dreux), 131–33
Robert the Illuminator, 270, 274. *See
    also* Illuminators
Robert the Wise of Naples, 9
Rodriguez de la Cámera, Juan, 311
Rodríguez Lopez, Amancio, 205–6,
    208–9, 226 (n. 80)
Roet, Payne, 258 (n. 71)
Roger (the hermite), 107, 112
Roger (*scriptor*), 178–79, 193 (n. 18)
Roger de Quincy (earl of Winchester),
    260–61 (n. 93), 264 (n. 119)

Roland, 200 (n. 62)

Rolandslied, 15, 40–41 (n. 59)

Rolle, Richard, 295

Romances, 4, 21, 23, 25–26, 33, 47
(n. 107), 176–79, 181–88 passim, 190
(n. 7), 194 (n. 24), 196 (n. 37), 199
(n. 53), 272–74, 302 (n. 10)

Roman de Guillaume le Conquerant,
176, 194 (n. 28)

Rome, 74, 76, 162, 206, 304 (n. 26),
310; Roman Empire, 61

Rossignos, 176, 187–88, 200 (n. 62)

Rotruda (daughter of Charlemagne).
See Alcuin, writings of

Rufinus, 74–75, 98 (n. 5)

Rupertsberg, 115, 117

Rutilius, 194 (n. 28); *De re rustica*, 195
(n. 30)

Sail d'Escola, 7

Saint Albans, abbey of, 112, 156, 158,
169 (n. 17), 242; Psalter, 107, 108–
12. *See also* Christina of Markyate;
Psalters

Saint Anthony of Padua, church of
(Lisbon), 311

Saint-Antoine of Paris, 211

Saint-Benoîte d'Origny, convent of, 13

Saint Bernard, abbey of
(Hemiksem), 21

Saint-Corneille de Compiègne, abbey
of, 42 (n. 68)

Saint-Denis, abbey of, 42 (n. 68), 44
(n. 76), 127, 129, 142, 211, 223
(n. 52)

Saint Edward Martyr, abbey of, 113

Saint Chapelle (Paris), 138

Sainte-Croix of Poitiers, Abbey of,
11–12

Saint-Etienne de Caen, 42 (n. 68)

Saint-Etienne de Troyes, 18–19

Saint Euphemia, church of
(Olybrius), 54

Saint-Evroul, abbey of, 16

Saint-Florent de Saumur, 42 (n. 68)

Saint Francis, convent of (Prague), 22

Saint Guilia, Benedictine abbey in
Brescia, 22

Sainte-Hilaire-le-Grand, Poitiers, 16

Saint Isidore, monastery of, 225 (n. 72)

Saint Jacques de Haut Pas, xi

Saint Jacques Hospital (Lille), 314

Saint John, Church of (Ephesus), 59

Saint John's College, Cambridge, 32

Saint Lawrence, Church of, 52

Saint Michael, Church of (Antioch), 61

Saint-Omer, abbey of, 127

Saint Peter, Church of (Jerusalem), 52

Saint-Pierre, Church of (Lille), 313

Saint Polyeuktos, Church of, 51, 53–54

Saint Salvatore, Brescia, 22

Saints' lives, 20, 176, 178, 229, 237,
240, 274; importance of female
saints, 21–22, 249 (n. 7). *See also*
Baudonivia; Bocking, Ralph;
Bokenham, Osbern; Capgrave, John;
Fortunatus, Venantius; Lydgate,
John; Wauchier de Denain; Winter,
Symon; *See also under individual
Saints' names*

Saints Sergius and Bacchus, church of,
58–60

Saint Stephen, Church of (Jerusalem),
52; chapel of, 53

Salian dynasty, 17

Salic Law, 47 (n. 114). *See also* Women:
legal status of

Salina. *See* Jerome, Saint

Salome, 142

Salter, Elizabeth, 228

Salthouse (scribe), 299

Sanchia of Provence (countess of
    Cornwall), 243
Sancho (king of Navarre), 43 (n. 73)
Sancia (queen of Naples), 9
San Miniato al Monte, Basilica of, 313
Sanson de Nantuil, 251 (n. 19)
Santa Chiara, Naples, 9
Santa Maria Regalis. See Las Huelgas
Santiago de Compostela, 314
San Vitale, church of (Ravenna), 50,
    62–64
Satan, 120, 250 (n. 10)
Scivias. See Hildegard of Bingen
Scribes, xii, 274
Scriptor, Matthew, 274
Scriptoris, Walter, 274
Scrope, Stephen, 241–42, 248, 260
    (n. 89)
Sculpture, patronage of, 142–43, 267,
    269
Seals, 28, 272, 302 (n. 12)
Sedulius, 83
Segrave, John, 235
Selby Abbey, 158
Seneca, 79, 308
Serlo, 101 (n. 30)
Shaftesbury, abbess of, 130
Shaftesbury Psalter, 113. See also
    Psalters
Sheba, queen of, 75, 94, 96
Sheen, Carthusian house at, 300
Siete partidas. See Alfonso X, the Wise
    (king of Castile and León)
Silvanès, abbey of, 7
Silverius (pope), 88
Simon of Crespy, Saint, 42 (n. 68)
Simon of Dammartin, 183, 199 (n. 53)
Sisara, 94
Socrates, 120
Soissons Cathedral, 138
Solomon, 54, 94, 249 (n. 6); Book of

Solomon, 251 (n. 19)
Song of Roland, 165
Sophia (virgin). See Bernard of
    Clairvaux, Saint
Sozomen, 65
Spaulding, Robert, 275
Speculum dominarum, 28–29, 48
    (n. 115), 48 (n. 121). See also Bouton
    of Corbeveau; Watriquet de Couvin;
    Ysambert de Saint-Léger
Speculum historiale. See Vincent de
    Beauvais
Speculum vitae, 239
Spryngold, Robert, 303 (n. 21)
Stafford, Anne (countess of March,
    daughter of Anne of Woodstock),
    237–38; and patronage of John
    Lydgate, 238, 247, 264 (n. 129)
Stafford, Anne (de Vere), 241–42, 260
    (n. 89); support for Christine de
    Pizan's Epistle of Othea, 242, 248, 265
    (n. 146)
Stafford, Anne Neville, 239–41, 247,
    259 (n. 81), 260 (nn. 85, 89), 264
    (n. 135)
Stafford, Edmund, 237–38
Stafford, Humphrey (duke of
    Buckingham), 240
Stafford, Philippa, 237
Stafford, Thomas, 237
Stained glass, 106, 128–31 passim, 138–
    40, 152 (n. 88), 214, 216, 227
    (nn. 82, 84), 314
Stapleton, Miles (of Ingham), 248, 265
    (n. 145)
Stapleton, Catherine de la Pole, 248,
    265 (n. 145)
Stephen, Roger, 279. See also Architects
Stephen of Blois, 3, 43–44 (nn. 69,
    73), 95
Strabo, Walafrid, 83, 101 (n. 28)

Sudbury, Simon (archbishop of
Canterbury), 276
Suger (abbot of Saint-Denis), 127
Susanna (biblical figure), 151 (n. 78)
Suso, Heinrich, 231, 311
Suzanne de Bourbon, 31
Swynford, Katherine Roet, 239, 258
(n. 71)
Syon, 257 (n. 70)

Taborer, W., 272
Talbot, John (earl of Shrewsbury), 234,
253 (n. 39)
Talbot, Thomas (viscount of Lisle), 235
Talbot, Margaret Beauchamp. See
Beauchamp, Margaret
Talbot Hours, 234
Tancred of Sicily, 200 (n. 62)
Tarquinius, 87
Templars, 33
Terence, 33
Termonde, 315
Textiles, 124, 140, 283 (nn. 33, 34), 302
(n. 11). See also Needlework
Thaïs, 250 (n. 10)
Thamyris, 95
Thaxted, 278
Thebaud, Nigel, 276
Theodatus, 88
Theodora (Byzantine empress), 50–72
passim, 70 (n. 58), 71 (n. 78), 72
(n. 82), 88
Theodoric, 88
Theodosius I, 50–53, 96
Theodosius II, 51–52
Theodulf, 83, 99 (n. 13)
Theophilus, 133, 250 (n. 10)
Theresa of Avila, Saint, 311
Thibaud le Grand (count of
Champagne), 43 (n. 73), 95

Thibaut III (count of Champagne), 18
Thibaut IV (count of Champagne), 18,
43 (n. 73)
Thomas (earl of Stafford), 237
Thomas à Kempis, 310–11; Imitation de
Jésus-Christ, 310
Thomas de Friskeneye, 276
Thomas de la Pole, 265 (n. 145)
Thomas le Purtreor, 270
Thomas of Chobham, 138
Thomas of Woodstock, 237, 256 (n. 60)
Toledo, cathedral of, 213–14
Tournai, 315; bishop of, 133
Toxotius, 249 (n. 6)
Translation, xiv, 26–28, 39–40 (n. 53),
46 (n. 103), 47 (n. 107), 48 (n. 115),
80–81, 86, 180, 184, 229, 263
(n. 115), 274, 284 (n. 69), 297,
310–12, 316–17
Treatises, 229, 245
Tree of Jesse, 113, 117, 131, 136;
Canterbury Cathedral, 129; Ingeborg
Psalter, 133 (fig. 24), 150 (n. 63);
Saint-Denis, 129; York Minster, 129
Trevet, Nicholas, 186, 199 (n. 55), 246,
257 (n. 63)
Trinity Apocalypse, 178, 190 (n. 7)
Trinity College, Cambridge, 276
Tristan (prose), 179, 199 (n. 53)
Tristán de Leonis, 177
Tristant und Isalde, 15, 40 (n. 59)
Troilus, 200 (n. 62)
Troilus frontispiece, 241
Tromper, Perot, 272
Troubadours, 7–8
Troyes, 19
Trumper, Martin, 272
Tulebras, abbey of, 207
Turgot, 18, 163, 185, 240
Tychemersch, William, 275
Tyson, Diana, 2, 27

Uclés, 216
Universities, women's patronage of, 32, 49 (n. 131), 52, 267, 277–78
University Hall, 276–77
University of Paris, 317
Usk Castle, Wales, 279
Uta (abbess of Niedermünster, Regensburg), 113
Uta Codex, 113

Valentinian, 88
Val-Sainte-Marguerite, Chartreuse du (Basel), 315
Van der Weyden, Rogier, 309, 315
Van Eyck, Jan: marriage portraits of Isabel of Portugal and Philip the Good of Burgundy, 315
Vasco de Lucena, 311, 316–17, 320 (n. 38). Translations of: Quintus Curtius's Faictz et gestes d'Alexandre le Grand, 316; Histoire d'Alexandre, 311; Xenophon's Traité des faiz et hautes promesses de Cyrus, 311
Vegetius, 184, 194 (n. 23), 195 (n. 30); De re militari, 180
Venus, 87
Vernacular language, xiv–xviii, 25–27, 33, 36 (n. 11), 40 (n. 57), 47 (n. 111), 79, 86, 175–77, 180–82, 186–87, 229, 292, 310
Vidulator, Patrick, 272
Vidulator, Richard, 272
Vie de Saint Bonaventure, 312. See also Saints' lives
Vie de Sainte Benoîte, 13. See also Saints' lives
Vie de Sainte Marthe, 21
Vie des Pères, 24, 273
Vienna Dioscurides, 54–55, 55 (fig. 1)
Vincent de Beauvais, xiii, xvi–xvii, 45–46 (n. 92); De eruditione filiorum nobilium, 22; Miroir de la salvation humaine, 312; speculum historiale, xi, xvi
Virgil, 33, 79; Aeneid, 91
Virgin Mary. See Mary, Virgin
Vita Aedwardi Regis, 185, 188, 201 (n. 62), 261 (n. 95). See also Saints' lives
Vita Beatricis, 18, 21
Vitae patrum, 24, 273
Vita Gundulphi, 170 (n. 20)
Volmar, 115, 117 (fig. 9)
Voyage of Godfrey of Bouillon, The, 239
Voyage of St Brendan, 162. See also Benedeit l'apostoïle

Wake, Lady, 278
Walafrid Strabo. See Strabo, Walafrid
Walden Abbey, 236
Walsingham Priory, 270, 276, 278, 282 (n. 21)
Walter de Bykerton, 275
Walter de Thaxted, 275
Walters Art Gallery, Baltimore, xi–xii, xvi–xvii
Waltham, abbey at, 158, 168 (n. 13)
Walton, John, 232–33, 246
Warin, Lord Lisle, 233
Warin de Munchensy, 263 (n. 113)
Waterbeach Abbey, 263 (n. 113), 279
Waterton, Hugh, 256 (n. 59)
Waterton, Katherine, 256 (n. 59)
Watriquet de Couvin, 28. See also Speculum dominarum
Wauchier de Denain: Vie de Sainte Marthe, 21. See also Saints' lives
Weingarten Abbey, 124
Westminster Abbey, 160, 176
Westminster Palace, 156, 168 (n. 15), 178
Wheel of Fortune, 240

Whitby, abbey of, 13, 27

White, William, 290–91, 302 (n. 9)

Widows, 7, 18; legal status of, 151 (n. 80), 244–45, 262 (n. 108). *See also* Patronage: of widows

Widukind of Corvey, 103 (n. 41); *Sachsengeschichte*, 88; dedication to Mathilda (abbess of Quedlinburg), 88

Wife of Bath, 302 (n. 13), 304 (n. 30)

William (duke of Suffolk), 243

William atte Hall (goldsmith), 269

William de Ferrers (earl of Derby), 243

William de la Pole, 244, 261 (n. 102)

William de Warenne (earl of Surrey), 242–43

William of Bourges, Saint (archbishop), 138, 139 (fig. 28)

William of Braine, 26. See also *Pseudo-Turpin Chronicle*

William of Malmesbury, 20, 44 (n. 81), 156–57, 159–60, 164–66, 173 (n. 48); *Gesta regum anglorum*, 102 (n. 37), 157, 164

William of Poitiers, 170 (n. 22)

William of Syracuse, 174 (n. 58)

William Rufus, 5, 165, 168 (n. 15)

William I, the Conqueror, 3, 83, 95, 102 (n. 33), 104 (n. 50), 163, 170 (n. 22)

William IX of Aquitaine, 127

Wilton, convent of, 18, 165

Winchester, 42 (n. 68), 125–27, 149 (n. 53); cardinal of, 308; countess of, 243

Windsor chapel, 275

Winter, Symon, 257 (n. 70)

Women: and activities with books, 289–301 passim; as cultural ambassadors, 15–16; legal status of, 8–9, 13–14, 38 (n. 25), 39 (n. 35), 48 (n. 114), 244–45; role in caring for the dead, 18, 199 (n. 52), 210, 212, 217, 270, 313; role in education, 289. *See also* Education; Patronage; Widows

Woodstock, Thomas (duke of Gloucester), 237, 256 (n. 60)

Wright, William, 294, 301 (n. 8)

Xenophon, 311

Ximénez de Rada, Rodrigo (archbishop of Toledo), 214; *De rebus Hispaniae libri IX*, 196 (n. 39), 218 (n. 9), 227 (n. 84)

Yolande of Flanders (countess of Bar), 32, 49 (n. 130)

Yolande of Flanders (countess of Saint-Pol), 26, 47 (n. 107)

Ysambert de Saint-Léger, 28, 48 (n. 121). See also *Speculum dominarum*

Yvain, 200 (n. 62)

Zouche, Alan, 264 (n. 119)

Zouche, Aline (Elena), 246, 264 (n. 119)